A History of
Modern Europe

A History of Modern Europe

Third Edition

Volume 2
From the French Revolution to the Present

John Merriman

Yale University

W. W. Norton & Company
New York · London

Copyright © 2010, 2004, 1996 by John Merriman

All rights reserved
Printed in the United States of America

Editor: Steve Forman
Project editor: Kate Feighery
Production manager, College: Eric Pier-Hocking
Composition: Westchester Book Group
Manufacturing: Courier Companies—Westford division

The Library of Congress has cataloged the one-volume edition as follows:

Merriman, John M.
   A history of modern Europe : from the Renaissance to the present / John
Merriman.—3rd ed.
      p. cm.
   Includes bibliographical references and index.
   ISBN: 978-0-393-93433-5 (pbk.)
   1. Europe—History—1492–   I. Title.

D228.M485   2009
940.2'1—dc22   2009027982

ISBN: 978-0-393-93385-7 (pbk.)

W. W. Norton & Company, Inc., 500 Fifth Avenue, New York, N.Y. 10110
                        www.wwnorton.com

W. W. Norton & Company Ltd., Castle House, 75/76 Wells Street, London
W1T 3QT

   4 5 6 7 8 9 0

For Laura Merriman and
Christopher Merriman

CONTENTS

CHAPTER 19 RAPID INDUSTRIALIZATION AND ITS
CHALLENGES, 1870–1914 742

CHAPTER 20 POLITICAL AND CULTURAL RESPONSES TO A
RAPIDLY CHANGING WORLD 783

PART SIX CATACLYSM

Maps

JOHN MERRIMAN is Charles Seymour Professor of History at Yale University, and regularly teaches the survey of modern European history at Yale. He received his Ph.D from the University of Michigan, and is the author and editor of many books on the history of modern France, including *The Margins of City Life: Explorations on the French Urban Frontier*, *The Red City: Limoges and the French Nineteenth Century*, *The Agony of the Republic: The Repression of the Left in Revolutionary France, 1848–1851*, and most recently *The Dynamite Club*.

PREFACE

Caught as we are in a global economic crisis, the interconnections of economies, nations, and societies around the world could not be clearer. The ongoing social and cultural turmoil of immigrant communities excluded from the mainstream by the former imperial powers demonstrates that history does not go away: the effects of Europe's imperial ambitions and vast empires, although they no longer exist, remain with us. The relatively recent disappearance in 1989–1992 of a more recent empire, that of the Soviet Union, has also had an enormous impact on Europe, and indeed much of the world, transforming international relations while presenting imposing challenges. Russia, to be sure, remains a major power, but it is commonplace now to consider the United States as the one remaining superpower, with an informal empire stretching across the globe through its great economic, political, and military influence.

Empires have greatly shaped European history since the Renaissance. Trade with Africa, Asia, and the Americas led to colonization and empire. Within Europe, rivalries between empires—such as those of England and Spain in the sixteenth and seventeenth centuries, the Ottoman Turkish Empire and the Austrian Habsburg and Russian Empires, and Britain and France in the eighteenth century—reflected both the consolidation and expansion of state power and also shaped the evolution of warfare. During the first fifteen years of the nineteenth century, Napoleon's empire extended through much of the European continent and led to conquests as far as Egypt.

The rise and fall of empires—Portuguese, Spanish, Dutch, Ottoman, British, French, and that of the Soviet Union—is a major theme developed in the third edition of *A History of Modern Europe*. More than ever, the history of Europe cannot be understood without attention to Europe's interaction with cultures in the rest of the world. Europeans, to be sure, have for centuries learned from Muslim, Asian, African, and American cultures. The influence of the Ottoman Empire in Eastern Europe and the Balkans commands additional attention in this volume. At the same time, through commercial contact, conquest, and intellectual, religious, and political influence,

xxiii

as well as, finally, decolonization, the European powers and cultures have affected the histories of non-Western peoples. The construction of stronger and more efficient states facilitated the development of national identities—consider, for example, the role of the British Empire in the emergence in the eighteenth and nineteenth centuries of the sense of being British, and of the wrenching bewilderment among many Britons when the empire ended after World War II. At the same time, national identities developed in the newly independent states that were once colonies. Reflecting recent scholarship, this third edition describes in greater detail the end of the British Empire in Africa, specifically the bloody story of decolonialization in Kenya.

The third edition emphasizes the dynamism of European trade, settlement, and conquest and their great impact not only on Asia, Africa, and the Americas, but also on the history of European peoples. Comparisons are made between the Spanish Empire in Latin America and the English colonies in the Americas. Unlike the Spanish Empire, trade was the basis of the burgeoning English Empire. The Spanish Empire reflected the combination of the absolutism of the Spanish monarchy and the determination to convert—by force if necessary—the indigenous populations to Catholicism. In sharp contrast, many settlers came to the North American English colonies in search of religious freedom. And, again in contrast to the building of the Spanish Empire a century earlier, the English colonists sought not to convert the indigenous peoples to Christianity, but rather to push them out of colonial areas of settlement. While the Spanish colonies reflected state centralization, their English counterparts evolved in a pattern of decentralization that would culminate in the federalist structure of the United States. British rule in India, particularly interesting because of the cultural interaction that took place there, receives more well-deserved attention. And so does the expansion of Dutch rule in Southeast Asia and the response of China and Japan to the Western powers.

Many of the chapters have been usefully reduced in size. There are other changes, as well. The section on the middle classes has been moved to Chapter 14, "The Industrial Revolution," so that "Liberal Challenges to Restoration Europe" stands alone as Chapter 15. In the twentieth century, Joseph Stalin and Stalinism have been moved from the chapter on "Revolutionary Russia and the Soviet Union" (Chapter 23) to the discussion of the Europe of dictators (Chapter 25). I have amplified the discussion of the National Socialism of the Nazis and fascism as a European-wide phenomenon during the inter-war period. The post–World War II chapters have been reorganized and streamlined. Decolonialization and the Cold War, certainly two of the major occurrences in the decades that followed the war, have been combined in Chapter 28. The final chapter has been shortened and brought up to date.

We move away from the traditional textbook strategy of continually contrasting Western and Eastern Europe. For example, the third edition of *A History of Modern Europe* places the emergence of the concept of political sovereignty not only in early modern England and the Dutch Republic, but also in the Polish-Lithuanian Commonwealth during the early modern period. We offer expanded coverage of the heroic rising of the Jews of the Warsaw ghetto against the Nazis in 1943, and of the Warsaw Uprising little more than a year later. We explore the roots of the economic and political problems that continue to beset Western and Eastern Europe, for example by demonstrating how the simmering ethnic tensions that burst into bloody civil war in Bosnia after the disintegration of Yugoslavia echoed the quarrels that eroded the stately Habsburg monarchy a century earlier.

The third edition draws on exciting studies in the social history of ideas, approaches that stand at the intersection of intellectual, social, and cultural history. Volume 1 explains how artistic patronage during the Renaissance and the Golden Age of Dutch culture reveals some of the social foundations of art. Recent studies on the family economy, village and neighborhood life, and the changing structure of work have all enriched this book's account of the transformation of European society from an overwhelmingly peasant society into an increasingly urban and industrial world. The account of the emergence of mass politics in the nineteenth century draws on recent studies of popular culture and the symbolism and power of language.

We retain a narrative framework with the goals of both analyzing the central themes of the European experience and telling a story. Each chapter can be read as part of a larger, interconnected story. Moreover, this book stresses the dynamics of economic, social, political, and cultural change, but within the context of the amazing diversity of Europe. The history of modern Europe and its influence in the world presents extraordinary characters, well known and little known. The text brings the past to life, presenting portraits of men and women who have played major roles in European history: religious reformers such as Martin Luther and Jean Calvin; Queen Elizabeth I, who solidified the English throne, and Maria Theresa, who preserved the Habsburg monarchy; King Louis XIV of France and Tsar Peter the Great, two monarchs whose reigns exemplified the absolute state; great thinkers like Kepler and Voltaire; Napoleon, heir to the French Revolution, but also in some ways a despot in the tradition of absolute rulers, and perhaps even an originator of total war. Inevitably, we discuss the monstrous Adolf Hitler, examining the sources of his growing popularity in Germany in the wake of World War I, and Joseph Stalin, discussing his Communist state and murderous purges. But ordinary men and women have also played a significant role in Europe's story, making their own histories. This book thus evokes the lives of both leaders and ordinary people in periods of rapid economic and political change, revolution, and war.

The growth of strong, centralized states helped shape modern Europe. Medieval Europe was a maze of overlapping political and judicial authorities. In 1500, virtually all Europeans defined themselves in terms of family, village, town, neighborhood, and religious solidarities. Over the next three centuries, dynastic states consolidated and extended their territories while increasing the reach of their effective authority over their own people. Portugal, Spain, England (and later as Great Britain), France, the Netherlands, and Russia built vast empires that reached into other continents. The European Great Powers emerged. With the rise of nationalism in the wake of the French Revolution and the Napoleonic era, demands of ethnic groups for national states encouraged the unification of Italy and Germany and stirred unrest among Croats, Hungarians, and Romanians, who were anxious for their own national states. Ordinary people demanded freedom and political sovereignty, with revolution both a reflection of and a motor for political change. The emergence of liberalism in the nineteenth century and the quest for democratic political structures and mass politics have transformed Europe, beginning in Western Europe. Even the autocracies of Russia and Central and Eastern Europe were not immune to change, and there the quest for democracy still continues.

While discussing dynastic rivalries and nationalism, the book also considers how wars themselves have often generated political and social change. French financial and military contributions to the American War of Independence further accentuated the financial crisis of the monarchy of France, helping to spark the French Revolution. French armies of military conscripts that replaced the professional armies of the age of aristocracy contributed to the emergence of nationalism in Britain and France in the eighteenth century. The defeat of the Russian army by the Japanese in 1905 brought political concessions that helped prepare the way for the Russian Revolution of 1917. The German, Austro-Hungarian, Ottoman, and Russian Empires disappeared in the wake of World War I and World War II; the economic and social impact of these wars generated political instability, facilitating the emergence of fascism and communism. World War I and the role played by colonized peoples gave impetus to movements for independence within the British, French, and Dutch Empires that would ultimately be successful, transforming the world in which we live.

Like politics, religion has also been a significant factor in the lives of Europeans and, at times, in the quest for freedom in the modern world. Catholicism was a unifying force in the Middle Ages; for centuries European popular culture was based on religious belief. Imperial missionaries carried their religions into Africa and Asia in the aggressive quest for converts. Spanish conquerors forced indigenous populations in the Americas to convert to Christianity. Religion has also been a frequently divisive force in modern European history; after the Reformation in the sixteenth century, states extended their authority over religion, while religious minorities demanded the right to practice their own religion. Religious (as well as racial and cultural) intolerance has scarred the European experience, ranging from the expulsion of Jews and Muslims from Spain at the end of the fifteenth century, to Louis XIV's abrogation of religious toleration for Protestants during the seventeenth century, to the horror of the Nazi Holocaust during World War II. Religious conflict in Northern Ireland and the bloody civil war and atrocities perpetuated in Bosnia in the 1990s recall the ravaging of Central Europe during the Thirty Years' War.

The causes and effects of economic change are another thread that weaves through the history of modern Europe. The expansion of commerce in the early modern period, which owed much to the development of the means of raising investment capital and obtaining credit, transformed life in both Western and Eastern Europe, and directly led to the European empires that followed. The Industrial Revolution, which began in England in the eighteenth century and spread to continental Europe in the nineteenth, depended on a rise in population and thus of agricultural production, but also manifested significant continuities with the past. As important as were inventions, the Industrial Revolution also drew on technology that had been in place for centuries. It ultimately changed the ways Europeans worked and lived. Here, too, European empires are an important, fascinating part of the story.

European history remains crucial to understanding the contemporary world. The political, religious, economic, and global concerns that affect Europe and the world today can best be addressed by examining their roots and development. Globalization has carried movement between the continents to new levels. For centuries, Europe sent waves of emigrants to other parts of the world, particularly North and South America. Now the pattern has been reversed. The arrival of millions of migrants from other continents, particularly Africa and Asia, has posed challenges to European states and Europeans. Moreover, the poverty of some of the states of Eastern Europe and the Balkans, and the tragic events in Bosnia in the 1990s, have increased immigration into Western European countries. Immigrants have added to the religious and cultural complexity of European states. As globalization continues to transform Europe and the world, it becomes even more important and exciting to study the continent's history. With the initiation of a new single currency within most of the member states of the European Union and the continued expansion of that organization, Europe has entered a new era, even as a daunting global economic crisis and the threat of terror in the post-9/11 world present some unprecedented challenges. This third edition enhances our understanding of Europe and the world today, as we contemplate not only the distressing failures and appalling tragedies of the past, but also the exhilarating triumphs that have been part of the European experience.

ACKNOWLEDGMENTS

Charles Tilly died during the time I was working on the third edition of *A History of Modern Europe*. His friends, colleagues, and former students—I am all three—miss him very much. He taught me that it is better not to see history as a series of bins that one opens and then shuts before getting on to the next topic, but rather to look for the big news, the major themes, that have been the dynamics of change and provide revealing continuities, even amid astonishing change. At the same time, he believed in keeping ordinary people fully in view by analyzing, describing, and evoking their histories.

I remain indebted to many colleagues and friends who shared their knowledge, expertise, and suggestions with me, including David Underdown, Laura King, Richard Brodhead, Daniel Orlovsky, Mark Steinberg, John Lynn, Mark Micale, Linda Colley, Roberto González-Echevarria, Ivo Banac, Vincent Moncrief, Laura Engelstein, Geoffrey Parker, David Marshall, David Bell, and my late friend Robin Winks. I also want to thank Jeffrey Burds, Harold Selesky, Leslie Page Moch, Richard Stites, David Cannadine, Jim Boyden, Paul Hanson, Michael Burns, Ivan Marcus, Thomas Kaiser, Christopher Johnson, Louise Tilly, Paul Monod, Judy Coffin, Mark Lawrence, John Sweets, Harold Nelson, Kathleen Nilan, Henry Hyder, Jim McClain, Alan Forrest, Martin Ultee, George Behlmer, Mary O'Neal, Mary Jo Maynes, Thomas Head, Jonathan Dewald, Johan Åhr, Margaret McLane, Jan Albers, Martha Hoffman-Strock, Tom Maulucci, Michael Levin, Daryl Lee, Max Oberfus, and my dear friend Peter McPhee. I am particularly grateful to Joel Mokyr for his many helpful suggestions. Special thanks also to Jeffrey Brooks, Eric Jennings, Christopher Reid, and Aristotle Kallis. I also greatly appreciate suggestions given by Doron Ben-Atar, Robert Brown, Alexander Ganse, Bradley Woodworth, David Goldfrank, Adel Allouche, Leon Plantagna, Michael Sibalis, James McMillan, Steven Wheatcroft, Rachel Fuchs, Kenneth Loiselle, and Maya Jasanoff.

For the third edition, my thanks to Elinor Accampo (University of Southern California), Paul Freedman (Yale University), Wayne te Brake (Purchase College), Timothy Snyder (Yale University), Anders Winroth (Yale University),

Andrew Devenney (Central Michigan University), Nicholas Murray (Adirondack Community College), Paul Deslandes (University of Vermont), Alex Porter, Zech Jonathan, Anne Riegert (Université de Rouen), Sven Wanegffelen (Université de Rouen), Steven Pincus (Yale University), Carol Merriman, Lindsay O'Neill (University of Southern California), Charles Beem (Michigan State University), Brian McClure (Michigan State University), Charles Keith (Michigan State University), Valerie Hansen (Yale University), Paul Bushkovitch (Yale University), Charles-Édouard Levillain (University de Lille), Robert Schwartz (Mount Holyoke College), Jay Winter (Yale University), Sarah Cameron (Yale University), Keith Wrightson (Yale University), Francesca Trivellato (Yale University), Steve Sawyer (American University of Paris), Steven Englund (American University of Paris), Michael Driedger (Brock University), Charles Lansing (University of Connecticut), Brian Peterson (Union College), Michael Mahoney (Yale University), Chuck Walton (Yale University), David Large (Montana State University), Frank Snowden (Yale University), Daniel Brückenhaus (Yale University), Jonathan Sperber (University of Missouri), and especially to Piotr Wandycz (Yale University), Victoria Johnson (University of Michigan), Christine Brouwer (Yale University), Michael Galgano (James Madison University), Bruno Cabanes (Yale University), and Gary Shanafelt (McMurry University). The third edition benefited greatly from conferences organized by the Civic Space Institute at the Larzowski School of Law and Commerce in Warsaw. Thanks to my colleagues and friends Andrzej Kaminski (Georgetown University and the Larzowski School of Law and Commerce), Jim Collins (Georgetown University), Wojciech Falkowski (University of Warsaw), Krzysztof Lazarski (Larzowski School of Law and Commerce), Daria Nałęcz (Larzowski School of Law and Commerce), Randy Roberts (Purdue University), Gabor Agoston (Georgetown University), Ashley Dodge, and Ted Weeks (University of Southern Illinois).

I have the greatest admiration for W. W. Norton, which remains a very special independent publisher. My friend Donald Lamm, former chairman of the board and former president of Norton, has always embodied the best in publishing. He and Steve Forman, a wonderful editor and valued friend, first proposed this project to me. Alan Cameron in London's Norton office has long provided support. Sandy Lifland's deft and patient work as developmental editor contributed greatly to the first edition. Sarah England, then Steve's assistant and now an editor at Norton, was extremely helpful throughout the preparation of the second edition, and Kate Feighery and JoAnn Simony were for the third edition. A special thanks to Carol Merriman, who has patiently lived with and encouraged this and other projects for many wonderful years.

The third edition of *A History of Modern Europe* is dedicated to Laura Merriman and to Christopher Merriman, with much love.

Balazuc (Ardèche),
March 5, 2009

A HISTORY OF
MODERN EUROPE

PART FOUR

REVOLUTIONARY EUROPE, 1789–1850

The French Revolution of 1789 struck the first solid blow in continental Western Europe against monarchical absolutism on behalf of popular sovereignty. The roots of revolution extend back to the second half of the seventeenth century, an era of hitherto unparalleled absolute monarchical authority. The monarchs of France, Russia, Prussia, Austria, Spain, and Sweden had reinforced their authority to the extent that they stood clearly above any internal challenge to their power. Compliant nobles served as junior partners in absolutism, acknowledging the ruler's absolute power to proclaim laws, assess taxes, and raise armies, in exchange for royal recognition of their noble standing and protection against popular revolts. The governments of Great Britain and the Dutch United Provinces stood in sharp contrast to absolute states. In the English Civil War in the 1640s, Parliament had successfully turned aside the possibility of absolute monarchy in England, leading to the execution of King Charles II, followed after some years of turmoil by the Restoration of constitutional monarchy. In the Netherlands, the Dutch revolt against absolutist Spain led to the establishment of the Dutch Republic. The theory of popular sovereignty developed not only as an alternative to absolute rule but also as an extension of constitutional rule. In the dramatic events of the French Revolution that began in 1789, the theory of popular sovereignty became reality as ordinary people helped bring about the downfall of absolute rule and then, three years later, the monarchy itself.

True popular sovereignty was a short-lived experiment, however, as counter-revolution and foreign intervention led to the dramatic centralization of state authority. In 1799, Napoleon Bonaparte helped overthrow the Directory, the last regime of

the revolutionary era in France. An admirer of the Enlightenment, Napoleon claimed that he was the heir of the French
Revolution. But while Napoleon saw himself as a savior who
carried "liberty, equality, and fraternity" abroad, his conquest of
much of Europe before his final defeat left a mixed legacy for
the future. More than a fifth of all the significant battles that
took place in Europe from 1490 to 1815 occurred between the
coming of the French Revolution and Napoleon's final defeat in
1815.

Following Napoleon's defeat in 1815 at the Battle of Waterloo,
the Congress of Vienna created the Concert of Europe, the international basis of Restoration Europe, in the hope of preventing
further liberal and nationalist insurrections in Europe. But liberal and nationalist movements could not so easily be swept away.
During the subsequent three decades, "liberty" became the
watchword for more and more people, particularly among the
middle classes, who came to the forefront of economic, political,
and cultural life. Liberal movements were in many places closely
tied to the emergence of nationalism, the belief in the primacy of
nationality as a source of allegiance and sovereignty.

In the meantime, during the first half of the nineteenth century, the Industrial Revolution slowly but surely transformed the
way many Europeans lived. Dramatic improvements in transportation, notably the development of the railroad but also road
improvements, expanded the market for manufactured and other
goods. Rising agricultural production, increasingly commercialized in Western Europe, fed a larger population. Migrants poured
into Europe's cities, which grew as never before. Contemporaries,
particularly in Western Europe, sensed profound economic,
social, political, and cultural changes.

CHAPTER 12

THE FRENCH REVOLUTION

In 1791, King Louis XVI decided to flee Paris and the French Revolution. A virtual prisoner in the Tuileries Palace by the first months of the year, he had secretly negotiated for possible intervention on his behalf by the Austrian king and other European monarchs. The royal family furtively left the Tuileries Palace late at night on June 20, 1791, disguised as the family and entourage of a Russian baroness riding in a large black coach with yellow trim. But in an eastern town, the postmaster recognized the king, whose image he had seen on a coin. He rode rapidly to the town of Varennes, where the National Guard prevented the king's coach from going on. Three representatives of the National Assembly brought the royal family back to Paris. Near the capital, the crowds became threatening, and national guardsmen stood by the roadside with their rifles upside down, a sign of contempt or mourning.

The French Revolution mounted the first effective challenge to monarchical absolutism on behalf of popular sovereignty. The creation of a republican government in France and the diffusion of republican ideals in other European countries influenced the evolution of European political life long after the Revolution ended. Issues of the rights of the people, the role of the state in society, the values of democratic society, notions of "left" and "right" in political life, the concept of the "nation at arms," the place of religion in modern society and politics, and the question of economic freedom and the sanctity of property came to dominate the political agenda. They occupied the attention of much of France during the revolutionary decade of 1789–1799. The political violence of that decade would also be a legacy for the future.

The revolutionaries sought to make the French state more centralized and efficient, as well as more just. Napoleon Bonaparte, whom some historians consider the heir to the Revolution and others believe to be its betrayer, continued this process after his ascent to power in 1799.

Modern nationalism, too, has its roots in the French Revolution. The revolutionaries enthusiastically proclaimed principles they held to be universal. Among these were the sovereignty of the nation and the rights and duties of citizenship. The revolutionaries celebrated the fact that the Revolution had occurred in France. But wars intended to free European peoples from monarchical and noble domination turned into wars of French conquest. The revolutionary wars, pitting France against the other great powers, contributed to the emergence or extension of nationalism in other countries as well, ranging from Great Britain, where the sense of being British flourished in response to the French threat, to central and southern Europe, where some educated Germans and Italians began to espouse nationalism in response to the invading French armies.

The Old Regime in Crisis

The French Revolution was not inevitable. Yet difficult economic conditions in the preceding two decades, combined with the growing popularity of a discourse that stressed freedom in the face of entrenched economic and social privileges, made some sort of change seem possible, perhaps even likely. When a financial crisis occurred in the 1780s and the king was forced to call the Estates-General, the stage was set for the confrontation that would culminate in the French Revolution.

Long-Term Causes of the French Revolution

The increasing prevalence of the language of the Enlightenment, stressing equality before the law and differentiating between absolute and despotic rule, placed the monarchy and its government under the closer scrutiny of public opinion. Adopting Enlightenment discourse, opponents accused Louis XV of acting despotically when he exiled the Parlement of Paris in 1771 and tried to establish new law courts that were likely to be more subservient than the *parlements*, the sovereign law courts, had been. Opponents believed that the king was trying to subvert long-accepted privileges. Following Louis XV's death in 1774, the young Louis XVI reinstated the parlements, which retained their right to register royal edicts.

As complaints mounted about noble privileges, guild monopolies, and corrupt royal officials, the implications of Enlightenment thought led to political action. In 1774, Controller-General of Finances Anne-Robert Turgot drew up a program to eliminate some monopolies and privileges that fettered the economy (see Chapter 11). However, the decree abolishing the guilds, among other decrees, generated immediate hostility from nobles, the Parlement of Paris, and from ordinary people, who rioted in Paris in 1775 because the freeing of the grain trade had brought higher prices in hard times. Two years later, Turgot's experiment ended. But some writers now began to contrast the freedoms Turgot had in mind with the corporate privileges that characterized the economy and society of eighteenth-century France.

France remained a state of overlapping layers of privileges, rights, traditions, and jurisdictions. Nobles and professional groups such as guilds and tax farmers (who generally had bought their offices and could pocket some of the taxes they collected) contested any plan to eliminate privileges. At the same time, the social lines of demarcation between nobles and wealthy commoners had become less fixed over the course of the eighteenth century. Despite increasing opposition from the oldest noble families who believed their ranks were being swamped by newcomers, in the fifteen years before 1789 almost 2,500 families bought their way into the nobility. Yet many people of means, too, resented noble privileges, above all the exemption of nobles from most kinds of taxes. Disgruntled commoners did not make the French Revolution, but their dissatisfaction helped create a litany of demands for reform. The monarchy's worsening financial crisis accentuated these calls.

The sharpest resistance to reform came from the poorer nobility. Among the "nobles of the sword," the oldest noble families whose ancestors had proudly taken arms to serve the king, some had fallen on hard times and clung frantically to any and all privileges as a way of maintaining their status. They resented the fact that the provincial parlements, in particular, had filled up with new nobles who had purchased offices—the "nobles of the robe"—and that power had shifted within the nobility from the oldest noble families to those recently ennobled.

The monarchy depended upon the sale of titles, offices, and economic monopolies for revenue and long-term credit. But by creating more offices—there were more than 50,000 offices in 1789—it risked destroying public confidence and driving down the value of offices already held.

Economic hardship compounded the monarchy's financial problems by decreasing revenue while exacerbating social tensions. Rising prices and rents darkened the 1770s and 1780s. A series of bad harvests—the worst of which occurred in 1775—made conditions of life even more difficult for poor people. The harvests of 1787 and 1788, which would be key years in the French political drama, were also very poor. Such crises were by no means unusual—indeed they were cyclical and would continue until the middle of the next century. Meager harvests generated popular resistance to taxation and protests against the high price of grain (and therefore bread). A growing population put more pressure on scarce resources.

Many peasants believed that their hardship was being increased by landowners. Something of a "seigneurial reaction" was under way as smaller agricultural yields diminished noble revenues, while inflation raised the costs of noble life. Noble landowners hired estate agents, lawyers, and surveyors to maximize income from their lands, and reasserted old rights over common lands, on which many poor peasants depended for pasturing animals and gathering wood for fuel. Many landlords raised rents and tried to force share-cropping arrangements on peasants who had previously rented land.

Although the feudal system of the Middle Ages had long since passed, remnants remained. Peasants were still vexed by seigneurial dues and cash owed to their lords. Many nobles still held some rights of justice over their peasants, which meant that they could determine guilt and assess penalties for alleged transgressions. Seigneurial courts were often used to enforce the landlord's rights over forests, lakes, and streams, and his exclusive rights to hunt and fish on his estate. The political crisis that led to the French Revolution would provide ordinary people with an opportunity to redress some of these mounting grievances.

The Financial Crisis

The serious financial crisis that confronted the monarchy in the 1780s was the short-term cause of the French Revolution. France had been at war with Britain, as well as with other European powers, off and on for more than a century. The financial support France had provided the rebel colonists in the American War of Independence against Britain had been underwritten by loans arranged by the king's Swiss minister of finance, Jacques Necker (1732–1804). Almost three-fourths of state expenses went to maintaining the army and navy, and to paying off debts accumulated from the War of the Austrian Succession (1740–1748) and the Seven Years' War (1756–1763), as well as from the American War of Independence. The monarchy was living beyond its means.

Where were more funds to be found? Nobles had traditionally enjoyed the privilege of being exempt from most, and the clergy from all, taxation. There was a limit to how many taxes could be imposed on peasants, by far the largest social group in France. In short, the financial crisis of the monarchy was closely tied to the very nature of its fiscal system.

The absolute monarchy in France collected taxes less efficiently than did the British government. In Britain, the Bank of England facilitated the government's borrowing of money at relatively low interest through the national debt. In France, there was no central bank, and the monarchy depended more than ever on private interests and suffered from a cumbersome assessment of fiscal obligations and inadequate accounting. French public debt already was much higher than that of Britain and continued to rise as the monarchy sought financial expedients.

The hesitant and naive Louis XVI was still in his twenties when he became king in 1774. Louis knew little of his kingdom, venturing beyond the region of Paris and Versailles only once during his reign. He preferred puttering around the palace, taking clocks and watches apart and putting them back together. He excelled at hunting. The unpopularity of Louis's elegant, haughty wife, Marie-Antoinette (1755–1793), accentuated the public's lack of confidence in the throne (whether or not she really snarled "Let them eat

(*Left*) Louis XVI. (*Right*) Marie-Antoinette.

cake!" when told that the people had no bread). The daughter of the Austrian queen Maria Theresa, Marie-Antoinette was married to Louis to strengthen dynastic ties between Austria and France. She never felt really at home in France. Unhappy in her marriage, Marie-Antoinette lived extravagantly and was embroiled in controversy. In 1785, she became entangled in a seamy scandal when a cardinal offered her a fabulous diamond necklace in the hope of winning favor. The necklace and some of the prelate's money were then deftly stolen by plotters, a strange scenario that included a prostitute posing as the queen. The "diamond necklace affair," as it was called, seemed to augment the public image of the king as a weak man, a cuckold. The queen's reputed indiscretions and infidelities seemed to undercut the authority of the monarchy itself. Her detractors indelicately dubbed her the "Austrian whore."

In the meantime, Necker continued to float more loans. But in 1781, some ministers and noble hangers-on convinced the king to dismiss Necker. Necker produced a fanciful account of the royal finances that purported to demonstrate that more revenue was coming to the state than was being spent. Necker hoped to reassure creditors that reform was unnecessary. Bankers, however, did not believe Necker's figures and some refused to loan the monarchy any more money until the state enacted financial reforms. The new finance minister, Charles-Alexandre de Calonne (1734–1802), demonstrated that Necker's calculations of royal finances were far-fetched. Yet Calonne spent even more money and put the royal treasury deeper in debt by borrowing from venal officeholders to pay off creditors now gathered at the royal door.

The parlements were certain to oppose fiscal reform, which they believed would lead to an increase in taxation through a general tax on land. They distrusted Calonne, whom they identified with fiscal irresponsibility and governmental arrogance that some believed bordered on despotism.

To sidestep the parlements, Calonne asked the king in February 1787 to convoke an Assembly of Notables consisting of handpicked representatives from each of the three estates: clergy, nobility, and the third estate (everybody else). The crown expected the Assembly to endorse its reform proposals, including new land taxes from which nobles would not be exempt. Calonne suggested that France's financial problems were systemic, resulting from a chaotic administrative organization, including the confusing regional differences in tax obligations. The monarchy's practice of selling the lucrative rights to collect, or "farm," taxes worsened the inefficiency. Calonne knew that the crown's contract with the tax farmers would soon have to be renegotiated, and that many short-term loans contracted by the monarchy would soon come due.

Denouncing "the dominance of custom" that had for so long prevented reform and encumbered commerce, Calonne proposed to overhaul the entire financial system. The Assembly of Notables, however, rejected Calonne's proposals for tax reform and refused to countenance the idea that nobles should be assessed land taxes. Moreover, the high clergy of the first estate, some of whom were nobles, also vociferously opposed Calonne's reforms. They, too, feared losing their exemption from taxation. The privilege-based nature of French society was at stake.

Nobles convinced the king to sack Calonne, which he did on April 8, 1788. Louis XVI replaced Calonne with the powerful archbishop of Toulouse, Étienne-Charles de Loménie de Brienne (1727–1794). Like his predecessor, Loménie de Brienne asked the provincial parlements to register—and thus approve—several edicts of financial reform, promising that the government would keep more accurate accounts. But the Parlement of Paris refused to register some of the edicts, including a new land tax and a stamp tax, which evoked the origins of the American Revolution.

The First Stages of the Revolution

Some members of the Assembly of Notables had been willing to accept fiscal reform and to pay more taxes, but only with accompanying institutional reforms that would guarantee their privileges. They wanted the king to convoke regular assemblies of the Estates-General—made up of representatives of the three estates—which had not been convoked since 1614. The king was in a difficult position. He needed to reduce the privileges of the nobles to solve the financial crisis, but to do so without their approval would lead to accusations of despotism, or even tyranny, the sometimes violent implementation of the structures of despotic authority. On the other hand, capitulating to the demands of the privileged classes in return for new taxes would compromise his absolute authority and suggest that his word was subject to the approval of the nation, or at least the nobility. The resolution of this dilemma would lead to the events that constituted the first stages of the French Revolution.

Convoking the Estates-General

The "noble revolt" began the French Revolution. In response to the refusal of the Parlement of Paris to register the land and stamp taxes, in August 1787 Louis XVI exiled its members to Troyes, a town east of Paris. Nobles and high clergymen protested vigorously. The provincial parlements backed up the Parlement of Paris. The Parlement of Grenoble refused to register the new stamp and land taxes and convoked its provincial estates (the assembly of nobles that represented the interests of the region) without royal authorization. The "revolt of the nobility" against the monarchy's attempt to force nobles to pay taxes spread. Provincial parlements demanded that the Estates-General be convoked. This revolt was not directed against the institution of the monarchy itself, but against what the nobles considered abuses of the rights and privileges of the nation committed by an increasingly despotic crown.

The monarchy sought compromise. Loménie de Brienne agreed to withdraw the new land and stamp taxes in exchange for maintaining the tax on income (the *vingtième* tax), which nobles and other privileged people had first been assessed in the late 1750s to pay for the Seven Years' War. He made clear, however, that the crown would be forced to settle its debts in paper money backed by royal decree. Louis XVI recalled the Parlement of Paris from exile in November 1787. But the king ordered new loan edicts registered without giving the parlement a chance to be heard. When the duke of Orléans, the king's cousin, interjected that such a procedure was illegal, Louis replied, "That is of no importance to me . . . it is legal because I will it." Louis XVI thus seemed to cross the line between absolutism and despotism.

In May 1788, the king ordered the arrest of two of the most radical members of the Parlement of Paris. He then suspended the parlements, establishing new provincial courts to take their place and creating a single plenary court that would register royal edicts. Resistance to the king's acts against the parlements came quickly. The Assembly of the Clergy, which had been summoned to decide on the amount of its annual gift to the crown, protested the abolition of the parlements. Riots in support of the parlements occurred in several towns, including Grenoble, where crowds expressed support for their parlement by pelting soldiers with stones and roof tiles.

On August 8, 1788, Louis XVI announced that he would convoke the Estates-General on May 1 of the following year. He hoped that he could avert royal bankruptcy if the Estates-General would agree to the imposition of the new taxes. Two weeks later, he reappointed Necker as minister of finance, a measure he believed would appease nobles, investors, and holders of government bonds, who had never objected to unrestrained borrowing.

But the convocation of the Estates-General helped unify public opinion against the king. That the nobles forced the crown to convoke the Estates-General became the first act of the French Revolution. Many people believed that the Estates-General, more than the parlements, would represent their interests and check royal despotism.

The question of how voting was to take place when the Estates-General met assumed increasing importance. Would each of the three estates—clergy, nobles, and the third estate—have a single vote (which would almost certainly quash any reform since the majority of nobles and clergymen were against reform), or would each member of the Estates-General be entitled to his own vote?

On September 25, 1788, the Parlement of Paris, which had been reinstated amid great celebration, ruled that voting within the Estates-General would take place by estate, as had been the case when the Estates-General had last met in 1614. Thus each of the three estates would have the same number of representatives and be seated separately. Henceforth, the parlements would be seen by many people as defending the prerogatives of their privileged members against the interests of the third estate, losing their claim to defend the nation against the king's despotism for having registered the royal decree that voting would be by estate.

Popular political writers now began to salute the third estate (which made up 95 percent of the population) as the true representative of liberty and of the nation against royal despotism. Others asked for some sort of representative assembly that would reflect "public opinion." The "patriot party," a co-alition of bourgeois members and some liberal nobles, began to oppose royal policies, which they contrasted with the rights of the "nation." "Patriots" denounced the vested interests of the court and the nobles close to it. Political publications transformed these debates into national political issues. The Society of the Thirty, a group that included liberal nobles from very old families—for example, the Marquis de Lafayette (1757–1834), French hero of the American War of Independence—as well as a number of commoner lawyers, met to discuss, debate, and distribute liberal political pamphlets. They proposed that the third estate be entitled to twice as many representatives in the Estates-General as the nobility and clergy.

In January 1789, Emmanuel Joseph Sieyès (1748–1836), an obscure priest, offered the most radical expression of a crucial shift in political opinion. "We have three questions to ask and answer," he wrote. "First, What is the Third Estate? Everything. Second, What has it been heretofore in the political order? Nothing. Third, What does it demand? To become something therein." He contrasted the "nation" against royal absolutism and noble prerogative, demanding a predominant role for the third estate in political life.

The vast majority of the men elected to the Estates-General were residents of cities and towns, and two-thirds of these had some training in the law. Two-thirds of those elected to the first estate were parish priests, many of whom were of humble origin and resented the privileges of the bishops

(*Left*) The Marquis de Lafayette. (*Right*) The Abbé Sieyès.

and monastic orders. Some of the younger noble representatives elected to the second estate were relatively liberal. They wanted institutional reforms in the organization of the French monarchy that would permit them to check the power of the king, in much the same way as the Parliament in England served as a check on the English crown. In December 1788, the king agreed to double the number of representatives of the third estate but declined to give all members an individual vote.

The king asked the local assemblies, along with the first two estates, to draw up lists of grievances (*cahiers de doléances*), which the Estates-General would discuss. Thousands of grievances offered the monarchy a wide variety of opinions, ranging from concrete suggestions for reform to the considered opinion that the foul breath of sheep was ruining pastureland in Lorraine. More important, *cahiers* criticized monarchical absolutism and the intransigence of seigneurs, asked for a more consistent and equitable tax structure, and called for the creation of a new national representative body. A few of the *cahiers* denounced as an abuse of royal power the so-called *lettres de cachet,* documents issued in the name of the king that allowed a person to be arrested for any reason and imprisoned indefinitely. For example, one *cahier* demanded "that no citizen lose his liberty except according to law." However, some *cahiers* also reflected continued reverence for the king, while denouncing the rapacity and bad faith of his advisers and ministers. Most *cahiers* never reached the king.

On May 5, 1789, the nearly 1,200 members of the Estates-General (about 600 of whom represented the third estate) assembled at Versailles. The king greeted the first two estates, but kept the commoners waiting for two hours. When he finished his speech, members of the third estate violated protocol by boldly putting their hats back on, a right reserved for the two privileged orders. On June 17, the third estate overwhelmingly approved a motion by Sieyès that declared the third estate to be the "National Assembly" and the true representative of national sovereignty. The third estate now claimed legitimate sovereignty and an authority parallel, if not superior, to that of the king of France.

But, on June 20, as rumors circulated that the king might take action against them, representatives of the third estate found that their meeting hall had been locked for "repairs." Led by their president, Jean-Sylvain Bailly (1736–1793), an astronomer, the members of the third estate took the bold step of assembling in a nearby tennis court. There they took an oath "not to separate, and to reassemble wherever circumstances require, until the constitution of the kingdom is established and consolidated upon solid foundations." With principled defiance, the third estate demanded that defined limits be placed on the king's authority.

The king declared the third estate's deliberations invalid. Yet on June 23 he announced some substantial reforms, agreeing to convoke periodically the Estates-General, to abolish the *taille* (the tax on land) and the *corvée* (labor tax), to eliminate internal tariffs and tolls that interfered with trade, and to eliminate the *lettres de cachet*. He also agreed that the Estates-General would vote by head, but only on matters that did not concern "the ancient and constitutional rights of the three orders." To the radicalized members of the third estate, the king's concessions were not enough.

The Tennis Court Oath, June 20, 1789.

Louis XVI had dismissed Necker on June 22, but reversed himself after learning that thousands of people in Paris had invaded the courtyard of the Tuileries Palace in Paris to demand that Necker stay on. Necker's contention in 1781 that the kingdom's finances could be put on an even keel without raising taxes had increased his popularity, as had the fact that nobles were pushing for his recall. During these days, most of the clergy and a number of nobles had joined the third estate. Now, after threatening to dissolve the Estates-General by force, on June 27 the king ordered the remaining clergy and nobles of the first two estates to join the third. The new gathering began to constitute itself as the National Constituent Assembly.

Storming of the Bastille

Amid a shortage of food and high prices, many ordinary people now believed that a conspiracy by nobles and hoarders was to blame. Furthermore, the number of royal troops around Paris and Versailles seemed to be increasing. Rumors spread that the National Assembly would be quashed. On July 11, the king once again ordered Necker, who remained unpopular with the court, into exile. He and other ministers were dismissed because the king was convinced they were unable to control the demands for change coming from the Estates-General. Bands of rioters attacked the customs barriers at the gates of Paris, tearing down toll booths where taxes on goods entering the city were collected, thus making foodstuffs more expensive.

On the morning of July 14, 1789, thousands of people—mostly tradesmen, artisans, and wage earners—seized weapons stored in the Invalides, a large veterans' hospital. Early that afternoon, the attention of the Paris crowd turned toward the Bastille, a fortress on the eastern edge of the city, where the crowd believed powder and ammunition were stored. For most of the eighteenth century, the Bastille had been a prison, renowned as a symbol of despotism because some prisoners had been sent there by virtue of one of the king's *lettres de cachet,* summarily and without a trial. On that hot summer day, the Bastille's prisoners numbered but seven, a motley crew that included a nobleman imprisoned upon request of his family, a renegade priest, and a demented Irishman, who alternately thought he was Joan of Arc, Saint Louis, and God.

The crowd stormed and captured the Bastille, which was defended by a small garrison. More than 200 of the attackers were killed or wounded. A butcher decapitated the commander of the fortress, and the throng carried his head on a pike in triumph through the streets. The Bastille's fall would be much more significant than it first appeared. The king entered "nothing new" in his diary for that day, July 14. But the crowd's uprising probably saved the National Assembly from being dissolved by the troops the king had ordered to Versailles and Paris. Now unsure of the loyalty of his soldiers, Louis sent away some of the troops he had summoned to Paris, recognized both the newly elected municipal government, with Bailly serving as mayor,

The taking of the Bastille, July 14, 1789.

and a municipal defense force or National Guard (commanded by the Marquis de Lafayette), and capitulated to the popular demand that he recall Necker to office.

On July 17, 1789, the king came to Paris to be received by the municipal council at the town hall, accepting and wearing an emblem of three colors, red and blue for the city of Paris, and white for the Bourbons. By doing so, Louis XVI seemed to be recognizing what became the tricolor symbol of the French Revolution.

The Great Fear and the Night of August 4

News of the convocation of the Estates-General had brought hope to many rural people that the king would relieve their crushing fiscal burdens. They had expressed such hopes in the grievances they sent with their third estate delegates to Versailles. Now, upon news of the fall of the Bastille, between July 19 and August 3 peasants attacked châteaux. In some places they burned title deeds specifying obligations owed to lords. These peasant rebellions helped cause a subsequent panic known as the "Great Fear." Fueled by the rumor of an aristocratic "famine plot" to starve or burn out the population, peasants and townspeople mobilized in many regions of France. To repel the rumored approach of brigands sent to destroy crops, townspeople and peasants formed armed units to defend themselves and save the harvest. New local governments and National Guard units were established to institute reforms and to restore order as the effective authority of the state disintegrated. These events brought to local influence lawyers, merchants, and other "new men" who had formerly been excluded from political life.

News of peasant violence galvanized members of the National Assembly. On August 4, 1789, in an effort to appease the peasants and to forestall further rural disorders, the National Assembly formally abolished the "feudal regime," including seigneurial rights. This sweeping proclamation was modified in the following week: owners of seigneurial dues, or payments owed by peasants who worked land owned by nobles, would receive compensation from the peasants (although, in general, such compensation was not forthcoming and was subsequently eliminated). The Assembly abolished personal labor servitude owed to nobles, without compensation. The members of the National Assembly thus renounced privilege, the fundamental organizing principle of French society. Other reforms enacted the following week included the guarantee of freedom of worship and the abolition of the sale of offices, seigneurial justice, and even of the exclusive right of nobles to hunt. The provinces and cities, too, were required to give up most of their archaic privileges. In these ways, the National Assembly enacted a sweeping agenda that proclaimed the end of what soon became known as the Old Regime.

CONSOLIDATING THE REVOLUTION

The Assembly's decrees destroyed absolutism by redefining the relationship between subject and king. No longer would the king rule by divine right, or buy allegiance by dispensing privileges to favorites. Instead, he would be constrained by powers spelled out in a constitution. The Assembly promulgated the Declaration of the Rights of Man and Citizen, a remarkable document that proposed universal principles of humanity. It next established a new relationship between church and state, creating a national church, making Catholic Church property "national property," and compelling the clergy to swear allegiance to the nation. The National Assembly then turned to the long process of framing a constitution for the new regime, and is therefore sometimes also known as the Constituent Assembly.

In the meantime, Marie-Antoinette denounced the revolutionaries as "monsters," and some of the king's most influential advisers balked at accepting any weakening in royal authority. Fearing the influence of nobles at the court, crowds early in October marched to Versailles, returning to Paris with the king and the royal family. Henceforth, while many nobles, among others, fled France for exile and sought the assistance of the monarchs of

Europe against the Revolution, the king himself became vulnerable to the tide of Parisian popular radicalism. As nobles and clergy led resistance to the Revolution, the Parisian clubs made more radical demands.

The Declaration of the Rights of Man and Citizen

As it set out to create a constitutional monarchy, the Assembly promulgated the Declaration of the Rights of Man and Citizen on August 26, 1789. This set forth the general principles of the new order and intended to educate citizens about liberty. One of the most significant documents in Western political history, the Declaration reflected some of the ideas that Thomas Jefferson had enshrined in the American Declaration of Independence of 1776. Article One proclaims, "Men are born and remain free and equal in rights." The Enlightenment's influence is apparent in the document's concern for individual freedom, civic equality, and the sense of struggle against corporatism, unjust privilege, and absolute rule, a discourse based upon a belief in the primacy of reason. All people were to be equal before the law. All men were to be "equally eligible to all honors, places, and employments . . . without any other distinction than that created by their virtues and talents." No person could be persecuted for his or her opinions, including those concerning religion.

Proclaiming universal principles, the Declaration of the Rights of Man and Citizen clearly placed sovereignty in the French nation. The notion of rights stemming from membership in the "nation," as opposed to that in any corporate group or social estate, was a fundamental change. Laws were to reflect the notion of the "general will," an Enlightenment concept, which would be expressed by national representatives. The nation itself, not the monarch alone, was to be "the source of all sovereignty." The assertion of equality of opportunity, however, was not intended to eliminate all social distinctions. The preservation of property rights assured that differences due to wealth, education, and talent would remain and be considered natural and legitimate. The Declaration thus helped make wealth, not birth, blood, or legal privilege, the foundation of social and political order in modern France.

The Declaration invoked "universal man," meaning mankind. But at the same time, its authors excluded women from the Declaration and did not espouse or foresee equality of the sexes. Nonetheless, many men and women now began to greet each other as "citizen." Indeed, some calls for women's rights arose from the beginning of the Revolution.

The abolition of feudalism and the proclamation of the Declaration of the Rights of Man and Citizen were such monumental achievements that already in 1790 people were referring to the Old Regime as having been that which existed before the representatives of the Estates-General constituted the National Assembly. It remained, however, for Louis XVI to accept the Assembly's work.

"The Baker, the Baker's Wife, and the Baker's Little Boy"

The political crisis was by no means over. The king's closest advisers, the "court party," rejected any constitutional arrangement that would leave the monarch without the power of absolute veto. Royal authority was at stake. Speaking for the patriot party, Sieyès insisted, "If the king's will is capable of equalling that of twenty-five million people . . . it would be a *lettre de cachet* against the general will." The majority of the Assembly, having defeated a motion that an upper chamber like the British House of Lords be created, offered the king in September the power of a "suspending" veto over legislation. The king would be able to delay a measure passed by the Assembly from becoming law for up to four years.

When the king refused to accept these provisions and the decrees of August 4, a flood of pamphlets and newspapers attacked his intransigence. The radical journalist Jean-Paul Marat (1743–1793) quickly found a popular following for his new newspaper, *The Friend of the People*. A physician beset by financial woes, Marat was like one of the ambitious, frustrated "scribblers" whom Voltaire, forty years earlier, had scathingly denounced as hacks. Marat captured with stirring emotion and the colorful, coarse slang of ordinary Parisians the mood of those for whom he wrote. The rhetoric of popular sovereignty, some of it borrowed from the philosophe Jean-Jacques Rousseau, came alive in the outpouring of political pamphlets that undermined popular respect for Louis XVI and even for the institution of monarchy itself.

By October, some "patriots" were demanding that the king reside in Paris, echoing a number of *cahiers*. Like many of the most important events in the French Revolution, the "march to Versailles" began with a seemingly minor event. The officers of the Flanders Regiment insulted the newly adopted tricolor emblem at a reception in their honor attended by the king and queen. According to rumor, they shouted, "Down with the National Assembly!"

On October 5, women from the neighborhoods around the Bastille, having found little at the market, gathered in front of the town hall. From there, some 10,000 people, mostly women, left on foot for Versailles, hoping to convince the king to provide them with bread. Some of them occupied the hall of the National Assembly, where they claimed power in the name of popular sovereignty. Later in the day, a large force of national guardsmen led by Lafayette also arrived at Versailles, hoping to keep order and to convince the king that he should return with them to Paris. Louis cordially greeted the women in the late afternoon, promising them bread. That night Louis XVI announced his acceptance of the Assembly's momentous decrees of the night of August 4.

Nonetheless, violence followed at dawn. When people tried to force their way into the château, royal guards shot a man dead, and the crowds retaliated by killing two guards and sticking their heads on pikes. The crowd insisted that the royal family join it on the road to Paris. Some of the women

à Versailles à Versailles du 5 Octobre 1789

Women of Paris leaving for Versailles.

sang that they were returning to Paris with "The Baker, the Baker's Wife, and the Baker's Little Boy," reflecting the popular notion that the king was responsible for providing bread for his people. The National Assembly, too, left Versailles for Paris. By putting the king and the Assembly under the pressure of popular political will, the women's march to Versailles changed the course of the French Revolution.

Reforming the Church and Clergy

As the National Assembly set about creating a constitution that would limit the authority of the king, it proclaimed Louis "the king of the French," instead of the king of France, a significant change that suggested that he embodied the sovereignty of his people. Alarmed by such changes, the king's brother, the count of Artois, went into exile after the October Days, and was soon followed by more than 20,000 other émigrés, most of whom were nobles, other people of means, and clergymen.

The Assembly turned its attention to reforming the Church. The decrees of August had ended the unpopular tithe payments to the Church, and now the Assembly looked to the Church's wealth to help resolve the state's mounting financial crisis. On October 10, Charles-Maurice de Talleyrand (1754–1838), who had entered the priesthood at the insistence of his family and had been consecrated bishop early in 1789, proposed that Church property become "national properties" (*biens nationaux*). After the Assembly narrowly passed Talleyrand's measure on November 2, some 400 million francs in Church property—roughly 10 percent of the nation's land—began to be offered for sale at auction. The primary beneficiaries of the sale were urban bourgeois and prosperous peasants who could marshal enough cash to buy the land put up for sale.

To raise funds immediately, the Assembly issued paper money (*assignats*), which was backed by the value of the Church lands. Although the law required everyone to accept *assignats* in payment of debts, their value fell dramatically because of a lack of public confidence, and those who used the *assignats* to purchase Church lands or pay debts received a windfall. Even poor peasants were thus able to reduce their debts with inflated currency. Among the consequences of the sale of Church lands, and later of lands owned by noble émigrés, was that more land was brought under cultivation by peasants. The clearing of trees and brush to make room for crops and small-scale farming also put increased pressure on the environment.

The Assembly then altered dramatically the status of the Church itself. On February 13, 1790, it decreed the abolition of the religious orders, deemed politically suspect by many reformers. On July 12, the National Assembly passed the Civil Constitution of the French Clergy. The Assembly redefined the relationship between the clergy and the state, creating, in effect, a national church. Bishops, who could now only publish pronouncements with the authorization of the government, were to be elected by local assemblies at the local level. Ten days later, the king reluctantly accepted these measures affecting the Church.

The Church became essentially a department of the state, which henceforth would pay clerical salaries, the expenses of worship, and poor relief. In November 1790, the National Assembly proclaimed that all priests had to swear an oath of loyalty to the Revolution, and thus accept the Civil Constitution of the French Clergy. His authority directly challenged, Pope Pius VI denounced the Declaration of the Rights of Man and Citizen in March, and in April 1791 he condemned the Civil Constitution of the French Clergy.

The Civil Constitution of the French Clergy altered the course of the Revolution, largely because it was widely resisted and contributed directly to the growth of a counter-revolutionary movement. Between one-half and two-thirds of parish priests refused the oath, and the Assembly prohibited these disloyal, "non-juring" priests from administering the Church sacraments. Nonetheless, many continued to do so with popular support. The issue of the oath split dioceses, parishes, and some households. In some provinces, violence mounted against "non-juring" priests; in others, refractory priests received popular support and protection. Such issues were no small matter, as many Catholics, Louis XVI among them, believed themselves obliged by faith to refuse to take sacraments from the "juring" clergy, that is, those who had taken the oath.

The Reforms of 1791

The Constitution of 1791 formalized the break with the Old Regime by substituting a constitutional monarchy for absolute rule. Although the king retained only the power of a suspending veto, he would still direct foreign policy and command the army. Acts of war or peace, however, required the Assembly's approval.

But France was far from being a republic. In sweeping away the Old Regime, the Revolution had redefined the relationship between the individual and the state by stripping away hereditary legal privileges. Although all citizens were to be equal before the law, when the Assembly abolished titles of hereditary nobility in June 1790, it carefully distinguished between "active" and "passive" citizens. Only "active citizens," men paying the equivalent of three days' wages in direct taxes, had the right to vote in indirect elections—they would vote for electors, wealthier men, who in turn would select representatives to a new legislature (see Map 12.1). Critics such as Marat and the populist orator Georges-Jacques Danton (1759–1794) denounced the restrictive franchise, claiming that the Assembly had merely replaced the privileged caste of the Old Regime with another by substituting the ownership of property for noble title as the criterion for political rights. Rousseau himself would have been ineligible to vote.

In Europe, religious discrimination still characterized many states. In Britain, English Dissenters and Catholics could not hold public office and were excluded from certain professions; in Hungary and the Catholic Rhineland, Protestants faced discrimination. Jews faced intolerance and persecution in much of Europe, excluded, for example, from certain occupations or forced to live in specially designated places. In some parts of Eastern Europe and Ukraine, they suffered violence as well.

Now the National Assembly granted citizenship and civil rights to Protestants and Jews by laws in 1790 and 1791 (Protestants had already been granted civil rights in 1787). The Assembly abolished guilds, declaring each person "free to do such business and to exercise such profession, art or trade as he may choose." It subsequently passed the Le Chapelier Law on June 14, 1791, prohibiting workmen from joining together to refuse to work for a master. This law was a victory for proponents of free trade. The Assembly also passed laws affecting the family: establishing civil marriage, lowering the age of consent for marriage, permitting divorce, and specifying that inheritances be divided equally among children.

The National Assembly abolished slavery in France, but not in the colonies. This exception led to a rebellion by free blacks on the Caribbean island of Hispaniola in October 1790 against the French sugar plantation owners, many of whom were nobles. It was led by Toussaint L'Ouverture (1743–1803), a former slave who had fought in the French army. The National Convention (which would replace the Assembly in September 1792) abolished slavery in the colonies in 1794, hoping that the freed slaves

MAP 12.1 FRANCE BEFORE AND AFTER 1789 The map on the left indicates the provinces and provincial capitals in France before the Revolution. The map on the right indicates the administrative districts (*départements*) created in France in 1790.

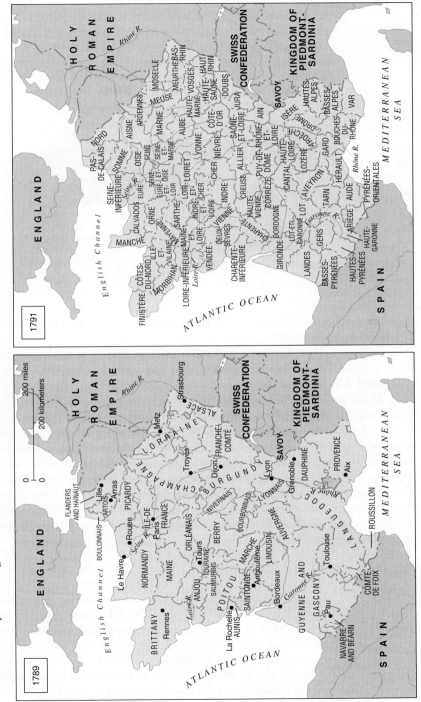

The Three Estates hammering out the next constitution.

would fight against Britain. Half of Hispaniola—modern-day Haiti—became the first free black state.

In 1791, the call for equal rights for women was first made explicit in France when Olympe de Gouges (1755–1793), the daughter of a butcher, published *The Rights of Women*. "The law," she wrote, "must be the expression of the general will; all female and male citizens must contribute either personally or through their representatives to its formation." Encouraging women to demand their natural rights—and thereby evidencing the influence of the Enlightenment—she called on the Assembly to acknowledge women's rights as mothers of citizens of the nation. She insisted on women's right to education and to control property within marriage and to initiate divorce proceedings. Olympe de Gouges defined the nation as "the union of Woman and Man," and suggested that men would remain unfree unless women were granted similar rights, stopping short of demanding full political rights for women.

Resistance and Revolution

On July 14, 1790, the first anniversary of the fall of the Bastille, an imposing Festival of General Federation took place on the Champ-de-Mars, a royal parade ground in Paris. But there was no revolutionary consensus in France. In the south, nobles had already begun to organize resistance against the Revolution, and militant Catholics attacked Protestants, who tended to support the Revolution. By the summer of 1791, as the Assembly promulgated its constitution, open resistance to the Revolution had broken out in parts of the south and west, and in Alsace.

Such resistance prompted further calls for even more radical changes. Some of the revolutionaries, who did not accept the distinction between active and passive citizens, called for more democratic participation in political life. From where did this democratic thrust come? The monarchical state had rested on an intertwining network of groups—each with a set of privileges—at virtually every level of society. These included judicial, professional, administrative, and clerical groups, ranging from provincial Estates to artisanal guilds. Participatory and sometimes even democratic procedures within such bodies (or *corps*) may have instilled a tendency toward democracy that affected the course of the Revolution and pushed France toward a republic.

The first clubs were established by political factions among the deputies to the National Assembly. Some of the Assembly's most radical members split off to form the Jacobin Club, so-called because it met in the house of the religious order of the Jacobins. The Cordeliers Club brought together the radicals of Paris, while supporters of the cause of constitutional monarchy, whose members broke with the Jacobins in July 1791, gathered at the Club of the Feuillants. Monarchists formed royalist clubs. Moreover, some women began their own political clubs, such as the Club of Knitters, or joined the Fraternal Society of Patriots of Both Sexes. By 1793, there were at least 5,000 clubs in France. During the first years of the Revolution, however, there was little in France that was not politi-cal, and the political clubs were not the only place where political debate occurred. In Paris, there were also meetings of neighborhood "sections," which had first been defined as electoral districts for the convocation of the Estates-General.

Parisian revolutionaries became increasingly known as *sans-culottes*. They defined themselves by what they were without—the fancy knee britches, or *culottes,* which were associated with the aristocracy. The sans-culottes were shopkeep-ers, artisans, and laborers who were not opposed to private property, but who stood against unearned property, and especially against those people who seemed to have too much property, or who did not work for a living. They demanded that a maximum price be placed on bread, which alone absorbed more than half of the earnings of the average working family. Sans-culottes were for "the people," as they put it. They were defined by their political behavior. Even aris-tocrats could be sans-culottes if they supported the Revolution. Likewise, laborers or peasants could be called "aristocrats" if they seemed to

A female sans-culotte.

King Louis XVI wearing the Phrygian cap.

oppose the Revolution. In a world in which symbols played a crucial political role, sans-culottes could be identified by the Phrygian cap, a symbol of freedom drawn from the Roman Republic—close-fitting, red in color, with a tricolor emblem—in contrast to the three-cornered hat that had been worn by urban social elites. The language of the sans-culottes also quickly indicated who they were; they called everyone "citizen" and used the familiar (*tu* and never *vous*), egalitarian form of address. The political ideal of the sans-culottes was that popular sovereignty had to be practiced every day in direct democracy, in revolutionary clubs and in the sections.

The Flight to Varennes

Fearing the growing violence of the Revolution and counting on the support of the other monarchs of Europe, Louis XVI and his family tried to flee France in June 1791. The king's goal was to throw his support behind the foreign enemies of the Revolution and return to France to revoke the concessions that he had made. Apprehended by the National Guard in Varennes, the royal family was prevented from continuing their journey into exile and freedom.

The king's attempt to flee turned public sentiment further against him, and strengthened support for a republic. The day after his flight, the Cordeliers Club called for the establishment of a republic, but the majority of the Assembly feared civil war. On July 17, 1791, at the Champ-de-Mars in Paris, people came to sign (or put their "X" on) a petition resting on the "Altar of the Fatherland" that called on the National Assembly to replace the king "by all constitutional means." The National Guard opened fire, killing fifty people. Bailly, the moderate mayor of Paris, and Lafayette, the commander of the National Guard in Paris, declared martial law. However, even Louis XVI's formal acceptance of the constitution on September 14, 1791, could not stem the popular tide against the monarchy.

WAR AND THE SECOND REVOLUTION

The Revolution now entered a new, more radical phase. The king's flight seriously weakened the constitutional monarchists within the Assembly.

(*Left*) Georges–Jacques Danton. (*Right*) Maximilien Robespierre.

The leaders of the Parisian population—Danton, Marat, and Maximilien Robespierre—were Jacobins who had given up on the idea that a constitutional monarchy could adequately guarantee the liberties of the people. Elections brought to Paris a Legislative Assembly, which met on October 1, 1791. It replaced the Constituent Assembly, which had dissolved following the proclamation of the constitution the previous month. Republicans—now identified with the "left" as monarchists were with the "right," due to the location of the seats each group occupied in the Assembly—became a majority in March 1792.

In the meantime, French émigrés at the Austrian and Prussian courts were encouraging foreign intervention to restore Louis XVI to full monarchical authority. The republican followers of Jacques-Pierre Brissot (1754–1793), former radical pamphleteer and police spy as well as a flamboyant orator, called for a war to free Europe from the tyranny of monarchy and nobility. The members of this faction became known as the Girondins because many were from the district of Gironde, in which the major Atlantic port of Bordeaux is located. Under Girondin leadership, the Assembly's proclamations took on a more aggressive tone. The French declaration of war against Austria led to the Second Revolution, the formation of a republic, and, ultimately, a Jacobin-dominated dictatorship, which imposed the "Terror."

Reactions to the French Revolution in Europe

The French Revolution had a considerable impact on the rest of Europe. The early work of the National Assembly, particularly the abolition of feudal rights and the establishment of a constitutional monarchy found considerable favor among educated people in Britain, the Netherlands, and some German and Italian states. Some lawyers and merchants in other lands applauded, for example, measures taken to reduce the independence of the Catholic Church. The promulgation of the principles of national sovereignty and self-determination, however, threatened the monarchies of Europe. The threat posed by the French Revolution brought about a rapprochement between Austria and Prussia, rivals for domination in Central Europe, as well as a wary alliance between Great Britain and Russia.

The Prussian government's first reaction to the Revolution had been to try to subvert the alliance between France and Austria and to undermine Austrian authority in the Southern Netherlands (Belgium). In Vienna, the Habsburg emperor Leopold II was initially preoccupied with demands from the Hungarian nobility for more power. In 1789, a rebellion drove Austrian forces out of the Southern Netherlands and led to the establishment of a republic that survived only until Austrian troops returned in force in 1790.

In London, some radical Whigs greeted with enthusiasm the news of the fall of the Bastille and the first steps toward constitutional monarchy in France. But in 1790, the British writer Edmund Burke attacked the Revolution in *Reflections on the Revolution in France.* He contended that the abstract rationalism of the Enlightenment threatened the historic evolution of nations by undermining monarchy, established churches, and what he considered the "natural" ruling elite.

The Englishman Thomas Paine (1737–1809; see Chapter 11) wrote pamphlets denouncing monarchical rule and unwarranted privilege. *The Rights of Man* (1791–1792) defended the Revolution against Burke's relentless attack. Political societies supporting the Revolution, in which artisans played a major role, sprang up in Britain during the early 1790s. A small group of English women also enthusiastically supported the Revolution. Mary Wollstonecraft (1759–1797), a teacher and writer, greeted the Revolution with optimism, traveling to France to view events firsthand. Angered that the Assembly limited the right to education to men only, she published *Vindication of the Rights of Woman* (1792), the first book in Britain demanding the right for women to vote and hold elected office.

The rulers of the other European states felt threatened by the proclamation of universal principles embodied in the Declaration of the Rights of Man and Citizen. The Revolution also posed the threat of French expansion, now on behalf of carrying the revolutionary principles of "liberty, equality, and fraternity" to other lands. Besieged by exiles from France eager to tell tales of their suffering, the rulers of Prussia, Austria, Naples, and Piedmont

Olympe de Gouges (*left*), whose book *The Rights of Women* was published in France in 1791. It detailed the notion of equal rights that Mary Wollstonecraft (*right*) would take up the next year in Britain with the publication of her *Vindication of the Rights of Woman.*

undertook the suppression of Jacobin sympathizers in their states. In Britain, the seeming threat of foreign invasion helped affirm British national identity (see Chapter 11). Popular respect for the British monarchy and probably also for nobles soared as anti-French and anti-Catholic feelings came to the fore. Pitt the Younger's government lashed out at the development of popular politics in Britain, suspending the freedoms of association, assembly, and the press, as well as the writ of *habeas corpus*. "Coercion Acts" facilitated the arrest of those advocating parliamentary reform.

Thus, Louis XVI's virtual imprisonment in the Tuileries Palace in Paris and the thunderous speeches in the Assembly proclaiming the necessity of "a war of peoples against kings" worried the crowned heads of Europe. On August 27, 1791, Emperor Leopold II of the Holy Roman Empire (brother of Marie-Antoinette, who had not seen him in twenty-five years) and King Frederick William II of Prussia promulgated the Declaration of Pilnitz. It expressed their concern about the plight of the French monarchy and stated the common interest of both sovereigns in seeing order restored in France. Despite Robespierre's speeches warning the deputies that the Revolution must first deal with its enemies within France before waging war abroad, the Assembly, egged on by General Charles François Dumouriez (1739–1823), minister of foreign affairs, in April 1792 declared war on Austria. The stated reason was fear that an Austrian invasion from the Southern Netherlands was imminent. The declaration of war soon seemed a rash move, as the army had been devastated by the desertion of two-thirds of its officers (85 percent of its officers had been nobles before the Revolution). Moreover, Prussia soon joined with Austria in fighting the French. The early stages of the war produced French defeats at the hands of Austrian and Prussian armies.

A Second Revolution

The war sealed the fate of the monarchy and the royal family. As France faced the possibility of foreign invasion by Austria and Prussia, the popular fear that aristocrats and clergymen were betraying the Revolution brought down the monarchy. Early defeats on the northern frontier by Austrian troops and soaring bread prices (in part due to the requisitioning of food for the army) compounded popular anxiety and led to a new revolutionary groundswell, particularly in Paris.

In early April 1792, women marched through the capital demanding the right to bear arms. On June 20, a crowd stormed into the Tuileries Palace and threatened the royal family, shouting, "Tremble, tyrants! Here come the sans-culottes!" Strident calls for the end of the monarchy echoed in clubs and in the sections. On July 11, the Assembly officially proclaimed the *patrie,* or nation, to be "in danger," calling on all citizens to rally against the enemies of liberty within as well as outside of France. The Assembly encouraged the sections to admit the "passive" citizens who had previously been excluded because they had failed to meet tax requirements. Troops from Marseille, among volunteers called up to defend the front, sang a new revolutionary song, "The Marseillaise," penned by Rouget de Lisle. It became the anthem of the Revolution. In the meantime, the Jacobins pressed their attack against the monarchy.

In the Brunswick Manifesto (July 1792), Austria and Prussia warned the French that they would be severely punished if the royal family were harmed. All but one of the forty-eight sections of Paris responded by demanding that the king be immediately deposed. Popular discontent and Jacobin agitation came together in August. A radical committee overthrew the city council and established a revolutionary authority, the Commune of Paris. On August 10, sans-culottes from the Paris sections attacked the Tuileries Palace. The invaders killed 600 of the king's Swiss Guards and servants after they had surrendered. The royal family escaped and found protection in the quarters of the Legislative Assembly. The Assembly immediately proclaimed the monarchy suspended and ordered the royal family's imprisonment.

The popular revolution doomed France's first experiment in constitutional monarchy. On September 2, 1792, a Prussian army entered French territory and captured the eastern fortress town of Verdun. The proximity of the allied armies and the fear of betrayal at home led to the imprisonment in Paris of many people suspected of plotting against the Revolution. When a rumor circulated that the prisoners were planning to break out of prison and attack the army, mobs dragged the prisoners from their cells and killed them. During these September Massacres, more than 1,200 people, includ-

The September Massacre of 1792 in the abbey of Saint-Germain-des-Prés in Paris.

ing 225 priests, perished at the hands of crowds who acted as judges, juries, and executioners.

But just as Paris seemed vulnerable to foreign invasion, a ragtag army of regular soldiers and sans-culottes stopped the Prussian and Austrian advance with effective artillery barrages on September 20, 1792, near the windmill of Valmy, near Châlons-sur-Marne. The German poet Johann Wolfgang von Goethe, amazed by the victory of such ordinary people over a highly trained professional army, wrote, "From this time and place a new epoch is beginning." An officer trained under the Old Regime called the resultant warfare of the revolutionary armies a "hellish tactic," which saw "fifty thousand savage beasts foaming at the mouth like cannibals, hurling themselves at top speed upon soldiers whose courage has been excited by no passion."

The Revolution had been saved by the same people who had first made it. Delegates to a new assembly called the National Convention were selected by universal male suffrage in elections. The Jacobins dominated. The delegates arrived in Paris to draft a republican constitution. Their first act was unanimously to abolish the monarchy and proclaim the republic on September 21, 1792, even before news of Valmy had been learned.

The revolutionary armies of proud, loyal citizen-soldiers, however badly armed, pushed Prussian troops back across the Rhine and entered Mainz in October. On November 6, Dumouriez defeated the Austrians at Jémappes in the Austrian Netherlands, which was soon controlled by the French revolutionary army (see Map 12.2). To supply French troops, arms manufacturers turned out 45,000 guns in one year, and a Parisian factory produced 30,000 pounds of gunpowder every day.

MAP 12.2 EXPANSION OF REVOLUTIONARY FRANCE, 1792–1799 The map indicates French revolutionary army offensives and foreign anti-revolutionary army offensives. It also shows areas annexed by the French, areas occupied by the French, and dependent republics established by revolutionary France.

Emboldened by these unexpected military successes, the National Convention on November 19, 1792, promised "fraternity and assistance to all peoples who want to recover their liberty." French troops captured Frankfurt and occupied much of the Rhineland. The Convention also declared the outright annexation of the Alpine province of Savoy, belonging to the Kingdom of Sardinia, and the Mediterranean town of Nice, captured at the end of September. They declared them within the "natural frontiers" of France—a claim that contradicted the principles of popular sovereignty and self-determination contained in the annexation decrees themselves. On December 15, 1792, the Convention abolished all feudal dues and tithes in those territories occupied by French armies.

The governments of Britain and the Dutch Republic viewed the occupation of the Austrian Netherlands as a great threat. When it appeared that both states were considering joining Austria and Prussia in taking action against France, the Convention on February 1, 1793, declared war on Britain and the Dutch Republic. Spain and the Kingdoms of Sardinia and Naples joined this First Coalition against France.

When correspondence between Louis XVI and the Austrian government was discovered, his trial became inevitable. Accused of treason, the king defended himself with grace and dignity. He called on the Convention to look after his family as he had tried to watch over those of France. But with the words "one cannot reign innocently" ringing in the hall, the Convention condemned the king to death. On the morning of January 21, Louis XVI was guillotined. The huge throng roared its approval as the executioner held up the severed royal head, symbol of the Old Regime, for all to see.

As the Convention and the more radical Paris Commune vied for authority, the French Republic, still at war, began to split apart. The Girondins and the Jacobins quarreled bitterly. The Girondins were popularly identified with the economic liberalism that characterized the port cities and with the desire to carry the Revolution aggressively beyond the frontiers of France. Opposed to centralizing power in Paris, they wanted a significant

The execution of Louis XVI.

degree of local political control. The deputies of the far left, principally the Jacobins and their followers, sat on the raised side of the Tuileries Hall where the Convention met. The far left became known as "the Mountain" (their followers the *Montagnards*). The political center became known as "the Plain." Backed by the Parisian sans-culottes, the Jacobins insisted on the necessity of centralizing authority in the capital to save the Revolution from internal subversion and foreign armies. The Girondins, more moderate, believed that the Revolution had gone far enough. The Jacobins accused them of secretly supporting the monarchy and demanded swift punishment for traitors.

From the point of view of the Jacobins, those who were not for them were against the Revolution. The sense of vulnerability and insecurity was heightened by reverses in the field. The armies of the First Coalition defeated the French in the Austrian Netherlands in March 1793. Dumouriez then betrayed the Revolution, preparing to march his soldiers to Paris to put Louis XVI's son on the throne as Louis XVII. When his army refused to follow him, Dumouriez fled across the border to join the Austrians and other émigrés. In the meantime, the allies recaptured the left bank of the Rhine River.

Counter-Revolution

The Counter-Revolution began in regions where religious practice still seemed strong and where the Civil Constitution of the French Clergy had met with considerable resistance (see Map 12.3). A full-scale insurrection against the Revolution began in March 1793. This revolt in the western part of France became known as the Vendée, after the name of one of the most insurrectionary districts (the old provinces having been divided into *départements* in 1790). In August 1793, the revolutionary government decreed mass conscription, the *levée en masse,* which initiated the concept of the nation at arms: "Young people will go to battle; married men will forge arms and transport supplies; women will make tents, uniforms, and serve in the hospitals; children will pick rags; old men will have themselves carried to public squares, to inspire the courage of the warriors, and to preach hatred of kings and the unity of the Republic." The unpopularity of military conscription in defense of the republic also generated resistance.

South of the Loire River, the counter-revolutionary forces principally emerged from the relatively isolated bocage, or hedgerow country, where the old noble and clerical elites had been relatively unaffected by the economic changes of the past few decades, specifically the expansion of the market economy. In Brittany, which had enjoyed a relatively light tax burden during the Old Regime, the revolutionary government was hated for having ended that privilege, thereby increasing taxes. Both sides fought with a brutality, including mass executions and systematic pillage, that recalled the Thirty

MAP 12.3 THE COUNTER–REVOLUTION The map indicates areas of federalism and counter-revolutionary activity, including major uprisings.

Years' War (1618–1648) in Central Europe. In insurrectionary areas during 1793–1794, perhaps a quarter of the population perished, as many as 250,000 people, in part because the revolutionary troops, facing guerilla warfare, saw local civilians as potential threats.

The Terror

Faced with foreign invasion and civil insurgency, the Jacobins further centralized government authority and implemented the "Terror" against those considered enemies of the Revolution. The Convention set aside a planned Constitution of 1793 (which was to have replaced the Constitution of 1791).

The rights of the accused were limited, and new special courts prosecuted anyone considered disloyal to the republic. On March 19, 1793, the Convention passed a law permitting the immediate trial of armed insurgents without a jury. The Jacobin-dominated Convention established a Committee of Public Safety of nine and then twelve members, which gradually assumed more and more power as it oversaw the Terror. The Convention also decreed a special war tax, including a forced levy on wealthy people, and in May 1793 imposed the "Maximum"—a maximum price on grain. These measures of centralization and government interference in the economy led to an irreversible break between the Jacobins, who believed in state controls, and the Girondins, who believed in economic freedom.

Military requisitions of foodstuffs accentuated hardship. Poor people rioted against the high price of grain. In Paris, the Society of Revolutionary Republican Women took to the streets, demanding laws against hoarding and calling for women to be granted citizenship. A group called the *enragés* (the "enraged") demanded that bakers be penalized if they charged more than the maximum price for bread.

In June, pushed on by crowds from the radical sections of Paris, the Convention expelled twenty-nine Girondin deputies, accusing them of supporting hoarders, and it ordered the arrest of some of them. Insurgents in Toulon turned over half of the French fleet to the British. In July, Charlotte Corday, a royalist noblewoman, stabbed Marat to death in his bathtub. Tax revenue and foreign trade fell by half. *Assignats,* more of which had rolled off the government presses as the financial crisis continued, plunged further in value.

Two young radical Jacobin leaders strode forward to take charge of the Terror. Louis Antoine Saint-Just (1767–1794), a precocious, icy young deputy whose mother had once had him incarcerated for running off with the family silver, waged war on royalists, hoarders, and Girondins. "Those who make revolutions by halves dig their own grave," he warned.

Jacques-Louis David's *The Death of Marat.*

Maximilien Robespierre (1758–1794) emerged as the leading figure on the Committee of Public Safety. He knew that the Mountain drew its support from the sans-culottes, some of whom supported the Terror. But he also believed that the popular movement remained a threat to the orderly transformation of political life in France. Historians have offered interpretations of Robespierre that range from the view that he was a popular democrat who saved the essence of the Revolution from counter-revolutionaries to the suggestion that he was actually a precursor of twentieth-century totalitarianism.

Robespierre was the son and grandson of lawyers from the northern town of Arras. After his irresponsible father abandoned his family, Robespierre depended on scholarships for his schooling. At age eleven, he was chosen to read an address in Latin to the royal family at his school in Paris. It was raining and the royal family, it was said, without acknowledging the young student, ordered their driver onward. The royal coach splashed Robespierre with mud.

After completing his law degree, Robespierre defended a number of poor clients, including a man unjustly accused of stealing from an abbey. After he was elected to the third estate, Robespierre gradually established a reputation in Paris for his well-organized and thoughtful but colorless speeches. Contemporaries noted the prissiness of the impeccably dressed, slight man with very pale skin and chestnut hair always perfectly powdered. A favorite of the Parisian sans-culottes, the man they nicknamed "the Incorruptible" called in 1793 for "a single will" of the nation to save the Revolution.

Insurrections by supporters of the Girondins against the Jacobins and the authority of the Convention broke out in Lyon, Marseille, Bordeaux, and Caen, where merchants and lawyers played prominent roles in failed "federalist revolts" against centralized revolutionary authority emanating from Paris. Lyon fell to Jacobin troops on October 9, 1793, and bloody reprisals followed.

The "Law of Suspects" promulgated by the Convention in September deprived those accused of crimes against the nation of most of their remaining rights. The Convention banned clubs and popular societies of women. Olympe de Gouges was among the Girondins guillotined. Marie-Antoinette, though hardly a feminist, also went to the scaffold.

The Jacobins were so intent on destroying the Old Regime and building a new political world that they instituted a new calendar in October 1793. The old calendar gave way to a new republican calendar based upon "weeks," or cycles of ten days, and "months" taking their names from more secular notions of the changing of the seasons (such as *Germinal*, meaning "the budding," *Ventôse*, meaning "windy," and so on). September 22, 1792, the first year of the republic, became, retroactively, day one of the "year I."

The Jacobins adopted new revolutionary symbols to take the place of Old Regime symbols and to help maintain revolutionary enthusiasm. Following the execution of Louis XVI, the revolutionaries chose a female image for liberty and the republic, which was ironic in light of their denial of political rights to women. The female image of the republic appears gentle, non-threatening, and virtuous, representing the abstract virtues of liberty, popular sovereignty, community, and nation. Contemporaries contrasted republican virtue with the abuses of power that seemed to have characterized the Old Regime. They did so even as Jacobin representatives of the Revolution imposed their will wherever they were resisted in the provinces.

During the "year II" (which began in September 1793), radical revolutionaries undertook an ambitious campaign of "de-christianization," a war on religious institutions and symbols. They closed down churches and removed crosses standing in public places. The campaign failed, unable to overcome centuries of firmly implanted beliefs and traditions, even among many people who supported the Revolution. It also turned many clergy who had accepted the Civil Constitution away from the Revolution, generating further resistance.

Outside of Paris, "representatives on mission," armed with dictatorial authority in the name of the Convention, tried to maintain order. They worked with local "surveillance committees" and "revolutionary tribunals" of Jacobins. Some of these revolutionary officials sent counter-revolutionaries to the guillotine. "Revolutionary armies" of artisans and day laborers guarded requisitioned provisions for the military and oversaw the melting down of church bells for war use.

Yet the Terror was never uniformly implemented. Between 11,000 and 18,000 people perished at the hands of the Committee of Public Safety (a fraction, by comparison, of the deaths that had resulted from the Thirty

A Revolutionary Tribunal during the Terror.

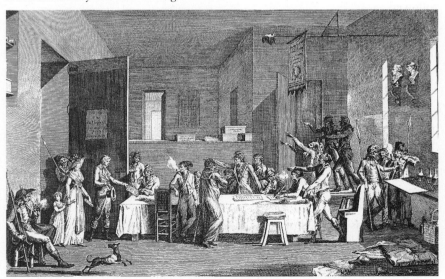

Years' War or the American Civil War). About 300,000 royalists, Girondins, or other "enemies of the Revolution" were imprisoned for some period during the Terror. About 15 percent of those killed were nobles or clergy. Thus, nobles and clergy suffered disproportionately in terms of their number in the population as a whole (5 to 8 percent). However, artisans and peasants constituted by far the largest number of those dispatched by the revolutionary tribunals. The majority of these were arrested near the northern and eastern frontiers that had been invaded by foreign armies or in the counter-revolutionary west where civil war raged. During the winter of 1793–1794, perhaps as many as several thousand prisoners—including priests and nuns—captured from the counter-revolutionary armies of the Vendée were taken out into the swirling waters of the Loire River in boats that had holes bored in them and drowned at the orders of a cruel revolutionary official. In all, several thousand people perished.

In the meantime, the tide of the war had turned in favor of the aggressive French armies. Significant French victories on the battlefield undercut the argument that the Terror was necessary because of the immediate external threat to the republic. A French army defeated the Austrians in the Austrian Netherlands in June 1794, forcing them out of Belgium. Another French force reached the Rhine River and captured Mainz. A third French army recaptured Savoy from the Kingdom of Sardinia. The Spanish army retreated across the Pyrenees Mountains.

The Terror then struck the *enragés* leaders in March 1794 after they demanded even more economic controls and an intensification of the "de-christianization" campaign. They were brought before the Revolutionary Tribunal of Paris, condemned, and guillotined. The Committee of Public Safety then went after Danton and his followers, who believed that the Terror was no longer necessary, and thus had been labeled the "Indulgents." They too were condemned and guillotined. Real and imagined conspiracies provided the justification for the Terror, which now seemed without end. "Who will be next?" was whispered among even those loyal to the most radical members of the Committee of Public Safety. In May, Robespierre survived an assassination attempt.

Robespierre sought to establish a secularized "Cult of the Supreme Being" that would serve as a "constant reminder of justice" to bind the people to the new values of republicanism. With the elimination of the *enragés* and Danton and many of his followers, Robespierre devoted his energies to creating a "Republic of Virtue." Early in June 1794, the republic celebrated the "Festival of Reason." The cathedral of Notre Dame in Paris became a "temple of reason." A popular female opera singer, dressed as Liberty, wearing a Phrygian cap and holding a pike, bowed before the flame of reason. The painter Jacques-Louis David constructed huge statues of monsters like Anarchy and Atheism made of pasteboard. After Robespierre set fire to them, a statue of Wisdom rose out of the ashes.

The Terror took on a momentum of its own. Saint-Just warned, "We must punish not merely traitors, but also the indifferent." The Jacobins arrested the Marquis de Condorcet (1743–1794) for alleged counter-revolutionary activity. Condorcet, an influential philosophe of the late Enlightenment, had been elected to the Assembly in 1791. He believed that all people should have a voice in approving acts of government, albeit indirectly, and that all citizens should be equal before the law. He had campaigned against the death penalty and slavery, and he defended political equality and the rights of women. Condorcet died of apoplexy—or committed suicide—in his cell in the spring of 1794, shortly before he was to be executed. The Revolution seemed to have turned on and destroyed the enlightened reason that had arguably helped bring it about.

THE FINAL STAGES OF THE REVOLUTION

Moderate Jacobins and other members of the Convention, fearing that they might be next in line to be purged, overthrew the Jacobin dictatorship. They established a new government called the Directory, which ended the Terror. Caught between staunch Jacobins on the left and monarchists on the right, the period of the Directory was marked by great political instability, ongoing wars abroad, and economic hardship at home. Although the Directory consolidated some of the gains of the Revolution, it too would be overthrown by conspirators led by the Abbé Sieyès and one of the rising stars of the revolutionary army, Napoleon Bonaparte.

Thermidor

The Revolutionary Tribunal of Paris used new powers granted by the Committee of Public Safety in June 1794 to send 1,376 people to their deaths over a period of six weeks. Afraid that they would be next on Robespierre's list, moderates in the Convention began to plot against Robespierre and his allies. They were led by Paul Barras (1755–1829), a follower of Danton, and Joseph Fouché (1758–1820). On July 27, 1794 (the 9th of Thermidor), Robespierre haltingly addressed the Convention, calling for one more purge. But, anticipating his own downfall, Robespierre also murmured, "I ask for death." That night, Robespierre and Saint-Just were arrested at the virtually unguarded town hall of Paris. Robespierre attempted suicide, shattering his jaw with a shot.

Robespierre and the others were executed without trial, their fate as swift and pitiless as that of the Terror's victims. They were followed to the scaffold by more than a hundred of their allies. In the provinces, particularly in the south, the revenge against the Jacobins by their enemies was swift and brutal. Lazare Carnot (1753–1823), a talented military engineer, brilliant administrator ("the organizer of victory"), and one of the twelve members of the Committee of Public Safety, survived because he had opposed Robespierre. Moreover, the continuing war effort desperately required his administrative talent.

After dismantling the Paris Commune, the victors of Thermidor—the name taken from the period in the revolutionary calendar in which Robespierre fell—set about establishing a new national government. Order was only slowly and incompletely restored in the countryside. The Thermidorians greatly reduced the powers of the Committee of Public Safety on July 31, 1794, and then abolished it completely. In November 1794, Jacobin Clubs were banned.

The Directory: Politics and Society

In 1795 the Thermidorians produced a constitution that created a bicameral (two-house) legislative assembly and a collective executive of five directors. The latter provided the name "the Directory" for this period of the Revolution. The two assemblies included the Council of the Ancients (250 members), which discussed and voted on legislation proposed by the second assembly, the Council of Five Hundred. Two-thirds of the members of the new councils were elected from among the members of the existing Convention. The two councils elected the five directors who formed the collective executive authority, or Directorate. Beginning in 1797, one-third of the members of each council and one of the five directors were to be replaced each year.

People with property benefited from the Thermidorian reaction. By the Constitution of 1795, all male taxpayers could vote, but they selected electoral assemblies for which only about 30,000 men were eligible, a smaller group than in the indirect elections of 1789–1791. But although about 2 million men could vote (out of some 7 million men of voting age), the system of indirect election favored the selection of the wealthiest citizens to serve in the assemblies.

The period of the Directory was marked by a decided turn against the asceticism associated with Robespierre's Republic of Virtue. The *jeunesse dorée,* or gilded youth, drawn from the bourgeoisie and old nobility, set the social and cultural tone of the day. Wearing square collars and fancy clothes, wealthy young men smashed busts of Marat. The red-colored symbols of the sans-culottes—such as the Phrygian cap—quickly disappeared. Women who could afford to do so wore long flowing white robes of opulence and sensuality, with plunging necklines that would have horrified Robespierre. The familiar (*tu*) form of address, identified with section and club meetings, gave way to the formal *vous* more characteristic of the Old Regime. Crowds in which women played a prominent part demanded that churches be reopened. Boisterous social events amused the middle class; among them the macabre "Dance of the Victims," a ball to which only those with a relative who had perished in the Terror could be admitted. Some revelers turned up with their

The return of high society during the Directory.

hair cut away from the back of their neck, mimicking the final haircut of those about to be sent to the guillotine.

Under the Directory, the comforts of the wealthy, some of whom had made their fortunes during the Revolution (by buying Church lands or supplying the military), contrasted sharply with the deprivations of the poor. The economy lay in shambles. The winter of 1795 was cruelly harsh. The abolition of the Maximum spelled the end of cheap bread, which rose in price by thirteen times that spring in Paris. The price of basic commodities soared. Near Paris, people scrambled to eat the carcasses of dead army horses, and in mountainous areas people searched for berries and edible roots while trying to stay warm. Peasants suffered the military requisition of food supplies.

Instability

The Directory may have ended the Terror, but it brought neither stability nor peace to France, despite peace agreements concluded with Prussia in April 1795. Prussia accepted the French annexation of the left bank of the Rhine River, the Austrian Netherlands, and the Dutch United Provinces (which became the "Batavian Republic"). In the meantime, French armies continued to press forward against the Austrian armies in Central Europe and Italy. Mass desertion and heavy casualties drastically reduced the size of the French army, which, after reaching a million men in the summer of 1794, fell to less than 500,000 a year later.

War compounded social and political instability in 1795. That spring, the Directory repressed two small popular demonstrations by crowds demanding a return to controls on the price of bread. Encouraged by the Convention's move to the right, royalists also tried to seize power. The king's son had died in a Paris prison in June 1795, and so the count of Provence, Louis XVI's brother, was now heir to the throne. An army of nobles supported by the British landed at Quiberon Bay in Brittany on June 27, but French forces turned back the invaders with ease. On October 5, 1795, royalists attempted an insurrection in Paris, where they found support in the more prosperous districts. The government called in Napoleon Bonaparte (1769–1821), a young Corsican general, who turned away the insurgents with a "whiff of grapeshot."

Instability continued. François-Noël Babeuf (1760–1797), who was called Gracchus, plotted to overthrow the Directory. Influenced by Rousseau and espousing social egalitarianism and the common ownership of land, Babeuf concluded that a small group of committed revolutionaries could seize power if they were tightly organized and had the support of the poor. Babeuf organized the "Conspiracy of the Equals," finding support among a handful of Parisian artisans and shopkeepers. In May 1796, Babeuf and his friends were arrested; they were guillotined a year later after a trial. The Directory took advantage of the discovery of this plot to purge Jacobins once again.

Caught between the intransigent, dogmatic followers of Robespierre and the Jacobins on the left and the royalists on the right, and lacking effective and charismatic civilian leaders, the Directory's difficult tightrope act grew more precarious in an atmosphere of uncertainty, intrigue, and rumors of coups d'état.

In 1797, elections returned many royalists to the Council of Five Hundred. Fearful that they might press for peace with France's enemies in the hope of obtaining a restoration of the monarchy, the Directory government annulled the election results. The coup d'état of the 18th Fructidor (September 4, 1797) eliminated two of the directors, including Carnot. In May of the next year, the directors refused to allow recently elected deputies to take their seats on the Council of Five Hundred.

For all of its failures, the Directory did provide France with its second apprenticeship in representative government. The Constitution of 1795 was an important transition between the political system of the Old Regime, based primarily upon monarchical absolutism and noble privilege, and modern representative government grounded in the sanctity of property.

The Directory had rejected cautious British suggestions that a workable peace might be forged without France having to give up its conquests of the Rhineland and the Austrian Netherlands. Perhaps fearful that a more bellicose ministry in Britain might replace that of William Pitt the Younger if such a peace were signed, the French fought on.

Napoleon Bonaparte, who had swept aside the royalist insurrection, now commanded the Army of Italy, checking in with Paris only when it suited him. His armies overwhelmed the Austrian troops in northern Italy. The Treaty of Campo Formio (October 17, 1797) left France the dominant foreign power in Italy. This victory, and Napoleon's boldly independent diplomatic negotiations in the Italian campaigns, made him the toast of Paris. The Austrians joined the Prussians in recognizing French absorption of the left bank of the Rhine River and annexation of the Austrian Netherlands. Reorganized in July 1797 as the Cisalpine Republic, much of the north of Italy became a feeble pawn of France.

Despite these victories, years of war had exhausted the French nation and damaged the economy. France's financial situation deteriorated even further. Inflation was rampant, and the collection of taxes was sporadic at best. *Assignats* were now virtually worthless. Many bourgeois were dissatisfied, having lost money when the Directory cancelled more than half of the national debt in 1797.

In May 1798, Napoleon sailed with an army to Egypt, over which Turkey was sovereign; he hoped to strike at British interests in India. Fearing that France sought to break apart the Ottoman Empire and extend its interests in an area Russia had always wanted to dominate, Russia allied with Britain. Austria also joined the alliance, which became the Second Coalition (1799–1802). Austria hoped to undo the Treaty of Campo Formio and to prevent further French expansion in Italy, where French forces had sent the pope into exile and established a Roman Republic.

The combined strength of the Coalition powers for the moment proved too much for the overextended French armies in Italy. In Switzerland, a combined Russian and Austrian army defeated a French force. When Irish rebels rose up against British rule in 1798, France sent an invasion force to aid the insurgents, in the hope of launching an invasion of England. After the defeat of the Irish insurgents and French troops who landed ashore, a French fleet attempting to land more soldiers was defeated off the coast. British troops crushed a series of Irish rebellions in a bloody struggle in which 30,000 people were killed, and the British navy captured one of the French ships and turned back the rest.

In the meantime, coalition members quarreled over strategy and eventual goals. Russian Tsar Paul (ruled 1796–1801) withdrew from the Second Coalition in October 1799, as he was irritated with the British for insisting that the Royal Navy had the right to stop and search any vessel on the seas.

The Eighteenth Brumaire

The wily Abbé Sieyès (who once replied "I survived" when asked what he had done during the Revolution) became a director in the spring of 1799. He believed France needed a government with stronger executive authority.

Because the role of the army had grown enormously, he concluded that it would emerge as the arbiter of France's political future. In the face of endemic instability, Sieyès decided in 1799 to overthrow the Directory. The go-between was Talleyrand, the foreign minister. The career of Talleyrand provides another remarkable example of revolutionary survival; a detractor once claimed that Brie cheese was "the only king to whom he has been loyal." Sieyès contacted General Napoleon Bonaparte. On November 9, 1799 (the 18th Brumaire), General Bonaparte announced to the hastily convened councils that another Jacobin conspiracy had been uncovered and that a new constitution had to be framed to provide France with a stronger executive authority. The deputies were justly dubious. Some demanded his immediate arrest. Napoleon's response was incoherent and ineffective, but the quick thinking of his brother, Lucien, president of the lower assembly, saved Bonaparte from one of his few moments of indecision. Lucien rejected the call for a vote to outlaw Napoleon, and he ordered troops to evict members who opposed him. Those who remained delegated complete power to Sieyès and General Bonaparte. Would Napoleon, whose rise to power would have been almost unthinkable without the French Revolution, be the heir of the French Revolution, or its destroyer?

A contemporary British caricature of the 18th Brumaire: "The Corsican Crocodile dissolving the Council of Frogs!!!"

Perspectives on the French Revolution

The French Revolution, which began in Paris, swept across Europe. In France, it marked a significant break with the past, although, to be sure, important continuities from the Old Regime helped shape the modern world. In other countries, too, the Revolution effected major changes. These included in some places the abolition of feudalism, curtailment of clerical privileges, and establishment of a more centralized governmental structure. But while some people welcomed the export of the French Revolution, others did not, viewing "liberation" by the French as indistinguishable from conquest. The French presence engendered a patriotic response in Russia, Spain, and some of the German and Italian states, contributing to the emergence of nationalist feeling there.

Like the contemporaries who witnessed the Revolution, modern historians also have had a variety of interpretations of it. Many of them still disagree as to the causes, effects, and significance of the Revolution, debating the dramatic events with some of the same passion as those who experienced it firsthand.

European Responses to the Revolution

In countries over which revolutionary armies swept, enthusiastic shouts for "liberty, fraternity, and equality!" echoed in German, Dutch, and Piedmontese, then disappeared in a sea of French muskets, military requisitions, and even executions. The revolutionary wave did bring about sweeping changes in some of the "liberated" territories, and these changes continued even as Napoleon consolidated his authority in France (see Chapter 13). Thus, in Piedmont, French control reduced the influence of the nobility and left a heritage of relative administrative efficiency. The abolition of feudalism in some of the conquered German states, northern Italy, and the Kingdom of Naples increased the number of property owners. The French conquerors proclaimed the rule of law and curtailed some of the influence of the clergy.

But the French faced the realities of almost constant warfare and, increasingly, local resistance. As the wars dragged on and the economic situations of the "republics" grew worse, the benefits brought by the French seemed increasingly less important. Ruined merchants and former officials joined nobles and clerics in opposing rule by France or its puppets. As the Civil Constitution of the French Clergy led to a violent reaction against the Revolution in France, anticlerical measures in the occupied territories had the same effect. The peoples of the Rhineland, the Netherlands, and Flanders bitterly resented the revolutionaries' de-christianization campaign. Increasingly, the French presence bred contempt and hatred. Bavarian, Dutch, Piedmontese, Austrian, and Swiss patriots found willing listeners. The French occupation gave rise to general opposition and a new wave of national feeling among the conquered. In Great Britain, the French Revolution also contributed to the accentuation of British nationalism in the face of a perceived threat by its old Catholic enemy in a new guise.

The French conquests in Europe were themselves an exercise in statemaking, largely unanticipated and unwanted by the local populations. Between 1795 and 1799, the Directory established satellite "sister republics" directly administered by France. The Helvetic Republic (Switzerland), the Batavian Republic (the Netherlands), the Cisalpine Republic (Milan), and the Parthenopean Republic (the Kingdom of Naples) were founded with the goal of shoring up alliances against the other great powers. But in the Italian states, only the Cisalpine Republic generated any local enthusiasm for the French invaders, and then only briefly. People "liberated" from the rule of kings and princes found themselves governed by a revolutionary bureaucracy administered from Paris.

The French found support and hired officials principally from the middle class, which had already provided officials in the old state structure. But the French invasions gradually generated a hatred for the revolutionary invaders and in some places a concomitant nationalist response. This was especially true within the German states, where many writers and other people in the upper classes hoped one day that "Germany"—300 states, 50 free cities, and almost 1,000 territories of imperial knights of the Holy Roman Empire—would one day be politically unified.

Historians' Views of the Revolution

Marxist historians long dominated the historiography of the French Revolution. They have described the Revolution as the inevitable result of a bourgeois challenge to the Old Regime, dominated by nobles. Thus, Marxists have interpreted the Revolution in terms of the rise of the bourgeoisie and its struggle for social and political influence commensurate with its rising economic power during the eighteenth century. Marxists have insisted that the nobility compromised the authority of the absolute monarchy by refusing to be taxed; then, according to this interpretation, the emboldened bourgeoisie allied with urban artisans and workers to bring down the absolute monarchy. They have described the emergence of the bourgeoisie as the dominant social class in France, insisting on its growing role in the country's increasingly capitalist economy.

This traditional Marxist economic interpretation of the French Revolution has been largely discredited. Some historians have noted that differences between aristocrats and bourgeois, and within both social groups, had become considerably blurred during the eighteenth century; that most of the "bourgeois" members of the Estates-General were not drawn from commerce and manufacturing but rather from law; and that, in any case, the upper middle class and nobles by the time of the Revolution shared a common obsession with money, not privilege. Thus, one cannot accurately depict the Revolution as having been simply a victory for the bourgeoisie.

Moreover, the Revolution did not expedite capitalism but may even have retarded it, by launching France and Europe into a long series of costly wars.

Views critical of the "bourgeois revolution" thesis have also emphasized that within France the complex nature of local political power, divided among provincial Estates and parlements, and among various groups enjoying formal privileges or monopolies and municipalities, limited the actual prerogatives of absolute monarchy. Many historians now see the Revolution as affirming the victory of men of property—a rubric that included both nobles and bourgeois—over titled nobles born into status and power.

A related interpretation has seen the Revolution as part of an essentially democratic "Atlantic Revolution" stretching across the Atlantic Ocean. By this view, the American War of Independence was the first manifestation of an essentially political quest for popular sovereignty. It influenced, in turn, the French Revolution and subsequent attempts in other European countries to gain political rights, as well as movements for independence in Spain's Latin American colonies early in the nineteenth century.

More recently, another revisionist school has argued that a new political culture was already in place in the last decades of the Old Regime. An extreme version of this interpretation sees the French monarchy as a state well on the way to reforming itself through the collaboration of liberal nobles before the Revolution interrupted this process. One view sees in the 1750s and 1760s the origins of this new, revolutionary political culture, seen in the political and ideological opposition to Louis XV and particularly in the rhetorical violence of the Revolution's first year.

None of these varying interpretations, however, diminishes the significance of the French Revolution in transforming the Western world by providing its first modern European democratic experience. This is why its origins and nature continue to generate excitement and debate today, well more than 200 years after the fall of the Bastille.

CHAPTER 13

NAPOLEON AND EUROPE

The royalist, religious writer François-René de Chateaubriand once called his enemy Napoleon "the mightiest breath of life which has ever animated human clay." In a rare moment of introspection, Napoleon once remarked, "It is said that I am an ambitious man but that is not so; or at least my ambition is so closely bound to my being that they are both one and the same."

Yet, far more than his imposing will, Napoleon's career was shaped by and reflected the breathtaking changes brought by the French Revolution. Statemaking and the emergence of nationalism, accompanied by the increased secularization of political institutions, slowly but surely transformed the European continent.

An admirer of the Enlightenment, Napoleon claimed that he was the true son of the French Revolution. He personally supervised the writing of the new constitution, which made wealth, specifically propertied wealth, the determinant of status. Napoleon's reign was also a watershed in statemaking: he further centralized the French state and extended its reach, making it more efficient by codifying laws and creating new bureaucratic structures and a new social hierarchy based upon state service.

Napoleon saw himself as a savior who carried "liberty, equality, and fraternity" abroad, freeing the European peoples from sovereigns who oppressed them. From his final exile on the distant Atlantic island of Saint Helena, Napoleon claimed to have created European unity. But in the process of "liberating" other nations from the stranglehold of old regimes, he also conquered them.

NAPOLEON'S RISE TO POWER

Napoleon's rise to power should be seen in the context of the French Revolution. With the emigration of most of the officer corps during the early stages of the Revolution, a generation of talented generals had risen rapidly through the ranks by virtue of their remarkable battlefield accomplishments during the revolutionary wars that had raged across much of Western and Central Europe since 1792. During the Directory, generals became increasingly powerful arbiters in political life. Napoleon manipulated the consuls and ultimately overthrew the Directory.

The Young Bonaparte

Of the strategically important Mediterranean island of Corsica, Jean-Jacques Rousseau in *The Social Contract* (1762) wrote, "I have a presentiment that one day this small island will astonish Europe." The year before, the Corsican patriot Pascale di Paoli (1725–1807) had managed to evict the Genoese from Corsica. But in 1768 the French took Corsica. Carlo Buonaparte, one of Paoli's followers, remained on the island rather than join Paoli in exile in England.

On August 15, 1769, Buonaparte's wife, whose family could trace its noble origins back to fourteenth-century Lombardy, gave birth to a son, Napoleon, named after a cousin who had been killed by the French. It is one of the strange ironies of history that Napoleon would have been British had his father followed Paoli into exile. In 1770, the French government accepted the Buonaparte family as nobles. The island's governor arranged for the young Buonaparte to receive an appointment to the royal military school at Brienne, in Champagne, which Napoleon entered as a boy in 1779. There he was exposed not only to a rigorous program of study but also to the humiliating condescension of the other students. He was an outsider, and the other students mocked his strong Corsican accent—Napoleon's first language was the patois of his island, a mix of Genovese and Tuscan—and his relatively humble economic situation. During the summer of 1789, he penned a history of his island in which the French were portrayed as murderous exploiters and tormenters, and Corsicans their victims. Unusually bright but also brooding, melancholy, and at least once even suicidal, he earned appointment to the artillery section of the national military academy in Paris, passing the examinations in a single year.

Antoine-Jean Gros's painting of the young Napoleon in *Bonaparte at Arcole* (1796).

Napoleon and the Revolution

With the outbreak of the Revolution, Napoleon returned to Corsica in September 1789. There he helped organize the National Guard and drew up a petition to the National Assembly in Paris asking that Corsica formally become part of France, with its people enjoying the rights of citizenship. In this way, Napoleon distanced himself from those Corsicans who wanted independence, thus parting ways with his hero Paoli, who had returned from England and joined the island's royalists. Napoleon favored the Revolution for three reasons: he wanted to see a curtailment of the abuses of the Old Regime; he hoped that the Revolution might end his island's status within France as little more than a conquered territory; and he thought the Revolution might provide him with an opportunity for promotion.

Napoleon became a Jacobin. He commanded a volunteer force that on Easter Sunday, 1792, fired on rioters supporting the cause of the Catholic Church. When Paoli's victorious forces turned the island over to the English, the Buonapartes were forced to flee. Sent by the Committee of Public Safety to fight federalist and royalist rebels and their British allies in the south, in December 1793 Napoleon planned the successful artillery siege of the port of Toulon, which was held by British forces.

Useful political connections and the lack of direct involvement in the bitter factional struggles in Paris may have saved Napoleon from execution in the Terror or during Thermidor. The result was that Napoleon's star continued to rise (with the help of his own determined campaign to construct a heroic public image of his exploits), while some of his Jacobin friends went to the guillotine. In the Paris of Thermidor, Napoleon helped put down a royalist uprising on October 6, 1795. He attracted the attention of—and soon married—Josephine de Beauharnais, the lover of the corrupt Paul Barras, one of the directors, and the widow of a member of the National Assembly who had been guillotined during the Terror. In 1796, the directors made Napoleon commander of the Army of Italy. It now seemed appropriate to eliminate the Italian spelling of his name; Buonaparte became Napoleon Bonaparte. Spectacular successes against the Austrians and their allies in Italy, including at the Battle of Arcole (November 1796), made him the toast of Paris. He later recalled that, after victory over Austrian forces at the Battle of Lodi (May 1796), which opened the way to Milan, "I realized I was a superior being and conceived the ambition of performing great things, which hitherto had filled my thoughts only as a fantastic dream. I saw the world flee beneath me, as if I were transported in air."

Napoleon was now conducting military and foreign policy virtually on his own, pillaging and looting Italy of art treasures as he pleased in the name of "liberty." His forceful and virtually independent pursuit of the war, and the subsequent peace he arranged with Austria at Campo Formio on October 18, 1797, gave France control of the Austrian Netherlands, Venetia, and the satellite Cisalpine Republic in northern and central Italy. For the moment, only Great Britain remained as an enemy.

Dreaming of an eastern empire, Napoleon then turned his attention to the Middle East. In 1798, he set off on a spectacular voyage to Egypt, part of the Ottoman Empire, thus undertaking the first try by a Western power to occupy a country in the Middle East. He was accompanied by 35,000 soldiers and a shipload of scientists, including mathematicians, physicians, zoologists, and engineers, a few of the latter already dreaming of carving a canal through the Isthmus of Suez that would give the French an overwhelming advantage in trade with the Far East. In Cairo he founded the Institute of Egypt, which greatly influenced the origins of Egyptology. Thus, Napoleon cloaked his invasion as a "civilizing mission."

After pausing en route long enough to capture the island of Malta, Napoleon defeated Egyptian forces at the Battle of the Pyramids in July 1798. But the tiny British admiral Horatio Nelson (1758–1805), who could see out of only one eye, had lost an arm, and had few teeth left, trapped and destroyed the French fleet on August 1, 1798, in the Battle of the Nile. Russia and Austria, their respective interests threatened by French campaigns in the east, now formed a Second Coalition against France, which Turkey also joined. Temporarily stranded in Egypt because of the naval defeat, and with his officers having to use the Greek historian Herodotus's *Histories* as their guide to Egypt, the undaunted Napoleon set off to conquer Syria. In Palestine his army stopped at Jaffa, where it massacred the population. Forced to retreat to Egypt by dwindling supplies and disease, Napoleon achieved a final victory there over the Turks with the annihilation of several more villages and their inhabitants. Napoleon then returned to France.

In Paris, Abbé Emmanuel Sieyès was plotting to overthrow the Directory. Such a venture now required the participation of one of the powerful, popular young generals whom the incessant warfare had catapulted to prominence. Napoleon, who could be portrayed as the potential savior of France, now helped piece together a political constituency from among the quarreling factions of the Directory. With the coup d'état of the 18th Brumaire (November 9, 1799), Sieyès and Napoleon overthrew the Directory.

CONSOLIDATION OF POWER

After the overthrow of the Directory, the conspirators established a new government, the Consulate. It brought political stability to France. It did so by concentrating strong executive authority in the eager hands of Napoleon, who oversaw the drafting of a constitution and made peace with the Catholic Church. Designated "consul for life" in 1802, Napoleon crowned himself emperor two years later. In the meantime, he continued to wage wars against Britain, Austria, Russia, and Prussia, four rivals driven into coalitions by French expansion. By 1809, although he had failed in his goal of bringing Britain to its knees, a series of remarkable victories enabled Napoleon to forge a great empire, the largest in Europe since that of Rome.

Establishment of the Consulate

With the fall of the Directory in 1799, Napoleon Bonaparte, at the age of thirty, became first consul, the most powerful man in France in a new, stronger executive authority of three consuls, replacing the five directors. The Constitution of 1799, promulgated in December, gave lip service to universal suffrage, but reflected the authoritarian character Sieyès intended. Indirect election for each political institution reduced the political body of the nation to a small number of notables. A Senate, appointed by the consuls, chose men from a list of 6,000 "notabilities" to serve in a Tribunate. A Council of State, whose members were appointed by the first consul, would propose legislation. The Tribunate would discuss the proposed legislation, and a Legislative Body would vote on the laws but could not debate them. There was more than a little truth to the oft-repeated story that one man who asked what was in the new constitution received the reply, "Napoleon Bonaparte." The constitution was submitted to voters in a plebiscite (voters could vote either yes or no). More than 99 percent of the all-male electorate approved the document. The plebiscite became a fundamental Napoleonic political institution, embodying his principle of "authority from above, confidence from below."

The Consulate provided political stability by institutionalizing strong executive authority. France's districts (*départements*) each received an appointed prefect, whose powers, delegated by the central government in Paris, surpassed those of the intendants of the Bourbon monarchs. Napoleon's brother Lucien, as minister of interior, extended effective executive authority to the most distant corners of the nation, curtailing royalist and Jacobin opposition. Napoleon ruthlessly suppressed the press, reducing the number of newspapers in Paris from seventy-three to thirteen, cowing survivors with threats, or winning their allegiance with bribes.

The Concordat

Napoleon made peace with the Catholic Church, bringing it under state supervision. Deep hostility remained between priests who had sworn allegiance to the nation during the Revolution—the "juring" clergy—and those who had refused. Influenced by the Enlightenment, Napoleon believed the Church should not have an institutional role in the affairs of state. But he was also a cynical pragmatist. "There is only one way to encourage morality," he once said, "and that is to reestablish religion. Society cannot exist without some being richer than others, and this inequality cannot exist without religion. When one man is dying of hunger next door to another who is stuffing himself with food, the poor man simply cannot accept the disparity unless some authority tells him, 'God wishes it so . . . in heaven things will be different.'" An agreement with the Church also was intended to undercut popular support for the monarchist cause by restoring some of the Church's prerogatives, but not any that would threaten the government's authority. Napoleon thus shrewdly sought to detach the Church from the quest for a restoration of the monarchy.

With the death in 1799 of Pope Pius VI (pope 1775–1799), who had refused any accommodation with the Revolution, his successor, Pius VII (pope 1800–1823), was eager to end a decade of religious turmoil. In 1801, Napoleon signed a Concordat with the papacy that helped solidify some of the changes brought by the Revolution, declaring Catholicism "the religion of the majority of citizens" in France. A majority of bishops refused to accept the Concordat. The pope would henceforth appoint new bishops, but on the recommendation of the first consul, that is, Napoleon. The Church also abandoned all claims to those ecclesiastical lands that had been sold as "national property" during the first years of the Revolution. The Concordat helped restore ecclesiastical influence in France, reflected by an increase in religious observance and in the number of people entering the clergy. Napoleon also pleased the Church by abandoning the confusing official calendar put in place in 1793, reestablishing Sundays and religious holidays.

The Organic Articles, which Napoleon promulgated without consulting the pope, regulated the Gallican (French) Church's status in France and reduced the pope's authority. The Church would now be subject to virtually the same administrative organization and policing as any other organization;

Napoleon and Pope Pius VII signing the Concordat in 1801, reconciling the Catholic Church with France after the Revolution.

a "minister of religion" would sit with the other ministers in Paris. The state would pay clerical salaries. No papal bull could be read in France's churches without permission of the government, and the clergy would have to read official government decrees from the pulpit. Under Napoleon, the Church gained the freedom of religious practice, but at the expense of some of its independence. Primary-school students were required to memorize a new catechism:

> *Question:* What are the duties of Christians with respect to the princes who govern them, and what are, in particular, our duties toward Napoleon . . . ?
> *Answer:* . . . Love, respect, obedience, fidelity, military service. . . . We also owe him fervent prayers for his safety and for the spiritual and temporal prosperity of the State.

Napoleon granted Protestants and Jews state protection to practice their religion. An article of the Concordat guaranteed freedom of worship for people in both religions (who together made up less than 5 percent of the population, the vast majority of whom were Protestants). One set of Organic Articles supervised Calvinists, another Lutherans. An imperial decree in 1808 organized Judaism into territorial consistories, although rabbis, unlike priests and Protestant ministers, were not to be paid by the state.

Napoleon's settlement with the Church alienated some of his cautious supporters on the left, notably the group known as the Ideologues. After a solemn ceremony at Notre Dame Cathedral in Paris celebrating the Concordat, one general put it bluntly to Napoleon—"A fine monkish show. It lacked only the presence of the hundred thousand men who gave their lives to end all that."

Napoleon's Leadership

One of his staff would later describe Napoleon as an "ever-restless spirit." He ate rapidly and could work days on end with very little sleep. He dictated more than 80,000 letters in his extraordinary career. Napoleon seemed to absorb every bit of information that arrived in his office or field headquarters and rapidly mastered subjects related to military or administrative concerns. But he often ignored matters that did not particularly interest him, such as economics and naval warfare, in which France lagged behind Britain.

Napoleon was more than just an optimist. He believed that his wildest dreams of conquest and empire would inevitably become reality. Everyone feared his rages, although he could be surprisingly understanding and generous toward subordinates when he believed they erred. He delegated very little meaningful authority, mistrusting even his closest advisers, but he tolerated opposing viewpoints. Napoleon's style of leadership became ever more tyrannical. He made up his own mind, and that mind invariably chose war.

Wars of Conquest and Empire

Napoleon had brought stability to France, but France was still at war with the Second Coalition: Great Britain, Austria, and Russia. In February 1800, when Austria turned down his overtures for peace on the basis of the Treaty of Campo Formio (1797), Napoleon returned to the battlefield, retaking Milan and defeating an Austrian army in June 1800. With the Treaty of Lunéville (February 1801), Austria reaffirmed the conditions of the Treaty of Campo Formio, accepting French gains in Italy, as well as French control over the Southern Netherlands (Belgium).

With Austria defeated and Russia tied up by a war against the Ottoman Empire, the British government signed the Peace of Amiens in March 1802. France kept all of its significant gains on the continent, and Britain returned all of the French colonies it had captured. Great Britain gained only the end of hostilities.

In Central Europe, Napoleon was now free to dismember the Holy Roman Empire and to dictate the territorial reorganization of the small German states. France had absorbed the left bank of the Rhine River, fulfilling the nationalistic dreams of a France extending to its "natural frontiers." Since this expansion came at the expense of Prussia and Austria, these two powers had to be compensated. By the oddly named Imperial Recess of 1803, the two most powerful German states absorbed a number of small, independent German states, ecclesiastical territories, and most of the free cities. The rulers of Baden, Bavaria, Hesse-Kassel, and Württemberg, the other largest German states, also added to their domains. France's position in Italy also was solidified. Piedmont remained a French possession, with Napoleon naming himself president of the Italian Cisalpine Republic. After imposing a Federal Constitution on the cantons of Switzerland that transformed them into the Helvetic Republic, Napoleon forced a defensive alliance on that strategically important country. By 1802, France was at peace for the first time in a decade. Napoleon had brought his nation to a position of dominance in Europe not seen since the time of Charlemagne a thousand years earlier.

No longer satisfied with the title "first consul," in 1802 Napoleon became "consul for life," a change approved by another plebiscite. Napoleon then prepared the establishment of a hereditary empire in France. Although thousands of émigrés took advantage of a declared amnesty to return to France, an alleged conspiracy against Napoleon's life by a group of royalists in 1804 led him to act against the Bourbons and to expedite his plan to become emperor. Napoleon accused Louis de Bourbon-Condé, the duke of Enghien (1772–1804)—a member of the Bourbon family who had emigrated to Baden—of involvement in the conspiracy. French troops moved into Baden to arrest him. The duke was hurriedly tried and executed near Paris, despite the lack of any evidence of his involvement in plans to assassinate Napoleon. Public opinion throughout much of Europe was outraged. The German composer Ludwig van Beethoven crossed out the dedication to Napoleon of his Third Symphony ("Eroica," meaning "heroic") shouting, "So he is also nothing more than an ordinary man? Now he will trample on the rights of mankind and indulge only his own ambition; from now on he will make himself superior to all others and become a tyrant!" One of the royalist conspirators, before his own execution, lamented, "We have done more than we hoped to do; we meant to give France a king, and we have given her an Emperor."

The Tribunate, Senate, and another plebiscite quickly approved the change from the Consulate to an empire. On December 2, 1804, Napoleon was anointed emperor by Pius VII. Instead of waiting for the pope to crown him, Napoleon snatched the crown from the pontiff and placed it on his own head. A new constitution presented a telling contradiction: "The government of the republic is entrusted to an emperor." Once an unknown officer who had scraped by with little money amid the spendthrift glitter of Thermidor, Bonaparte began to wear a coat of red velvet that would have been fit for Louis XIV.

Napoleon was no more temperamentally suited to live with peace than with defeat. Jealous of Britain's naval and commercial supremacy in the

Jean-Louis David's *Emperor Napoleon Crowning the Empress Joséphine in the Cathedral of Notre Dame* (1805–1808).

Mediterranean and the Western Hemisphere, he began to goad Britain into a new war. Haiti, the western side of the island of Hispaniola, had proclaimed its independence from France in 1801 under the leadership of Toussaint L'Ouverture (see Chapter 12). In 1802, in response to pressure from sugar planters, Napoleon restored French control of Haiti and reinstituted slavery in the French colonies. French troops captured L'Ouverture and took him to France, where he soon died. However, tropical disease killed most of the French troops occupying Haiti, and the British prevented the arrival of reinforcements. The French army surrendered, and in 1804 Haiti, which had been France's richest colony, again became independent. With his plans to extend France's empire to the Caribbean having come to naught, Napoleon shouted "Damn sugar, damn coffee, damn colonies!"

Seeking to recoup the financial losses France had incurred from war, Napoleon sold the huge Louisiana Territory to the United States in 1803 for 60 million francs (then about 11 million dollars). In retrospect, this was a paltry sum for a territory that virtually doubled the size of what was then the United States. Napoleon's hope that its former colony would emerge as a rival to Britain also lay behind the sale.

In July 1805, Russia and Austria joined Britain to form the Third Coalition against Napoleon. Undaunted, Napoleon readied an army and ships at the port of Boulogne on the English Channel for an invasion of Britain. A French decoy fleet lured Horatio Nelson's fleet into pursuit, hoping to inflict a crushing defeat on the Royal Navy. But the hunter soon became the hunted. When the French fleet sailed from the Spanish Mediterranean port of Cádiz on October 21, 1805, it sighted the Royal Navy. Turning to sail back to port, the French vessels were left vulnerable to attack by two columns of ships that succeeded in breaking the French line. As Nelson lay dying of a wound (which might have been avoided, had he covered up his shiny medals and epaulets that attracted a French marksman's eye), his fleet earned one of naval history's most decisive victories at Cape Trafalgar, not far from Gibraltar. Any chance for a French invasion of England evaporated. Great Britain controlled the seas.

The French armies were more successful on the continent. They defeated the Austrians at Ulm in October 1805, capturing 50,000 troops. Napoleon finally coaxed the Russians and Austrians into open battle. At Austerlitz on December 2, 1805, Napoleon tricked his opponents into an attack on his intentionally weakened right flank. He then divided the two armies with a crushing attack at their vulnerable center. When the dust cleared after the battle, the Russians and their Austrian allies had suffered 30,000 casualties, the French fewer than 9,000. Austria asked for peace, giving up the remnants of imperial territories in Italy and Dalmatia. Napoleon's allies, Bavaria, Baden, and Württemberg, once again gained Habsburg territories.

In the wake of Austerlitz, the hesitant King Frederick William III (ruled 1797–1840) of Prussia abandoned his tentative agreement to join the Third Coalition, instead signing an alliance with France. In July 1806,

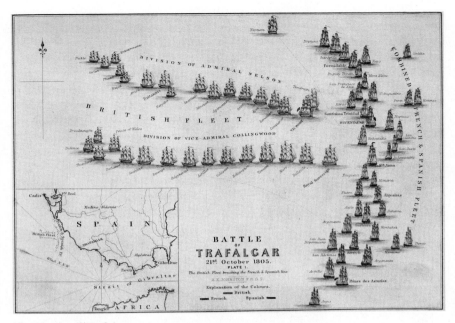

The Battle of Trafalgar.

Napoleon organized the Confederation of the Rhine, composed of sixteen German states, excluding Prussia and Austria (see Map 13.1). Napoleon named himself "Protector" of the Confederation, whose members agreed to accept French garrisons in southern Germany and to support Napoleon if war broke out again. This made the Holy Roman Empire even more irrelevant than it had been for a very long time. In 1806, Francis II (Francis I of Austria) simply dissolved the clumsy entity by abdicating as Holy Roman emperor.

As French power in Central Europe grew, the British government convinced Frederick William to join the alliance against Napoleon. But Napoleon's forces humiliated the Prussian army at Jena near Nuremberg on October 14, 1806, and then occupied Berlin. In February 1807, the French and Russian armies fought to a bloody draw in a Polish snowstorm. Had Austrian and British troops been sent to support the Russians, Napoleon might well have been soundly defeated. But Austria was still reeling from the defeat at Austerlitz, and the British were preoccupied with defending their commercial interests in the Western Hemisphere. Napoleon sent for fresh troops from France and added 30,000 Polish soldiers, some attracted by speculation that the emperor might create an independent Polish state.

After defeating the Russian army at the Battle of Friedland (June 1807), Napoleon met with Tsar Alexander I (ruled 1801–1825) on a raft in the middle of a river. Frederick William, the king of Prussia, paced anxiously on

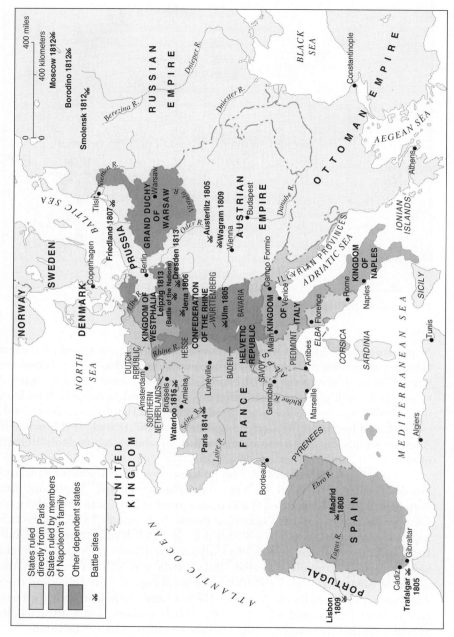

MAP 13.1 THE EMPIRE OF NAPOLEON   This map shows the areas conquered by Napoleon, including dependent states and states incorporated directly into France or ruled by Napoleon's relatives.

States ruled directly from Paris

States ruled by members of Napoleon's family

Other dependent states

⚔ Battle sites

the shore as he awaited the outcome. The news was indeed bad. By the Treaty of Tilsit (July 1807), Prussia lost territory in western Germany and in Poland, which became, respectively, the Kingdom of Westphalia and the Grand Duchy of Warsaw, the latter annexed by Napoleon's ally, Saxony. The king of Saxony became the grand duke of Warsaw by virtue of a personal union. Russia was forced to accept the territorial settlements in Western Europe as definitive. In return, the tsar received a promise of French support in Russia's current quarrel with the Ottoman Empire. France thus tacitly agreed to back Russia's long-standing ambitions in southeastern Europe. Finally, the tsar agreed to close Russian ports to British ships.

When Austria challenged Napoleon by invading Bavaria in 1809, Napoleon moved rapidly against Vienna, capturing the Habsburg capital. He then crossed to the left bank of the Danube River and defeated the Habsburg army in July at Wagram, a battle in which 300,000 men participated and 80,000 were killed or wounded. Defeat forced Austria to surrender Illyria to France and other territory to Bavaria and Russia, which was still technically but uneasily allied to France. With Austria defeated and weakened, Prussia discouraged and dismembered, Russia neutralized, and Britain once again left alone to challenge France, Napoleon's position in Europe seemed invincible. Through conquest, the establishment of satellite states, and alliances with smaller powers, Napoleon had constructed a vast empire.

The Corsican Warrior

Napoleon has been considered one of the most brilliant military leaders in modern history. Yet his talents lay not in originality but in his stunningly innovative adaptations of military strategies and tactics developed in the eighteenth century and during the Revolution. Before mass military conscription, warfare had usually involved relatively limited numbers of soldiers. Armies had not moved rapidly. Since the beginning of the Thirty Years' War (1618–1648), wars had been fought over dynastic honor, commercial rivalry, and disputed territories (see Chapters 7 and 11). Old Regime armies had consisted largely of mercenaries commanded by nobles. Most battles had been fought in precise, drilled ranks, by two relatively small armies in line formation directly facing each other.

In the eighteenth century, technological and tactical improvements in artillery augmented its importance in warfare. Artillery pieces became lighter and therefore could be moved more easily. Improvements in roads also helped expedite the movement of cannon, as well as troops. Properly positioned artillery, launching powerful shells, could now play a decisive role against infantry. The artillery became a more respected part of the army; talented officers, Napoleon not the least of them, found a chance for promotion that they would not have had elsewhere.

Warfare changed when armies were no longer made up of mercenaries but rather of "citizen-soldiers" with greater commitment to their cause. Thus, during the French Revolution, committed sans-culottes were first mobilized as citizen-soldiers in the *levée en masse* proclaimed in August 1792. They fought to defend the nation, winning the stunning victory over the Austrian army at Valmy (September 1792; see Chapter 12). The Revolution inaugurated a period of warfare in Europe in which more soldiers entered battle than ever before. Between 1800 and 1815, perhaps as many as 2 million men served in or allied with Napoleon's armies. Napoleon harnessed French nationalism to win the commitment of his armies.

The Prussian general and military writer Karl von Clausewitz (1780–1831) described how warfare, which he defined as "an extension of state policy by other means," had changed. Whereas the wars of most of the eighteenth century had been those of kings and of states, not entire peoples, now "war had again suddenly become an affair of the people, and that of a people numbering thirty million, every one of whom regarded himself a citizen of the state."

Napoleon's genius was his ability to organize, oversee, and assure the supplying of and communication between larger armies than had ever before been effectively assembled, and to move them more rapidly than anyone before him. "Everything is in the execution," as he put it. He built on the French innovation in 1792–1793 of using combat divisions that combined

French citizens drawing lots to determine who would be conscripted to fight in Napoleon's wars.

infantry, cavalry, and artillery, and he subdivided his armies into corps, each with its own sense of pride.

Napoleon founded a military school in 1803 that produced 4,000 officers by 1815—there were lots of vacancies as the wars took their toll. As in the administration of the empire, however, Napoleon refused to delegate responsibility for crucial strategic and tactical decisions to his subordinates. In the long run, this would cost him dearly.

The infantry remained the heart of Napoleon's armies and his military planning (there were never more than 4 artillerymen for every 1,000 foot soldiers). Napoleon perfected the "mixed order" formation developed in the eighteenth century, which combined stretching troops across the field in a thin line about three men deep and bunching them in columns not only for marching but also for attack. Napoleon kept some battalions in columns, others in lines, which allowed battlefield flexibility. When he saw the opportunity, he launched an attack by outflanking his opponent and striking against the enemy's lines of communication. When he confronted an army stretched out before him, skilled marksmen threw the opponent's advance forces into disarray. Napoleon then brilliantly assessed the opposing army's weakest point. The concentration of deadly artillery fire—Napoleon once referred to the twelve-pound cannons as his "beautiful daughters"— prepared the way for the assault of the infantry columns. The speed of his army's movements was such that Napoleon could rapidly attack and defeat part of an enemy army before reinforcements could arrive. Instead of stopping to celebrate victory, Napoleon sent his troops, particularly the cavalry, to pursue the enemy. Victory became a rout.

Napoleon's armies, unlike the professional armies of the Old Regime, lived off the land, simply requisitioning what they needed. This did not make the French troops very popular, even in those lands officially incorporated into the empire. But it did allow the imperial army to travel far afield, in great numbers, marching up to twenty miles a day. Such speed seemed incredible for the period, since each infantryman carried with him about sixty pounds of equipment.

Finally, Napoleon enjoyed intense loyalty from his officers and troops, even up to the bitter end. He took to the field with his troops and rewarded good work with promotions and decorations, sometimes given on the field of battle. The emperor's own courage was also a source of inspiration to his troops. During one battle, the Imperial Guard refused to fight until Napoleon had moved to a safer place. He treated his soldiers with demonstrable respect and even affection because they seemed willing to die for him. At least 400,000 did just that.

The Napoleonic adventure offered even the most humble soldier a chance for glory. Yet the risks of injury and death were considerable. Disease sometimes killed more soldiers than battlefield wounds. (Napoleon had the good fortune to be wounded only twice in his long military career.) Soldiering was a tough life. In good times, soldiers ate reasonably well—bread, vegetables,

Napoleon used titles and awards as pillars of the empire. Jacques-Louis David's *Oath of the Army after the Distribution of Standards* shows the eagerness of the army to defend Napoleon and the empire.

even some meat, and drank wine or rum. But after defeat, or when they were far inside inhospitable territory, soldiers were fortunate just to find enough to eat. Medical care remained inadequate, despite improvements that included caring for wounded soldiers while the battle was still raging, rather than afterward when it often was too late. Major surgery—including the countless amputations occurring after each major battle—was often fatal. Napoleon, however, remained far more concerned with able-bodied soldiers than with the wounded or sick.

THE FOUNDATIONS OF THE FRENCH EMPIRE

The Napoleonic empire was a significant episode in the long story of statemaking in Europe. Continuing the tradition of eighteenth-century monarchs, Napoleon sought to make state administration more efficient and uniform. His aggressive conquests brought centrally controlled, bureaucratic government and a centralized legal system to much of the continent. For this reason, it is possible to see him as the embodiment of "enlightened absolutism" awaited by the philosophe Voltaire.

Napoleon created a new social hierarchy based not on blood but on service to the state, particularly in the army and bureaucracy, and on ownership of property. Beyond French borders, the empire was based on an imperial system in which Napoleon made his relatives and marshals heads of state. Thus, he gave the throne of Westphalia to his brother Jérôme, as earlier he had transformed the Cisalpine Republic in northern Italy into a monarchy ruled by his stepson, Eugène de Beauharnais. He named his brother Louis king of Holland. His brother Joseph became king of Naples and later king of Spain. Everywhere that French armies conquered, Napoleon's daunting will imposed change.

Institutional Foundations: Imperial Centralization

Napoleon's Council of State, the most prestigious and important administrative body of the empire, oversaw finance, interior affairs, and war. Members advised the emperor and drew up laws and regulations for approval by the Legislative Body. Napoleon attached to the council a corps of young, bright, apprentice bureaucrats who would assume important administrative posts in the future. The Senate, Legislative Body, and Tribunate lost all but their ceremonial roles, and Napoleon completely eliminated the Tribunate in 1807. Even the members of the Council of State found their influence on the emperor increasingly reduced.

Napoleon established the Bank of France in 1800, which facilitated the state's ability to borrow money. He followed the Directory's policy of abandoning the grossly inflated paper money of the Revolution. This stabilized France's currency. He facilitated the assessment and collection of taxes, ordering a land survey of the entire country upon which direct taxes were to be based. And he expanded the number of indirect taxes collected on salt (which had also been a principal source of revenue for the Old Regime monarchy), tobacco, and liquor, as well as on goods brought into any town of over 5,000 inhabitants.

The empire followed the Revolution, and particularly the Directory, in making higher education the responsibility of the state. With about half the population illiterate, Napoleon believed that schools could create patriotic and obedient citizens through teaching secular values that would ultimately link education to nationalism. In 1802, Napoleon established state secondary schools (*lycées*), thirty-seven of which were operating six years later, for the relatively few boys who went to secondary school. Students read only textbooks approved by the emperor. In 1808, Napoleon created France's first public university system, charging it with "direct[ing] political and moral opinions."

Legal Foundations: The Napoleonic Code

Napoleon wanted to be known to history as the new Justinian, the Roman lawgiver. The Civil Code of 1804, which became known as the Napoleonic Code, may have been the emperor's most lasting legacy. Many of the *cahiers*, or lists of grievances submitted to Louis XVI on the eve of the Revolution, had asked that French laws be uniform. During the constitutional monarchy, the Convention had begun the process of codifying French laws, but it had been interrupted by the vicissitudes of the Revolution. While the fundamental division in French law had been between the written Roman law in the south and customary law based upon regional and local traditions in the north, there were many different legal codes in France. Napoleon ordered the Council of State to seek advice from a battery of lawyers to codify the laws of the land. Napoleon personally participated in many critical discussions and debates. The Napoleonic Code made the rights of property owners sacrosanct: the majority of the articles concerned private property.

The code, over 2,000 articles long, enshrined the equality of all people before the law and granted the freedom of religion. The subsequent Penal Code of 1810 proclaimed the "freedom of work," reaffirming the Le Chapelier Law of 1791 that forbade the formation of workers' or employers' associations (the latter were extremely rare). The "freedom" guaranteed in relations between employers and workers left workers legally subordinate to their employers and unable to strike. Furthermore, workers were required to carry small passports that had to be handed over to municipal officials, police, or employers when requested.

The Napoleonic Code reflected Napoleon's traditional attitudes toward the family. He considered the family the most important intermediary between the state and the individual, a means of guaranteeing social order. Rejecting scattered demands during the Revolution for the equality of women, the code reaffirmed the patriarchal nature of the traditional family. It made women and children legally dependent on their husbands or fathers. The code granted men control of family property. A woman could not buy or sell property or begin a business without her husband's permission, and any income she earned would pass to his descendants, not hers. A woman worker's wages, too, went to her husband, and women had no control over their children's savings. As during the First Republic, the state recognized divorce, but it was now more difficult to obtain. More articles in the Napoleonic Code established conditions for the sale of cattle than addressed the legal status of women. In cases of adultery, women risked penalties that were far more severe than those for men. Only adult males could officially witness a legal document. Napoleon complained: "In France women are considered too highly. They should not be regarded as equal to men. In reality they are nothing more than machines for producing children."

As in the Old Regime, parents could put their offspring in jail and retained authority over their children's marriages. The code required equal inheritance of all children (the parents could dispose of a certain percentage, based on a sliding scale, as he or she wished), ending primogeniture (inheritance by the eldest son) in northern France, where it still existed. Yet siblings often found ways to keep the family property together; one brother could buy out his brothers' shares in an inherited property. The end of primogeniture also may have provided an impetus for French couples to have fewer children in an effort to avoid further division of property.

The Napoleonic Code—despite its obvious inequities, imperfections, and the fact that it was sometimes promulgated by a conquering army—served as the basis for the codification of laws and the reorganization of judicial systems in Switzerland, Piedmont-Sardinia, and the Netherlands. At the end of his life, Napoleon claimed, "My glory is not to have won forty battles . . . but what nothing will destroy, what will live eternally, is my Civil Code."

Social Foundations: The Imperial Hierarchy

Napoleon once wrote, "My motto has always been: a career open to all talents." He considered the end of social distinctions by birth to be one of the most lasting accomplishments of the French Revolution. The empire favored the aspirations of the middle classes. The elimination of legal barriers to social ascension left wealth, largely defined by the ownership of property and service to the state (rewarded by grants of property, titles, and pensions), as the main determinant of status. Yet imposing obstacles to social mobility remained. It took wealth to acquire the background, education, and reputation to take one's place in the imperial hierarchy.

The army and the bureaucracy were the two pillars of the empire. Napoleon created an elite of "notables," as they were called, rewarding those who served him well with prestigious titles and lucrative positions. At the pinnacle of the new hierarchy were eighteen marshals, appointed in 1804 from the ranks of the Senate and including generals who had earned fortunes waging war. Napoleon began to restore titles abolished by the Revolution: prince in 1804, duke two years later, followed by count, baron, and chevalier. But unlike the titles of the Old Regime, these titles, which could be hereditary, did not stem from the ownership of a certain estate or château, but rather were awarded for service to the state.

Between 1808 and 1814, Napoleon created 3,600 titles. Yet Napoleonic notables totaled only one-seventh of the number of the nobles in France on the eve of the Revolution. Some of the new notables had already become rich through purchase of ecclesiastical and émigré lands sold during the Revolution. More than half of all men granted titles by the emperor had rendered service in the military. The emperor often repeated that "in the backpack of each soldier, there is a marshal's baton." The civil service was the second most important avenue to a Napoleonic title. Some Italians, Dutch, Germans, and others from conquered lands found that the French Empire offered them dignified and sometimes even lucrative careers.

In May 1802, Napoleon established the Legion of Honor to reward those who served the nation with distinction. It was, predictably enough, organized along military lines, with commanders, officers, and knights. Indeed 97 percent of those so decorated by Napoleon served in his military forces. Yet a former Jacobin member of the Council of State complained that the award, a decorated cross that could be displayed prominently on one's coat, was nothing more than a "bauble." Napoleon replied, "You may call them baubles, but it is by baubles that mankind is governed." The subjects of territories incorporated into the empire were eligible to receive the Legion of Honor. When Rome became part of Napoleon's immense empire, the following parody on the Legion of Honor appeared on the walls of the Eternal City:

> In fierce old times, they balanced loss
> By hanging thieves upon a cross.
> But our more humane age believes
> In hanging crosses on the thieves.

THE TIDE TURNS AGAINST NAPOLEON

French rule generated resistance in countries absorbed into Napoleon's empire through conquest. Napoleon manipulated factional splits in some countries, co-opted local elites where he could, brushed aside rulers as he pleased, and tried to establish compliant new regimes, some handed over to his brothers. But ultimately French rule over such an extended empire collapsed. Napoleon's failure to force British submission by strangling its economy with his "Continental System," which aimed to cut off Britain from its continental markets, kept his major enemy in the field, or more appropriately, on the high seas. In Spain, resistance against French rule became a full-fledged rebellion (the Peninsular War) that, with British assistance, sapped imperial resources. Moreover, French occupation of some of the German states gave rise to German nationalism, solidifying resistance. Prussian and Austrian military reforms led to stronger opponents in the field. And in a final ill-considered expansion of imperial aggression, Napoleon in 1812 decided to invade Russia. The destruction of his "Grand Army" in the snowdrifts and howling winds of Russia was the beginning of the end.

The Continental System

Knowing that the war was costing the British government huge sums (between 60 and 90 percent of the state's annual revenue), in November 1806 Napoleon announced his Continental System. It prohibited trade with Britain, which he hoped would strangle the British economy by closing all continental ports to British ships. French merchants and manufacturers, as well as the state, would earn fortunes supplying the captive markets of the continent. Increased hardship might even cause damaging unrest in Britain.

But the blockade of the continental ports was far easier said than done. The continental coastline is enormous, the British navy was strong (despite the loss of 317 ships between 1803 and 1815), and the merchants and smugglers resourceful. British merchants continued to find American markets for their goods. The banning of British imports did lead to the development of some important innovations in France (for example, the Jacquard loom for silk weaving and the planting of the sugar beet to compensate for the loss of sugar from the West Indies). But France's relative lack of available coal and iron ore, its lack of capital accumulation and investment, and the overwhelming allocation of the nation's material and human resources to war prevented French merchants from taking up the slack left by the absence of British goods in continental markets.

In response to Napoleon's Continental System, the British government's "Orders in Council" of November and December 1807 demanded that trading ships under all flags purchase a license in a British port. This decision placed Britain at loggerheads with the United States, one of France's principal trading partners. Napoleon retaliated with the Milan Decrees, threatening to seize any ship that had traded with Britain or that had even accepted a search by British authorities. Yet, in 1809, British imports could still be readily found on the continent. The French, suffering a sharp decline in customs revenue, began tolerating violations of the Continental System, even selling special licenses and placing hefty taxes on the importation of British goods to bring in more revenue. The blockade came completely apart in the midst of an economic depression that began in 1811.

Napoleon counted on Britain's deepening crisis with the U.S. government, which opposed the boarding and searching of its vessels by British

British Prime Minister William Pitt the Younger and Napoleon carve up the world.

inspectors, to bring Anglo-American relations to a breaking point. But even the War of 1812 between the British and the United States, which ended with the exhausted British capitulating, could not destroy the British economy. Moreover, the fact that French agents had encouraged an Irish insurrection against British rule in 1798 lingered in the memory of the British upper class, adding to their resentment of France. Tory governments, which governed Britain throughout the entire revolutionary and Napoleonic periods, remained committed to defeating Bonaparte (and repressing dissent at home), despite the staggering economic cost of the war.

The Peninsular War

Napoleon's obsession with bringing Britain to its knees led him into the disastrous Peninsular War (1808–1813) in Spain. In 1807, Napoleon had reached an agreement with Charles IV (ruled 1788–1808), the incompetent king of Spain, that permitted French troops to pass through his kingdom to conquer Portugal, Britain's ally (an arrangement that had functioned to guarantee Portugal's independence from Spain and had also provided Portuguese wine with a ready market for thirsty British people of means). A French army marched on Lisbon, and the Portuguese royal family fled to Brazil. An insurrection in March 1808 led to the abdication of Charles IV and the succession of his son Ferdinand VII (ruled 1808, 1814–1833) to the throne. Believing that the kingdom of Spain was on the verge of falling like an apple into his hands, Napoleon forced Ferdinand to abdicate that same year, and summoned his older brother, Joseph Bonaparte (1768–1844), from his wobbly throne in Naples to become king of Spain.

But Napoleon did not count on the resistance of the Spanish people. Ecclesiastical reforms imposed by Joseph and Napoleon, including the reduction in the number of monastic convents by two-thirds and the abolition of the Inquisition, angered the Church, which remained a powerful force in Spanish life. Napoleon found some allies among the urban middle class, but the Spanish nobility joined their old allies, the clergy, in opposition to the invaders. French forces were easy targets for the small, mobile groups of Spanish guerrillas, who attacked and then quickly disappeared into the Spanish landscape. British troops led by Arthur Wellesley, later duke of Wellington (1769–1852), arrived to help the Spanish and Portuguese fight the French. By 1810, about 350,000 French troops were tied up in the Iberian Peninsula. Fighting for "Church and king," Spaniards sustained what arguably was the first successful guerrilla war in modern Europe. Napoleon's "Spanish ulcer" bled France.

Stirrings of Nationalism in Napoleonic Europe

One of the lasting effects of the Napoleonic period was the quickening of German and, to a lesser extent, Italian national identity. The French revolutionaries had called for a war against the tyrants of Europe. But Napoleon

Francisco Goya's *The Third of May, 1808* depicts the execution of citizens of Madrid by French soldiers after the fall of the city during the Peninsular War.

seemed blind to the fact that the exportation of the principles of the French Revolution might encourage resentment and even nationalist feeling against the French in those countries conquered by his armies. Gradually the French discovered that nationalism was a double-edged sword. Some people in states conquered by French armies not only resented the occupation of their lands but they also began to long for the existence of a territorial state organized around their own nationality.

In any case, Napoleon sought to curry favor in each conquered state in exchange for support against his enemies. Napoleon may indeed have intended that Westphalia, created by the Treaty of Tilsit (1807) out of former Prussian territories and other smaller states that had fought against him, would become a model state. He ended serfdom and gave peasants the right to own land, to move through the kingdom as they pleased, and to send their children to school. But his principal goal was to bolster the Confederation of the Rhine's north flank against possible attacks against his interests.

Napoleon considered conquered territories sources for military conscripts and raw materials, or as potential markets for French goods. In Italy, French authorities forbade the importation of textile machinery and imposed disadvantageous tariffs, fearful of competition with their own industries. With the exception of Jacobin anti-clericals, intellectuals, and merchants who stood to profit from the French occupation, most people expressed little enthusiasm for the Napoleonic regime. In the Netherlands, the French occupation virtually brought the prosperous Dutch trading economy to a standstill. Poles soon began to doubt Napoleon's promise to reestablish Polish independence; some Polish nobles began to look to the Russian tsar for help, others to the king of Prussia. Among those territories conquered by Napoleon, open insurrections were relatively rare, although in the Austrian Tyrol, peasants sang nationalist songs as they fought against the French in 1813. The French armies waged war brutally against those who dared oppose them, burning villages and executing civilians, particularly in Spain, Tyrol, and southern Italy.

The impact of the French invasions on nationalism was perhaps clearest in the numerous German states. At first, some German intellectuals had praised Napoleon, but that soon changed. Attacks by German writers against French occupation mounted in 1807. That year, the French executed a Nuremburg bookseller accused of selling anti-French literature. Two years later, Napoleon escaped an assassination attempt by a young German student, the son of a Lutheran minister, who shouted "Long live Germany!" as he was executed. Gradually German writers espoused the view that people of the German states shared a common culture based upon language, tradition, and history. Only in the middle of the eighteenth century had German writers begun to write in their own language; before then, they considered French the language of culture. Like some composers, they began to discover elements of a common culture, drawing on language, literary texts, folk traditions, and other German cultural traditions to express themselves. This emotional quest for cultural and political institutions that would define "Germany" reflected some rejection of the rational tradition of Enlightenment thought identified with France.

Some German nationalists believed that the multiplicity of states in Central Europe stood in the way of eventual German unification. The Holy Roman Empire had been swept away in 1806. Napoleon destroyed the religious settlement imposed by the Treaty of Westphalia, which in 1648 had ended the Thirty Years' War. Napoleon may have helped the cause of German nationalism by eliminating some tiny states, increasing the territory of the middle-sized states at the expense of the former. About 60 percent of the population of the German states passed from one ruler to another during the revolutionary and Napoleonic eras. Yet in states such as Hanover and Württemburg, German particularism—local identity—was considered part of being German. Forty separate German states survived. Baden, Bavaria, and Württemberg, although much smaller and less powerful than Austria and Germany, emerged from the period with their independence and separate traditions for the most part intact.

Even though any possible political unification of Germany seemed distant, if not impossible, German nationalism nonetheless contributed to the determination with which the people of the German states resisted Napoleon. Johann Gottlieb Fichte (1762–1814) called on "the German nation," which he defined as including anyone who spoke German, to discover its spiritual unity.

In Spain, as we have seen, people of all classes came to view the French as invaders, not liberators. A constitution proposed by the Spanish Cortes in 1812 at Cádiz, which was not under French control, nonetheless reflected the influence of the French Revolution. It proclaimed freedom of the press, established an assembly to be elected by a relatively wide electorate, and abolished the Inquisition. But the constitution, although never implemented because of the eclipse of Spanish liberals in the wake of conservative reaction, was also a self-consciously nationalist document. Some Spaniards, too, were becoming more aware of their own shared linguistic, cultural, and historical traditions.

Military Reforms in Prussia and Austria

The successes of Napoleon's armies led Prussia (particularly in view of the devastating Prussian defeat at Jena in 1806), and, to a lesser extent, Austria, to enact military reforms. In 1807, a royal decree abolished serfdom in Prussia, with military efficiency in mind. Peasants were now free to leave the land to which they had been attached and to marry without the lord's permission. A decree three years later allowed peasants to convert some of the land they worked into their own property. Other reforms removed class barriers that had restricted the sale of land between nobles and non-nobles and that had served to keep middle-class men from assuming the military rank of officer (and had also prevented nobles from taking positions considered beneath their status). The Prussian military commander Baron Heinrich Karl vom und zum Stein (1757–1831) appointed some commoners to be officers and cashiered some of the more inept noble commanders. Stein established a ministry of war, taking away some important decisions from the whims of the king and his inner circle. In 1807, the Stein ministry abolished serfs' ties to the land, but the labor obligations and seigneurial dues of serfs remained in effect. This reform improved the loyalty of peasant-soldiers to the state. Stein called for greater patriotic participation in the national affairs of Prussia. Thus he and many other statesmen who resisted Napoleon continued to think in Prussian, not "German" terms. The elimination of most forms of corporal punishment enhanced troop morale, as did the rewarding of individual soldiers who served well. Stein also organized a civilian militia, which provided a proud, patriotic reserve of 120,000 part-time soldiers.

The Empire's Decline and the Russian Invasion

Napoleon now confronted the fact that he still had no legitimate children to inherit his throne. Although he loved his wife Josephine, he was as unfaithful to her during his lengthy absences as she was to him. Napoleon arranged for a bishop in Paris to annul his marriage—the pope having refused to do so—allowing him to remarry with the Church's blessing. Napoleon then considered diplomatically useful spouses. When the Russian tsar would not provide his younger sister, Napoleon arranged a marriage in 1810 with Marie-Louise (1791–1847), the daughter of Austrian Emperor Francis I. She had never even met Napoleon, but that in itself was not as unusual as the fact that the French emperor had an old enemy, the Archduke Charles (brother of Francis I and Napoleon's opponent during the 1809 war with Austria), stand in for him at the wedding ceremony, while he remained in Paris. Napoleon thus entered into a *de facto* alliance with the Habsburgs, Europe's oldest dynasty. Within a year, Marie-Louise presented Napoleon with a son and heir.

For the first time since Napoleon's remarkable rise to power, dissent also began to be heard openly inside France. Deserters and recalcitrant conscripts dodged authorities in increasing numbers beginning in about 1810. Royalist and Jacobin pamphlets and brochures circulated, despite censorship. Royalists objected to Napoleon's disdainful treatment of the pope, who excommunicated the emperor after France annexed the Papal States in 1809. Napoleon responded by simply placing Pius VII under house arrest, first near Genoa, and then near Paris in Fontainebleau.

Napoleon had become increasingly unable to separate options that were feasible or possible from those that were unlikely or indeed impossible to achieve. One of the emperor's ministers remarked: "It is strange that Napoleon, whose good sense amounted to genius, never discovered the point at which the impossible begins. . . . 'The impossible,' he told me with a smile, 'is the specter of the timid and the refuge of the coward . . . the word is only a confession of impotence' . . . he thought only of satisfying his own desires and adding incessantly to his own glory and greatness . . . death alone could set a limit to his plans and curb his ambition."

Napoleon's advisers now expressed their doubts about the emperor's endless plans for new conquests. Talleyrand had resigned as foreign minister in 1807, after the execution of the duke of Enghien. Talleyrand now symbolized the "party of peace," which opposed extending the empire past limits that could be effectively administered. In 1809, he began to negotiate secretly with Austria about the possibility of a monarchical restoration in France should Napoleon fall.

Napoleon's interest in expanding French influence in the eastern Mediterranean and his marriage to a Habsburg princess virtually assured war with Russia, which had reopened its ports to British and neutral vessels carrying English goods. Believing that he could enforce the continental blockade by defeating Russia, Napoleon prepared for war, forcing vanquished Austria and Prussia to agree to assist him. In the meantime, the tsar signed a peace treaty with the Ottoman Empire, freeing Russia to oppose Napoleon. Alexander I lined up the support of Sweden. There Jean-Baptiste Bernadotte

(1763–1844), once one of Napoleon's marshals, had been elected crown prince in 1810 and thus heir to the Swedish throne by the Swedish Estates (he would succeed the childless Charles XIII in 1818 as King Charles XIV). In return, the tsar offered Sweden a free hand in annexing Norway.

In June 1812, Napoleon's "Grand Army," over 600,000 strong, crossed the Niemen River from the Grand Duchy of Warsaw into Russia. Napoleon hoped to lure the Russian armies into battle. The Russians, however, simply retreated, drawing Napoleon ever farther into western Russia in late summer.

The Grand Army may have been the largest army ever raised up to that time, but the quality of Napoleon's army had declined since 1806 through casualties and desertions. Some of his finest troops were tied up in Spain. Half of the Grand Army consisted of Prussian, Italian, Austrian, Swiss, or Dutch conscripts. Officers now were by necessity more hurriedly trained. As the Grand Army was almost constantly at war, there was no chance to rebuild it to Napoleon's satisfaction.

In Russia, disease, heat, and hunger took a far greater toll on Napoleon's army than did the rearguard action of enemy troops. The Grand Army finally reached the city of Smolensk, 200 miles west of Moscow, in the middle of August; there the emperor planned to force the tsar to sign another humiliating peace. However, the Russian troops continued to retreat deeper into Russia. Napoleon's marshals begged him to stop in Smolensk and wait there. Tempted by the possibility of capturing Moscow, Napoleon pushed on until his army reached Borodino, sixty miles from Moscow. There the two armies fought to a costly draw in the bloodiest battle of the Napoleonic era, with 68,000 killed or wounded before the Russian army continued its retreat. Napoleon entered Moscow on September 14, 1812. He found it virtually deserted. Fires, probably set by Russian troops, spread quickly through the wooden buildings. Almost three-quarters of the city burned to the ground. The tsar and his armies had fled eastward.

Over 1,500 miles from Paris, without sufficient provisions, and with the early signs of the approaching Russian winter already apparent, Napoleon decided to march the Grand Army back to France. The retreat, which began on October 19, was a disaster. Russian troops picked off many among the retreating forces, forcing them to take an even longer route to Smolensk, 200 miles away. The Russians were waiting for Napoleon's beleaguered armies at the Berezina River, where they killed thousands of French soldiers. The emperor himself barely escaped capture by the Cossacks. The freezing winter then finished off most of what was left of Napoleon's Grand Army.

The retreat from Moscow was one of the greatest military debacles of any age. A contemporary described some of the French troops as "a mob of tattered ghosts draped in women's cloaks, odd pieces of carpet, or greatcoats burned full of holes, their feet wrapped in all sorts of rags . . . skeletons of soldiers went by, . . . with lowered heads, eyes on the ground, in absolute silence. . . ." Of the more than 600,000 men who had set out in June from

The retreat of the Grand Army in Russia, November 1812.

the Grand Duchy of Warsaw (Napoleon's defeat ended the hopes of Polish nationalists for independence), only about 40,000 returned to France in December. (Indeed, a mass grave of frozen soldiers of the Grand Army was discovered in Lithuania in 2003.) After racing ahead of the groans of the dying and the frozen corpses, Napoleon issued a famous bulletin that was sent back to Paris: "The health of the emperor has never been better."

Napoleon arrived at the Tuileries Palace in December 1812. In the wake of a military disaster of such dimensions that press censorship and duplicitous official bulletins (the expression "to lie like a military bulletin" became current) could not gloss over it, the mood of the French people soured.

Undaunted, Napoleon demanded a new levy of 350,000 more troops. This call, coming at a time of great economic hardship, was greeted with massive resentment and resistance. Instead of negotiating a peace that could have left France with the left bank of the Rhine River, Napoleon planned new campaigns and further expansion.

The Defeat of Napoleon

Napoleon now faced allies encouraged by his devastating defeat. In February 1813, Russia and Prussia signed an alliance, agreeing to fight Napoleon until the independence of the states of Europe was restored. Napoleon earned two costly victories over Russian and Prussian troops in the spring of 1813, but his casualties were high. Great Britain, still fighting the French in Spain, formally joined the coalition in June. Napoleon rejected Austrian conditions for peace, which included the dissolution of the Confederation of the Rhine, and Austria joined the coalition in August 1813. Napoleon's strategy of winning the temporary allegiance, or at least neutrality, of one of the other four European powers had failed.

In August 1813, Napoleon defeated the allies at Dresden, but then learned that Bavaria had seceded from the Confederation of the Rhine and joined the coalition against France. In October, his troops outnumbered two to one, Napoleon suffered a major defeat at Leipzig (in the Battle of the Nations) and retreated across the Rhine River into France. His armies, ever more filled with reluctant, raw recruits, lacked adequate supplies. An insurrection in the Netherlands followed by an allied invasion restored the prince of Orange to authority there. Austrian troops defeated a French army in northern Italy. The duke of Wellington's English forces drove the French armies from Spain and back across the Pyrenees. Forced to fight on French soil for the first time, Napoleon's discouraged armies were greeted with hostility when they tried to live off the land as they had abroad. Opponents of Napoleon, including some for whom a Bourbon restoration seemed a possibility, now spoke more openly in France.

Early in 1814, the allies proposed peace (perhaps insincerely, assuming the French emperor would refuse) if Napoleon would accept France's natural frontiers of the Rhine River, the Alps, and the Pyrenees. Napoleon stalled. An allied army of 200,000 moved into eastern France. In Paris, the Legislative Body approved a document that amounted to a denunciation of the emperor, though it never reached the public. Even Napoleon's normally dutiful older brother Joseph encouraged the members of the Council of State to sign a petition calling for peace.

The allies were determined not to stop until they had captured Paris. After overcoming stiff French resistance, the main allied force swept into the

(*Left*) Arthur Wellesley, the duke of Wellington. (*Right*) Charles Maurice de Talleyrand.

French capital in March 1814. Tsar Alexander I of Russia and King Frederick William III of Prussia rode triumphantly into the city. At Fontainebleau, Napoleon's marshals refused to join in his frantic plans for an attack on the allies in Paris and pressured him to abdicate. Talleyrand called the Senate into session. It voted to depose Napoleon. The allies refused to consider Napoleon's abdication in favor of his three-year-old son. Without an army and, perhaps for the first time, without hope, Napoleon abdicated on April 6, 1814, and then took poison, which failed to kill him. The long adventure finally seemed at an end.

MONARCHICAL RESTORATION AND NAPOLEON'S RETURN

The allies sought the restoration of the Bourbon monarchy. The French Senate, too, expressed its wish that Louis XVI's brother, the count of Provence, return to France as Louis XVIII. By the Treaty of Fontainebleau (April 11, 1814), the allies exiled Napoleon to a Mediterranean island off the coast of Italy. Bonaparte would be emperor of Elba. Marie-Louise refused to accompany him, preferring to be duchess of Parma, receiving the title by virtue of being a member of the Austrian royal family.

The Bourbon Restoration

The count of Provence entered Paris on May 3, 1814, as King Louis XVIII (ruled 1814–1815; 1815–1824). With more than a little wishful thinking, he announced that this was the nineteenth year of his reign (counting from the death of the son of Louis XVI, who had died in 1795 in a Paris prison without ever reigning). The allies worked out a surprisingly gracious peace treaty with France, largely thanks to Talleyrand's skilled diplomacy. The Treaty of Paris, signed on May 30, 1814, left France with Savoy and small chunks of land in Germany and the Austrian Netherlands—in other words, the France of November 1, 1792. France could now rejoin the monarchies of Europe.

Louis XVIII, king of the French. Note the perhaps unconscious Napoleonic pose.

Louis XVIII signed a constitutional "Charter" that granted his people "public liberties," promising that a legislature would be elected, based on a very restricted franchise. Although the document affirmed monarchical rule by divine right, it confirmed some of the important victories of the Revolution, including equality before the law and freedom of expression and religion, although Catholicism would be the religion of the state (see Chapter 15). A coterie of fanatical nobles and their followers (the Ultra-royalists) convinced the king to enact some measures, however, that were highly unpopular. Many in France disapproved of the substitution of the white flag of the Bourbon family for the tricolor, the description of the Charter as a "gift" from the king to the French people, the retiring of 14,000 officers at half pay, the restoration of returned émigrés to high positions in the army, and the return to their original owners of national lands that had not been sold. But most of the French were simply exhausted from years of wars and sacrifice.

The 100 Days

In March 1815, just months after his exile, Napoleon boldly escaped from Elba and landed near Antibes on the French Mediterranean coast. He knew that he retained considerable popularity in France. Furthermore, so much time had passed and so many dramatic events had occurred since the execution of Louis XVI that one of the monarchy's staunchest supporters claimed, with some exaggeration, "The Bourbons were as unknown in France as the Ptolemies."

The word that Napoleon had landed in France stunned everyone. Marshal Ney, who had offered his services to the Bourbons, promised to bring Napoleon back to Paris in a cage. But upon seeing Napoleon, Ney fell into his arms. Regiment after regiment went over to Napoleon as he marched north. With Bonaparte nearing Paris, Louis XVIII and his family and advisers fled to Belgium, which had become part of the Kingdom of Holland. Soon Napoleon again paced frenetically through the Tuileries Palace, making plans to raise new armies.

It was not to be. The allies quickly raised an enormous army of more than 700,000 troops. Napoleon led an army of 200,000 men into the Austrian Netherlands, engaging Prussian and British forces south of Brussels on June 16, 1815. He forced the Prussians to retreat and ordered one of his generals to pursue them with his army. Napoleon then moved against the British forces commanded by Wellington, his old nemesis. The armies met near the village of Waterloo on June 18, 1815. Wellington had skillfully hidden the extent of his superior infantry behind a ridge. Napoleon watched in horror as a Prussian army arrived to reinforce Wellington. The general sent in pursuit of the Prussians, like all Napoleon's commanders, had been taught to follow Napoleon's directives to the letter and not to improvise. He held back until it was too late. When the imperial guard broke ranks and retreated, much of the rest of the French army did the same. The defeat was devastating and total.

BATTLE OF WATERLOO.

The Battle of Waterloo, June 18, 1815.

Napoleon abdicated a second time. He surrendered to British forces near the western coast of France, while hoping to find a way to sail to America. This time the exile would be final. The allies packed Napoleon off to the small island of Saint Helena, in the South Atlantic, 1,000 miles away from any mainland. The closest island of any size was Ascension, a British naval base, some 600 miles distant. Louis XVIII returned to take up the throne of France a second time, 100 days after fleeing Paris.

On Saint Helena, Napoleon's health gradually declined. He died on May 5, 1821, his last words being "France, army, head of the army, Josephine." He died of an ulcer, probably a cancerous one, despite stories to this day that he was poisoned by arsenic.

NAPOLEON'S LEGACY

Napoleon's testament, a masterpiece of political propaganda, tried to create a myth that he saved the Revolution in France. "Every Frenchman could say during my reign,—'I shall be minister, grand officer, duke, count, baron, if I earn it—even king!'" And in some ways, Napoleon was indeed the heir to the French Revolution. He guaranteed the survival of some of its most significant triumphs. Napoleon considered his greatest achievement "that of establishing and consecrating the rule of reason." His Napoleonic Code proclaimed the equality of all people before the law (favoring, however, men over women), personal freedom, and the inviolability of property. Napoleon furthered the myth, and to some extent the reality, of the "career open to talent," which aided, above all, the middle class, but even peasants in some cases. He consolidated the role of wealth, principally property ownership, as the foundation of the political life of the nation. This increased the number of citizens eligible to participate in political life, however limited by imperial strictures. Furthermore, Napoleon helped turn nationalism into an aggressive secular religion, manipulating this patriotic energy and transforming it into an ideology inculcated by French schools.

Napoleon's reforms, built upon those of the French Revolution, extended into states conquered by his imperial armies. The French imposed constitutions and state control over the appointment of clergy, standardized judicial systems, and abolished ecclesiastical courts. Napoleon created new tax structures, standardized weights and measures, ended internal customs barriers, abolished guilds, and established state bureaucracies that were extensions of French rule in the "sister republics" founded by the Directory. In addition to abolishing serfdom and proclaiming equality before the law in Poland, the French occupation also ended residual peasant seigneurial obligations (such as the requirement to provide labor services to the lord) virtually everywhere, and abolished noble and ecclesiastical courts in northern Italy and the Netherlands. The Napoleonic Code proclaimed freedom of worship, and the French conquest of other European states, including Baden, Bavaria, and the Netherlands, helped remove onerous restrictions on Jews. But under pressure from French planters, Napoleon also reestablished slavery in Haiti in 1802.

Yet Napoleon's success in implementing reforms varied from place to place, depending on existing political structures, the degree of compliance by local elites, and the international situation. In southern Italy, for example, which Napoleon's armies conquered relatively late and where the structures of state authority had always been particularly weak, the French presence had little lasting effect. As the Napoleonic wave subsided, nobles and clergy regained domination over the overwhelmingly rural, impoverished local population.

Napoleon claimed from Saint Helena that he was trying to liberate Europe, but he had actually replaced the old sovereigns with new ones—himself or his brothers. "If I conquered other kingdoms," he admitted, "I did so in order that France would be the beneficiary." Wagons returned from Italy full of art and other treasures, which became the property of Napoleon and his family, his marshals, or the state. French conquests helped awaken nationalism in the German states and Spain.

To the writer Germaine de Staël (1766–1817), the daughter of the Swiss banker Jacques Necker, Louis XVI's minister, Napoleon "regarded a human being as an action or a thing . . . nothing existed but himself. He was an able chess player, and the human race was the opponent to whom he proposed to give checkmate." In the end, his monumental ambition got the best of him.

About 2 million men served in Napoleon's armies between 1805 and 1814; about 90,000 died in battle and more than three times that number subsequently perished from wounds or disease; over 600,000 were later recorded as prisoners or "disappeared." Reflecting in 1813, Napoleon put it this way: "I grew up on the battlefield. A man like me does not give a damn about the lives of a million men." Indeed, Napoleon's armies may have suffered as many as 1.5 million casualties. The Napoleonic Wars killed about one in five of all Frenchmen born between 1790 and 1795.

Napoleon's final legacy was his myth. From Saint Helena, he claimed, "If I had succeeded, I would have been the greatest man known to history." The rise of romanticism helped make the story of Napoleon, the romantic hero, part of the collective memory of Western Europe after his death. Long after Waterloo, peddlers of songs, pamphlets, lithographs, and other images glorified Napoleon's life as earlier they had the lives of saints. "I live only for posterity," Napoleon once said. "Death is nothing, but to live defeated and without glory is to die every day." Rumors of his miraculous return to France were persistent long after his death. So powerful was his legend that even the most improbable seemed possible.

Of the changes in the post-Napoleonic period that profoundly transformed the way Europeans lived, none arguably had more important social, political, and cultural consequences than the Industrial Revolution. Having begun in England in the middle decades of the eighteenth century, it accelerated in that country during the first decades of the nineteenth century. It spread to Western Europe in particular, but affected regions in other places as well. The Industrial Revolution and its critics would help shape the modern world.

CHAPTER 14

THE INDUSTRIAL REVOLUTION

$\sim$

Manufacturing on a small scale had been part of the European experience for centuries. The economy of every region had depended to some extent on the production of clothes, tools, pots, and pans. Most production was carried out by men and women working in small workshops, hammering and shaping household goods, or by country women weaving or knitting clothes.

During the first half of the nineteenth century, the Industrial Revolution slowly but surely transformed the way many Europeans lived. In Western Europe, it became easier for entrepreneurs to raise money for investment as banking and credit institutions became more sophisticated. Dramatic improvements in transportation, notably the development of the railroad and steamship but also the construction of more and better roads, expanded markets. Rising agricultural productivity, increasingly commercialized in Western Europe, fed a larger population. Western Europe underwent a period of rapid urbanization: the number of people living in cities and towns grew more rapidly than did the percentage of people residing in the countryside, although the latter still predominated.

As the population expanded, demand increased for manufactured goods. The number of people working in industry rose. Mechanized production slowly revolutionized the textile and metallurgical industries, increasingly bringing together workers, including women and children, in large workshops and factories. Rural industry declined and, in some regions, disappeared. Rural producers in much of France, the uplands of Zurich in Switzerland, and Ireland, among others, lost out to more efficient urban, factory-based competitors. Slowly but surely factory production transformed the way Europeans worked and lived.

While many contemporaries were amazed and impressed by factory production of goods and watched and rode trains in wonderment and appreciation, others were shocked at what seemed to be the human costs of such a transformation. Poor migrants flooded into towns and cities,

A factory town in Germany in the 1830s.

which burgeoned as never before. Conditions of life in gritty industrial towns were appalling. At the same time, large-scale industrialization undercut many artisans, who lost protection when guilds were abolished under the influence of the French Revolution. Mechanization undercut their livelihood. At the same time, lurid but not inaccurate accounts of the awful conditions of workers (men, women, and children) in factories and mines began to reach the public. Calls for state-sponsored reform from state officials and middle-class moralists echoed far and wide. Moreover, many skilled workers in Western Europe not only protested harsh conditions of work and life but began to see themselves as a class with interests defined by shared work experience. During the 1830s and 1840s, workers began to demand social and political reform. Proclaiming the equality of all people, the dignity of labor, and the perniciousness of unrestrained capitalism, the first socialists challenged the existing economic, social, and political order.

PRECONDITIONS FOR TRANSFORMATION

We have come to call the transformation of the European economy the "Industrial Revolution." It began in England and parts of northwestern Europe during the eighteenth century (see Chapter 10). Early histories of the Industrial Revolution tended to emphasize the suddenness of the changes it brought; historians sought to identify the exact period of industrial "take-off" in each country, underlining the role of inventions, mechanization, and factories in the process. This led to an emphasis on "victors" and "laggards," "winners" and "losers" in the quest for large-scale industrialization, a preoccupation that blinded historians to the complexity of the manufacturing revolution.

Recent work, however, has de-emphasized the suddenness of these changes. Despite the importance of inventions such as those that gradually transformed textile manufacturing, the first Industrial Revolution was largely the intensification of forms of production that already existed. Most industrial work still was organized traditionally, using non-mechanized production. Rural industry and female labor remained essential components of manufacturing. Not until the mid-nineteenth century, when steam power came to be used in many different industries in Western Europe, did industrial manufacturing leave behind traditional forms of production. Handicraft production remained fundamental to manufacturing, as did domestic industry (tasks such as spinning, weaving, and product finishing done for the most part, but not exclusively, by women in the countryside). For example, the growth of the linen industry in Porto, Portugal, stemmed not from factories, but from the work of villagers in the countryside who were paid for spinning and weaving per piece. Even in England, the cradle of large-scale industrialization, craft production and rural "outwork"—work farmed out to cheap labor—remained important until the second half of the nineteenth century. Even in Britain at mid-century, the majority of British industrial workers were not employed in factories. In Germany there were twice as many "home workers" as workers employed in factories. In the Paris region in 1870, the average manufacturer still employed only seven people.

The Industrial Revolution could not have occurred without increased agricultural productivity, which sustained a dramatically larger population. In turn, an increase in population generated greater consumer demand for manufactured goods, now transported in many places by trains and steamships.

Demographic Explosion

The rise in population in Europe that began in the eighteenth century accelerated during the first half of the nineteenth century. Europe's population grew from an estimated 187 million in 1800 to about 266 million in 1850, an increase of 43 percent. Europe was then the most densely populated of the world's continents, with about 18.7 people per square kilometer in 1800 (compared to approximately 14 people in Asia and fewer than 5 in Africa and the United States), rising to about 26.6 fifty years later.

Industrializing northwestern Europe—Britain, Belgium, and northern France—had the greatest population increases (see Table 14.1). Britain's

Table 14.1. Estimated Populations of Various European Countries from 1800 to 1850 (in millions)

Country	1800	1850
Denmark	0.9	1.6
Norway	0.9	1.5 (1855)
Finland	1.0	1.6
Switzerland	1.8	2.4
Holland	2.2	3.1
Sweden	2.3	3.5
Belgium	3.0	4.3 (1845)
Portugal	3.1	4.2 (1867)
Ireland	5.0	6.6
Great Britain	10.9	20.9
Spain	11.5	15.5 (1857)
Italy	18.1	23.9
Austria-Hungary	23.3	31.3
The German states	24.5	31.7
France	26.9	36.5

Source: Carlo M. Cipolla, *The Fontana Economic History of Europe: Vol. 3, The Industrial Revolution* (London, 1973), p. 29.

population tripled during the nineteenth century. The population of predominantly agricultural societies rose as well. Sweden's population more than doubled over the course of the nineteenth century. Russia's population also grew substantially, from about 36 million in 1796 to about 45 million in 1815 to at least 67 million in 1851. The population of the Balkans rose from about 10 million in 1830 to four times that ninety years later.

Nonetheless, disease and hunger continued to interrupt cycles of growth well into the twentieth century. Cholera tore a deadly path through much of Europe in the early 1830s and reappeared several times until the 1890s. During the Irish potato famine in the late 1840s, between 1 and 2 million people died of hunger in Ireland. Tuberculosis (known to contemporaries as "consumption") still killed off many people, especially workers and particularly miners.

Overall, however, the mortality rate fell rapidly in the first half of the century. Vaccination made smallpox, among other diseases, somewhat rarer. Municipal authorities in some places paid more attention to cleanliness, sewage disposal, and the purity of the water supply, although the most significant improvements did not come until later in the century. Sand filters and iron pipes helped make water more pure. Improvements in reservoirs, the first of which was built in 1806, increased the availability of clean water.

Life expectancy increased in all classes. Individuals surviving their first years could anticipate living longer than their predecessors. Fewer women died young, thus prolonging the period during which they could bear children. Furthermore, wives were less likely to suffer the loss of their partner during this same period, and therefore were more likely to become pregnant. Yet poor people—above all, in cities—remained far more vulnerable than people of means to fatal illness. In Liverpool, half of all children born to the poorest families died before the age of five. In eastern and southern Europe, mortality and birthrates continued to be quite high until late in the century.

Despite the fact that infant mortality rates remained high until the 1880s, the chances of a baby surviving his or her first year of life rose because of rudimentary improvements in sanitation, such as a safer water supply and better waste disposal. "Wet-nursing," a common practice in which urban families sent babies to women in the countryside to be nursed, traditionally had taken a heavy toll on infants because of illness and accidents. Mothers, particularly poor ones, would not have sent their babies to wet nurses if keeping them at home did not also pose a risk. Many mothers needed to work to help keep the family economy afloat, and not all were, in any case, healthy enough to breast-feed or able to supply enough milk. Substituting cow's or goat's milk could be lethal, and also had been a cause of high mortality rates during the warm summer months. Now the practice of wet-nursing slowly declined. Fresh milk became more readily available, and by the end of the century people were aware that it must be sterilized.

The decline in mortality, particularly among infants, preceded and encouraged a fall in the birthrate in Western Europe. With more adults surviving childhood, the subsequent decline in birthrates had much to do with choice. The French birthrate, in particular, gradually fell, and then plunged dramatically beginning with the agricultural crisis of 1846–1847. Many farming families in France had fewer children so that inheritance would not be spread too thin.

Europe also enjoyed nearly a century of relative peace, broken only by brief and limited wars. A Swedish bishop, then, was not wrong to describe the causes of his overwhelmingly rural country's rise in population during the first half of the century as "peace, vaccine, and potatoes."

The Expanding Agricultural Base

Agricultural production sustained the rise in population (although more easily in western than in eastern or southern Europe). It also permitted the accumulation of capital, which could be reinvested in commercialized farming or in manufacturing. Capital-intensive production (larger-scale and market-oriented farming) underlay the agricultural revolution. More land gradually came under cultivation as marshes, brambles, bogs, and heaths gave way to the plow. Between 1750 and 1850 in Britain, 6 million acres—or one-fourth of the country's cultivable land—were incorporated into larger farms.

Farm yields increased in most of Europe. England produced almost three times more grain in the 1830s than in the previous century. The elimination of more fallow land (land left untilled for a growing season so that the soil could replenish itself) helped. Some farmers raised cattle or specialized in vegetables and fruits for the burgeoning urban market. Farmers increased yield by using more intensive agricultural techniques and fertilizers, which, in turn, accentuated demand for sturdier manufactured agricultural tools.

During the first half of the century, continental visitors to England were surprised to find that, in contrast to the world they knew, relatively few small family farms remained. With the ongoing consolidation of plots, the number of rural people dependent on wage labor for survival rose. Farm work in 1831 remained the largest single source of adult male employment in Britain, employing almost a million men. Thus, the English countryside was peopled by a relatively small number of "gentlemen"—including British nobles—of great wealth who owned most of the country, landed gentry of considerable means, many yeomen (independent landowners and tenant farmers of some means), and landless laborers, who moved from place to place in the search for any kind of farm work. The tough lives of the latter reflected a too-often forgotten human dimension of the agricultural revolution, which increased the vulnerability of the rural poor.

On the continent, there was not as much consolidation of land as in England, but there, too, productivity rose as more land was brought into cultivation and fertilizers became more widely used. French agricultural production rose rapidly after 1815, as northern farmers with fairly large plots began to rotate their crops three times a year. In the south, where the soil was of a generally poorer quality, the land more subdivided, and much of it rocky, peasants planted vineyards, although the wine they produced hardly caused the owners of the great vineyards of Burgundy or the Bordeaux region to lie awake at night worrying. Farmers terracing hillsides, goats climbing up steep slopes, and the sounds of silkworms munching mulberry leaves as peasants anticipated the harvest of raw silk characterized some Mediterranean regions.

In Central Europe and parts of Eastern Europe, too, a modest increase in agricultural production occurred. In the German states, agricultural productivity rose more than twice as fast as the population between 1816 and 1865. Prussian agricultural productivity jumped by 60 percent during the first half of the century, partly because of improved metal plows and other farm implements, as well as because of information disseminated by new agricultural societies. As in Britain and France, root crops, such as turnips and the potato, added nutrition to the diet of the poor. Even in the impoverished Balkans, some peasants began to grow corn, potatoes, and tomatoes.

Yet in much of Europe, including Portugal, where two-thirds of the land was not cultivated, and the Balkans and Greece, subsistence agriculture continued as it had for centuries. In Russia, the rich Black Earth region, covering the middle Volga River area and much of Ukraine, still was undeveloped. During the first half of the nineteenth century, some of the larger estates, benefiting from fertilizer and even some farm machinery, began to produce and export more wheat and rye. The yield of potatoes and sugar beets increased dramatically during the 1830s and 1840s. Yet Russian farms could barely feed the empire's huge population in good times, and their output was grossly inadequate in bad times. Serfdom still shackled Russian farm productivity.

Trains and Steamboats

Besides the growth in population and the expansion of the agricultural base, remarkable improvements in transportation also contributed to the transformations of the Industrial Revolution. The first railroad train began hauling coal in northern England in 1820, and passenger train service began between Liverpool and Manchester in 1830. (It was macabre testimony to the novelty of the train that the British minister of commerce was run down and killed by a train after stepping out of a carriage.) Britain had about 100 miles of rail in 1830 and 6,600 in 1852. Railway construction employed 200,000 men by mid-century. Some observers compared the building of rail lines to the construction of the pyramids of ancient Egypt, as embankments, tunnels, and bridges transformed the countryside. The wonders of modern science were now clearly applied to daily life. In England railroad terminology was swiftly incorporated into the teaching of the alphabet, and board games and puzzles quickly embraced the train. Paintings, lithographs, drawings, and engravings took the magic of the railroad and the wonders of travel as themes. Giant railway stations became centers of urban activity, attracting hotels and commerce (see Map 14.1).

The railroad's development served as a significant catalyst for investment, catching the imagination of the middle classes, which identified the railway with progress that could be seen, heard, and experienced. Private investment completely financed British railways during this period. Whereas earlier investments in businesses had been largely the preserve of patricians, smaller companies undertaking railroad construction attracted middle-class investors. Railway booms accustomed more middle-class people to the benefits (up to 10 percent annually in 1846), as well as the risks, of investment. The value of the stock-in-trade of the London and North Western Railway had outstripped that of the East India Company by the mid-nineteenth century.

MAP 14.1 PRINCIPAL BRITISH RAILWAY LINES, 1851

The construction and operation of railroads also brought other benefits to the expanding British economy. Railroad construction spurred the metallurgical industry. Rail transport reduced shipping costs by about two-thirds, dramatically increasing consumption and, in turn, production. Trains carried "railway milk" from the countryside and frozen meat from the port of

The opening of the Stockton and Darlington Railway in 1825.

Southampton to London. Yet, at the same time, railways also entailed the destruction of large swaths of major city centers, displacing about 50,000 people in Manchester during a seventy-five year period, and many times that in London. Railway construction also brought continental states into the realm of economic decision making; in France, the government and private companies cooperated in building a railway system. In Belgium and Austria, the railway system was state owned from the beginning (see Map 14.2).

Railways became part of the social and cultural landscape. The relatively rapid pace of travel arguably helped spread the sense of being "on time," and in the 1850s Greenwich time, or "railway time," had become standard in Britain. Trains brought places much closer together, carrying newspapers and mail more rapidly than could ever have been imagined. The first trains could speed along at twenty-five miles an hour, three times faster than the finest carriages. An English clergyman described his first train ride in 1830: "No words can convey an adequate notion of the magnificence (cannot use a smaller word) of our progress . . . soon we felt that we were GOING. . . . The most intense curiosity and excitement prevailed." Railroad companies were quick to divide their cars into first-, second-, and third-class service, although at first the luxuries were limited to foot-warmers in winter. For people of more modest means, second- or even third-class carriages (called "penny a mile" travel in Britain, with train wagons not even sheltered from the elements until the mid-1840s) had to suffice. English seaside resorts lured middle-class visitors and some craftsmen and their families. Trains ran

MAP 14.2 PRINCIPAL CONTINENTAL RAILWAY LINES, 1851 More railway lines existed in the north than in the south of Europe, as industrialization proceeded more quickly in northern France, Belgium, the German states, and the northern Italian states than in southern France or southern Italy.

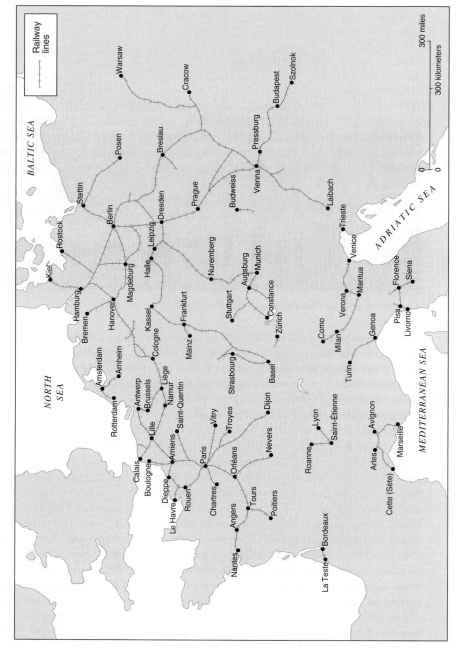

to German health spas and casinos, whose clientele a century earlier had been limited to princes and noblemen.

Yet some contemporaries already feared the environmental costs of the iron tracks and black soot pouring from locomotives. Fearing for nature, the British poet William Wordsworth (1770–1850) denounced the plan to build a line into the Lakes District: "Is then no nook of English ground secure / From rash assault?" In the 1870s the English writer John Ruskin (1819–1900) lamented railways that "slashed like a knife through the delicate tissues of a settled rural civilization. . . . Your railroad mounds, vaster than the walls of Babylon, they brutally amputated every hill on their way." Yet after mid-century the use of steel rails, more powerful locomotives, and innovations in engineering eliminated enormous excavations and earthworks, meaning less damage to the landscape.

Speed—at least relatively speaking—was also brought to rivers and oceans. In 1816, a steamship, combining steam and sail power, sailed from Liverpool to Boston in seventeen days, halving the previous best time for the journey. Steamboats, which began to operate on Europe's rivers in the 1820s and 1830s, revolutionized travel and transport. By 1840, the transport of Irish cattle and dairy products to England alone fully engaged eighty steamships. A constant procession of steamships traveled the Rhine River from Basel, Switzerland, to the Dutch seaport of Rotterdam.

At the same time, the contribution of improved, paved roads to the Industrial Revolution should not be forgotten. Here, too, the story of European economic development involved continuity as much as innovation, reminding us that in some significant ways the Industrial Revolution was based upon an innovative expansion of technologies and ways of doing things that were already in place.

The Great Western leaving Bristol in 1838 for its maiden voyage to New York. Steam power reduced the trip to nineteen days.

A VARIETY OF NATIONAL INDUSTRIAL EXPERIENCES

During the first half of the nineteenth century, the Industrial Revolution affected Western Europe more than the countries in southern or eastern Europe. Furthermore, within states some regions underwent significant shifts toward a manufacturing economy: Catalonia, but not Castile in Spain; the Ruhr and Rhineland in the German states, but not East Prussia; Piedmont and Lombardy in northern Italy, but not southern Italy and Sicily (see Map 14.3).

Some regions that developed modern industries had the advantage of building on long-standing economic bases (see Table 14.2). This was true in Belgium, newly independent since 1831, which emerged with continental Europe's greatest concentration of mechanized production and factories. While Belgium's northern neighbor, the once-great trading power of the Netherlands, continued its relative economic decline, Belgium seemed to offer a blueprint for rapid industrial development. Like the Netherlands, it was densely populated and urbanized, which provided demand for manufactured goods and labor. Flanders had for centuries been a center of trade and the production of fine textiles. Belgian manufacturing boomed. Blessed with rich coal deposits, Belgium's railroad construction advanced rapidly, facilitating the transport of goods from Belgian ports to Central Europe.

TABLE 14.2. MANUFACTURING CAPACITY THROUGHOUT EUROPE (THOUSANDS OF HORSEPOWER OF STEAM POWER)

Country	1800	1850
Great Britain	620	1,290
The German states	40	260
France	90	270
Austria	20	100
Belgium	40	70
Russia	20	70
Italy	10	20
Spain	10	20
The Netherlands	—	10
Europe	860	2,240

Source: Carlo M. Cipolla, ed. *The Fontana Economic History of Europe: Vol. 4(1), The Emergence of Industrial Societies* (London, 1973), p. 165.

In the Vanguard: Britain's Era of Mechanization

Why did the Industrial Revolution begin in England? Britain was well on the way to becoming the "workshop of the world" in the second half of the eighteenth century. Capital-intensive commercialized farming began to trans-

MAP 14.3 THE INDUSTRIAL REVOLUTION IN EUROPE, 1815–1860 Areas of industrial concentration and growth in Britain and on the continent.

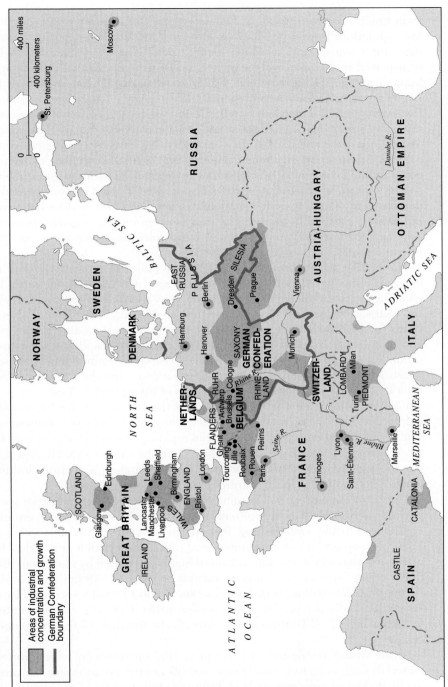

Areas of industrial
concentration and growth
German Confederation
boundary

form English agriculture earlier than anywhere else, feeding Britain's growing population. Britain was blessed with coal and iron ore deposits located near water transportation, which made it possible for raw materials to be transported to factories with relative ease. British commercial domination, built in part on its rich colonial trade, provided capital for investment in manufacturing. British entrepreneurs relied heavily on self-finance, and at first banks played a relatively small role in long-term investment. However, the government did encourage a precocious banking system that would assume a greater role later in the century. It was far easier to begin a company in Britain than on the continent; after 1840, any number of people could form a company in Britain simply by registering with the government.

The structure of British society also proved conducive to economic development. There were fewer social barriers between wealthy landowning nobles, prosperous gentry, and eager entrepreneurs. Dissenters (non-Anglican Protestants) were afforded basic toleration, and some became manufacturers.

The British government adopted a general policy of non-interference in business. But Parliament, which had protected British manufacturers by enacting tariffs in the eighteenth century, now was able to reduce tariffs in the 1820s, shrugging off foreign economic challenges. Parliament allocated funds for England's burgeoning transportation network, aiding merchants and manufacturers. Parliamentary acts of enclosure (facilitating the consolidation of arable strips of land and the division of common lands) helped wealthy landowners add to their holdings, augmenting the productivity of their land and permitting the accumulation of investment capital.

English cotton manufacturing, gradually transformed by mechanization, led the Industrial Revolution and carried along other industries in its wake. The popularity of cotton clothing spread rapidly, allowing poor people to be more adequately clothed. Cotton fabric could be more easily cleaned and was less expensive than wool, worsted, and other materials. Cotton clothing joined silks and linens in the wardrobes of the wealthy.

The cotton manufacturer became the uncrowned king of industrial society in Britain, revered as the epitome of the successful entrepreneur, enriching himself while embellishing Britain's reputation. Between 1789 and 1850, the amount of raw cotton imported into Britain (much of it picked by plantation slaves in the southern United States) increased by more than fifty times, rising from about 11 million pounds per year to 588 million pounds. During the same period, British production of cotton textiles increased from 40 million yards per year to 2,025 million yards. Cotton goods accounted for about half of all British exports through the first half of the nineteenth century.

In the British textile industry, spinning (the operation by which fibrous materials such as cotton, wool, linen, and silk are turned into thread or yarn) gradually had become mechanized during the last decades of the eighteenth century (see Chapter 10). The advent of power looms and power weaving

Power looms in a British cotton factory, 1830.

(the process by which threads are interlaced to make cloth or fabric) removed the last bottleneck to fully mechanized production. The number of power looms in England multiplied rapidly, from 2,400 in 1813 to 85,000 in 1833 to 224,000 in 1850.

Industrialization in France

France was the world's second leading economy, although the wars during the revolutionary and Napoleonic periods had interrupted economic development. The revolutionary government had eliminated some hurdles for French businessmen by ending the tangle of regional customs barriers and tax differences. But France's coal deposits were less rich and more dispersed and were far from iron ore deposits and canals. Thus, transportation costs kept up the prices of raw materials. Demand was also less in France than in Britain because the French population rose by only 30 percent during the first half of the nineteenth century; in Britain the population had doubled during the same period. French agricultural production developed more slowly than that of Britain; small family farms remained characteristic. High agricultural tariffs did not encourage agricultural efficiency.

French banking facilities remained relatively rudimentary compared to those in Britain and the Netherlands. The primary function of the Bank of France, created by Napoleon in 1800, was to loan money to the state. The handful of private banks, which were run out of the deep pockets of wealthy families, preferred to make what appeared to be safer loans to governments.

Furthermore, banks—like investors—faced unlimited liability in the event of bankruptcy. Deposit banks were specifically denied the right to invest in private industry, except for investment in companies enjoying state concessions, such as those building the railways. Even normal business transactions were complicated by the fact that more than 90 percent of payments had to be made in specie (gold or silver). Until the late 1850s, the smallest banknote was worth 500 francs (the equivalent of almost a year's earnings for an unskilled worker). Banks thus had considerable difficulty attracting ordinary depositors.

The French state shared investors' suspicions of companies of any size, limiting the number of investment "joint-stock companies" that could be created. Furthermore, many companies were cautious family firms that invested profits in land rather than in the expansion of their businesses. With many peasant families still hiding their money in their houses or gardens, it was difficult to raise investment capital.

In France, too, textile production provided the catalyst for industrial development. At the same time, between the end of the Napoleonic Wars in 1815 and the beginning of the economic crisis of 1846–1847, the production of coal tripled, and that of pig iron doubled. But the reputation of French industry proudly rested on the production of luxury products, "articles of Paris" such as gloves, umbrellas, and boots, as well as fine furniture. Workshop production—for example of barrels, pipes, and watches—expanded into

A rural joiner's workshop in France.

many rural areas in response to increased demand, spurred by a modest level of urban growth. Rural industry, characterized by low capital investment, remained essential to French economic growth.

French manufacturers benefited from increased state assistance. The July Monarchy (1830–1848), the constitutional Monarchy brought by the July Revolution of 1830 (see Chapter 15), encouraged business interests, sometimes maintaining high tariffs that protected special interests—for example, those of textile manufacturers, who feared outside competition from British imports. Taxes on commerce and industry remained extraordinarily low. The government provided a decisive push in the launching of railways in France, purchasing the land and bridges along which the tracks were to pass and guaranteeing a minimum return on investments in railway development. Bankruptcy laws became less onerous, eliminating the humiliation of incarceration as a penalty. New legislation made it easy for investors to join together to form new companies with people to whom they were not related or, in some cases, did not even know—hence their name, "anonymous societies" (*sociétés anonymes*). The government also pleased businessmen by crushing insurrections by republicans and by silkworkers in Lyon in the early 1830s. Furthermore, strikes, legalized in Britain with the repeal of the Combination Acts (1799–1800) in 1824, remained illegal in France until 1864.

Industrialization in the German States

In the German states, industrialization lagged behind that of Britain and France. Three main factors undercut manufacturing in the German states: the multiplicity of independent states; the labyrinth of tolls and customs barriers, a veritable financial gauntlet through which any wagon or boat carrying merchandise had to pass; and virtual monopolies held by guilds over the production and distribution of certain products. The German states remained as a whole overwhelmingly rural, their percentage of rural population barely declining at all between 1816 and 1872. Furthermore, the harvest failure and subsequent agricultural depression of 1846, compounded by the Revolutions of 1848 (see Chapter 16), temporarily halted German economic development, like that of France, in its tracks.

Yet beginning in the mid-1830s, textile manufacturing developed in the three most demographically dynamic regions—the Rhineland, Saxony, and Silesia (see Map 14.3). Berlin emerged as a center of machine production. Coal mining and iron production developed in the Ruhr Basin, which had half of the coal riches of the entire continent. The Prussian state appointed directors to serve on the boards of private companies, brought technical experts from Britain to help develop industries, encouraged technical education, and founded associations for the encouragement of industrialization. In the 1840s, the Bank of Prussia began operating as a joint-stock credit bank to provide investment capital, the lack of which limited industrial development in the other German states.

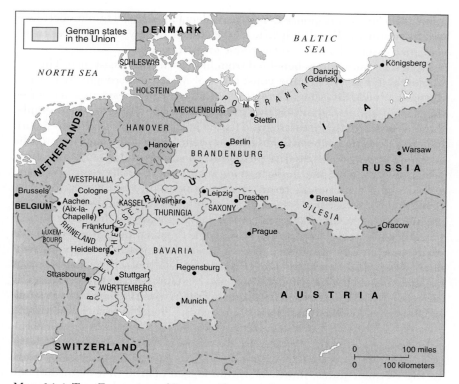

Map 14.4 The Zollverein (German Customs Union), 1834   States and cities within the German Customs Union. Led by Prussia, it was the first attempt by the German states to reduce customs duties and to coordinate economic activity.

The German states took a major step toward an expansion of commerce and manufacturing when they formed the Zollverein, a customs union, in 1834 (see Map 14.4). The Zollverein was the brainchild of economist Friedrich List (1789–1846), a tanner's son who became an outspoken proponent of railway building. Calling a customs union within the German states and railway construction the "Siamese twins" of economic expansion, List proposed in 1819 the abolition of all tariffs within the German states, although, unlike many other liberal economists, he insisted that protective tariffs be raised to shield German industries from British imports. List, a fiery advocate for the political unification of the German states, believed that only through tariff reform could Germans save themselves from being "debased to be carriers of water and hewers of wood for the Britons . . . treated even worse than the downtrodden Hindu." The Zollverein included four-fifths of the territory of the German states. It contributed modestly to German economic and industrial growth, expanding markets for manufactured goods.

In the Ruhr Basin, young Alfred Krupp (1812–1887) began to manage his late father's small steel manufacturing firm in Essen at the age of fourteen. He served, in his words, as "clerk, letter-writer, cashier, smith, smelter, coke-pounder, [and] night watchman at the converting furnace." In 1832, his firm nearly closed for lack of business. In 1848 he melted down the family silver in order to pay his workers. Finally, an order from Russia arrived for machinery to produce knives and forks, followed by another for steel springs and axles for a German railway. In 1851 at the Crystal Palace in London, he exhibited axles for train coaches and cannon with a gleaming cast-steel barrel (his newest and ultimately most successful product). Thereafter, Krupp's steelworks became enormously successful, turning out guns of increasing size and quality. Krupp employed 72 workers in 1848, 12,000 in 1873.

Sparse Industrialization in Southern and Eastern Europe

Eastern and southern Europe remained sparsely industrialized, hampered by inadequately developed natural resources and insufficient government attention. Entrepreneurs faced the difficulty of raising investment capital in poor agricultural societies. There were regional exceptions, to be sure, such as the increasingly mechanized textile production of Piedmont and Lombardy in northern Italy and Catalonia in Spain, and pockets of industrialization in Bohemia and near Vienna.

Industrialization in Spain was slowed by inadequate transportation and laws that discouraged investment. Lacking navigable rivers, Spain also suffered the absence of a railway system until after the middle of the nineteenth century. A commercial code in 1829 established the right of the state to veto any proposed association of investors. Following the continent-wide economic crisis in 1846–1847, the state placed banking under the control of the Cortes (assembly) and forbade the creation of new companies unless investors could demonstrate that they would serve "public utility."

Russia had a relatively tiny middle class—with only about 160,000 merchants out of a population of about 57 million people at mid-century. However, the majority of the population were serfs (see Chapter 18) bound for life to land owned by lords. Their bondage made it difficult for entrepreneurs to recruit a stable labor force; industrial workers were among the hundreds of thousands of serfs who fled toward the distant eastern reaches of the empire.

Transportation in the Russian Empire remained rudimentary. The minister of finance from 1823 to 1844 opposed the building of railway lines, believing that they would encourage needless travel. Moscow and Saint Petersburg were joined by rail only in 1851. Serviceable roads—only about 3,000 miles of them—had been built with military, not commercial or industrial, considerations in mind. Rivers provided arteries of transportation, but the boats were not steam-driven and travel was slow. Three hundred thousand boatmen pulled barges up the Volga River, a trip of seventy-five days.

Early in the nineteenth century several major canals were constructed, including one joining Saint Petersburg to the Volga River. Internal and foreign trade expanded markedly in the first half of the nineteenth century, including grain and timber, much of it through Black Sea ports. However, coal and iron ore deposits lay thousands of miles from Saint Petersburg, Moscow, and Kiev and could be transported to manufacturing centers only with great difficulty and at daunting cost.

Some hostility toward industrialization—and toward the West in general—remained entrenched in Russia, in part orchestrated by the Orthodox Church. In the 1860s, there still was no generally accepted word in Russian for "factory" or even "worker." Industrial workers remained closely tied to village life. The state undertook only feeble efforts to encourage industrial development. The Council of Manufacturers was created in 1828, trade councils organized in the largest towns, and several technical schools were established.

Overall, despite these factors, the growth of Russian industry was significant during the first half of the nineteenth century, if only in and around Saint Petersburg, Moscow, and the Ural Mountains. The cotton industry developed rapidly, as did a number of traditional manufacturing sectors in response to population growth. The number of Russian industrial workers—a fifth were serfs who had to pay some of what they earned to their lords—increased from 201,000 in 1824 to 565,000 in 1860 out of a population of about 60 million. At the same time, Russia began to import and construct more machinery. However, spinning and weaving remained overwhelmingly cottage industries.

THE MIDDLE CLASSES

One should not exaggerate the cohesiveness of the European middle class. The size and influence of the middle class was far greater in Britain, France, Belgium, the German states, and the northern Italian states, whose economies and politics were slowly being transformed by the Industrial Revolution, than in Spain, the Habsburg monarchy, or Russia, which still were dominated by nobles.

In liberalism, the middle class found an economic and political theory that echoed the way they viewed the world, with the family as the basis of social order. Within the family, men and women occupied, at least in theory, separate spheres. Religion and education played privileged roles in middle-class families. At the same time, for all the frugality sometimes ascribed to the nineteenth-century middle class, bourgeois prosperity found expression in the development of a culture of comfort.

The family concert.

Diversity of the Middle Classes

The middle class expanded in size and diversity amid the ongoing economic transformation of Europe. It included all people who neither held noble title nor were workers or peasants depending on manual labor for economic survival. The terms "bourgeois" and "burghers" had first emerged in the Middle Ages to refer to residents of towns like Lübeck, Bremen, and Hamburg that enjoyed specific rights (such as immunity from some kinds of taxation) or even independence granted by territorial rulers. By the nineteenth century, the middle class made up roughly 15 to 25 percent of the total population in Western Europe but a far smaller percentage in Sweden, Eastern Europe, and the Balkans. The Russian middle class at the beginning of the century accounted for no more than about 2 percent of the population, including some intellectuals and Orthodox priests.

The nineteenth-century middle class encompassed a great range of economic situations, occupations, education levels, and expectations. It can be imagined as a social pyramid, topped by a small group of well-connected banking families, industrial magnates, and the wealthiest wholesale merchants, as well as a few top government ministers and ambassadors. Below this extremely wealthy group came lawyers and notaries (both part of what became known as "the liberal professions") and families drawing more modest incomes from businesses, rental properties, and lucrative government posts. In general it required some resources, connections, and access to credit to make money. Four out of five Berlin entrepreneurs were the sons

A middle-class couple out on a walk in Vienna.

of bankers, manufacturers, or merchants; their fathers brought them into the business or loaned them enough money to get started on their own. At the bottom of the pyramid stood the "petty bourgeoisie," at whose expense nobles and wealthy bourgeois made cruel jokes. This stratum included shopkeepers of modest means and expectations, wine merchants, minor officials, schoolteachers, café owners, and some craftsmen—especially those in luxury trades, such as goldsmiths and silversmiths—who proudly considered themselves middle class.

Many wealthy merchants and industrialists hungered for social prestige, which was still closely tied to owning land. The proportion of land owned by the middle class increased rapidly during the first half of the nineteenth century in Britain, France, and the German and Italian states. Since ownership of land (specifically the taxes paid on it) remained the basis of electoral enfranchisement in much of Western Europe, this further increased the political influence of the middle classes.

The landed elite—noble and non-noble—remained at the pinnacle of social status in Britain, although its share of the nation's wealth fell from about 20 percent to about 10 percent between 1800 and 1850. Some English "country gentlemen" still looked down their noses at those they scorned as mere "calico printers" and "shopkeepers," even if some peers now owed their titles to family fortunes made in commerce or industry a century earlier. Likewise, because in Britain the eldest son still inherited the entire family fortune, some second and third sons left country life to become businessmen, without feeling the sense of humiliation that their counterparts might have felt in Prussia. Many noble families were delighted to have their offspring marry the sons and daughters of wealthy businessmen.

The Entrepreneurial Ideal and Social Mobility

The entrepreneur emerged as a man to be revered and emulated. The Scottish philosopher and economist James Mill (1773–1836) became the political champion of the middle class, which he called "both the most wise and the most virtuous part of the community." Mill's 1820 *Essay on Government* denounced nobles for selfish attention to their landed interests: "They grow richer as it were in their sleep, without working, risking, or economizing. What claim have they, on the general principle of social justice, to this accession of riches?" In Spain, the middle class—bankers, manufacturers, and merchants in the prosperous port of Barcelona, and lawyers and civil servants in Madrid—considered themselves "the useful classes," in contrast to noble "idleness." Many middle-class families in England, the Netherlands, and some of the German states were influenced by evangelical Protestantism, which stressed the redeeming nature of hard work. In 1847, a Parisian newspaper defined what it meant to be bourgeois: "The bourgeoisie is not a class, it is a position; one acquires that position and one loses it. Work, thrift, and ability confer it; vice, dissipation, and idleness mean it is lost."

The notion of "respectability" gradually changed in Europe. Even in Prussia, schoolbooks that had early in the nineteenth century emphasized immutable social hierarchy and the necessity of obedience gradually shifted to discussions of the virtues of hard work, self-discipline, and thrift. Middle-class families viewed the expansion of their fortunes as the best assurance of respectability. Bankruptcy seemed a fate worse than death.

The ideal of the self-made man was born. Yet rapid social ascension remained difficult and fairly rare. There were, to be sure, spectacular success stories. The son of an ironmonger and saddler, the Welshman Robert Owen (1771–1858) began his career as a clerk and then sold cloth. Borrowing money to start up his own textile business, he became part owner of the large and prosperous New Lanark Mills in Scotland. Robert Peel (1788–1850), a British prime minister, is another case in point. His family had owned some land, his grandfather sold goods door to door, and his father became one of the most successful entrepreneurs in Lancashire. By 1790, Peel sat in Parliament as Sir Robert Peel, one of England's wealthiest men. To be sure, some degree of social mobility was also possible from the ranks of relatively prosperous master artisans. Yet hard times could cause petty bourgeois to tumble into the working class. The possibility of being afflicted by economic crises or personal disasters haunted such families.

Rising Professions

Urban growth swelled the ranks of lawyers, doctors, and notaries. For the most part, however, the aspirations of those in these professions remained higher than their incomes and prestige. In the novels of Honoré de Balzac (1799–1850), young middle-class men "kill each other, like spiders in a jar." Lawyers had less than sterling reputations even as their numbers increased. In the 1830s and 1840s, the French caricaturist Honoré Daumier (1808–1879) depicted lawyers as arrogant, self-satisfied, insensitive men far more interested in extracting fees than serving justice. However, in Britain—and

Daumier depicts a lawyer pleading his case.

elsewhere—the "pettifogging attorney" of the eighteenth century gradually was replaced by the "respectable lawyer" of the nineteenth. Notaries, too, gained in wealth and status with the growth of cities. They earned—though some of their clients would not choose that particular verb—fees that sometimes amounted to more than 10 percent of the value of property by registering and storing deeds of title. They prepared marriage documents, dowries, and wills. Notaries thus remained in most countries the financial equivalent of father-confessors, knowing—or at least guessing—most of the deepest secrets concerning their clients' fortunes.

The number of doctors rose rapidly in nineteenth-century Western Europe, although they still struggled to be recognized as professionals rather than members of a trade. While some brilliant researchers labored in obscurity, some notorious hacks received public plaudits. Among the latter was the decorated French doctor who claimed that he had proved that syphilis was not communicable—thus reassuring clients who paid for his soothing words. Doctors were limited in the treatments at their disposal, which also contributed to their profession's minimal prestige. Popular belief in age-old cures rooted in superstition persisted. The vast majority of the hospitals that existed in London at mid-century had been founded since 1800.

In Western Europe, doctors began to form professional associations. The British Medical Society began in 1832 with the goal of encouraging standardized training and professional identity. For the first time, in some countries surgeons now needed to have studied medicine in order to take up a scalpel, at least legally. The British Medical Act of 1858 standardized credentials for doctors, but did not require them.

Other professions also gradually commanded respect. In 1820, the Scottish writer Sir Walter Scott, assessing the future of a nephew, said that if the young man seemed fit for the army, he might well make his way there, but, if not, "he cannot follow a better line than that of an accountant. It is highly respectable." Newer professions in such fields as veterinary science and pharmacology were open to sons of artisans and peasants. Clergymen and schoolteachers were increasingly drawn from the middle classes. The growing reach of the state also required more officials and bureaucrats, providing attractive careers for middle-class sons.

Middle-Class Culture

The middle classes believed that the family offered the best guarantee of social order. Most bourgeois held fast to the idea of separate spheres for men and women. Education and religious practice (however varied) provided a common culture for the middle classes. A wave of evangelical fervor swept over Britain in the late eighteenth and early nineteenth centuries, and a revival of religious enthusiasm was apparent in some places on the continent as well.

Marriage and Family

An astute choice of a marriage partner could preserve and even enhance a family's wealth and position through the acquisition of handsome dowries and wealthy daughters- and sons-in-law. There were fewer noblemen to go around. The disasters of what were considered ill-advised or inappropriate marriages ("misalliances")—that is, a union between two people far apart on the social ladder—continued to be a popular theme in novels and the theater.

Love could—and increasingly did—happily play a role in the choice of a mate. Prospective partners were more likely to insist that their views be taken into consideration in the arrangement of marriages. A Parisian woman told her father that she could not marry "someone that I do not love . . . in order to give myself a lot in life. . . . How could I hold onto him, if I do not love him and desire him?"

With an eye toward assuring the future of their progeny, some middle-class families began to practice contraception after about 1820, limiting their children to two. The economist Jean-Baptiste Say (1767–1832) encouraged family planning, warning that "one must increase savings accounts more than increase the number of children." Coitus interruptus certainly became more common, as well as other rudimentary forms of birth control.

The concepts of childhood and adolescence developed within middle-class families. The "children's room" and the "children's hour," when the young came forward to see their parents or meet guests, were middle-class concepts. In working-class and peasant households, there was no space for a separate room or quarters for children. Most working-class and peasant children had to begin work as soon as it was physically possible for them to do so. Many children who were apprentices did not live with their families, but with the masters of their chosen trade.

Because children, too, were an investment—and much more, of course— parents had to prepare them to take over family responsibilities, passing on self-discipline and self-reliance to their offspring. Germans called it *Bildung,* the training of cultivation and character, the subject of many nineteenth-century novels.

Separate Spheres and the Cult of Domesticity

To the nineteenth-century middle class, the family was the basis of order, what the English called the "nursery of virtue." Many men considered women "virtuous" when they remained in their domestic sphere, "angels" whose obligation was to provide comfort, happiness, and material order to their families. However, although many bourgeois insisted that women should work only when dire necessity left them with no alternative, many middle-class women worked in commerce, as unpaid clerks in their husbands' shops or as receptionists and secretaries in their spouses' law, medical, or notarial offices.

At the same time, the cult of domesticity also became increasingly fundamental to concepts of masculinity: men were to provide for and assure the future of the family. Yet during the middle decades of the nineteenth century the concept of British "manliness" came to emphasize physical strength. Men increasingly joined sports clubs. Oxford and Cambridge Universities evolved into defiantly masculine spaces that privileged athletic prowess. This trend perhaps reflected a response to the perceived threat of gradually increasing possibilities for women in British society, as well as a homosexual subculture at universities and in Britain's burgeoning urban world.

A woman's status remained closely tied to that of her father and her husband. In France, the Napoleonic Code made all men legally equal but left each woman subordinate to her husband's (or father's) will. On his accession to the throne in 1820, King George IV of Britain (ruled 1820–1830) tried to prevent his wife, Caroline, from becoming queen by blocking her return from Italy under threat of prosecuting her for adultery. But the king was forced to abandon his plan and accept his queen when women— particularly middle-class women—petitioned on her behalf, denouncing the king for promoting a double standard, since his own liaisons were notorious. A ballad urged women to rally behind Caroline:

Attend ye virtuous British wives
Support your injured Queen,
Assert her rights; they are your own,
As plainly may be seen.

A woman's separate sphere was inside the household and included supervising children and servants.

Middle-class women cared for their children, planned and oversaw the preparation of meals, supervised the servants, and attended to family social responsibilities. They exercised great influence over the education of their children, supplementing formal school instruction and taking responsibility for providing some religious instruction.

Middle-class British feminists began to challenge female legal and political subordination, debating the issue of "separate spheres" for women and men. Some women now demanded the right to vote. In *The Enfranchisement of Women* (published anonymously in 1851), Harriet Taylor Mill (1807–1858) stressed the injustice of considering anyone inferior, and therefore not deserving of the right to vote, by virtue of gender. Eighteen years later, her long-time companion and future husband John Stuart Mill (1806–1873) published *The Subjection of Women* (1869). Mill argued that women, like men, should be able to compete as equals in a society defined by market relations. Feminists demanded that married women be allowed to continue to have control over property they had brought with them into marriage. However, opponents of women's rights identified feminist movements with the violence of the French Revolution, or with surges of working-class militancy. Many upper-class Britons continued to view feminism as "unrespectable."

A Culture of Comfort

The European middle classes gradually shaped a culture based on comfort and privacy. Most bourgeois families were able to employ one or more servants and had apartments of several rooms. The wealthiest usually occupied the first floors of apartment buildings—but rarely the ground floor, where the concièrge lived—while less well-off neighbors had to hike further up the stairs.

A cross section of a Parisian apartment building, about 1850. Note that with the exception of the concierge's apartment on the ground floor, the farther you had to walk up the stairs, the less well off you were.

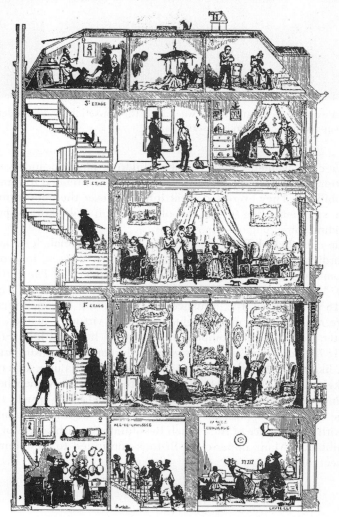

Kitchens and even dining rooms became separate rooms, as did attached offices for notaries, lawyers, and doctors. A distinct middle-class style of interior design slowly emerged, with national and regional variations. The accoutrements of the salon were likely to include an armoire or two, a chest of drawers, an elegant table and chairs, Limoges porcelain in France, Wedgwood china in England, crystal glasses, a clock, candelabras, a painting or print or two on the walls, all passed down from one generation to the next. The German decorative style offered wallpaper and sparse, austere furnishings and ornamentation. Pianos and other musical instruments became more common in the home and accompanied family singing. Flush toilets with running water began to replace outdoor privies and the chamber pots that had caused many unfortunate mishaps when emptied unceremoniously out windows.

Victorian Britons in particular embraced household possessions with a passion that verged on obsession. Leaving the simplicity of decoration behind, they began to fill up their residences with china, carpets, mantelpieces, statues, and garishly decorated fire-screens and teapots. They ascribed to furniture and items of interior decoration a kind of moral quality they believed suggested that their owners were living good lives. The Victorians' identification with their homes also arguably reflected the threat to class distinctions that was indeed very real in a century of enormous social change. Some of these novelties—such as antiques of fairly dubious origin or copies of colonial items purchased in curiosity shops—may seem to us in hindsight to be remarkable for their bad taste. But they enabled their owners to defy the trend of mass manufactured items, and try to reflect their status in Victorian society.

The old Roman saying that "clothes make the man" rang true of the nineteenth-century bourgeoisie. Middle-class men wore black suits, perhaps enlivened by a cashmere scarf. Their wives dressed only somewhat less simply; it was left to jewelry to suggest family wealth.

Expanding readership during the first half of the century encouraged a proliferation of novels, histories, poetry, literary reviews, newspapers, and political pamphlets, reflecting the diversity of middle-class interests. Reading clubs and bookshops flourished. Balzac's novels were first published in France as installments of lengthy serials—authors were often paid by the word—that appeared at the bottom of the front page of newspapers. Charles Dickens (1812–1870), too, first reached his public in monthly installments. *The Pickwick Papers* (1836–1837) attracted 40,000 regular readers in Great Britain.

Travel for pleasure became more common among the middle class. It also became a business. In 1835 in the German Rhineland, a young publisher named Karl Baedeker (1801–1859) published a guide to sites along the Rhine River. He soon published similar guides to Paris, German states, Austria, Belgium, and the Netherlands. In Britain, Thomas Cook (1808–1892) organized his first collective excursion in 1841 when he chartered a special train to transport a group of workers to a temperance meeting. Four years later, he began the first travel agency, building on demand for his services at the time of the Great Exposition of 1851 in London. Soon Cook was transporting groups as far as classical ruins in Italy and Greece. Middle-class families began to view travel as a means of self-improvement. They took in museums and other sights. In London, the National Gallery first opened its doors in 1824, about the same time as Berlin's Old Museum.

Education

Secondary education increasingly provided a common cultural background for the middle classes. Prussia's secondary schools (*Gymnasien*, or high schools) were arguably Europe's finest, offering a varied curriculum that included considerable religious instruction. In Britain, the victory of the entrepreneurial ideal was reflected in a gradually changing secondary-school curriculum. The English elite had long been exposed to a classical curriculum, as well as to Spartan discipline featuring corporal punishment. Reforms undertaken by Thomas Arnold (1795–1842), headmaster at Rugby School, were intended to spur students on to better performances by stimulating academic competition through examinations and prizes. Arnold's reforms reinvigorated the existing English "public"—in the United States they would be considered private—secondary schools, and new ones were established.

Many businessmen, however, still believed that experience was the best preparation to carry the family torch. Prosperous French shopkeepers sometimes pulled their children out of school at age eleven or twelve, viewing what they learned there as irrelevant to the tasks that lay ahead. Some entrepreneurs of family firms preferred to send sons to other companies, sometimes even in other countries, to obtain practical experience.

Secularized education, sponsored by states, only slowly undermined the role of religion in public life. In France, the Chamber of Deputies approved a law in 1833 (the Guizot Law, named after the French politician who sponsored it) specifying that each village was to have a primary

The Reading Lesson, by Jean-François Millet.

school. Private schools operated by the clergy continued to exist, and in many places provided the only schooling. In Catholic countries, middle-class families sent girls to convent schools to learn about drawing, music, and dance. However, state educational systems, staffed by lay teachers, gradually eroded ecclesiastical control of education. In France, liberals and republicans opposed a pronounced role for the Church in public life, demanding public schools that would teach secular, nationalistic values. In the German states, ecclesiastical and secular authorities battled it out, but the established churches retained greater influence over public education. The clergy still controlled schools in Spain and the Italian states. Yet in 1847 Piedmont became the first European state to establish a ministry of public education.

The educational systems of early nineteenth-century Europe did provide many more people than ever before with basic reading and writing skills. The literacy rate in Western Europe moved well above 50 percent. But social barriers remained daunting. Relatively few families could afford to send their children to secondary schools, which could provide them with more advanced skills needed for better-paying employment. In France in the early 1840s, only two of every thousand people attended a secondary school. Some working-class families still resisted even sending their children to primary school, not only because they could ill afford the modest costs involved, but because they needed their children's wage contributions, however small, to the family income. For women, very few formal opportunities existed for secondary schooling.

More young men went to university in order to prepare for careers in law, medicine, the church, or the civil service. Even in Russia, the number of university students tripled, from 1,700 in 1825 to 4,600 in 1848—still precious few in a population of more than 50 million.

Religion

Religious ideals still played an important part in the middle-class view of the world. Although disenchantment with organized religion permeated novels in Britain, France, and the German states, contemporary writing rarely challenged common assumptions that closely linked Christianity and morality. Biblical references abounded even in the treatment of secular subjects, because they were understood by all literate people. In the German states, as in the Scandinavian countries, the middle classes were more likely to go to church than other social groups. Throughout Europe, women manifested a much higher rate of religious observance than did men.

Many middle-class men and women deplored the materialism that seemed to have lured some of their own away from church. The novels of Jane Austen (1775–1817), the daughter of a clergyman, were highly successful at least partially because she affirmed that character, moral rectitude, and proper conduct, including control of the passions (in short, "respectability"), were not the preserve of wealthy landowners and titled nobles, many of

Evening prayer in a Viennese middle-class household.

whom were concerned only with wealth and status. Virtue could also be found among the men and women of the middle class.

The English middle class also viewed religion as a way of "moralizing" workers by teaching them self-respect. By the mid-nineteenth century, more than 2.6 million children attended Sunday schools, many created by the working-class communities they served. They provided the children of workers with educational, social, and recreational opportunities not otherwise available. Indeed the middle class did not have a monopoly on "respectability" and the virtues of hard work and discipline.

THE AMBIGUITIES OF LIBERALISM: VOLUNTARISM VERSUS STATE INTERVENTION

Clubs, societies, and other voluntary associations became part of middle-class life. Some, organized exclusively for leisure activities, manifested an upper-class sense of social distinction, such as the exclusive clubs of west London and the Anglophile Jockey Club of Paris. French bourgeois increasingly joined sociable "circles," and German university students formed dueling fraternities (*Burschenschaften*). Middle-class women formed their own clubs, among the few public opportunities open to them.

Charitable activities emerged as an important facet of middle-class life in nineteenth-century Europe, in many places remaining closely tied to organized religion. Growing public awareness of the appalling conditions in which many workers and their families lived engendered impressive charitable efforts among the more privileged. Such associations joined manufacturers, merchants, and members of the professions in northern English industrial towns in seeking to "moralize" the lower classes by shaping their conduct (for example, by encouraging them to attend church and to drink less). In 1860, there were at least 640 charitable organizations in London alone, more than two-thirds of which had been established since the beginning of the century.

Despite the growing tradition of voluntarism and liberal rejection of state interference, fear of popular insurgency could temper liberalism. Anxious bourgeois were reassured by the greater professionalization of police forces both in France and in Britain, where Home Secretary Robert Peel (a future prime minister) organized an unarmed municipal police force in London. They became known as "bobbies" in his honor. At mid-century Berlin had only 200 policemen to watch over a population of 400,000, which they did with military precision and occasional brutality. In British, German, French, and Italian cities, and in the United States, as well, civilian national guards were established, with membership limited to property owners. Such forces on occasion supplemented the police, national police, and regular

A charity providing halfpenny dinners to children in London.

HALFPENNY DINNERS FOR POOR CHILDREN IN EAST LONDON.

army units, and could be called upon to quell local disturbances and protect property.

By about 1830, some Western European liberals became aware of some of the social consequences of laissez-faire economic policies. They did not object to the wealthy becoming even wealthier, but worried that the poor were becoming too poor. Some of Jeremy Bentham's followers, among others, began to espouse government-sponsored social reform. Liberals crusaded against slavery, portraying the institution as incompatible with morality and British freedom. Such campaigns also reflected evangelical Christianity.

Differing views circulated on education for the poor. The British writer Hannah More (1745–1833) believed that poor children should learn how to read so that they could study the Bible, but not to write, because such a skill might make them reject their social subordination. Thomas Malthus (1766–1834), the English clergyman who predicted that the rise of population would rapidly outdistance the ability of farmers to provide enough food, believed that education would make ordinary people "bear with patience the evils that they suffer," while realizing the "folly and inefficacy of turbulence." Middle-class liberal reformers, however, shared far more optimistic views of education. The National Society campaigned for universal education in Britain. Henry Lord Brougham (1778–1868) believed that progress would be served if working men were educated. In 1826, he founded the Society for the Diffusion of Useful Knowledge, which made available to ordinary people cheap pamphlets and other publications of "improvement literature." Brougham and his followers founded a number of schools called Mechanics Institutes, most of them short-lived, which hammered home the entrepreneurial ideal to artisans and skilled workers. But educational reform in Britain proceeded slowly, at least partially because the state provided little direction.

Many poor children in Britain attended Sunday schools, charity schools, or "dame" schools (essentially day-care centers that charged a fee). The state did no more than provide inspectors for schools built by towns or parishes that could afford to do so or that had received random government grants. On the continent, compulsory primary education existed only in Switzerland, beginning in the 1830s.

The English philosopher John Stuart Mill became a forceful proponent of greater government intervention on behalf of social reform. He was appalled that relatively few people of means seemed concerned about the awful conditions of working-class life. In his *Principles of Political Economy* (1848), Mill rejected Adam Smith's cheery optimism about the "invisible hand," and called on the state to assist workers by encouraging their cooperative associations. Mill's *On Liberty* (1859) argued that the individual is the best judge of his or her own interests, but he encouraged a retreat from pure economic liberalism even in his spirited defense of individual freedom. Moreover, John Stuart Mill's espousal of causes such as women's rights and his participation in union campaigns for economic justice reflected this evolution of liberalism away from laissez-faire principles to a political theory concerned with economic, social, and political justice.

IMPACT OF THE INDUSTRIAL REVOLUTION

The Industrial Revolution, to be sure, changed the way people lived. Yet one should not overestimate either the speed or the extent to which these fundamental changes occurred in the nineteenth century. Even in Britain, France, and Prussia, the three most industrialized European powers, factory workers comprised between only 2 and 5 percent of the population in 1850. In many places, industrial workers—particularly miners—returned home to work in the fields part of the year, or even part of the day.

Continuities on the Land

Most rural people in Europe were not landowners. Landless laborers outnumbered any other category of the rural population, and their numbers increased dramatically in nineteenth-century Europe. Agricultural wages fell, and rural under- and unemployment became chronic. Landlords hired workers on a disadvantageous short-term basis. The abolition of serfdom in 1807 on the Prussian great estates east of the Elbe River increased the number of rural laborers scrambling to find farm work there. The increase in population put more pressure on the rural poor. Yet, even when peasants owned land, they were by no means guaranteed a decent life, because many plots were too small to be profitable, or the land was of poor quality. In Prussia and southern Spain, the number of landless laborers soared as owners of small farms were unable to survive and sold off their land.

Rural protest increased in the first two decades of the nineteenth century. In 1830, a hard year, travelers found people who had died of hunger on the roads, nothing in their stomachs but dandelions. In southern and eastern England, wealthy landowners had begun to use threshing machines, which left many hired hands without work. Grain passed through the rollers of these portable machines and then into a revolving drum. Threshing machines could be set up in any barn or field and operated by one or two horses. Farm workers, whose labor as threshers or "flailers" was no longer needed, began to smash threshing machines. The protesters were sometimes supported by local artisans, whose own livelihoods were threatened by mechanization, or by small landowners who could not afford the machines and were being driven out of business by their wealthier colleagues who could.

Some of the scrawled threats landowners received were signed "Captain Swing" (for example, "Revenge for thee is on the wing, from thy determined Captain Swing!"). Swing emerged as a mythical figure symbolizing popular

Bread riots in England, 1830.

justice, created to give the impression that the laborers were numerous and organized enough to force the landowners to renounce—as a few did—use of the machines. Authorities weighed in to make arrests, exiling some people to Australia, and executed nineteen men. Other similar attacks occurred between 1839 and 1842 in Wales when poor people attacked tollgates and tollhouses in the "Rebecca riots," which were also named after an imaginary redresser of social wrongs. In Portugal, women played a major role in an uprising in 1846 that followed a government attempt to enclose land and force peasants to register land they owned.

Rural poverty weighed heavily, especially on the continent. The Prussian political theorist Karl von Clausewitz, traveling in the Rhineland during the brutal winter of 1817, came upon "ruined figures, scarcely resembling men, [prowling] around the fields searching for food among the unharvested and already half rotten potatoes that never grew to maturity." Conditions of rural life in Eastern Europe may even have worsened since the eighteenth century. Russian serfs and Balkan peasants still lived in wooden huts. In Sweden, the small red cottages of farming families were notoriously cramped; many people depended on their parishes to provide assistance in hard times. Rural people drew warmth from fireplaces during the day and from animals with which many shared quarters at night. There were few windows because they let in wind and rain (in Sweden, some windows were still covered with animal membrane), or because farmhouses had been built that way to reduce the tax on doors and windows, as in parts of France. A traveler described the hovels in which Romanian peasants lived: "holes dug in the earth, over which a propped roof is thrown—covered rarely with straw, generally with turf."

The farther east one went in Europe, the more peasants remained fettered by obligations to lord and state. Russian serfs needed permission to leave their villages. In Silesia, peasant families still owed lords more than a hundred days of labor a year, for which they were to provide a team of animals; they were obligated to repair roads and to make various payments in kind. Peasants also paid the equivalent of a third of their produce to the lord or to the state in taxes. Such obligations, particularly to lords, were often deeply resented. More than a hundred Russian landlords or their stewards were murdered by their peasants and serfs between 1835 and 1855. In 1846, peasants in Austrian Galicia rose up and slaughtered their lords. Even when entrepreneurial landlords began commuting such payments in labor and in kind into cash, this did not end subsistence agriculture in parts of Central Europe and most of Eastern Europe and the Balkans.

The rural poor ate rye bread, porridge, and vegetables such as potatoes in northern Europe, cabbage in Central and Eastern Europe and in Russia, and onions and garlic in France. For many people, meat was little more than a distant memory of a wedding feast. When they could afford to eat meat, poor people were most likely to eat tripe, pigs' ears, or blood sausage. Most peasants who owned animals could not afford to slaughter them. Fish was relatively rare on peasant plates, except near the sea or a lake or pond in which they were allowed to fish or could get away with it (although even the English and Scandinavian poor could afford herring, fished in enormous quantities in the Baltic Sea). Water, however contaminated, remained the drink of necessity for the poor; in southern Europe they drank poor-quality wine, and in northern Europe they drank beer when they could, or cider, although both were relatively expensive.

Urbanization

The first half of the nineteenth century brought about a marked urbanization of the European population, as the percentage of people living in towns and cities rose rapidly (see Table 14.3). In 1750, two British cities had more than 50,000 inhabitants (London and Edinburgh); in 1801 there were eight, and by mid-century, twenty-nine. London's population rose from about 900,000 in 1800 to 2,363,000 in 1850. At mid-century, half of the population of Britain resided in towns. French and German urbanization proceeded at a significantly slower pace than that of Britain and Belgium. In 1851, only a quarter of the French population lived in urban areas, which were then defined as settlements of at least 2,000 people.

Yet Paris grew from about 550,000 in 1801 to a million inhabitants in 1846. Stockholm's population multiplied by four, from 75,000 in 1800 to 350,000 at the end of the century. Smaller towns grew rapidly, as well, such as Porto in Portugal, which doubled in size in sixty years. Industrial towns grew most rapidly, but commercial and administrative centers, too, gained population.

TABLE 14.3. Population of Major European Cities

City	1800	1850
London	900,000–1,000,000	2,363,000
Paris	547,000 (1801)	1,053,000 (1851)
Vienna	247,000	444,000
Naples	350,000	415,000 (1871)
Saint Petersburg	200,000	485,000
Moscow	200,000	365,000
Berlin	172,000	419,000
Liverpool	77,000	400,000
Birmingham	73,000	250,000
Leeds	53,162	172,023
Manchester	25,000 (1772)	367,000

In general, the farther north and particularly east one went in Europe, the fewer and smaller the towns. In Austria, more than four of every five people lived in the countryside, and in Sweden, nine of ten. In Russia, serfdom tied peasants to the land. Furthermore, there was in general less manufacturing in Eastern Europe, and therefore fewer manufacturing towns and trading ports. The Russian Empire had only three cities of any size—Saint Petersburg, Moscow, and Kiev; parts of Moscow were still indistinguishable from the rural world, dotted with wood or mud huts inhabited by peasant workers. Yet even in the Russian Empire, the percentage of people living in towns and cities almost doubled during the first half of the century.

As cities grew, streets may have been better illuminated than ever before, thanks to gas lighting, but poorer districts became much more crowded. Only a fifth of the buildings in Paris were connected to the city's water supply, and in these only the first floor or two (carriers hauled tubs of water up and down staircases). Crimes against property increased rapidly with urban growth, especially during periods of hardship. Between 1805 and 1848, indictable offenses in England and Wales multiplied by six, although part of this dramatic jump may reflect the result of better policing, and thus reporting. To the upper classes, rapid urban growth itself seemed threatening.

As urban centers became ever more densely packed, industrial suburbs developed. The urban periphery offered more available land; proximity to railways, canals, and rivers; and a ready labor supply perched on the edge of the city, where the cost of living was cheaper. After the Revolution of 1830, one of French King Louis-Philippe's ministers warned that the factories and industrial workers of the periphery "will be the cord that wrings our neck one day." Within cities, the European middle classes withdrew into privileged elite quarters, leaving workers and other poor people in separate, disadvantaged neighborhoods.

Social segregation intensified within cities. Industrial pollution, including smoke and other smells, altered residential patterns, driving some middle-class families to new quarters. At the same time, some people of means in industrial cities moved to newly developing middle-class suburbs. Country-side secondary residences, retreats from the bustle of urban life, became more common. Although most European suburbs were plebeian, in England some middle-class people of means moved to exclusive suburbs, such as the villa neighborhoods on the edge of London and Manchester. A poem in 1851 described a suburb of Birmingham, England: "See Edgbaston, the bed of prosperous trade, Where they recline who have their fortunes made; Strong in their wealth, no matter how possessed, There fashion calls, and there at ease they rest." The wealthy in London enjoyed vast public gardens, comfortable theaters, and elegant shopping arcades, a jolting contrast to the misery of the East End. Public gardens like Copenhagen's Tivoli and Berlin's Tiergarten, as well as Paris's Champs-Elysées, developed so middle-class denizens could observe and be seen. Cafés catered to people of means—coffee was expensive—while cabarets, selling cheap drink, attracted more ordinary people.

On the Move

As more people died than were born in most large cities, immigration of peasants and unskilled workers accounted in almost every case for urban growth. Thus, only about half of the residents of London and Paris and only about a quarter of those in the even more rapidly growing northern English industrial towns had been born there. The majority of immigrants were poor.

Most migrants moved to town because they knew someone there, usually relatives or friends from home who might be able to help them find a job, and perhaps put them up until they found a job and their own place to live. People tended to live in the same neighborhood as others from their regions, such as the sooty "Little Ireland" in the midst of the largest factories of Manchester in which many of the 35,000 Irish of the city lived in cellars, or the infamous Irish "rookery" of St. Giles in central London. The discrimination faced by the Irish in London was reflected in Elizabeth Gaskell's *North and South* (1855), in which the villains are Irish. Among the English of all social classes, "Paddy" became a racist stereotype of the Irish character, depicted as ignorant, superstitious, lazy, drunken, and potentially violent. Anti-Irish feeling in Victorian England was linked to anti-Catholicism, which, after generating violence and riots in the 1850s and 1860s, only slowly declined in the last part of the century.

Between 1816 and 1850, at least 5 million Europeans booked passage across the seas, particularly during the "hungry forties," which struck Central and Eastern Europe and Ireland particularly hard. One and a half million people of Ireland's population of approximately 8 million left their homeland between 1835 and 1850 (and somewhere between 1 and 2 million people died of hunger on the Emerald Isle), particularly during the potato famine in the 1840s. An Irish migrant to London remembered:

> I had a bit o' land, yer honor, in County Limerick. . . . It was about an acre, and the taties was well known to be good. But the sore times came, and the taties was afflicted, and the wife and me—I have no children—hadn't a bit nor a sup, but wather to live on, and an igg or two. I filt the famine a-comin'. I saw people a-feedin' on the wild green things. . . . The wife and me walked to Dublin . . . and we got to Liverpool. Then sorrow's the taste of worruk could I git, beyant oncete 3 [shillings] for two days of harrud porthering, that broke my back half in two. I was tould, I'd do betther in London, and so Glory be to God! I have—perhaps I have.

Following the Irish, Germans were the next largest group of emigrants. After 1820, Norway sent more emigrants to the United States than the number of people living in the country in that year. At the same time, hundreds of thousands of Russian migrants pushed toward the eastern reaches of the empire in the quest for land.

Improvements in transportation expanded the distance people could travel to find work. Seasonal migration took men greater distances to work in towns

This British cartoon from 1850 depicts the expectations of migrants.

HERE   AND   THERE;
Or, Emigration a Remedy.

and cities during the warmer months of the year, while their wives cared for the children and whatever land they might have at home. Before the middle of the nineteenth century, seasonal workers still may have accounted for as much as a third of the workforce.

INDUSTRIAL WORK AND WORKERS

The English novelist Charles Dickens dubbed the grim, sooty industrial cities of England "Coketown." After completing his novel *Hard Times* (1854), an account of working-class life, Dickens wrote that "one of Fiction's highest uses" is to "interest and affect the general mind in behalf of anything that is clearly wrong—to stimulate and rouse the public soul to a compassionate or indignant feeling that *it must not be.*"

Middle-class socialists and workers themselves also began to criticize passionately some of the consequences of large-scale industrialization. The growing awareness among some workers that they formed a class apart followed directly from their growing sense that they were vulnerable to the vicissitudes of capitalism.

Gender and Family in the Industrial Age

In Western European nations, domestic service remained the largest category of female employment at the middle of the century, employing in Britain 1.3 million women, nearly 40 percent of women workers. Working up to eighteen hours a day, servants slept under staircases and in attics, but ate relatively well. They had a higher rate of literacy than did working-class women in general and better prospects of marrying above their social class.

Country women spun and wove wool, linen, and cotton; sewed, embroidered, and knitted stockings by hand; and worked in fields or gardens, while looking after children. Such cottage work on the continent allowed country people to maintain the traditional rural family economy well into the nineteenth century. Urban women worked as laundresses, seamstresses, or street merchants and peddlers, and some kept boardinghouses.

Female labor remained central to large-scale industrialization. Women were employed in many of the industries, both rural (where their labor had long been predominant in cottage industry) and urban, that expanded during the industrial age. Although only a relatively small percentage of women worked in factories, a gradual shift to larger textile and clothing workshops and factories occurred in England, above all, as well as in parts of France, Belgium, and the Prussian Rhineland. In France, women accounted for 35 percent of the industrial workforce. With the expansion in power-loom weaving, women with experience as cottage laborers found employment in textile mills. While there were a number of important predominantly male industries, such as iron production, the leather trades, building, and mining, women did work in these industries as well. The textile industry was the second largest employer of women (hiring 22 percent of all female workers). In general, women everywhere worked for about half of what their male counterparts earned. As in the pre-industrial period, many, if not most, female factory workers were young and single.

Many male workers bitterly resented the arrival of women in the workplace. This challenged traditional gender roles, including that of patriarchy, in that women's work had long been assumed to be at home. What came to be called the "struggle for the breeches" began in Britain. One of the significant developments brought about by the Industrial Revolution may have been the slow change from the conception of gender as hierarchical to one as representing different but complementary spheres.

Thus, despite significant continuities, wage labor altered family life and the structure of communities. Wage labor made young women and men less dependent on their parents, enabling many to marry earlier. But marriage still remained to some extent an economic relationship; moreover, some couples delayed wedlock until both partners could accumulate the skills or assets to maintain an independent household. A sharp rise in illegitimate births (in Paris, about 33 percent of all births, 45 percent in Stockholm) seems to have been another effect of the rise in employment opportunities and wages for unmarried couples in "free unions," or common-law marriages, although many women who gave birth were unattached.

Working-class families were presented with a dilemma: with the growth of factories and the consequent separation of home and work, women had to balance the need for the additional income factory work could provide with caring for young children. Many mothers left the workforce to care for children for at least a time. But since the family economy also depended on their wages, they generally returned to work as quickly as possible.

Hundreds of thousands of European women worked full- or part-time as prostitutes. Prostitution presented a hierarchy of conditions of life and wages, ranging from confident high-class courtesans to poor girls beckoning clients from dark doorways. Some women, including many who were married, were able to earn much more money selling sexual favors than they could earn in textile mills or in domestic service.

To middle-class moralists, prostitutes symbolized moral failure and the dangers of modern life. Yet it was the increase in middle-class male demand for prostitution that increased the number of prostitutes in Europe's burgeoning cities. Governments therefore accepted prostitution as a "necessary evil." They sought to police brothels and the comportment of prostitutes in order to keep the profession hidden as much as possible from public view, while trying to limit the ravages of venereal disease by ordering prostitutes to have regular medical checkups. The number of prostitutes in London was so difficult to determine that estimates for the 1840s vary from 7,000 to 80,000. In Saint Petersburg, there were over 4,000 registered prostitutes in 1870.

Child Labor

Children had always worked in agriculture, given such tasks as caring for farm animals, scaring birds away from crops, and gleaning at harvest time. At a very young age, many had also learned to assist in domestic textile production, preparing wool for spinning and raising silkworms. Now in factories, their smaller size made children useful for certain tasks, such as mending broken threads or climbing on machinery to extract something impeding its operation. Teenage girls were particularly adept at calico printing. In Britain during the early 1830s, youths less than twenty-one years of age made up almost a third of the workforce.

As in cottage industry, factory work often employed entire families, with adult males supervising other family members. Children's low wages—about a quarter of what their fathers earned—nonetheless represented a significant contribution to the family economy. One man recalled "being placed, when seven years of age, upon a stool to spread cotton upon a breaker preparatory to spinning," an elder brother turning the wheel to put the machine in motion.

Factory work was often dangerous. An English factory inspector reported that the children working at a punching machine risked losing their fingers: "'They seldom lose the hand,' said one of the proprietors to me, in explanation, 'it only takes off a finger at the first or second joint. Sheer carelessness . . . sheer carelessness!'" An eight-year-old girl who worked as a "trapper" in the mine pits, opening ventilation doors to let coal wagons pass, related, "I have to trap without a light, and I'm scared. I go at four and sometimes half-past three. . . . Sometimes I sing when I've light but not in the dark. I dare not sing then."

Young children working in a factory.

Some contemporaries believed that long days of labor instilled discipline, whereas idleness would turn children into sinners and criminals. But Methodists, among other British evangelical Protestants, wanted to save children from exhausting and sometimes dangerous work. A British law passed by Parliament in 1833 forced employers to start part-time schools in factories employing children, although in some cases the owners simply designated a worker to be "teacher," whether or not he could read or write very well. The 1833 Factory Act in Britain banned work by children less than nine years of age and limited labor by older children to eight hours (subsequent legislation in 1847 limited older children and women to a ten-hour day). In 1841, France's first child labor law banned factory work for children under eight years of age and limited the workday to eight hours for those eight to thirteen years old and to twelve hours for those thirteen to sixteen years old, banning child labor at night and on Sundays and holidays. The law, however, was extremely difficult to enforce, and was routinely circumvented by employers and ignored by parents who needed the additional family income, however small.

The Laboring Poor

In 1838, a British member of Parliament described a cotton mill:

> [It was] a sight that froze my blood. The place was full of women, young, all of them, some large with child, and obliged to stand twelve hours a day. Their hours are from five in the morning to seven in the evening, two hours of that being for rest, so that they stand twelve hours a day. The heat was excessive in some of the rooms, the stink pestiferous, and in all an atmosphere of cotton flue. I nearly fainted. The young women were all pale, sallow, thin, yet generally fairly grown, all with bare feet— a strange sight to English eyes.

The northern industrial cities of England in particular attracted the attention of horrified observers. There were, to be sure, people of means in Manchester, but Friedrich Engels (1820–1895), a German Rhinelander, sought and found the grim face of unrestrained capitalism there:

> At the bottom flows, or rather stagnates, the Irwell, a narrow, coal-black, foul-smelling stream, full of debris and refuse. . . . Above the bridge are tanneries, bonemills, and gasworks, from which all drains and refuse find their way to the Irk, which receives further the contents of all the neighboring sewers and privies . . . here each house is packed close behind its neighbor and a bit of each is visible, all black, smoky, crumbling, ancient, with broken panes and window-frames. The background is furnished by old barrack-like factory buildings. . . . [Beyond] the background embraces the pauper burial ground, the station of the Liverpool and Leeds railway, and, in the rear of this, the Workhouse . . .

of Manchester, which, like a citadel, looks threateningly down from behind its high walls and parapets on the hilltop, upon the working people's quarter below.

The satanic mills of Manchester.

The "cheerful" school of historiography has argued that the Industrial Revolution, at least during the first half of the century, by increasing employment and lowering the price of some goods, almost immediately improved the way ordinary people lived. By contrast, other historians have embraced the view that industrial capitalism was making conditions of life even worse for workers and their families as the number of people depending on wage labor increased faster than did job possibilities and pay.

During the first half of the century, the incomes of many artisans, as well as women workers, fell as trades were flooded with the end of guild restrictions and increasing mechanized production. Women workers such as spinners were often the first to experience unemployment because of the new technology. Wages in many industries were extremely volatile; boom periods could come and go with numbing suddenness. Even good years were broken in many industries by "dead seasons" when there was no work. The gap between the rich and the poor increased. In England, many middle-class heads of household earned three or four times as much as even a skilled worker. In the late 1820s in Paris, more than three-quarters of people who died left virtually nothing to heirs, because they had next to nothing and, in any case, they could not afford to have a will drawn up by a lawyer.

On the continent, the poorer a family was, the greater the percentage of its income that was spent on food, primarily bread. Clothing accounted for the second largest category of expense, followed by lodging. All other expenses, including heat, light, tools, supplies, and recreation, had to come out of less than 10 percent of the family income. Most migrants to cities no longer benefited from the kind of community support they had received during hard times in their villages. Recourse to the neighborhood pawn shop was part of the experience of the majority of urban working-class families.

English workers tended to be better off than most of their continental counterparts. Paternalism, the tradition by which employers took some responsibility for helping their workers by providing some supplementary assistance in addition to their salaries, seemed rare in the new factory towns. But some manufacturers did pay slightly higher wages, provided decent housing, and insisted that their workers' children attend school. However, such laudable efforts affected the lives of relatively few workers.

The nineteenth-century urban poor probably lived in more miserable housing than their counterparts in the previous century. Buildings in industrial cities, built hurriedly and as cheaply as possible, quickly became dilapidated tenements. Many workers lived amid terrible smells from raw sewage, garbage, industrial pollution such as sulfurous smoke, and putrid rivers and streams. Warm summers brought outbreaks of serious diseases like typhus and dysentery. Between 1848 and 1872 in Britain, a third of all people died of contagious diseases. Despite attempts to improve water supplies and construct sewer systems in several large English cities, the decline in mortality was barely felt in the heart of industrial cities, where tuberculosis remained a great killer.

Many children either died or were abandoned at an early age. At midcentury, about 26,000 infants were abandoned each year in both Moscow and Saint Petersburg, and about a fifth of all babies in Warsaw. The most fortunate of the abandoned were left at the doors of charitable organizations created by states, municipalities, and churches. Some babies were left with notes such as this one found in Rouen in 1831: "It is with the greatest pain that I separate myself from my son, after the great suffering I have gone through to keep him in his present state. . . . I hope to see him again as soon as I can take him back for good." Sadly, this would usually not be the case.

A poor family blocks their landlord from invading their cellar apartment, which they share with a donkey and some rats.

Foundling homes were overcrowded and notoriously unhealthy. In four towns in one Russian province, more than 90 percent of all of the children taken in by orphanages died within a few years.

Great Britain was the first state to have a national policy of poor relief. Against the background of the French Revolution, the Speenhamland system established in 1795 supplemented the wages of laborers with funds generated from property taxes ("poor rates"). Doles were based on the price of bread and the number of dependents for whom each head of a poor family had to provide. But this arrangement had the drawback of encouraging landowners to pay lower wages, while assuring them of an inexhaustible supply of cheap field hands. It also may have encouraged poor families to have more children, as payments were adjusted to family size.

The Poor Law Amendment Act of 1834 ended the Speenhamland system. It established workhouses in which poor people without jobs would be incarcerated. Workhouses were organized like prisons, their occupants exposed to harsh discipline in the hope that they would find any kind of possible work in order to avoid being sent back. Towns enforced laws against begging in order to force the unemployed poor into workhouses. When families were taken in, husbands were separated from their wives, children from their parents, and all were herded into dormitories. Inmates were forced to work at simple tasks and were given used clothes and dreadful food. The stigma of being poor was such that one influential official even tried to stop the ringing of church bells at pauper funerals. In 1841, despite organized opposition and although application of the law varied greatly, more than 200,000 people were workhouse inmates in Britain.

Class Consciousness

During the first half of the nineteenth century, many workers began to consider themselves members of the working class, with interests that were different from those of their employers and the middle class. They began to have a sense of community based on a belief in the dignity of labor. This class consciousness did not spring up overnight, and it is difficult to fix a certain point in time when it did develop. Moreover, certainly not all workers became conscious of themselves as a class apart. Great differences in skills and work experience remained among workers in different countries and even among workers in the same region, or city, and between male and female workers. Other identities continued to be important to workers, such as those of family and motherhood, cultural identity (Flemish, Venetian, Welsh, etc.), religious adherence, and village and neighborhood solidarity.

Urban artisans were the first workers to begin to express class consciousness, sharing the frustrations and goals of other workers. This process began early in the nineteenth century in England, although it was not until the early 1830s that one can speak of a cohesive class identity; it began in the

1840s in France and in some areas of the German states, and later in other countries.

Large-scale industrialization had deleterious consequences for many trades, threatening the control craftsmen had maintained for centuries over their work. Changes in artisanal production were a Europe-wide phenomenon. Artisans had traditionally organized themselves by trades into guilds, which enabled them to control entry into their trades, the training of apprentices, and production, even if guild controls had not been able to protect all workers from market forces (for example, from rural cottage production). Shoemakers, masons, and tailors, among those in other trades, retained their own craft organizations. Rival associations within the same trade sometimes engaged in bitter, violent battles. Furthermore, even within trades, hierarchies of skill and remuneration remained.

As a number of states followed France's lead in 1791 by banning guilds in the name of economic liberalism, the number of artisans expanded rapidly because there were no legal restrictions to entering a given craft. Journeymen, having completed their apprenticeships, were more uncertain than ever before about whether they would become masters and would employ their own journeymen and take on apprentices. In Prussia, the number of masters increased by only about half between 1816 and 1849; the number of journeymen and apprentices aspiring to a mastership more than doubled during the same period. Artisans' confraternities and trade associations (some of which governments tolerated, even if they were technically illegal) facilitated the emergence of working-class consciousness (although in places where they helped to maintain trade exclusiveness, they may have delayed its emergence).

"De-skilling" reduced the income and status of workers like tailors and skilled seamstresses by taking away opportunities for them to work for piece rates and wages they had once earned. For example, competition buffeted tailors as never before. Merchant-manufacturers, some of them former tailors who had been able to save some money, put work out to master and journeymen tailors, but asked them to perform a single task, such as making sleeves, in return for less money than if they had tailored an entire suit. Tailors' incomes plunged during the 1830s and 1840s. Many master tailors were driven out of business or forced by necessity to become subcontractors in their own trade. Mechanization also gradually began to undercut tailors by producing ready-made clothes.

The gradual mechanization of some trades brought protest. Already in 1811 and 1812, glove makers in Nottingham, England, smashed a thousand stocking-frames that deprived them of work. One of their leaders—perhaps fictitious—was a man called Ned Ludd. Machine-breaking "Luddites" yearned for a return to the old economic and social order, before mechanization, as had the "Captain Swing" rebels in 1829–1830.

In 1836, a mob burned down a textile factory in Barcelona, Spain, denouncing machinery as "the devil's invention." Mechanical looms reduced Silesian hand-loom weavers to desperate poverty. Movements of social protest and gradual political involvement infused communities of workers with a sense of moral struggle against economic and political forces they could not control.

Workers' views of themselves drew upon a corporate language of the Old Regime that gave primacy to the idea of work as a value in itself and of the community of workers as a moral entity. Many workers concluded that they, not entrepreneurs with capital, were the source of wealth and were being exploited. Other workers also began to feel a sense of class consciousness because they collectively suffered unemployment or reduced wages. Residential patterns and leisure haunts (pubs, cabarets, music halls) contributed to solidarities among such workers.

Workers' Associations and Social Protest

Workers' associations helped shape working-class consciousness and militancy. In Britain, craft-based "friendly societies" had more than a million members in 1815. More than 32,000 such organizations existed in 1872. Their counterparts were journeymen's associations and "mutual aid societies" in France and in the German states.

Fledgling trade unions developed in Britain, particularly after 1824 when Parliament repealed the Combination Acts (1799–1800), which had banned unions. Members sought to protect wage rates and conditions within their trades. Yet, even in prosperous periods when workers could afford dues, less than a fifth of workers belonged to such associations during the first half of the century, and the vast majority of these were more skilled craftsmen. Many of these men believed they had little in common with unskilled workers, who, in any case, could not afford union dues and who lacked job stability.

Some trade associations, including a minority organized by and for women, provided assistance when a member fell sick (paid out of membership dues) and assured members that they would be spared the indignity of a pauper's grave. They also provided funds to assist workers who refused to agree to conditions imposed by employers or masters. These payments had to be made covertly because strikes remained illegal in most places.

Artisans led movements of social protest. They had a much higher level of literacy than did unskilled workers—printers were an obvious example, but tailors and shoemakers were often literate, as well as many seamstresses, who were often self-educated. Literate workers read newspapers and brochures and related the news to those who could not read. The emergence of political movements seeking universal male suffrage (or even universal suffrage) and significant social reforms aided the development of a sense of class by emphasizing the language of "liberty, fraternity, and equality," a heritage of the French Revolution.

Francis Place (1771–1854), a tailor who had been a member of one of the workers' associations sympathetic to the French Revolution, became a

Socialism as a symbol of hope for the working poor, about 1848.

leader of the English workers' movement. Some workers began cooperative stores, hoping to put aside funds to finance cooperative villages. Trade unionism made considerable headway between 1829 and 1836. In the latter year, the first national union, made up of spinners, was founded. Some trade union members undertook producers' cooperatives within their trades, but most of these were short-lived.

The period from 1815 to 1850 was arguably the most socially turbulent period in modern British history. Skilled workers joined with middle-class radicals to demand political reform. William Cobbett (1763–1835) helped galvanize radical opinion with his journal, the *Political Register*. Artisans and skilled workers led massive demonstrations in 1831 and 1832, which pressured Commons and the House of Lords to pass the Reform Bill of 1832 (see Chapter 15). By expanding the number of those eligible to vote, the Reform Bill temporarily diffused middle-class dissatisfaction. The continued exclusion of working men from voting contributed to working-class consciousness in Britain, because in this way Parliament had legally defined workers as a separate, inferior class. At about the same time, middle-class and working-class support for factory reform, marked by public meetings, petitions, and demonstrations, led to the acts of Parliament in the 1830s limiting work hours for children and then women. Amid hardship, more workers took to the streets in protest to demand political reform.

Yet, even in Britain, the most industrial nation, major impediments limited working-class militancy. Methodism (see Chapter 9), which won thousands of converts among workers, preached discipline and the acceptance of one's fate on earth. More important, solidarities within specific trades remained stronger than those that cut across trades. Furthermore, unskilled workers lacked the organization and resources of craftsmen, some of whom continued to do very well, the English "aristocracy of labor." Gradually, too, the utopian vision of rebuilding British political life while bringing social justice faded. Many if not most workers came to accept capitalism as inevitable, while demanding a fairer share of its benefits.

French and German artisans were more militant than their British counterparts, who accepted the tradition of the politics of reform. German craftsmen desperately struggled to try to protect their trades from being flooded by newcomers. Many French workers, now seeing themselves as members of a "confraternity of proletarians," struck against employers in the 1830s and 1840s. They also supported bourgeois republicans in their push for electoral reform, in the hope that a republic would enact reforms on their behalf.

THE ORIGINS OF EUROPEAN SOCIALISM

As large-scale industrialization gradually transformed economy and society in Western Europe, the 1830s and 1840s brought lively discussion, heated debate, and startling transformations in thought. The rapid increase in wage labor influenced the emergence of new political forces that, proclaiming the equality of all people, sought dramatic social and political change. One of the most salient results of the growing preoccupation with the condition of workers was the birth of the movement known as socialism.

Utopian Socialists

Utopian socialists, most of whom were French, provided an original critique of the changes brought by the Industrial Revolution. Their ideas were in part shaped by their reaction against the social consequences of economic liberalism. The name "utopian" reflectes their dreams of creating a perfectly harmonious way of life. But their importance comes not from their sometimes quirky theories, however intriguing they may be, but from the fact that many workers found an explanatory power in the critical reaction of the utopians to liberalism and capitalism. This accentuated their determination to put forward demands for social and political reform.

Utopian socialists agonized over the living conditions of the laboring poor. The "social question" was the miserable living conditions of many if not most workers. Rejecting the "egotistic" individualism of the spirit of acquisition, utopian socialists envisioned a gentle world of cooperation. In some ways children of the Enlightenment, utopian socialists were also optimistic champions of the power of science and technology to construct new social and political institutions.

Count Claude-Henri de Saint-Simon (1760–1825) posited a "religion of humanity," arguing that religion should "direct society toward the great end of the most rapid amelioration possible of the lot of the poorest class." In 1820, Saint-Simon published a provocative parable. Speaking hypothetically, he asked what the consequences for France would be if all of its dukes and duchesses, princes and princesses, bishops and priests, and other luminaries of altar, throne, and château sank in a terrible shipwreck. As tragic as that event would be, he had to admit that the loss to society would be inconsiderable. However, if France, in a similar tragedy, were to lose all of its most learned men, talented bankers, artisans, and productive farmers, the result would be disastrous. The timing of his parable was most unfortunate, because soon after its publication in 1820 the heir to the throne of France, the duke of Berry, fell to an assassin's knife (see Chapter 15). Saint-Simon was charged with offending the royal family, but he was acquitted by a jury.

Saint-Simon postulated a hierarchy, or order of status, based not on blood, but on productivity. Believing that history moves through discernible stages, he asserted that mankind could anticipate a future in which science would solve the material problems of humanity in harmony with an era of moral improvement. For this to happen, people of talent must be freed from the fetters of restraint imposed by uncaring, unproductive monarchs, nobles, and priests.

Contemporary and historical appraisals of Charles Fourier (1772–1837), Saint-Simon's mystical rival, have ranged from sanctifying him as a genius of great insight to ridiculing him as a paranoid crackpot. Fourier claimed that at a very early age he discovered that the art of selling was the practice of lying and deception. At his father's insistence, he went off to Lyon as a young man to start a business that quickly failed. Fourier spent the rest of his life preparing a grand scheme for improving the condition of humanity. His cosmology rested upon his conclusion that history moved in great cycles toward a more perfect future. This planet's next stage would be based upon mankind's discovery that the principles of cooperation and harmony would free everyone from the repression of bourgeois individualism. Having determined that there were 810 distinct personality types, Fourier proposed that they be organized into "phalanx" communities made up of 1,620 people, one man and one woman of each personality type. The phalanx would channel the "passions" of each person in socially productive ways, while individuals would benefit from the opportunity to express their deepest proclivities. In the "phalanstery," the place where the utopians would live, crime would become a distant memory, because criminals' supposed penchant for blood would be safely fulfilled in certain occupations, such as by becoming butchers. With everyone so satisfied, it would not matter that differences in wealth would remain. Fourier sat in his apartment everyday at noon, await-

A drawing of a phalanstery contemplated by Charles Fourier.

ing the wealthy man who would come, he hoped, to finance the first phalanstery. No one ever showed up.

While Fourier dreamed and waited, the wealthy British industrialist and philanthropist Robert Owen acted. Believing that education and environment could shape a spirit of cooperation, Owen built a mill in New Lanark, Scotland. He provided decent housing for his workers and established schools for their children. Like Fourier, for whom human progress demanded the emancipation of women, Owen espoused the equality of women, although he emphasized not political rights but rather the special qualities of motherhood. Likewise, an Englishman named William Thompson penned in 1825 the *Appeal of One Half of the Human Race, Women, Against the Pretentions of the Other, Men.*

No utopian socialist had a greater popular following than Étienne Cabet (1788–1856) in France. Cabet, too, sought to apply the principles of Christianity to the extreme social problems of the day. His novel *Voyage to Icaria* (1840) described an imaginary city of wide streets, clean urinals, and social harmony, a vision of organized economic and social life so attractive that even the bourgeoisie would be converted peacefully to the principles of cooperation and association. Cabet's "communist" newspaper had 4,500 subscribers in the early 1840s, and almost certainly reached twenty times that number. Artisans, their livelihoods threatened by the abolition of the guilds and mechanization, were particularly intrigued by Cabet's ideas. A few of them set sail with Cabet for the New World, founding several utopian colonies in Texas and Iowa.

Another group of utopian socialists represented the scientific, or technocratic and even authoritarian tendencies inherent in Saint-Simon's overwhelming respect for science and insistence that the state lead the way toward material progress. Prosper Enfantin (1796–1864)—called "Father" by his followers—left Paris for Egypt with a small group in search of the Female Messiah; one of the traveling party, Michel Chevalier, came back with the idea of building a canal through the Isthmus of Suez, thus joining the Red Sea and the Mediterranean, a project later achieved in 1869 by Ferdinand de Lesseps, another Saint-Simonian.

Practical Socialists

Some utopian socialists carried Saint-Simon's analysis a crucial step further. They relegated the bourgeoisie into the category of non-producers, because they possessed capital, while workers seemed to them to be the real producers by virtue of their labor. In France, a group of Saint-Simonian women in 1832 founded a newspaper, *La Tribune des Femmes,* that vowed only to publish articles by women, proclaiming that the emancipation of women would come with the emancipation of the worker.

Gender discrimination led Flora Tristan (1801–1844) to socialism. When the French government confiscated her Peruvian father's fortune upon his death and declared Flora to be illegitimate because it refused to recognize her parents' marriage in Spain, she had to take a series of makeshift jobs. When she separated from her abusive husband, French law decreed that he receive custody of their children, although she later won custody when he started to abuse them, too. Tristan campaigned against women's inequality within marriage and before the law. Linking feminism and socialism, she campaigned for female emancipation with impassioned speeches and forceful prose.

Louis Blanc (1811–1882) looked to governments to give scientists a free hand in applying their talents to the betterment of the human condition. The state should also guarantee workers the "right to work," that is, employment in times of distress and a decent wage in the face of unchecked competition. The state should provide credit to workers so that they could form producers' associations within their trades, thereby eliminating the middleman who skimmed off profits that he had not earned. Blanc believed that these workshops would serve as the basis for the reorganization of society along cooperative lines. Blanc's socialism was predicated on increasing workers' influence on government through the establishment of universal suffrage.

In sharp contrast to Blanc, Pierre-Joseph Proudhon (1809–1865) looked not to the strengthening of the state but to its abolition to create a better world. Proudhon, a typesetter, had grown up among landowning peasants in eastern France. He believed that the very existence of the state itself was a principal reason why capitalism exploited workers. In 1840, he published a fiery pamphlet that answered the question "What Is Property?" with the resounding reply "Theft." Not surprisingly, this frightened property owners in France, even though Proudhon defined property as unearned profit that came to employers from the labor of their workers, and not property per se. Proudhon wanted workers to organize themselves into small, autonomous groups of producers that would govern themselves. By preaching the abolition of the state, Proudhon was arguably the first anarchist.

Karl Marx and the Origins of "Scientific Socialism"

The economic and political theorist Karl Marx (1818–1883) also read the utopian socialists, but although admiring their critique of capitalist society he found them naive and "unscientific." Born in 1818 in the Rhineland, Marx studied philosophy at the University of Berlin. When in 1843 his career as a journalist came to an abrupt halt after his radical newspaper ran afoul of the Prussian government, he went to Paris. There he read the histories of the French Revolution and the utopian socialists.

Proudhon destroying property as seen by a hostile caricaturist.

After Marx lambasted the French monarchy in a series of articles, the French police expelled him. He befriended Friedrich Engels, the Rhineland German whose prosperous, conservative family owned a cotton mill in Manchester, England. Marx visited industrial Lancashire, then the greatest concentration of industry in the world. His observation of evolving capitalist society led him to conclude that capitalism was but a stage in world history.

Marx applied the concept of dialectical stages of the development of ideas and institutions, developed by the German philosopher Georg Wilhelm Friedrich Hegel (1770–1831), to the progression of world history. The French Revolution had marked the definitive overthrow of feudal society, represented by the power of the aristocracy and the Church; for Marx, this was a bourgeois revolution. Just as the nobility and the bourgeoisie had battled in the eighteenth century, so the victorious bourgeoisie, who controlled the means of production (capital, raw materials, and equipment needed to produce goods), and the proletariat were in the process of fighting it out in the middle decades of the nineteenth century. English commercial capitalism had brought the bourgeoisie to power, which in turn had facilitated the growth of industrial capitalism. By creating a proletariat, however, capitalists had sown the seeds of their demise. Inevitably, socialism would replace capitalism when the proletariat seized power. The end of private property and pure communism would follow.

But that moment, Marx thought, lay in the future, awaiting the further concentration of capitalism and the development of a larger, class-conscious proletariat aware of its historical role. Marx called his socialism "scientific socialism" (in contrast to utopian socialism), because he thought that it was inevitable, based on what he considered the scientific certainty of class struggle.

Marx believed that a revolution by workers would be prepared by the organizational efforts of a group of committed revolutionaries, so he formed the Communist League. In 1848, he published the *Communist Manifesto,* which resounds with the provocative exclamation, "The proletarians have nothing to lose but their chains. They have a world to win. Working men of all countries, unite!"

Conclusion

Europeans could not help but be impressed with the rapid pace of economic change during the first half of the nineteenth century. Trains truly revolutionized commerce and travel, bringing distant places closer together. Cities grew rapidly, their railway stations bringing in more agricultural goods produced with capital-intensive farming. More people worked in industry than ever before. Factories now dotted the landscape, although traditional workshop and cottage production remained essential.

Yet many upper-class contemporaries were worried by what seemed to be teeming, increasingly disorderly cities. The Industrial Revolution, to be sure, had generated material progress—indeed, opulence for some people—but it also seemed to have increased wrenching poverty and dissatisfaction among workers.

In the meantime, having defeated Napoleon at Waterloo, the European powers—Britain, Prussia, Austria, and Russia—set about trying to restore the prerogatives of ruling dynasties, nobles, and the established churches. Liberal and national movements struggled against conservative ideology in Restoration Europe. Liberalism, above all, seemed to reflect the desires of the middle classes, whose numbers and influence expanded so rapidly in the decades following the end of the Napoleonic era.

CHAPTER 15

LIBERAL CHALLENGES TO RESTORATION EUROPE

At the Congress of Vienna of 1815, representatives of the allies who had defeated Napoleon—Austria, Russia, Prussia, and Great Britain—came together to reestablish peace in Europe. They hoped that by imposing a treaty on France and creating an international mechanism, the Concert of Europe, they could prevent Europe from again being shaken by revolution in France or elsewhere. The Congress represented conservative impulses, standing against the liberalism and nationalism that espoused organizing states along ethnic or national lines and demanded reforms in the name of the popular sovereignty that conservatives blamed for the French Revolution and Napoleonic era.

Early nineteenth-century Vienna was a perfect setting for a gathering of the representatives of Europe's sovereign powers. The Schönbrunn Palace on the outskirts of the Habsburg capital and Vienna's own elegant baroque buildings still reflected the grandeur of absolutism and traditional court life, despite the years of warfare that had virtually bankrupted the Austrian monarchy.

At the Congress, which met between September 1814 and June 1815, the Austrian hosts staged elaborate dinners, elegant balls, and festive fireworks displays, and organized hunts helped relieve boredom. Artists stood ready to paint the portraits of the members of the diplomatic delegations. Aristocratic guests amused themselves by trying to guess which of the hundreds of maids and porters were spying for the Austrians. The antics of some representatives provided as much comic relief as irritation. A Spanish diplomat insisted that his country should have the right to several small Italian states. The other representatives were so annoyed by this demand that they invited him to go on a ballooning excursion, and sent him off in the general direction of the Alps.

What the English poet George Gordon, Lord Byron (1788–1824), called "that base pageant," the Congress of Vienna provided an opportunity for the informal discussions that had always been an important part of traditional

The Congress of Vienna.

European diplomacy. In fact, the Congress met officially but once, to sign the final treaty, which had been negotiated in smaller formal and informal gatherings of the various delegations. In the wake of the many territorial changes that had occurred during the previous twenty-five years, the representatives redrew the map of Europe, particularly of Central Europe, putting old rulers back on their thrones.

After Napoleon's final defeat in 1815—the Congress of Vienna continued to meet during the 100 Days—a protracted struggle among the conservative forces, monarchies, nobles, established churches, and liberals took place in Europe. "Liberalism" as an economic and political philosophy implied the absence of government constraints that could interfere with the development of the individual. It was a philosophy perfectly suited to the middle classes in "the bourgeois century." The middle classes were an extremely diverse social group that ranged from merchants and manufacturers of great wealth to struggling shopkeepers (see Chapter 14). Rapid population growth swelled the number of lawyers, notaries, and other middle-class professionals. The entrepreneur came to be revered. Moreover, the middle classes' liberal emphasis on individual freedom found expression not only in economics and politics but also in the literature, art, and music of romanticism, which celebrated individual fulfillment through subjectivity and emotion. Boasted one German liberal, "We are the times."

Liberal movements were in many places closely tied to the emergence of nationalism as a source of allegiance and sovereignty. Nationalism was usually defined by language and cultural traditions, and the quest to establish national states whose borders would correspond to patterns of ethnic residence. Nationalism threatened the territorial settlements effected by the Congress of Vienna. The Habsburg Austrian monarchy itself ruled eleven major nationalities without a state of their own, including Hungarians and Poles, who had once had fully independent states. In the meantime, German and Italian nationalists began to call for national political unification.

THE POST-NAPOLEONIC SETTLEMENT

The allied representatives to the Congress were determined to ensure that France could not again rise to a position of domination in Europe. Thus, even before Napoleon's first defeat and abdication in 1814, representatives of Prussia, Austria, Russia, and Great Britain formed a coalition, the "Quadruple Alliance," intended to prevent France or any other state or political movement from threatening the legitimate sovereigns of Europe.

The Treaty of Paris

The Treaty of Paris was signed in March 1814, thus before the Congress of Vienna. Charles-Maurice de Talleyrand (1754–1838), who had served Napoleon with flexibility rooted in an uncanny sense of survival, became the intermediary. He exploited tensions among the allies, especially between Prussia and Austria. The victorious powers agreed to restore the Bourbons to the throne of France in the person of the count of Provence, brother of the executed Louis XVI, who took the throne as Louis XVIII. The allies might well have forced the French to sign a draconian treaty. But they were dealing not with the defeated Napoleon but with the restored Bourbon monarch, whose throne they wanted to solidify against liberal challenges within France.

France retained lands incorporated before November 1, 1792, including parts of Savoy, Germany, and the Austrian Netherlands, as well as the former papal city of Avignon. France gave up claims to the remainder of the Austrian Netherlands, the Dutch Republic, the German states, the Italian states, and Switzerland. It lost to Britain the Caribbean islands of Trinidad, Tobago, Santa Lucia, and part of Santo Domingo. The allies demanded no reparations from France. Yet difficult territorial issues remained to be resolved in central and southern Europe.

Diplomatic Maneuvering at the Congress of Vienna

The Congress of Vienna was almost entirely the work of diplomats representing Austria, Prussia, Great Britain, and Russia. The goals were threefold: to redistribute territory in the wake of the French revolutionary and Napoleonic Wars, to achieve a balance of power that would prevent any one

British Foreign Secretary Viscount Robert Castlereagh.

state from becoming too powerful and potentially aggressive, and to make future revolutionary movements impossible. At the beginning, defeated France played only the role of a very interested observer (although French was the official language of the conference). But Talleyrand's wily off-stage negotiations gradually brought France to the position of a full-fledged participant in the deliberations.

The dominant figure in Vienna was the Austrian chancellor Prince Klemens von Metternich (1773–1859). Born in the German Rhineland, Metternich was the son of a noble who had served at the court of the Habsburg monarch. Forced to flee his homeland by the French invasion in 1792, he subsequently entered the diplomatic service in Vienna, rising to become the minister of foreign affairs in 1809. Metternich was a handsome dandy with immaculately powdered hair as at home in the social whirl of formal receptions and magnificent balls as in the petty intrigues of high society. He could bore people in five languages. But he was a determined, calculating practitioner of tough-minded diplomacy. Metternich dominated international affairs of the continent until 1848.

Foreign Secretary Viscount Robert Castlereagh (1769–1822) represented Britain. Aloof and painfully shy, Castlereagh, whose passion was sheepherding, went to Vienna in the hope of establishing Britain as the arbiter of European affairs. Now Europe's greatest power, the British Empire included one of every five people in the world. The British government sought the elimination of the French threat to its commercial interests as well as security. Moreover, Castlereagh and Metternich both viewed the prospect of Russian expansion in Central Europe with anxiety. Only Russia now seemed in a position to disrupt Europe through unilateral acts.

Tsar Alexander I of Russia (ruled 1801–1825) wanted the allies to affirm formally what he considered the religious basis of the European alliance. Alexander I was, above all, a deeply religious man who occasionally lapsed into an intense mysticism and overwhelming unhappiness as he became increasingly reactionary. Alexander I drafted a document that became the basis for the Holy Alliance. It asserted that the relations of the European sovereigns, "the delegates of Providence," would thereafter be based "upon the sublime truths which the Holy Religion of Our Savior teaches." Emperor Francis I of Austria and Frederick William III of Prussia signed the document, but the British prince regent—the future George IV (ruled 1820–1830)—begged off. Castlereagh called it "a piece of sublime mysticism and nonsense." Prussia, Russia, and Austria promised mutual assistance wherever established religions and peace were threatened. In the moral claims of the Holy Alliance lay justification for the repression by the allies of any liberal and national movements in Europe.

The Congress System

The Congress of Vienna drew a map of Europe that lasted for several generations (see Map 15.1). Under Metternich's stern leadership, what became known as the Congress system restored the principle of dynastic legitimacy and the balance of international power in Europe. The future of Poland, which had lost its independence when it was last partitioned by Russia, Prussia, and Austria in 1795, stood at the top of the list of contentious issues. Russian troops occupied much of Poland, which Tsar Alexander wanted to annex to the Russian Empire. Great Britain, France, and Austria, fearing increased Russian and Prussian power in Central Europe, formed an alliance to head off any attack in Central Europe by Russia or Prussia. In May, the Kingdom of Poland was proclaimed by the Congress. It was to include lands Austria and Prussia had seized during the earlier partitions. But "Congress Poland," as it came to be known (made up of about 20 percent of Poland's territory before the first partition of 1772; see Chapter 11), was despite a constitution nothing more than a Russian protectorate, with the tsar himself occupying the Polish throne. Moreover, large parts of what had been independent Poland remained in Prussia and in the Austrian Empire. Russia also held on to Finland, which it had conquered during the Napoleonic Wars. To balance Russian gains in the east, Prussia received the northern half of Saxony, which had cast its fate with Napoleon, as well as Polish-speaking Posen and the port city of Gdańsk.

In comparison with the debates over Poland and Saxony, the resolution of remaining territorial issues seemed easy. Prussia received territories on the left bank of the Rhine River to discourage French aggression to the east. The Prussian Rhineland was now separated from the eastern Prussian provinces by the states of Hanover and Hesse-Kassel. Prussia also received Swedish Pomerania and parts of Westphalia, but lost its outlet to the North Sea with the return of East Friesland to Hanover. Other buffers against France along its eastern border included Switzerland, reestablished as a neutral confederation of cantons, and the Kingdom of Piedmont-Sardinia, enlarged to include Genoa, Nice, and part of Savoy.

Most territorial settlements were made without the slightest consideration of local public opinion. Although the allies emphasized the principle of legitimacy in the territorial settlement, they never hesitated to dispense

MAP 15.1 EUROPE AFTER THE CONGRESS OF VIENNA, 1815 Changes in boundaries of states after the Congress of Vienna.

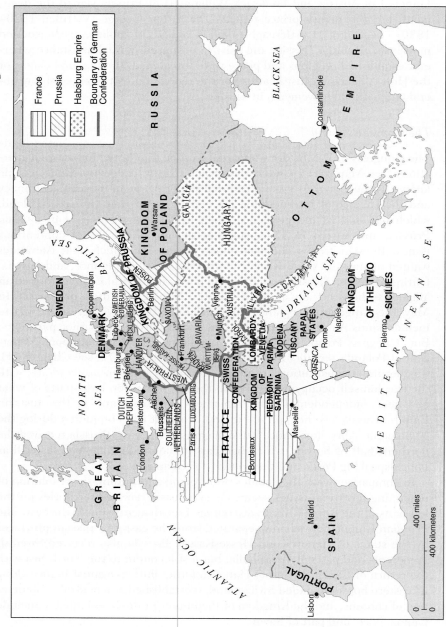

with a number of smaller legitimate princes whose claims would have interfered with the creation of buffers against France. The republics of Genoa and Venice disappeared from the map.

The Congress placated Britain by awarding the former Austrian Netherlands (Belgium) to the Dutch, leaving a state friendly to Britain on France's northern border. The former stadholder of the Dutch Republic became King William I. But Castlereagh's plan to link the Dutch throne to the British monarchy by engineering the marriage of a British princess to the Dutch royal family failed, at least in part because the intended groom became royally drunk in the presence of the intended but most unwilling bride.

Austria was well compensated for the loss of the Austrian Netherlands with Lombardy and Venetia in Italy, much of Galicia, and Illyria on the coast of Dalmatia. The grand duchies of Parma, Modena, and Tuscany, too, had close family links to Vienna. The Congress restored the Bourbon dynasty to the throne of the Kingdom of the Two Sicilies (Naples and Sicily). There, Ferdinand I introduced a constitution, but signed an alliance with Austria and promised not to introduce any further reforms without the latter's permission. Austrian garrisons and secret police in each Italian state helped assure Austrian domination of northern Italy.

Napoleon's remarkable escape from Elba in March 1815 and the dramatic episode of the 100 Days (see Chapter 13) did not change the most important aspects of the Congress's shuffling of European territories. The second Treaty of Paris, signed in November 1815 following Napoleon's defeat at Waterloo in June, however, pushed France back from its 1792 borders to those of 1790. Furthermore, the allies now exacted reparations totaling 700 million francs from France. Their armies would occupy France until the debt was settled.

Napoleon's victories in Central Europe had led to the end of the Holy Roman Empire in 1806. On June 9, 1815, the Congress created a German Confederation of thirty-five states loosely joined by a Federal Diet (Bundestag), or governing body, that would meet in Frankfurt. In addition to Prussia and Austria, the Confederation also included the states of Bavaria, Hanover, Württemberg, the two Hesses, and Baden, and the independent, or "free," cities of Hamburg, Frankfurt, Bremen, and Lübeck. The Confederation did not, however, include the non-German lands of the Austrian Empire. Members of the Confederation pledged to assist each other if any of them were attacked or in any way threatened. But it was unlikely that unanimity could ever be achieved among the member states, or that states could be compelled to obey a decision made by the Confederation. The Diet merely afforded Metternich a means of bullying the smaller states. The German Confederation was anything but an affirmation of a move toward German national unification. German states, large and small, were proud of their traditions of autonomy, or what was known as "German particularism." By virtue of its Rhineland acquisitions, Prussia emerged as a rival for Austria's leadership of the Confederation and for dominance in Central Europe.

The Concert of Europe

To preserve the settlements enacted at Vienna, the five major European powers (Great Britain, Prussia, Austria, Russia, and France) formed a "Concert of Europe." In this extension of the Congress of Vienna, representatives of the powers would meet annually. If necessary, they would join together to put down movements that could threaten the *status quo*. Metternich's Austria had the most to fear from national claims for independent states. Austria was both a state in the German Confederation and the most important province within its empire of many nationalities. The Austrian Empire stretched from the stately elegance of Vienna through the plains of Hungary, to isolated Romanian and Croatian villages. German was the language of the imperial bureaucracy, and of many of the towns, but one could find eleven major languages within the borders of the empire. The Habsburg monarchy depended on the support of the nobles of the favored nationalities—principally Austrian, Hungarian, and Croat—and the German-speaking middle classes. Metternich exploited the fear that the upper classes of the favored nationalities felt toward any awakening from the lower classes, particularly of other ethnic groups. This kept most Magyar (Hungarian) nobles loyal to the Habsburg dynasty, although some desired ultimate independence.

Tensions remained between the allies. Prussia and particularly Austria feared that Russia was seeking to expand its influence in the Balkans, especially among peoples of the Orthodox faith. Metternich therefore was willing to use Austrian armies to maintain the *status quo,* but he sought to avoid any joint Congress military action that might bring Russian armies into Central Europe or the Balkans. He thus wanted to keep alive the Austrian alliance with Britain against any future French, Prussian, or Russian aggression.

Castlereagh, on the other hand, was less concerned by Russia's expanded interests in Central Europe than about containing France. But he had reservations about the appropriateness of the Quadruple Alliance's intervention in the internal affairs of European states. The British participated in the annual gatherings of representatives of the Concert powers, but gradually withdrew from the Congress system. At Aachen in 1818, the allies agreed to withdraw their remaining troops from France, which, having paid off the war debts, now joined the Holy Alliance.

RESTORATION EUROPE

The monarchs, diplomats, and nobles at the Congress of Vienna were guided by conservative principles of monarchical legitimacy, with the right to the thrones of Europe to be determined by hereditary succession, and by close ties to the prerogatives of the established churches.

The Restoration of Monarchs, Nobles, and Clergy

Monarchs, nobles, and clergy returned to power, prestige, and influence. In the Kingdom of Piedmont-Sardinia, the members of the ruling House of Savoy came back wearing powdered wigs in the style of the eighteenth century, and the religious orders returned in force. In Lombardy-Venetia, consultative assemblies were established in Milan and Venice, but they did little more than assess taxes. With the exception of Baden, in the German states such bodies routinely approved legislation without limiting the power of the sovereign. The governments of the German states that had been occupied by France completely purged the remnants of Napoleonic administration, annulled French-inspired legislation, and imposed strict censorship.

When the French left the Papal States, Pope Pius VII immediately tried to exorcise all traces of French influence. Administrative reforms undertaken during the occupation ended; so did street lighting and even vaccinations, which were identified with the godless French. The clergy reclaimed most public offices. In Tuscany the duke ordered the colors of Giotto's portrait of Dante altered, fearing that observers would see in them the French tricolor flag.

The French Revolution had by no means eliminated noble influence in the states of Europe. Even in Britain, where the lines between landed and business wealth were more blurred than anywhere else, nobles still dominated the House of Commons. In France, the Bourbon monarchy restored nobles to political primacy. An electoral system based on landed wealth gave them a disproportionate advantage. In Spain, nobles were particularly numerous, although many of them were relatively poor. Sweden still counted about 12,000 nobles in the middle of the nineteenth century. In the Italian states, nobles still held sway in declining or stagnant walled towns like Palermo, Naples, and Rome, as they did in the countryside. Even in industrializing Milan and in Turin, nobles dominated the civic administration.

The farther east one went, the more nobles still dominated economic, social, and political life. Nobles (Junkers) owned 40 percent of the land of Prussia and retained their stranglehold over the officer corps. The army defiantly brushed aside possible competition from the Landwehr, the civilian reserve force commanded by mere commoners—merchants, teachers, and bureaucrats. In Russia, the officer corps remained a noble stronghold, reinforced by the aristocracy's near monopoly on appointments to military academies and to important posts in the civil service. In Austria, where the greatest 300 to 400 hereditary aristocratic families remained close to the Habsburg throne, 70 percent of those in top official posts had noble titles in 1829, and twenty years later the percentage had grown even more. Austrian Chancellor Metternich warned Tsar Alexander I about the dangers of the "intermediate class," which prospered by adopting "all sorts of disguises."

Postcard depicting the Houses of Parliament in Budapest.

Indeed, noble style and distinction retained great influence. In the archi-tecture of public buildings and palaces, noble taste still predominated, as in the enormous neo-Gothic Parliament in Budapest, where nobles held sway as for centuries. In much of Europe, public buildings and statues affirmed aristocratic values and moral claims that had characterized the old regimes. European nobles retained close ties to the established churches, which still deferred to aristocratic status.

During the revolutionary era, the established churches, particularly the Catholic Church, had suffered. Europe now witnessed a marked religious revival, as in the Lutheran northern German states. In France, the old reli-gious confraternities were revived; pious families contributed money to rebuild churches, monasteries, and convents destroyed or damaged during the Revolution. In Britain, the Established (Anglican) Church rejected the notion of divine-right or absolutist monarchy, yet most British conserva-tives believed the existing social order represented by the Anglican Church to be God-given and immutable. They strongly opposed (Protestant) Dis-senters and, above all, Catholics.

Conservative Ideology

The conservative ideology of Restoration Europe drew on several sources. A theory of organic change held Christian monarchies to be, as a French writer put it, "the final creation in the development of political society and of religious society." Conservatives insisted that states emerged through gradual growth and that monarchical legitimacy stemmed from royal birthright, confirmed by the sanction of religion. Catholic and Protestant conservatives insisted that the established churches provided a moral authority that complemented that of traditional monarchical institutions of government, which alone could maintain order. In Russia, the mystical Tsar Alexander I believed fervently that the Orthodox Church had an important role in keeping his people subservient. In the German states, Pietism broke with Protestant orthodoxy to teach that mankind was essentially sinful and required a repressive state to keep in line. Europe's conservative monarchies, depending on noble support, therefore sought to reestablish the privileges that the French Revolution and Napoleon had swept away.

A French writer, Joseph de Maistre (c. 1754–1821), emerged as a theorist of the alliance of throne and altar. Rejecting the concept of "natural rights" associated with Enlightenment thought, de Maistre argued that a king's power could never be limited by his subjects, because that power came only from God. De Maistre blamed the Revolution on the philosophes who had shaken the faith that underlay the absolutism of hereditary monarchy. To de Maistre, "the first servant of the crown should be the executioner." Most conservatives saw no difference between reform and revolution, believing that reform would inevitably lead to revolution and radical change. They stood adamantly opposed to political claims stemming from any notion of individual freedom, popular sovereignty, or membership in any particular national group.

Yet conservatives confronted the problem that their support was limited to a very narrow social and political base in a Europe that was slowly being transformed by the Industrial Revolution. It was testimony to the influence of the revolutionary era that the restored monarchy in France under Louis XVIII granted a Charter to the French people promising essential liberties. Moreover, the French monarchy, as well as that of Piedmont-Sardinia and even Metternich's Austria, utilized the bureaucratized state apparatus inherited from Napoleon to repress liberals, instead of restoring the less-centralized ruling structure that had typified Old Regime Europe.

LIBERALISM

Nineteenth-century liberalism was more than an economic and political theory: it was a way of viewing the world. Liberals—the term became current in the late 1830s—shared a confidence that human progress was inevitable, though gradual. From the Enlightenment, the bourgeoisie inherited a faith in science, which they held to be a motor of progress. Liberalism reflected middle-class confidence and economic aspirations.

Liberals and Politics

"Liberty" became the watchword for the increasingly liberal middle classes, who protested their exclusion from political life in most European states. Liberals believed that all individuals should be equal before the law because—reflecting Enlightenment influence—they held that individuals are born good, free, and capable of improvement. Economic liberals for the most part believed in "laissez-faire," that the economy should be allowed to operate freely without state interference. (In contrast, liberals in more recent times want states to protect and assist ordinary people, particularly the poor.) Nineteenth-century liberals wanted government by constitution and by elected legislative bodies (such as the British Parliament and the French Chamber of Deputies) that would reflect some degree of sovereignty, with authority resting to some extent in the popular will rather than from monarchical legitimacy. Moreover, liberals demanded such civil liberties as freedom of the press and of assembly, and education for the lower classes, so that individuals could develop to their full capacities.

Liberals gradually replaced the discourse emphasizing the rights of man— which had emerged from the Enlightenment of the eighteenth century and the French Revolution—with that of the legally defined rights of the citizen or subject. They put their faith in political and social rights embodied in constitutions, defined by law, and guaranteed by the state. Middle-class voters trusted elected legislative bodies to ensure that their rights as property owners could not be trampled by monarchs and aristocrats. They opposed electoral systems that were so narrowly constructed that only the wealthiest men were allowed to vote, as in Britain, France, and Prussia. Their goal was the expansion of the electoral franchise. But most liberals during the first two-thirds of the nineteenth century did not believe that all people should vote, but rather that eligibility to vote should stem from the amount of property owned, and that only such men—and not women—of property should hold the electoral franchise.

Laissez-Faire

Adopting the maxim that "that government is best which governs least," liberals sought to place limits on state authority. In particular, they rejected government interference in the operations of the economy. Many liberals therefore opposed protectionism—state-imposed duties on imports. They followed the theories of Adam Smith (1723–1790), author of *The Wealth of Nations* (1776). Their motto was "laissez-faire" ("let do as one pleases"), which meant that government should allow the "invisible hand" of supply and demand to bring change. Smith had argued that the unrestricted functioning of the free economy would ensure the pursuit of private interests. This would, in turn, serve the public interest by creating more wealth. Smith contended that a new social hierarchy would emerge if the economy were allowed to follow its natural course. With their investments augmenting the general good, businessmen would supplant nobles and churchmen as the men to whom ordinary people deferred. Indeed, this was increasingly what was occurring in Western Europe.

Utilitarianism formed another cornerstone of the entrepreneurial ideal, indeed of liberalism in general. Jeremy Bentham (1748–1832) was its most influential exponent. In 1776, he posited that laws should be judged by their social utility, or whether or not they provided "the greatest good for the greatest number" of people. His famous standard question about any law or government institution was "Does it work?" Bentham's utilitarianism reflected the relatively decentralized government of Britain and a pervasive belief among the king's subjects that a government that made few demands and that served efficiently counted among the "liberties" of freeborn Britons.

Adam Smith's successors gradually made a science out of speculations about the operations of the economy, insisting that the laws they postulated about the development of capitalism were based on scientific certainty. They optimistically pointed to the ongoing economic and social transformation of Britain in the manufacturing age. The theories of Smith and Bentham had a great impact on British businessmen. The social status of an individual increasingly came to be measured in terms of utility.

In 1817, the British economist David Ricardo (1772–1823) published *Principles of Political Economy and Taxation*. Ricardo assumed the existence of an "iron law of wages," which held that, if wages were left to the laws of supply and demand, they would fall to near subsistence level. This was certainly more cheering news for manufacturers than for workers. Elected to Parliament in 1819, Ricardo became a hero to the middle class. He reassured liberals by telling them that the "invisible hand" of the economy would bring continued economic growth, with the bulk of entrepreneurial profits going into employers' pockets. Through the Political Economy Club, the *Westminster Review* (first published in 1824), and newspapers, the ideas of Bentham and other liberals reached a wide audience. Liberal economists earned academic appointments at the University of Edinburgh and the University of London (founded in 1828 by religious Dissenters). Economic liberalism found proponents in France and the German states.

Middle-class entrepreneurs did not always agree on what specific economic policies they favored. In the 1820s, Tory governments in Britain bored the first holes in the wall of protectionism by reducing the duty collected on Baltic timber, which had been kept high to favor Canadian exporters, and by establishing sliding scales for tariffs tied to the price of wheat in England. Many French industrialists demanded that the government maintain high tariffs to keep out British manufactured goods and machinery. Businessmen everywhere demanded improved transportation networks. Most liberals like Ricardo demanded the "freedom of work," that is, that nothing constrain free agreements between employers and their workers. Many industrialists opposed state-imposed limits to their authority within the workplace, including regulations concerning safety and child labor. They considered their factories to be their castles, in which they could do what they pleased.

British liberals believed that a strong state compromised political freedom. The French Revolution had, after all, culminated in Jacobin state centralization and Napoleonic despotism. Continental liberals remained more "statist," accepting a more active role by government, particularly in the German states, and in Spain, where they relied on a powerful state to counteract the influence of nobles and clerics.

Romanticism

Romanticism, emphasizing imagination and emotion in personal development, began to emerge as a literary, artistic, and musical movement in the late eighteenth century. In 1798, the English poets Samuel Taylor Coleridge (1772–1834) and William Wordsworth (1770–1850) penned a manifesto calling on poets to abandon the classical style based on Greek and Roman models that characterized eighteenth-century court and aristocratic life and instead express their emotional response to nature. During the romantic era, swooning and fainting came into vogue because they seemed to be honest expressions of emotion.

Conservative Origins

Romanticism first contributed to the conservative revival. After initially being intrigued by the French Revolution's apparent victory over the strictures of the Old Regime, the early romantic writers had become disillusioned by its violent turn. Coleridge had been among the first to sing the praises of the Revolution, but turned against it when French armies began pouring across the frontiers more as conquerors than as liberators.

Many of the early romantic writers were individuals of religious faith who rejected Enlightenment rationalism. "I wept and I believed," wrote the French writer François-René de Chateaubriand (1768–1848), relating his re-conversion to Catholicism after the turmoil of the revolutionary and Napoleonic eras. Disillusionment with the French Revolution helped German romantic writers discover in nationalism a means of individual fulfillment. Nationalism, too, marked a reaction against Enlightenment rational tradition. Johann Gottfried von Herder (1744–1803), the son of a Prussian schoolteacher, was one of the impassioned leaders of the *Sturm und Drang* (Storm and Stress) movement, a rebellion by young German writers against Enlightenment thought. Calling for the study and celebration of German literature and history, Herder argued that it was through the passionate identification with the nation that the individual reached his or her highest stage of development. All Germans would be bound together by an awareness of and identity in a common history, culture, and above all, language as part of a *Volk*, or living and evolving "national community." Herder thus helped invent the idea of a national culture. At the same time, his insistence on the existence of different racial types, shaped by climate, history, and cultural traditions, would influence the evolution of racism later in the century. In Central and Eastern Europe, which was constituted in many areas by a patchwork of nationalities, romanticism celebrated the historical authenticity of the cultural traditions and languages of ethnic peoples. From there it would be a short step to argue that nationalities should have their own independent state.

Romantic Literature and Painting

Romantics defined freedom as the unleashing of the senses and passion of the soul. They searched for the "heroic genius" who fulfills himself in spite of constraints placed on him by the state, religion, or societal convention. Johann Wolfgang von Goethe (1749–1832) evoked the impassioned battle raging in the mind of the heroic individual. Goethe's hero in *Faust* (1790) struggles to make his way against a society that fails to understand him.

Like Faust, romantic writers and artists were, at least at the beginning, literary and academic outsiders. Many were loners, without established professional positions, overwhelmed by what they considered the tragedy of their unrequited search for individual fulfillment because less-gifted people did not comprehend their brilliance. Romantics bared the suffering of their souls. The English poet Percy Bysshe Shelley (1792–1822) penned his loftiest tribute to the poet (and, thus, himself) in "Hymn of Apollo":

> I am the eye with which the Universe
> Beholds itself and knows itself divine;
> All harmony of instrument or verse,
> All prophecy, all medicine is mine,
> All light of art or nature;—to my song
> Victory and praise in its own right belong.

Romantic painters sought to convey feeling through the depiction of the helplessness of the individual confronted by the power of nature—gathering storms, surging seas, and immense, dark forests, portrayed with deep, rich colors. In France, Théodore Géricault (1791–1824) reached the public eye with his *Officer of the Chasseurs Commanding a Charge* (1812), p. 584, an almost worshipful painting of a Napoleonic officer in the heat of battle. Géricault became obsessed with shipwrecks, a subject that reflected his volatile personality. He sought out real-life survivors of such tragedies in order to paint his powerful *The Raft of the Medusa* (1818–1819), depicting a shipwreck off the West African coast.

Théodore Géricault's *Portrait of an Officer of the Chasseurs Commanding a Charge* (1812).

Romantic Music

The romantics also believed that music, like painting, was poetry capable of releasing torrents of emotion in listeners. Whereas romantic literature sought and achieved a sharp break with the rules of classical literature, romantic musical compositions built on the traditions of the eighteenth-century masters, helping the public rediscover them. The compositions of Ludwig van Beethoven (1770–1827) bridged the classical and romantic periods, with a foot firmly in each. The son of an alcoholic court musician in the Rhineland town of Bonn, Beethoven was a homely, isolated, brooding man.

Beethoven's music followed classical rules of structure and harmony. The German romantic composer Richard Wagner would later say that, as Beethoven became increasingly deaf, he was "undisturbed by the bustle of life [hearing only] the harmonies of his soul." Beethoven's audiences struggled to understand his music, which increasingly seemed to defy traditional structures and harmonies. A critic reacted to one of Beethoven's symphonies, "The composer . . . takes the majestic flight of the eagle, then he creeps along rock-strewn paths. After penetrating the soul with a gentle melancholy he immediately lacerates it with a mass of barbarous chords. I seem to see doves put in together with crocodiles!" Beethoven's symphonies and string quartets were widely played in Europe, and his sonatas helped popularize the piano. The instrument, which continued to be improved, became more resonant and was established as a single solo instrument. Part of the growing popularity of the piano may have stemmed from contemporary fascination with fast-moving machines. Whereas only two decades earlier Mozart had struggled to make ends meet, Beethoven enjoyed wealth and fame, freeing himself from the old patronage system of court and church.

Although opera remained the most popular form of musical expression, drawing crowds with its extravagant staging and elaborate, expensive costumes, romantic music grew in popularity during the first half of the nineteenth century. The public flocked to public concerts, and more musicians could now make a living from their performances. Musicians wrote music for public concerts. The musical "virtuoso" became a phenomenon, going on

The celebrated Niccolò Paganini in concert, early nineteenth century.

concert tours and traveling by train. No one was more popular than the Italian composer and violinist Niccolò Paganini (1782–1840). Paganini's performances, the musical effects he produced, and his frenzied appearance suggested to one observer that he was engaging in witchcraft. Music also assumed a greater role in private life. Not only did more people play the piano, but concerts in middle-class homes became common.

STIRRINGS OF REVOLT

The Congress of Vienna resembled the Dutch boy gamely trying to dam the deluge by plugging up the holes in the dike with his fingers. During the first half of the century, virtually every country in Europe experienced a confrontation between the old political order, represented by the Congress of Vienna, and nascent liberalism.

In France and the German states, liberal bourgeois demanded political rights for a wider number of people. Newspapers and political pamphlets deftly sidestepped the heavy hand of censorship to challenge the restored prerogatives of conservative regimes. In Britain, middle-class spokesmen confronted conservatives and what conservatism's enemies referred to as "Old Corruption," a political system based upon the patronage and influence of wealthy landowners. On the continent, the middle classes clamored for constitutions.

In the German and Italian states and Belgium, liberalism was closely associated with emerging groups of nationalists. Intellectuals, lawyers, and students called for the creation of independent states based upon ethnicity. This was anathema to the powers represented at the Congress of Vienna, particularly the leaders of the polyglot Russian and Austrian Empires. Demands for new states organized around the principle of nationality—as opposed to monarchical or princely sovereignty—would threaten the very existence of these empires.

Liberal Revolts in Spain, Portugal, and Italy

The first test for the Congress system came in Spain. Upon his return to Madrid in 1814, King Ferdinand VII (ruled 1808–1833) declared that he did not recognize the liberal constitution that had been drawn up by the Cortes (assembly) in 1812. It provided ministers responsible to the Cortes and defined sovereignty as residing "essentially in the [Spanish] Nation," the union of all Spaniards in both hemispheres. It guaranteed the right of property, freedom of the press, and freedom from arbitrary arrest.

Ferdinand VII imposed strict censorship, welcomed back the Jesuit religious order, and repressed Masonic lodges. Furthermore, he refused to convoke the Cortes, which he had promised to do upon his return. Ecclesiastics and nobles reclaimed land they had lost during the Napoleonic period. The Inquisition, the Catholic Church's institutionalized apparatus to maintain religious orthodoxy, returned to Spain, and the police again began to arrest alleged heretics.

Thus the Spanish monarchy remained inextricably allied with noble and ecclesiastical privilege. The clergy accounted for about 30 percent of adult Spanish males, many living in monasteries that dotted the countryside. The aristocracy and the Church owned two-thirds of the land, much of it as unproductive as its owners, who collected revenue from those tilling the soil. Yet the vast majority of peasants supported the established order, believing the word of the village priest to be that of God. The small number of nobles and bourgeois who read the country's few newspapers—the majority of the population remained illiterate—found little except, as one traveler put it, "accounts of miracles wrought by different Virgins, lives of holy friars and sainted nuns, romances of marvelous conversions, libels against Jews, heretics and Freemasons, and histories of apparitions."

The allies were delighted to have a "legitimate" sovereign back on France's southern flank, although Spain had long since ceased to be a European power. Moreover, the Spanish Empire had begun to disintegrate. French occupation and the Peninsular War, with the king in exile (see Chapter 13), had weakened Spain's hold over its Latin American colonies. Rebellions against Spanish rule broke out in the colonies, beginning in Argentina in 1816. Simón Bolívar (1783–1830), a fiery Creole aristocrat educated in European Enlightenment ideals, led an army that liberated his native

Venezuela in 1821 and defeated Spanish troops in Peru in 1824. The example of the War of American Independence in North America provided inspiration. Spanish forces, lacking resources and badly led, were obliged to fight over enormous stretches of wildly varying territory. Spain recognized the independence of Mexico in 1821. Of the overseas empire that had stretched from North America to the southern tip of South America in the sixteenth century, Spain retained only the Caribbean islands of Cuba and Puerto Rico, as well as the Philippines in Asia.

Against this background, a revolt broke out in Spain in 1820. Army officers who led the insurrection against Ferdinand were soon joined by merchants and lawyers. The king now agreed to convoke the Cortes and abide by the liberal constitution of 1812. Metternich and Tsar Alexander I of Russia, supported by Prussia, demanded allied armed intervention; so did Louis XVIII of France, eager to prove himself a reliable ally. Great Britain, however, remained adamantly opposed to any intervention in Spanish internal affairs, first as a matter of principle, and secondly because of fear that the presence of foreign troops in Spain might jeopardize British commerce or increase French influence on the Iberian Peninsula.

Meanwhile, the fires of liberalism also spread to Portugal. Liberal army officers took advantage of the continued absence of King John VI, who had fled to Brazil during the Napoleonic Wars, to rise up against the British-backed regent in 1820. They drafted a liberal constitution, based on that penned in Spain in 1812. That same year, a military coup d'état led to the return of King John from Brazil as a constitutional monarch. The constitution proclaimed that year guaranteed religious toleration, civic rights, and the sanctity of property. The influence of this revolution, which undercut the influence of the Church, led to civil war from 1832 to 1834 between royalists and an alliance of liberals and radicals, and then in 1851, after some forty different governments and another coup d'état, to the establishment of a

A secret meeting of the members of the Carbonari, Italy c. 1815–1830.

parliamentary system of government based on a restricted electoral franchise.

In 1820 an insurrection also broke out in Italy. Army officers and merchants in Naples and Sicily revolted against the rule of King Ferdinand I, another monarch who had been restored to his shaky throne by the allies. Some of the revolutionaries were members of a secret society, organized along military lines, known as the "Carbonari." These "charcoal-burners" took their name from their practice of swearing each new member to secrecy by tracing a charcoal mark on his forehead. The Carbonari, originally formed to fight Napoleon's armies, now directed its fervor against the monarch placed on the throne by the Austrians. However, Austrian troops put down the revolt, and another in the Kingdom of Piedmont-Sardinia.

In response to what they perceived as the liberal threat, in 1820 the Russian, Prussian, and Austrian governments signed an agreement at the Congress of Troppau in Austrian Silesia. Based on the "principles of the [Holy] Alliance," it proclaimed the right of the signatories to intervene militarily in any country in which political changes were brought about by revolution. Following the suicide of Castlereagh (who suffered unpopularity and perhaps also blackmail over a sexual matter) in 1822, Britain further distanced itself from the Congress system. That year, the remaining Congress powers reconvened in the northern Italian town of Verona. Britain's withdrawal cleared the way for military action in Spain to restore King Ferdinand VII to his throne. With the support of Russia, Prussia, and Austria, a French army took to the field for the first time since Waterloo, but in very different circumstances. It crossed the Pyrenees Mountains in 1823 and captured Madrid. The grateful king of Spain renounced the Constitution of 1812 and ordered the torture and execution of his opponents.

In December 1823, U.S. President James Monroe, fearing that the Concert powers might try to help Spain restore its authority over its former Latin American colonies, issued a proclamation that became one of the bases of subsequent American foreign policy. Stressing that the political systems of the European powers were different from its own, the Monroe Doctrine warned that the United States would "consider any attempt on their part to extend their system to any portion of this hemisphere as dangerous to our peace and safety."

Stirrings in Germany

In the German and Italian states, liberals and nationalists were often the same people. Members of student fraternities demanded a united Germany. In 1817, a large convocation of student associations celebrated the three-hundredth anniversary of Martin Luther's revolt against the papacy by burning books deemed anti-patriotic. In 1819, a German student murdered an arch-conservative historian and dramatist commonly believed to be in the pay of the Russian tsar. Metternich persuaded Emperor Francis I

Nationalist German students in 1817 burning books and other objects deemed anti-patriotic.

of Austria and Frederick William III of Prussia to impose the Carlsbad Decrees, which the Diet of the German Confederation unanimously accepted. These muzzled the press and dissolved the student fraternities. Teachers fired in one state were to be blacklisted in other member states. Metternich convinced Frederick William to renounce any form of "universal representation" in his kingdom. The episode seemed to clinch Metternich's victory over constitutionalism in the German states.

Cracks in the Congress of Europe: The Greek Revolt

The Greek revolt in 1821 against the Ottoman Turks shattered the Congress system. Austria and, above all, Russia hoped to extend their influence in the Balkans at the expense of the Ottoman Empire. In the late eighteenth century, Catherine the Great had seen Russia's role in the Balkans as protecting Christians there against the Islamic Turks. Moreover, Russian nationalists coveted Constantinople, the gateway to Asia and the Black Sea. Britain feared a potential threat to British control of India and was wary of Russian influence in Afghanistan. Austria, threatened by Russian interest in the Balkans, also feared Russian designs on Constantinople. The Greek revolt put the Congress powers in a bind. Christian Europe traditionally considered the Turks savage infidels. But, at the same time, the Congress powers had to recognize the Ottoman Empire as the historically "legitimate" sovereign of the Greeks. Support for the Greek rebels would represent a renunciation of the *status quo*, a principle upon which the Congress system had been based.

The Greek revolt grew out of a small Greek nationalist movement that had developed at the end of the eighteenth century. Prince Alexander Ypsilantis (1792–1828), a former general in the Russian army, founded a secret nationalist organization in 1814, the "Society of Friends." He counted on the tsar's support for a Greek uprising. (Russia had encouraged a Greek insurrection in 1770, one that had been crushed by Turkish forces.) In 1821 Ypsilantis organized a revolt in Turkish Moldavia, hoping that Romanians would also rise up against Ottoman domination and that Russia would aid the cause of the insurgents. But when Romanians did not rebel and the tsar disavowed the rebels, the Turks crushed the initial Greek uprising. Several weeks later, further revolts against the Turks broke out in mainland Greece and on several Aegean islands. The Congress powers, including Russia, immediately condemned the insurrection.

However, the Greek revolt caught the imagination of writers in Western Europe. Romantic writers espoused national self-consciousness. Members of the philhellenic movement (scholars and intellectuals who had become passionately interested in classical Greece) embraced the Greek revolt as a modern crusade for Christianity and independence against what they con-

Eugène Delacroix's *Massacre at Chios*, 1824.

sidered Turkish oppression of the birthplace of Western civilization. The English poets Byron and Shelley took up the cause of Greek independence. Shelley, who called the poet the "unacknowledged legislator of the world," also supported Irish independence from Britain.

The Greek insurgents massacred thousands of Turks in 1821, but it was the brutal Turkish repression of the Greeks that caught the attention of Western conservatives and liberals alike. In 1822, the Turks massacred the entire Greek population of the island of Chios, after having executed a year earlier the patriarch of Constantinople in his ecclesiastical robes on Easter Sunday. The French romantic painter Eugène Delacroix (1798–1863) celebrated the Greeks' struggle for national sovereignty in his painting *The Massacre at Chios* (1824), p. 590. The British government also had come to the view that peace could best be maintained by the creation of an autonomous Greek state. In 1827, Britain, France, and Russia signed the Treaty of London, threatening the Turks with military intervention if they did not accept an armistice. When the Turks refused, a combined naval force destroyed the Turkish fleet at Navarino.

Russia declared war on the Ottoman Empire in 1828 and occupied the Balkan territories of Moldavia and Eastern Wallachia. However, military obstacles and the self-interested disapproval by Britain and France of Russian plans for dismembering the Ottoman Empire forced Russia to agree to the Treaty of Adrianople (1829). Moldavia and Wallachia became protectorates of Russia, further pushing back the Ottoman Empire's European territories and expanding Russian influence in the Balkans. In 1832, the Greeks finally gained independence. The treaty between Britain, France, Bavaria, and Russia placed Greece under the "guarantee" of "protecting powers" and selected a young Bavarian prince to be king of Greece (Otto I, ruled 1833–1862).

The Decembrist Revolt in Russia

At his succession to the throne after the assassination of his autocratic father in 1801, Tsar Alexander I seemed liberal and idealistic. Scarred by the hatred between his father, Tsar Paul, and his grandmother, Catherine the Great, and by the assassination of Paul, Alexander had at least been aware of the plot. Because he was somewhat familiar with Enlightenment thought, some Russian liberals welcomed Alexander's accession to the throne, seeing him as a potentially charming reformer. He surrounded himself with a committee of advisers who advocated reform and began his reign by granting amnesty to thousands of people condemned by his father, relaxing censorship, abolishing torture in judicial investigations, and allowing more Russians to travel abroad. During the Napoleonic Wars, Tsar Alexander had taken steps to make his regime more efficient, including the creation of a council of state, the formation of centralized ministries directly responsible to the tsar, and the organization of local governments. Yet, an enormous social, economic, and legal gulf separated the Russian aristocracy from the millions of destitute serfs bound to the lands of their lords. Most Russian nobles feared that any reform would threaten their prerogatives. Early in his reign in 1803, the tsar gave permission to the nobles to free their serfs but few chose to do so.

However, Tsar Alexander I became increasingly reactionary. In 1809, he rejected a proposed constitution. Conservative elements regained power and introduced coercive measures. Universities and schools were closely monitored to root out liberals; study abroad was banned; and censorship was applied with ruthless efficiency. At the same time, he continued the aggressive policies of Peter the Great and Catherine the Great in the late seventeenth and eighteenth centuries, expanding the empire by adding Georgia at the expense of the Turks.

But liberal reform had advocates in Russia, including some young nobles who had been educated in Western Europe (before foreign study was prohibited) and a handful of army officers who had lived in France during the allied military occupation after Napoleon's fall. They were bitterly disappointed by Alexander I's reactionary turn. By 1820, two loosely linked conspiratorial "unions," as they were called, had been formed. The educated nobles of the Northern Union hoped that Russia might evolve toward British constitutionalism. The military officers of the Southern Union had a more radical goal: to kill the tsar and establish a republic.

Tsar Alexander's sudden death in December 1825 seemed to offer the conspirators their chance. The tsar had two brothers. Constantine, the eldest, had quietly yielded his succession to the throne in favor of his younger, more

Decembrists gathering in December 1825 at Senate Square in Saint Petersburg.

reactionary brother Nicholas. The Northern Union nonetheless convinced the Saint Petersburg garrison to support the succession of Constantine. Troops occupied a central square in the capital, shouting the name of their favorite, until Nicholas ordered troops loyal to him to fire. A hastily planned insurrection by the Southern Union was also put down. The leaders of the Decembrists, as they came to be known, were executed.

Hard-working and willful, Nicholas I (ruled 1825–1855) believed that his power to govern came directly from God. Nicholas tightened the grip of the police on education in an attempt to exclude Western ideas from Russia. In 1833, the minister of education proclaimed the doctrine of "Official Nationality": autocracy, orthodoxy, and official [Russian] nationality were the intertwined principles of the state. The new tsar did not approve of serfdom because it was inefficient, but he feared that its abolition could lead to peasant insurrection. Nicholas did, however, order the codification of Russian laws in the first decade of his reign and encouraged reforms improving the conditions of state serfs. The arrival of liberal ideas from the West encouraged debate and calls for reform within the Russian intelligentsia, encouraging a group of reform-minded men within the imperial bureaucracy.

France: The Bourbon Restoration and the Revolution of 1830

In a contemporary French lampoon of the return of the Bourbons to the throne, a majestic eagle—the symbol of Napoleon—sweeps out of the Tuileries Palace in Paris as a somewhat plump, unsightly duck waddles in, followed by its ungainly brood. The contrast between the image of Napoleon's bold achievements and the stodgy and pious Restoration was sharp indeed. The Bourbons returned "in the baggage of the allies," as it was said.

Upon the return of the Bourbons to power in May 1814, Louis XVIII promulgated a Charter that, in effect, made France a constitutional monarchy. The Charter recognized equality before the law and accepted the Napoleonic Civil Code. It established an assembly consisting of a Chamber of Deputies and a Chamber of Peers. The king would name members (whose appointment would be for life and hereditary) of the Chamber of Peers, as well as ministers, who would be responsible only to him. The Chamber of Deputies would be elected in a complicated two-stage process, based on an extremely narrow electoral franchise.

The restored Bourbon monarchy maintained the centralized state bureaucracy; recognized all Napoleonic titles, decorations, and even pensions; and promised that property purchased during the Revolution as "national" would remain in the hands of the new owners. Moreover, the Charter offered freedom of the press. The government could levy no taxes without the consent of the Assembly.

The Catholic Church would still be subject to Napoleon's Concordat (see Chapter 13), but was returned to its privileged position, and Catholicism again became the official state religion, although the Napoleonic

Code's guarantee of the free practice of religion to Protestants and Jews was reaffirmed. The religious orders returned to France in force, and the observance of Sunday and Church holidays became obligatory.

Ultra-royalists, or "Ultras," the most fanatical royalist enemies of the Revolution, had after Waterloo launched the "White Terror," so called because of the color of the Bourbon flag, against those who had supported Napoleon. In the election for the Chamber of Deputies in August 1815, the Ultras easily defeated more moderate royalists sponsored by the government. Some of the Ultras referred contemptuously to Louis XVIII as "King Voltaire" because of his Charter, which they viewed as a compromise with the Revolution. They demanded that the "national property" be returned to its original owners.

Louis XVIII dissolved the Ultra-dominated Chamber of Deputies in 1816, and new elections produced a somewhat more moderate Chamber. In 1820, a madman assassinated Charles, the duke of Berry, the king's nephew and the only member of the Bourbon family capable of producing an heir to the throne. France was plunged into mourning. The Ultras cried for revenge, accusing the liberals of being ultimately responsible for the assassination. The king dismissed the moderate government, restored more stringent censorship, and altered the electoral system to reduce the influence of bourgeois voters living in towns.

Soon, however, the church bells stopped their mournful cadence and rang out in joy. It turned out that the duke's wife had been pregnant at the time of his death. Royalist France celebrated the birth of a male heir, "the miracle baby," as he came to be called, the duke of Bordeaux (later known as the count of Chambord). Confident that God was with them, the Ultras, at least for the moment, retained the upper hand.

Upon Louis XVIII's death in 1824, his reactionary brother, the count of Artois, took the throne as Charles X (ruled 1824–1830). Rumors spread that the pious king was going to allow the Catholic Church to collect the tithe, that is, require French subjects to pay 10 percent of their income to the Church. The Chamber of Deputies passed a law making sacrilege—any crime committed in a church—a capital offense. That no one was ever executed for such an offense did not diminish public outrage. The government financed the indemnification of those who had lost land during the Revolution by reducing the interest paid to holders of the national debt, most of whom were middle class.

Many in France retained an allegiance to Napoleon's memory. Former Napoleonic soldiers, particularly those officers pensioned off on half pay, looked back on the imperial era as their halcyon days. In 1820–1821, some joined the Carbonari, a secret society named after its Italian equivalent, and plotted to overthrow the Restoration. Some merchants and manufacturers believed that the Restoration monarchy paid insufficient attention to commerce and industry, listening only to rural nobles.

Honoré Daumier's caricature of the less-than-inspiring members of the French Chamber of Deputies.

Amid an economic crisis that had begun with the failure of the harvest the previous year, elections in 1827 increased liberal strength in the Chamber of Deputies. Two years later, Charles X threw caution to the wind, appointing as his premier the reactionary Prince Jules de Polignac (1780–1847), one of only two members of the Chamber of Deputies who had refused an oath of allegiance to the Charter granted by Louis XVIII.

The opposition to the government of Charles X received a boost from a new generation of romantic writers. In the preface to his controversial play *Hernani* (1830), the production of which caused a near riot outside the theater, Victor Hugo (1802–1885) clearly set liberalism and romanticism against the established order of the restored monarchy:

> Young people, have courage! However difficult they make our present, the future will be beautiful. Romanticism, so often badly defined, is . . . nothing less than *liberalism* in literature. . . . Literary liberty is the daughter of political liberty. That is the principle of this century, and it will prevail.

In 1828, liberals formed an association to refuse to pay taxes in protest of the government's policies and worked to ensure that all eligible to vote registered to do so. Benjamin Constant (1767–1830), a Swiss novelist, political essayist, and member of the French Chamber of Deputies, demanded that the electoral franchise be extended. He espoused a philosophy of liberalism based on a separation of powers and "a government of laws and not men" that would protect property and other freedoms from tyranny (he had both Napoleon and arbitrary monarchical rule in mind).

In response to Charles's bellicose speech opening the 1830 session of the Chamber, 221 deputies signed an address to the throne that attacked the government in no uncertain terms. When the king dissolved the Chamber, the liberal opposition won a majority in the new Chamber. In the meantime, Charles had sent an army to conquer Algeria, whose ruler was a vassal of the sultan of Turkey. But not even news of the capture of Algiers on July 9, 1830, could end vociferous opposition. The king and Polignac then settled on a move that they hoped would bring an end to the crisis. Instead, it brought revolution.

On July 26, 1830, Charles X promulgated the July Ordinances, shattering the principles of the Charter of 1814. He dissolved the newly elected Chamber of Deputies; disfranchised almost three-quarters of those currently eligible to vote; ordered new elections under the newly restricted franchise; and muzzled the press. Demonstrations on July 27 led to skirmishes with troops. Parisians blocked the capital's narrow streets with barricades. Fired upon in the street and pelted by rocks and tiles thrown from rooftops, the king's soldiers became increasingly demoralized.

Early on July 30, liberals put posters around Paris calling for Louis-Philippe to be the new king. From the family of Orléans, the junior branch of the royal Bourbon family, Louis-Philippe, the duke of Orléans, had the reputation for being relatively liberal, having fought in the revolutionary armies. His father (known as Philippe Égalité) had in the National Assembly voted for the execution of Louis XVI. Louis-Philippe had expanded his horizons by drinking bourbon in Kentucky. Liberals offered the throne to Louis-Philippe (ruled 1830–1848), who became "king of the French"—the title, rather than "king of France," was intended to convey that the king's authority came from the people. Charles X abdicated on August 2. Louis-Philippe agreed to a revised version of the Charter, and the tricolor flag of the Revolution replaced the white flag of the Bourbons.

Despite its revolutionary origins, the new liberal monarchy won relatively quick acceptance from the other European powers. Catholicism ceased to be the official religion of the state, although it remained the nominal religion of the vast majority of the population. The new Orleanist regime almost doubled the number of voters, but France was still far from being a republic. Many of those enfranchised by the revised Charter were drawn from the middle class. Lawyers and men of other professions significantly increased middle-class representation in the legislature. The government helped stimulate economic growth and industrial development by improving roads and implementing other policies that benefited manufacturers and merchants. The rallying cry of François Guizot, historian and prime minister (1787–1874, prime minister 1840–1848), to the middle class was "Enrich yourselves!" Known as the "July Monarchy," after the month of its

Eugène Delacroix's *Liberty Leading the People* (1830). Note the female image of liberty and the presence of the top-hatted bourgeois and the heavily armed street urchin, neither of whom actually fought in the Revolution.

founding, the Orleanist reign also came to be known and lampooned as "the bourgeois monarchy." The portly Louis-Philippe himself contributed to this image, surrounding himself with dark-suited businessmen and carrying an umbrella, that symbol of bourgeois preparedness.

The Orleanist monarchy could claim neither the principle of monarchical legitimacy asserted by the Legitimists (supporters of Charles X's Bourbon grandson) or that of popular sovereignty espoused by republicans. Legitimists launched several small, failed insurrections in western France. In Paris, crowds of workers, disappointed by the government's lack of attention to their demands, sacked the archbishop's palace in 1831. Silk workers in Lyon rose up against their employers and the state in 1831 and 1834. Following an uprising by republicans in Paris, the Chamber of Deputies passed a law in 1835 severely restricting the right to form associations, and the next year it passed another law again fettering the press.

Louis-Philippe survived an assassination attempt in 1835; a plot by a secret organization of revolutionaries, the "Society of the Seasons," to overthrow him in 1839; and another attempt to kill him in 1840. Less serious—for the moment—seemed attempts in 1836 and 1840 by Louis Napoleon Bonaparte, Napoleon's nephew, to invade France with a few loyalists and

Louis-Philippe receiving black-suited members of the Chamber of Deputies, who present him with the act by which they confered the crown on him.

rally support. The cult of Napoleon, accentuated by the vogue for the literature of romanticism, served only to highlight what seemed to be the mediocrity of the July Monarchy.

OTHER LIBERAL ASSAULTS ON THE OLD ORDER

The French Revolution of 1830 directly encouraged liberal and national movements in other countries. Liberal successes followed in Belgium and Switzerland, but not in Spain.

Independence for Belgium

The Dutch Netherlands had achieved independence from Spain in the seventeenth century. The Southern Netherlands was Belgium, largely Catholic, and divided between Flemish speakers in the north and French-speaking Walloons in the south (see Map 15.2). Brussels, the largest city in Belgium, lies within Flemish Belgium, but had many French speakers.

What Belgians called "Dutch arithmetic" left Belgium with fewer seats in the Dutch Estates-General than its population should have warranted. Catholics had to contribute to Protestant state schools and paid higher taxes. In the late 1820s, Belgian liberals allied with Catholics against the Protestant Dutch government demanding that ministers be responsible to the Estates-General and taxes be reduced. Dutch King William I (1772–1843) granted only more press freedom.

MAP 15.2 THE BIRTH OF BELGIUM, 1831–1839   The boundaries of the Dutch Republic and Belgium, including within Belgium the areas that were Protestant and Catholic, as well as Flemish and Walloon areas. The Grand Duchy of Luxembourg was created in 1831 and united with the Netherlands in the person of the grand duke, King William I of the Netherlands.

Following the arrival of news from France of the July Revolution, the Brussels opera presented a production about an insurrection in Naples in 1648 against Spanish rule. So inspired, the audience left the theater to demonstrate against a government newspaper and other symbols of Dutch authority. Workers, suffering unemployment and high prices, put up barricades, and were soon joined by units of bourgeois militia from outside Brussels. A halfhearted military attack floundered when inexperienced Dutch troops panicked as the ranks of the defenders swelled. After three more days of fighting, the Dutch troops withdrew to the north. The Dutch bombardment of Antwerp convinced more Flemish to support the rebels.

In early October 1830, a provisional government declared Belgium independence. A Belgian Congress offered the throne to one of Louis-Philippe's sons, but he was forced to decline because Britain would not tolerate such French influence in Belgium. The Congress then offered the throne to a German prince, Leopold of Saxe-Coburg (who was a British subject, the widower of Princess Charlotte of England). Leopold was crowned King Leopold I (ruled 1831–1865) in July 1831. The European powers guaranteed Belgium's independence, and when the Dutch took Antwerp in August 1831, French military intervention returned that city to the new nation. Belgium became a constitutional monarchy with a parliament of two houses, both elected by about one of every thirty males.

Liberal Successes in Switzerland

Another liberal success came in Switzerland, which the Congress of Vienna had reestablished as a federation of semi-autonomous cantons. Because of Switzerland's long tradition of decentralized government, the allies had been willing to tolerate a constitution that allowed relatively extensive political freedoms. However, fearing that some cantons might become havens of liberalism, the Congress powers forced the Swiss cantons in 1823 to restrict freedom of the press and curtail the activities of foreign political exiles.

The 1830 revolution in France inspired the quest for constitutional guarantees of freedom, more efficient government, and limits on the political influence of Protestant and Catholic clergy in Switzerland. In December 1830 the federal Diet initiated a period of "regeneration." The constitutions of ten cantons were liberalized, guaranteeing freedom of expression and giving all adult men the right to vote, a victory unique at that time.

But Metternich was not far away. Austria pressured the German-speaking Swiss cantons to oppose secularization. During the winter of 1844–1845, when the canton of Lucerne announced that the Jesuit order would again be welcome within its borders, liberals rebelled. Seven Catholic cantons withdrew from the Swiss Confederation, forming a separate league (Sonderbund). In 1847, the other cantons declared war on the Sonderbund and, in what amounted to little more than a skirmish, defeated the Catholic cantons within a month. In 1848, Switzerland adopted a new liberal constitution, becoming a federal state with universal male suffrage.

NATIONALIST DREAMS

Nationalism also gradually emerged as a force for change in Central and Eastern Europe within the context of multinational empires. Nationalism was closely tied to liberalism in that exponents of both ideologies demanded far-reaching political change that threatened the state systems (see Map 15.3).

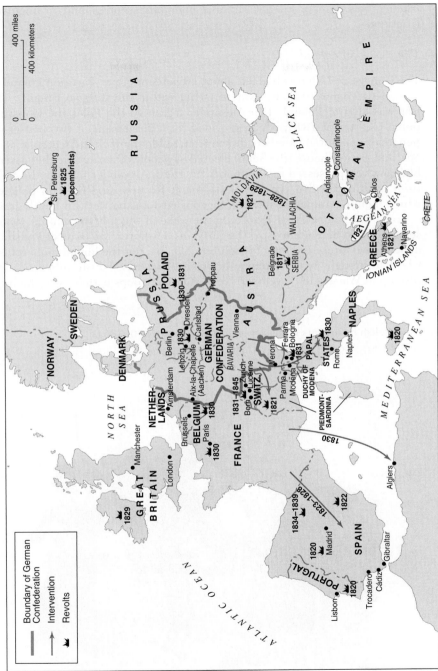
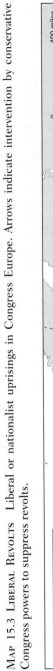

MAP 15.3 LIBERAL REVOLTS   Liberal or nationalist uprisings in Congress Europe. Arrows indicate intervention by conservative Congress powers to suppress revolts.

Intellectuals demanded that national boundaries correspond to linguistic frontiers.

The Revolt in Poland

The Congress of Vienna had left about 20 percent of pre-Partition Poland as "Congress Poland" with its own army, but within the Russian Empire. The tsar was king of Poland. Tsar Alexander I granted the Poles the Constitutional Charter of 1815, which provided for a parliament of two houses—a Senate of appointed members drawn from noble families and Catholic bishops, and a lower house (the Sejm) elected by people of means. Neither assembly, however, possessed real authority. In 1820, Alexander forbade the Sejm from meeting for five years as punishment for opposing Russian policies, which included imposing disadvantageous customs barriers on Polish grain.

Some Poles hoped that France, in the wake of the July Revolution, would send forces to help them expel the Russians. However, the issue of Polish independence interested only French republicans, not the liberal monarchists who had brought Louis-Philippe to power. However, Polish military cadets rose up in Warsaw in November 1830. Russian troops withdrew in the hope

Polish insurgents rising up against Russia in 1830–1831.

that the municipal government could restore order. In January 1831, a large crowd surrounded the Sejm, which declared that the Russian tsar (Nicholas I) was no longer king of Poland. A provisional national government formed. The Sejm, however, refused to attempt to mobilize peasants in support of the insurrection, fearing that they might demand land reform and attack their lords instead of the Russians. In August 1832 the tsar's troops surrounded Warsaw. Tensions between moderates and radicals erupted into violence, making its defense even more difficult. Warsaw fell to Russian troops in the autumn, and about 10,000 Poles fled Russian oppression. Émigré Polish artists and musicians enriched cultural life in Western Europe capitals. The composer Frédéric Chopin (1810–1849) moved to Paris in 1831, hoping to make his fortune. Although he was not really a political refugee, ardent nationalism infused his music, as he drew upon Polish folk themes and dances.

The privileges that had been accorded "Congress Poland" disappeared. Nicholas I abolished the constitution that Poland had enjoyed within the Russian Empire, as well as the Sejm and the Polish army. Encouraged by Russian measures against the Poles, Prussia and Austria withdrew concessions they had earlier given to the Poles in the territories they had absorbed in the 1790s.

Uprisings in Italy and Spain

Popular stirrings in the Italian states, beginning with movements in Bologna and the Duchy of Modena, started as protests against inefficient and corrupt rule. Rebels in Parma literally locked Duchess Marie-Louise out of the city by shutting the gates until an Austrian army arrived in March 1831 to let her back in. Several cities in central Italy that declared their independence from the Papal States proclaimed the "United Provinces of Italy."

Like the Poles, insurgents against Austrian rule in several towns within the Papal States unrealistically counted on help from French armies, who again would march with a tricolor flag since the fall of the Bourbons. With Austrian troops approaching from the north, an army of volunteers marched toward Rome, defeating the pope's army. But by then Austrian forces had taken Modena, Parma, and Ferrara. A papal army mopped up resistance, sacking several towns, and Austrian troops had to return to save the local populations. The Italian insurrections collapsed without winning popular support.

Giuseppe Mazzini (1805–1872), a lawyer by training and an energetic revolutionary by temperament, emerged as a guiding spirit in the quest for Italian unification under a republic. Mazzini wanted to bring peace to Europe by liberating all peoples. He was one of the first to suggest that the states of Europe might evolve into a loose federation of democratic states based on the principle of nationality. Mazzini believed that a defeat of Austria in northern Italy would serve as a first step toward creating a federation of European democratic republics. Rejecting the Carbonari's conspiratorial tradition, he was convinced that he could expand his nationalist organization, Young Italy, whose membership was limited to individuals under forty years of age. Jailed and then expelled from one country after another, he launched futile insurrections in 1834–1836 and in 1844. However, Mazzini kept the cause of Italian nationalism alive.

Some Italian nationalists began to look to the liberal Kingdom of Piedmont-Sardinia, Italy's strongest state, to effect national unification. But Austria still dominated the Italian peninsula, which included small states that were proud of their independence. The dream of Italian unification remained for the most part limited to a small number of middle-class intellectuals.

In Spain, King Ferdinand VII married Maria Christina, a liberal Neapolitan princess, in 1830. Their daughter Isabella became the heir to the Spanish throne. But nobles and churchmen insisted that a woman could not rule Spain. After the king's death in 1833, civil war broke out between liberals and conservatives (the Carlists), who supported the cause of the late king's brother, Don Carlos. Maria Christina, ruling as regent, promulgated a constitution in 1834 modeled on the French Charter of 1814. In 1843, General Ramón Narváez (1800–1868) seized power, promulgating a conservative constitution and stifling the press. On his deathbed he boasted, "I have no enemies, I have shot them all."

German Nationalism in Central Europe

In the German states, liberals faced an uphill battle. Constitutions implemented during the Napoleonic period had been gradually weakened or withdrawn. Electoral assemblies were selected by limited franchise and had almost no power. However, the wave of liberal and nationalist movements encouraged by the revolutions of 1830 reached Central Europe. Popular disturbances forced the rulers of Hanover and Hesse-Kassel to make political concessions. In Saxony, a liberal constitution was enacted following uprisings in Leipzig and Dresden, and liberals won a constitution in the northern German state of Brunswick.

The Polish revolt against Russia in 1831 fueled the imagination of German university students. The movement culminated in a huge meeting in 1832 of 30,000 people at the ruins of a château near the University of Heidelberg, where speakers saluted popular sovereignty. Police foiled an attempt by students to seize Frankfurt, the meeting place of the Federal Diet of the German Confederation. The Confederation's Diet responded by passing "Ten Articles," which brought the universities under surveillance, coordinated police repression of liberals in the German states, prohibited public meetings, and stipulated that any state threatened by revolution would be assisted by the others.

Yet liberalism in the German states slowly gained momentum among professors, students, and lawyers during what later became known as the

Vormärz ("Before March") period, that is, the period of ferment that preceded the Revolution of March 1848 (see Chapter 16). The French Revolution of 1830 influenced these "Young Germans." The poet Heinrich Heine (1797–1856) had rushed to Paris after the fall of the Bourbon dynasty. His *French Conditions* sharply contrasted the mood of apparent intellectual freedom and optimism of Paris with that of the repression and gloomy resignation liberals faced in the German states, which had no revolutionary tradition. German liberals remained political outsiders, confronting a pervasive respect for ideological conformity.

Yet German liberalism became increasingly linked to the pursuit of German unification, despite the challenge posed by German particularism, the tradition of many small, independent states. The philosopher Georg Wilhelm Friedrich Hegel (1770–1831) made explicit the close connection between the development of German nationalism and the reverence for a strong state as the embodiment of national sovereignty, which characterized German liberal thought. For Hegel, nationalism was the equivalent of a secular religion that had the potential of shaping a new morality. Hegel's state is overwhelming, even frightening, subsuming individual rights to its power.

Liberal economic theory attracted German merchants and manufacturers, who objected to the discouraging complexity of customs tariffs that created a series of costly hurdles along roads and rivers. As German manufacturing developed, particularly in the Rhineland, businessmen supported a proposed German Customs Union (Zollverein), which, following its creation in 1834, removed some tariff barriers in seventeen states. To liberal nationalists, the Zollverein seemed to offer a basis for the eventual political unification of Germany. It breathed life into the movement for political reform. But those who hoped that Prussia and the other German states would move toward constitutionalism were disappointed. Prussian King Frederick William IV (ruled 1840–1861) refused to establish a Diet representing all of Prussia. When he finally did convoke a United Diet in 1847, it was not popularly elected and was to serve the king only in an advisory capacity.

CRISIS AND COMPROMISE IN GREAT BRITAIN

In Britain, demands for political reform, specifically the expansion of the electoral franchise to include more middle-class voters, would be the true test of the ability of the British elite to compromise in the interest of social and political harmony. Three hundred thousand soldiers demobilized after Waterloo found little work, and many of them depended on poor relief. Amid popular protest, working people joined clubs organized by radicals demanding universal suffrage. Poor harvests in 1818 and 1819 brought high prices and grain riots and machine breaking. The popular radicalism of the 1790s had led to the government's dissolution of radical "corresponding societies" and the suspension of *habeas corpus*, which made it possible to arrest people

The Peterloo Massacre in Manchester, 1819.

without charging them with anything. The Combination Acts (1799–1800) made strikes illegal while reinforcing existing laws against trade unions. Ordinary people now demanded political reform. On August 16, 1819, a crowd of some 60,000 men and women gathered near Manchester to demonstrate for the right to form political organizations and to assemble freely. Deputized local constables moved in to arrest the main speaker. Then soldiers gunned down protestors, many dressed in their Sunday best, killing eleven and wounding hundreds of others. The ugly incident entered history as "Peterloo," a shameful victory not over Napoleon at Waterloo but over Britain's defenseless laboring poor. Parliament passed Six Acts that, reviving the repressive legislation of the era of the French Revolution, included suspending *habeas corpus* and imposing further restrictions on the press. That year the government broke up the "Cato Street Conspiracy," a plot by radicals to assassinate members of the Cabinet as they attended a dinner in London.

The late 1820s were also bleak years for the English poor. Crimes increased in Britain, particularly against property, reflecting hard times. Artisans and skilled workers demanded higher wages and organized more unions within crafts—for example, those representing skilled engineering workers. Parliament abolished the Combination Acts in 1824, making strikes legal. Workers formed more "friendly societies," which, in exchange for modest fees, offered minimal assistance when a member became ill, or paid for burial upon death to avoid the indignity of a pauper's grave. The friendly societies and other clubs of workingmen generated interest in reform, against a backdrop of hardship, industrial disputes, demonstrations, and the wave of food riots and machine breaking that spread in 1829–1830 through southern England.

Religious and Electoral Reform

However, there would be no revolution in nineteenth-century Britain. The landed elite, which dominated Parliament, supported by manufacturing interests, enacted reforms that defused social and political tensions by bowing to middle-class demands. Even if many Tories believed that electoral reform would be a dangerous precedent, the fear of popular protest and perhaps even revolution led them to compromise. Reforms passed by Parliament contributed to the emergence of a liberal consensus in Victorian Britain that lasted throughout the century. Religion, too, may have played a part. The government allocated funds for the construction of more Anglican churches in working-class areas. At the same time, Methodism, along with other churches within the "New Dissent," won many converts, arguably reducing social tension. Bible societies and other evangelical associations interested in the plight of the poor increased dramatically in number.

In 1828, despite vociferous opposition from the Established Church, Parliament repealed the Test and Corporation Acts, which had forced anyone holding public office to take communion in the Anglican Church. Catholic emancipation had emerged as a major political issue at least partly because it was linked to the problem of Catholic Ireland. There a reform movement had begun and organized protests against English Protestant domination. Insurgency seemed endemic. Catholics of means had not been able to vote until 1793 in Ireland (and the franchise was subsequently made even more restrictive). The Irish Parliament had been eliminated in 1800, although Ireland was represented in British Parliament. Finally, in 1829, Parliament passed the Catholic Emancipation Act, which removed the legal restrictions that had kept Catholics from holding office or serving in Parliament.

In Britain, political liberalism continued to be closely linked to the movement led by Whigs, the party most attached to constitutional monarchy and the rights of Parliament, for electoral reform. Only one of fifteen men in Britain had the right to vote. Businessmen resented being underrepresented in the House of Commons. The electoral system remained a patchwork that reflected the interests of local elites and particular communities that had gradually developed in England since the fourteenth century. The industrial north sent few men to Parliament because electoral districts had not changed since before the Industrial Revolution. No one represented the industrial centers of Manchester and Birmingham in Parliament. Wealthy merchants in those cities were no longer content with indirect, "virtual representation" through members of Parliament who claimed to have their interests in mind. In contrast, some sparsely populated rural districts still were represented in Parliament. Dunwich, the most notorious of these "rotten boroughs," had been covered over by the sea since the twelfth century. "Pocket boroughs" were electoral districts "in the pocket" of a wealthy landowner routinely returned to Parliament (see Chapter 11).

With news of France's Revolution of 1830, the British upper classes rallied together, fearful, as they used to say, that when France sneezed, the rest of Europe might catch a cold. Amid shows of armed force by the government, organized protest was limited to an enthusiastic rally in the Scottish city of Glasgow to celebrate the news of the French and Belgian revolutions. In England, crowds gathered to hear the popular radical William Cobbett (1763–1835), whose weekly newspaper, the *Political Register*, aimed at "journeymen and labourers" spoke on behalf of the extension of the electoral franchise to all men.

The Reform Bill of 1832

The general election following George IV's death in 1830 reduced the conservative majority in Parliament. A broadly based campaign for electoral reform swept the country; some of the 5,000 petitions that were brought to Parliament attacked in patriotic language the selfishness of the landed elite. The new prime minister, Earl Charles Grey (1764–1845), a Whig, knew that any reform bill that passed the House of Commons would never get through the House of Lords as then constituted. In 1831, Lords rejected a bill sponsored by the government that would have eliminated many "rotten" and "pocket" boroughs. Public meetings protested this defeat, particularly in the cities of the industrial north and Scotland, which had no representation in Commons. When the House of Lords rejected a second reform bill in October 1831, demonstrators massed in London and a riot in Bristol ended in twelve deaths.

By this time, more Tories had come around to Grey's view that only the passage of some sort of electoral reform bill could save Britain from a revolution. They feared an alliance between frustrated businessmen and radicals, supported by workers, as had occurred in France in 1830. The Whigs proposed a third bill, which Commons passed in March 1832, and sent it on to Lords. The duke of Wellington tried and failed to form a ministry. Grey, who again became prime minister, convinced the new king, William IV (ruled 1830–1837), to threaten to create enough new peers to get the reform bill through the House of Lords, whose peers did not want to see their ranks contaminated by "instant lords." Wellington agreed not to oppose its passage, and the bill passed.

The Reform Act of 1832 was a turning point in the history of modern Britain. The landed magnates agreed to lower the minimum franchise requirement, almost doubling the size of the electorate. Britain was far from a democracy—only about one of every five adult male citizens was now eligible to vote—but the British Parliament now more accurately reflected

Britain's emerging industrial society. In the early 1840s, 15 percent of the members of the House of Commons were businessmen, and 35 percent had some other connection to commerce and industry, such as serving on the board of directors of enterprises. A larger percentage of men could now vote in Britain than in France, Belgium, the Netherlands, or Spain.

The new electorate, as the Tories had feared, increased Whig strength. Commons passed two reforms in 1833 influenced by the Reform Act. In part a response to growing opposition to slavery by religious Dissenters, Evangelical Protestants, and political radicals, anti-slavery societies launched a nationwide campaign against slavery in the British Dominions. Britain had withdrawn from the slave trade in 1808, and six years later 750,000 people had signed petitions in Britain calling for the abolition of slavery. However, in 1830 there were still 650,000 slaves in the British West Indies, and slaves in British colonies in Africa and Asia (as well as in the United States). Ladies' associations distributed campaign literature and organized a boycott of sugar produced by slaves in the West Indies. The campaign was successful. In 1833, Parliament abolished slavery in the British Empire.

The second reform measure, also passed in 1833 (see Chapter 14), prohibited work by children under nine years of age, limited the workday of children from nine through twelve years to eight hours a day (and a maximum of forty-eight hours per week), and that for "young persons" ages thirteen to eighteen to twelve hours a day (to a maximum of sixty-nine hours per week).

The Poor Law followed in 1834. Able-bodied individuals would no longer receive assistance from parishes, but would be incarcerated in "well-regulated" workhouses. And the Municipal Corporations Act of 1835 eliminated the old, often corrupt borough governments, creating elected municipal corporations responsible for administration. This again reflected the growing political influence of the English middle classes, particularly in industrial areas. These reforms allowed many more Whigs, including Dissenters, to assume positions of responsibility in local government, another blow to the domination of public life by the old aristocratic oligarchy and the Established Church.

Chartism and the Repeal of the Corn Laws

The Chartist movement reflected the strength of reformism in Britain. Whereas some French and German workers dreamed of revolution, their English counterparts took out their quill pens. In 1836, William Lovett (1800–1877), a cabinetmaker, founded the London Workingmen's Association for Benefiting Politically, Socially, and Morally the Useful Classes. Two years later, Lovett and Francis Place, a London tailor, prepared the "Great Charter." It called for the democratization of political life, including universal male suffrage, annual elections, equal electoral districts, the secret ballot, and salaries for members of Parliament, so that ordinary people could serve if elected. Chartists objected to the monopoly of wealth and political influence in Britain by a small percentage of the population, wealthy landowners and the captains of industry. The Chartist movement remained overwhelmingly peaceful, its members committed to acting as a "moral force" in British life. Chartism was in some ways a movement that looked back into a past its members imagined as being more moral than the period in which they lived. Chartist leaders attempted to attract women to the movement by recognizing the contributions of women workers to the family economy—despite the resentment of many male craftsmen in working-class families that the gender roles of many women seemed to be changing and that some men now found themselves working alongside them. Some Chartists sought to convince hard-drinking and often wife-beating male workers to be more respectable. (However, Chartist leaders rejected feminist pleas that their movement include demands for the rights of women.) A small "Physical Force" group emerged within the Chartist movement in northern England, threatening strikes and even insurrection if Parliament did not yield, but this group remained small and relatively unimportant.

In 1839, Parliament summarily rejected a Chartist petition with almost 1.3 million signatures. Undaunted, the Chartists tried again in 1842 when the National Chartist Association carried a giant scroll with 3.3 million signatures to Westminster. Once again, Parliament turned the Great Charter away. Thereafter, Chartism declined as a movement, despite a brief revival in 1848.

Yet Parliament enacted another significant reform. Passed by a conservative-dominated Parliament in 1815 and 1828, the Corn Laws had

Photograph of the final Chartist demonstration at Kensington Common, April 10, 1848.

imposed a sliding tariff on imported wheat (then known as "corn"). When the price of wheat produced in Britain fell below a certain level, import duties would keep out cheaper foreign grain. Foreign grain could be imported virtually free of import taxes only when the price of wheat stood at or above a certain level. The laws protected landowners, but were detrimental to the interests of businessmen who imported or sold imported grain and, above all, to ordinary people, who were forced to pay higher prices for bread. Failed harvests in 1839–1841 brought great deprivation, as parishes cut back on allocations to the poor. The "Great Hunger" in Ireland, caused by the potato famine that began in 1845, brought mass starvation (see Chapter 14).

The issue of the repeal of the Corn Laws pitted proponents of laissez-faire economic policies against wealthy property owners, Whigs against Tories. British manufacturers and spokesmen for the poor denounced the entrenched "bread-taxing" and "blood-sucking" oligarchy. In 1839, the Anti–Corn Law League started up, joining businessmen, Whig politicians, and political radicals, who believed that the repeal of the Corn Laws would be a major step toward universal male suffrage. John Bright (1811–1889) argued that the repeal of the Corn Laws would be a major step toward political democracy. The son of a Quaker cotton mill owner, Bright, although not an MP, incarnated British liberalism, as he thundered against aristocratic privilege and its close ties to the Established Church. He warned, "Until now, this country has been ruled by the class of great proprietors of the soil. Everyone must have foreseen that, as trade and manufactures extended, the balance of power would, at some time or other, be thrown into another scale. Well, that time has come."

SEARCHING FOR POTATOES IN A STUBBLE FIELD.

A destitute, hungry Irish family searching for potatoes in a stubble field during the potato famine.

As with the 1832 Reform Act, it took a change of heart by a Conservative government to get a repeal bill passed. Prime Minister Robert Peel, whose smile it was said resembled the gleam of silver plate on a coffin, was himself the conservative son of a cotton manufacturer. Believing in free trade, he had pushed through reductions in and even the elimination of some tariffs, including those on imported raw cotton. The Irish potato famine helped push him to undertake the dismantling of the Corn Laws. Repeal would be an act of political courage, as he was bound to fall from power. Peel now believed only such a move could forestall a popular insurrection. In 1846, Parliament repealed the Corn Laws, reducing duties on wheat and other imported agricultural products. Having bitterly divided the Conservative Party, Peel was forced to resign the same day, a victim, his supporters insisted, of doing the right thing.

Conclusion

Between 1820 and 1850, liberals and nationalists challenged the conservative post-Napoleonic settlement. Revolutions brought a liberal monarchy to France and independence to Belgium. In Great Britain, political and economic liberalism triumphed within the context of the nation's reformist tradition. The Reform Act of 1832 incorporated many more middle-class men into the political arena. British workers remained committed to peaceful protest. Liberals also gained ground in the German and northern Italian states, where middle-class proponents of German and Italian national unification became more vocal.

At the same time, cultural and nationalist movements began to develop among Czechs, Serbs, and other peoples within the Habsburg domains. However, the Prussian and Austrian monarchies, to say nothing of the Russian tsar, whose troops had crushed the Polish insurrection in 1831, stood as formidable obstacles both to reform and national movements. Nonetheless, the Concert of Europe no longer existed. Political momentum was with those seeking to break down the bastions of traditional Europe, as the dramatic Revolutions of 1848 would clearly demonstrate.

16

THE REVOLUTIONS OF 1848

~~~~~~

The year 1848 was the year of barricades in Europe, the "springtime of the peoples." Few took note when an uprising occurred in January 1848 in Palermo, Sicily, against King Ferdinand II of Naples. But when a revolution drove Louis-Philippe from the throne of France in February, nationalists exiled in London, Brussels, Paris, and Zurich excitedly returned to their native lands, convinced that their time had come. Everything seemed possible.

The establishment of a republic in France became the catalyst for revolutionary movements in Central Europe. In the face of clumsy attempts by governments to repress opposition by force, street insurgency and barricades forced the rulers of Prussia, Austria, and several other German and Italian states to accept more liberal constitutions when confronted by determined crowds. The existence of the Habsburg monarchy was threatened by insurrections against its rule. People in Lombardy and Venetia in northern Italy, and Czechs, Poles, and South Slavs put forth demands for autonomy. In Austria, liberals demanded political reforms, while some German speakers sought inclusion in a unified Germany. Magyar nobles forcefully asserted demands for Hungarian autonomy. Turkish and Russian troops put down an uprising by Romanian nationalists in Bucharest. Of the European powers, only Britain (the most economically and politically advanced) and Russia (the most economically backward) did not experience revolutions. Yet in Britain, the Chartist petition campaign for the extension of political rights revived in 1848 with news from the continent. Daniel O'Connell (1775–1847), a barrister, had stimulated national awareness among Irish peasants. The radical Irish Confederation grouped militants determined to work for independence. The government feared an Irish uprising and searched ships arriving from the United States for weapons. In several countries, monarchs capitulated to liberal demands. In Sweden, the king appointed a new, more popular government. Danish nationalists pressured their king to grant a liberal constitution. The Netherlands received a new constitution in October

1848, and popular pressure forced the expansion of the Belgian electoral franchise.

A common process was present in the revolutions in France, the German states, and in the Habsburg lands: initial mobilizations of liberals, republicans, and nationalists coalesced into movements against existing regimes (see Map 16.1). In each revolution, the hard times of the 1840s, marked by harvest and business failures, had increased popular dissatisfaction with conservative or moderate regimes. Essentially middle-class movements, they drew on the support of artisans and craftsmen, members of trade organizations who believed that political change would lead to social reforms that would benefit their trades. Following initial victory, ranging from the overthrow of the Orleanist monarchy in France to political concessions in Austria and Prussia, however, the ensuing struggle to implement change led to a split between moderates and radicals. Then followed the gradual but convincing victory of counter-revolution, in which the armies of the reactionary Tsar Nicholas I of Russia would play an important role.

REVOLUTIONARY MOBILIZATION

The late 1840s brought food shortages in Europe, including the tragic Irish potato famine. Unemployment plagued manufacturing towns. Yet, however widespread, economic discontent was not enough in itself to bring about the wave of revolutions that occurred in 1848 (if this was the case, the Irish would have risen up). Rather, hard times provided an impetus to political opponents of existing regimes, which were preoccupied with food riots and other popular protest.

Critics and political opponents included liberal reformers asking for moderate political changes, such as a lessening of restrictions on the press, or, in states with elected assemblies, an expansion in the electoral franchise so that more men could vote. German nationalists stood ready to push for the unification of the German states. Republicans and socialists demanded more radical reforms, including universal male suffrage and social reforms to ameliorate the condition of the laboring poor. Radical reformers also included nationalists within the Austrian Habsburg lands, principally Hungarians, who wanted their own independent state. When a spark ignited the fires of protest, moderates and radicals joined forces in revolution. The sudden overthrow of the July Monarchy in France provided that spark.

The February Revolution in France

In France, the liberal Orleanist monarchy, which had been established by the Revolution of 1830, seemed to have more enemies than friends. It was caught between nobles insisting that the monarchy lacked dynastic legiti-

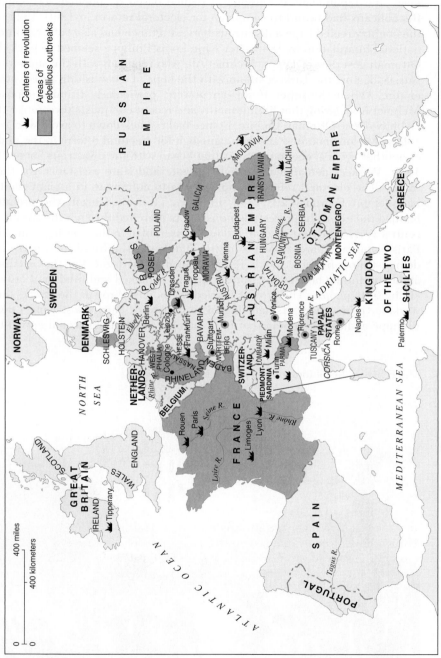

MAP 16.1 MAJOR REVOLUTIONS, 1848–1849   The map shows areas of rebellion and centers of revolution during the turbulent period of 1848–1849.

macy and republicans demanding a regime based on popular sovereignty. Republicans had begun to campaign for electoral reform in 1840–1841, as the country reeled from a disastrous harvest. France had also suffered international humiliation in 1840 after King Louis-Philippe seemed to back the Ottoman governor of Egypt, Mehmet Ali, who rebelled, with the support of Russia, against the Turkish sultan with the hope of establishing an Egyptian empire. When the other European powers, particularly Britain, opposed Mehmet Ali, fearing that his autonomy and recent conquests threatened the stability of the Ottoman Empire, France had to back down to avoid war.

Republicans mounted another campaign for electoral reform in the midst of another cyclical economic crisis that began with the disastrous harvest of 1846. Workers demanded the right to vote and state assistance for their trades. The electoral reform campaign was to culminate in a giant reform banquet on February 22, 1848, in Paris. François Guizot, the premier, banned the event. In protest, demonstrators marched through the streets of central Paris. The next day, large crowds assembled in the pouring rain. The Paris National Guard, drawn from the middle class, refused to disperse the demonstrators by force. Louis-Philippe dismissed Guizot. But that evening, amid continuing boisterous protests, troops panicked and fired on a crowd, killing forty people. The crowds carried the bodies through the streets, and workers (primarily craftsmen) began to construct barricades. King Louis-Philippe abdicated, hoping that the Chamber of Deputies would crown his

The February Revolution of 1848 in Paris.

young grandson, the count of Paris. It was too late. The victorious crowd proclaimed the Second French Republic at the town hall.

The Chamber of Deputies selected a provisional government, headed by nine republicans. A crowd at the town hall pressed for the addition of two well-known socialists supported by the radicals: the socialist Louis Blanc and a worker. The provisional government immediately proclaimed universal male suffrage and abolished slavery in the French colonies.

The revolution spread to the provinces. Enthusiastic crowds planted "liberty trees," intended to commemorate a new era, a ritual borrowed from the French Revolution. Legitimists wanted a Bourbon Restoration. Nor could the Orleanists be counted out, for Louis-Philippe had several able sons in exile. Both shades of monarchists could count on the support of local notables (nobles or wealthy bourgeois). Furthermore, Napoleon Bonaparte's nephew, Louis Napoleon Bonaparte (1808–1873), had a coterie of supporters who honored his uncle's memory. At a time when the prominent poet Alphonse de Lamartine (1790–1869) complained that "France is bored," the legend of Napoleon remained strong among many former soldiers, peasants, and students.

Republicans were themselves divided between staunch republicans, who had opposed the Orleanist regime all along, and moderates, who accepted the republic only after its proclamation. Socialists hoped that the republic would be but the first step toward a "democratic and social republic." Louis Blanc and other socialists were committed to the "right to work," as they put it, believing that the government should assume responsibility for providing employment in times of economic crisis, as well as encouraging or even subsidizing workers' associations.

Because of France's revolutionary tradition, the fledgling republic had to reassure the other powers of Europe that the French would not try to export their revolution, as had occurred in the 1790s. The other powers feared that the new regime might publicly support Polish independence or Italian or German nationalism, spurred on by the presence in Paris of political exiles advocating these causes. Some French nationalists called for the annexation of Savoy and Nice (parts of the Kingdom of Piedmont-Sardinia), which France had claimed off and on for centuries. Volunteers formed a ragtag army with this acquisition of territory in mind. But Lamartine, the new republic's minister of foreign affairs, assured the European powers that the French had only peaceful intentions.

With elections for a constituent assembly approaching, political interest was widespread among people previously excluded from political life. In Paris, more than 200 political clubs, mostly republican and republican-socialist, began to meet, and almost that many newspapers began publication, joined by others in the provinces. When George Sand (the pen name of Amandine Dudevant; 1804–1876), a writer and activist for women's rights, was locked out of her apartment, she discovered that all three of the neighborhood locksmiths were at club meetings. Representatives from the clubs went into the provinces with the goal of wooing the overwhelmingly rural electorate away from the influence of local notables who favored a monarchy.

The economic crisis immediately widened the gap between moderate republicans and socialists. Unable to secure credit, many businesses closed. Government bonds plunged in value, and the Paris Stock Exchange temporarily shut down. Artisans were left without clients, laborers without work. More than half of the workforce in the capital was unemployed. Younger and more marginal workers were enrolled in an auxiliary paramilitary police force, the Mobile Guard, organized by the provisional government to help maintain order. Short of funds, the provisional government raised direct taxes on an emergency basis by 45 percent, the 45 centimes tax.

With more provincial workers arriving in Paris every day looking for assistance, the provisional government opened "National Workshops," paying unemployed workers to repair roads and level hills. Many well-off Parisians began to grumble about the new government having to support unemployed workers. The government finally agreed to restrict the workday to a maximum of ten hours in Paris and twelve hours in the provinces. At the request of the socialists, the government also established the "Luxembourg Commission" to study working conditions.

By undermining existing political structures, the 1848 revolution called into question all social institutions, including the existing gender hierarchy. In Paris, women formed a number of clubs. *The Women's Voice* and several other newspapers begun by women called for reforms, including equality of women before the law, the right to divorce, and better working conditions. Petitioners demanded that the republic extend the electoral franchise to

A Paris women's club in 1848.

women. This groundswell of demands for change frightened the upper classes.

April elections brought a conservative majority, including many monarchists, to the Constituent Assembly, which would draw up a new constitution. Radical republicans and socialists won only about 100 of 900 seats. The republicans were hurt in the countryside by the provisional government's tax hike. Many rural people resented the demands of urban workers, including low bread prices and the maintenance of National Workshops. The euphoria of February gave way to anxiety.

Revolution in the German States

Unlike the Revolution of 1789, that of 1848 spread rapidly from France into Central Europe. While liberals bided their time, young German radicals, few in number, became more restive. During the "hungry forties," in which perhaps 50,000 people died of disease in Prussian Silesia alone, riots against grain merchants and tax collectors occurred in many German states. Craftsmen formed trade associations and mutual aid societies. Although these organizations offered only minimal assistance during times of unemployment and strikes, they provided an apprenticeship in political ideology.

The differences in tactics between German liberals and radicals were clear and significant. Both groups, sometimes sharing newspaper offices, political clubs, and even associations of gymnasts and rifle enthusiasts, demanded an end to all remaining feudal obligations owed by peasants to nobles, the end of political repression, the granting of a constitution, freedom of assembly and the press, and expansion of the electoral franchise. Liberals, however, rejected universal male suffrage. Radicals, some of whom were socialists, believed that only revolution could move the German states along the path to a new, more liberal political order, and perhaps to unification.

The news in late February 1848 of revolution in France convinced rulers of the German states to make concessions to liberals. In Bavaria, word of the February Revolution arrived at a time when students had begun protesting the rule of Ludwig I (ruled 1825–1848). As Bavarian demonstrators built barricades and demanded a republic, Ludwig granted freedom of the press and other liberties. When this failed to placate his opponents, the king abdicated in favor of his son. The sovereigns of several smaller states, including Hanover, Württemberg, Saxony, and Baden, also named prominent liberals to ministerial positions. These were the "March governments" of 1848, formed not out of conviction but rather from fear of revolutionary contagion.

Everyone waited to see what would happen in Prussia and Austria, the two largest and most powerful German states. In the Prussian capital of Berlin, demonstrators agitated for liberal political reforms and in favor of German nationalism. Prussian King Frederick William IV responded by convoking the United Diet (Parliament). On March 18, 1848, he replaced his conservative

Germans putting up barricades in the streets of Altenburg during the Revolution of 1848.

cabinet with a more liberal one. The king promised to end press censorship and grant a constitution. He further stated that the Prussian monarchy would take the lead in pushing for a joint constitution for the German states.

But as troops moved in to disperse the throngs, someone on one side or the other fired shots. Students and workers put up barricades. The next day the army attacked the insurgents, killing 250 people. As in Paris, the shooting of civilians by troops drove the situation out of control. Women were among the casualties. The king sent the troops out of the capital and appealed for calm. Intimidated by the disturbances, he met with representatives of the crowd, authorized the formation of a civic guard, and ordered the release of imprisoned liberals. He paid homage to those killed in the "March Days" and announced that "Prussia is henceforth merged with Germany."

Most of the Berlin insurgents had been artisans, as in the February Revolution in Paris. Although some of them were vaguely nationalist and wanted Prussia to lead the way toward the unification of Germany, most had economic goals. During the "hungry forties," mechanized production had undercut tailors, whose handmade clothes could not compete with mass-produced garments. Cabinetmakers and shoemakers had lost the security afforded by guilds. Now these artisans demanded state protection. Workers in other German states, too, mounted protests, principally in the more industrialized

Rhineland. Transport workers who had been put out of work attacked railroads and steamships on the Rhine River, forcing temporary government concessions.

As in Paris, clubs and workers' associations began meeting in several German cities in March. A Club of Democratic Women and a congress of workers both demanded equal rights for women. The German political theorist and revolutionary Karl Marx hurried back to the Rhineland from Belgium, convinced that the revolution he awaited was at hand.

Disturbances broke out in the German countryside. In the Black Forest, peasants attacked noble manors. In early March, the rural poor defied laws forbidding them to use royal and noble forests, and now hunted game and pastured their flocks as they pleased. Some peasants seized and destroyed old documents that had recorded feudal obligations and forced lords to sign formal renunciations of old privileges. Outbreaks of violence occurred even in Brandenburg, where the iron will of the Prussian nobles, the Junkers, had rarely been tested. Several wary German princes formally relinquished long-held rights. Armies, militias, and police hesitated to enforce the laws or obligations that affected the peasantry for fear of sparking a bloody uprising like the one that took place in Polish Galicia in 1846.

Revolution in Central Europe

There were relatively few liberals to trouble the sleep of the feeble-minded Habsburg ruler, Ferdinand I (ruled 1835–1848), who could barely sign his name to the reactionary decrees put before him. Liberals, most of whom were Austrians seeking political change or Czechs desiring more rights for their people, opposed Habsburg autocracy, not Habsburg rule itself. They wanted constitutional reform, the complete emancipation of the peasantry, greater efficiency in the administration of Habsburg lands, and, like Western liberals, freedom of the press and expansion of the electoral franchise.

Although Hungary, over which Ferdinand ruled as king, had an even smaller middle class than Austria, it did have several prominent Hungarian nobles who espoused liberalism and supported constitutional reform. Their chief goal, however, was the creation of an independent Hungary. Lajos Kossuth (1802–1894), a lawyer from a lesser noble family, emerged as the leader of Hungarian liberals who had been influenced by British and American constitutional liberalism. Whereas some Magyar leaders believed that Hungary could survive as a nation only within the Austrian monarchy, Kossuth saw Hungary's junior partnership with Austria as an obstacle to liberal reform and to Magyar nationalism. Most nobles were unwilling, however, to support reforms that would inevitably undercut their special privileges. Elsewhere in the Austrian monarchy, small nationalist groups, such as the Polish Democratic Society, Young Italy, and the Italian Carbonari, also demanded national independence from Habsburg rule.

News from Paris encouraged liberals and radicals in the imperial Habs-burg capital of Vienna. On March 13, 1848, crowds composed largely of students and artisans demanded reform. Troops opened fire, killing several demonstrators, by now a familiar scenario. Klemens von Metternich, the seventy-five-year-old Austrian premier, was not optimistic: "I am not a prophet and I do not know what will happen, but I am an old physician and can distinguish between temporary and fatal diseases. We now face one of the latter." The Imperial Council advised Ferdinand to sacrifice Metternich. The guiding light and symbol of the post-revolutionary restoration left Vienna in a rented carriage, beginning his journey to the safety of London amid the spectacle of joyous crowds parading through the streets in tri-umph. The crown capitulated to protesters' demands and authorized the for-mation of a National Guard, with a separate battalion (the Academic Legion) for Vienna's students. Workshops, similar to those in Paris, provided many workers with temporary employment.

The emperor then announced several important political concessions, including freedom of the press and the expansion in the narrow electorate for the Diet. Ferdinand hurriedly granted constitutions to Austria, Moravia, and Galicia, adding lower houses to the Diets that were to be elected indi-rectly by men wealthy enough to pay taxes. When demonstrators protested these requirements, the crown reversed itself, creating a single house of par-liament to be elected by universal male suffrage in each province. In the elected Austrian parliament, the monarchy's ethnic minorities combined would outnumber German speakers.

Vienna explodes in the Revolution of 1848.

Ferdinand then attempted to renege on his promises and ordered the universities closed and abolished the Academic Legion within the National Guard. But again barricades went up in Vienna, and again Ferdinand was forced to relent.

The Habsburg realm had remained under the grip of feudalism, particularly in Galicia and Transylvania. Now fearing rural rebellions on which liberals and nationalists might capitalize, the emperor in September decreed the abolition—effective the following year—of all remaining feudal and seigneurial obligations, including the onerous *robot,* the yearly obligation of labor service—sometimes a hundred days working in the fields or on roads—that peasants owed lords. The crown would compensate the lords for their losses. Many landowners had already converted the labor obligation into peasant cash payments. The Austrian parliament also took credit for these dramatic changes.

Meanwhile, the Hungarian nobles proceeded as if the Habsburg monarchy no longer existed. Kossuth demanded virtually complete Hungarian autonomy. He and his allies proclaimed the "March Laws," under which the delegates to the Hungarian Diet were to be elected by male property holders. The cabinet would be responsible to Hungary's Diet. The emperor of Austria would remain the king of Hungary, but Hungary would maintain a separate army and conduct its own foreign policy. The Habsburg court, reeling from reverses on all sides, had little choice but to approve the changes. The new Hungarian government immediately proclaimed freedom of the press, established a civilian guard, and affirmed the abolition of the *robot* for peasant landowners, while maintaining it for landless peasants.

Although asserting its own autonomy from the Habsburg Empire and abolishing serfdom, the Hungarian Diet virtually ignored the autonomy of the other nationalities within the Hungarian domains, including Croats, Slovaks, Serbs, and Romanians, some of whose intellectuals viewed the revolutions of 1848 as the victory of the idea of the nation. Croats, the largest of the non-Magyar nationalities in Hungary, were particularly resentful at not having been consulted. The narrow electoral franchise, based on property owned and taxes paid, excluded most people of the poorer nationalities from election to the Diet. So did the requirement that each representative speak Hungarian, one of Europe's most difficult languages (although Latin had remained the official language of Hungary until 1844).

The Magyars' problem of national minorities became the Habsburg dynasty's hope for holding its empire together. The imperial government began to mobilize the Croats against the Hungarians, whom the Serbs and Romanians also resented. In March, the emperor appointed Joseph Jelačić (1801–1859) as the new governor-general for Croatia. Jelačić refused to cooperate with the Hungarians. In retaliation, the Hungarians refused to send troops to help the imperial army battle Italian insurgents. Ferdinand then withdrew the concessions he had made in March to Hungarian autonomy.

Another challenge to the monarchy, again revealing the complexity of Central Europe, came in Bohemia, populated by both Czechs and Germans. In March, Czech nationalists revolted in Prague, demanding that Bohemia, like Hungary, become an autonomous state only loosely tied to the old monarchy. They wanted the Czech language to be made equal to German, which remained the language of the army, the bureaucracy, and commerce. They also wanted to expand the borders of Bohemia eastward into Moravia, where many Czechs lived. At the same time, many Bohemian Germans looked eagerly toward possible unification with the German states to the north. In the meantime, Emperor Ferdinand left Vienna for Innsbruck in May 1848, fearing that revolutionary students and workers might make him a prisoner in his own palace.

Revolution in the Italian States

In the Italian states, March brought insurrections against Austrian rule in Lombardy and Venetia, and against conservative regimes in the other states, notably the Papal States. In Tuscany, the grand duke bowed to reformers by promulgating a constitution. King Charles Albert (ruled 1831–1849) of Piedmont-Sardinia met some liberal demands by creating a bicameral parliament to be selected by a small minority of adult males, easing press censorship, and establishing a civilian guard in Italy's strongest state. The revolutions in the Italian states, too, were animated by different goals: bourgeois liberals called for political reform and Italian unification, radicals wanted a republic, and workers demanded some tangible benefits for themselves.

On March 18, 1848, 10,000 people marched to the palace of the Austrian governor-general in Milan carrying a petition calling for liberal reforms, echoing those in Paris, Berlin, and Vienna. Barricades went up, and five days (known as the "Five Glorious Days") of bitter street fighting followed. The poorly armed people of the city, whose arsenal included medieval pikes taken from the opera house, drove away the Austrian army of Count Joseph Radetzky (1766–1858). Radetzky became a major figure in the counter-revolution at age eighty-one (and was energetic enough to have fathered a child only two years before). Now in Milan, as insurgents established a provisional republican government, he found his army weakened by the desertion of many Italian soldiers.

Suddenly, much of Italy, particularly the Austrian-controlled north, seemed on the verge of a liberal and national revolution. Other towns in Lombardy rose up against Austrian rule. Venetians forced Habsburg troops to leave their city and declared a republic. In Naples, liberals forced a constitution on King Ferdinand II (ruled 1830–1859).

Many Italian nationalists now looked to King Charles Albert of Piedmont-Sardinia for leadership in the political unification of Italy. Yet, despite pleas for armed assistance from Lombardy and Venetia, Charles

Albert hesitated to send his army against the Habsburg forces. He felt that if the Italian peninsula were to be unified, it should be on his terms, not as a result of rioting commoners. The Piedmontese king feared the specter of popular insurgency in northern Italy. He also worried that if Piedmont launched a war against Austria, the new French republic might take advantage of the situation to invade Savoy and Nice.

The outpouring of anti-Austrian sentiment in Piedmont and the opinions of his advisers convinced Charles Albert to change his mind. The Piedmontese army, swollen by volunteers from Tuscany, Naples, and Parma, and even the Papal States, marched unopposed through Lom-

Giuseppe Mazzini dreaming of a unified Italy.

bardy, defeating the Austrian army. But instead of crossing the Po River and cutting off Radetzky from supplies in Venetia, Charles Albert decided to consolidate his gains in Lombardy, with an eye toward annexing that territory to Piedmont.

In Lombardy itself, no one seemed able to agree on what should happen next. Wealthy landowners wanted little more than a loose union of Lombardy with Piedmont. Middle-class nationalists hoped to drive the Austrian army from Italy and establish a unified state, perhaps even a moderate republic. Radicals were disappointed when the charismatic nationalist leader Giuseppe Mazzini supported Charles Albert, instead of forcefully arguing in favor of a republic. In a hurried plebiscite, the people of Lombardy approved union with Piedmont.

The other Italian states hesitated. Some rulers mistrusted Charles Albert, fearing (with reason) that he wanted to expand Piedmont at their expense. Traditional tensions between northern and southern Italy surfaced. Furthermore, the pope helped stymie the movement for Italian unification. Before the revolutions, the new pope, Pius IX (pope 1846–1878), had initiated a few modest reforms in his territories, releasing some liberals jailed by his predecessor. Some nationalists had even begun to think that Italy could be unified around papal authority. But the pope was hardly about to oppose the Catholic Habsburg dynasty on which the papacy had depended for centuries. Pius IX then announced that he would not support the war against Austria.

Meanwhile, the newly elected French Constituent Assembly unanimously approved a motion calling for the liberation of the Italian states. A French volunteer legion stood ready on the frontier, hoping that its help against Habsburg armies would bring French annexation of Savoy and Nice, as

Charles Albert had feared. But facing British opposition and with enough to worry about at home, the new French republic for the moment stayed out of the Italian fray. Nonetheless, the beleaguered Austrian court seemed resigned to losing Lombardy, and willing even to abandon its claim on Venetia, provided that Piedmont would not directly annex either territory.

Benefiting from better troop morale and reinforced by soldiers arriving from Austria, Radetzky believed he could defeat the nationalist armies of the Italian states, which fought with more enthusiasm than experience and lacked effective organization and supplies. One Piedmontese commander complained that the nationalists did "nothing, except to drown themselves with flowers, dancing, singing, shouting, and calling each other 'sublime,' 'valorous,' and 'invincible.'" Radetzky's army defeated the Piedmontese-led army of Italian nationalists at Custoza near Milan in early August 1848. The people of Milan then scornfully turned against Charles Albert, who slipped out of the city late at night and returned to his capital of Turin. From safer ground, the hesitant king negotiated an armistice with Austria, hoping in vain that he could retain Lombardy for his Kingdom of Piedmont-Sardinia.

THE ELUSIVE SEARCH FOR REVOLUTIONARY CONSENSUS

The Revolutions of 1848 generated resistance almost immediately from the political and social forces that had the most to lose from their success. In Prussia, the king and nobles feared being toppled from their privileged positions. In the Habsburg lands, where nationalism was the most significant factor in the revolution, the emperor and his army resisted. In France, the upper classes generally opposed radical changes. The ultimate success of the counter-revolution throughout Europe was aided by the revolutionaries' mixed aims. The split between liberals and radicals worked to the advantage of those who wanted a return to the way things had been before the spring of 1848.

Crisis in France

In France, the political crisis intensified as the provisional government faced competing demands. On May 15, 1848, an attempt by the political clubs of the far left to dissolve the Constituent Assembly and declare a "social" republic of the people failed. The provisional government now began to arrest radical republicans. With the provisional government rapidly running out of money and credibility, on June 23, 1848, the Assembly announced that the National Workshops would be closed in three days. Enrolled unmarried men were to be drafted into the army and married workers sent to work in the provinces. Parisian workers rose up in rebellion.

For three days the "June Days" raged in the workers' quarters of central and eastern Paris. General Louis Cavaignac (1802–1857) put down the

ATTAQUE DE LA BARRICADE PLACE MAUBERT

Troops attacking a barricade in Paris during the June Days, 1848.

uprising with brutality, using regular army soldiers, the Mobile Guard, and National Guard units, some of whom arrived from conservative provinces by train and steamboat, symbols of a new age. More than 1,500 insurgents were killed, some summarily executed. The provisional government deported more than 4,000 workers to Algeria or other colonies, and sent thousands of people to prison.

Karl Marx believed that the June Days were a dress rehearsal for a future proletarian revolution that would pit workers against the bourgeoisie. The short, bloody civil war, however, was more complicated than that. Some younger workers, including artisans, fought alongside unskilled proletarians in the Mobile Guard, which helped put down the uprising. Some radical bourgeois supported the workers.

The Assembly immediately passed legislation to curtail popular political movements. New laws limited freedom of the press and assembly and closed political clubs, specifically banning women from membership. The Luxembourg Commission was quickly disbanded. Cavaignac became provisional chief executive of the republic.

Attention now focused on the presidential elections instituted by the new republican constitution that was finally promulgated in November 1848.

Louis Napoleon Bonaparte quickly emerged as a leading candidate, largely because of the reputation of his uncle, Napoleon. Although one wag cruelly dubbed him "the hat without the head," it was testimony to the magic of the Napoleonic legend that Louis Napoleon had been elected to the Constituent Assembly in April 1848, after returning from exile. Many people believed that he could restore political stability. Cavaignac, the other major candidate, was the favorite of those who wanted to combine social order with a very moderate republic. The minister of the interior of the provisional government, Alexandre-Auguste Ledru-Rollin (1807–1874), was the principal candidate of the socialists, while Lamartine, a moderate, also ran, but both were identified with the provisional government and the unpopular 45 centimes tax. Outside of Paris many people had never heard of either one of them, but just about everyone had heard of Napoleon. Louis Napoleon also won the support of many people who were for the republic. Like his uncle, he was assumed to have good will toward all people in France. On December 10, 1848, Louis Napoleon was overwhelmingly elected president of the Second Republic. Some skeptics were already wondering whether he, like his uncle, would serve as the heir to a revolution, or its executioner.

The Frankfurt Parliament

In the German states, liberals and radicals gradually split as conservative forces gathered momentum. Shortly after the February Revolution in Paris, a group of German liberals, meeting in Heidelberg, invited about 500 like-minded figures to form a preliminary parliament to prepare elections for an assembly that would draft a constitution for a unified Germany. Most liberals wanted the German states to be united under a constitutional monarchy. Radicals, however, wanted nothing less than a republic based on universal male suffrage, and some of them joined a brief insurrection in the Rhineland state of Baden. To conservatives, and to some of the liberals as well, this insurrection raised the specter of "communism," amid rumors that radicals would divide the great estates among landless peasants.

The remainder of the members of the preliminary parliament announced elections for a German Constituent National Assembly, the Frankfurt Parliament. But, distinguishing their liberalism from that of the departed radicals, only male "independent" citizens in the German states would be eligible to vote; some states used this vague qualification to exclude men who owned no property. The Diet of the German Confederation accepted the plans for the election of the Frankfurt Parliament.

In May 1848, more than 800 elected delegates of the German Constituent National Assembly filed into Frankfurt's St. Paul's Church, which was decked out in red, black, and gold, the colors of early German nationalist university student organizations. State, municipal, and judicial officials, lawyers, university professors, and schoolteachers comprised about two-thirds of the Frankfurt Parliament. Since about a third of the delegates had some legal training, many people began to refer to the gathering as a "parliament of lawyers," whose members debated far into the night, confident that their deliberations would shape the future of the German states. Many were oblivious to the fact that poor acoustics rendered their speeches inaudible to people sitting in the back.

In electing Heinrich von Gagern (1799–1880) president, the delegates chose a man who symbolized the liberal and nationalist idealism of 1848. He had been one of the founders of the nationalist fraternities and a leader of the liberal opposition in his

The Frankfurt Parliament in 1848.

native Hesse. Although not of great intellect, Gagern offered an imposing physical presence and carried out his difficult tasks with dignity. He confidently gave the false impression that the unity of the delegates was assured and that German unification lay just ahead.

The Frankfurt Parliament operated outside any state structure. It lacked the support of the rulers of Prussia and Austria, and, for that matter, of Bavaria and Württemberg. Without an army, it could not impose its will on any of the German states. Furthermore, considerable division existed over what shape the proposed unified Germany would take. Would it be a centralized state, or only an expansion of the German Confederation? How would sovereignty be defined? Who would have the right to vote?

Amid flowery speeches celebrating German national destiny, the problem of nationality immediately surfaced. Some delegates wanted Austria excluded from a united Germany, leery of the problem posed by non-German speakers within their state. Among these exponents of this "smaller German" (*Kleindeutsch*) solution, some wanted German unification around Protestant Prussia, fearing the inclusion of Catholic Austria. The more liberal "greater German" (*Grossdeutsch*) group wanted a unified Germany to include all states and territories within the German Confederation. Some wanted Austria's inclusion to counter possible Prussian domination, as well as that of northern Protestants.

After months of debate, a compromise solution appeared to be a victory for the "smaller German" plan. On October 27, 1848, the Frankfurt Parliament voted that any German state could join the new Germany, but only if it did not bring with it territories having non-German populations. Unless Austria was willing to separate itself from Hungary, it would have to remain outside a united Germany. For the moment, the Austrian government, struggling against resistance to its authority from Hungary and the northern Italian states of Lombardy and Venetia, regarded the Frankfurt Parliament's German nationalism as another threat to its survival.

The Frankfurt Parliament put aside its liberalism when it came to the question of Poland. When a Polish uprising against Prussian rule broke out, a parliamentary delegate rose to denounce Polish nationalism, insisting on "the preponderance of the German race over most Slav races" and calling for "[German] national egotism" and "the right of the stronger." The Frankfurt Parliament voted overwhelmingly in favor of armed Prussian repression of the Polish uprising, also expressing support for the Habsburg monarchy's crushing of the rebellious Czechs.

The Prussian parliament (which had been elected by universal male suffrage after the March insurrection in Berlin) had also gathered in May 1848 to begin to draft a constitution for Prussia. Amid urban and rural unrest, the parliament voted to make the civic guard a permanent institution, which challenged noble control of the army officer corps. It also abolished the Junkers' special hunting privileges and banned the use of all noble titles in anticipation of the abolition of formal class distinctions.

The Junkers, however, were not about to stand by and watch Prussia drift toward a constitutional monarchy or republic. They vowed to defend "God, the King, and the Fatherland," which they identified with their immunity from taxation and other prerogatives. Encouraged by the reaction to the June Days in France, Frederick William dismissed his liberal cabinet, sent troops to Berlin, and then in December dissolved the parliament. He declared martial law and disbanded the civic guard. Prussian troops crushed opposition in the Rhineland and Silesia.

While counter-revolution gathered momentum in Prussia, the middle-class liberals of the Frankfurt Parliament, powerless to effect German unification on their own, failed to build a base of popular support among workers and peasants. They feared the lower classes perhaps even more than did the Prussian nobles: one member of the Parliament described universal male suffrage as "the most dangerous experiment in the world." Thus, the Frankfurt Parliament rejected craftsmen's demands for protection against mechanization and an influx of new practitioners into their trades as being incompatible with economic liberalism. Since the eighteenth century, German guilds had gradually lost their autonomy to the regulatory authority of the states. The influx of apprentices and journeymen into trades had reduced the opportunity for journeymen to become masters. By turning a deaf ear to workers' demands, the Frankfurt Parliament lost a significant source of popular support. Furthermore, any hope of winning the allegiance of German peasants probably ended when the Parliament proclaimed that peasants must compensate their former lords in exchange for their release from remaining obligations.

Frustrated by the Parliament's moderation and general dawdling, in September 1848 several hundred workers charged into St. Paul's Church and tried to persuade the Parliament to declare itself a national convention of republicans. Austrian, Prussian, and Hessian troops had to rescue the delegates.

After six months of debate, the Frankfurt Parliament proclaimed in December 1848 the Basic Rights of the German People. Influenced by the American Declaration of Independence and the French Declaration of the Rights of Man and Citizen, it proclaimed the equality of "every German" before the law; freedom of speech, assembly, and religion; the end of seigneurial obligations; and the right to private property. Jews gained legal equality. The support of Prussia and/or Austria would be necessary to implement the Basic Rights of the German People and to form a united Germany. "To unite Germany without [Prussia and Austria]" would be, as a contemporary put it, "like two people trying to kiss with their backs turned to one another." But Austria's opposition to the Frankfurt Parliament became even stronger. Nationalism was antithetical to the monarchy's existence. The Frankfurt Parliament could do nothing as the Austrian government executed one of its delegates for having led an uprising in Vienna in October 1848. The Habsburgs encouraged other German states to disregard the Parliament and to proceed with their own counter-revolutions. The emperor made it clear that Austria would only consider joining a united Germany if the entire Habsburg monarchy, with its many non-German nationalities, was included. The Parliament had already rejected such a possibility.

In April 1849, the Frankfurt Parliament promulgated a possible constitution for a united Germany. It proposed the creation of a hereditary "emperor of the Germans" and two houses of Parliament, one representing the individual German states, the other elected by universal male suffrage. Austria, Bavaria, and Hanover rejected the proposed constitution.

The only chance for the constitution to succeed was to convince the king of Prussia to become king of a unified Germany. Frederick William had occasionally voiced vague support for German nationalism. The Parliament sent a delegation to Berlin to offer Frederick William the German crown. A Prussian noble shouted: "What, you bring an imperial crown? You are beggars! You have no money, no land, no law, no power, no people, no soldiers! You are bankrupt speculators in cast-off popular sovereignty!" When the head of the delegation asked for a glass of water in the royal palace, he was denied even that. Frederick William refused to accept a "crown from the gutter," a "dog collar" offered "by bakers, and butchers, and reeking with the stench of revolution."

Before the Prussian parliament could approve the constitution proposed by the Frankfurt liberals, the king dissolved it on April 28, 1849, declaring a state of emergency. He then implemented new voting restrictions that greatly favored the conservatives in subsequent parliamentary elections. Henceforth, the wealthiest 3 percent of the Prussian population elected one-third of the representatives; the next wealthiest 10 percent elected another third; and the remaining 87 percent of men elected the final third of the Prussian parliament. Liberal abstentions and popular indifference further assured conservative domination of the new parliament, which created an upper house of nobles, officials, churchmen, and other members to be selected by the king. Divided by indecision, lacking popular support, and facing Prussian and Austrian opposition, most of the Frankfurt parliamentarians went home. The Frankfurt Parliament, which embodied the hopes of German liberals and nationalists, ended in abject failure. Germany would not be unified by liberals.

COUNTER-REVOLUTION

With the lack of consensus among the revolutionaries, counter-revolution now gained the upper hand in the Habsburg Empire and in the German and Italian states. In the Habsburg lands, the initial period of optimism gave way to a grim realization of the complexity of Central Europe. Ethnic conflicts broke out among Hungarians, Croats, and Serbs, as well as between landowners and peasants.

Counter-Revolution in Habsburg Central Europe

The confusion of competing national claims and rivalries within the Habsburg lands eased the task of counter-revolution within the Austrian Empire. If freedom was a central concern of the revolutionaries, it meant different things to different people. Magyar nobles wanted more autonomy for Hungary; Viennese journalists wanted freedom from press censorship; artisans wanted freedom from the competition of mechanized production; peasants wanted freedom from labor obligations owed to nobles. Czechs demanded freedom from German domination as well as their own national autonomy within the Habsburg domains.

Czechs hosted a Pan-Slav Congress in Prague in June 1848 to promote the rights of and bolster a union of Slavs within the Habsburg Empire and Central Europe. The assembled national groups could agree only on their common dislike for Habsburg policies. Each group had a different plan for the reorganization of the empire, one that would favor its own interests. Frantisek Palacký (1798–1876), a Czech historian, declared that if Austria did not exist, it would have to be invented, because otherwise small ethnic peoples such as the Czechs would be submerged by Germans or Russians. Often considered the father of Czech nationalism, Palacký therefore supported increased autonomy for the Czechs within a strong Habsburg state. Finally, the Pan-Slav Congress issued a vague statement in June 1848 that

Croatian regiments loyal to the Habsburg emperor attack Viennese revolutionaries, October 1848.

condemned the Germans for having oppressed the Slavic peoples and called for the reorganization of the Austro-Hungarian monarchy into a federation that would take into consideration the rights of each nationality.

While the Pan-Slav Congress, like the Frankfurt Parliament, was discussing lofty national questions, ordinary people were hungry. On June 12, 1848, barricades went up in Prague, manned by artisans and the laboring poor. Prince Alfred Windischgrätz (1787–1862), the Habsburg imperial governor, ended the insurrection four days later, bombarding Prague with cannon fire. Meanwhile, in northern Italy, the Habsburg imperial army defeated the Piedmontese forces, which had moved to assist the revolutions against Austria-Hungary, and Jelačić's Croatian army defeated Hungarian revolutionary forces.

In August, Emperor Ferdinand returned to Vienna and was welcomed by the middle classes. When he began to shut down the workshops, which had been established to provide work for the unemployed, the workers rose up, as they had in Paris, before being crushed by the National Guard. Two months later, workers rebelled again. Ferdinand fled Vienna for a second time, taking his court to Moravia. The imperial armies under Windischgrätz bombarded Vienna, killing more than 3,000 people. Once again, enthusiastic revolutionaries proved no match for the professional armies of the established powers. The emperor imposed martial law, closed the political clubs, dissolved the National Guard, and reestablished censorship. Arrests, trials, and executions followed. The emperor appointed a council of advisers (the *Reichsrat*), but was under no obligation to consult it.

Emperor Ferdinand appointed Prince Felix zu Schwarzenberg (1800–1852) as head of government on November 21, 1848. This ended the period of political uncertainty within Austria that had followed the March insurrection. Schwarzenberg convinced the hapless emperor to abdicate his throne in December 1848 in favor of his eighteen-year-old nephew, Francis Joseph (ruled 1848–1916). Placing his faith in the army, the new emperor was determined to assure the dynasty and its empire's survival.

Prince Schwarzenberg enhanced the effectiveness of the imperial bureaucracy by appointing able commoners to important posts. He hoped to win the support of Hungarian moderates, albeit without recognizing the rights of nationalities. Alexander Bach (1813–1893), a lawyer of noble origins, was first appointed to be minister of justice and then of the interior, and reformed the Habsburg legal system. At the same time, he implemented a system of carefully coordinated bureaucratic surveillance, spying, and repression—known as the "Bach system"—that helped root out political opposition.

But the Schwarzenberg government still had to deal with the Austrian parliament. That body, from its exile in the town of Kremsier, had produced a draft for a liberal constitution. The constitution approved the emancipation of the peasantry and sought to establish a decentralized, multinational state under a constitutional monarchy that would recognize all languages. It would have made ministers responsible to parliament. But the liberal Kremsier constitution was never implemented. Schwarzenberg suddenly dissolved the parliament in March 1849, ordered the arrest of some of the deputies, and imposed his own constitution. It made virtually no concessions to the non-German nationalities within the Habsburg domains and restored Hungary to its pre-1848 position. Furthermore, Schwarzenberg, with the young emperor's consent, intended to delay putting his constitution into effect until the revolutionary crisis had passed.

In April 1849, the Hungarian Diet refused to recognize Francis Joseph's ascension to the Habsburg throne and thus his sovereignty over Hungary. In turn, the young emperor refused to recognize Ferdinand's concessions to Hungary. The liberal Hungarian leader Kossuth tried to rally support in Hungary against Austria. The Hungarians defeated the imperial forces twice in the spring, taking Budapest and driving the Habsburg army out of Transylvania.

On April 14, 1849, the Hungarian Diet proclaimed Magyar independence and made Kossuth president of the newly formed Hungarian republic. As the Habsburg Empire's survival was now defiantly threatened, Francis Joseph called on the Russian tsar for help. The recent European revolutions had made Nicholas I even more reactionary. Having previously granted small reforms (see Chapter 15), he now forbade Russian students from traveling abroad, drastically reduced the number of government scholarships, ordered that philosophy and constitutional law be dropped as university subjects, and reinforced censorship of all publications. Thus without hesitation the Russian tsar sent 140,000 troops into Hungary and Transylvania. Kossuth frantically implored the Frankfurt Parliament for assistance, but that body had no army. The British government disliked the Russian intervention in Central Europe, but it wanted to preserve the Habsburg monarchy as a buffer against French and, above all, Russian interests. Hungarian resistance ended in August as Russian and Austrian forces advanced. Kossuth escaped to Turkey, never to return to Hungary. Austria executed thirteen Hungarian generals for treason, imprisoned thousands of people, and imposed martial law. The "Patent" of December 31, 1851, officially restored imperial absolutism.

An early photograph of the Hungarian noble, lawyer, and patriot Lajos Kossuth.

One by one in the other German states, the "March ministries" of 1848 fell from power as rulers abrogated constitutions granted that spring. Even where constitutions remained on the books, the counter-revolutions orchestrated by rulers with the help of nobles left parliaments and assemblies with little or no effective power. Scattered radical insurrections failed. After being chased from his duchy in June 1849, the grand duke of Baden returned to oversee the trials of more than 1,000 people. The German Revolution of 1848 was over. On August 23, 1851, the German Confederation annulled the Basic Rights of the German People, the major work of the Frankfurt Parliament.

Prussian-Austrian Rivalry

Now that the German revolutionaries had been swept away by the juggernaut of counter-revolution, Prussian King Frederick William IV proposed the creation of a "Prussian Union." It would consist of two "unions": the larger would include the states of the defunct German Confederation, as well as non-German Austrian territories; the smaller would be a confederation of all German-speaking lands, including those of Austria. In proposing these clumsy structures, a loose confederation based both on conservative political premises and an expansion of Prussian influence, Frederick William took advantage of the insurrections against Austrian authority in Hungary and northern Italy. Austria, Bavaria, and Württemberg all expressed immediate opposition to the plan. The Habsburg dynasty no more wanted to see an expansion of Prussian influence in Central Europe than it had desired German unification under the liberal auspices of the Frankfurt Parliament. On September 1, 1849, Austria unilaterally proclaimed the revival of the old German Confederation, pressuring member states to withdraw all the concessions to constitutionalism and liberalism they had made in 1848.

As Prussia and Austria both sought to assure the victory of counter-revolution as well as to secure a dominant position in Central Europe, relations between the two powers deteriorated further. In September 1849, the prince of Hesse asked the reconstituted German Confederation for assistance when his own people rebelled against the withdrawal of a liberal constitution he had earlier granted. The government of Prussia, however, objected to the involvement of the Confederation in Hesse because Hesse stood between two parts of Prussia. Prussia, which had the right to move troops through Hesse, threatened to send an army there if the Confederation tried to intervene. But the Russian tsar, now wary of a possible expansion of Prussian power in Central Europe, forced Prussia to back down. In October, the German Confederation, with secret Russian backing, sent Bavarian and Hanoverian troops to Hesse, but Prussian forces blocked their way. However, the Prussian government backed away from war, agreeing to drop plans for a Prussian Union. The Prussian government signed the "humiliation of Olmütz" (November 29, 1850), in which Prussia agreed to demobilize its army.

The Counter-Revolution in the Italian States

The counter-revolution in Central Europe and particularly in Austria spelled doom for Italian revolutionaries. And as in the German states and in the Habsburg Empire, those espousing liberal reforms and the cause of nationalism were too few, scattered, and divided by divergent and even conflicting goals. When Habsburg forces were fighting in Hungary, a nationalist "war party" in Piedmont-Sardinia pushed King Charles Albert toward a resumption of hostilities with Austria. The Piedmontese army crossed into Lombardy, but Austrian forces under General Joseph Radetzky defeated it at Novara in March 1849. Fearing that Radetzky's strengthened army would invade Piedmont, Charles Albert asked for peace and abdicated in favor of his son, Victor Emmanuel II. The new king signed an armistice with Austria in Milan in August, renouncing Piedmontese claims to Lombardy.

In 1848, revolutionaries had challenged the authority of the pope in the Papal States. In August, workers in Bologna rose up against Pope Pius IX. But the pope's forces prevailed. The next outbreak of opposition to papal authority came in Rome itself. Fearing an insurrection, Pius named a new, more liberal government, which announced the imposition of a tax on Church property. After one of the government's leaders was assassinated in November 1848, crowds stormed into the streets, calling for a declaration of war against Austria. Pius appointed more liberals to his government and called for parliamentary elections, before fleeing in disguise. From Naples, he called for the overthrow of the government he had appointed under duress.

In Rome, the new cabinet met many of the workers' demands, setting up charity workshops and ending the grain tax. The new government confiscated Church property, turning some buildings into apartments for poor workers. In elections for a Constitutional Assembly, the radicals won an overwhelming victory. On February 9, 1849, the Assembly proclaimed

Pope Pius IX puts aside the liberal mask of Christ, revealing his true conservative face.

the Roman Republic. The pope immediately excommunicated from the Catholic Church some of the republic's officials. The republic, in turn, abolished the Inquisition and proclaimed freedom of the press and the secularization of university education.

Some Italian nationalists now were beginning to think of the Roman Republic as a center around which the peninsula could be unified. Mazzini's arrival in Rome in early March 1849 to join the revolutionary government confirmed the pope's fears in this regard. With the armies of the Habsburgs tied up with struggles in Central Europe, the pontiff had to look elsewhere for a strong army to come to his rescue. Although Piedmont, the strongest Italian state, did not want a Roman Republic, the pope did not solicit Piedmontese assistance, fearing that if its forces came to the rescue, they might never leave.

Beset by severe economic shortages and inflation and discouraged by the news of the Piedmontese defeat at Novara in March, leaders of the Roman Republic now learned that the French were coming to try to restore the pope's temporal power. Louis Napoleon Bonaparte was eager to consolidate the support of French Catholics. He also did not want Austrian influence in Italy to go unchallenged. With the approval of the French Constituent Assembly, an army of 10,000 French troops disembarked near Rome, and then, embarrassingly enough, had to retreat when they met fierce resistance.

Giuseppe Garibaldi (1807–1882), a more strident—and organized—republican nationalist than Mazzini, arrived with a corps of volunteers from Lombardy to help the besieged republic. As pro-papal forces sent by the king of Naples and the Spanish government approached Rome, the French army began to shell the Eternal City in early June 1849. The Constitutional Assembly capitulated a month later. French troops then occupied Rome, dissolving the Assembly and the clubs and reviving press censorship. The pope returned to Rome in April 1850.

Of all of the governments formed by revolutions and uprisings in the Italian states in 1848, only the Venetian Republic now survived. But having defeated the Piedmontese in March 1849, the Austrians blockaded and bombarded Venice. The Venetian Republic capitulated on August 22, 1849.

The Italian revolutions were over. The only liberal regime that remained was in Piedmont. Austria retained Lombardy and Venetia. The king of Naples, the grand duke of Tuscany, and the pope were back in power. Italian unification remained a dream of northern middle-class nationalists. The multiplicity of states and lack of strong popular support for unification—reflected by the gap between liberals' and workers' goals—had for the moment proven too powerful.

The Agony of the French Second Republic

In France, the election of Louis Napoleon as president in December 1848 seemed to guarantee a return to political stability. Yet even as better economic times gradually returned, the "democratic-socialists," whose supporters had been primarily drawn from France's largest cities and some smaller market towns, expanded their appeal in the countryside. They particularly gained followers in the south, winning support among many peasants, for whom the low prices of agricultural depression had brought hard times. Taking the name of the far left during the French Revolution, the Montagnards called for the establishment of progressive taxation, higher wages, the abolition of the tax on wine, the creation of credit banks for peasants, and free and obligatory primary schools. The democratic-socialists effectively used written political propaganda to reach ordinary people; stories, songs, lithographs, and engravings spread the popularity of radical candidates. In the legislative elections of May 1849, the left won almost a third of the seats in the Constituent Assembly, harnessing the heritage of the French Revolution in regions in which it had found enthusiastic support.

Encouraged by the strength of the left in the Chamber of Deputies and in Paris, Ledru-Rollin, who had been a candidate in the presidential election, attempted to provoke an insurrection on June 13, 1849. His pretext was the Assembly's readiness to send a French army to support the pope, which the left claimed violated the new constitution, because French troops would be violating the freedom of the Romans. However, intervention in Rome earned Louis Napoleon the gratitude of conservative Catholics; Ledru-Rollin's

Uprooting a liberty tree in Paris.

uprising discredited the left among the upper classes. But by-elections in the spring of 1850 reflected the growing popularity of the democratic-socialist program in some places.

Backed by the "party of order," Louis Napoleon's government claimed that a massive plot threatened social order. Symbols of the French Revolution itself, including singing "The Marseillaise," became illegal. The government also outlawed red caps and belts, because red was identified as the color of the left. The police felled liberty trees one by one. The government curtailed the freedoms of assembly and association and banned many workers' associations, including some that had been granted state funds in 1848 to establish producer and consumer cooperatives. National Guard units in many towns were disbanded. Mayors and schoolteachers were replaced if they supported the left, and cafés identified with the democratic-socialist cause were closed. Many radical republican and socialist leaders were jailed. These included Jeanne Deroin (1810–1894), a socialist seamstress and feminist, who in 1849 had tried to run for election despite the fact that women were ineligible for election and could not vote. In March 1850, the Assembly passed the Falloux Law, which allowed the Catholic clergy to open secondary schools and permitted them to serve on education committees. One of the practical consequences was that villages now could turn operation of their schools over to the clergy.

In May 1850, the Constituent Assembly ended universal male suffrage by adding a residency requirement that disqualified many workers who traveled from place to place to find work. This reduced the electorate by one-third, eliminating 3 million voters. Many of the disenfranchised lived in the larger cities, where Napoleon and his candidates had not fared well. The repression succeeded in smashing the left in much of France.

In some southern and central regions, the repression drove the left into secret societies, whose members, mostly artisans and peasants, swore an oath of allegiance to defend the "democratic and social Republic." These societies, which started in towns, gradually spread into the surrounding countryside. This occurred particularly where economic growth during the preceding two decades, including cash-crop agriculture and rural handi-crafts, had brought more rural artisans and peasants regularly into market towns.

The constitution limited the presidency to one term of four years. Although Louis Napoleon's term as president was, in principle, nearing an end, he had no intention of stepping aside. On December 2, 1851, the anniversary of his uncle's victory at Austerlitz and the coronation of Napoleon Bonaparte as emperor, Parisians awoke to read an official poster that announced the dissolution of the Constituent Assembly. The secret societies then undertook the largest national insurrection in nineteenth-century France. More than 100,000 people took up arms in defense of the republic. But the ragged forces of artisans and peasants armed with rusty rifles and pitchforks were easily dispersed by troops before they got very far. Military courts tried over 26,000 democratic-socialists, and almost half that many went into exile.

Yet support for the coup by Louis Napoleon was overwhelming in France as a whole. The plebiscite that followed the coup approved the takeover by more than 10 to 1. The Paris stock market soared. Louis Napoleon proclaimed a new constitution. On December 2, 1852, he took the title Napoleon III, emperor of the French.

The Legacy of 1848

The glacial winds of reaction brutally chilled the "springtime of the peoples." The wave of repression dashed the hopes of liberals, republicans, and nationalists throughout Europe. It has often been said, with the advantage of hindsight, that in 1848, at least with reference to Prussia and the other German states, European history reached its turning point and failed to turn.

European states became even stronger after the Revolutions of 1848. The revolutions had succeeded at first because the French, Prussian, and Austrian authorities lacked sufficient military preparedness. All three quickly learned their lessons. With the defeat of the revolutionaries came the end of

The generals who crushed the insurgency within the Habsburg Empire: Jelačić, Radetzky, and Windischgrätz.

the era of civic or national guards, which had been demanded by the people of Berlin, Vienna, and Paris. Professional armies enforced the counter-revolution, restoring Habsburg authority in Bohemia, Hungary, and northern Italy; the Prussian army crushed the last gasps of revolution in the German states; and the French army put down subsequent resistance to Louis Napoleon's coup d'état. Louis Napoleon's plebiscite reinforced the centralized character of the French state.

Nonetheless, the Revolutions of 1848 marked the first time workers put forward organized demands for political rights. Moreover, radical peasants in southern France helped dispel the myth of the inevitably conservative peasant. Although the Revolutions of 1848 ultimately failed, they left crucial political legacies. The period was one of political apprenticeship for republicanism in France and nationalism in the German and Italian states. Portugal completed a liberal revolution begun in 1820 with the establishment of a parliamentary government. The revolutions were not only separate national phenomena but also part of a common process that anticipated the emergence of mass politics in the last decades of the nineteenth century. While many of the goals of the revolutionaries centered on middle-class demands for liberal reforms, such as freedom of the press, the Revolutions of 1848 also had a popular quality characterized by demands for universal male suffrage, as well as by a few calls for political rights for women. Hundreds of thousands of ordinary people participated, if only somewhat briefly, in political life. The mid-century revolutions influenced the subsequent political evolution of each country that had had a revolution in the spring of 1848.

Great Britain provides the counterexample. However, in Britain, too, the experience of 1848 was revealing in that there was no revolution in 1848. In Britain, political reform followed compromise, not revolution. In contrast to their French counterparts before the Revolutions of 1830 and 1848, English middle-class liberals avoided at all costs prodding workers into street confrontations with authority, fearful of unwittingly unleashing an uncontrollable insurrection. Chartism, the mass petition movement in the 1840s for universal male suffrage, had its last gasp in 1848. The British government arrested suspected radicals, sent 8,000 troops into London in anticipation of a movement on April 10 that never occurred, and appointed 150,000 civilian "special constables." Businessmen, anticipating trouble from a Chartist demonstration, hauled out hunting rifles and barricaded their offices. In any case, with the exception of a very small radical component in favor of the use of "physical force," the Chartists were gradualists. The Irish nationalist movement, dormant since a failed insurrection in 1798, reawakened in 1848, in part because of the revolutionary enthusiasm of Irish immigrants then living in the United States. British authorities searched ships arriving from the United States for weapons and funds intended for potential insurgents. But the presence of the British army, as well as the emigration of great numbers of Irish to the United States, limited Irish nationalists' efforts in that revolutionary year to one minor uprising. A possible alliance between the radical Irish Confederation and "physical force" Chartists never took place. At the same time, elite fears of Irish insurgency contributed to the persistence of anti-Catholicism in British national identity, as the press denigrated the Irish "Paddy" as drunken, untrustworthy, and potentially revolutionary.

The counter-revolution in Europe scattered a generation of committed republicans, nationalists, and socialists throughout much of the world. Thousands of Frenchmen were exiled to Algeria, while German and Italian political exiles left for the United States. They spread the ideas of republicanism, nationalism, and socialism.

The Habsburg monarchy, too, survived the liberal and nationalist challenges of 1848. The young Habsburg Emperor Francis Joseph bragged to his mother, "We have thrown the constitution overboard and Austria has now only one master." The Austrian government had adroitly manipulated ethnic tensions, using a Croatian army against a Hungarian uprising. The situation was so complicated that a Hungarian noted "the King of Hungary declared war on the King of Croatia, and the Emperor of Austria remained neutral, and all three monarchs were the same person." Hungary, in which perhaps as many as 100,000 people were killed during the fighting in 1848–1849, remained within the monarchy as Austria's junior partner. But peasants were now free from labor obligations previously owed to landowners. Although the liberal Kremsier constitution had been tossed aside, the Austrian constitution of March 1849 did establish a parliament. Yet the goals of many Hungarians, Czechs, Poles, and other ethnic groups remained unachieved. On the Italian peninsula, Habsburg control of Lombardy and Venetia, the existence of many other separate states, and the indifference of most people to Italian nationalism remained daunting obstacles to Italian unification. Even in failure, however, the revolutions in the Italian states had only made Italian nationalists more determined to work for national unification. Likewise, the defeat of the Hungarian and Bohemian revolutions, as well as the failure of the radical revolution in Vienna, by no means ended challenges to the Habsburg monarchy.

The Revolutions of 1848 accentuated support for German nationalism. A Prussian minister recognized that "the old times are gone and cannot return. To return to the decaying conditions of the past is like scooping water with a sieve." The revolution did produce a Prussian constitution and an elected assembly, however, which the king only slightly modified in 1849–1850, when he again took control. The failure of the Revolutions of 1848 in Central Europe suggested to many Germans that unification could only be achieved under the auspices of either Prussia or Austria. German unification under any auspices would potentially entail a drastic change in the European state system, altering the balance of power, especially in Central Europe.

PART FIVE

THE AGE OF MASS POLITICS

In 1850, Great Britain, France, and Russia were the three major European powers. However, the unification of Italy and Germany during the 1860s and early 1870s shifted the balance of power in Central Europe and dramatically changed international dynamics. Moreover, amid rising national consciousness, ethnic minorities within the Habsburg Empire, in particular, demanded more rights, setting the stage for further conflict in Europe.

During the nineteenth century's last three decades, much of Europe entered a period of remarkable economic, social, political, and cultural change. During the Second Industrial Revolution, scientific and technological advances ushered in a period of rapid economic growth. Steel and electricity transformed manufacturing. Cities grew rapidly, their wide boulevards lined with department stores, cafés, and newspaper kiosks. The emergence of spectator sports and flashy cabarets symbolized the fin-de-siècle period. However, some of the rebellious writers and artists of the avant-garde worried that Western civilization was moving too rapidly and seemed out of control.

On the continent, political parties developed, which helped bring about the age of mass politics. Despite a general improvement in the quality of life, the difficult conditions of the laboring poor encouraged the creation of Socialist parties. Socialists were elected to many European parliaments. Trade unions put forth demands and engaged in strikes. In Britain, the Labour Party started up early in the twentieth century, supported by workers demanding social reform. In Russia, liberal critics of the tsarist autocracy became bolder. The humiliating defeat of Russia by

Japan led to the Russian Revolution of 1905. This forced short-lived political reforms and encouraged reformers and revolutionaries alike.

For more than half a century, liberals had championed the interests of the middle class, basing the right to vote on the ownership of property. They did so in the context of constitutional government, pushing for the rights of legislative assemblies. In the three decades following the largely unsuccessful 1848 revolutions, liberalism prevailed in Great Britain, France, Austria, Italy, Greece, and Sweden. The British Parliament, which in 1867 had greatly extended the right of men to vote, approved the secret ballot in 1872, and in 1884 enfranchised almost all remaining adult males. France became a republic early in the 1870s, and universal male suffrage subsequently was adopted in Germany, Belgium, Spain, Austria, and Italy. Without the liberals' determination to expand the franchise, universal male suffrage in much of Western Europe, followed by political democracy in many states, would not have occurred. Liberal democracy emerged as the dominant form of European politics from the second half of the nineteenth century to the present day.

However, in the last decades of the century, liberalism was on the defensive, attacked from left and right. Nationalism increasingly became part of the expanding contours of political life within states and between them. During the French Revolution and Napoleonic era, nationalism had been an ideology identified with the political left. Liberals had believed that laissez-faire economic policy and parliamentary government combined with an expansion of the right to vote (but not necessarily universal male suffrage) would provide a firm base for the establishment of nation-states. During at least the first half of the nineteenth century, liberalism and nationalism were closely entwined; liberals and nationalists were often the same people, as in Britain, France, and Italy.

By the end of the century, many nationalists, convinced that their people were superior to any other, trumpeted the primacy of the nation over claims of popular sovereignty or belief in human equality. Nationalism became an ideology championed, above all, by right-wing parties. Cheap newspapers glorified the nation for eager readers. "Jingoism" came to define the swaggering self-assurance of nationalists committed to expanding the power of their nation. At the same time, waves of strikes and demonstrations frightened conservatives from Norway and Sweden to Austria and Spain. The fear of socialism, espousing internationalism, pushed social elites and some in the middle class to the nationalist right. Anti-Semitism fed on aggressive nationalism.

Nationalism merged easily with imperialism, which was predicated on the assumption that the people of one nation were superior to others, and therefore entitled to dominate "inferior" peoples through the expansion of empire. The "new imperialism" of the powers began in the 1880s. By 1914, they had divided up three-quarters of the world's surface. Imperialism helped sharpen international rivalries. Entangling alliances led the European powers into two heavily armed camps, linking Germany and Austria-Hungary against Britain, France, and Russia. The growth of nationalism in the Balkans fueled the rivalry between Russia and Austria-Hungary, each backed by strongly committed allies.

CHAPTER 17

THE ERA OF NATIONAL UNIFICATION

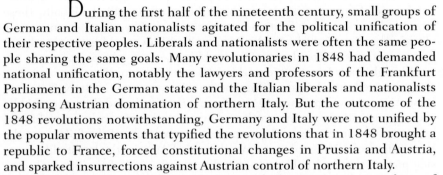

During the first half of the nineteenth century, small groups of German and Italian nationalists agitated for the political unification of their respective peoples. Liberals and nationalists were often the same people sharing the same goals. Many revolutionaries in 1848 had demanded national unification, notably the lawyers and professors of the Frankfurt Parliament in the German states and the Italian liberals and nationalists opposing Austrian domination of northern Italy. But the outcome of the 1848 revolutions notwithstanding, Germany and Italy were not unified by the popular movements that typified the revolutions that in 1848 brought a republic to France, forced constitutional changes in Prussia and Austria, and sparked insurrections against Austrian control of northern Italy.

Italian unification came, not because of the utopian nationalism of Giuseppe Mazzini nor because of the frenzied dashes of Giuseppe Garibaldi and his followers into the south, but rather largely as a result of the expansion of Piedmont-Sardinia, the peninsula's strongest and most liberal state. Italy was unified politically under the liberal auspices of the Piedmont-Sardinian monarchy, the House of Savoy.

The case of Germany was very different. German unification was effected by autocratic Prussian King William I and Chancellor Otto von Bismarck through shrewd manipulation of both diplomacy and warfare. "Most countries have an army," it was said, but "Prussia is an army with a country." The German Empire, like the Prussia that forged it in "blood and iron," was defiantly reactionary, flying in the face of currents of European liberalism.

Without question, the emergence of Italy in the 1860s and of Germany in 1871 changed the history of modern Europe. Germany emerged as a great power, Italy as a would-be great power. And the Austro-Hungarian monarchy increasingly was confronted by demands from its ethnic minorities for their own independence, which remained a factor for instability in its domestic and international politics. In some ways, the Habsburg monarchy seemed an anachronism, out of place in the age of nationalism.

THE POLITICAL UNIFICATION OF ITALY

The Austrian statesman Klemens von Metternich once whimsically remarked that Italy was "a mere geographical expression." Since the end of the Roman Empire, Italy had been politically disunited, a cacophony of competing voices from different regions and peoples.

Marked differences in economic development compounded political fragmentation. Northern Italy has always been considerably more prosperous than the south. The Habsburg monarchy also presented a formidable obstacle to Italian unification, as it retained Venetia and Lombardy, and dominated Parma, Tuscany, and Modena in north-central Italy (the rulers of the latter two states were members of the Austrian royal family). The pope's influence and temporal control over the Papal States around Rome posed another barrier to Italian unification. Furthermore, Italy lacked a tradition of centralized administration. Powerful local elites dispensed patronage, constituting unofficial parallel governments in much of the south and Sicily. Finally, these structural barriers to unification were accompanied by disagreement among elites and nationalists about whether a unified Italy would be governed by a monarchy (constitutional or not), a republic, or even by the pope.

Although many forces were working against Italian unification, some factors promoted the ultimate Risorgimento ("Resurgence") of Italy. Nationalist sentiment developed among the liberal aristocracy and the upper middle classes, particularly among northern lawyers and professors. It was fanned by nationalist brochures and newspapers, the memory of the failures of the Revolutions of 1848, and a common hatred of Austria, the latest of the outside powers that had held parts of Italy since the end of the fifteenth century. Most Italian nationalists envisioned a Risorgimento independent of the pope and the Catholic Church.

Leadership for Italian Unification

There seemed to be two possible sources of leadership for Italian unification. First, Victor Emmanuel II (ruled 1849–1878) of the House of Savoy, king of Piedmont-Sardinia (the Kingdom of Sardinia), wanted to unify Italy by gradually extending his control over the peninsula. Piedmont-Sardinia was far and away Italy's most prosperous region, boasting a significant concentration of industrial production, fine sources of water power, and accessible markets. It had inherited from the French revolutionary and Napoleonic eras a relatively efficient bureaucracy.

King Victor Emmanuel II, poorly educated and uncouth, loved horses and hunting more than anything else, with the possible exception of his sixteen-year-old mistress, the daughter of a palace guard. In 1852, Victor Emmanuel at least had the good sense to appoint Count Camillo di Cavour (1810–1861) to be his prime minister.

(*Left*) King Victor Emmanuel II of Piedmont-Sardinia. (*Right*) Count Camillo di Cavour.

Born into a family of Piedmontese nobles during the Napoleonic occupation, Cavour was a pampered child who grew up to be headstrong, somewhat lazy, and bad tempered. His older brother inherited the family title of marquis, and Cavour entered a military academy, where he did well in mathematics and engineering. In the army, he became enamored of political radicalism. Upon hearing of the July Revolution of 1830 in France, Cavour ran through his barracks in Genoa waving a paper knife, shouting "Long live the Republic! Down with all tyrants!" Cavour's political radicalism was unlikely to win him promotion in the army. He resigned his commission as a military engineer, pleading poor eyesight and bad health, the latter at least partially due to a lifelong pattern of eating and drinking too much.

Cavour read widely in economics and politics and traveled to France and England, both of which impressed him with their prosperity and efficient administration. Cavour's first language remained French, although his command of Italian improved. On his property, he made a good deal of money by utilizing crop rotation, land drainage, and mechanized farm machinery. Triumphs in banking and business followed, but none brought the morose Cavour happiness. In his early twenties, he wrote in his diary that he thought of suicide because he believed his life was "without purpose, without hope, without desire." Yet he found a compelling goal: the unification of the Italian peninsula.

Cavour came to espouse aristocratic liberalism. He became determined to effect political unification by gradually expanding the constitutional monarchy of Piedmont-Sardinia. An idealist of vision and courage, Cavour was also capable of ruthlessness and unscrupulous trickery, all of which would be necessary to achieve Italian unification. He bragged that he liked to reduce political problems to graphs on which he had plotted all possible factors and outcomes.

Elected to the Piedmontese Parliament in 1849 in the new constitutional government, named minister of commerce and agriculture the following year and prime minister in 1852, he initiated the first of a series of loose coalition liberal governments based on the political center, standing between the noble and clerical right and the republican left.

Cavour's policies helped stimulate the Piedmontese economy. He facilitated the availability of credit for businessmen, helped attract foreign capital by lowering tariffs, built railways, and strengthened the army. Reflecting Piedmontese liberal secular values, Cavour made the clergy subject to the same civil codes as everyone else and taxed Church property. Like the liberalism of the French Orleanist monarchy and the early Victorians in Britain, however, Cavour's liberalism stopped well short of republicanism.

A second, more popular nationalist tradition survived the broken dreams of "the springtime of the peoples," the Revolutions of 1848. Giuseppe Mazzini remained its spokesman. The Genoese-born Mazzini had as a boy watched Piedmontese patriots leave for exile after an ill-fated revolutionary uprising in 1820–1821. Mazzini frequently dressed in black (often in the company of his pet canaries, who wore yellow), vowing to remain in mourning until Italian unification could be achieved. The failure of conspiratorial uprisings led him to espouse a nationalist movement that had a wider range of support, with the goal of establishing a republic that would implement social reforms. While he was a determined enemy of monarchism and aristocratic privilege, Mazzini believed that classical liberalism was devoid of moral values, and he rejected socialism as overly materialistic. He embraced unification as a moral force that would educate and uplift the people of Italy, providing a common faith and purpose that would unlock their potential and make them worthy of democracy.

Mazzini believed that the unification of Italy had to be the work of the people themselves, and should not be achieved merely through the expansion of the Kingdom of Piedmont-Sardinia. Drawing on the conspiratorial tradition of the Carbonari, Mazzini's secret society, "Young Italy," hoped to mobilize the European masses, beginning in the Italian states, to rise up for nationalism and democracy. He thus supported the goals of other nationalist groups in Europe, including Hungarians, Poles, and Slavs in the hope that "Young Europe," a brotherhood of nations, would eventually come into existence.

Mazzini was undaunted by the failures and repression that followed the Revolution of 1848, including the ill-fated attempt to proclaim the Roman Republic in 1849. However, these debacles discredited his movement among the middle classes. Four years later, Cavour tipped off the Austrians that Mazzini was planning an insurrection in Lombardy. King Victor Emmanuel II congratulated Austrian Emperor Francis Joseph on the success of the subsequent repression. Yet Mazzini's effective propaganda kept the Italian question alive in European diplomatic circles while attracting the interest of lawyers and liberal landowners in some of the northern Italian states.

Alliances and Warfare to Further Italian Unification

Italian unification would be impossible as long as Austria dominated much of northern and central Italy. Having first concentrated on reforms within Piedmont-Sardinia, Cavour next began a series of diplomatic moves that he hoped would bring the support of Great Britain and France. Specifically, he wanted to form an alliance with France against Austria that would further the cause of Italian unification. Austria was not about to withdraw from Lombardy on its own, and Piedmont-Sardinia was too weak to defeat the Habsburg army alone. Cavour initiated commercial agreements with France, as well as with Great Britain, trying to impress both powers with Piedmont-Sardinia's political and economic liberalism.

In March 1854, France and Great Britain joined the Ottoman Empire in opposing Russia in the Crimean War (1853–1856). The cagey Cavour worked to make the war serve the interests of Piedmont-Sardinia and Italian unification. Cavour informed the French and British governments that Piedmont-Sardinia would be willing to join the coalition against Russia in exchange for a role in determining new frontiers in Eastern Europe at the war's end. Knowing that Britain needed more troops for the fight, Cavour sent 15,000 soldiers to Crimea in January 1855. Mazzini, on the other hand, bitterly opposed intervention as irrelevant to his vision of a united republican Italy. Piedmont-Sardinia signed the Peace of Paris in 1856, which ended the Crimean War, an occasion Cavour used to focus diplomatic attention on the Italian situation.

Cavour was now eager to ally with imperial France in the interest of working toward Italian unification. Despite a failed assassination attempt against him by an Italian nationalist republican in 1858, French Emperor Napoleon III was eager to extend his country's influence in Italy and hoped to annex Savoy and Nice from Piedmont-Sardinia. He proposed marriage between Victor Emmanuel's fifteen-year-old daughter and his own young cousin, Prince Napoleon Bonaparte. Such an alliance would help cement relations between France and Piedmont-Sardinia, not a happy situation for the Austrians (nor necessarily for the young bride).

Cavour devised an agreement with France against Austria, which was signed in July 1858 at Plombières, a spa in eastern France. Napoleon III now agreed to support Piedmont-Sardinia in a war against Austria. In January 1859, Piedmont-Sardinia and France formalized the Plombières agreement in a treaty. Then the ruling dynasties were united in youthful marriage (the princess had agreed to marry the young Frenchman if "he is not actually repulsive to me"). Russia, Austria's rival in the Balkans, was happy to sit this one out in exchange for French acceptance of a possible revision of the

Pope Pius XI on the special train given to him by Napoleon III, who protected papal temporal independence.

Peace of Paris, which had in 1856 deprived Russia of the right to have a fleet in the Black Sea. In turn, Russia would look the other way if events in Italy altered the settlements enacted by the Congress of Vienna in 1815.

Austria provided an excuse for war, announcing that it would draft men from Venetia and Lombardy into the imperial army. Piedmont-Sardinia, in turn, made it known that it would accept deserters from Austrian conscription, and it mobilized troops in March. But the British government lobbied so effectively for a peaceful solution that Cavour denounced a "conspiracy of peace" and threatened to resign. Napoleon III hesitated, asking Piedmont-Sardinia to demobilize its troops. Austria saved the situation for Cavour by issuing an ultimatum to Piedmont-Sardinia on April 23, 1859, hoping that other German states would support it. With Austria now appearing as the aggressor, Prussia and the other German states felt no obligation to come to its aid. After Piedmont-Sardinia rejected the ultimatum, Austrian troops invaded Piedmont, which brought France into the war. Napoleon III himself led 100,000 troops into northern Italy; many of the troops went by train, the first time that a railway played a major part in warfare.

The French and Piedmontese defeated the Habsburg army at Magenta and then at Solferino in June 1859, driving the Austrians out of Lombardy (see Map 17.1). But the French feared that a crushing defeat of Austria might yet bring Prussia and other German states into the war against France, with the bulk of the French armies still in northern Italy. Furthermore, Cavour

MAP 17.1 THE UNIFICATION OF ITALY, 1859–1870   The unification of Italy by Piedmont-Sardinia included territory acquired in 1859, 1860, 1862, and 1866.

had sparked several nationalist insurrections against the Austrians in Tuscany, Bologna, Modena, and Parma, whose rulers fled, leaving the duchies under Piedmontese control. Further revolts in the Papal States failed; the pope's Swiss mercenaries recaptured Perugia, looting the city and shooting unarmed civilians. It became apparent to the French emperor that if Piedmont-Sardinia were *too* successful, Victor Emmanuel's expanded kingdom might become a rival instead of a grateful, compliant neighbor. Without consulting Cavour, Napoleon III arranged an armistice at Villafranca with Emperor Francis Joseph of Austria in July.

Cavour and Victor Emmanuel now believed that France had betrayed them. Austria lost Lombardy to Piedmont-Sardinia but would retain Venetia. By the Treaty of Turin on March 24, 1860, Napoleon III agreed to Piedmont-Sardinia's annexation of Tuscany, Modena, Parma, and Bologna, in addition to Lombardy. In exchange, Piedmont-Sardinia ceded Savoy and Nice, which passed to France after a plebiscite. With the exception of Venetia, almost all of northern and central Italy had now been united under the constitutional monarchy of Piedmont-Sardinia.

Garibaldi and the Liberation of Southern Italy

The colorful republican revolutionary Giuseppe Garibaldi (1807–1882) now leapt onto the stage. Born in Nice (and, like Cavour, a French speaker), the charismatic and courageous Garibaldi had joined Mazzini's Young Italy movement in 1833. After twelve years in exile in South America, he fought against the Austrians in Lombardy in 1848 and against the French in Rome in 1849. The war of 1859 provided him with another opportunity to fight Austria. Angered that the Villafranca armistice had cut short what he considered a war for Italian unification, Garibaldi formed an army of volunteers, hoping to drive the Austrians from Venetia and the French from Rome. But an ill-prepared attack on Rome failed completely.

In April 1860, a revolt began against Francis II, the Bourbon monarch of the Kingdom of the Two Sicilies (Naples and Sicily), as a protest against the milling tax and the high price of bread. Secretly encouraged by Cavour (who

planned to send Piedmont-Sardinia's army to Rome later to rescue the pope) and openly urged on by Mazzini, Garibaldi landed in Sicily with an army of 1,000 "Red Shirts." Sicilians welcomed him as a liberator. Garibaldi's followers outfought the larger Neapolitan army, taking Palermo on May 27, 1860. This success swelled Garibaldi's ragtag army of nationalists and adventurers.

Garibaldi then announced that he was assuming dictatorial power in Sicily on behalf of King Victor Emmanuel II of Piedmont-Sardinia. In August, Garibaldi's army returned to the Italian peninsula. Aided by a popular insurrection, the Red Shirts took Naples, Italy's largest city, in September. Garibaldi's victories now put Piedmont-Sardinia in a difficult

Giuseppe Garibaldi.

situation. If Garibaldi marched against Rome, France might declare war because of the threat to the pope. If Garibaldi moved against Venetia, which seemed inevitable, Austria would almost certainly fight again, perhaps this time with Prussia's support. Cavour sent Piedmontese troops into the Papal States the same day that Garibaldi's troops took Naples. The ostensible goal was to join Garibaldi, but the real intention of the expedition was to stop the adventurer's dramatic independent operations. The combined forces of Piedmontese troops and Garibaldi's army put an end to papal resistance and that of the royal Bourbon family of Naples.

Italy Unified

Plebiscites in October in Naples, Sicily, and the Papal States demonstrated overwhelming support for joining the expanding Italian state of Piedmont-Sardinia. The annexation of these states angered Napoleon III, as Cavour had promised that an international conference would provide arbitration. Now only Venetia—still Austrian—and Rome and its region—the shrinking kingdom of the pope—remained unincorporated into the new Italy.

Victor Emmanuel II of Piedmont-Sardinia triumphantly entered Naples with Garibaldi in November 1860. He took the title King Victor Emmanuel II of Italy in March 1861. Garibaldi, whose daring exploits had made these events possible, retired in semi-exile. On June 6, 1861, Cavour died at age fifty-one, depriving Italy of his effective decision making and political acumen. Depending on one's point of view, Italy had lost either the great hero of the Risorgimento or a scheming Machiavellian—probably something of both.

Two more conflicts completed the political unification of Italy. In 1866, Austria went to war with Prussia, its rival for the leadership of the German states. Italian troops, allied with Prussia, moved into Austrian Venetia. When Prussian forces defeated the Austrians in July (see pp. 666–67), Venetia became part of Italy.

The final piece in the Italian jigsaw puzzle fell into place when French troops left Rome in 1870 at the beginning of the Franco-Prussian War. Italian troops occupied Rome, making it the capital of the new Italian state. On May 13, 1871, the Italian Parliament passed the Law of Papal Guarantees, which reduced the holdings of the pope to the Vatican, barely larger than Saint Peter's Basilica and its adjoining ecclesiastical buildings.

Limits to Unification

During the next decades, the limits to Italian unification became increasingly apparent. The Italian state, despite its phalanx of civil servants and police, seemed irrelevant to many, perhaps even most, of the people now called Italians. Most remained loyal to their families, towns, regions, and to the Catholic Church (particularly in central and southern Italy), as well as to powerful local leaders, families, or factions. Almost 70 percent of the population was illiterate in 1871 and 50 percent in 1900, even though the peninsula now shared a common written Italian language. In 1860, almost 98 percent of the population of Italy spoke dialects in daily life and not Italian. Schoolteachers sent to Sicily from the north were taken for Englishmen. A French writer related that in Naples in 1860 he heard people shout "Long Live Italy!" and then ask what "Italy" meant.

Resistance to the Italian state came naturally. In southern Italy, the crime organizations of the Camorra of Naples and the Mafia of Sicily, with similar codes of honor, served as the real basis of authority. Family feuds and vendettas, often accompanied by grisly violence, went on as before. "Italy" was seen as a northern ploy to bilk money through taxes, or to draft the sons of southern Italians into the army, or to undercut what seemed to be legitimate local influence and ways of doing things. To the poor farmers and impoverished laborers trying to scratch out a living, local notables at least could provide what they considered "justice" for the poor. Moreover, brigands had traditionally received assistance from the local population, who viewed them as fellow resisters to the state, if not Robin Hoods. The state managed to drive bands of brigands out of business in the 1870s, but only through a savage repression that killed more Italians than all the wars of the Risorgimento combined, intensifying suspicion and mistrust of the state.

The liberal free-trade policies of Cavour, who had never been farther south in Italy than Florence, further served to concentrate industry in the triangle formed by Milan, Turin, and Genoa by driving out smaller and less efficient manufacturers, accentuating the gap between north and south. The south became even more dependent on poor agriculture. Northerners dominated Italian politics, as they had Italian unification, treating the people of the south as colonial underlings. Far fewer southerners were eligible to vote than northerners. Mass emigration, principally to the United States and Argentina, could only partly resolve the problems of overpopulation and poverty.

In the meantime, the popes portrayed themselves as Roman prisoners of a godless state. The Church had refused to accept the Law of Papal Guarantees of 1871, which gave it title to the Vatican and the authority to make ecclesiastical appointments within Italy. The popes not only refused to recognize Italy's existence, but they banned the faithful from running for electoral office or even voting. While some Italian Catholics simply ignored such stern papal warnings, others systematically abstained from casting a ballot. The state paid the salaries of the clergy, but it also confiscated Church property. Secular reforms removed the teaching of theology from the universities, closed convents and monasteries, made priests eligible for military conscription, banned public religious processions, and made civil marriage obligatory. The attitude of the Church hierarchy and prominent laymen to the Italian state was reflected by the headline of a Catholic newspaper after the death of King Victor Emmanuel II in 1878: "The king is dead, the pope is well."

Italian Politics

The king of Italy ruled through a premier and parliament. The electoral franchise was small: only about 600,000 men (2.5 percent of the population) were eligible to elect members of the Chamber of Deputies before the expansion of the franchise in 1882, after which 2 million men, about 10 percent of the population, could vote, and in 1912, when the number eligible to vote was doubled. Italian governments lurched from one political crisis to another in the 1880s, buffeted by rampant corruption as well as rapidly changing coalitions—a process that became known to critics as *trasformismo*—"transforming" political opponents into allies. King Umberto I (ruled 1878–1900) stood aside until his intervention became absolutely imperative. Italy's king was lazy, so uneducated that he did not even like to sign his own name if someone was watching, and considered himself above politics.

The arrogant Premier Francesco Crispi (1819–1901) built political alliances between northern industrialists, who were anticlerical and wanted high tariffs, and southern landowners, who also favored protectionism. Crispi used the army against strikers and demonstrators and used the police to cow opponents daring to organize electoral opposition against him. In 1894, he ordered the disfranchisement of nearly a million voters and banned the Italian Socialist Party. His authoritarian methods angered even the king, who wryly admitted, "Crispi is a pig, but a necessary pig."

In 1901, King Victor Emmanuel III (ruled 1900–1946) signed a decree granting the premier authority over cabinet posts. Upon becoming premier in 1903, Giovanni Giolitti (1842–1928) brought relative stability to Italian political life. Giolitti was a master of *trasformismo*, making party labels essentially meaningless by building a series of makeshift but effective coalitions. Giolitti won the loyalty of enough deputies to remain in office through negotiations, cajoling, promises of jobs and favors, threats, and outright bribery. With the motto "neither revolution nor reaction," the premier's balancing act depended on votes from the anticlerical Radicals, a party based in the north, who supported increased administrative efficiency and liked the premier's opposition to socialism. But Giolitti also depended on southern Catholic moderates, and therefore opposed any land reform on behalf of the rural poor that would break up large estates. His government also had to appease the Church by refusing to meet the anticlerical demands of the Radicals. (In 1904, the Church relaxed its anti-republican stand enough to allow practicing Catholics to vote in elections if their participation would help defeat a Socialist candidate.) Giolitti also sponsored legislation that turned over education in southern Italy to the clergy. The premier left the Mafia and Camorra alone because they could bring him votes in any region or town they controlled, ordering on one occasion the release of more than a thousand *mafiosi* from prison in exchange for their votes.

The Rise of Italian Nationalism

In a country wrought by political division, aggressive nationalism appeared as one means of bringing Italians together. Crispi had favored a policy of forceful colonialization, fearful that Italy would be left out while the other powers snatched up territory (see Chapter 21). He prepared an invasion of the East African state of Abyssinia (now Ethiopia) from the Italian colony of Eritrea in 1896, circumventing parliamentary opposition and refusing to heed the warning of generals that such a move might fail. When the Abyssinian tribesmen Crispi had referred to as "barbarians" crushed the Italian army at Adowa, he resigned. Italian nationalists then began to claim the territory of Trentino in the Austrian Tyrol and the Adriatic port of Trieste as "Unredeemed Italy" (*Italia Irredenta*). In 1911, while Giolitti was premier, Italy launched a war of conquest in Libya, establishing a colony there (see Chapter 22). Giolitti's social reforms had frightened employers and many other conservatives, and the ranks of the anti-parliamentary right swelled. Nationalist candidates demanded further aggressive moves in the Mediterranean. Although the war in Libya went reasonably well for Italian troops, the right objected to the fact that it seemed mismanaged, and the left did not want the invasion at all. Both left and right moved farther away from Giolitti's Liberal center. The Libyan war thus directly undid Giolitti's political system. With the Socialists divided by the Libyan war and unwilling to be "transformed" into temporary political partners, Giolitti now had to turn to Catholic leaders. Giolitti convinced Catholics to support his Liberal candidates if the Liberals agreed to end the campaign against Church schools and for legalized divorce. Angered by Giolitti's promises to the Church, the left tripled its vote, forcing him from office in March 1914. A nationalist proclaimed that the role of his new party was to teach Italians to respect "international struggle," even if the result was war. The Italian liberal state had survived many challenges, but even greater ones lay ahead.

THE UNIFICATION OF GERMANY

The unification of Germany would not come through liberal auspices. In the German states, too, growing nationalist sentiment existed within the middle class. Yet, as in the case of Italy, there were also formidable obstacles to German unification. First, in the wake of the Revolution of 1848, the upper classes were wary of any change that might threaten the *status quo*. They particularly feared the strong nationalist feeling unleashed by revolution, the extension of which might lead to, they reasoned, the proclamation of the equality of all citizens. Second, it was still not clear around which power, Austria or Prussia, Germany could achieve national unification. Some believed in the "small German" solution in which Prussia might effect German unification and exclude Austria. Other German nationalists supported the "big German" ideal, whereby Austria would dominate an expanded German Confederation. Third, in both Prussia and Austria, the 1850s brought repression that made it clear to most nationalists that German unification would not come under liberal auspices. The repression following the Revolutions of 1848 had scattered thousands of German democrats and socialists across Europe and as far as the United States.

As in the case of Italy, where unification had been achieved primarily through the efforts of one relatively strong and prosperous state, in the German states Prussia held several trump cards toward achieving German unification, including territorial additions in the industrializing Rhineland after the Napoleonic Wars and a relatively strong economic position, which had been bolstered by the Zollverein customs union. Furthermore, Prussia's population was quite homogeneous, as it was almost entirely German-speaking and Protestant. The Prussian royal family, the Hohenzollerns, benefited from the internal stability brought by an effective administrative bureaucracy and were supported by an ambitious, powerful landed nobility, the Junkers, who dominated the officer corps of the Prussian army. Prussia already represented an example of successful statemaking. The expansion of Prussian power therefore seemed to many Prussians to be perfectly natural. Catholic Austria, on the other hand, dominated a multinational population. The Habsburg monarchy had much to lose by the encouragement of national movements that might catch fire among the varied peoples within the imperial boundaries.

All German nationalists, however, did not agree on what political form a unified Germany should take. Most Prussian Junkers had been unrelenting in their opposition to the liberal movements that had championed popular sovereignty during the 1848 revolutions. They rejected the liberalism of Rhineland industrialists, eager to enhance their own political power. Many liberals, particularly republicans from the more liberal southern German states, wanted a unified Germany to have a parliamentary government free from domination by either autocratic, aristocratic Prussia or imperial Austria. Yet, despite Prussia's autocratic and militaristic traditions, some nationalistic republicans still hoped Prussia, not Austria, would lead Germans to unification. Prussian Junkers also feared that if the "big German" plan for unification came to be, their influence would be greatly diluted by Austrian influence. Nonetheless, Austria continued to attract the interest of German nationalists who mistrusted Prussia. Many southern Germans wanted the Habsburg monarchy to champion the cause of the smaller German states, leading to a decentralized federation, not domination by Prussia.

William I, Bismarck, and the Resolution of the Constitutional Crisis

The first step in the unification of Germany was the ascension to power of a monarch equal to the task. In 1858, the pious William I (1797–1888) became regent for his brother, Frederick William IV, who was declared insane. Crowned following Frederick William's death in 1861, William I made clear from the outset of his reign that, unlike his predecessor, he would look beyond the small group of reactionary Prussian Junkers and bring some more moderate conservatives into his cabinet. William I promised to rule constitutionally. Voters—men of at least moderate wealth—responded by turning out in unprecedented numbers to vote. Liberals won a clear victory in the 1858 elections to the Prussian Parliament, which brought to that assembly a good number of men enriched by the economic boom in the early 1850s. Liberals who favored German unification now had a public forum in which to be heard. Many businessmen believed that German unification would be good for them, as the Zollverein customs union had benefited them in the 1840s.

In the meantime, the Austrian war against Piedmont-Sardinia and France in 1859 divided Prussians. Some were torn between dislike for Austria and irritation with French Emperor Napoleon III for helping engineer the outbreak of war. Austria was a member of the German Confederation and had the right to expect assistance from fellow members. But Austria was also Prussia's major rival for power within the German states. Prussia remained neutral in the war, but Italy's move toward unification greatly impressed German nationalists. Those who looked to Prussia to forge German unity welcomed Austria's defeat.

In 1858, several "Pan-German" associations had been formed as pressure groups supporting German unification. The largest and most influential, the National Union (*Nationalverein*), wanted a constitutional and parliamentary German state. The Prussian government remained suspicious of the National Union because many of its members favored the extension of political freedom within the German states. As in the old Frankfurt Parliament, its members were overwhelmingly middle class, including intellectuals, lawyers, officials, and small businessmen, but also included several industrialists. The National Union rebuffed an attempt by workers' organizations to join in 1863, but contributed to the resurgence of political liberalism within Prussia by demanding an effective constitution that would limit the domination of the monarchy and the Junkers.

William I.

The question of army reform raised the issue of parliamentary control over the budget. The Prussian constitutional crisis that followed became a critical step in the unification of Germany along lines that turned out to be anything but liberal. The Prussian military mobilization in 1859 during the Austrian war against Piedmont and

France had revealed serious inadequacies in the Prussian army. The minister of war proposed expensive reforms of the army: expansion of the officer corps, increasing the number of recruits, and an extension of the time of service to three years. Prussian liberals wanted all citizens to serve in the army, but also hoped that the National Guard (*Landwehr*) would replace the professional, Junker-dominated army as the foundation of the Prussian military, thus forging a link between the army and the people.

The Prussian Parliament did not enjoy many prerogatives in autocratic Prussia, but it did have the right to approve new taxes. In response to government pressure, in 1861 the parliament, despite its liberal majority, passed a provisional bill that gave the army the money it needed until the reform could be considered. Liberal approval of the provisional bill was a fateful event in German history because it provided parliamentary sanction to the virtually unchallenged power of the Prussian army.

Some leaders among the liberal opposition then formed the German Progressive Party. Liberals declined to vote for the new military budget when the minister of war refused compromise. After William dismissed parliament, new elections returned another liberal majority, which rejected a second army budget. Seeking to overcome parliamentary opposition, the king turned to a strong-willed and intransigently conservative Junker, Count Otto von Bismarck (1815–1898), appointing him prime minister in 1862.

Bismarck was the son of a dull Junker father and a lively, intelligent mother from a family of middle-class bureaucrats. In his Berlin school, Bismarck was more noted for dueling scars earned in student fraternities than for academic success. After receiving his law degree, he passed the entrance examination for the Prussian bureaucracy. Bismarck was appointed Prussian representative to the German Confederation in Frankfurt in 1851. He was sent to Saint Petersburg as ambassador in 1859, perhaps to mute his noisy denunciations of Austria.

As prime minister of Prussia, Bismarck was convinced that he could create a new German state that would not be too large for Prussia to dominate, nor too democratic for the tradition of the Hohenzollern monarchy. He wanted to create a modern, bureaucratic state that would be strong and secular. He cleverly used political parties when it suited his purposes. For the next three decades, he doggedly held on to personal power. Bismarck's shrewd manipulation of domestic and international politics dominated relations among the European powers. The "iron chancellor" patiently made uncanny assessments of every possible option and then moved with determination to strengthen Prussia's position. Bismarck's type of politics came to be known as *Realpolitik,* the pursuit of a nation's self-interest based on a realistic assessment of the costs and consequences of action. Inherent in *Realpolitik* was an absence of moral or ethical considerations, overrun by Bismarck's unshakable determination to enhance the power of the Prussian monarchy and nobility, and therefore of Germany.

Bismarck was a very complex man, both a man of iron and one easily moved to tears. He once said of himself: "Faust complains of having two souls in his breast. I have a whole squabbling crowd. It goes on as in a republic." A large man, he looked like a senior military officer stuffed into a uniform that was too small. At times outgoing and charming, Bismarck could also lapse into moods of intense, gloomy isolation. He was unforgiving toward those who crossed him: "If I have an enemy in my power, I must destroy him." He once said that he sometimes spent whole nights hating. Bismarck could never contain his disdain for parliamentary liberalism: "The position of Prussia in Germany will be determined not by its liberalism but by its power. . . . Not through speeches and majority decisions are the great questions of the day decided—that was the great mistake of 1848 and 1849—but through blood and iron."

Bismarck now announced that the government would operate without constitutional authorization. It did so for four years, using tax money previously voted to finance army reforms. In June 1863, Bismarck struck against the liberal Progressives by restricting freedom of the press, refusing to confirm the election of Progressive mayors, and banning discussion of political issues in municipal council meetings. The fact that both public opinion and even Crown Prince Frederick William opposed these measures did not dissuade him in the least. Nor did the election of even more liberals to the parliament in October 1863. In the meantime, Bismarck's stridently anti-Austrian policy helped split the liberal parliamentary opposition.

Alliances and Warfare to Establish Prussian Leadership

Russia and France were the two powers that would be most threatened by a unified Germany. The 1863 Polish revolt against Russian domination presented Bismarck with a perfect opportunity to ingratiate himself to the tsar. Whereas the other major powers sympathized with the Poles, Bismarck immediately voiced support for Russia. "Hit the Poles so hard that they despair for their lives," Bismarck advised. The Prussian government then signed an agreement with Russia, in which they agreed to assist each other in pursuing insurgents across their respective frontiers. Austria, which also had a sizable Polish population within its borders, found its relations with Russia soured.

Bismarck's first war was fought against the Danes in 1864 over Schleswig-Holstein, two duchies that included the Baltic port of Kiel (see Map 17.2). British Prime Minister Lord Palmerston (Henry John Temple, 1784–1865) once said that only three men truly understood the problem of Schleswig-Holstein: one was dead, one had gone mad, and the third, Palmerston himself, had forgotten it all. The duchies were ruled by the king of Denmark although not incorporated as part of the kingdom of Denmark. Holstein, which lies between Prussia and Schleswig, was almost entirely German-speaking and belonged to the

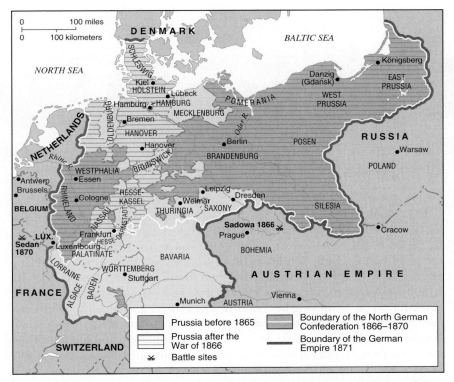

MAP 17.2 THE UNIFICATION OF GERMANY, 1866–1871   The unification of Germany by Prussia included territory acquired after the Austro-Prussian War (1866) and the Franco-Prussian War (1870–1871).

German Confederation, whereas both German and Danish speakers lived in Schleswig, which was not part of the Confederation. In 1848, the king of Denmark had declared the union of Schleswig with Denmark, and revolution broke out in both duchies. The Danish army occupied Schleswig. During the summer, a Prussian army on behalf of the German Confederation intervened in defense of the revolutionary provisional government in Holstein, which demanded autonomy. International opinion (particularly in Britain and Russia) rallied to the cause of the Danes. After some fighting, the Prussian forces withdrew. Following Swedish mediation, the provisional government of Holstein was dissolved by the Armistice of Malmö (August 1848). Although they were administered by a Danish-German commission, the two duchies essentially retained their former status. Prussia's defeat seemed a defeat for the cause of German nationalism. A small war followed in 1849–1850 between Prussian and Danish troops, ended by another armistice that left the status of Schleswig and Holstein up in the air.

Prussian coastal battery during the war against Denmark, 1864.

The London Protocol of 1852 placed Schleswig-Holstein under the authority of the Danish king, but forbade their incorporation into Denmark. In March 1863, however, the Danish king enacted a new constitution that seemed to incorporate Schleswig into his kingdom. Bismarck, capitalizing on the wave of nationalistic support, then found an ally in Austria. Prussia issued Denmark an ultimatum in January 1864, demanding that the new constitution for Schleswig be redrawn. The Danish government, incorrectly assuming that because of Schleswig's strategic importance, France and Britain would rush to its defense, rejected the ultimatum and found itself at war with Prussia and Austria. To no one's surprise, the Danes were easily beaten. The Treaty of Vienna (October 1864) established the joint administration of Schleswig-Holstein by Prussia and Austria—Austria would administer Holstein, and Prussia would administer Schleswig. This awkward arrangement left Prussia with a military corridor and communications line through Austrian-controlled Holstein and use of the port of Kiel.

Bismarck now viewed a military showdown with Austria as inevitable, even desirable. Yet, while preparing for that eventuality by currying the favor of the smaller German states and working to isolate Austria further from the other European powers, he blithely tried—and failed—to tempt Austria into making an agreement that would formally divide their influence in the German states into north-south spheres. Bismarck persuaded Napoleon III that France would receive territorial compensation in the Rhineland if it would stay out of an Austro-Prussian war. The French emperor tried to play both sides. Convinced that Austria could defeat Prussia, he signed a secret treaty with the Habsburg monarchy that would give the French Venetia and establish a French protectorate in the Rhineland after an Austrian victory.

Bismarck then drew Italy into a secret alliance, signed in April 1866, by promising it Venetia in the event of a Habsburg defeat. Italy promised Prussia assistance if there was war with Austria, knowing that a Prussian victory would add the last large chunk of the Italian peninsula to Italy (see p. 657).

Exaggerating reports of Austria's military preparations, Bismarck denounced Austria's "seditious agitation" against Prussia in Schleswig-Holstein. After Bismarck had secured the temporary alliance with Italy and assured France's neutrality, Prussian troops entered Holstein. Austria allied with some of the smaller states (including Hanover, Saxony, and Hesse-Kassel) of the German Confederation. Prussia left the German Confederation, which then voted under Austria's leadership to send troops against the Prussian army.

Within three weeks, Prussian troops had defeated the South German and Hanoverian armies in the Austro-Prussian War (1866). The Prussian army bested the Austrian forces in the Battle of Sadowa (or Königgrätz) in eastern Bohemia on July 3, 1866. Almost 1 million soldiers fought in the battle. Superior military planning as well as the rapid mobilization, deployment, and concentration of troops, talented officers, and more modern weapons—particularly the breech-loading "needle gun"—brought the Prussian army success.

The North German Confederation

In the aftermath of a victory most people did not expect, Bismarck restrained the Prussian officer corps, many of whom wanted to push on to Vienna. Bismarck realized that he would ultimately need the support of the South German states, some of whom had been allied with Austria, if Germany was to be unified under Prussian auspices. Moreover, the chancellor did not want to provide France or Russia with an opportunity to enter the conflict. The Treaty of Prague (August 1866) eliminated Austria as a rival for the domination of the German states. The German Confederation was dissolved. The Habsburg monarchy recognized the North German Confederation (see Map 17.2), a new union of twenty-two states and principalities north of the Main River, with a constitution and a parliament (Reichstag), which Prussia would dominate with William I as president and Bismarck as federal chancellor. Bavaria signed an alliance promising to join Prussia if it were attacked by France, which had been alarmed by the relatively easy Prussian victory. Schleswig-Holstein became part of Prussia. By virtue of the annexation of Hanover, Frankfurt, Nassau, and Hesse-Kassel, Prussia was no longer divided into two separate provinces. The Berlin government intimidated, bribed, or cajoled these smaller states into compliance.

Bismarck left no doubt that he considered the North German Confederation a provisional solution until Germany could be united under Prussian leadership. In the meantime, the old Zollverein customs union, which included the South German states, was expanded to include an assembly of elected delegates. Bismarck received support from Prussian businessmen who would profit from the removal of customs barriers and the centralization of railway networks. As long as unification brought material progress, it did not seem to matter to them that the traditional class system and restricted political life that characterized Prussia would form the basis of a united Germany. Bismarck was the man of the hour, the Prussian state a dynamic force with which to be reckoned.

Bismarck's bitter quarrel with the liberals over the military budget disappeared in the enthusiasm. Some members of the Progressive Party and other liberals still espoused "a vigilant and loyal opposition" at home. But liberal newspapers willingly accepted the triumphs of Prussian foreign policy and military might. Some liberals were so elated by the prospect of German unification that they left the more hesitant Progressive Party and formed the nationalistic National Liberal Party, which supported Bismarck. At the same time, some of the South German states were moving closer to Prussia through economic and military alliances.

The Franco-Prussian War and German Unification

Prussian victory in the Franco-Prussian War of 1870–1871 completed the unification of the German states, with the exception of Austria. Napoleon III foolishly seized upon the issue of the Hohenzollern candidacy for the vacant Spanish throne as an occasion to go to war against Prussia. Bismarck fanned the embers of the crisis he had hoped would lead to a war he considered inevitable and necessary. His carefully planned diplomacy was never more evident. The Russian tsar warmly remembered Prussian support during the Polish rebellion of 1863. The Austrian government had not forgiven France for joining Piedmont-Sardinia in the war of 1859. Italy still resented the loss of Savoy and Nice in 1860 to France. Bismarck played his real trump card with the British, coolly revealing documents proving that the French emperor had in 1866 demanded Belgium and Luxembourg as compensation for Prussia's increased power. This ended any chance of support for Napoleon III by the British government, which would never tolerate a potentially hostile power in Belgium. France went alone to war against Prussia. Following the surrender of French armies at the end of August and the beginning of September, Prussian forces besieged Paris. French resistance continued until January 28, 1871 (see Chapter 18).

Bismarck signed a convention with the provisional French government, awaiting the election of a National Assembly in France that could conclude a peace treaty. Bolstered by a surge of nationalist sentiment in the South German states as well as in Prussia, Bismarck demanded the annexation of Alsace, where German speakers predominated (although they did not necessarily want to be incorporated into a united Germany), and much of Lorraine.

The German Empire was officially proclaimed at Versailles on January 18, 1871. King William I of Prussia became Emperor William I of Germany. The North German Confederation and its constitution provided the framework for German unification. The German Empire took on the auto-

Prussian troops move to cut a French railway line in the Franco-Prussian War.

cratic political structure of Prussia, dominated by Prussian nobles and military officers. For their part, industrialists and merchants trusted that unification would provide a boost to large-scale industrialization in the new Germany. Hamburg merchants thus traded the traditional independence of their city for the economic advantages of operating within a centralized state. Bismarck had harnessed economic liberalism to the goals of conservative political nationalism. Although many Germans remained indifferent to unification and others preferred the particularism of their region, over the long run, most Germans came to accept with growing enthusiasm the politically unified state that had been forged by Bismarck's spectacularly successful statemaking. The result was a critical shift in the balance of power in Europe.

The empire had a parliament, but the Reichstag had little real authority. Its members, elected by a franchise system that in Prussia grossly overrepresented landed interests, could not hold cabinet posts. The chancellor was responsible not to the Reichstag, but rather to the emperor. The Reichstag could not propose legislation. Foreign policy and military affairs remained in the hands of the emperor and the chancellor. The Reichstag's control over the budget could not limit the prerogatives of the throne. Each of Germany's twenty-five states sent a delegate to a federal council (*Bundesrat*), over which the chancellor presided. Although each German

William I and Bismarck celebrate the proclamation of the German Empire in the Hall of Mirrors at Versailles.

state—for example, Bavaria, which had a relatively liberal constitution—retained considerable administrative autonomy, as well as in some cases its own prince, the nature of the German imperial government remained authoritarian. Germany's growing economic power was therefore unaccompanied by the evolution toward effective parliamentary government that characterized Britain and then France, as well as to some extent Italy.

Junkers dominated the army and civil service. In exchange for loyalty, they were exempt from most taxation, receiving what amounted to state subsidies for their immense estates. Inevitably, as in England, noble economic clout declined with the agricultural depression and with the remarkably rapid industrialization of Germany, but Prussian Junkers retained their full measure of political power.

Unlike their counterparts in Victorian England and France, the German middle class largely remained outside political life in the German Empire, as they had been in Prussia before unification. Most middle-class Germans willingly acquiesced to imperial authority and noble influence. The subsequent rise of the German Social Democratic Party, founded in 1875 (see Chapter 20), was, in most cases, enough to keep the German middle class loyal to the empire.

Nationalist versus Internationalist Movements

Chancellor Bismarck hated the Catholic Center and Social Democratic parties, doubting their loyalty. The Catholic Center Party was founded in 1870 to lobby for the rights of Catholics, who made up 35 percent of the German population, most living in Bavaria and the Rhineland. In 1870, the pope asserted the doctrine of papal infallibility. To Bismarck, this meant that one day the pontiff might simply order German Catholics to not obey the government. In 1873, Bismarck launched a state campaign against Catholics, the *Kulturkampf* ("cultural struggle"). Priests in Germany henceforth had to complete a secular curriculum in order to be ordained, and the state would now recognize only civil marriage. Subsequent laws permitted the expulsion from Germany of members of the Catholic clergy who refused to abide by discriminatory laws against Catholics. An assassination attempt against Bismarck by a young Catholic in 1874 and papal condemnation of the *Kulturkampf* the following year only hardened the chancellor's resolve.

Gradually, however, Bismarck realized that he might in the future need the support of the Catholic Center Party against the Social Democrats. The chancellor quietly abandoned the *Kulturkampf*, although Catholics were still systematically excluded from high civil service positions, as were Jews. The state helped German Protestants purchase bankrupt estates in Prussian Poland so that they would not fall into the hands of Catholics, who made up most of the population there. Alsace and the parts of Lorraine annexed from France, where Catholics formed a solid majority, were administered directly from Berlin instead of being considered a separate state of the Reich.

Bismarck became obsessed with destroying the socialists, who improved their gains in the elections, although they still held only a couple of seats in the Reichstag. Two attempts to kill Emperor William I in 1878 provided Bismarck with an excuse for his war on the socialists, although neither would-be assassin had even the slightest contact with socialist leaders. The Reichstag obliged Bismarck by passing antisocialist legislation that denied socialists the freedoms of assembly, association, and the press. The police arrested socialists, shut down their newspapers and periodicals, and intimidated workers into quitting trade unions.

A contemporary image of Bismarck pitted against the pope in the German chancelor's campaign against German Catholics.

William II and German Nationalism

Following William I's death, Frederick III, a man of foresight and tolerance, reigned for only 100 days, tragically dying of throat cancer. In 1888, William II (ruled 1888–1918) became emperor. William held that "a society is only strong if it recognizes the fact of natural superiorities, in particular that of birth." He boasted, "We Hohenzollerns derive our crowns from Heaven alone and are answerable only to Heaven."

The German emperor compensated for a withered left arm with a love of military uniforms and swords. His education had proceeded in a hit-or-miss fashion that mostly missed. William's favorite reading included the pseudo-scientific racist ramblings of the English writer Houston Stewart Chamberlain. William II considered himself an expert on military affairs, but was not. He was lazy, yet talked at great length superficially about any conceivable subject, rushing to conclusions without reflection. His lack of tact—he invariably referred to the diminutive King Victor Emmanuel III of Italy as "that dwarf"—was a common topic of conversation in imperial circles.

Bismarck lasted two years as William's chancellor. When Bismarck in 1890 sought a pretext to launch another campaign of repression against the Social Democrats, the emperor, wanting to cultivate as much popularity as possible, preferred to win mass support by sponsoring more legislation that would improve working conditions. After an unpleasant confrontation, Bismarck resigned.

William II (*left*) and Emperor Francis Joseph of Austria-Hungary (*right*).

The iron chancellor's less able successors were unable to keep William from impulsively antagonizing Germany's rivals. The emperor's personal foibles became increasingly important as international relations entered a new and dangerous stage. He personally contributed to the rise of aggressive German nationalism and the Anglo-German naval rivalry. William zipped around Germany and the North Sea eagerly reviewing troops and christening ships. He enthusiastically supported the expansionist goals of the Pan-German and Naval Leagues. He asserted, "I believe, as it is written in the

Bible, that it is my duty to increase [the German heritage] for which one day I shall be called upon to give an account to God. Whoever tries to interfere with my task I shall crush."

The alliance between Conservatives, National Liberals, and the Catholic Center Party provided the German emperor with a conservative base within the Reichstag. The National Liberals wanted a strong, secular state, and mistrusted parliamentary democracy. The resulting alliance between industrialists and agriculturists ("iron and rye") led to protectionist economic policies that began in 1879 and culminated in 1902 with a tariff that imposed a 25 percent duty on manufacturing and food imports. Liberalism continued to be closely tied to the defense of small-town interests.

In the meantime, the German conservatives became increasingly nationalistic and anti-Semitic. Following the economic crash of 1873, two years after Jews had received full legal emancipation with the proclamation of the empire, newspapers selected Jewish bankers, industrialists, and rival publishers as scapegoats. The operatic composer Richard Wagner and his circle of friends were outspokenly anti-Semitic. Wagner believed that the theater (and composers) stood as a center of German emotional national culture, which he did not believe included Jews. Some Germans identified Jews with liberalism and socialism. In 1892, the German Conservative Party made anti-Semitism part of its party platform, despite the fact that most Jews were fully assimilated into German society. A Jewish industrialist remembered in 1911 that "in the youth of every German Jew there comes a painful moment that he never forgets, the moment when he realizes for the first time that he has entered the world as a second-class citizen and that neither his efforts nor his accomplishments will free him from this status."

Yet, the Social Democrats won more seats in the Reichstag in 1912 than any other party. But many Social Democrats also were engulfed by the mood of aggressive nationalism that swept much of Germany, heightened by rivalry with Great Britain and by the Second Moroccan Crisis of 1911, which brought Germany and France close to war (see Chapter 22). Socialist deputies voted for the prodigious augmentation of funds for naval expansion, but did so in part because the issue of direct versus indirect taxation was at stake, and they wanted to establish the principle of direct taxation so as to end the tax privileges of wealthy families. Unlike French or Italian socialists, German socialists manifested little anti-militarism, giving every sign that they would support the government in time of war, particularly against Russia. The German Empire embodied the decline of liberalism and the rise of aggressive nationalism in late nineteenth-century Europe.

NATIONAL AWAKENINGS IN THE HABSBURG LANDS

Whereas Germany and Italy were politically unified when astute leaders mobilized nationalist feeling within the upper classes and successfully carried out an aggressive foreign policy, nationalism threatened the very existence of the Habsburg monarchy. Ethnic tensions within the Austro-Hungarian Empire, the second largest European state, were in many ways those of Europe itself. In the meantime, the unification of Germany, as well as that of Italy, altered the balance of power in Central Europe. Unified Germany, not Austria, was now unquestionably the strongest state in Central Europe. Moreover, the absorption of Lombardy and Venetia into the new Italian state had come at the expense of the Austrian Habsburgs.

Diversity and Cohesion in the Habsburg Empire

The provinces that formed the Habsburg domains represented extraordinary linguistic, cultural, and historical diversity (see Map 17.3). Eleven

MAP 17.3 Nationalities in the Habsburg Empire   The diverse nationalities and lands encompassed by the Habsburg Empire during the 1860s and 1870s.

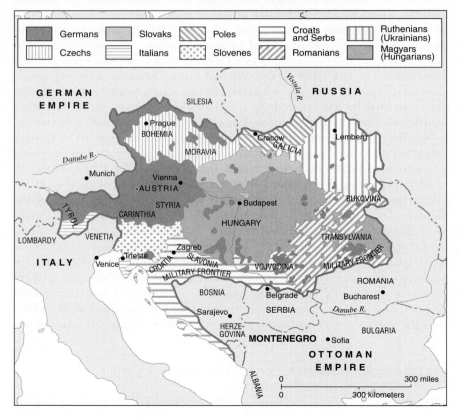

TABLE 17.1. ETHNIC COMPOSITION OF THE AUSTRO-HUNGARIAN EMPIRE IN 1910 (IN MILLIONS)

Ethnic Group	Population	Ethnic Group	Population
Germans	12.0	Serbs	2.0
Magyars	10.1	Slovaks	2.0
Czechs	6.6	Slovenes	1.4
Poles	5.0	Italians	0.8
Ukrainians	4.0	Bosnian Muslims	0.6
Romanians	3.2	Others	0.4
Croats	2.9		

major nationalities lived within the territorial boundaries of the empire; these included Czechs in Bohemia and Slovaks to their east; Poles in Galicia; Slovenes, Croats, Muslim Bosnians, and Serbs in the Balkans; Romanians and Ukrainians in the southeast; and Italians in the Alpine Tyrol, as well as Jews and Gypsies. But by far the two largest national groups were the Germans (35 percent of the population), living principally in Austria but numerous also in Bohemia, and the Hungarians, or Magyars (23 percent). The traditional Hungarian crown lands formed the largest territory in the empire, divided into Hungary, Croatia, Transylvania, the Vojvodina, and the Military Frontier. Yet the Germans and Hungarians were outnumbered by the various Slavic groups, who together accounted for about 45 percent of the empire's population. Czechs comprised 23 percent of Austria's population. In Hungary, Romanians (with 19 percent of the population) formed the next largest group after the Magyars (see Table 17.1). Inadequate transportation networks accentuated the insular and overwhelmingly rural nature of many ethnic regions—for example, there was no railroad between Vienna and the Croatian capital of Zagreb.

How did this polyglot empire hold together as long as it did among all of the competing ethnic rivalries and demands? The answers tell us something of the process of statemaking from the point of view of the nonnational state. First, the tradition of the Habsburg monarchy itself was an important force for cohesion, rooted in centuries of Central European history. Emperor Francis Joseph, who was eighteen when he came to power in 1848, had taken the second part of his name from his enlightened ancestor Joseph II to invoke the tradition of the House of Habsburg in those revolutionary times. As a Hungarian statesman put it during the Revolutions of 1848, "It was not the idea of unity that had saved the monarchy, but the idea of the monarchy that saved unity."

Second, the Habsburgs depended on the support of the German middle class and of the enormous German-speaking bureaucracy. The most salient cultural traditions (for example, music) of the imperial capital, Vienna, were overwhelmingly German. Viennese liberals celebrated their domination of

Austrian political and cultural life during the 1850s and 1860s by building a broad modern boulevard, the Ringstrasse. The grand artery was built on the traces of the city's fortifications, which Francis Joseph had ordered dismantled in 1857, since they had long since lost all military function except to separate the wealthy center of the city from the proletarian suburbs. The new boulevard also took shape with military motives in mind—troops could be moved rapidly in the event of a working-class rebellion. The architecture of central Vienna reflected the taste of the aristocracy and the Catholic Church. In contrast, public buildings (including the university, the opera, and the parliament building) and residences of manufacturers and bankers that bordered the Ringstrasse reflected the secular cultural tastes of the Viennese upper classes.

The empire's largest Czech and Austrian towns were largely German-speaking; in Prague, Germans outnumbered Czechs by more than three to one, although the percentage of Germans there declined during the second half of the century with the migration of more Czechs to the city. German was also the official language of the army (and of the secret police). To get anywhere, one had to speak German, a fact learned by non-German migrants to the cities. The German middle class also benefited from free-trade policies, and profited from the beginnings of industrial concentration in Bohemia.

Third, the monarchy enjoyed the support of Austrian and Hungarian nobles, as well as their Croatian, Polish, and Italian counterparts, landed nobles of ethnic groups with long histories of political sovereignty. The latter three nobilities depended on the Habsburg monarchy to maintain their

A view of Vienna and its Ringstrasse, 1873.

prerogatives vis-à-vis ethnic minorities within their territories and against the peasants of their own nationality. Thus, the small Croatian nobility, which needed the cooperation of the Habsburgs for the retention of their own privileges in Croatia, had a long tradition of military service to the dynasty. (In 1868, Croatia received semi-autonomous status within the empire.) The monarchy therefore depended on the preservation of the status of the favored nationalities, above all, the Germans and Magyars, from the challenges of other national minorities within the lands of their domination, such as Slovenes, Slovaks, Ukrainians, Serbs, and Czechs.

Fourth, Catholicism, the religion of the majority of the peoples of the Habsburg domains, was another factor for unity in Austria. The centuries-old support of the Catholic Church for the Habsburg dynasty also undercut nationalist movements among predominantly Catholic nationalities like the Slovaks, Croats, and above all, the Poles. In the newly unified Germany, by contrast, the religious division between the Protestant north and the Catholic south represented at least a potential force for disunity.

Fifth, the imperial army retained considerable prestige (although, lacking adequate funds, it had proved more dashing on the parade ground than on the battlefield, as defeats by the French in 1859 and the Prussians in 1866 had demonstrated). The army helped hold the monarchy together. German speakers dominated the officer corps, as they did the bureaucracy, holding 70 percent of military positions. Habsburg officers prided themselves on an esprit de corps (addressing each other by the familiar *Du* form, and not the more formal *Sie* that persisted in the German army). Soldiers drawn from the different nationalities continued to serve loyally in the army, which rarely intervened in local strikes, in contrast to the situation in France, where the army was unpopular with workers. Francis Joseph, whose long rule was shaped by the fact that he had come to power as his monarchy seemed to be breaking apart, was as devoted to the army as it was to him.

Repression of Nationalism in the Habsburg Empire

In the 1850s and 1860s, nationalism among the ethnic minorities remained limited to a relatively small number of intellectuals and people from the liberal professions, particularly Poles and Hungarians. As a Czech nationalist put it at a meeting of writers in Prague, "If the ceiling were to fall on us now, that would be the end of the national movement." Most nationalists at first aimed at a cultural and linguistic revival.

The Habsburg monarchy feared that demands for autonomy, or even outright independence, would pull the empire apart. Nationalism, which had frequently been tied to political liberalism, could also challenge the empire's authoritarian structure. The success of German and Italian nationalism also threatened the empire's territorial integrity by raising the possibility that the very small Italian and, above all, the German-speaking parts of the empire might prefer inclusion in Italy or Germany, respectively.

Alexander von Bach

Furthermore, Hungarians, the second-largest ethnic group within the empire, demanded political influence commensurate with the size of the Magyar territorial domains.

After the mid-century revolutions, the Habsburg monarchy, like the German states and France, continued an unrelenting repression of liberal and national movements. Beginning with Francis Joseph's accession to the Habsburg throne, the monarchy entered a period of "neo-absolutism," codified in the "Patent" of December 1851. Alexander von Bach (1813–1893), the minister of the interior (and essentially prime minister without the title), put some of the most potent tools of the state to work, including a hierarchy of officials and police sent out from Vienna into the imperial provinces. The nobles, some of whom resented the abrogation of peasant obligations after 1848, in general welcomed the restoration of Habsburg authoritarianism. But they also had lost some of their regional privileges and prerogatives to the state.

In 1855, Bach signed a Concordat with the Catholic Church, restoring many of its privileges and extending ecclesiastical authority, including the right of prelates to judge the clergy. As in France, the Church made a comeback. The monarchy eliminated civil marriage and restored the Church's *de facto* control over education. Protestants were not allowed to teach in Catholic schools, and new restrictions limited the right of Jews to acquire property. A contemporary cynically described the Bach system: "The administration was run by a standing army of soldiers, a kneeling one of those praying in church to be acceptable to the government, and a crawling one of informers."

Political Crisis and Foreign Policy Disasters

In the wake of the defeat of Austrian forces in Italy and amid mounting hostility between Germans and non-Germans and the growing unpopularity of neo-absolutism, in August 1859 Francis Joseph dismissed Bach as the head of government. He then promulgated a new constitution, the October Diploma of 1860, which reestablished a form of conservative federalism. The provincial assemblies received new authority, placating the nobles. Nonetheless, the October Diploma did not satisfy the Hungarian aristocrats, who lacked the influence and political role enjoyed by German speakers who had benefited from the Bach system.

Anton von Schmerling (1805–1893), minister of the interior, drafted the February Patent of 1861, a constitution that established a bicameral parliament in which all the empire's nationalities were to be represented. Yet the number of non-German representatives, as elected by the diets of the respective crown lands, would not equal those of the Germans, as electoral restrictions favored urban elites. Magyars, Croats, and Italians refused to participate in the first election, and Schmerling dissolved the regional parliaments. The February Patent perpetuated the most salient elements of Bach's neo-absolutism, placing virtually no constitutional limitations on the emperor's power. Francis Joseph even suspended the constitution in 1865.

While Bach's neo-absolutism made internal enemies, foreign policy failures seriously undermined the monarchy's international position. The Habsburg monarchy's status as a power in European affairs declined as relations with Russia and Prussia deteriorated. In 1863, Schmerling expressed sympathy for the Poles in their struggle against Russia (in contrast to Bismarck's response, as we have seen). This pleased the Poles within the Habsburg Empire but angered Tsar Alexander II. When Francis Joseph went to war with Prussia in 1866, he could not look for support from the tsar, or from the British or French, who resented the fact that Austria had joined Prussia against Denmark two years earlier.

Prussia's victory over Austria cast doubt on the efficiency of Bach's neo-absolutism and encouraged the other preeminent nationalities—particularly the Magyars, but also the Croats and Poles—to demand a greater share of political power, since the monarchy seemed to be floundering under the domination of German speakers. Humiliated twice in seven years on the field of battle, some of Francis Joseph's subjects blamed the authoritarian structure of neo-absolutism for the defeat. Liberals called for the implementation of constitutional government.

Creation of the Dual Monarchy

The empire's military defeats heightened Magyar demands for more power. Fearing the possible alliance of German liberals with the Magyars, Francis Joseph in 1865, a year before the defeat at the hands of Prussia, met the Magyar demand for the reincorporation of Transylvania into Hungary. He had already asked Ferenc Deák (1803–1876) to propose a solution that would reconcile Magyar demands with imperial power. Deák, a wealthy Magyar noble and lawyer, believed that Hungary's identity as a nation depended on the continued existence of the Habsburg monarchy. The emperor realized that as long as the Magyars remained dissatisfied and uncooperative, he could not contemplate a war of revenge against Prussia.

The Compromise (*Ausgleich*) of 1867 created the Dual Monarchy of Austria-Hungary. The Hungarian Parliament proclaimed Francis Joseph constitutional king of Hungary, as well as emperor of Austria. The bureaucracy in Vienna would continue to carry out matters of finance, foreign policy, and defense. Hungarian now became the language of administration in Hungary, and the Magyar domains henceforth had their own constitution, parliament, and bureaucracy. The halves of the Dual Monarchy would negotiate economic tariffs every ten years. The parliaments of Austria and Hungary elected representatives to the Imperial Assembly, or Delegation.

The *Ausgleich* left intact the dominance of German speakers in Austria and of Magyars in Hungary. While in principle recognizing the equality of all nationalities, the new constitution nonetheless maintained the disproportionate advantage enjoyed by Austria's Germans in the Austrian Imperial Council (Reichsrat) in Vienna. The emperor routinely appointed Germans to important ministries, and he could easily circumvent parliamentary opposition by ruling by decree when parliament was not in session, or by refusing to sign any piece of legislation he did not like.

The Hungarian Constitution of 1867 allowed the Magyar nobles to hold sway in the Hungarian Parliament, since the emperor's powers as king of Hungary were now more limited. Hungarian ministers were not responsible to Francis Joseph, but rather to the Hungarian Parliament's lower house, which was elected by leading Magyar property owners. Thus the *Ausgleich* was a victory for Hungarian liberalism. The Nationality Law of 1868 gave the peoples of each nationality the right to their own language in schools, church, and in government offices, but it did not recognize any separate political ethnic identity. The Croats and the South Slavs particularly resented the settlement. Growing tensions were reflected by the claim of one of the Austrian architects of the *Ausgleich* that "the Slavs are not fit to govern; they must be ruled." Many Serbs increasingly identified with Russia, which saw itself as the protector of all Slavs.

Ethnic Tensions and Nationalist Movements in the Dual Monarchy

In Austria-Hungary, ethnic tensions generated continued political division, stemming principally from Hungarian resentment of Austrian preeminence within the Dual Monarchy and the demands of subordinate nationalities. Beginning in the 1870s, Croatia, which was technically part of Hungary, sent five representatives to the sixty-member imperial Delegation, while the Slovaks, Serbs, and other minorities were left out. The Hungarian government relentlessly carried on with a program of Magyarization, ranging from dissolving non-Magyar cultural societies to banning non-Magyar names for villages and streets. Hungarian remained the official language and the government refused to allow administrative or cultural autonomy of the other nationalities. To an extent, the Magyarization campaign in Hungary was a reaction by Hungarians to this growing Pan-Slavist movement, combined with Hungary's resentment of its junior status in the Dual Monarchy.

An image in a Pan-Slav journal published in Vienna, *Slavic Papers.*

Count Eduard von Taaffe (1833–1895), Austrian prime minister from 1879 to 1893, balanced off the competing interests of the varied nationalities. Czech nobles and intellectuals earlier in the century had worked toward a literary and linguistic revival, compiling and publishing Czech dictionaries and books of Czech grammar. Czech nationalists demanded recognition of the historic Kingdom of Bohemia. But opposition from German speakers in Bohemia, and from Magyars, who feared similar demands from minorities within Hungary, led Francis Joseph to refuse such recognition. While ignoring demands by Slovenes and other smaller national groups for concessions to their languages, Taaffe placated the Czechs, the third largest ethnic group, by declaring their language on an equal footing with German in the state administration in Bohemia and Moravia in 1880. He also encouraged Czech schools and established a university in Prague (1882). But intellectuals within the "Young Czech" movement wanted national independence. In 1893 Taaffe resigned over the issue of increasing the number of eligible voters in Austria. One of his successors would later resign after the government had to declare martial law when Czechs demonstrated against the withdrawal of an edict, following protests by German speakers, that ordered officials to know both German and Czech.

As movements of cultural nationalism grew, they almost inevitably added the goal of national independence. Since the Third Partition in 1795, Poles had been a subject people in the empires of Germany, Austria-Hungary, and Russia, where troops had crushed the Polish insurrection of 1863 (see Chapter 18). Polish nationalism revived during the 1880s, but the relatively favored position of Poles in Austrian Galicia (where they held sway over Ukrainians in eastern Galicia) and the dispersion of the Polish people in three empires reduced any immediate Polish threat to the Habsburgs.

The absorption in 1878 of Bosnia and Herzegovina into the Habsburg Empire added a large Serb, as well as Muslim, population at a time when the Pan-Slav movement was growing in Russia and the Balkans. This increased demands from South Slavs—principally Serbs, Croats, and some Slovenes—that they be allowed to form an integral third part of the monarchy. Serbia had been virtually independent within the Ottoman Empire since 1828, when a Serb official who had put down a Serb insurrection was named hereditary prince of Serbia. Now, with Serbia's independence formalized in 1878, many Serbs in Austria-Hungary wanted to be attached to Serbia.

Hungarians demanded that their language be put on an equal footing with German in the army. At the turn of the century, Emperor Francis Joseph threatened to dissolve Hungary's parliament and to declare universal suffrage, believing that giving in to Hungarian demands would have meant the end of the Dual Monarchy. Relations between the aging Habsburg emperor and the Hungarian Parliament deteriorated, just as the Balkan Wars (1912–1913; see Chapter 22) and rampant South Slav nationalism soured relations between the Austro-Hungarian Empire and Russia. A visitor to the lower house of the Austrian Parliament in March 1914 recalled in amazement: "About a score of men, all decently clad, were seated or standing, each at his little desk. Some made an infernal noise violently opening and shutting the lids of these desks. Others emitted a blaring sound from little toy trumpets; others strummed Jew's harps; still others beat snare drums. . . . The sum of uproar thus produced was so infernal that it completely drowned the voice of a man who was evidently talking from his seat in another part of the house, for one could see his lips moving, and the veins in his temple swelling. Bedlam let loose! That was the impression on the whole."

CONCLUSION

The unification of Italy and that of Germany had both largely been effected by the expansion of the most powerful of the states that would become part of the unified state that resulted. Yet the two cases were different, despite appearances. Camillo di Cavour first had transformed Piedmont-Sardinia into a liberal monarchy through reforms, before achieving the unification of Italy. Liberal Italy then struggled from one political crisis to the next, despite reforms, its expanding electoral franchise—which more than doubled in 1912—arguably adding even more divisions to those provided by the gap between north and south. The advent of Giovanni Giolitti as premier in 1903 stabilized Italian politics. At the same time, socialists, growing in strength, opposed the liberal regime from the left, while nationalists attacked from the right.

Whereas Cavour had achieved Italian unification through liberal political means, Otto von Bismarck had harnessed economic liberalism to the goals of conservative political nationalism in achieving the unification of Germany. Liberals had relatively little influence in unified Germany. Although having universal male suffrage, Germany remained dominated by reactionary monarchs supported by reactionary Junkers, its Reichstag almost powerless against autocracy, despite the growth of a mass socialist party.

In the wake of the Revolutions of 1848, nationalism had proven itself a major force for unification in both Germany and Italy. In the Habsburg lands, in sharp contrast, nationalism was a force that came to challenge the very existence of the empire. In the age of militant nationalism, ethnic tensions within the Austro-Hungarian Empire would become those of Europe. In contrast, each of Europe's three other powers had been politically unified for centuries. Of the three, Britain and Russia had had no revolution in 1848. In contrast, France, the third, emerged from the tumultuous period with an authoritarian empire. In the next chapter, we will consider Britain, Russia, and France during the great period of change, 1850–1914.

CHAPTER 18

THE DOMINANT POWERS IN THE AGE OF LIBERALISM: PARLIAMENTARY BRITAIN, TSARIST RUSSIA, AND REPUBLICAN FRANCE

The Crystal Palace, a vast structure built of glass and iron in London's Hyde Park, housed the Exposition of 1851, the first world's fair. It stood 1,848 feet long, 408 feet across, and 66 feet high, and included a million square feet of glass, 3,300 columns, and 2,300 girders, all of identical size so they could be prefabricated. Gaslight provided illumination, and, for the first time, public toilets were installed for the convenience of visitors. The machinery on exhibit, above all, captured the attention and imagination of observers, including Queen Victoria herself. To the British subjects of Queen Victoria, the Great Exposition of 1851 represented the ascendancy of the British constitution, free trade and manufacturing, and Christianity.

Great Britain was the quintessential liberal state. Britain's long tradition of constitutional monarchy, with the remaining authority of the monarch more than balanced by Parliament, reflected its liberalism and economic prosperity. There had been no revolution in 1848 in Europe's most liberal

The Crystal Palace, symbol of the new industrial age.

nation. In the parliamentary constitutional monarchy, reform in 1867 expanded the number of those males eligible to vote.

Besides Britain, the other dominant powers during the age of liberalism were France, which was more slowly entering the industrial age, and Russia, which despite some significant reforms remained an autocracy antithetical to liberalism. France during the period 1852–1870 was a highly centralized empire, with Emperor Napoleon III determined to bring economic progress through the strong involvement of the state. Napoleon III implemented universal male suffrage in the first year of his reign. Following a disastrous war against Prussia (1870–1871), the empire fell, replaced by the Third Republic, another liberal regime in which executive authority was left weak, in this case out of fear that yet another Napoleon might emerge.

In contrast, Russia remained an autocracy, a state in which the absolute authority of the tsar was limited only by bureaucratic inefficiency and the impossibility of reaching into every corner of the vast empire. Russian nobles dominated the peasant masses, and unlike Britain and France, Russia had no representative political system and only a tiny middle class, despite economic growth. Tsar Alexander II shocked many of his own nobles by emancipating the serfs in 1861. But unlike the political reforms enacted in Britain and France, the tsar's reforms did not significantly alter the autocratic nature of the Russian Empire. Yet Russia, too, was transformed by new ideas and increasingly courageous opponents of autocratic authority. And, like France, imperial Russia also had to worry about the consequences of a unified Germany.

Victorian Britain

In 1840, young Queen Victoria (1819–1901) married the German Prince Albert (1819–1861) of Saxe-Coburg-Gotha. They were happily married, although she described sex as "giving way to the baser passions." She warned one of her daughters who was about to be married that a bride was "like a lamb led to the slaughter," and that there would be times when she would simply have to submit to her husband's urges and "think of England." Victoria bore children only because she thought it part of her duties as queen. She raised her children with little visible affection, as if managing a business from afar. Yet the queen projected a maternal image both in Britain and in the colonies over which she also ruled.

Albert's tendency to be narrow-minded, socially awkward, and tactless irritated cabinet ministers and other highly placed people. He hovered about the government, dashing off letters and memoranda when the mood struck him, meddling when he could. Although Victoria made clear from the beginning that she would serve as a queen without a king, her devotion to Albert sparked some anti-German feeling in Britain.

Prince Albert organized the Great Exposition of 1851 in London. In his opening prayers, the Anglican archbishop made the connection between Britain's prosperity and the era of relative peace that had prevailed since the end of the Napoleonic Wars in 1815. More than this, Great Britain seemed special. The historian Thomas Macaulay wrote in the wake of the Revolutions of 1848 on the continent: "All around us the world is convulsed by the agonies of the great nations. . . . Meanwhile, in our island, the course of government has never been for a day interrupted. We have order in the midst of anarchy."

At the Great Exposition of 1851, more than 6 million visitors—most from Britain but a good many from the continent and beyond—could choose among more than 100,000 exhibits (half from Britain and its colonies) put forward by 14,000 exhibitors. The exhibits were categorized into raw materials, machinery, manufactured goods, and fine arts, and ranged from useful household items to huge guns exhibited by the Prussian industrialist Krupp. These seemed somewhat out of place in a venue where many assured themselves that science and industry offered hope for continued peace in Europe.

The Great Exposition celebrated the industrial age, Britain's primacy in manufacturing, and the "working bees of the world's hive." Its catalogue intoned, "The progress of the human race . . . we are carrying out the will of the great and blessed God." Most of the visitors to the Great Exposition, ranging from the wealthy and famous to the poor folk paying just one shilling to enter, arrived by railroad.

When Albert died of typhoid in 1861 at age forty-two, Victoria was devastated. She retreated into lonely bereavement and isolation, ignoring most public duties. Only gradually did Victoria reemerge to provide a focal point for a nation in the midst of a great transformation during the second half of the century.

Victoria knew virtually nothing about the lives of her subjects and instinctively disapproved of factory reforms and increased opportunity of education for the lower classes (fearing that it would lead them to want to raise their station in life). But the queen remained the personification of the "respectability" that gave her name to the Victorian age. "Respectability"—inculcated by education and contemporary literature—centered on the family and strict rules about public comportment. But it meant different things to families of different strata: three servants for a comfortable middle-class family, a parlor off the kitchen for breakfast for a lower-middle-class family, and avoiding a pauper's funeral for a lower-class family.

The Victorian Consensus

"Victorian," a term first used in 1851, the year of the Great Exposition, evokes a sense of the contentment and confidence that middle-class Britons enjoyed. The Victorian consensus was formed around the capitalist entrepreneurial ethic, emphasizing self-reliance and faith in progress. In the Victorian entrepreneurial ideal, the individual demonstrated his moral worth through hard work, in contrast to the evils of the old system of patronage. Competition would determine those who were fit to rule, not aristocratic monopoly or unearned privilege, and not working-class demands for a greater share in the prosperity of the nation that middle-class Britons believed their hard work had created.

In 1859, the belief in the virtues of rugged individualism received a boost from the publication of *On the Origin of Species* by Charles Darwin (1809–1882). Darwin, the son of a domineering father, overcame chronic anxiety, self-doubt, and severe depression to undertake determined, systematic research and analysis on the evolution of living organisms. His bold book argued that some animal species survived and evolved by virtue of being better adapted to existing conditions, while others disappeared because they were less "fit." By implication, Darwin's work seemed to suggest that the state should stand back and let individuals alone to compete on the playing field of life. This was more good news for many confident Victorians, but not for churchmen, for Darwin's book taught that mankind evolved from other animal forms over millions of years, thus challenging the Bible's description of God having created the world in seven days. Darwin's research and analysis were a major event in the battle between science and religion in nineteenth-century Europe.

Religious images and references permeated Victorian social and political discourse. Entrepreneurs believed that they were doing God's work by becoming successful and rich. Many Victorians insisted that the pervasive influence of religion more than prosperity explained the apparent social harmony of their age. Thus, many Britons were surprised and even shocked by the

A contemporary impression of Darwin looking at human ancestry.

results of a government survey of every church in England and Wales on a Sunday morning in 1851. Out of a population of almost 18 million people, only slightly more than 7.2 million had attended church. Moreover, if everybody in England and Wales had decided to attend church, only 58 percent of the population and only 30 percent of Londoners could be accommodated. Between 1841 and 1876, the Anglicans built 1,727 new churches and restored more than 7,000 old ones; among their rivals, Congregationalists and Catholics doubled the number of their churches, and Baptists multiplied their churches by five.

The Church of England, closely identified with the British elite, remained a target for liberal reformers. Parliament had repealed the Corporation and Test Acts in 1828, eliminating two significant discriminatory laws that had kept Dissenters (non-Anglican Protestants) who refused to take communion in the Anglican Church from holding office. Parliamentary decrees in 1854 and 1856 allowed non-Anglicans to attend Cambridge and Oxford Universities. Catholics, most of whom were Irish immigrants—in addition to a small number of nobles whose families had converted to Catholicism—still faced popular suspicion, however, reflecting the deep roots of anti-Catholicism in British national identity.

Many middle-class Victorians wanted to make the lower classes more "moral." Congregationalist and Baptist evangelicals (as well as Methodists) won converts among the lower classes, perhaps because leaders of these churches demonstrated far more interest in the conditions of the poor than did the Church of England. Temperance movements proliferated in a wave of concern about lower-class drunkenness—one-third of all arrests were for drunk and disorderly conduct. The Charity Organization Society, founded in 1869, promoted charitable giving to those who steered clear of drink. And in 1875, the Salvation Army began its work, offering assistance to those who would participate in religious revival services.

The Crimean War

In 1854, Britain found itself involved in a major war that ended the long peace that had lasted almost without interruption since Napoleon's defeat in 1815. (Indeed the period is sometimes known as the Pax Britannia, in part because Britain's naval domination helped discourage conflict.) Britain entered the Crimean War (1853–1856) to support the Turks against Russia, which had intervened in 1841 against Mehmet Ali, the governor of Egypt (see Chapter 16). In 1853, Russian forces occupied the Ottoman Danubian principalities of Moldavia and Wallachia (see Map 18.1) to solidify Russia's position in the Balkans.

The Russian Empire had since the late eighteenth century sought control over the Straits of Constantinople, which divide Europe from Asia and could provide the Russian navy with access to the Aegean and Mediterranean Seas. Such ambitions inevitably brought conflict with the Ottoman Empire, which had controlled virtually the entire Balkan region until the early nineteenth century.

Following defeat after the Greek revolt in the 1820s, Ottoman rulers had undertaken a series of major reforms of the army (after having replaced the janissary corps—the Turkish sultan's militia that had originally been formed of Christians who converted to Islam, slaves, and members of other nationalities—with a more European army in 1826) and

MAP 18.1 THE CRIMEAN WAR, 1853–1856   Russian, British-French-Piedmontese, and Austrian troop movements involved in this war between the great powers.

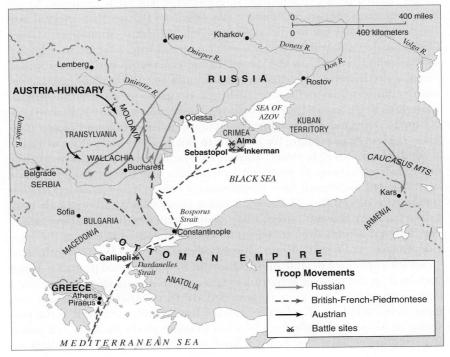

imperial administration. Sultan Mahmud II (ruled 1808–1839) had reorganized the treasury and ordered a census of the empire in 1831. Mahmud II's successors decreed further reforms during the period known as Tanzimat—the "Reorganization"—that lasted from 1839 to 1878. By the Rose Chamber (Gulhane) Decree of 1839, the sultan guaranteed the life and property of all Ottoman subjects and their equality before law, while initiating military conscription and a more organized system of taxation. Other changes followed: the establishment of penal and commercial codes, the reform of justice, and the implementation of more central government control over regions, reducing the autonomous power of the governors through the creation of a more modern bureaucracy. Such reforms pleased the governments of Britain and France, in part because Ottoman markets were now more open to foreign trade, but also because these governments viewed the stability of the Ottoman Empire as necessary to tempering Russian dreams of further expansion toward Constantinople and the Bosporus and Dardanelles straits.

A century earlier, perhaps as much as 80 percent of the population of the Ottoman Empire in Europe had been Christian. Each religion had the right to worship freely, and non-Muslims had access to Islamic courts. Christians and Muslims got along for the most part very well. The structure of the empire had for centuries encouraged the conversion of Christians to Islam, because Christians were considered second-class subjects and faced a heavier tax burden then did Muslims. Intermarriage was fairly frequent. In the late eighteenth century, the sultans had begun to tighten their control over the various religions in the empire. Each religious community—Greek Orthodox, Jewish, and Armenian—was organized into what became known as the "millet" system. In the middle of the nineteenth century, the sultan brought the hierarchy of Muslim religious and cultural leaders (the *ulema*) under administrative control. In addition, stories of persecution of Muslim minorities in Russia and suspicion of the Western powers toward Islam contributed to the gradual emergence of Islamism in the Ottoman Empire. Religious leaders began calling for a return to the fundamental values of Islam.

At the same time, however, Turkish economic development brought the emergence of a group of prosperous merchants who turned away from and even rejected the organization of communities along religious lines. Officials (*memurs*) replaced the old Ottoman ruling class, which had originally been drawn from the servants of the sultan's household, who had held positions in the imperial administration and army. The Ottoman ministries of the interior, finance, and foreign affairs, among others, reflected Western influence.

Yet the continued decline of the Ottoman Empire seemed probable. Egypt appeared on the verge of achieving independence. Russia stood poised like a vulture to profit from its once-powerful rival's weakness, a situation that came to be called the "Eastern Question." Russia presented itself as the protector of Slavic and Orthodox Christian interests in the Balkans, encouraging agitation against the Turks. Christian minorities within the Ottoman

Empire in the Balkans began to exert nationalist claims, dreaming of their own independent states. This challenged the Islamic character that had existed for centuries as an essential part of the empire.

With interests in Afghanistan, Britain was ill disposed to the expansion of Russian influence. Increased British trade with the Ottoman Empire had become another factor in British support for the Turks. Napoleon III of France, eager for a military victory to solidify support for his regime, also stood ready to stop Russian expansion by supporting the Ottoman Empire. The French emperor saw himself as the protector of the Catholic Holy Places of Judea, which were under Ottoman authority. To placate Catholic supporters, Napoleon III demanded at least Catholic equality with the Orthodox religion in Jerusalem's Church of the Holy Sepulcher. This Russia refused, demanding the right to veto any changes in the status not only of the Holy Places but also in the situation of the entire Ottoman Christian population.

The Ottoman Empire declared war on Russia in October 1853. Russian Tsar Nicholas I's fleet defeated the Ottoman fleet in the Black Sea, setting fire to the sultan's wooden ships with incendiary shells. But the tsar's confidence that Britain and France would soon quarrel because of conflicting interests proved ill founded. With British public opinion eager for the flag to be shown even after the withdrawal of Russian troops from Moldavia and Wallachia, the British Royal Navy sailed into the Black Sea. Not to be outdone, Napoleon III, too, sent warships.

Britain and France declared war on Russia in March 1854. British and French forces first moved against the Russian port of Sebastopol on the peninsula of Crimea on the edge of the Black Sea. Invulnerable to sea attack, Sebastopol could only be stormed from land. The rusty invading armies lay siege to Sebastopol. The French army seemed better trained, as well as better fed and supplied than that of the British. The senior British commander, a veteran of Waterloo forty years earlier, persisted in referring to the Russians as "the French." Most British officers owed their commissions to the fact that they were aristocrats, not because of particular competence. One commander spent each night on his private yacht anchored offshore, dining on meals prepared by a French chef while his men shivered in the wind and mud of the Crimean winter and ate ghastly rations.

Far more men died (about 600,000) of disease than in battle, although Alfred Tennyson (1809–1892), Britain's poet laureate, helped make famous the "Charge of the Light Brigade," in which British cavalry rode into "jaws of death" at Balaklava. The first war correspondents sent dispatches by telegraph to eager readers in Britain and France, where interest in the distant siege dramatically increased newspaper circulation.

Into this maelstrom ventured Florence Nightingale (1820–1910). The daughter of a prosperous family, she had shocked her parents by becoming a nurse, an occupation that had a reputation as providing a refuge for "disorderly" women. Nightingale volunteered for service in a Constantinople hospital after hearing of the appalling conditions endured by the

(*Left*) The charge of the Light Brigade at Balaklava. (*Right*) Florence Nightingale.

wounded and those sick with cholera and dysentery. She bombarded the government with highly detailed information on what was wrong and what was needed. Raising funds through private contributions, she succeeded in improving conditions in the hospital. Nightingale had to overcome the conviction of officers that she would "spoil the brutes," that is, the sick and wounded enlisted men, as well as overcoming prejudices against a woman making forceful demands on the government. The government several years later enacted a series of reforms to improve food and health care for the men in its army. In part a result of Florence Nightingale's highly publicized work throughout the remainder of her career, nursing emerged as a more respected profession.

The Crimean War ground to a halt after Sebastopol finally capitulated in September 1855. The Peace of Paris (March 1856) guaranteed the autonomy of the Danubian principalities of Moldavia and Wallachia (which became independent Romania in 1878), the independence of Turkey, and the neutrality of the Black Sea. The Crimean War left little doubt that Victorian Britain remained Europe's strongest power.

The Liberal Era of Victorian Politics

Britain entered a period of relative social harmony. The repeal of the Corn Laws in 1846 convinced many workers that they could place their trust in political reform, which is one reason there was no revolution in Britain in 1848 (see Chapter 16). Middle-class reformers had broadened their appeal to include the most prosperous segments of the working class. Most British workers seemed to accept the belief that hard work and savings would inevitably be rewarded. Most Victorians of all social classes increasingly felt themselves part of a nation with which they could identify.

British workers, including many union members, joined "friendly societies," or as they were increasingly called, "self-help associations." Membership in such groups rose from less than a million in 1815 to 3 million in 1849 and 4 million in 1872, four times that of unions. They provided members with minimal assistance in times of unemployment or illness and a decent burial. Preaching individual self-help and respectability, such organizations did not offer the socialist vision common among workers in France, Belgium, or the Rhineland. They helped inculcate a sense of what the British called "respectability," which discouraged militancy.

Like the friendly societies, Britain's "new model unions" also embodied the concept of self-help. Members of these unions first and foremost saw their organizations as representing craftsmen and skilled workers of specific crafts, such as carpenters and printers from the "aristocracy of labor" who could afford dues. They constituted about 15 percent of the working class, standing apart from the mass of unskilled laborers. Some of them taught in Sunday schools, working men's colleges, reading rooms, and improvement societies. Even when local unions within a single trade joined to form national organizations, there was no talk of revolution or even of eventually restructuring British economic, social, and political life. Strikers in the 1860s were increasingly willing to accept arbitration boards and to compromise to achieve limited goals.

Benefiting from the 1832 enfranchisement of more middle-class men, the Whigs governed Britain for most of the 1850s and 1860s. Henry John Temple (1784–1865), the Viscount Palmerston, who began his political career as a Conservative, led the Whigs. The notorious philandering of the shrewd and feisty "Lord Cupid," as he was known to his detractors, stood out in an age of public prudishness. Palmerston outraged Queen Victoria by trying to seduce one of her ladies-in-waiting in Windsor Castle.

Palmerston held together a coalition of Whigs who were determined to uphold laissez-faire economic policies. Dissenters, Catholics, and liberal Anglicans wanted the Anglican Church to lose its status as the Established Church of England. Gradually these Whigs began to be referred to as the Liberal Party.

Palmerston's bellicose saber-rattling won him personal popularity. Crowds cheered when he ordered the blockade of the Greek port of Piraeus in 1850 to enforce claims against the Greek government by Don Pacifico, a British-born Portuguese Jew whose house an Athens mob had destroyed. Palmerston boastfully compared the might of classical Rome and Victorian Britain, which had remained one of the "protecting powers" of Greece since its independence in 1832. Following the overthrow of King Otto in 1854, Britain, France, Bavaria, and Russia selected a Danish prince to rule Greece as King George I, while placating Greek nationalists by awarding one of the Ionian islands to Greece.

After glorying in Britain's victory in the Crimean War, Palmerston then lurched into a short war against China in 1857, after the Chinese government seized a pirate ship that had formerly been registered under the British flag. Rebuffed by a majority in Commons and opposed by pacifist political radicals outside of Parliament, Palmerston refused to resign and called for a general election. Basing his campaign on an appeal to patriotism, he won the day.

William Gladstone (1809–1898) then became the leader of the Liberal Party. Gladstone was the son of a wealthy and unscrupulous merchant who had made a fortune in trade with India and the West Indies. The young Gladstone was deeply religious and wore his moral vision of the world on his sleeve, going out into the night to try to convince prostitutes to abandon their trade. Gladstone sought to impose his own self-discipline and sense of Victorian Christianity on the nation. During his early years in government, he worked to assure laissez-faire economic policies, campaigning for the abolition of even the very modest income tax.

As chancellor of the exchequer, Gladstone had waged war against extravagance and waste in government. In contrast to his Conservative rivals, he opposed colonization as being too expensive. Queen Victoria loathed Gladstone, blaming him for almost every domestic and international problem. She resented his *de facto* campaign to reduce the already limited role of the monarchy in the constitutional government of Britain. Having supported the repeal of the Corn Laws in 1846, he wanted to make the Liberals the party of reform.

Robert Peel had split the Conservatives by supporting the repeal of the Corn Laws in 1846. After Peel's death in 1850, Benjamin Disraeli

(*Left*) William Gladstone, Liberal prime minister. (*Right*) Benjamin Disraeli.

(1804–1881) became the leader of the Conservatives and Gladstone's great rival. A Jew who had been baptized into the Anglican Church, Disraeli seemed an unlikely leader of a party dominated by landed wealth. But he was an energetic, skilled politician and an impressive orator who had the good sense to realize that further Conservative attempts to revive economic protectionism were doomed. Unlike Gladstone, Disraeli got along famously with the queen, whom he flattered on every possible occasion. Victoria depended upon Disraeli for advice much as she had on Albert. (As Disraeli lay dying, the queen wrote to ask if she might visit the Conservative leader. "It is better not," Disraeli replied. "She'd only ask me to take a message to Albert.")

The Reform Bill of 1867

Since 1832, the majority of British subjects had regarded further political reform as a certainty. A growing number of middle-class voters, hoping to end disproportionate aristocratic influence in British political life, supported some expansion of suffrage. Workers wanted universal male suffrage. As for Queen Victoria, she insisted that she "cannot and will not be the queen of a democratic monarchy." John Bright (1811–1889), who represented Manchester and then Birmingham in the House of Commons, campaigned for electoral reform. In 1866, the National Reform Union, whose membership was overwhelmingly middle class, and the Reform League, which many craftsmen joined, allied with Bright's parliamentary radicals. Their goal was household suffrage, that is, the right of the adult male head of family to vote.

Gladstone, typically, was convinced that political reform was not only expedient but also moral. "You cannot fight against the future," the Liberal leader taunted Conservatives in Parliament. "Time is on our side. The great social forces . . . are against you." But he wanted to let down the electoral drawbridge only long enough to let in artisans and skilled workers, the "aristocracy of labor," but not all males.

Conservatives feared that the enfranchisement of more people would add to the ranks of the Liberals and eventually lead to subsequent legislation that might weaken the political influence of wealthy landowners. The Liberal government proposed a bill to reduce the minimum amount of tax one had to pay to be eligible to vote both in the countryside and in towns, where the rate would be set lower. The proposed reform would still exclude ordinary workers and other poor people. However, the House of Lords rejected the bill because a majority of members opposed any change.

Disraeli, who had predicted that "pillage, incendiarism, and massacre" would follow universal male suffrage in Britain, now believed that electoral reform that maintained some exclusions was not only inevitable but that his Conservative Party could benefit from it. Disraeli took a "leap in the dark," proposing that the vote be given to each head of a household and that the minimum countryside tax requirement be further lowered. Under Conservative auspices, the Reform Bill of 1867 passed, like that of 1832. This doubled the ranks of voters but still left Britain short of universal male suffrage.

In France at the same time, every adult male could vote during the Second Empire, to be sure. But there Emperor Napoleon III cynically manipulated universal male suffrage by presenting government-sponsored candidates and utilizing that old Bonapartist tool, the plebiscite. The German Empire, too, had universal male suffrage, but the Reichstag (assembly) had little real authority. In Russia, there were no national elected bodies at all, and local assemblies (zemstvos) initiated in 1864 were elected by local electoral colleges but were dependent upon officials named by the tsar. In Italy, only a small percentage of adult males were eligible to vote, by virtue of their ownership of property. The reformed electoral system in Britain not only enfranchised many more voters, but gave them more influence, because the House of Commons exercised great authority in Britain's constitutional monarchy. Here, too, Britain seemed to lead the way in the gradual emergence of democratic politics.

Disraeli's Conservatives, however, failed to woo many of the new voters. The Liberals won a large majority in Parliament, boosted by support from workers who now could vote. The major goal of the Chartist campaign more than two decades earlier had been reached.

Another act of reform in 1884 added 2 million more voters to the rolls by enfranchising agricultural laborers. With women still excluded from the vote, the only adult males who could not vote were those without a fixed residence, sons living at home with their parents and not paying rent, and domestic servants. The Redistribution Act of 1885 disenfranchised some underpopulated districts while increasing representation of many urban areas. However, the establishment of single-member constituencies compensated Conservatives, balancing potential Liberal gains in urban areas.

Other Victorian Reforms

The Victorian consensus rested upon a strong belief that the "invisible hand" of the economy would generate economic growth. Many Victorians had believed the Poor Law of 1834 was self-defeating because it provided minimal resources to the poor for which they had not worked. But increasingly aware of the devastating poverty of millions of workers, most middle-class Victorians by mid-century had changed their minds about the role of government in society. Edwin Chadwick (1800–1890), a journalist and associate of Jeremy Bentham, had drafted the Poor Law. His *Report on the Sanitary Condition of the Laboring Population of Great Britain* (1842) served as an impassioned plea for government action after cholera had ravaged poor urban neighborhoods. Largely thanks to Chadwick's efforts, Parliament passed laws facilitating the inspection of rooming houses, where many poor workers resided. Thereafter, parliamentary commissions began to call upon experts to gather information and assess conditions of British life. The age of statistics had arrived.

Regulatory agencies began to spring up. In 1848, Parliament created the national General Board of Health. Chadwick's revelations about public health—or rather, the lack of it—encountered ferocious opposition from those who were against any government intervention as a matter of principle. "We prefer to take our chance on cholera and the rest than be bullied into health," groused *The Times*. Yet, by the time Chadwick was driven to resign from the General Board of Health in 1854, the right of the state to intervene in matters of health had been established. Parliamentary acts in the 1860s extended regulations of working conditions in mines and in factories with more than fifty employees and where women and children worked. The Public Health Act of 1866 gave local government more authority to assure a cleaner water supply. Five years later, state inspectors for the first time obtained legal access to workplaces. Parliament soon established health boards in towns and country districts, even if local business and political interests often combined to foil the efforts of reformers. Yet, reform leagues, such as the National Education League became part of British political life.

Victorious in elections following the passage of the Reform Act of 1867, the Liberals ended the purchase of army commissions, enacted land reform in Ireland, and the government recognized the legal existence of trade unions. When the Conservatives returned to power in 1874, they, too, sought to woo the allegiance of workers from the Liberals by getting Parliament to approve a number of reforms, including a law that forbade labor by

Street disinfectors in London, 1875.

uneducated children. Yet considerably more than altruism lay behind a shift in middle-class attitudes. Manufacturers also knew that demand for their products depended on workers having money to spend. In Great Britain, the "age of optimism" became the "age of improvement."

Queen Victoria once asked someone to define "bureaucracy," a term she did not know. "That, Madam," came the reply, "is something that they have in France." Yet the Victorian state expanded. In 1841, the British government— the least centralized of the major European powers—had employed 40,000 men and 3,000 women; by 1911, 271,000 men and 50,000 women worked for the state. The administration of the Poor Law itself served to strengthen the role of government in local affairs. Municipal councils took over the task of administering local government from the justices of the peace, who had served in such capacity since the sixteenth century. Municipalities were now responsible for education, as well as for health, housing, roads, and policing. Service in local government, once little more than another honor awarded a landed gentleman, now required the participation of paid officials.

With increased responsibilities, the British civil service became professionalized. The government administered competitive examinations on which appointment and promotion depended. However, these exams did not democratize entry into the civil service. Applicants who had attended one of the expensive, elite public schools (so called because they accepted students from all over Britain, provided their families could afford the steep tuition) had a far greater advantage on the examinations than those who had not.

As the role of the British state thus expanded considerably during the middle decades of the century, the era of laissez-faire liberalism came to a close. Speaking of her father, Gladstone's daughter remembered, "I was accustomed to hear him utter the word 'Government' in a tone that charted it with awe and made it part of my effective religion."

Mass Politics Come to Britain

Out of office following passage of the 1867 Reform Act, Benjamin Disraeli sought to accommodate Conservatives to the era of mass political life. Realizing that his party, long closely tied to the British landed elite and the Anglican Church, would have to outbid their Liberal rivals for votes, he created a modern national party organization. Disraeli made British nationalism and imperialism part of the Conservative Party platform, suggesting that the Liberals would weaken Britain. When the Turks and Russians began to quarrel over the Balkans, Disraeli supported the Turks, despite the massacre of about 10,000 to 15,000 Bulgarians in 1876 by Turkish troops. Gladstone, however, was horrified by the bloodbath and made a political issue of the Balkans. It was easy enough for him to do so: Britain had less to fear from the Ottoman Empire in decline than from an aggressively expansionist Russia.

The Conservative Party now reflected an important change in modern British political life. The traditional split between "city" and "country," which had characterized politics since the seventeenth century, had largely ended. The Conservatives now found new support among some of the wealthiest businessmen, who abandoned the Liberals. Furthermore, many aristocrats were themselves now actively involved in the management of banks and modern industries. The English business elite that had been formed during the first decades of Victoria's reign became as conservative as the aristocrats they emulated. A contemporary assessed this evolution when he wrote: "Our territorial nobles, our squires, our rural landlords great and small, have become commercial potentates; our merchant princes have become country gentlemen." Some wealthy businessmen deserted the Dissenters to join the Established Anglican Church. This new Conservative political culture, supported by a faithful minority of nationalist "Tory workers," survived the economic and social changes that were transforming Britain.

Gladstone himself embarked on whistle-stop "Midlothian" campaigns— so named for one of his first stops in 1879. His audiences were made up of anyone who wanted to come to the railroad station to hear him. This forced Conservatives even more to put aside their feelings that such appeals to ordinary people were vulgar, or too "American."

Yet the Conservative Party remained the party of great landed wealth. The law of primogeniture helped keep huge estates intact. Because of parliamentary districting, the countryside remained overrepresented in Parliament, again to the advantage of landed gentlemen. In 1871, about 1,200 people owned a quarter of the land of England, and the holdings of 7,000 families amounted to half of the country. Landed gentlemen dominated the House of Commons until 1885, the cabinet until 1893, and the aristocratic House of Lords well into the twentieth century.

Irish Home Rule

The Liberals continued to be faced with the problem of Ireland, which reflected the dilemmas of national identity in late nineteenth-century Europe. In 1868, William Gladstone had announced that the most pressing mission of his new government was to "pacify Ireland." A year later, the Liberal prime minister pushed through both houses of Parliament a bill that disestablished the Church of Ireland (which had become part of the United Church of England in 1800), since Ireland was 80 percent Catholic. This meant that the Episcopal Church in Ireland no longer received state support.

To many Irish, it seemed that only by owning land could Irish peasants reach any degree of prosperity. The Irish Land Act of 1870 provided tenants with compensation for improvements they had undertaken and protected them from being evicted from property without just cause. But English

Protestant landlords were not about to turn over land in Ireland to the peasants who rented from or worked for them. The fall in the price of agricultural commodities made it more difficult for tenant-farmers to meet their rent payments. In 1879, the Irish Land League, drawing on the remnants of the secret Irish Republican Brotherhood (known in Gaelic as the Fenians) and sworn to win independence, began to pressure Parliament for land reform.

Gladstone's determination to make Ireland his ongoing moral crusade met with opposition within his own Liberal Party, which depended on support from Whig landowners in Ireland to maintain a parliamentary majority. Charles Stewart Parnell (1846–1891), a Liberal Irish Protestant, began to build a small parliamentary coalition in favor of Home Rule, which meant the establishment of a separate Irish Parliament, but not outright independence. The Irish Catholic Church supported Home Rule. Parnell's program, however, fell short of the demands of the Land League, which wanted immediate and sweeping land reform, and the revived Irish Republican Brotherhood, which insisted on complete Irish independence.

During 1879–1882, Irish farmers undertook a "land war" of protest. Irish tenants and laborers began to shun farmers who took over the leases of peasants evicted for nonpayment of rent. A certain Captain Boycott, the agent of a large landowner, was one of the first targets; his name became synonymous with such a strategy. The British government replied with repression, suspending the writ of *habeas corpus* in Ireland in 1881. However, that same year, Gladstone also pushed through a bill (by threatening to dissolve Parliament) protecting any Irish tenant from eviction who could pay one year's back rent. Parnell was sent to prison for his violently anti-British speeches. Moreover, opposition to Home Rule mounted in Parliament among MPs who argued that concessions had encouraged violence. A year later, the British government ordered Parnell's release from prison, in the hope that he would help end disorder in Ireland in exchange for the future passage of another bill to help Irish tenants.

In 1882, Irish republicans hacked to death two British officials who had been walking in Phoenix Park in Dublin. The assassinations shocked the English public. In response to the murders, and to more than thirty other deaths in Ireland at the hands of Irish republicans, a Coercion Act facilitated the British government's repression of the republicans by eliminating some rights of those arrested. Five of those responsible for the Phoenix Park assassinations were arrested and hung.

Gladstone (who served as prime minister four different times) proposed Home Rule in 1886, but the issue divided the Liberal Party and the bill failed. Joseph Chamberlain (1836–1914) led the defection of the "Liberal Unionists" over Home Rule. Parnell fell into disgrace three years later when news broke of his affair with Kitty O'Shea, the wife of a Liberal Irish MP active in the campaign for Home Rule. Another bill failed in 1893, defeated in the House of Lords.

New Contours in British Political Life

Queen Victoria's longevity—she ruled the vast British Empire with dignity from 1837 until 1901—symbolized British social and political stability. She endeared herself to her people on the occasion of her silver jubilee in 1887 by wearing a simple bonnet (albeit one with diamonds) instead of her crown. The Prince of Wales inherited the throne as King Edward VII (ruled 1901–1910). Edward could not have been more different from his mother, with whom he constantly battled and whom he often embarrassed. Edward "the Caresser" indulged his extravagant tastes in beautiful women, prize horses, good food, fine wines, and gambling.

The Conservatives returned to power in 1895. Like their counterparts in France and Germany, the British Conservative Party became even more aggressively nationalist, imperialist, and resolutely antisocialist. The Liberal Unionists had allied with the Conservatives over Home Rule. In 1895, their leader Joseph Chamberlain joined the Conservative government as colonial secretary.

Frustrated by the Conservative government's refusal to initiate parliamentary bills of social reform and by employers' attempts to weaken the unions by hiring non-union labor, British trade unionism entered a more aggressive phase during the last two decades of the nineteenth century. The Trades Union Congress (created in 1868) had provided a forum for organized labor, although the financial resources of unions became even more depleted.

Now, a more militant "new unionism" was characterized by the organization of semiskilled workers, including many iron and steel factory workers. In 1887, for the first time since the last Chartist marches in London in 1848, English workers went into the streets in great numbers to protest, demonstrating against unemployment and the high cost of living. On November 13—"Black Monday"—store owners slammed their doors shut amid a "red fear" in central London, again the first since 1848. The police attacked crowds of workers, killing 2 and wounding about 100 protesters.

In 1889, following a victory by gas workers in a London strike that achieved the eight-hour workday, dockworkers struck for a minimum wage. They were led by Ben Tillett (1860–1943). Born in Bristol, Tillett had at the age of seven begun cutting slabs of clay in a brickyard, then ran away with Old Joe Barker's Circus as an acrobat, before joining the merchant marine and then the navy. Finding work as a dockyard laborer, he helped organize thousands of unskilled laborers in a massive strike. Australian workers sent funds that helped tide the strikers over. After five weeks, the dockworkers won a minimum wage and overtime pay. Tillett's dockworkers' union soon had 30,000 members.

But hundreds of thousands of casual laborers, including those living in London's teeming East End, still were not unionized, nor in friendly societies. For them the independence of the skilled worker remained only a

(*Left*) Ben Tillett, organizer of the Docker's Union. (*Right*) James Keir Hardie, founder of the Independent Labour Party.

dream. Strikes in 1897–1898 (including Britain's first national walkout, which ended in the workers' defeat) revealed the growing reach of the new unions.

The state went on the offensive against the unions. In 1901, in resolving a railway case in Wales, the Taff Vale decision of the House of Lords made unions and their officers legally responsible for losses sustained by companies during strikes. This encouraged the creation of the Labour Party. First organized in 1900 (taking its name in 1906), the Labour Party had its origins in the small Independent Labour Party, which had been founded in 1893 by MP James Keir Hardie (1856–1915). This rough-hewn Scottish miner had provoked the House of Commons by chiding members for sending a congratulatory message to the queen on the birth of a great-grandson instead of a message of condolence to the families of several hundred miners killed in an accident in a mine shaft in Wales. The Labour Party now vowed to represent workers in Parliament and specifically to bring about the repeal of the Taff Vale decision.

A split within the Liberal-Unionist-Conservative bloc brought ten years of Conservative government to an end. Some political leaders, including Joseph Chamberlain, campaigned for protective tariffs, believing that they would increase British prosperity by creating a large imperial market. Many Conservatives, including Prime Minister Arthur Balfour (1848–1930), believed that voters preferred traditional free trade policies, identified with lower food prices. Unable to resolve the split within his party, Balfour resigned in December 1905, and the Liberals swept to victory the following year. Promising to repeal the Taff Vale decision, they garnered many working-class votes. The Labour Party, which had managed to win only one seat in 1900, now sent twenty-nine MPs to the House of Commons. Under the Liberal government, Parliament reversed the Taff Vale decision with the Trade Disputes Act of 1906, which legalized picketing and relieved unions of the legal responsibility for financial losses caused by strikes.

In 1908, Herbert Asquith (1852–1928) became Liberal prime minister. Like the Conservatives, he supported British imperial causes. But the dynamic, ambitious, and charismatic Welshman David Lloyd George (1863–1945) was the rising star of the Liberals. A man of modest origins who preferred to speak his native Welsh than English, Lloyd George had come into the public eye for his opposition to the Boer War (see Chapter 21), although in general he supported the empire. While crusading against the Conservative Party, Lloyd George worked to continue the Gladstonian reformist tradition. He wanted to counter the drift of union members toward the Labour Party by bringing workers, middle-class men, and businessmen into an alliance that would support Liberal social and political reforms. The Liberal government established local boards to set minimum industrial wages, involving the British government in bargaining between employers and workers to an extent hitherto unseen.

In 1909, Lloyd George (who was chancellor of the exchequer) proposed a budget that called for increased public benefits to be partially funded by taxes on inheritance and on unearned income and uncultivated land. These "supertaxes" (which were in fact quite small) would fall on the richest families of the nation. He compared the costs of maintaining "a fully-equipped duke" to that of a new battleship, depicting the aristocratic families as parasitical leeches maintained at public expense.

In the Osborne judgment of 1909, the House of Lords had ruled in favor of a railway worker who had sued his union with the goal of keeping union funds from being used to support Labour candidates for the House of Commons or to pay them while they served. (MPs began to receive salaries several years later.) Like the Taff Vale case, the Osborne judgment struck a damaging blow against the unions. In a climate of social confrontation, the House of Lords then provocatively vetoed the 1909 budget, which it viewed as an attack on the wealthy, thus exercising a right that it had not used for decades. Asquith called the House of Lord's veto a "break with the constitution and a usurpation of the rights of the Commons." He dissolved Parliament, confident of winning the new elections.

The Liberals did indeed return to power early the next year with the help of Irish nationalists and the Labour Party. Asquith's Parliament Act of 1911 proposed to eliminate the right of the House of Lords to veto any financial bill. Many Britons viewed the passage of such a bill as a final blow to noble privilege. The act also specified that any bill that the House of Lords did not pass after it had been approved on three occasions by the House of Commons would become law if two years had passed since it had first been introduced in Parliament.

When Asquith threatened to ask King George V (who had succeeded to the throne in 1910) to create enough new peerages to pass the bill, the House of Lords, despite the opposition of intransigents, the so-called Die-hards, approved the Parliament Act in 1911. The House of Lords thus eliminated its own constitutional veto, completing the long revolution in British political life that had begun with the passage of the Reform Act of 1832, which had first reduced the disproportionate power of British nobles. The House of Lords then reversed the Osborne judgment.

In 1911, a walkout by seamen, stevedores, bargemen, and ship repairers spread rapidly in London, Manchester, and Liverpool. The prospect of a food shortage forced the government's hand. Through binding arbitration, the strikers won raises. A national rail strike ended in compromise settlements. When the Miners' Federation called the first general coal strike, more than 800,000 men went out, which left another 1.3 million without work. The miners gained a minimum wage, but when dockers failed to achieve their strike goals in 1912, Britain's largest wave of strikes to date ended in failure. That many strikes ended in defeat may have helped turn British workers further toward parliamentary reformism. In any case, collective bargaining had become commonplace in the 1890s, with conciliation and arbitration boards established in many localities.

Irish Home Rule, still a major political issue, now seemed almost inevitable. Irish politicians, peasants, and poets shared the burst of nationalist sentiment characteristic of the first decade of the twentieth century. The Gaelic League popularized Irish music and encouraged people to speak Gaelic, not English. The poet William Butler Yeats (1865–1939), who helped create a native Irish theater in Dublin, contributed to a literary nationalism that sometimes glossed over class differences among the Irish: "Parnell came down the road and said to a cheering man: / 'Ireland will get her freedom, and you shall still break stone.'" Such literature also tended to romanticize the Irish as peasants made virtuous by poverty and hard work. In the collection of short stories *Dubliners* (1912) by James Joyce (1882–1941), the countryside appears as an idyllic escape from the confusion of Ireland's rapidly growing, impoverished metropolis, which had once been his home.

If some Irish nationalists would accept nothing less than complete independence from Britain, others advocated Home Rule. Irish Protestants living in Ulster, who outnumbered Catholics there by two to one, opposed any measure of Home Rule, which they identified with Catholic "Rome Rule." In 1913, Ulster Protestants formed a paramilitary army of volunteers. At the same time, an Irish Republican Army added men and arms. Century-old wounds split open again, and Ireland seemed on the verge of civil war. In September 1914, Parliament passed a Home Rule Bill, despite the intransigent opposition of the House of Lords. But with Britain—and all the powers of Europe—going to war, the details were left for the uncertain future. Liberal Britain, too, was being swept into international events it could not control.

TSARIST RUSSIA

Autocratic Russia—an absolutist state based upon an alliance of the tsar and the nobles—in the nineteenth century presented a particularly sharp contrast with Great Britain, with its long tradition of parliamentary rule and commercial and manufacturing prosperity. Since the sixteenth century, the Russian tsars had slowly expanded their empire through the conquest of vast stretches of territories and peoples to the south and into Asia. Like the Austro-Hungarian Empire, the much larger Russian Empire was multinational. Ethnic Russians formed less than half of the population. Ethnic resistance to the empire and to the Orthodox Church—for example, from Polish Catholics—increasingly challenged Russian domination.

Since the brief and ill-fated Decembrist uprising of 1825 (see Chapter 15), Russia had seen no major reforms, except the emancipation of state-owned serfs in the 1840s. The structure of the state remained the same, with no institutional constraints on the tsar's authority. Yet liberal ideas from the West had begun to filter into Russia via intellectuals. Alienated from a society built upon serfdom, which legally bound most peasants to the land of their lords, some of them believed revolution inevitable. Moreover, serfdom not only was inhumane, it was also economically inefficient. This helped convince the tsar that only through reform and the emancipation of the serfs could Russia compete with the West.

Stirrings of Reform in Russia

Serfs lived in villages in which patriarchs served as intermediaries between the lords and the community and, like the gentry, administered harsh physical punishments to serfs who failed to obey. Only about 5 percent of the empire's population resided in towns. Russia had a very small middle class and a tiny group of intellectuals and educated commoners. The intelligentsia believed that only revolution could bring change.

Nicholas I (ruled 1825–1855), who had become tsar just after the Decembrist revolt of 1825, was obsessed with keeping Russia sealed off from Western ideas, which he blamed for the rebellion of military officers. The Revolutions of 1848 in Western and Central Europe increased the determination of the Russian autocracy to stifle internal dissent. The ministry of education oversaw a policy of tight censorship and repression by the fearsome Third Section, the political police. But the police found it impossible to seal off the colossal empire entirely. More than 2 million foreign books entered Russia just in the 1847–1849 period, most ending up in Saint Petersburg and Moscow.

In Eastern and eastern Central Europe, the Russian and Polish intelligentsia stood as separate social groups who felt responsible for leading the fight for social and political change and for national independence. Many were gentry who could survive well enough without a university position or government post. Part of an educated elite, they could afford to write, even if the public audience they reached was small indeed. Unlike their counterparts in Western countries, they were not absorbed into the liberal professions and maintained their identity as a group.

During the 1830s and 1840s, some gentry were overwhelmed with guilt that they were well off while the masses suffered. Alexander Pushkin (1799–1837), whose mother exiled two serfs to Siberia with a nod of her head after they failed to bow as she passed by, attacked serfdom in his short stories. Steeped in a variety of intellectual currents, the intelligentsia brooded in small groups, or "circles," in Saint Petersburg and in Moscow over how Russia might emerge from autocracy and relative backwardness.

Several important writers emerged from this underground hotbed of intellectual and creative ferment. Fyodor Dostoyevsky (1821–1881), who adhered to populism and the Pan-Slavist cause, presented brilliant psychological depictions of his characters. These included disturbing portraits of troubled individuals like himself whose actions reflected not rationality but aberration, even madness, in such novels as *Crime and Punishment* (1866) and *The Brothers Karamazov* (1879–1880). Sentenced to death by the authorities in 1849 for participation in a reading circle that discussed socialism, he was hauled out of jail early one morning, blindfolded, placed before a firing squad, and then, after a cruelly staged mock execution that understandably shattered his nerves, sent to prison in Siberia. He described his own suffering, but also that of Russian society, in the crucial years following defeat in the Crimean War. Count Leo Tolstoy (1828–1910), another great Russian realist writer, was a wealthy landowner who served in the Crimean War. He emerged as a moral voice against violence. His monumental *War and Peace* (1869) depicts the struggle between his country and the West.

Pyotr Chaadayev's *Philosophical Letters* slipped by the censors in 1836. Chaadayev (1794–1856) presented a thinly veiled condemnation of Russia's cultural history. Officials declared him to be mad, and the police hounded him for the rest of his life. He pessimistically provoked heated discussion by suggesting that cultural backwardness would keep Russia from joining the ranks of civilized nations. *Philosophical Letters* opened the debate between "Westernizers"—those Russian intellectuals who, like Tsar Peter the Great in the seventeenth century, looked to the West for a model for progress—and "Slavophiles," who believed that Russia could never be reconciled with Western values. Like Westernizers, most Slavophiles were social critics of autocratic Russia. Westernizers like Chaadayev regarded the development of parliamentary institutions and industrialization in Britain,

France, and the German states as a model for Russia to emulate. In contrast, Slavophiles cherished the specificity of Russia's defining institutions: the Orthodox Church, the village commune (the *mir*), and even tsardom itself. They argued that Russia could avoid the traumas of Western industrial development because in the village it already possessed the basis for a future socialist society. The peasant commune, with a variety of communal buildings (a wind or water mill, a grain supply store, tavern, and a workshop), enabled peasants to adapt their lives to unbelievably difficult conditions imposed by nature, the state, and the lords. The *mir* seemed to provide both a moral vision and revolutionary potential.

Vissarion Belinsky (1811–1848) and Alexander Herzen (1812–1870) forcefully made the case that Russia had to follow the example of the West to emerge from backwardness. Belinsky, the son of a doctor, had been expelled from university for writing an article denouncing serfdom. When the writer Nikolay Gogol (1809–1852) refused to criticize the autocracy, Belinsky circulated his *Letter to Gogol* (1847), which helped define the Westernizer position by blasting Gogol's respect for "orthodoxy, autocracy, and nationality," the dominant triad of the Russian Empire: "Advocate of the knout [whip], apostle of ignorance, champion of obscurantism and reactionary mysticism, eulogist of Tartar customs—what are you doing? Look at what is beneath your feet; you are standing at the brink of an abyss."

Herzen, a landowner's son, had vowed to carry on the work of the Decembrist martyrs. Arrested and exiled for participation in a student discussion group, Herzen traveled to France. Returning to Moscow in 1840, he espoused the French Jacobin and socialist tradition and the belief in the inevitability of progress. In *From the Other Shore* (1855), written in voluntary exile in Paris after the Revolution of 1848, Herzen expressed confidence that Russia, even while following the lead of the West, would take its own path to socialism. Socialism could be easily established in Russia because the village commune already existed as a community of social equals in the face of autocratic and noble exploitation. Herzen implored Russian officials to struggle for peaceful liberal reform. Interestingly enough, both radical reformers and the men of the tsarist state shared a suspicion of Western "bourgeois" political and social life. The Slavophile current of reformism thus had much more in common

Alexander Herzen.

with the tsarist autocracy than it cared to admit. Unlike the Westernizers, the Slavophiles celebrated the religious faith of the Russian masses, believing that an era of social harmony and equality had existed in Russia before Peter the Great transformed the Russian state in the late seventeenth century by importing Western ideals and bureaucracy. "We are a backward people," wrote one young Slavophile, "and therein lies our salvation. We must . . . not repeat the stale old lessons of Europe."

The Emancipation of the Serfs

The emancipation of the serfs in 1861 by Tsar Alexander II (ruled 1855–1881) was the most ambitious attempt at reform in Russia during the nineteenth century. Serfdom dictated the organization of taxation, the army, the courts, and virtually every other institution of government. Indeed, the state had little active presence in the village—as the peasants put it, "God is in heaven and the tsar far away." Because landowners had a virtually unlimited source of labor, many showed little inclination to try to increase agricultural yields.

Alexander II, who succeeded his father Nicholas I as tsar in 1855, was shocked by Russia's defeat in the Crimean War. The tsar and some of his officials began to believe that his country could not compete with the West if the serfs were not emancipated. Despite an increase in agricultural laborers hired for wages, Russian industrial development and effective agricultural production required free wage labor that could be taxed. Even if some lords had attempted to increase the productivity of their land, serfs only worked halfheartedly—and who could blame them. Most Russian peasants still used the wasteful three-field system (with one field left fallow each year).

Serf rebellions—more than 1,500 during the first half of the century—periodically shook the empire. Many serfs had joined the army during the Crimean War, believing that they would be freed upon returning home. The flight of thousands of serfs toward the open spaces of the east, or to Crimea, undermined the agricultural economy upon which Russia depended. As rumors spread that the tsar, whom many peasants considered the father of his people, would end Russia's "peculiar institution," peasant rebellions became even more widespread. Intellectuals continued to denounce serfdom, as did bureaucrats, at least in private. Tsar Alexander II told assembled landowners, "It is better to abolish serfdom from above than to wait until serfs begin to liberate themselves from below." Some nobles now believed emancipation inevitable. In 1858, a Slavophile noble wrote the tsar that the "abolition of the right to dispose of people like objects or cattle is as much our liberation as theirs."

On April 5, 1861, Russia became the last European state to abolish serfdom. Alexander II emancipated the 22 million serfs by a proclamation made through the Orthodox Church. For two years, however, the old sys-

Peasants hailing Tsar Alexander II after the emancipation of the serfs in 1861.

tem remained essentially in place. But serfs then received land through the commune—the *mir*—which was administered by male heads of household. The state compensated nobles for their land, and peasants had to repay the state through annual redemption payments. Yet nobles lost in the emancipation, as in many cases they received bonds of little value, as well as losing the value of the serfs. Peasants were no longer dependent upon the whims of landlord justice. Yet many peasants, who had wanted complete and immediate freedom without compensation ("We are yours," went an old serf proverb, "but the land is ours.") were disappointed by the terms of their freedom. Furthermore, as the villages were collectively responsible for land redemption payments and taxes (although the lords' household serfs were freed without land and owed no payments), former serfs were rather like hostages to their own villages. Instead of owing labor to the lords, they now owed taxes to the state, which would be collected by the communes. They were dependent upon the village patriarchs for permission to go find work elsewhere. Peasants flocked to the cities, which grew by leaps and bounds.

In tsarist Russia, the serfs were freed practically without bloodshed, while in the United States the slaves found freedom only after one of the most violent struggles—the Civil War (1861–1865)—of the nineteenth century. Unlike the southern landed elite in the United States, who went to war in defense of slavery, the Russian nobility capitulated without resistance to emancipation. Despite the vast expanse of the Russian Empire, the tsarist state exercised more centralized authority than did the relatively weak central government in the United States. Moreover, Americans considered private property more of an absolute right than did even Russian nobles, who wanted, above all, to extract services from peasants. After emancipation, the vast wealth of the Russian nobles could still pay for such services.

More reforms followed. Alexander II rooted out some incompetent ministers and officials and asked the ministry of finance to keep regular budgets. In 1864, the tsar decreed the establishment of district or village assemblies called *zemstvos*. These would elect delegates to regional assemblies. Six years later, he created similar urban institutions called *dumas* (councils), with the authority to assess taxes and to organize public services and education. But the ministry of the interior controlled the *zemstvos*, and provincial governors ignored them, some treating their members as seditious agitators. Moreover, wealthy landowners elected the members of the *zemstvos*; their votes were given more weight than those of townsmen and peasants, yet the *zemstvos* provided some political apprenticeships to ordinary people.

Russian law had been codified in the 1830s, but the emancipation of the serfs necessitated an expanded administrative apparatus, since millions of people were now subject to the justice of the state. The tsar introduced regional and lower courts modeled on those of Britain, as well as public trial by jury. In 1864, for the first time, a separate judicial branch of government came into existence in Russia, although the tsar could override any court decision. A jury system was established, along with the possibility of appeals. Yet peasants were not judged in the same courts as social elites.

Thus, the essential structure of the Russian Empire remained the same. The army was no longer made up of loyal, poorly supplied, illiterate, beaten serfs but rather of loyal, poorly supplied, illiterate, beaten peasants. In the past, few soldiers had been expected to survive the twenty-five-year term of service. Indeed, wives of soldiers had the right to remarry three years after their husbands left for military service. Alexander II established a Prussian-style general staff, took steps to modernize weapons, and reduced the term of military service to six years, followed by nine years in the reserves and five years in the militia. Alexander also ordered the elimination of some forms of corporal punishment, including the brutal—and often fatal—floggings.

However, the arbitrary power of the tsarist state and its Third Section police to repress dissent remained largely intact. Most political cases were handed over to trial by secret court-martial. Alexander restored the censorship apparatus, which was temporarily weakened in the years before the emancipation, to full strength. Moreover, the tsar had no intention of creating any kind of national representative institution that would undercut his authority. Russian reform had its limits.

The Expansion of the Russian Empire

Following defeat in the Crimean War and as stipulated by the Peace of Paris (1856), Russia relinquished Moldavia, Wallachia, and Bessarabia and had to accept the neutrality of the Black Sea, further frustrating imperial designs in southeastern Europe (see Map 18.2). Russia now confronted nationalist movements among peoples within the empire. After two years of public demonstrations, an uprising in Poland occurred in 1863. Rebels proclaimed a "national government" before being crushed by Russian troops. Tsar Alexander II cracked down, ordering the confiscation of some Polish lands as punishment for participating in the revolt, closing most monasteries, and not permitting the creation of *zemstvos* (elected councils) or juries in law courts, reforms he had applied to Russia. Poland was transformed into a province with all illusions of autonomy ended. Poles felt the effect of the repression even in Prussia, where the government forbade the sale of lands to Poles or Catholics (priests had been among the insurgents). In the Ukraine, Polish national consciousness helped inspire emerging Ukrainian identity. In response, in 1863 the state forbade the publication of nonfiction works in the Ukrainian language.

In the Ottoman Balkans, Russian troops intervened on behalf of Bulgarians, who were fellow Slavs. The rising of pan-Slavism as an ideology was increasingly apparent. Pan-Slavism enthusiastically proclaimed that all Slavs were in the same family. In Herzegovina, peasants had rebelled against Ottoman tax collectors and soldiers. In the subsequent Russo-Turkish War (1877–1878), a Russian army drove toward Constantinople. Austro-Hungarian forces and the British navy readied to prevent the Russians from reaching the Dardanelles strait. Defeat forced the Ottoman Empire to sign the Treaty of San Stefano (1878) with Russia. Then the other powers called for an international conference to discuss the matter. German Chancellor Otto von Bismarck presided at the Congress of Berlin (1878). Bulgaria became a principality, but remained a vassal state of the sultan of Turkey. At Disraeli's insistence, the Congress of Berlin reduced the size of Bulgaria. Greece received Thessaly, which it had claimed, thus moving the Greek border to the edge of Macedonia, claimed by Bulgaria, Serbia, and Greece. There were then few Bulgarian nationalists, despite the fact that Bulgaria received its own Orthodox Church in 1870; not many decades earlier most educated people there had considered themselves Greek. The fact that Russia would clearly dominate Bulgaria—Russians held key government posts— and the rising mood of Pan-Slavism (a movement aimed at promoting the interests and unity of all Slavs) in the Balkans alarmed Austria-Hungary and Britain. The Congress of Berlin also recognized Serbia, Montenegro, and Romania as independent states, further reducing Ottoman territory in Europe. Russia received a small part of Bessarabia, which allowed it to control the mouth of the Danube River. But Russian Pan-Slavs, in particular, believed themselves aggrieved by Britain and betrayed by Bismarck's

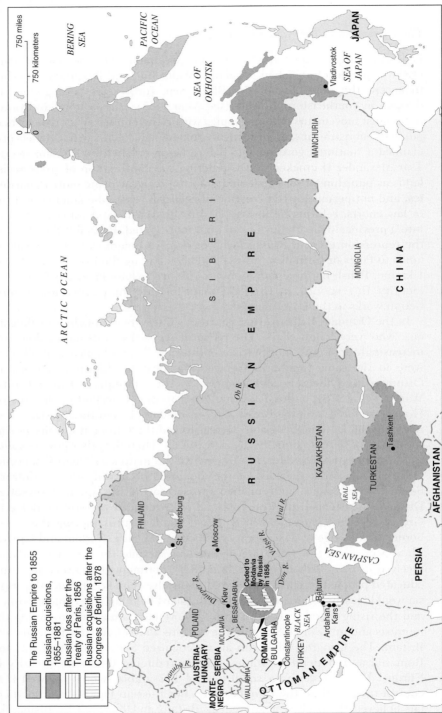

MAP 18.2 THE EXPANSION OF RUSSIA   After territorial losses under the Peace of Paris (1856), Russia turned eastward, expanding through Central Asia toward the Far East and its port at Vladivostok.

Germany. Likewise, Bulgarian nationalists would increasingly feel that they had been cheated out of land in Macedonia that they believed Bulgaria had been promised by Russia.

Alexander II then turned his attention toward Central Asia and the Middle East. Russian armies conquered Turkistan in 1859–1860, annexed Tashkent in 1866, and then reached Afghanistan. The wars that subdued the Muslim mountain people of the Caucasus ended in 1860. The expansion added about 5 million Muslims to the empire. Russian expansion now seemed to impinge upon British interests near India, the gem of its empire. The British army invaded Afghanistan, and in 1881 put a puppet ruler on the throne. In the Far East, Russian forces moved across Siberia, where the discovery of gold in the 1830s had attracted tens of thousands of settlers, to go with the ever-expanding convict population, giving the Russian navy access to the Pacific Ocean at Vladivostok.

The Russian Empire now included about one-seventh of the world's land mass. This eastward expansion eventually brought conflict with China. The Chinese emperors would be powerless in the face of Russian demands, as they were when confronted by those of Britain. Surprisingly, Japan, which emerged from centuries of isolation following the Meiji Restoration in 1868, would prove to be a far tougher adversary for Russia.

Nihilists and Populists

Revolutionaries replaced the conscience-stricken gentry of the 1830s and 1840s as the principal critics of the Russian autocracy. They were drawn from a variety of social backgrounds, including the sons and daughters of nobles, merchants, peasants, and Orthodox priests. Convinced that one spark might ignite a wave of rebellion, they struck out on their own or in very small groups.

Some Russian revolutionaries found the old debates between the Westernizers and Slavophiles irrelevant. Nihilists accepted no dogmas, but above all rejected the materialist doctrines of the West. They also disavowed many Russian traditions, and thus repudiated the Slavophiles. Some of them viewed the Orthodox Church as an institution of oppression, whereas others remained fervent believers.

Nihilists saw in the Russian masses an untapped revolutionary force, believing that the emancipation of the serfs had aided their cause by creating an independent peasantry, which might be more likely to rise up against its oppressors. Like the conscience-stricken gentry before them, the nihilists believed in the power of literature to effect change. In 1863, Nikolay Chernyshevsky (1828–1889), a former seminarian, published *What Is to Be Done?*, a novel that had an enormous impact on several generations of intellectuals. Chernyshevsky described committed people of action as "rational egoists" who would form a disciplined vanguard of change. Because nihilists did not feel bound by moral codes, they believed they could take whatever

(*Left*) Michael Bakunin, professional anarchist. (*Right*) Karl Marx, founder of Communism.

action seemed necessary to achieve their goals. In the 1860s, groups of nihilists turned to violent revolution, plotting the assassination of state officials and the tsar. The police infiltrated and drove groups like "Land and Freedom" and "The Organization"—with its central committee called "Hell"—underground, particularly after a student attempted to kill Tsar Alexander II in 1866.

In the meantime, Michael Bakunin (1814–1876) became the most famous anarchist of his or any other time. Anarchists rejected the very existence of the state, thereby quarreling bitterly with socialists, who wanted not to destroy the state but to take it over. A professional revolutionary who complained, "Karl Marx is ruining the workers by making theorists out of them," Bakunin left behind comfortable noble origins. He was a man of enormous energy who slept only a couple of hours a day, eating, drinking, and smoking cigars almost constantly, organizing and plotting between bites, gulps, and puffs. Once calling himself "the devil in the flesh," Bakunin defined the "social question" as "primarily the overthrow of society." That he set out to do. He led the police on a chase from Paris in 1847 to Dresden and other stops in Central Europe in 1848, that year of revolution. Arrested and imprisoned in Russia, he was exiled to Siberia, managed to escape in 1861, reached Japan, and then arrived in London via the United States.

Bakunin believed that "destruction is a creative passion" and, like the nihilists, that the peasant masses had untapped revolutionary potential. Marx insisted that peasants, unlike the industrial proletariat, could never be truly revolutionary because they could not be class-conscious. Anarchists, in turn, rejected Marx's belief that a militant working class organized in a centralized party could make a revolution, fearing that Marxists wanted to replace a bourgeois state with a proletarian state, a state all the same.

Unlike revolutionary nihilists and anarchists who dreamed of a spontaneous peasant uprising, Sergei Nechayev (1847–1882) held that a small, tightly organized revolutionary group could begin the peasant revolution that would sweep away autocratic oppression. "The revolutionary is," Nechayev wrote, "a doomed man. He has no personal interests, no affairs, sentiments, attachments, property, not even a name of his own. Everything in him is absorbed by one exclusive interest, one thought, one passion—the revolution." After murdering one of his colleagues, Nechayev was arrested and sent to prison, where he died.

During his anguished life, Nechayev had battled the populists (*narodniki*). The populists developed their doctrine in response to nihilism and retained the Slavophiles' faith in the Russian peasantry. They were romantic collectivists who idealized the Russian peasant community. In contrast to Chernyshevsky, who wanted to teach the peasants, the populists wanted to learn from them. In the early 1870s, several thousand young Russians, who had been members of circles of intellectuals, went from Saint Petersburg and Moscow into the countryside. Many had been influenced by Peter Lavrov (1823–1900), who lamented in his *Historical Letters* (1869) that the gap between the intellectuals like himself and peasants had become even greater over the previous decades. These upper-class Russians resembled the conscience-stricken gentry of the 1830s and 1840s. "Going to the people" and dressing like peasants, they also wanted to prepare revolution by helping to educate the peasants. Some of those attracted to direct revolutionary action worried that the emancipation of the serfs might create a class of conservative peasant proprietors. Time seemed to be running out for Russia to take its own path to socialism before capitalism became entrenched in Russia, as it had in Western Europe.

In 1878, a revolutionary populist shot and wounded the governor-general of Saint Petersburg. Another attack that year, carried out by the "disorganization section" of Land and Freedom, struck down the head of the Third Section police. A wave of strikes by industrial workers convinced the terrorists that revolution was not far away.

Twice more, Tsar Alexander II escaped assassination attempts. In the hope of placating his enemies without destroying the foundations of the autocracy, Alexander disbanded the Third Section. He dismissed the minister of education, whose restrictive policies on university admission were unpopular, and announced the formation of a new consultative assembly. But in 1881, members of "People's Will" struck, hurling a bomb near Alexander's sleigh. When the tsar foolishly stepped from the sleigh to inspect the damage, another man threw a bomb that killed him. However, the assassination did not prove to be the revolutionary spark anticipated by those who carried it out. Millions of the tsar's subjects mourned the ruler who had freed them.

Alexander III's Empire

Following his father's assassination, Alexander III (ruled 1881–1894) was in no mood to contemplate any liberalization of imperial institutions. Public opinion existed in the Russian Empire, but mass political life did not. The assassination led to a curtailment of the powers of the *zemstvos*. Judicial authority shifted to the police, putting political trials in the hands of military courts. For the moment, exile was the only safe place from which to criticize the autocracy. Small colonies of political refugees, most of whom were socialists, lived in Geneva, Paris, and London.

Professors and teachers were brought under stricter state control, and tuition was increased to discourage commoners from going to school. The police could arrest and imprison anyone without reason. The resulting political trials may have actually helped the cause of reformers and revolutionaries by serving as tribunals where the autocratic regime was discussed and political issues were brought into the open. What went on in courtrooms helped shape Russian opinion, even when political trials were moved into military courts.

The Russian Empire late in the nineteenth century was enormous. More than a hundred times the size of Great Britain and three times larger than the United States (to which Russia had sold Alaska in 1867), its population doubled from about 74 million inhabitants in 1861 to about 150 million by 1905. It was now comprised of almost 200 nationalities who spoke 146 languages. Russians made up 40 percent of the population of the empire. Ukrainians, Poles, and Belorussians made up the next largest national groups, followed by Lithuanians, Latvians, Estonians, Finns, Romanians (in Bessarabia), Crimean Tatars, Armenians, Georgians, Azeri (in the Caucasus), and the Muslim peoples of Central Asia.

Alexander ordered a vigorous campaign of "Russification" in the western empire. The tsar banned the use of languages other than Russian in school, and forbade publication in, for example, the Ukrainian language, despite the fact that it was spoken by 25 million people. At the same time, the Russian Orthodox Church launched campaigns against non-Orthodox religions, which held the allegiance of almost a third of the people of the empire. New laws enforced restrictions against Jews, who in principle where supposed to be confined to the "Pale of Settlement" in Poland. In 1899, the Finnish Assembly was reduced to a "consultative" voice, and Russians replaced Finns in most key administrative positions.

"Russification" firmed the resolve of nationalist groups to persevere in their demands for recognition. In Russian Poland, opposition grew more daring. Poles were linked by long-standing cultural bonds, based on language and Catholicism. Polish identity had survived the end of an independent Poland with the Third Partition of 1795 by Russia, Austria, and Prussia. Moreover, the cause of Polish independence had been kept alive by Poles forced to flee abroad after the ill-fated insurrections of 1831 and

1863. Two strong movements then developed. National Democrats sought to build up the strength of the Polish nation within the context of the Russian Empire, viewing Prussia and then Germany as the principal enemy. Polish Socialists, in contrast, wanted to organize another uprising, one that they hoped one day would lead to an independent and socialist Poland in which the rights of non-Poles would also be recognized.

Unrest, Reform, and Revolution

The majority of the population of the Russian Empire was poor: the average per capita income was more than four times higher in Britain, three times higher in Germany, and twice as high in the Balkan states. If by 1910, 70 percent of children aged 7 to 11 were likely to attend school for at least one year, about 60 percent of the population remained illiterate. In 1897, only 1 percent of the population had attended secondary school for any amount of time.

Yet literacy in European Russia and the Baltic region, in particular, was rising, and with it the number of people who wanted reform. The reading public grew dramatically in size around the turn of the century, especially in Saint Petersburg and Moscow. Even seasonal workers and peasants migrating to Siberia began to carry books with them. The taste for literature expanded from religious books and the emerging classics of the Russian literary tradition (above all, Gogol and Tolstoy) to relatively liberal magazines and newspapers.

Liberals had played a role in the expanding domain of Russian public opinion since the heady days of the 1860s and the emancipation of the serfs. The Russian army's poor performance in the war against Turkey (1877–1878) proved that military reforms instituted following the Crimean War had been inadequate. Expanding opportunities for education, increased government bureaucratization, and industrial development increased the professional middle class. This, combined with the expansion of heavy and light industry, and urban growth, seemed to make autocracy an anachronism.

Liberals included a smattering of gentry, leaders of local assemblies (the *zemstvos* and the municipal *dumas*), and, above all, members of the professional classes, including economists, *zemstvo* agronomists, physicians, lawyers, teachers, and students. Some state bureaucrats, too, sought a middle way between state and noble intransigence and revolutionary insurgency, hoping that the tsar would grant political reforms to complement the gradual modernization of the Russian economy. Some were encouraged by laws slightly reducing the long work day (1897) and providing the first factory insurance law (1903). Liberals in the Union of Liberation demanded an extension of the powers of the *zemstvos*, whose limited authority had been curtailed in 1890, but imagined little more than active consultation between those bodies and the tsar.

New revolutionary groups, however, still believed the autocracy incapable of reforming itself and that only revolution could bring reform. The populist Socialist Revolutionaries became the largest radical group, with growing support among peasants, whom Socialist Revolutionaries, like some of their optimistic predecessors, believed would one day overthrow the tsar. In the meantime, national movements developed in Poland, Finland, Ukraine, and the Baltic region. In the distant Muslim reaches of the empire, religion provided a new cohesiveness.

Marxists founded the Russian Social Democratic Workers' Party in 1898. They were confident that one day, though probably not in their lifetimes, the Russian proletariat would be sufficiently numerous and class-conscious to seize power. But this seizure of power could only occur, they believed, after a democratic revolution had successfully overthrown the Russian autocracy. Marxists claimed vindication for their view that peasants had no true revolutionary potential when, despite the terrible suffering and deaths of millions of peasants during the famine that followed the severe drought and epidemics of 1891–1892, the countryside remained quiescent.

By 1900, the tsar's police had succeeded in disbanding most of the revolutionary groups within the empire, deporting their leaders to join the groups in exile, sending them to Siberia, or putting them in prison. Most revolutionaries shared a belief that their country was far from revolution.

Lenin and the Bolsheviks

Vladimir Ilyich Ulyanov, known as Lenin, was born in the Volga River town of Simbirsk on April 22, 1870, more than 400 miles east of Moscow. His father served as the director of primary schools for the province and, as a result of loyal service, he obtained non-hereditary membership in the nobility; Lenin's mother, whose family had originally been German, was the daughter of a doctor. Older brother Alexander, who joined the revolutionary group "People's Will," was executed in 1887 for participation in a plot to kill Tsar Alexander III. Lenin briefly attended university, but was expelled for participating in a student demonstration. During the next six years, Lenin read widely in history and philosophy, including the works of Marx and Friedrich Engels, and received a degree in law from the University of Saint Petersburg.

In 1895, Lenin went to Austria, France, and Switzerland, meeting Russian political exiles and socialists from many countries. Back in Saint Petersburg two years later, he was charged with organizing and writing articles in a clandestine newspaper (*Iskra*, or *Spark*) and exiled to Siberia. When his term of banishment ended in 1900, he moved to Switzerland. As a virtually penniless exile, he bore his situation with good humor. Lenin's few interests outside of politics and revolution included chess, hunting, bicycling, and mountain hiking. But he viewed most recreational activities—even, at times, simple conversation—as interfering with revolutionary struggle. There was nothing about Lenin's appearance that would have attracted the attention of tsarist spies or Swiss and French police. An Englishman said that "he looked more like a provincial grocer than a leader."

Lenin combined a powerful ability to theorize with a facility for adapting to changing circumstances. His steely resolve would carry him to cold fury when colleagues or rivals failed to agree with him. "He who does not understand this does not understand anything!" was a typical Lenin rejoinder. A vigorous polemicist, he could be impatient and churlish in speech, cutting and sarcastic with his potent pen.

In 1902, Lenin, who had taken his name as a pseudonym the previous year, published *What Is to Be Done?* In this pamphlet (with the same title as the work by Chernyshevsky), Lenin established what would become the basic tenets of a new revolutionary party. Lenin believed that Marxist analysis could be applied to a backward, authoritarian nation with a relatively undeveloped working class and a small bourgeoisie. "The one serious organizational principle for workers in our movement must be strictest secrecy," he wrote, and "the strictest choice of members and the training of professional revolutionaries." He rejected all compromise with liberals and reform socialists, viewing as self-defeating the struggle of workers for small economic gains, crumbs tossed from the posh table of the ruling class. Rejecting the common Marxist view that the social experiences of workers would lead them to revolutionary consciousness, Lenin believed that only a minority of workers would achieve consciousness and that these should join with intellectuals in a party that would direct the masses.

Lenin and his followers became known as the "Bolsheviks," or "majority" (although much of the time in the years that followed they were not), and their rivals were known as the "Mensheviks," the "minority." The Mensheviks believed that a proletarian revolution lay in the future, but not until a bourgeois uprising had first succeeded in overthrowing the tsarist state. Mensheviks believed that their role was to mobilize support for their party through propaganda, while undertaking timely alliances with liberal groups. They objected to the high degree of party centralization upon which Lenin insisted.

The Russo-Japanese War (1904–1905)

In the meantime, the Russian Empire lurched toward war with Japan. It had begun to covet Chinese Manchuria and the peninsula of Korea. The acquisition of Manchuria would permit Russia to construct a more direct rail link to the ice-free Russian port of Vladivostok; that of Korea would protect the new port from possible attack and provide still more ports. In 1894, Japan goaded China into a war. By the Treaty of Shimonoseki (1895), the victorious Japanese took the island of Formosa (Taiwan) and gained Chinese recognition of Korea's independence. This placed the peninsula under direct Japanese influence. Japan also acquired the Liaodong (Liaotung)

Three Manchurian men crouch before the hulks of Russian ships sunk during the Russo-Japanese War.

peninsula in southern Manchuria but was forced by Russia, Germany, and France to return it.

Russia viewed the expansion of Japanese interests in the Far East with concern. In 1898, Tsar Nicholas II (ruled 1894–1917) signed a treaty with China and obtained a concession to build the Manchurian railway and to construct a port at Port Arthur on the tip of the Liaodong peninsula, providing a source of conflict between Japan and Russia. Japan, in turn, signed a treaty in 1902 with Great Britain, Russia's rival for influence in Afghanistan. Britain would remain neutral if Japan and Russia went to war against each other. But Britain would join Japan in any conflict that allied Russia with any other power in a war against Japan.

In February 1904, Japanese torpedo boats launched a surprise attack on the Russian fleet at Port Arthur, destroying a number of ships while the Japanese army drove Russian forces away on land. In March 1905, Japanese troops defeated the Russians in the bloody Battle of Mukden where, for the first time, two armies faced each other across trenches dug for protection. Two months later, the Japanese navy pounced on the Russian fleet, which had spent nine months at sea. The Battle of Tsushima ended with nineteen Russian ships sunk, five captured, and six forced to neutral ports. Only three ships of the Russian fleet reached Vladivostok.

How could the Russian Empire be defeated by a small island nation in Asia? Only a single-track railway line stretching across thousands of miles supplied the Russian forces. The Russian army was poorly commanded and fought with outdated artillery and rifles. By the Treaty of Portsmouth (New Hampshire), signed in September 1905 at a conference hastily arranged by U.S. President Theodore Roosevelt, Japan took over Russia's lease of the Liaodong peninsula and Chinese concessions in Manchuria. Russia accepted Japanese influence over Korea. A new world imperial power was born.

The Revolution of 1905

Many of the tsar's subjects had blamed government inaction for the murderous famine of 1891–1892, which had captured world attention. In 1902, peasants attacked noble property in some districts, and a wave of industrial strikes followed the next year. Liberals organized support for political reform by sponsoring banquets similar to those employed by French republicans just before the Revolution of 1848. Dissent mounted against forced Russification among subject nationalities, most notably the Poles and the Finns. Marxist groups were particularly active in Poland—where the issue of Polish nationalism versus internationalism was hotly debated—and in the Jewish Pale—those provinces where Jews were allowed to settle and where they faced endemic anti-Semitism and occasional bloody pogroms.

Shocking defeats in the distant Russo-Japanese War increased calls for liberal reform. A wide-ranging social and political alliance for change extended across classes. For the first time, liberals and socialists (except for Bolsheviks and Mensheviks), gentry, intellectuals, professionals, and workers, and both Russians and non-Russians came together in common opposition to autocracy, embracing a loose ideology of reform. After the assassination of his minister of the interior in July 1904 by a Socialist Revolutionary, Nicholas II appointed a more moderate successor in the hope of calming dissent. Moreover, the tsar allowed a national congress of *zemstvos* and *dumas* to take place. It called for the establishment of a national parliament.

In the meantime, the Russian labor movement remained small and faced constant police harassment. Skilled factory workers supplied the majority of labor militants. At the turn of the century, the police had authorized government-controlled labor associations in the hope of undercutting revolutionaries by encouraging workers to concentrate on economic grievances and achieve some small victories through negotiation or conciliation, as strikes remained illegal. But such halfway measures gave workers useful organizational experience.

In January 1905, a strike by 100,000 factory workers brought Saint Petersburg to a standstill. In Warsaw, a general strike brought violence and reprisals by troops. On January 22, an Orthodox priest, Father Gapon, led a march of workers to the tsar's Winter Palace, carrying a petition asking for "justice" and political reform. Troops blocked their way. When the marchers locked arms and refused an order to disperse, a commander barked out the order to fire.

More than 300 marchers, including women and children, fell dead, and perhaps 1,000 or more were wounded. "Bloody Sunday" helped shatter the myth that the tsar was the Holy Father manipulated by selfish nobles and wicked advisers. Bolsheviks and Socialist Revolutionaries, the latter particularly influential in the countryside, encouraged more strikes. A violent faction of the Socialist Revolutionaries carried out a particularly bloody series of terrorist attacks and assassinations. Nicholas dismissed his liberal minister of the interior. The tsar's uncle fell to an assassin's bullets. Strikes spread to Poland, where they were bolstered by the nationalist movement, and to Ukraine, Latvia, and Estonia. In some parts of Russia and in the Baltic provinces, peasants attacked the homes of wealthy landowners. In the southeastern borderlands, Muslim leaders announced the formation of an All-Russian Muslim League. Workers began to organize trade unions in huge numbers and newspapers appeared in open defiance of censorship. In June, sailors on the battleship *Potemkin* mutinied on the Black Sea, killing the captain and several officers.

With the bulk of the army fighting the Japanese in Manchuria, Nicholas appeared to choose the path of reform, appointing Sergei Witte (1849–1915) as prime minister. Witte was eager to make Russia a modern industrial power, and he believed that he could do so if the tsar granted minimal reforms. He persuaded Nicholas to rescind redemption payments to the state for land acquired when the serfs were emancipated in 1861, to allow Poles and Lithuanians to use their own languages, to allow religious toleration in Poland, to return political trials to regular courts, and to abolish some restrictions on Jews.

Russian troops fire on the workers, Bloody Sunday, January 1905.

Even more important, Nicholas's October Manifesto of 1905 created a national representative assembly, the Duma, to be chosen by universal male suffrage, and promised freedom of the press. Some state officials and most nobles, however, viewed these particular reforms as unacceptable, associating them with the parliamentary regimes of the West. But progressive nobles and businessmen were encouraged by the sudden, unexpected turn of events. Some staunch liberals, some of whom had participated in the *zemstvos*, took the name of the Constitutional Democratic Party (known as the Kadets). They demanded constitutional rule, insisting that even the promised reforms left the essential structures of autocracy unchanged. In the meantime, the Mensheviks had championed the establishment of Saint Petersburg workers' councils, known as *soviets*. These were neighborhood councils made up of delegates from factories, shops, trade unions, and political parties who helped organize strikes, which became legal in December. The Mensheviks now were willing to collaborate with the liberals to bring further reforms to workers and peasants.

But a violent uprising in Moscow in December 1905 brought on vigorous counter-revolution. Witte ordered the arrest of many of the workers' leaders. The *soviets* no longer were free to meet. Army units returning from Manchuria crushed nationalist demonstrations in Poland and Georgia and brutally restored order in the Russian and Ukrainian countryside. In the Baltic provinces of Latvia and Estonia, punitive expeditions ordered by the tsar killed over 1,000 people while crushing strikes and rural unrest. Fanatical Russian nationalists known as the Black Hundreds, perhaps instigated by Orthodox priests, unleashed a wave of violence against Jews (and against Russian, German, and Polish property owners, as well) which lasted more than a year. The Black Hundreds were led by small traders and agricultural laborers who feared that economic change would cost them what limited security they had and by police who opposed political reform. In the Black Sea town of Odessa, drunken mobs aided by the local police murdered 800 Jews, injured more than 5,000 others, and left twice that number homeless. The tsar himself intervened to prevent Witte from prosecuting the police there, praising the "mass of loyal people"; they had struck out against "troublemakers." Jews could be conveniently blamed for agitating against autocratic rule.

Against this turbulent backdrop, the Duma had met for the first time in April 1906. The U.S. ambassador described the gathering in the Winter Palace of the members of the Duma, who were dressed "in every conceivable costume, the peasants in rough clothes and long boots, merchants and tradespeople in frock coats, lawyers in dress suits, priests in long garb and almost equally long hair, and even a Catholic bishop in violet robes." The majority of the Duma members were Kadets (Constitutional Democrats), largely because the Marxist Mensheviks and Bolsheviks and the Socialist Revolutionaries refused to participate in the election.

As the Duma debated land reform, an issue on which the tsar refused any compromise, Nicholas decreed the establishment of an upper assembly, the State Council. With members to be drawn from the high clergy, the army, or other loyal institutions, it would counteract the influence of the Duma. The tsar then dismissed Witte and announced that he would promulgate any decree he pleased while the Duma was not in session. When the Kadets petitioned Nicholas to abolish the State Council, make ministers responsible to the Duma, and turn over some noble estates to the peasants, he dissolved the first Duma.

The Revolution of 1905 ended in failure, but its memory could not be effaced. The tsar had been forced to grant a parliament and the promise of limited civil rights. Many people within the Russian professional class, particularly bureaucrats and lawyers, remained sympathetic to the reforms after they had been undone by the tsar.

The Revolution of 1905 heightened the divisions among exiled Russian socialists. Mensheviks contended that compromise with bourgeois reformers would increase socialist support within Russia. Lenin and the Bolsheviks, on the other hand, believed that the failed revolution had clearly demonstrated that the Russian proletariat in the large cities was already a revolutionary force, and that the first stage of Marx's promised revolution could be achieved if workers and peasants joined together.

Nicholas II named Peter Stolypin (1862–1911) prime minister, and in June 1907 ordered the dissolution of a second elected Duma even though it was more conservative than the first. The tsar established military field courts

Tsar Nicholas II presides over the opening of the Duma.

that could summarily convict and sentence civilians accused of violent political crimes. This law resulted in nearly 1,000 hangings before it expired six months later. Liberals dubbed the ropes of the gallows "Stolypin's neckties."

After Nicholas changed the rules of election to increase the power of noble votes at the expense of peasants, workers, and non-Russians, a third Duma was elected in 1907 that was more to the tsar's liking. It was dominated by the "Octobrists," who believed that the tsar's promises in the October Manifesto of 1905 represented sufficient reform and wanted to stop at that. The repression and Russification campaign went on.

Stolypin nonetheless undertook rural reforms beginning in 1906, hoping that they might defuse the political intensity of the agrarian question and reduce unrest without the confiscation of land owned by the gentry. His goal was to create a class of prosperous peasants (*kulaks*) while increasing agricultural production by allowing peasants to leave their villages and set up independent farms. He hoped that the enclosure of common lands and a consolidation of holdings would expand the number of peasant plots. Indeed, a considerable amount of land passed from communal to private ownership. The number of prosperous peasants increased. Yet prices for farm products fell, and even peasants with fairly large plots of land still had to struggle to survive. By 1914 more than 5 million Russians had crossed the Ural Mountains, most of them peasants attracted by the possibility of land—Siberia thus became something of the equivalent of the American West.

In 1911, Stolypin was assassinated. Although the government of course claimed the assassin was a Jew, the minister may have been killed with the approval of the tsar at the instigation of noble advisers who considered him too liberal and rejected any agrarian reforms.

A surge of industrial strikes and peasant violence over the next three years demonstrated continued popular dissatisfaction. With political parties now legal, although facing police constraints, and the press in principle free, Liberals, Socialist Revolutionaries, and Menshevik and Bolshevik Social Democrats mobilized support against the regime. Indeed, the growing popularity of Bolsheviks among organized urban workers—revealed in their victories in trade union elections—reflected deepening impatience with the path of moderate reform.

FRANCE: SECOND EMPIRE AND THIRD REPUBLIC

In the meantime, Europe's traditionally most revolutionary country remained France. Following the Revolution of 1848, Louis Napoleon Bonaparte completed his destruction of the Second Republic with his coup d'état on December 2, 1851. The following year he proclaimed himself emperor as Napoleon III, with the overwhelming support of the upper classes and many peasants.

Emperor Napoleon III was a small man with a prominent nose who appeared lethargic. He reminded some people of a sphinx, and a contemporary of "a melancholy parrot." An unimpressed visitor from the United States described the French ruler as "a long-bodied, short-legged man, fiercely mustached, old, wrinkled, with eyes half closed, and such a deep, crafty, scheming expression about them!" Indeed, like his legendary uncle Napoleon Bonaparte, Napoleon III consistently demonstrated considerable energy when it came to behind-the-scenes intrigue and the pursuit of women.

During the Second Empire (1852–1870), wealthy businessmen became the equivalent of an imperial aristocracy in France, money standing as the measure of value that blue blood had been in the early modern period. Enjoying access to the emperor, some of them lived in Parisian residences and owned country houses that would have made eighteenth-century aristocrats drool with envy. The empress set the tone for Parisian fashion, while critics condemned the "triumphant vulgarity and appalling materialism" of the "imperial festival."

Yet Napoleon III set out to pull the nation together. France was the only European power with universal male suffrage, however distorted by government pressure. The emperor promoted economic growth, encouraged urban rebuilding projects (see Chapter 19), created institutions that provided credit, and constructed more railways. Moreover, in 1859 Napoleon III initiated the "liberal empire," encouraging a series of reforms, including authorizing a liberal trade treaty with Britain in 1860 and permitting the legalization of strikes in 1864.

The Authoritarian Empire

Napoleon III ruled with the help of a handful of worldly, trusted cronies who held ministries or who served on the Council of State. Ministers were responsible to the emperor, who alone could propose legislation. The state clamped down on the remnants of political opposition, maintained press censorship, and sponsored "official" candidates in the elections held every six years for the Legislative Body, the lower house of the National Assembly. Hand-picked notables made up its upper chamber, the Senate. Napoleon III's men built a Bonapartist party from the remnants of Orleanism, that is, from those conservative bourgeois who had supported the July Monarchy (1830–1848). They rallied to Napoleon III, who promoted economic growth and promised to maintain social and political order. The French state, more than its decentralized British counterpart, could buy political support by dispensing patronage, through prefects, the most powerful local officials. The Second Empire thus further centralized economic and political power in France.

A good many Legitimists—that is, the supporters of the Bourbon royal family and its exiled pretender, the count of Chambord—supported the emperor. Like his uncle, Napoleon III had made peace with the Church.

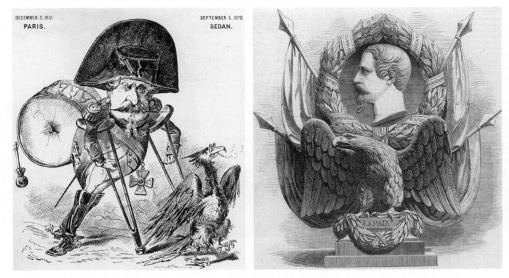

A cartoon critical of Napoleon III, shown limping behind a vulture after his defeat in the Franco-German war (*left*), stands in stark contrast to the Bonapartist propaganda early in his dictatorship declaring "The Glory of Napoleon III" (*right*).

The clergy remained grateful that during the Second Republic over which Napoleon had presided as president and then destroyed, the Falloux Law of 1850 had returned much control over education to them.

Economic Growth

The rate of French economic growth was such during the 1850s that economic historians sometimes use it as an example of an industrial "take-off." French exports doubled between 1853 and 1864. Never before had any state taken such a direct role in stimulating the economy through encouragement and investment. Government officials coordinated the efforts of the ministries of agriculture, commerce, and public works, while keeping in close touch with wealthy bankers and industrialists who backed the regime.

French entrepreneurs had often found it difficult to raise investment capital. Most companies remained family concerns, hesitant to open investment possibilities to outsiders. Napoleon III encouraged the creation of state mortgage banks. In 1852, the Péreire brothers, who were Protestants like many French bankers, created the Crédit Mobilier, an investment bank. Selling shares to raise capital until its collapse in 1867, it provided loans to businessmen. Other smaller deposit banks, too, attracted large and medium-sized investors. A mortgage bank (the Crédit Foncier), another one of Napoleon III's pet projects, aided the development of the agricultural sector.

At the same time, some major French industries reached a scale of production and concentration comparable to that of their British rivals. The

The opening of the Suez Canal, 1869.

metallurgical industry, in particular, underwent unprecedented growth. But most French industries remained relatively small in scale, producing luxury goods such as gloves, umbrellas, silk, jewelry, and fine furniture.

France became a major exporter of capital. French investors financed the construction of Russian, Spanish, and Italian railroads, as well as providing other timely loans to Portugal, Austria-Hungary, and Mexico. Ferdinand de Lesseps (1805–1894), an engineer, raised enough money through loans (half through public subscription) to finance the construction of his brain-child, the Suez Canal, which opened with suitable fanfare in 1869. Yet the chief beneficiary of the canal was not France but Britain, the world's leading trader, which had by far the most to gain by considerably reducing the journey to and from India and the rest of Asia (see Chapter 20).

State encouragement of economic development may be most clearly seen in the French railways. The Bank of France, which had seventy-four branches by 1870, provided financial aid to the companies that for the most part completed the main railway lines that helped stimulate the country's commercial and manufacturing boom. The state guaranteed investors a minimum profit. Between 1851 and 1869, the railway network expanded by five times, reaching almost 10,000 miles of track. French railroads became one of the largest employers in Europe.

The "Liberal Empire"

In 1859, Napoleon III announced his intention to "crown the [imperial] edifice with liberty." He would diffuse opposition by implementing some of the very reforms his opponents on the left desired. Five republicans had been elected to the Legislative Corps two years earlier. In 1860, the

National Assembly received the right to discuss the emperor's annual address—an exercise in sheer boredom, as he was a notoriously poor speaker. That same year, France and Britain signed a liberal trade agreement lowering tariff barriers between the two nations. In France the Cobden-Chevalier Treaty of 1860 was the idea of the emperor himself and an adviser, Michel Chevalier (1806–1879), who had been a utopian socialist as a young man. The treaty provided a sliding scale on import duties, aiding, for example, Bordeaux wine producers selling to England. The National Assembly received the right to approve the imperial budget. The liberalization of political institutions helped republicans increase their support. Press controls were relaxed, and the right to strike was established in 1864. Also in 1864, several French artisans were among the founders in London of the first international workers' organization, the First International, in the hopes of strengthening socialist movements within individual countries.

Foreign policy ultimately undid Napoleon III. In 1859, he joined with Count Camillo di Cavour of Piedmont-Sardinia to draw Emperor Francis Joseph of Austria into a war (see Chapter 17). The French army defeated the Austrians in northern Italy at Magenta and at Solferino, where the emperor himself commanded the French troops on horseback, if at a safe distance from the actual fighting. By the Treaty of Turin (1860), France gained Savoy and Nice (the latter after a plebiscite), both long coveted. Napoleon III then ordered the expansion of French control in Senegal and sent troops to protect missionaries in Lebanon and distant Indochina, annexing Cochin-China as a colony.

An imperial adventure in Mexico, which was in the midst of a civil war, ended in fiasco. The emperor believed that Mexico could become a profitable market for French exports of textiles and wine, and in 1861 he sent troops to protect French financial interests there. When order was restored, the French troops stayed. In 1864, Napoleon III proclaimed his protégé, Austrian Archduke Maximilian (1832–1867), the brother of Habsburg emperor Francis Joseph, to be emperor of Mexico. The United States protested that French intervention represented a violation of the Monroe Doctrine (1823), which had declared the Western Hemisphere off limits to the European powers. The Mexicans, understandably enough, did not want an Austrian emperor. Three years later, Mexican patriots defeated the French forces, who disembarked, leaving Napoleon III's hapless protégé to his own devices. Maximilian was executed in June 1867, a blow to the French emperor's international prestige.

A year earlier, the French emperor had made an error in foreign policy that would come back to haunt him. As Prussia and Austria drew closer to war in 1866, Napoleon III believed that Habsburg Austria would prevail. Bismarck quickly rejected Napoleon III's demand that Prussia compensate France with Rhineland territory. The French emperor then boldly insisted that Prussia go along with a possible French annexation of Belgium and Luxembourg (see Chapter 17). After an international conference a year

Edouard Manet's *Execution of Maximilian* (1867).

later guaranteed Luxembourg's independence, Napoleon III's dreams of territorial compensation from Prussia disappeared. But the cagey Bismarck had the French emperor's written demand tucked away in a drawer.

In June 1868, the emperor's authorization of a law permitting freedom of assembly helped mobilize opposition among monarchists, republicans, and socialists alike. Napoleon III's advisers wondered aloud if he had not sown the seeds of imperial demise by granting liberal reforms. Early in 1870, strikes spread. The emperor invited opponents to join the government and to begin drafting a more liberal constitution, one that would make ministers in some way "responsible" to the Legislative Corps. Napoleon III then reverted to a plebiscite, with a craftily worded statement in May 1870 by which those who wanted more extensive changes were forced to abstain, or to vote "yes" as if they approved of the emperor's policies. The plebiscite, in which "yes" overwhelmed "no," thus partially concealed the depth of opposition to imperial policies.

To the end, Napoleon III manifested a bizarre combination of perceptive foresight and bad judgment. When the Spanish throne fell vacant after a military coup deposed Queen Isabella II of Spain in 1868, one of the candidates was Prince Leopold, a Catholic prince of the ruling Prussian dynasty, the Hohenzollerns (see Chapter 17). Napoleon III threatened war with Prussia if it did not withdraw the Hohenzollern candidacy, which risked, if successful, leaving France with Hohenzollerns on two sides. He then ordered his ambassador to extract a letter from the king of Prussia apologizing to France and promising that Prussia would never revive the candidacy of

Prince Leopold. In July 1870, the French ambassador harangued Prussian King William I in a garden in the spa town of Ems. The king sent Bismarck a telegram stating what had occurred. After learning that the Prussian army was ready to fight, Bismarck embellished the king's telegram—the Ems Dispatch—to make the graceless diplomacy of the French seem positively insulting. Prussian public opinion reacted with anger. Bismarck's expectation that it would "have the effect of a red cloth on the Gallic bull" was justified; the incident increased popular support for war against France, which declared war on July 19, 1870. Württemberg, Hesse, Baden, and, more hesitantly, Bavaria joined the Prussian side. Napoleon III went to war against Prussia without allies.

The Franco-Prussian War and the Siege of Paris

The Franco-Prussian War was a French debacle. As French troops slowly mobilized, Prussian armies moved quickly into northeastern France. The speed of the Prussian attack and the competence of its generals more than made up for superior French rifles and recently developed machine guns. In August, Prussian troops cut off the fortress of Metz from the rest of France. When Marshal Marie-Edme de MacMahon (1808–1893) moved north in an attempt to relieve Metz, the Prussians cut him off. At the end of August, the main French force foolishly retreated to the fortress town of Sedan not far from the Belgian border. Sedan was soon surrounded by Prussians, who captured the emperor, so sick that he could barely sit on his horse. In Paris on September 4, 1870, crowds proclaimed a republic, and a provisional government was formed. Prussia allowed Napoleon III to leave for exile in Britain.

The Prussian army besieged Paris, its population swollen with soldiers and national guardsmen. As hunger invaded the capital, dogs and cats disappeared from the streets, finding their way to some of the finest tables. Zoo animals, too, were eaten, including two elephants admired by generations of Parisian children. An attempt to break through the Prussian lines north of the city at the end of October failed miserably. Still, Paris hung on.

In the meantime, Louis-Adolphe Thiers (1797–1877), who had served as Orleanist prime minister during the 1830s, wanted Bismarck's help in facilitating the establishment of a very conservative republic at the war's conclusion, or even a monarchy. The provisional government negotiated with Bismarck in the hope of obtaining an armistice on favorable terms. On January 28, 1871, ten days after the proclamation of the German Empire at Versailles (see Chapter 17), Bismarck and Thiers signed an armistice.

Some French leaders protested, demanding that the French army keep fighting. In February 1871, French voters elected a monarchist-dominated National Assembly, charged with making peace with Prussia and with establishing a new government. The newly elected National Assembly officially elected Thiers to be chief executive of the provisional government.

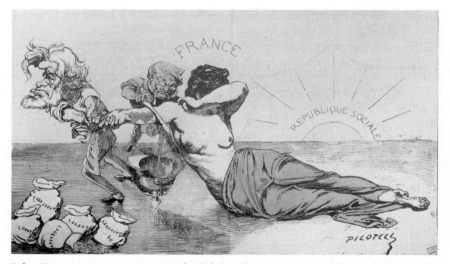

Jules Favre, peace negotiator, and Adolphe Thiers, provisional head of the government, accede to the loss of Alsace-Lorraine, France's right arm. They drag the weeping female image of France away from the "social republic."

By signing the Treaty of Frankfurt (May 10, 1871), France lost Alsace and some of Lorraine to the new German Empire. Prussian troops would occupy Paris and retain garrisons in eastern France until a large indemnity had been paid off. The National Assembly's choice of Versailles, the home of the Bourbon monarchs, as the temporary capital stirred popular anger and suspicion. Parisians, who had held out against the Prussians for four months, resented the ease with which the provinces had seemed to capitulate. Wealthy Parisians who had left Paris at the beginning of the siege returned from the safety of the countryside. Landlords insisted that back rents be paid immediately, angering renters, many of whom were unemployed workers who had managed to hang on during the siege.

The Paris Commune

Early in the morning on March 18, 1871, Thiers sent a small detachment of troops to the butte of Montmartre in Paris to seize cannon that had belonged to the National Guard, many of whose members were socialists, during the siege. Women at the market alerted the neighborhood; a crowd surrounded the detachment and put two generals up against the wall and shot them. Thiers ordered his troops to surround the capital. A second siege of Paris began, this one a civil war.

During the Prussian siege, socialists had placed bright red posters on the walls of the capital calling for the establishment of the "Paris Commune" to defend Paris. The leaders of the Commune were drawn from a variety of political persuasions: Jacobins, socialists, and republicans who wanted Paris to become again the capital of an anticlerical republic. Some Communards had been democratic-socialist activists during the Second Republic; others were followers of the revolutionary Auguste Blanqui (1805–1881), who believed that revolution could be achieved only by a small cell of determined men seizing power. There were also a good many anarchists, who hoped that independent Paris would serve as a model for a society of producers existing without the tyranny of the state.

Revolutionary clubs sprang up. The Communards organized Paris's defense and enacted a number of significant social reforms. These included the creation of a Labor Exchange, a place for workers to gather and find out about jobs; the abolition of night baking (a grievance of bakers) because of long hours and little sleep; the establishment of nurseries for working mothers; and the rights of workers' organizations to receive preference when the

A cartoon dedicated to the National Guard during the Paris Commune. Note the woman standing tall.

municipality contracted work. The Commune recognized women's unions—indeed the role of women in the Commune exceeded that of any previous revolutionary movement in France. Given the severity of the circumstances, with cannon shelling the city, it is remarkable how much the Communards accomplished in such a short time.

Much smaller uprisings occurred in Lyon, Marseille, and several other towns. These movements reflected a combination of middle-class dissatisfaction with Bonapartist centralization, republican enthusiasm, and socialist mobilization. But the provinces provided no help to the Paris Commune; rather, conservative regions sent volunteers to fight for the Versailles forces.

On May 21, 1871, the troops of Thiers's Versailles government poured into Paris through the western gates, left open for them by monarchist sympathizers. During the "bloody week" that followed, Thiers's army, aided by the recently constructed boulevards (see Chapter 19), overwhelmed neighborhood after neighborhood, blasting through barricades. Summary executions occurred throughout Paris, particularly after a rumor began that female incendiaries were burning banks and the homes of the wealthy. The Communards retaliated by executing some hostages, including the archbishop of Paris. About 15,000 to 25,000 Parisians were summarily executed or dispatched after hurried military trials.

For the left, the Commune seemed to be a glimpse of the future proletarian revolution (although Paris largely remained a city of artisans and skilled workers). To conservatives, the Commune offered a frightening glimpse of plebeian insurrection, affirming their resolve to oppose movements for social and political change with force.

REPUBLICAN FRANCE

The National Assembly elected in February 1871 had a monarchist majority. Yet most people in France wanted a republic. Gradually the Third Republic took hold, at first extremely conservative, then moderate, and beginning in 1899, radical, under the guidance of the socially moderate but stridently anticlerical Radical Party. Yet the republic had to overcome dramatic challenges from the far right, which rejected parliamentary rule and dreamed of recapturing Alsace-Lorraine from Germany.

Monarchists and Republicans

The Bourbon pretender to the throne of France was the count of Chambord, a lazy man of mediocre intelligence who lived in an Austrian castle and amused himself by playing cards and telling dirty jokes and anti-Semitic stories to his cronies. The Orleanist pretender to the throne was the relatively dashing count of Paris. Yet Chambord seemed to hold the upper hand, for his was the old Bourbon royal line. But, unlike the count of Paris, he was childless. A compromise, by which Chambord would become king with the count of Paris as his heir, fell through when the former refused to be king under the tricolor flag, which he identified with the French Revolution.

The close association of monarchism with the Catholic Church led many people to agree with the assessment of the radical republican Léon Gambetta (1838–1882) that "clericalism, there is the enemy." Republicans opposed the political domination of the "notables," the wealthiest men in France. The republic found a groundswell of support from those Gambetta called "the new social strata," the shopkeepers, café owners, prosperous peasants, craftsmen, and schoolteachers. The charismatic Gambetta's whistle-stop tours of the provinces reflected the rise of mass politics in France.

Thiers resigned under monarchist pressure as provisional head of state in 1873. Prussian troops marched out of France that year after the French government finished paying off the war indemnity, raised by loans and a public subscription. The monarchists, seeing their majority in the National Assembly eroding with each by-election, elected as president Marshal MacMahon, a hero of the Crimean War and the Italian War of 1859, who favored a monarchist restoration. The new government of "Moral Order," closely tied to the Church, undertook a massive purge of republican mayors, censored newspapers, closed hundreds of cafés, and banned public celebration of the French Revolution on July 14.

For the moment, the government of France was a republic with monarchist political institutions. In January 1874, the National Assembly passed the Wallon Amendment by one vote, stating that henceforth "the president of the Republic" would be elected by the Senate and the Chamber of Deputies. The lower house drafted a republican constitution in 1875, but one that seemed so vague that the state could easily enough have been converted into a monarchy.

Universal male suffrage determined the composition of the Chamber of Deputies. Each district elected a single representative. This gave monarchists an advantage, as local notables would be the most likely beneficiaries from last-minute political negotiations before the second ballot in each election. The Senate would be elected indirectly through a system that was radically tilted to over-represent conservative rural interests. Yet, despite heavy-handed governmental and ecclesiastical pressure on voters, more than twice as many republicans were elected as monarchists to the Chamber of Deputies in 1876. MacMahon was therefore forced to select a moderate republican, Jules Simon (1814–1896), as premier.

The republican majority in the National Assembly sought to limit the power of the president who was, after all, a monarchist. In 1877, MacMahon initiated a political crisis (the Crisis of May 16) by forcing Simon's resignation and naming a monarchist in his place. When the Chamber of

Deputies withheld its approval, MacMahon dissolved it and called for new elections. He embarked, with the help of the Church, on a bitter campaign to defeat Gambetta and the republicans.

However, France's voters returned republicans again, although with a smaller majority. MacMahon named a republican premier, and then resigned in 1879. Henceforth, the role of the executive authority would be weak because republicans feared that some Napoleonic character might try to impose his rule—indeed that threat lay ahead. With the constitutional privilege of dismissing government cabinets that had lost the confidence of the majority of its members, the Chamber of Deputies would dominate the political life of the French Third Republic. In 1881, the Chamber of Deputies passed a bill granting full amnesty to exiled Communards.

The Third Republic

The governments of the new republic reflected the center of the political spectrum, that of the "Opportunists," so called because many of them accepted a very conservative republic while preferring something more to the center. Resolved to hold the center against the monarchists and the Church on the right, and the anticlerical Radicals and the socialists to their left, the Opportunists retained the support of peasants by implementing high agricultural tariffs. The Méline Tariff, supported by industrialists and farmers, went into effect in 1892.

The Opportunist republic guaranteed freedom of the press, legalized public gatherings without prior authorization, and gave municipal councils the right to elect their own mayors (with the exception of Paris, not allowed to have a mayor—until 1977—for fear he might become too powerful). The president served as something of a chairman of the board to the Chamber of Deputies. He shook hands with everybody, intrigued pleasantly, and helped form coalitions. Governments came and went, giving an exaggerated image of parliamentary instability and impotence.

Because the republic had only gradually taken root in the 1870s and had been strongly contested by conservatives, the educational reforms of the 1880s had the goal not only of making France more literate but also more republican. Jules Ferry (1832–1893) sponsored laws that made primary education free and obligatory. The state allocated money to build village schools. Although some priests and nuns stayed on to teach in what were technically lay schools, the debates over the laicization of public schools ensured the animosity of many prelates and practicing Catholics against the "godless" republic.

General Boulanger and Captain Dreyfus

Amid growing social and political division, during the 1880s the parliamentary center began to melt under pressure from right and left. Nationalism became a potent political ideology. Bonapartists emerged from obscurity to tout Napoleon III's cousin, Prince Napoleon Bonaparte (1822–1891), as a potential savior. Some nationalists began to think that the republic was too weak to ever recapture Alsace and much of Lorraine from Germany. This concern with "revenge" against Germany reflected the passing of nationalism from the liberal left to the right wing in France.

The Boulanger Affair was in some ways the birth certificate of the new right in France, the Dreyfus Affair its baptism. In 1887, French rightists began to place their hopes of overthrowing the republic on the dashing figure of General Georges Boulanger (1837–1891), who had risen rapidly through the ranks to become minister of war. His bellicose noises about recapturing Alsace-Lorraine pleased nationalists while irritating Bismarck. Conservatives now were convinced that they had found the man who could overthrow the republic, restore the monarchy, or establish a dictatorship. Flattered by all of the attention, Boulanger allowed his name to be put forward as a candidate for the Chamber of Deputies.

The political movement on behalf of Boulanger was arguably the first mass political campaign in France. Funds provided by a wealthy royalist widow helped inundate the country with electoral posters and busts and statues of the dashing general. His supporters battled their political enemies in the streets, bringing unprecedented violence into an electoral campaign and drawing on rising nationalist anti-Semitism, although there were only about 80,000 Jews in a population of 40 million in France. For example, Parisian shopkeepers, frustrated by the economic depression, fearful of workers' consumer cooperatives, and losing clients to department stores, swung their support to right-wing nationalist parties, convinced by right-wing polemicists that "Jewish capitalists" were responsible for their plight.

Boulanger was elected in by-elections in several districts, but because he was in the army, he was ineligible to serve in the Chamber of Deputies. At this point, no one was sure what exactly Boulanger represented, no one probably less than the general himself. If his campaign money came from the right, many of his votes at first came from the left. The Opportunist government sent Boulanger to central France to remove him from the political limelight of the capital.

A political scandal cast a further shadow on the government, giving another twist to the term "opportunist." A prostitute revealed that the Legion of Honor medal was being peddled to the highest bidder. It turned out that one of the most successful salesmen was Daniel Wilson, the ruthless son-in-law of President Jules Grévy, who resigned.

All of this added to a feeling among some observers that the Third Republic was already at the end of its rope. The government declared General Boulanger retired. But this now left him free to run for the Chamber of Deputies, and he was elected deputy from Paris. To his right-wing followers, it seemed that a perfect occasion for a coup d'état had arrived. In January 1889, triumphant crowds gathered in the street, calling out Boulanger's name while he sat in a restaurant quietly eating dinner. But his moment passed. Two years later, government officials convinced the naive general that they held evidence that could lead to his conviction on charges of state treason. Boulanger caught a train to Belgium and, on the grave of his late mistress, took out his army pistol and blew out his brains.

Having survived Boulanger, the republic then received an unexpected boost from its old enemy, the Catholic Church, whose "rallying" (the *Ralliement*) to the republic began with an archbishop's toast in 1891 in Tunisia. Henceforth, the moderate republicans could draw on political support from the Catholic right against the socialist parties.

Another scandal gave the anti-parliamentary right a new focus for opposition. In 1881, a French company had begun to dig the Panama Canal under the direction of Ferdinand de Lesseps, who had overseen the construction of the Suez Canal. This canal proved to be even more challenging to build because of difficult terrain and malarial conditions. Company officials bribed government officials in the hope of gathering sufficient support to get the Chamber of Deputies to approve a loan that would be financed by a national lottery. The Chamber of Deputies obligingly approved the plan, but the financial campaign fell short. When the company went broke in 1889, more than half a million investors lost their money.

In 1892, Édouard Drumont's right-wing newspaper *La Libre Parole* published a series of revelations about the scandal. Drumont had earlier published a book in which he claimed that Jewish financiers were conspiring to dominate France. Now, the fact that some of the directors of the defunct company had been Jewish helped generate support for the League of Patriots, founded in 1892, a nationalist and anti-Semitic organization of the extreme right. The next year an indulgent court acquitted all but one of those implicated in the scandal.

The next scandal was such a series of dramatic events that it became known for years simply as "the Affair." It pitted right against left; the army, Church, and monarchists against republicans and, in time, socialists; and family against family.

Alfred Dreyfus (1859–1935) was the son of an old Jewish family from Alsace. His family had been peddlers and then textile manufacturers. They were assimilated Jews, proudly considering themselves French. Fol-

The suicide of General Boulanger.

lowing the annexation of Alsace by Germany in 1871, the Dreyfus family moved to Paris. In 1894, evidence surfaced—from a wastepaper basket in the office of a German military attaché—that someone in the French army had been passing secret information to the Germans about French military operations. Circumstantial evidence pointed to Captain Dreyfus—the writing on a list of documents that had been prepared to be handed over to a German contact resembled Dreyfus's handwriting. Maintaining his innocence, Dreyfus refused the arresting officer's offer of a loaded pistol with which he could kill himself. A hurriedly convened and secret court-martial found him guilty of treason. Dreyfus was stripped of his rank and sent to Devil's Island off the coast of South America.

However, confidential documents continued to disappear from French army offices. Two years later, a new chief of army intelligence, Lieutenant Colonel Georges Picquart, determined to his own satisfaction that the original list of documents had not been penned by Dreyfus, but by Major Walsin Esterhazy. Picquart, who was an unlikely hero in this case because he made no secret of his anti-Semitism, presented his evidence. But high-ranking officers believed that it was better to have an innocent Jew languishing in increasing depression on Devil's Island than to compromise the army's public image. The army packed Picquart off to a post in Tunisia, and a military court acquitted Esterhazy, despite overwhelming evidence of guilt.

(*Left*) Édouard Drumont's anti-Semitic newspaper *La Libre Parole* (*The Free Word*), 1893. (*Right*) Captain Alfred Dreyfus.

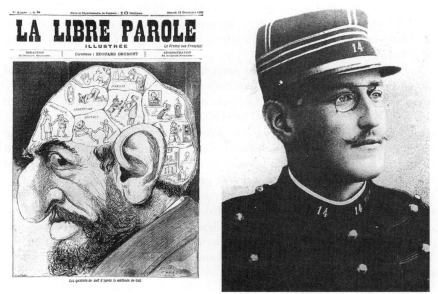

The novelist Émile Zola now took up Dreyfus's case. In January 1898, he wrote an article in a daily newspaper with the bold headline *"J'accuse!"* ("I accuse!"), denouncing the army and the government for covering up the reality of the case. The political right and the Church hierarchy jumped in on the side of the "anti-Dreyfusards," seeing the Dreyfus Affair as a conspiracy of Jews and Freemasons to destroy France by undermining the prestige of its army. A Catholic newspaper demanded that all Jews be deprived of their citizenship. Action Française, a right-wing nationalist and monarchist organization led by Charles Maurras (1868–1952), an anti-Semitic novelist, jumped into the fray against Dreyfus. Socialists demanded a new trial.

Another officer soon discovered that some new documents had been added to the Dreyfus file. They had been quite badly forged by Lieutenant Colonel Hubert Henry, who hoped they would lead to a new conviction of Dreyfus. Confronted with the evidence, Henry committed suicide in a military prison. In 1899, the army retried Dreyfus, once again finding him guilty, but with "extenuating circumstances." Dreyfus returned, a broken man, to Devil's Island. However, the president of France gave Dreyfus a presidential pardon that year, which allowed him to return to his family, although Dreyfus was not fully exonerated until 1906, when his military rank was restored.

The Radical Republic

Dreyfus's return to France provided the republic with a badly needed period of stability and boosted the Radical Party. The Dreyfus Affair had helped forge a working alliance between the Radicals, who were anticlerical moderate republicans, and socialists, which moved the republic to the left. In the Radical government formed in 1899, Alexandre Millerand (1859–1943), a reform socialist, became minister of commerce, despite the bitter opposition of many socialists who objected to a socialist serving in a "bourgeois" government.

In contrast to Britain, where the Anglican Church had always stood behind the government, in France the dominant religion had—at least until 1891—stood against the regime. The Radicals moved to separate church and state against conservative opposition. In 1902, the Chamber of Deputies, with socialist support, passed legislation exiling religious orders from France. In 1905, church and state were formally separated in France. During the next two years, the state took possession of all ecclesiastical property and assumed responsibility for paying the salaries of priests. Despite papal condemnation and the resistance of some clergy and parishioners, a *modus vivendi* evolved, with parish councils leasing churches from the state.

The Radical Premier Georges Clemenceau (1841–1929) embodied aggressive French nationalism. The man who later became known as "the Tiger" had been born into a family of modest noble title. His father was a prominent republican who had been exiled by Napoleon III. Clemenceau was a wealthy bully and a formidable dueler who hated socialists, unions, and the Catholic Church as much as he did his American ex-wife, whom he had followed by a detective, jailed, and deported. In 1907, he sent troops to crush a determined strike by small property owners and vineyard laborers in the south.

In 1911, Radical Premier Joseph Caillaux (1863–1944), unlike Clemenceau, sought accommodation with Germany. The French Socialist Party launched a campaign against militarism and particularly against the extension of the term of military service from two to three years. Anti-militarism remained popular among workers because of the role of troops in the repression of strikes. But the Second Moroccan Crisis between Germany and France that same year (see Chapter 22) gave rise to another wave of nationalism. Besieged by the press for his pacific stand, Caillaux's government fell the following year. Raymond Poincaré (1860–1934), an outspoken nationalist, became premier in 1912 and then president a year later. He eagerly anticipated the chance to win back Alsace and Lorraine, and he firmed up French support of a Russian role in the Balkans. Poincaré's nationalism seemed in tune with the times.

CONCLUSION

The second half of the nineteenth century brought about significant political change to the three European powers that had been the strongest at mid-century. In Britain, the second Reform Bill of 1867 expanded the electoral franchise, and another law in 1884 followed suit. After the collapse of the Second Empire in 1870 and the Paris Commune the following year, France emerged as a republic. In Russia, Tsar Alexander II's emancipation of the serfs in 1861 did not change the fundamental institutions of autocracy. Yet some reforms did follow, even as critics of the tsarist state grew more vocal, and the Revolution of 1905 challenged the foundations of autocracy. In the meantime, Britain's economic strength and great navy left it in a position to dominate international affairs. Having defeated Austria and then France, Prussia emerged as the leader of a unified and powerful Germany, dominant in Central Europe. At the same time, the Second Industrial Revolution brought remarkable technological advances, increased mass production, and ever larger cities now bathed in electric light.

CHAPTER 19

RAPID INDUSTRIALIZATION AND ITS CHALLENGES, 1870–1914

Jeanne Bouvier was a peasant girl born in 1865 in southeastern France. Her father earned his living by tilling the fields and as a barrel maker, an occupation closely tied to wine production. But in 1876, disease began to destroy the vineyards of the Rhône River Valley. Jeanne's family was forced to sell its land and possessions and travel to find work, pushed along by poverty and unemployment. From age eleven to fourteen, Jeanne worked thirteen hours a day in a silk mill. Four other jobs in various towns and villages in her region followed until Jeanne's mother took her to Paris, where the first job she found lasted only a week. Like so many other single, female migrants to city life, she then worked as a domestic servant. A cousin showed her how to do hat-trimming work. When that trade collapsed because of changes in style and the economic depression, she became a skilled dressmaker in a Parisian workshop and then developed her own clientele. Jeanne Bouvier became a Parisian. When she returned home to her native village, Jeanne spoke French, and not the patois in which her old friends conversed. She had become an urban woman.

In 1900, the French Catholic writer Charles Péguy expressed the opinion that Europe had changed more in the previous thirty years than it had since the time of Jesus Christ. The period 1870–1914 was indeed one of rapid economic and social change in much of Europe. Rail networks extended their reach into the countryside, carrying manufactured goods and returning with meat, vegetables, fresh milk, and fruit for burgeoning cities. The speed and capacity of steamships brought American cereal grains, cattle, and meat to Western European ports, reducing their prices.

Technological advances helped propel the Second Industrial Revolution, which beginning in the 1850s and 1860s swept across much of northern, western, and central Europe, as well as the United States, and some of southern and eastern Europe. New manufacturing processes spurred the emergence of the chemical, electrical, and the steel industries. "Big business" took shape as larger companies controlled a greater share of markets.

Technological advances and mechanized factory production transformed the way millions of people worked and lived. Electric lights turned night into day in cities and towns. A permanent working class that had broken its ties with the countryside developed. However, rural areas were also changing as agricultural productivity increased. Large, productive farms whose lands were enriched by chemical fertilizers and cultivated with mechanized equipment encouraged more efficient regional agricultural specialization. Improvements in agriculture were less apparent in the Russian Empire, Eastern Europe, and the Balkans, although in Hungary, where the great magnates and other nobles still owned much of the land, the use of agricultural machinery, the rotation of crops, and product specialization also brought greater yields.

Declining mortality rates led to an increase in Europe's population. Longer life expectancy followed better nutrition—a more varied diet with greater caloric consumption—as well as improved sanitation and purer water supplies. Living conditions gradually improved for most people. Wages continued to rise. Mass education elevated rates of literacy. The middle class expanded in size and complexity. An expansion in white-collar jobs—including positions as clerks, tram ticket collectors, and schoolteachers, among many others—offered peasants and workers chances for social mobility, particularly in Western Europe.

An elegant London department store, late nineteenth century.

Many workers now had a little money and time left over for leisure activities. Bicycles, sports, and, early in the new century, movies became part of the lives of millions. Nonetheless, in many regions—including much of southern Italy, Spain, Portugal, Russia, and the Balkans—wrenching poverty remained common, and mobility into the middle class remained exceptional at the turn of the century.

Emigration to other countries emerged as one of the most significant social phenomena of the age, particularly during the depression that lasted from 1873 into the mid-1890s. Peasants and laborers, in particular, left Europe in hope of economic opportunity in the United States, Canada, and Latin America. Great Britain, Germany, and Ireland had provided most of the earlier waves of emigrants—for example, during the "hungry forties" marked by the Irish potato famine. Now Italians, in particular, headed overseas in great numbers, along with Scandinavians.

The last years of the nineteenth century—the fin de siècle—would be remembered after World War I as the "Belle Époque"—the "good old days"— a period of material progress and cultural innovation. New inventions like the telephone and automobile promised an even better life ahead.

The Second Industrial Revolution

Steel led the Second Industrial Revolution. Then electricity accelerated European economic growth, providing, in the century's last two decades, power for industry. The Second Industrial Revolution brought a stunning variety of technological innovations that ultimately improved the everyday lives of most Europeans. In large cities, subways and, increasingly, automobiles made people more mobile. At the same time, new discoveries in the physical sciences—particularly chemistry—and the development of germ theory and bacteriology led to advances that improved agriculture, as well as public health, making possible longer lives.

The Second Industrial Revolution seemed impervious to an economic depression that began in 1873 and lasted until the mid-1890s. It was marked by falling prices and punctuated by financial panics, although not by prolonged unemployment or economic stagnation. Following a fever of speculation, particularly in Germany, banks failed in Vienna. The speed with which the crisis spread to other financial capitals reflected the extent to which improvements in transportation and communication had extended the links of an increasingly global economy. British foreign investment doubled between 1900 and 1914, and within Europe the volume of trade increased by twenty-five times between 1820 and 1913. Increasingly, the price of grain and other essential commodities became more constant with the development of a global market for foodstuffs. Agricultural prices fell virtually everywhere in Europe, in part because imported grain from the

United States and Canada flooded markets. In industrialized countries, tariffs became the focus of impassioned political debate, even in Britain, where economic liberalism remained the prevailing credo. Governments responded to the depression by imposing protective tariffs, in the interest of native industries and agriculture, in Austria (1874), Russia (1875), France (1892), Italy (1887), and Germany (1902).

New Technology and Scientific Discoveries

In 1856, the English inventor Henry Bessemer (1813–1898) developed a new method for forging steel from pig iron by forcing air through the molten metal to reduce its carbon content. The result was steel that was less expensive to produce than it had been by the old method and that could be turned out in greater quantities (see Table 19.1). Other related discoveries over the next twenty years permitted the production of steel of a more consistent quality, lowering its price by two-thirds.

Steel's strength, durability, and flexibility gave it a marked advantage over iron. Steel improved the size, quality, standardization, and precision of machinery. Just three years after Bessemer's discovery, the first British ship constructed of steel slid into the sea. Larger, sturdier, and faster than their predecessors, steel ships transformed naval warfare.

Medical advances enhanced the already soaring prestige of science and the professional stature of its practitioners. In much of Europe, a trip to the doctor was no longer seen as the first stop on the way to the undertaker. Anesthesia, which had already been discovered in the United States in the 1840s, made surgery less painful. The French scientist Louis Pasteur (1822–1895) discovered that just as various types of fermentation were caused by different kinds of germs, so were many diseases. His development of germ theory in the 1860s brought a virtual revolution in health

TABLE 19.1. ANNUAL OUTPUT OF STEEL (IN MILLIONS OF METRIC TONS)

Year	Britain	Germany	France	Russia
1875–1879	0.90	—	0.26	0.08
1880–1884	1.82	0.99	0.46	0.25
1885–1889	2.86	1.65	0.54	0.23
1890–1894	3.19	2.89	0.77	0.54
1895–1899	4.33	5.08	1.26	1.32
1900–1904	5.04	7.71	1.70	2.35
1905–1909	6.09	11.30	2.65	2.63
1910–1913	6.93	16.24	4.09	4.20

Source: Carlo Cipolla, ed., *The Fontana Economic History of Europe*, vol. 3(2) (London: Collins/Fontana Books, 1976), p. 775.

Louis Pasteur in his laboratory.

care. Pasteur's experiments demonstrated that the spoilage of food could be avoided by destroying microbes that were already present and preventing the arrival of others (thus, the "pasteurization" of milk). Pasteur's studies of specific bacteria and viruses led to the immunization of animals and helped end a silkworm blight. Wilhelm Röntgen (1845–1923), a German scientist, discovered the X-ray in 1895. Then another German, Robert Koch (1843–1910), discovered and isolated the tuberculosis bacillus.

The development of bacteriology, which infused the hygienic movement with the certitude of science and helped create preventative medicine, reduced mortality by encouraging, for example, sewage works. Sewer systems ensured a cleaner water supply, reducing some contagious diseases. People became less tolerant of foul smells. Rat poison killed off disease-carrying rodents.

The Electric and Chemical Revolutions

Electricity made possible the invention of the electromagnetic telegraph, the undersea cable, and the telephone. Yet electricity remained little more than a scientific curiosity until relatively late in the century. The bottleneck remained the generation of electricity. Werner von Siemens (1816–1892), a German, invented the first self-excited electromagnetic generator in 1867, which made possible the production of electrical energy, and three years later the first generator of direct current (a ring dynamo) followed. Germany took the lead in the production of power generators. Thomas Edison (1847–1931), an American scientist, invented the incandescent lamp in 1879. Two years later, the first electric power stations began operation in England, and during the following decades electricity gradually entered European homes. Electric alternators and transformers and improvements in cable and insulation provided means by which electric power could be generated and diffused. Yet, well into the twentieth century, in many parts of Europe electricity still remained a luxury.

For all their efficiency, water power, coal, and gas had placed limits on the location of factories. Electric power, however, could be transported with relative ease, which ultimately enabled countries not well endowed with natural resources to industrialize partially. The steel, textile, shoe-making, and construction industries, among others, came to depend upon electric power. In Europe, as in the United States, the first results of the electric age were particularly striking in heavy industry—for example in electrochemistry (aluminum) and metallurgy (electric furnaces). The burgeoning German electrical manufacturing industry helped Germany to challenge Britain for European manufacturing primacy.

The sewing machine, developed by the American Isaac Singer (1811–1875), began to be found in industry and homes in the 1850s, well before the use of electricity became common. The mechanization of the production of ready-made garments rapidly extended consumer markets, setting styles and reducing the price of clothing. But the impact of the sewing machine also demonstrated continuities in industrial work. For the garment industry—attracting Jewish immigrants to Paris and, above all, New York—remained largely tied to home work, as well as to sweatshops. Women, and some men, too, turned out ready-made cloaks and dresses. Machines that could do band stitching, make buttonholes, or embroider led to a further specialization of labor. Singer marketed his machine as a device that would liberate women from tedious work. But the sewing machine also bound many women to the hectic pace of piecework, and to payments for the machine itself, usually purchased on time-payment plans.

By 1900, other electrically powered household appliances—refrigerators, fans, and vacuum cleaners—were generally available to those families that could afford to have their houses wired for electricity and could pay for the appliances.

The development of chemistry also brought lasting advances. In Germany, university chemical research and teaching developed precociously. German companies benefited from synthetic organic chemistry, manufacturing dyes, soaps, and pharmaceuticals, further improving sanitation and public health. Fritz Haber (1868–1934) discovered the nitrogen-fixing process, by which atmospheric nitrogen could be converted into compounds. By 1913, he and his colleagues were able to transform ammonia into nitric acid by oxidation, which made possible the industrial production of fertilizers and explosives. Advances in chemistry helped transform agriculture, the textile industry, and engineering.

In Western Europe, powerful industrial giants began to emerge. The development of economic cartels dealt a blow to the liberal era of free trade. Cartels are formal agreements by which competitors within the same industry protect profits by sharing markets, regulating output, fixing prices, and taking other measures to limit competition. Cartels permitted a few large companies to dominate production and distribution, enabling heavy industries to protect themselves during periods of falling prices and high unemployment by controlling production and setting prices. In Germany, mining cartels set production goals and kept prices artificially high. In France and Great Britain, informal agreements among industrialists achieved virtually the same results as formalized cartels. The return to protective tariffs aided

Women working on a sewing machine and sewing by hand.

cartels, protecting them from competition from abroad. Even where there were no cartels, the concentration of business in larger companies continued, in part because in industries such as metallurgy and chemicals, expensive machinery made "start-up" costs prohibitive for smaller firms.

Regional Variations

The industrial boom of the Second Industrial Revolution was perhaps most dramatic in Germany. By 1890, both Germany and the United States had surged ahead of Britain in metallurgical production. By the turn of the century, German factories turned out more steel than Britain and France combined, and Germany's chemical industry was the most modern in the world. In 1900, Britain produced twice as much sulphuric acid as Germany; in 1913, the proportion had been reversed. Germany's national product more than tripled between unification in 1871 and 1914.

Germany enjoyed the advantage of starting to industrialize after its rivals, thereby being able to employ the most modern equipment in factories specially built to accommodate technological advances. By contrast, some British factories, most of which had been built early in the century (and some even before), seemed to be crumbling.

German banks played a more direct role in German industrialization than did their counterparts in other countries. While providing investment capital, large investment banks acquired large blocks of industrial shares, particularly in heavy industries like coal mining, electricity, and railways. Having entered industry to assure proper business management of companies to which they loaned money, the banks earned big profits and paid high dividends to those who had invested in them. German banks themselves became industrial entrepreneurs. This also favored the trend of German industry toward cartels, which controlled production and prices.

German universities were more numerous and of better quality than any others in Europe at the same time, despite their authoritarian structure and their acquiescence in discrimination against Jews, Catholics, and socialists. They emerged as centers of scientific research, particularly in chemistry. By contrast, English employers tended to look down their noses at academic training as a poor substitute for work experience, just as universities in Britain were relatively slow to adopt a more practical curriculum.

Great Britain remained the world's greatest economic power, but British manufactured goods stacked up at the docks as demand declined abroad and prices fell. By the mid-1880s, some of the countries that had purchased British goods were able to meet consumer demand at home with their own production. In the century's last decades, shiploads of foreign-made goods began to undercut British production, which was unprotected by tariff walls. Instead of depending upon British shipping, German, Italian, and French merchants now took advantage of the Suez Canal, opened in 1869, to send their own ships to Asia to make purchases and sell goods directly.

In the Russian Empire, the economy remained overwhelmingly agricultural. Despite the development of Ukraine as a major producer of wheat, the famine of 1890–1891, to which the novelist Leo Tolstoy helped focus international concern, killed millions of peasants. Absentee ownership of large estates, peasant plots that continued to be farmed at subsistence level as they had been for centuries, and village communal lands hindered agricultural development. Farmers in some places lacked even enough horses to pull plows. Yet Russian agriculture gradually increased its productivity, doing so without the capital-intensive farming that characterized much of Western Europe. Russian increases in harvest yields were comparable to those of France and Germany by 1900, making possible the increased export of grain and other foodstuffs. The Peasant Land Bank, created in the 1880s, helped thousands of peasants purchase land, and a thriving cooperative movement beginning at the turn of the century brought some prosperity.

Russian industries still confronted the serious physical impediment of sheer distance between resources, manufacturers, and markets. Coal deposits lay far from centers of manufacturing. Weak banking structures limited the accumulation of investment capital, and the Orthodox Church viewed investment as usurious and therefore dishonest.

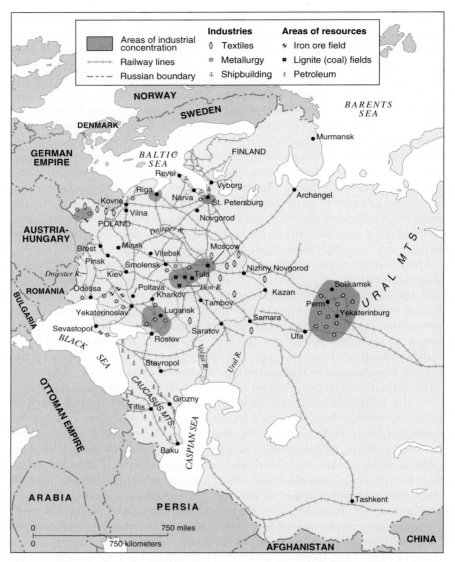

MAP 19.1 RUSSIAN INDUSTRIALIZATION, 1870–1914   Areas of industrial concentration, including kinds of industry and resources.

Yet Russian industry also developed rapidly beginning in the mid-1890s, benefiting from advanced technology imported from Western Europe (see Map 19.1). Foreign investment in Russia, above all from France, more than doubled during the 1890s. Although textiles still represented the largest branch of Russian industry, heavy industries, particularly metallurgy, boomed. The state helped develop heavy metals and fuel production,

TABLE 19.2. PRODUCTION OF COAL AND STEEL IN RUSSIA (IN THOUSANDS OF TONS)

Year	Coal	Steel
1860	695	257
1880	3,276	289
1890	6,015	857
1900	16,155	2,711
1910	25,000	3,017
1913	36,038	4,918

Source: Arcadius Kahan, *Russian Economic History: The Nineteenth Century* (Chicago: University of Chicago Press, 1989), p. 21.

including oil. The output of steel increased fourfold during the last decades of the century (see Table 19.2). By 1914, Saint Petersburg had become one of the largest concentrations of industry in Europe, with more than 900 factories. The growth of light industry and the expansion of the market contributed considerably to the country's economic growth, permitting exports to Asian neighbors. Russian foreign trade tripled between 1885 and 1913. The length of Russia's rail lines increased by three times between 1881 and 1905, and its banks developed in size and scale. By the turn of the century, railroads at last linked Russia's major cities and facilitated the shipping of grain to the empire's northern ports.

The Russian working class grew from about 2 million industrial workers in 1900 to about 3 million by 1914 (compared to over a 100 million peasants). Yet many Russian industrial workers still labored part-time in agriculture. In 1900, peasants made up two-thirds of the population of Saint Petersburg, a city of more than 1.4 million people. They retained strong ties to their villages, which remained their legal residences. The rural commune still carried out functions of local authority, including many fiscal obligations (assuring the payment of taxes and redemption payments on land gained at the time of the emancipation of the serfs in 1861), policing (including overseeing the division of communal lands), and rudimentary welfare functions.

In most of Europe's industrializing countries, the growing manufacturing sector coexisted with small-scale production (see Map 19.2). In France, the production of high-quality handicrafts, centered in Paris, continued to dominate industry. Traditional small-scale manufacturing also persisted alongside regionally specific heavy industries in Spain (Catalonia and the Basque region), Austria-Hungary, and Italy, where little large-scale industry could be found south of the triangle formed by Milan, Turin, and the port of Genoa. As in Russia, most of the investment in Spanish industry came from abroad because agriculture generated inadequate surpluses for significant industrial investment. In the Austro-Hungarian monarchy, the dynamism of

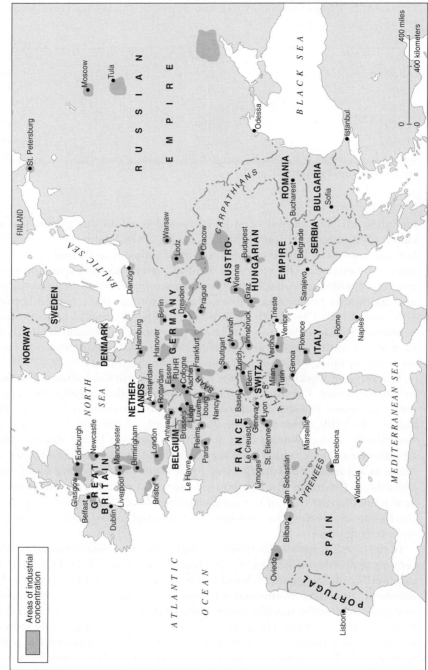

Map 19.2 Areas of Industrial Concentration, 1870–1914   Various regions industrialized more quickly than others, with industrial concentration likely to be found where there were coal fields and rivers.

Bohemia and Moravia contrasted sharply with the small-market ways of Austria and the Hungarian plain. In the Balkans, where major rail lines were not in place until the late 1880s, poor roads and the daunting mountains limited the emergence of vibrant regional market economies. In many places, mules remained the best way to transport goods. Yet even in overwhelmingly rural Bulgaria, the value of industrial production multiplied by three times just between 1904 and 1911, and the railway network increased rapidly after 1880.

Travel and Communications

Electric power led to the construction of modern public transportation systems, first trams and then subways. Mass transportation transformed residential patterns in large cities. The London underground railway had already opened without electricity in 1863, making it possible for employees and workers to live much farther from their jobs. In 1900, the first Paris subway—the *métro*—began operation on the right bank of the Seine River, and other lines soon followed. Four years later, the first sections of New York City's subway began operation.

In 1885, Carl Benz (1844–1929), a German engineer, built upon the invention of the internal combustion engine. He added a primitive carburetor and constructed a small automobile. The first automobiles were very expensive, the tires alone costing more than an average worker's annual wages. In 1897, Rudolf Diesel (1858–1913), a German, produced the first successful engine fueled by kerosene, which could power larger vehicles. By the turn of the century, four-cylinder engines powered automobiles.

Automobile manufacturing quickly became a major catalyst for industrial growth and the implementation of new production methods, stimulating the production of steel, aluminum, rubber, and tools. The petroleum industry slowly developed, although at the time only the oil reserves in Romania were known and exploited (the first oil refinery in Europe had been built there in 1857). Little by little some industrialists and statesmen began to grasp the economic and strategic significance of oil, particularly after the discovery in 1908 of rich oil fields in Persia (Iran).

Automobile manufacturers shifted from the limited production of elite cars, above all, the British Rolls Royce, to less expensive models. Henry Ford (1863–1947), who began his company in Detroit in 1903, produced more than 15 million "Model T" Fords, which even some of his own workers could afford to purchase. Worried by American competition, the French car manufacturer Louis Renault (1877–1944) looked for ways to cut production costs. Assembly-line production made it possible to construct cars in segments. Workers mounted components on stationary chassis frames lined up along the factory floor. They used hand files to shape engine parts for expensive cars since interchangeable parts were not yet available. The assembly

An early automobile assembly line.

line reduced the time it took to produce each car from twelve hours to one and a half hours.

The automobile transformed travel. Elegant horses and fancy carriages owned by people of means no longer monopolized travel. However, until it was repealed in 1896, the British "Red Flag Act" restricted the speed of motor vehicles to two miles per hour and required three people carrying red warning flags to accompany each vehicle, a decided inconvenience. In 1896, the speed limit was raised to fourteen miles per hour.

Car travel necessitated better roads. Early drivers required not only thick goggles to protect themselves against dust but also whips to keep away startled dogs. Gradually, government authorities ordered the paving of roads, and gas stations began to dot the landscape. In 1900, the Michelin Company in France, one of the first to shift from producing bicycle to automobile tires, published its first guide for travelers, listing garages, hotels, and restaurants. Michelin successfully lobbied for signs along roads indicating distances. The number of cars in Paris tripled between 1906 and 1912. Traffic jams became a way of urban life. Motorized taxis and then motorized fire engines raced by their horse-drawn predecessors.

The cult of speed next took to the air, after centuries of dreams had brought only balloon ascents and short glider flights. In 1900, a retired German general, Count Ferdinand von Zeppelin (1838–1917), built the lumbering dirigible airship that still bears his name. After years of experimentation with propellers and small engines, Orville and Wilbur Wright, two American bicycle manufacturers, launched the first successful flight in 1903. They then took their air show to England, France, and Germany, where the crown prince of Prussia began to consider the military uses of the airplane.

More Europeans could now travel for leisure than ever before. Middle-class vacations became more common. The travel business boomed. Health spas and resorts, which had developed since the mid-1800s, became even more popular in Western Europe. Spas claimed that their thermal waters offered healing and sustaining properties that facilitated the circulation of blood, attacked gout—the encumbering malady of people who were too well fed—or in some other way restored to equilibrium the human body victimized by modern life.

Mediterranean, North Sea, and English Channel resorts offered casinos and beachfront promenades. English coastal towns like Brighton and Blackpool attracted visitors oblivious to the rain. The tourist pier and arcade took shape. English nobles, who could afford to flee the British winter, "discovered" Nice. Upper-class Italians began to frequent their own Riviera, Belgians the port of Ostend, and Germans the Baltic resorts. Vacationers from many countries discovered the Alps and sent the first postcards back to envious friends. Partially spurred on by tourism, photography emerged as a major visual art. The relatively light Kodak camera appeared in 1888. Bretons began to refer to French-speaking tourists as "Kodakers."

A revolution in communications also slowly transformed life. The telegraph had already increased the availability of news from around the world, with the help of press agencies like Havas, the Associated Press, and Reuters. The telephone, invented by Alexander Graham Bell (1847–1922) in 1876, reached private homes. Germans made 8 million telephone calls in 1883, 700 million in 1900. Fifteen years after Thomas Edison invented the gramophone in 1876, a number of virtuosos had made their first scratchy recordings. The Italian Guglielmo Marconi (1874–1937) pioneered the first wireless voice communication in the 1890s; by 1913, weekly concerts could be heard on the radio in Brussels. Silent motion pictures, first shown in 1895, became an immediate hit, sometimes accompanied by a piano. Early viewers watched brief scenes of modern life, such as a train beginning to move. Longer films with plots and action followed. The Austro-Hungarian army began to experiment with motion pictures, using cameras to study the flight of artillery shells.

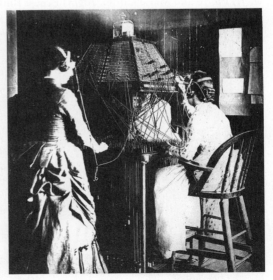

Women at work at a telephone switchboard.

*Further Scientific Discoveries: "A Boundless Future"
and Its Uncertainties*

The astonishing advances of late nineteenth-century science led one researcher to exude that "science strides on victoriously towards a boundless future." The creation in 1883 of a worldwide system for patenting reflected a veritable torrent of new inventions. Scientists had already concluded that cells form the basis for life. This knowledge led scientists to understand more about the principles of heredity. At the same time, new discoveries revealing nature's complexity began to temper the infectious optimism of the age. Fin-de-siècle scientists realized that the more they understood about the world, the more there was left to know about such basic principles as matter, light, and energy. Mathematicians and especially physicists began to rethink fundamental assumptions about the universe.

Radioactivity was discovered in Paris in 1896. Marie Curie (1867–1934), a Polish-born chemist carrying out research with her husband, Pierre Curie (1859–1906), isolated radium, a radioactive element, in 1910. Marie Curie, who was refused entry to the French Academy of Science because of her gender, won two Nobel Prizes. Her rival, Ernest Rutherford (1871–1937), a New Zealander, discovered two kinds of radiation, which he called the alpha and beta rays. He posited the disintegration of radioactive atoms, which is the phenomenon of radioactivity. Rutherford used this discovery to

(*Left*) Pierre and Marie Curie. (*Right*) Ernest Rutherford, who is holding the apparatus that he used to break up the nucleus of the nitrogen atom.

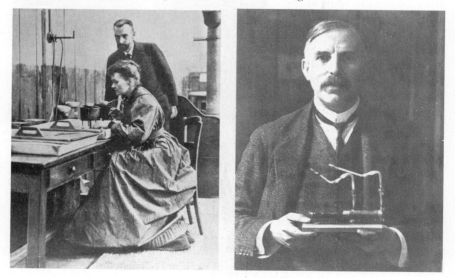

postulate the structure of the atom, with a positively charged nucleus and negatively charged electrons circling around it.

"Particle theories" in physics cast doubt on contemporary assumptions about the universe. They demonstrated the complexity of motion, light, and matter, which appeared to consist of electrically charged particles. Since the time of Sir Isaac Newton in the seventeenth century, scientists had believed that any two objects, whether the sun and the earth, or a coffee cup and a bowl of sugar, acted on each other through gravitational force. There seemed no mechanism for transmitting action but rather only empty space between the two. James Maxwell (1831–1879), a British scientist, solved the "action at a distance" problem for the case of electromagnetic forces. His theory of electromagnetic fields postulated that one object creates an electrical field around particles, which in turn exerts forces on electrically charged objects, and that light itself consists of electromagnetic waves. The German scientist Max Planck (1858–1947) discovered that radiant energy is emitted discontinuously in discrete units, or quanta. Planck's quantum theory, not finalized until 1925, challenged the fundamental scientific understanding of energy that had survived almost intact since Newton's day. More than this, it seemed to add an element of chance to the story of the universe, suggesting that its operations were not absolutely predictable. Here, too, scientists now realized that they knew considerably less about the nature of matter and about the universe than they had long assumed.

These discoveries were only a beginning. The much more difficult problem of gravity remained. In Switzerland, German-born Albert Einstein

Albert Einstein explaining his theories to a stunned audience.

(1879–1955), whose modest position as a patent examiner of other people's discoveries belied his genius, sought to carry physics beyond Newton's theory that space and time were absolute quantities. In 1905, Einstein postulated a special theory of relativity, arguing that the velocity of light was both constant and independent of the velocities of the source and observer of light.

Einstein also postulated the relationship between mass and energy in his equation: $E = mc^2$ (energy equals mass multiplied by the square of the speed of light). In the mid-twentieth century, this formula would provide the key for the controlled release of energy from the atom. Einstein's search for an exact description of the laws of gravitation led him in 1915 from his relatively simple special theory of relativity to his general principle of relativity, which postulated that the laws of nature operated in exactly the same way for all observers. His theory supplanted traditional theories of gravitation, which saw gravity as a property of objects interacting with each other. Rather, Einstein believed that they interacted with space. Yet Einstein and other scientists remained ill at ease with the element of chance suggested by Planck's quantum theory. Trying to explain his conclusion that the universe could not operate in a random way, Einstein later insisted: "God does not play dice." Both Planck's theory, by suggesting a role for chance, and Einstein's staggering achievements themselves left open as many questions for the future as they resolved, not the least of which would later be terrifying new applications of the German scientist's famous formula to the hydrogen and atom bombs.

Social Change

Between 1870 and 1914, the population of Europe increased by half, rising from 290 to 435 million (see Table 19.3). By the end of the nineteenth century, one of every four people in the world was a European. The urban population of most countries grew rapidly. More "white-collar" positions,

Table 19.3. Population Growth in Major States between 1871 and 1911 (population in millions)

	c. 1871	c. 1911	% increase
German Empire	41.1	64.9	57.8
France	36.1	39.6	9.7
Austria-Hungary*	35.8	49.5	38.3
Great Britain	31.8	45.4	42.8
Italy	26.8	34.7	29.5
Spain	16.0	19.2	20.0

*Not including Bosnia-Herzegovina.
Source: Colin Dyer, *Population and Society in Twentieth Century France* (New York: Holmes and Meier, 1978), p. 5.

such as clerks and salespeople, became available, and service employment drew migrants to cities. Increased factory production altered the physical structure of industrial cities, which were characterized by greater social segregation within their limits. Working-class suburbs grew rapidly on the outskirts of towns. Overseas emigration, particularly to the Americas, rose rapidly and did not slow down even with the end of the economic depression in the mid-1890s.

Demographic Boom

Europe's population grew rapidly because the continent passed from the traditional pattern of high birthrates and high death rates to low rates of both births and deaths. Mortality rates fell during the second half of the nineteenth century, particularly among children. Births outnumbered deaths, despite the fact that fertility rates fell beginning in the 1860s, or even before. Infant mortality declined, particularly in Western and Central Europe, because of greater medical understanding of chest and stomach infections, as well as a general improvement in the standard of living. Many poor people now lived in warmer, drier accommodations, although improvements still lagged behind in large, dirty, industrial cities.

With infant mortality greatly reduced, more couples sought to control the number of children they had (see Table 19.4). Although Britain's Queen Victoria had nine children, poor families often had more children than upper-class couples, who limited themselves to two or three offspring because they wanted to devote more resources to the education and inheritance of each child. In France, officials and nationalists worried about their country's unique plunging birthrate. The French population grew by only about 15 percent from mid-century until 1914. The division of farmland into small plots may be a partial explanation—another child ultimately meant a further subdivision of land because France no longer had primogeniture (inheritance by the eldest son).

Contraception became more widespread, although the methods were very traditional ones. Coitus interruptus was the most common method, although

TABLE 19.4. THE DECLINE IN FAMILY SIZE (NUMBER OF CHILDREN) IN ENGLAND AND WALES

Year	Family Size
1861–1869	6.16
1871	5.94
1876	5.62
1890–1899	4.13
1900–1909	3.30
1910–1914	2.82

Source: E. A. Wrigley, *Population and History* (New York: McGraw-Hill, 1969), p. 197.

it was hardly flawless. Rudimentary condoms made of animal intestines were superseded in the 1880s by rubber condoms, although these still were relatively expensive, and were used primarily for protection against disease rather than for birth control. As families sought to limit the number of children and single women encountered unplanned pregnancies, abortion became more common, in part because contraception methods remained very hit or miss. A quarter of pregnancies probably ended in abortion, even though abortions were both illegal and extremely dangerous. Women seeking to terminate a pregnancy took all sorts of concoctions rumored to be effective, or put themselves at the mercy of quacks.

In some places, however, births to unmarried couples or to single mothers increased rapidly. Young female migrants to the city were vulnerable to the advances of men promising marriage or promising nothing at all. Unplanned pregnancies followed. A sizable percentage of the population of most countries—about 10 to 15 percent—never married or entered into permanent or long-term relationships. Unmarried women were especially common in Scotland, Ireland, and in Brittany in France, from which more males than females migrated to urban, industrial regions.

Improving Standards of Living

Living standards improved for ordinary people in every industrialized country. Standards of living were far higher in northern Europe than in southern and eastern Europe, greater in Britain than in France, with Germany closing the gap with both of its rivals. In Britain, real wages (taking inflation into account), which had increased by a third between 1850 and 1875, again rose by almost half during the last three decades of the century. Workers enjoyed higher levels of consumption because the price of food fell as agricultural production increased and transportation improved. Working-class families still spent half of their budget on food, but this was less than during previous centuries. This left more money to spend on clothes, with something occasionally left over. Small-town shops were better supplied than ever before, and ready-made clothes sold on market day alongside manufactured household utensils.

More grain and meat, arriving in refrigerated ships, reached Europe from Australia, Canada, the United States, and Argentina. Meat ceased to be a luxury. The average German had consumed almost 60 pounds of meat in 1873, 105 pounds in 1912. Germans consumed on average three times more sugar at the end of the century than thirty years earlier. People who lived a good distance inland—and who were of some means—found that fish reached them before the ice keeping the fish fresh had melted. The poor, too, now enjoyed a more varied diet, consisting of more vegetables, fruit, and cheese. As the diet of ordinary people improved, and thus their nutrition, people gradually became taller. Still, workers almost everywhere remained chronically undernourished and vulnerable to childhood diseases.

The average European laborer was still shorter than the average middle-class person.

Migration and Emigration

European migration was part of a worldwide movement of men and women in what was becoming a global labor force. Migration—both permanent and seasonal—within Europe continued to be significant. In France, in particular, many rural regions of marginal agriculture lost population to cities and towns. Seasonal work took hundreds of thousands of laborers across borders for part of the year as construction and harvest workers. Some Italian laborers known as "swallows" spent four weeks a year traveling to and from Argentina to work the harvests.

Permanent migration to the city did not end the contact between the migrants and their rural origins. Many industrial workers still went back to their villages to help with the harvest, and many miners were also part-time farmers. Thus, migration was a two-way street, at least when patterns of movement involved relatively short distances. When migrants returned home for visits, they brought with them not only stories about what they had experienced in the cities and towns where they now lived, but different ways of speaking, knowledge of birth control, the habit of reading, a taste for sports, and greater political awareness and interest.

Immigrants from Europe await a ferry for New York City, having passed through the entry point at Ellis Island.

Overseas emigration increased dramatically during the nineteenth century's last decades, the result of economic stagnation, marginal and overcrowded agricultural regions, religious persecution, and the hope of finding a better life. Between 1850 and 1880, about 8 million Europeans emigrated, most to the United States. Russia and Eastern Europe sent an increasing number of impoverished people abroad. Between 1890 and 1914, about 350,000 Greeks—one-seventh of the population of Greece—left their country, most for good. Emigration from Europe was itself facilitated by the transportation revolution, as steamships carried millions of people to a new life across the oceans.

With improving economic times in the late 1890s, emigration slowed down from Germany, while remaining high from Ireland and increasing dramatically from Italy. During the first decade of the twentieth century, emigration from Europe rose to between 1 and 1.4 million people each year. Most of those packing themselves onto overcrowded steamers went to the United States: Italians and Irish to New York, Boston, and Philadelphia; Portuguese to Providence and New Bedford; Germans and Bohemians to Chicago, Milwaukee, and Philadelphia (see Table 19.5); Poles to Chicago and Detroit. In 1907, due to their sheer number, Italian emigrants sent back enough money to cover half the commercial deficit of their native country. Pushed by crop failures and pulled by the U.S. Homestead Act of 1862 (which virtually guaranteed land in the American West), waves of Swedes, along with Norwegians and Finns, began to emigrate to the northern United States. By the 1930s, 3 million Swedes had changed countries, leaving a population of about 6 million at home. Hundreds of thousands of Portuguese left for Brazil in search of jobs as laborers, following the abolition of slavery in that country in 1888.

Between 1871 and 1914, more than 1.5 million Jews left Russia and Polish Russia for the United States, fleeing poverty and periodic anti-Semitic violence. Many left their homes with little more than a few cherished items and great hopes. One Jewish emigrant from a village in Belarus remembered that his family carried empty suitcases as they left home—they did not want the

TABLE 19.5. EMIGRATION TO THE UNITED STATES, 1871–1910

	1871–1880	1881–1890	1891–1900	1901–1910
Germany	718,000	1,500,000	505,000	341,000
Ireland	437,000	656,000	388,000	339,000
England/Scotland/Wales	548,000	807,000	272,000	526,000
Scandinavia	243,000	655,000	372,000	505,000
Italy	56,000	307,000	652,000	2,000,000
Austria-Hungary	73,000	363,000	574,000	2,145,000
Russia/Baltic states	39,000	213,000	505,000	1,597,000

Source: Leonard Dinnerstein and David M. Reimers, *Ethnic Americans: A History of Immigration and Assimilation* (New York: Harper and Row, 1977), p. 11.

other people they met along the way to know that they owned virtually nothing to carry. Tens of thousands of Jews moved westward to European capitals, such as London, where they lived in the East End. Most Jews retained their cultural traditions and religion and spoke Yiddish as their first language. They were considered outsiders by many people in Vienna, Berlin, Budapest, Paris, and other cities (even in some cases by assimilated Jews). The Zionist movement for the establishment of the Jewish homeland in Palestine emerged partially in response to the rising tide of anti-Semitism in Europe. The movement's founder was Theodor Herzl (1860–1904), a gifted journalist and German-speaking Jew from Budapest who had moved to Vienna.

Although many families left together for overseas destinations, many married men went alone, hoping either to send for their families when they could afford to do so, or to return after saving some money. In new homes, migrants forged new collective identities, a process shaped not only by their own ethnic backgrounds and solidarities but also by conditions in their new homelands. Many never saw their families again. Migrants to the United States from southern Italy were the most likely to return permanently, with almost two-thirds eventually going back.

The Changing World of Work

By 1900, more than half of all industrial workers in Britain, Germany, and Belgium were employed in firms with more than twenty workers. Artisans, skilled workers, and unskilled workers often found themselves in the same factory. Most industrial workers came from proletarian families and grew up with few or no illusions about finding a more secure way of earning a living. But "proletarian" was also a state of mind. Many workers took pride in their work and in their social class. "I was born in the slums of London of working-class parents," a contemporary recalled, "and although I have attained a higher standard of living, I still maintain I am working class." Yet enormous differences in skill, remuneration, and quality of life continued to exist among workers.

Mechanization eliminated or reduced demand for some trades. Skilled glassworkers were no longer needed when the Siemens furnace, which permitted continuous production, was adapted to the production of bottles in the 1880s. Porcelain painters lost their jobs to unskilled female laborers when factory owners started using decals that could be applied to plates and then baked on. Steam laundries left many washerwomen without clients.

New professions brought some workers higher status. Engineers, capable of designing, overseeing, and repairing machinery, became fixtures in factories. In the 1880s, some engineers still had received training as apprentices, but by the first decades of the twentieth century, many had received university training in their chosen profession.

Women's work remained closely tied to their stage of life. Many young, unmarried women became servants upon arrival in the urban world, trying to

Derbyshire pit boys outside the mines in Britain.

save enough money for a modest dowry, in the hope of marrying someone of a slightly higher social class. By the end of the century, servants accounted for more than half of female workers in Britain.

Most female industrial workers were still employed in small workshops or at home, but more women became factory workers. Even in the Habsburg Empire, which was much less industrialized than Germany or Britain, about 900,000 women worked in factories, largely in unskilled jobs. Most earned only about half the wages of their male counterparts for, in some cases, the same jobs. Women workers were usually the last hired and the first fired. Despite harsh working conditions and relatively low wages, some women saw factory work as bringing an improvement in wages and conditions over agricultural labor, cottage industry, or domestic service. A Belfast woman in 1898 remembered her time in a linen mill: "Wonderful times then in the mill. You got a wee drink, got a join [pooled money with others to buy food], done your work and you had your company."

Industrialization and the Working-Class Family

Moralists bemoaned the effects of industrial work, arguing that the uprooting of families from villages put them at risk in cities and factories characterized by vice and immorality. Despite laws controlling child labor (see Chapter 14), at the turn of the century many thousands of children, including those between the ages of eight and fourteen, were still working in factories (the young above age fourteen worked as adults). Moralists believed that only education, marriage, the habit of saving money, and a return to the old ways could save family life. Women, they claimed, were being taken away from their reproductive function, and from family life itself. Working-class families in cities were indeed much less likely to live with their extended families—that is, with parents and sometimes grandparents and in-laws—than were country people. More families tended to be broken up early when children sixteen years or younger left villages in search of work in the cities, leaving aging parents to fend for themselves as best they could. Furthermore, long hours in the factory for parents and children alike seemed to erode parental authority. Moralists blamed increasingly homogeneous working-class neighborhoods, where drinking and domestic violence seemed rampant.

Many women of child-bearing age who could afford to do so, or who had no other choice, tended children full time. But once their offspring were old enough to care for themselves, many working-class mothers returned to factory work. Others worked at home, doing piecework and caring for their children at the same time. Many women thus alternated between industrial wage labor and child rearing.

As ever in the European experience, many women still were forced by economic circumstances into prostitution, in large cities, towns of modest size, and even villages. Some of the tens of thousands of prostitutes in Paris, London, Berlin, and Vienna worked in elegant brothels, under the direction of a "madam," who allowed them only a couple days off per year. Others worked on their own, waiting for customers in bars, doorways, windows, and parks. Most prostitutes were working-class women—some of whom were married—unable to find industrial work. Many were young, having had to leave school early to support younger siblings.

Henri de Toulouse-Lautrec's *In the Salon at the Rue des Moulins* (1894) depicts French prostitutes.

Prostitutes began to be perceived more than ever before as a chronic danger to public health. Complaints from the middle class increased (which was ironic, since middle-class men constituted a significant portion of the clientele for prostitutes). Socialist parties, however, expressed little interest in prostitution as an issue of reform, although they blamed capitalism for the low wages or unemployment that forced many women into prostitution.

In 1864, the British Parliament had passed the Contagious Diseases Act, which required medical examination of prostitutes. The goal was to stop the spread of venereal disease, particularly syphilis, by hospitalizing prostitutes found to be infected. If a woman refused medical examination, she could be prosecuted. The Contagious Diseases Act had the ironic effect of transforming prostitution from a temporary profession for many struggling working-class women to a dead-end, permanent job because the law publicly branded them as prostitutes.

Josephine Butler (1828–1906), the devoutly religious wife of a clergyman and president of an association encouraging higher education for women, led a well-organized, determined campaign in Britain and then on the continent against the Contagious Diseases Act. Some opponents of the act objected that the law called only for the inspection of prostitutes, not their clients; others opposed extensive police regulatory authority. Butler espoused the right of women to regulate their own sexuality. Parliament repealed the Contagious Diseases Act in 1886, and passed a law that banned brothels, forcing prostitutes to operate in tolerated "red-light" districts, where they were often subject to violence. Almost all of the victims of the still unidentified London killer "Jack the Ripper" were prostitutes.

In France, too, laws placed prostitutes under greater regulatory control. Gradually, the belief that morality could be legislated ebbed in Europe. Charitable institutions more willingly provided assistance to unwed mothers and their offspring, increasingly considering their sad situations as a social, not a moral, problem.

Teeming Cities

In 1899, an American statistician—the profession itself was another sign of the times—noted that "the concentration of population in cities [is] the most remarkable social phenomenon of the present century." Britain and Germany led the way, but France, Austria, Switzerland, Italy, Sweden, and even Spain and Serbia also had high rates of urban growth. Classic "factory towns" such as Manchester, Saint-Étienne, and Essen grew rapidly in size, but so did the population of other towns, swollen by service workers and state and commercial employees.

Rural industry, which had provided spinning, weaving, and finishing work for hundreds of thousands of people—above all, women—on a full- or part-time basis, gradually disappeared during the last half of the century. Manufacturing, including home production in the garment industry, now became overwhelmingly concentrated in urban centers. Mechanized agriculture and falling agricultural prices reduced demand for farm laborers, encouraging migration to towns in search of work in the booming service sector or in industry. The population of Istanbul doubled in forty years, reaching 850,000 by 1886, swollen by the influx of Muslim refugees from Russia and the Balkans. Warsaw's population grew by more than four times from about 160,000 in 1850 to almost 800,000 people in 1911; two-thirds of the Polish city's buildings had been built in the nineteenth century. In Central and Eastern European cities like Prague and Tallinn, Czechs and Estonians, respectively, arrived in greater numbers from the countryside, changing the ethnic composition of these places.

Although some working-class families now lived in marginally more spacious lodgings, many densely packed urban neighborhoods became ghastly slums. London had its infamous "back to back" row houses, with little or no space between the houses and room for little more between the rows than outdoor toilets, if that, and garbage heaps. For most British workers, a parlor (a family room), a sign of "respectability," remained only a dream. In Glasgow, Scotland, a third of the city's families lived in one room, as more and more highlanders crowded into tall tenement dwellings.

As Paris became ever more crowded, Emperor Napoleon III had undertaken a massive rebuilding project in Paris during the 1850s and 1860s. He entrusted the planning to Baron Georges Haussmann (1809–1891). Together they planned the most extensive project of urban renewal since the rebuilding of London following the great fire in the seventeenth century and that of Edo (Tokyo) in Japan at about the same time following the great conflagration of 1657.

Napoleon III and Haussmann wanted to facilitate the expansion of commerce and industry through the creation of long, wide boulevards, which would be lined by symmetrical apartment buildings. It was not a coincidence

(*Left*) Tenement housing in Glasgow. (*Right*) Company housing near mines in northern France.

that some of the new arteries cut through some of the most traditionally revolutionary neighborhoods, providing troops quick access into the narrow streets in eastern Paris where ordinary people had risen up during the June Days in 1848, as well as during the French Revolution. This made it more difficult to erect barricades. The impressionist painter Auguste Renoir (1841–1919) would lament the transformation of these old Parisian neighborhoods and the new symmetrical buildings that lined the boulevards, "cold and lined up like soldiers at review." It seemed an appropriate image to accompany the further consolidation of state power. Glittering department stores and fancy cafés stood along the elegant boulevards, showcases to imperial monumentalism but also to modern life. Large iron structures provided space for Les Halles, the refurbished market of central Paris.

Napoleon III also wanted to make Paris a healthier place. Some of the broad boulevards replaced narrow, winding streets, cutting through unhealthy neighborhoods. Aqueducts were built to provide cleaner water for residents. Four hundred miles of underground sewers (which emptied into the Seine River northwest of Paris) improved health conditions in a city that had been recently ravaged by cholera.

Although the massive rebuilding provided jobs for many workers, it also forced many thousands of workers and their families to leave the central city for the cheaper rents of the inner suburbs, particularly those to the north and northeast—which were annexed to Paris in 1860—or to increasingly industrialized suburbs farther out, themselves emerging symbols of the Sec-

Emperor Napoleon III (*left*) and Baron Georges Haussmann, viewed as either the rebuilder of Paris or the "Alsatian Attila" (*right*).

ond Industrial Revolution. The cost of all these projects was enormous and far exceeded original estimates. Speculators made a fortune, tipped off as to where the next demolitions would take place.

Paris had already reached well over a million inhabitants. By 1900, nine European cities had populations that large. London dwarfed them all, growing from 1.9 million in 1841 to 4.2 million in 1891. Between one-fifth and one-sixth of the population of Britain lived in London, which was larger than the next seven largest English cities and Edinburgh combined. The

Paris before Haussmann: Charles Marville's photograph of the Rue Traversine. Notice the drainage ditch in the center of the cobblestone street.

sprawling imperial city seemed almost ungovernable, an imposing labyrinth of different jurisdictions with 10,000 people exercising varying degrees of authority. Unlike Paris, which was for the most part administered by the centralized French state, London only had an effective local government after the establishment of the London City Council in 1889.

The largest port in the world, London also remained a center of international banking, finance, and commerce, and the administrative nerve center of the British Empire. The influence of "the City"—London's banking and finance district—extended around the world, channeling investment capital to innumerable countries within and beyond the empire. Half the capital that left Europe passed through London. The largest merchant marine fleet in the world carried woolens and other textiles to China, machine parts and hardware to Russia, toys to New York, settlers to Canada, and soldiers and sailors to India, and it imported Australian wool, Chicago beef, Bordeaux wines, Portuguese port, and Cuban cigars.

London was also a center of small-scale production and finishing in shops usually employing only a few skilled and semiskilled workers each, such as in the clothing industry, furniture making, engineering, and printing. The bustling East End docks employed a vast force of "casual labor"— that is, semiskilled and unskilled laborers who worked when work could be found. Two million people lived in the East End. There, and elsewhere, the homeless slept where they could, in empty or half-collapsed buildings, under bridges and railroad viaducts. To upper-class Londoners, the East

End, about which they knew nothing except "from hearsay and report," was a morass of tangled slums "as unexplored as Timbuktu." Residents of these districts spoke a cockney dialect that was difficult for outsiders to understand, or with a thick Irish brogue, or in Yiddish.

The Hungarian capital of Budapest revealed not only the social and ethnic complexity of the Austro-Hungarian Empire but also the increased social segregation characteristic of the modern city. This city on the Danube River grew from a population of about 120,000 in 1848 to 280,000 inhabitants in 1867 and almost 900,000 people in 1914. By then, Hungarian, which had been spoken by a minority of the population of the capital at mid-century, had become the language spoken by the vast majority of people. Many Germans and Jews had emigrated or been assimilated. The complexity of social differences was such that five forms of salutation were current, depending upon whom one was addressing. These ranged from the ultimate deference of "Gracious Sir," through the only slightly less groveling "Dignified Sir" or "Great Sir," all the way down to the considerably more common "Hey, you!"

Many social theorists were convinced that the rapid growth of cities bred crime (see Chapter 20). But, in fact, urban growth in some places seems to have significantly increased only crimes against property. Crime rates in Glasgow fell during the last half of the century, despite the petty extortion carried out by youth gangs like the Penny Mob, the Redskins, and the Kelly Boys. Many contemporary observers inveighed against cities as promoting an anonymous, alienated mass of people. Yet relatives and friends who had the same dialect or accent or religion encouraged others to move to the city and served as conduits for information about jobs and lodgings. The resulting "chain" migration created "urban villages" that mitigated against uprooting and lawlessness. Neighborhoods of Irish in Liverpool and London, and Italians and Irish in Boston and New York, provided solidarities that made the city seem less anonymous to newcomers.

Social segregation within European cities became more pronounced. Elevators carried wealthy occupants of apartment buildings to refurbished dwellings in the upper stories, where poorer people had once lived. Families of means lived along Vienna's Ringstrasse and near the parks of west London. As more suburbs developed around the edge of Europe's larger cities, some, particularly outside London, catered to middle-class people who could commute into the city, happy to live in small houses that offered more room and fresh air. These suburbs, unlike most center cities, reflected some degree of planning and improved water and gas supply, among other municipal services.

But European suburbs became even more mostly a plebeian phenomenon. Factories were constructed on the edge of cities so that manufacturers could take advantage of more space, proximity to railways and canals, somewhat lower cost of land and raw materials (avoiding the taxes that were still levied on goods brought into some cities), and the availability of cheap labor (see Chapter 14). Railway lines and factories on the edge of town were surrounded by poor-quality, low-rent housing, usually owned by absentee landlords. More and more workers commuted daily into town to work—some still on foot, others by tram, subway, train, and later bus. Modest suburbs even developed around the small Estonian capital of Tallinn in the Russian Baltic provinces, where peasant workers settled on the edge of town.

With urban growth in cities came civic pride. Municipal governments built celebratory historical monuments, constructed new hospitals and town halls, sponsored bands, and created beautiful parks complete with ornate bandstands. They prided themselves on an increasingly diverse municipal cultural life, including occasional music festivals and perhaps even a museum. The proliferation of voluntary associations, such as clubs and choral societies, also came to be taken as symbols of urbanity as cities and towns continued to grow, transforming the lives of millions of Europeans.

At the same time, homosexual subcultures developed in most large cities, and in some smaller places (a German writer first used the term "homosexuality" in 1868). Same-sex acts had first been decriminalized in France in 1791, but gays and lesbians largely remained in the shadows, although readily identifiable hotels, restaurants, bars, parks, and gardens provided places for them to meet. If the prostitution of women was very much out in the open, that of men was always less obvious. Public attitudes toward homosexuality remained generally intolerant. This was reflected by the fact that the English philosopher Jeremy Bentham (1748–1832) penned many pages defending same-sex relations, but never dared publish them, and by occasional high-profile trials. The Scientific-Humanitarian Committee, established in Berlin in 1897, was the first organization founded to support homosexual rights.

Social Mobility

The middle classes swelled during the Second Industrial Revolution, taking their places in Europe's burgeoning cities. Lower-middle-class occupations, in particular, expanded rapidly. (That the lower middle class had some degree of self-awareness was revealed by the fact that in 1899 the first—and last—World Congress of the Petty Bourgeoisie took place in Brussels.) Architects required draftsmen; companies needed accountants and bookkeepers; and the London underground and Paris subway had to have agents. Furthermore, the expansion of governmental functions generated thousands of jobs: tax collectors, postal workers, food and drug inspectors, and recorders of official documents. The number of schoolteachers increased dramatically between the 1870s and 1914—five times more in Italy, thirteen times more in England. (Table 19.6 represents the rapid growth in the number of state employees.) In Britain, the proportion of the population classified as lower middle class grew from about 7 percent in 1850 to 20 percent in 1900. Clerks working for banks, railroads, utility companies, and

Table 19.6. Number of Public Servants (Non-Military)

	1881	1901	1911
Great Britain	81,000	153,000	644,000
France	379,000	451,000	699,000
Germany	452,000	907,000	1,159,000

Source: Norman Stone, *Europe Transformed 1878–1919* (Cambridge, Mass: Harvard University Press, 1984), p. 130.

insurance companies considered themselves above the working class and therefore "respectable." With the optimism of the age, they viewed such employment as a first step to one day owning their own store. They did not wear work clothes and did not do manual labor and they made a little more money than workers.

In European cities, women found jobs as department store clerks, stenographers, and secretaries. There were twelve times as many secretaries in 1901 as there had been two decades earlier; women, who held only 8 percent of post office and government clerical positions in 1861, accounted for more than half in 1911. They now used metal pens that replaced the age-old quill, and then the typewriter, invented in the 1880s. Nursing became a respected profession. Cafés and restaurants employed hundreds of thousands of women.

Gains made by workers seemed paltry when compared to the fortunes being made by industrialists, and even the salaries earned by management personnel. These gnawing disparities aided unions and socialist parties in their quest for the allegiance of workers, many of whom walked to and from work while horse-drawn cabs raced by, carrying well-heeled occupants. Indeed, during the mid-1890s, real wages, which had risen for several decades, entered a period of decline.

Dizzying "rags to riches" tales (especially popular in the United States and Russia) suggested that hard work could lead to better conditions of life. Emigrants to the United States arrived with fantastically high expectations of what life would be like. Inflated expectations often brought disappointment, as social mobility was extremely limited, particularly for first-generation immigrants. During the last decades of the century, 95 percent of American industrialists came from upper- or middle-class families, and not more than 3 percent were the sons of poor immigrants or farmers. Among immigrants and native-born workers in the United States, the most common form of social advancement was within the working class, not into a higher social group.

Despite movement in Western European countries into clerical and other lower-middle-class jobs, however, there were fewer possibilities of movement by workers into the middle class during the hard years of the 1880s than there had been during the middle decades of the century. Low wages and periodic unemployment for industrial workers made saving and the ownership of apartments or houses, both essential components of

Clerical work toward the end of the nineteenth century.

mobility, extremely difficult to achieve. Craftsmen and skilled workers had a far better chance for social ascension than did unskilled workers. As in the United States, those who did move up to middle-class employment were the exceptions. The vast majority of marriages in Europe took place between partners considered social equals. Working-class women were more likely than their brothers to achieve some social mobility—for example, by marrying a clerk or railroad station employee.

CULTURAL CHANGES: EDUCATION AND RELIGION

In every country, states took enormous strides to bring education to more people. More children went on to secondary school, now including some girls. The state's increased role in education in Western Europe contributed to a growing secularization of public life. At the same time, the established churches lost the allegiance of many ordinary Europeans.

Education

Literacy rose rapidly during the last decades of the century in Europe as more governments enacted educational reforms. Literacy rates were higher in western—above all, northwestern Europe—than in southern and eastern Europe, although progress was notable in Russia around the turn of the century.

In Britain, Parliament passed, over Anglican opposition, the Education Act of 1870, which placed education in the hands of the state by permitting local education boards to create schools in districts where neither the Established Church nor its Dissenting Protestant rivals had established a school. (With the help of state grants, the Anglicans had far outdistanced their competitors in building new schools; only ten years earlier they had controlled 90 percent of the elementary schools in England and Wales.) In 1880, Parliament passed a law requiring that all children between five and ten years of age attend primary school, up to age twelve beginning in 1899, and in 1891 primary education became free. Truancy officers in working-class neighborhoods encountered resistance from parents who preferred the supplementary income from their children's work to their schooling. State inspectors maintained educational standards, requiring villages to provide better facilities for their schools and accommodations for teachers. Besides familiarizing young people with "the letters," primary schools in late Victorian Britain sought to teach them how to be "good Englishmen" and "good English wives," idealizing social harmony in Britain while espousing British "superiority" over the indigenous peoples of the empire (see Chapter 21).

In France, the Ferry Laws (passed 1879–1881, named after Minister of Education and then Premier Jules Ferry) made primary schools free, obligatory, and secular for all children from age three to thirteen. Each region was required to operate a teacher-training school. Bretons, Provençaux, Gascons, Basques, Catalans, and people speaking regional patois learned French, which became spoken by most people, although bilingualism remained common. In Italy, Italian ceased to be a language spoken only by the upper class.

The percentage of people able to read and write still varied considerably from country to country. More men could read and write than women, more urban residents than rural people. In France, where 40 percent of military conscripts had not been able to read or write at mid-century, the percentage had fallen at the turn of the century to only 6 percent. In contrast, in Dalmatia, on the Adriatic coast, only 1 of every 100 conscripts could read and write in 1870, and in Spain 70 percent of electors were illiterate in 1890. In 1860, 75 percent of Italian men and almost 90 percent of women could neither read nor write and depended on public letter writers to pen what correspondence they required. By 1914, 75 percent of all Italians were literate. Yet in southern Italy and Sicily, more than half of the children in many places still did not attend school regularly or at all. In Germany, by the turn of the century less than 1 percent of the population remained illiterate. In Russia, illiteracy fell from about 90 percent of the population in the 1860s to about 75 percent by 1910. Whereas the older, illiterate generation of Russians mistrusted education ("You can't eat books"), fearing that literacy would erode village religious culture (and perhaps also deference to elders), younger peasants ridiculed their superstitious parents and welcomed self-improvement through education.

During the 1870s and 1880s, the issue of female education surged to the forefront in Western Europe. Only women whose families were able and willing to pay the required fees received secondary education. In France, women were allowed to teach boys, but men were not permitted to teach girls. Both lay teachers and nuns instructed girls in the domestic mission of women, stressing gender differences and promoting deference to their future husbands, as in other countries. A female German Social Democrat later recalled that the education she had received had been so "that I might one day be able to provide my husband with a proper domestic atmosphere." Schooling for boys and girls alike emphasized patriotic, secular, and politically conservative themes. Female teachers of girls were to be considered morally irreproachable and thoroughly secular mother figures within their communities.

In Western Europe, more young people attended secondary schools, the number tripling in Germany and quadrupling in France between 1875 and 1912. Many families viewed education as a way of improving the employment and marriage possibilities for their daughters.

Yet secondary education in general remained possible only for families of some means. Moreover, existing educational systems reinforced social distinctions of class, counseling "patient resignation" to one's economic and social condition. Secondary schools taught skills that led to good jobs, but they drew very few children from the lower classes. In England, boarding schools founded in the 1860s and 1870s catered to middle-class students, while the sons of "gentlemen" attended the nine old elite "public"—that is, private—schools.

Although the number of university students tripled in Europe during this period, university education remained limited to a tiny proportion of the population drawn from the upper classes. At the University of Cambridge at mid-century, 60 percent of the students were sons of landowners or clergy. In all of Britain, there were only 13,000 university students in 1913 in a total population of 36 million people, although the percentage of university students drawn from the middle classes had greatly increased and technical colleges began to attract more students. In Prussia, for example, only 1 in 1,000 university students had parents who were workers. The Russian tsars reversed the European trend during the course of the century, making it more difficult for non-nobles to attend secondary school and university. Yet, overall, the number of universities increased—for example, in Hungary, where three new ones opened their doors.

Despite this, only very slowly were women admitted to universities. In the 1860s, a few women were medical students in Paris, and the first female students appeared at the University of Zurich in 1867. In the 1870s, there were already women's colleges in England and women began university study in Denmark and Sweden. In Germany, where professors constituted the "intellectual bodyguard" of the Hohenzollern dynasty, women did not attend university until the late 1890s. Upon seeing a woman in his lecture course, the historian Heinrich von Treitschke stopped speaking. He escorted her out the door. Only in 1909 did women obtain the right to study in any German university. At the University of Cambridge, the Senate in 1897 voted overwhelmingly to deny women the right to take a Cambridge

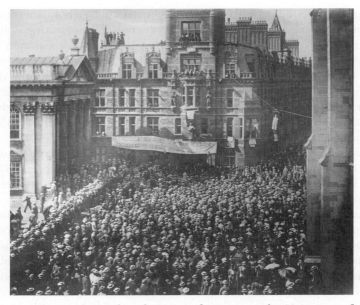

A protest opposing the admission of women to the University of Cambridge in 1881 demonstrates the unwillingness of many to erase gender distinctions in education.

degree. Women could not receive degrees or have full privileges as students at Oxford until 1920 and at Cambridge until 1948.

The Decline of Religious Practice

In a century of vigorous state secularization, particularly in Western Europe, many clergy viewed the period of rapid social change at the turn of the century with anxiety. The institutional influence of churches on states had declined dramatically in most of Europe. More than this, in some places, the influence of organized religion on society continued to wane. Secular education, espousing the cult of the nation, accelerated this trend, even though many people in Catholic countries still attended Church schools. However, fewer people went to church than earlier in the century. In London a survey at the turn of the century revealed that less than 20 percent of the population regularly attended services, a marked decline. In Spain, Galicia, the Basque provinces, and much of Castile remained devout, while much of southern Spain did not.

The first Catholic sociologists of religion found a sharp rise in "dechristianized" regions, as demonstrated by rates of couples not having church marriages or being slow to have their children baptized, or the decline in religious vocations. By the 1890s, the Church considered some

Catholic faithful at the Grotto of Lourdes.

regions in France, and most working-class districts of large European cities, to be "missionary" areas, in this way defined like China or the Congo. The loss of the Church's hold on ordinary people was reflected in the decline in the birthrate, explicable in part by increased use of birth control. Furthermore, an increasing number of French people called upon the clergy only at the time of baptism, marriage, and death (and thus were sometimes referred to as "four-wheeled Catholics," in reference to the wagons that carried an individual to each important occasion).

Yet the decline of religious practice in Europe was neither linear, nor did it occur everywhere. A revival of popular religious enthusiasm occurred in some places between 1830 and 1880, particularly among the upper classes. In Sweden the "Great Awakening" brought the revival of popular religion. In Catholic countries, lithography and printing presses helped rekindle devotion, spreading the news of religious shrines. Women were more apt to attend church than men (although in part this resulted from the fact that women live longer than men). The cult of the Virgin Mary also contributed to the feminization of religion in Catholic countries, perhaps encouraging more young women to enter convents.

The growing cult of miracles was part of a revival of popular religion, particularly in France, Italy, and Spain. Near the French town of Lourdes in the central Pyrenees, Bernadette, a peasant girl later canonized by the Church, announced in 1858 that the Virgin Mary had appeared to her.

Churchmen and their followers believed that the apparition explained the miraculous cures that seemed to occur at Lourdes, despite the skepticism of scientists. Religious pilgrimages by train to sites of miracles became big business. In the first decade of the new century, more than a million people came to Lourdes each year, many hoping to be cured of illness and disease. The popularity of pilgrimages reflected the resiliency of the Catholic Church, even in a time of growing doubt.

The Consumer Explosion

During the last decades of the nineteenth century, consumerism developed in the countries of Europe, again with considerable country-to-country variation. The new leisure activities of the Belle Époque themselves reflected the Second Industrial Revolution. Sports—principally soccer and rugby, bicycle and automobile races, and track and field—attracted participants and spectators and encouraged the formation of clubs.

Department stores reflected and helped shape the burgeoning consumer culture. First in London, Paris, and Berlin, department stores transformed the way many families shopped. They attracted prosperous clients in search of quality ready-made clothes that were less expensive than those stitched by tailors. The stores were monuments to the dynamism of bourgeois culture, displaying in their windows products that reflected material progress. Seeking to increase the volume of sales, department stores also stocked more inexpensive clothing, while adding umbrellas, toothbrushes, stationery, and much more. All of this required the organization into departments overseen by trained managers, which typified the Second Industrial Revolution. The expanding clientele of department stores included the families of shopkeepers, civil servants, and clerks of more modest means, and gradually workers as well. On an average day in the 1890s, 15,000 to 18,000 people entered the "Bon Marché"—still a Parisian landmark. Glossy catalogues in color, advancing advertising techniques, permitted shoppers to make purchases in the comfort of their homes. Advertisers began to direct their appeals at the "new woman," the housewife of taste, who had the time to create the model home and had some money to spend.

The owners of department stores wanted shopping to become an experience in itself, like a visit to a world's fair—except that one could now buy some of the displayed wonders of human innovation. Architects aimed at monumental and theatrical effects. The great department stores were enormous, stately structures topped with cupolas, with iron columns and an expanse of glass giving shoppers a sense of space and light. Shoppers could walk up grand staircases to observe the crowds below. Department stores became tourist sights, with dazzled visitors themselves becoming part of the spectacle. To Émile Zola, department stores had become the "cathedrals of modernity." For women of means, the commercialization represented by the department stores of the West End of London became a liberating experience, a veritable zone of pleasurable consumerism.

Leisure in the Belle Époque

During the Belle Époque, there was more to do than ever before for those with time for leisure and money to spend. The French capital set the tone for style in Europe, if not the world. Dance halls, cafés, and café-concerts, the latter offering the performances of musicians, singers, poets, comedians, jugglers, acrobats, female wrestlers, and snake charmers, lined the *grands boulevards,* attracting throngs of Parisians and tourists alike. Hundreds of thousands of Londoners and Parisians attended the theater at least once a week. The tango and the turkey trot, imported from the Americas, were banned in some establishments. German Emperor William II forbade officers from dancing these steps while in uniform.

The actress Sarah Bernhardt dramatically laid out in the Art Nouveau style in a coffin.

The talented and beautiful actress Sarah Bernhardt (1844–1923) embodied images of fin-de-siècle Europe. The daughter of a Dutch immigrant, she became famous for her dramatic expressiveness and ability to communicate tears to an audience through her supremely evocative voice. Bernhardt learned her trade from the traditions of the popular boulevard theater. Renowned for her dramatic gestures (as a young woman she asked a photographer to take a picture of her in a coffin) and for a variety of sexual liaisons, Sarah Bernhardt's worldwide fame was such that the American circus entrepreneur P. T. Barnum, upon hearing that she risked the amputation of a leg, offered her a fortune if she would allow him to take it on the road and exhibit it with his famous circus.

Sports in Mass Society

Sports emerged as a prominent feature of mass society during the last decades of the century, a phenomenon linked to modern transportation and to a general increase in leisure time. The first automobile race was held in 1894 in France. Some of the cars were powered by electricity, others by gasoline or even steam. Cycling competitions also generated enormous public interest. Sporting newspapers catered to fans. Competition between two cycling clubs led to the first Tour de France race in 1903, in which riders covered almost 1,500 miles in nineteen days.

Not only did people watch bicycle races, many rode bicycles themselves, both for leisure and as a source of transportation. A simple mechanism, the bicycle nonetheless reflected the technological innovation and mass production of the Second Industrial Revolution. By the late 1880s, bicycles were lighter, more affordable, and more easily repaired or replaced. Their manufacture became a major industry, with 375,000 produced in France by 1898 and 3.5 million in 1914.

Both men and women rode bicycles. But some men complained that the clothes women wore while riding bicycles were unfeminine. Some worried that female cyclists might compromise the middle-class domestic ideal of the "angel of the house." Moralists were concerned that the jolts of rough paths and roads might interfere with childbearing, or even lead to debauchery by generating physical pleasure. The president of a feminist congress in 1896, however, toasted the "egalitarian and leveling bicycle." It helped free women from the corset, "a new Bastille to be demolished." The bicycle may have also changed what some people considered the feminine ideal from plumpness to a more svelte line.

Team sports also quickly developed as a leisure activity during the second half of the nineteenth century. The two most popular team sports in Europe, football (soccer in the United States) and rugby, both began in England. Rugby, which developed at Cambridge and Oxford Universities in the 1860s, was an upper-class sport. Football had much earlier origins, perhaps going back to when Vikings and Russians used to "kick the Dane's head around"—literally. But football, which also had university origins, evolved into a plebeian sport, like boxing, which was to English workers what rowing, cricket, and golf became to the upper classes. Professional football began in England in 1863; eight years later, there were fifteen clubs playing for the championship. The new century brought the first major brawl between supporters of rival teams: a match between the Catholic Celtics and the Protestant Rangers of Glasgow ended with the stadium burned to the ground. In 1901, 111,000 spectators watched the English Cup Final.

Baron Pierre de Coubertin (1863–1937), a French noble who feared that the young men of his country were becoming soft, organized the first modern Olympic Games, held in Athens in 1896 in homage to the Greek creators of the Olympiad. An Anglophile, he revered the contemporary image of hard-riding, athletic upper-class Englishmen playing sports at Eton and Cambridge and then going on to expand the British Empire.

There was more to the rise of sports and the cult of physical vigor than simply games and fun. The development of sports culture also reflected the mood of aggressive nationalism. The popularity of Darwin's theory of the evolution of species led to a growing preoccupation with the comparative

characteristics of specific races, or peoples. "Social Darwinists" misapplied the
theory of "survival of the fittest" to society, including international sports competition. Games became hotly competitive.
Moreover, the development of feminism
in Western Europe may have contributed
to what has been called a "crisis of masculinity," by which many men saw the
strengthening of the "weaker sex" as the
weakening of men. By this view, growing
interest in sports competition was an
affirmation of masculinity. Furthermore,
the emerging interest in the times it took
to run distances may have reflected fascination with scientific management.

The burgeoning interest in sports
touched, above all, the young. In Germany,
"wandering youth" clubs (*Wandervogel*)
became popular, sending young boys out to
camp under the stars. In Great Britain,
Robert   Baden-Powell   (1857–1941)

Robert Baden-Powell, founder of
the Boy Scouts.

founded the Boy Scouts. After being rejected for admission to the University
of Oxford and finding his vocation among young men in the army, Baden-
Powell in 1908 organized the Boy Scouts in the hope of developing "among
boys . . . a spirit of self-sacrifice and patriotism, and generally to prepare
them to become good citizens." The uniform Baden-Powell had worn in
South Africa—a Stetson hat, neckerchief, and khaki shorts—became that
of the Boy Scouts, and their motto, "Be prepared."

Interest in sports touched all classes and reflected class differences. The
poet Rudyard Kipling (1865–1936), who disliked sports in general, called
cricket players (who tended to be from a loftier social class than his own)
"fools." Football players, most of whom were from the working class, he
dismissed as "oafs." People of great means were no longer the only people
able to enjoy sports. While the upper classes had their own sporting associations, which retained a preference for horse racing—"the sport of
kings"—working-class cycling and gymnastic clubs also began to spring up
in the 1880s in Western Europe, particularly as workers won a shorter
workweek and workday.

CONCLUSION

The Second Industrial Revolution transformed the way many Europeans
lived. Electricity brought light to growing cities and towns, along whose

boulevards, tramways and automobiles now carried passengers. Most Europeans could now read and write, but they were—at least in Western Europe—less likely to go to church regularly than earlier generations. Most people lived longer and better than ever before. At the same time, economic and social inequalities generated union organization, the growth of mass political parties—notably a variety of socialist movements—and waves of social protest. Nationalism became a political force in many countries during the last three decades of the nineteenth century and the beginning of the twentieth century, engulfing not only the industrialized constitutional monarchies and republics of western and southern Europe but also the empires of central and eastern Europe.

The rapid pace of material progress and scientific and technological advances generated innovative, complex cultural responses during the remarkable years that brought the nineteenth century to a close and saw the dawning of the modern world in the first years of the twentieth century.

CHAPTER 20

POLITICAL AND CULTURAL RESPONSES TO A RAPIDLY CHANGING WORLD

As European economies were being transformed by the Second Industrial Revolution, states faced organized challenges from political movements that rejected the economic, social, and political bases of those states and demanded sweeping changes. Government officials, social reformers, and politicians had to confront the difficult conditions of many workers and their families—"the problem of problems," as it was called in Britain. Some states began to enact social reforms to improve the quality of life for workers and other poor people.

At the same time, the growth of large socialist parties that wanted to capture control of the state was one of the salient signs of the advent of mass political life. Marxist socialists believed that inevitably a working-class revolution would bring down capitalism. Reform socialists, in contrast, believed that electoral victories could lead to a socialist state, and that along the way to ultimate victory socialists could exert pressure on states to improve conditions of life for ordinary people. Anarchists did not want to seize the state, but rather to abolish it. Believing that violent acts would provide a spark that would unleash a social revolution, a number of anarchists launched a campaign of terrorism at the turn of the century, carrying out political assassinations. In parts of Europe, trade unionists known as syndicalists (from the French word *syndicats,* trade unions) believed that trade unions would provide not only the means by which workers could take control of the state but also a blueprint of how society would be organized after a successful revolution.

The late nineteenth and early twentieth centuries also brought remarkable cultural achievement in Europe from Britain to Russia, as writers and artists reacted to and against changes in the world they saw around them. Beneath the tangible progress and increased prosperity of late-nineteenth- and early-twentieth-century Europe lurked cultural pessimism and artistic rebellion, a modernist critique of the idea of progress itself. In 1904, the German sociologist Max Weber wrote that "at some time or another the color changes, the importance of uncritically accepted viewpoints is put in doubt, the path is lost in the twilight." To some, the fin de siècle seemed to be such a time.

State Social Reform

In general, Karl Marx's gloomy prediction that workers' wages and overall conditions of life would continue to decline had not been borne out in late-nineteenth-century Europe. Yet economic uncertainty and grinding poverty seemed to have engendered a social crisis of unmatched proportions. Descriptions of the dreary slums of blackened manufacturing towns reached many readers through novels and surveys of working-class life. Beginning in about 1870, as a result of the far-reaching, visible impact of large-scale industrialization, states gradually began to intervene to assist the poor. States and charitable organizations increasingly came to consider poverty a social and not a moral problem. The political left in Western European states demanded measures of social reform. In France and Italy, programs of subsidies for unwed mothers overcame the opposition of the Catholic Church. Germany, Austria-Hungary, and Sweden then implemented short paid maternity leaves for women who had insurance. Unpaid maternity leaves were made possible in some other places. Organized assitance for the elderly lagged behind, in part because of the traditional assumption that families were responsible for their care.

Confronted with the increased militancy of workers, some Western European employers sought to maintain worker loyalty through paternalistic policies. They encouraged workers to form savings associations by matching whatever small sums the working-class families could put aside for the future. A minority of manufacturers started funds for insurance and pension plans, or provided basic company housing (especially in mining communities). Yet such paternalistic policies, largely confined to Western Europe, were far from being generalized. Some social reformers, many politicians, and most workers demanded state intervention to protect workers from some of the uncertainties and hardships of their labor.

Imperial Germany, not republican France or parliamentary Britain, first provided workers some protection against personal and family disaster stemming from work-related accidents. Germany's domineering Chancellor Otto von Bismarck sought to outbid the Catholic Center Party and the

Social Democrats for working-class support. Determined to preserve his own power and the autocratic structure of the empire, Bismarck carried out domestic policies based upon compromise and conciliation between middle-class political interests and working-class demands. The German chancellor thus placed socialists in the delicate position of either opposing bills that would benefit workers or appearing to compromise their ideologically based refusal to collaborate with the autocratic imperial government. The Sickness Insurance Law of 1883 covered all workers for up to thirteen weeks if their income fell below a certain level. Deductions withheld from workers' wages provided most of the funds. A year later Bismarck announced a state-run insurance program that would incorporate existing voluntary plans. It would compensate workers for injury and illness, as well as provide some retirement funds. Other laws required that all workers be insured against accidents and disability, with half of the funds paid by employers, and provided pensions for workers who lived until seventy years of age. By the turn of the century, many German workers received medical care, small payments when they were ill or injured, and, if worse came to worse, a decent burial. By 1913, 14.5 million German workers had insurance.

In comparison to Germany, Britain's social policies were out of an earlier era. Workhouses, which had been created by the Poor Law of 1834, still carried a social stigma, even if conditions had somewhat improved by the end of the century. Families were separated, and inmates were forced to wear uniforms, attend chapel, participate in group exercises, and sustain periods of silence, all with the goal of learning "discipline." A contemporary surveyor of working-class life noted that "aversion to the 'House' is absolutely universal, and almost any amount of suffering and privation will be endured by the people rather than go into it." The vast majority of the inmates of the workhouses were not the able-bodied unemployed, but were children, the infirm, single mothers, the aged, or the insane. But although public opinion had already turned against workhouses, the Poor Law, slightly reformed, remained on the books until 1929.

The first Victorian social reforms had been largely limited to establishing minimum health standards. The Factory Act (1875) then reduced the workweek in large factories to fifty-six hours. The Artisans' Dwelling Act, passed the same year, defined unsanitary housing and gave the state the right to order the demolition of slum buildings that fell below a minimum standard. However, these laws were only very randomly enforced.

By the turn of the century, many Conservatives, most Liberals, and virtually all members of the new Labour Party (founded in 1900, but taking its name only six years later) accepted the right and the obligation of government to undertake reforms, thus ending classic liberal government non-interference in the working of the economy. The Workmen's Compensation Law (1897) made employers responsible for bearing the cost of industrial accidents; another act extended the same protection to agricultural workers. Liberal governments provided lunches to poor children and passed the Old

Dinnertime in an English workhouse, which provided relief for unemployed workers experiencing the dislocation and social transformation accompanying the Second Industrial Revolution.

Age Pension Act (1908), which provided some income for workers over seventy years of age whose incomes fell below a paltry sum per week. In 1908 the "deserving" poor in Britain could receive small old-age pensions. As a result of the National Insurance Bill (1911), workers' friendly societies administered insurance payments based on voluntary (and thus unlike the German case) employee wage deductions. The law's most salutary effect was to provide more workers and their families with direct medical treatment. Yet a third of the British poor still received no assistance of any kind. Moreover, government assistance to unemployed workers in Britain was less well organized and less generous than that in France.

In France, pushed by Radicals and Socialists, the Chamber of Deputies between 1890 and 1904 passed laws that eliminated obligatory special identity papers, or internal passports, for workers, created a system of arbitration for strikes, banned female night work, established employers' legal liability for industrial accidents, reduced the workday to ten hours for women and children, established a minimum age for industrial workers, and mandated an obligatory weekly day of rest. It also affirmed the right of the state to monitor conditions of work and hygiene in factories (although inspection was in many areas nonexistent), passed a workmen's compensation law with modest pension benefits, and provided limited medical care for working-class families. With the exception of Belgium, Sweden, and a smattering of other countries, in most of Europe workers could only dream of such reforms.

The Trade Union Movement

The trade union movement grew rapidly in Western Europe, above all among male skilled workers. The goals of unions were to raise wages and improve conditions, while increasing the number of members. By 1914, 3 million workers had joined unions in Britain, 1.5 million in Germany, and 1 million in Italy. The number of white-collar unions also increased, such as those organizing schoolteachers and postal clerks. In 1913, there were more than 400,000 union members in Austria, a country of only 6 million inhabitants. French unions proliferated after they were legalized in 1884. In 1895, French unions formed the General Confederation of Labor (C.G.T.), with the goal of unifying the trade union movement. The C.G.T., to which about a third of French unions belonged, renounced participation in politics and espoused revolutionary principles. Union membership in France reached 2.6 million in 1914. May Day demonstrations and festivals, with red flags flying, vigorous political debates, consumer cooperatives, and informal networks provided by factory work and cafés, also helped maintain solidarity among workers.

However, most European workers did not belong to unions, although many supported strikes and believed in union goals. The 1875 Trade Union Act ended many limitations on unions in Britain, but by the turn of the century only about 25 percent of British workers were organized, 10 percent were in France, and even less in Italy. Several factors limited the expansion of union membership. Considerable gaps remained between the work experience, salary, organizations, and expectations of skilled and unskilled workers. Many workers moved from place to place, following employment opportunities. Those with urban roots were far more easily organized than recently arrived migrants from smaller towns or villages. Differences and tensions between workers of different national groups also served to divide workers, such as between Irish and English workers in London, German and Czech workers in Prague, or Belgian and French workers in northern France.

The union organization of female workers lagged far behind that of men. Women made up 30 percent of the British labor force, but only about 7 percent of union members. Almost all female workers were relegated to relatively unskilled and low-paying jobs and confronted chronic vulnerability to being dismissed. Most women worked in unskilled jobs, such as making boxes, knotting fish nets, making buttonholes, and doing food-processing work. Furthermore, many male workers refused to accept women as equals and claimed that they were taking jobs away from men (a French union that admitted women as members included the following regulation: "Women may address observations on propositions to the union only in writing and by the intermediation of two male members"). Women also had to take responsibility for their children, something male union members often failed to recognize. Yet women workers also struck in the face of tougher working conditions, low wages, and, occasionally, sexual harassment.

Between 1890 and 1914, strikes increased dramatically, particularly in Western Europe, becoming a social fact of modern life. Workers hoped that they could force government officials to pressure employers to bargain with them. They struck when employers seemed most vulnerable; for example, when they had recently received relatively large orders for products. The vast majority of strikes were undertaken by skilled, organized workers in large-scale sectors such as textiles, mining, and metallurgy, whose unions had resources upon which to fall back. Strike movements reflected a more generalized sense of class consciousness among many—but hardly all—workers.

Strikes reflected not only growth in union membership but also changes in the organization of industrial work. In addition to low wages and the length of their workday, workers also resented factory foremen. Representing the company's interests, the foremen sought to impose industrial discipline on workers, some of whom had worked on farms or in domestic industry and had more or less controlled their own time. Now they were forbidden to enter and leave the factory as they wished when they had nothing to do, or in some cases even to talk on the job.

Techniques of scientific management of assembly-line production—"Taylorism," after Frederick W. Taylor (1856–1915), the American engineer who developed them—included careful counting of the number of units assembled by each worker in an hour. Many workers objected. Such industrial discipline placed factory workers more directly under the control of factory managers by measuring worker performance, tying pay scales to the number of units produced, which put more pressure on workers. Taylorism wore out workers. Noting that virtually all the factory workers employed by a Philadelphia manufacturer who had become enamored of scientific management were young, a British visitor asked repeatedly where the older workers were. Finally, the owner replied, "Have a cigar, and while we smoke we can visit the cemetery."

Socialists

The Socialist First International Workingmen's Association was founded in 1864 in London. Members represented a bewildering variety of experiences and ideologies. Karl Marx emerged as the dominant figure in the International. He was convinced that the unprecedented concentration of capital and wealth meant that the final struggle between the bourgeoisie and the working class was relatively close at hand. Marx's inflexible beliefs ran counter to the views of the majority of French members, some of whom were anarchists, and to the moderate, reformist inclinations of the more prosperous British workers, as well as their German colleagues.

The First International was dissolved in 1876 amid internal division, having been weakened by repression in many countries. Nonetheless, socialism emerged as a major political force in every major European nation. In 1889, at the centennial of the French Revolution in Paris, delegates to a socialist congress founded the Second International. At its congresses, socialists discussed strategies for pushing governments toward reform and for coordinating international action (for example, to achieve a shorter workday), while debating differences over doctrine and strategy.

During the last two decades of the nineteenth century, mass socialist parties developed in France, Germany, Italy, and Belgium. By the end of the first decade of the twentieth century, every Western European state had working-class representatives in their national assemblies.

Socialists proclaimed themselves internationalists. Contending that workers in different nations shared common interests, they believed a revolution would put the working class in power. But socialists remained divided. For Marxist adherents of his "scientific socialism," emancipation of the workers from capitalism could only be achieved by the conquest of the state through revolution and the subsequent establishment of a socialist society. Reform socialists believed that political participation could win concrete reforms that would improve conditions of life for workers until socialists could take power. Reformists participated in the political process, even at the cost of being accused by revolutionary socialists of propping up "bourgeois" regimes by doing so. Legislation in many countries had brought improvement in conditions of work, however unevenly felt. The extension of the franchise also offered hope that progress might come without a revolution that, given the strength of states, seemed to even some revolutionaries to be increasingly unlikely.

A gathering of members of the British Independent Labour Party, founded by James Keir Hardie in 1893.

The emergence of socialists as contenders for political power reflected economic, social, and political changes in individual countries and had relatively little to do with the influence of the Second International. Yet the debates and divisions that obsessed European socialists revolved around common questions. What should be the relationship between socialism and nationalist movements? Could socialists, proclaiming international solidarity among workers, support demands for Polish independence from the Russian, German, and Austro-Hungarian Empires, or those by Czechs and other nationalities for independence from the latter? Czech socialists with national aspirations for their people challenged the domination of the Austrian Social Democrats by German speakers who seemed oblivious to Czech demands. Should socialists oppose imperialism in all its forms (see Chapter 21), or should they hope that the colonial powers might gradually improve the conditions of life of Africans and Asians, who might become adherents to socialism? Finally, amid rising aggressive nationalism, socialists were divided on what response they should take in the event of the outbreak of a European war.

In the Russian Empire, Marxists were "Westernizers," in that they looked to "scientific socialism" as a model for political change in their country (see Chapter 18). They counted on Russia's industrial workers to launch a revolution, but only after Russia had undergone a bourgeois revolution anticipated to bring the middle class to power. In the 1880s, socialists formed reading groups of intellectuals and students—and at least one that was made up of workers—in the imperial capital of Saint Petersburg. Exiles began to publish socialist newspapers abroad, smuggling them into Russia.

Reformism dominated socialist movements in much of northern Europe. Great Britain's handful of socialists were virtually all intellectuals and reformists. In 1884, a group of intellectuals formed the Fabian Society, which took its name from the Roman dictator Fabius, known for his delaying tactics. Committed to gradualism, the Fabians took the tortoise as their emblem. The Fabians were influenced by an American writer, Henry George. The author of the best-selling *Progress and Poverty,* George argued that the great gulf in Britain between rich and poor could be lessened by the imposition of a "single tax" on land, which would force wealthy landowners to pay more taxes. The "single taxers" believed that socialism could be gradually implemented through reform.

Most German socialists did not accept Marx's contention that the working class could only take power through revolution. In 1863, Ferdinand Lassalle (1825–1864), the son of a Prussian merchant, had formed the first (very small) independent workers' party in any of the German states. Lassalle only lived a year more—killed in a duel at age thirty-nine by the fiancé of the woman he loved. In 1875, the German Social Democratic Party (SPD), was founded. Despite official proscription in 1878, it slowly grew into a mass political party. The SPD's program included reformist demands such as proportional representation, political rights for women, and the eight-hour workday for workers. Eduard Bernstein (1850–1932), the son of a Berlin plumber who became a railway engineer, helped the reformists carry the day by forcefully rejecting in his *Evolutionary Socialism* (1898) the Marxists' insistence that capitalist society was on the verge of final collapse. He thus became a leading socialist "revisionist" who believed that the party should continue to push for reforms, not revolution. The SPD became a major reform socialist party.

The SPD's popular vote in the elections for the Reichstag rose from less than 10 percent in 1884 to almost 35 percent in 1912, and the SPD was the largest German political party in 1914. Women, who could join the party following the passage of a national law on associations in 1908 but who still were not permitted to vote, added to the ranks of the SPD, which had more than a million members in 1914. The SPD worked to build cradle-to-grave social institutions that would give members a sense that they belonged to a special culture, establishing consumer cooperatives, choral societies, and cycling clubs. Unlike French socialists, the SPD not only developed a close alliance with the trade union movement but also helped found some unions.

The SPD became the largest and best-organized socialist party in Europe; it published more than a hundred newspapers and magazines, and it held regular political meetings and social events. The party's organization and reformism influenced the evolution of similar parties in Belgium, Austria, and Switzerland. The SPD remained, however, caught in the paradox of struggling for social and political reform in a society—that of imperial Germany—that remained in many ways undemocratic.

In France, that country's revolutionary tradition and, above all, the memory of the Paris Commune of 1871, encouraged some French socialists to believe that revolution would bring them to power. The Parisian socialist Jules Guesde (1845–1922), rigid, humorless, and doctrinaire—he was known as "the Red Pope"—espoused Marxist socialism. In 1883, Guesde formed a defiantly Marxist political organization, the French Workers' Party, the first modern political party in France. Guesde viewed electoral campaigns as an opportunity to propagate Marxian socialism, although his followers joined the battle for an eight-hour workday and other reforms. The rival reform socialists espoused political pressure to win all possible social reforms through the ballot box. During elections, revolutionary and reform socialists often put their differences behind them, winning control over the municipal governments of several industrial cities. But the results in France of "municipal socialism," while subsidizing some services for ordinary people, were limited by the strongly centralized state.

When the reform socialist Alexandre Millerand (1859–1943) accepted a cabinet post in 1899, the split between revolutionary and reform socialists again lay bare. In 1905, Jean Jaurès (1859–1914), a former philosophy professor whose energy, organizational skills, and stirring oratory swept him to national prominence, achieved the unification of French socialists with the formation of the French Section of the Working-Class International (SFIO), although the differences between Guesdists and reformists could not be swept under the rug. The socialists became the second largest party in France, holding in 1914 a fifth of the seats in the Chamber of Deputies.

In Italy, socialists had to overcome the entrenched power of local elites, repression (including the jailing in 1887 of the first Italian socialist deputies), and the strong attraction of anarchism, particularly in southern Italy. The Italian Socialist Party, founded in 1892, made few inroads in Italy's impoverished south. By 1912, the revolutionary faction had gained control of the party.

In Spain, real power still lay in the hands of powerful local government officials and landowners, men of great local influence (the *caciques*) who rigged elections to the Cortes, backed by the Catholic Church and the army. The Spanish Socialist Party, founded in 1879, gained a sizable following only in industrial Asturias and the Basque region. In contrast to Germany, France, and Italy, the first Spanish socialists were not elected to Parliament until 1909.

Christian Socialism

In Catholic countries, the Church still provided an alternative allegiance to the nation-state. However, the secularization of state and social institutions, along with nationalism itself, reduced the Church's influence in some Catholic countries. Papal pronouncements seemed to stand steadfastly against social and political change, and particularly against the emergence of the nation-state and parliamentary forms of government. In a papal encyclical, the *Syllabus of Errors* of 1864, Pope Pius IX had condemned the very idea that "the Roman Pontiff can and ought to reconcile himself and come to terms with progress, liberalism and modern civilization." In 1870, the Church proclaimed the doctrine of papal infallibility, which stated that in matters of faith and morals the pope's pronouncements would have to be taken as absolute truth. The Church backed monarchical regimes in Spain and Portugal, opposed the newly unified state in Italy, and, at the beginning of the French Third Republic, lent tacit support to monarchist movements in France.

Breaking with his predecessors, Pope Leo XIII (pope 1878–1903) accepted the modern age. His encyclical *Rerum Novarum* (1891) called attention to social injustice, recognizing that many workers were victimized by "the inhumanity of employers and the unbridled greed of competitors." One of the unintended effects of *Rerum Novarum* was the development of "Christian Socialist" movements in France, Germany, Belgium, and Italy in the 1890s, although the Church itself generally repudiated them. Christian Socialists hoped to bring employers and workers back to the Church. Some clergy and laymen and -women organized clubs, vacation colonies, sporting clubs, and charities, and helped workers rent gardens so that they could grow vegetables and fruit. And many Catholics took the pope's encyclical as authorization to participate in national political life. Catholic unions tried to counter socialist influence by bringing together workers, employers, and honorary members drawn from local elites. These "mixed" or "yellow" unions drew the unrestrained opposition of most trade unions.

The Anarchists

While socialists wanted to take over the state, anarchists wanted to destroy it. Anarchism was never more than a minority movement. Yet the dramatic increase in the reach of European states in the nineteenth century encouraged the development of anarchism, a philosophy with few roots in earlier periods. Anarchism was the very antithesis of a philosophy of political organization because anarchists associated politics itself with a tacit recognition of the state's existence.

While many anarchists like Michael Bakunin (see Chapter 18) believed in the violent overthrow of the state, others believed that voluntary mutualism would eventually make the state superfluous. Peter Kropotkin (1842–1921), a geographer and the son of a Russian prince, held a vision of a gentle society of equals living in harmony without the strictures of the state. Kropotkin's desire for anarchist communism was rooted in his firsthand views of the misery of the Russian masses and his own experience living in the Jura Mountains of Switzerland and France in the 1860s, where watchmakers and peasants seemed to coexist in relative prosperity and the state seemed distant. Kropotkin, like Jean-Jacques Rousseau, espoused the primitive as a natural end in itself. He believed that each person was born a *tabula rasa* (blank slate)—an idea theorized by John Locke—and then corrupted by society and, above all, by the state.

Anarchism gained some adherents in France, the most centralized state in Europe, but above all in Italy and Spain, two countries in which the nation-state appeared to many people as a foreign intruder, and in Argentina, influenced by Spanish and Italian immigrants. Improvements in transportation and increased immigration brought anarchists, including some exiles, to new countries, with London serving as a particular place of refuge for continental anarchists. Anarchists were among recent immigrants in the United States during the last decades of the century, four of whom were hung after the Haymarket riots in Chicago in 1886. In contrast, anarchism found very few followers in Germany, where socialists as well as supporters of the imperial monarchy respected the state, and in Great Britain, the least centralized but also one of the most nationalist states in Western Europe.

A loose organization of anarchists, the International Working-Class Alliance, known as the "Black International" because of the color of the anarchist flag, maintained contacts among anarchists in France, Spain, Italy, and the United States. But, for the most part, anarchists formed small groups or struck out on their own. Among poor peasants in the rugged

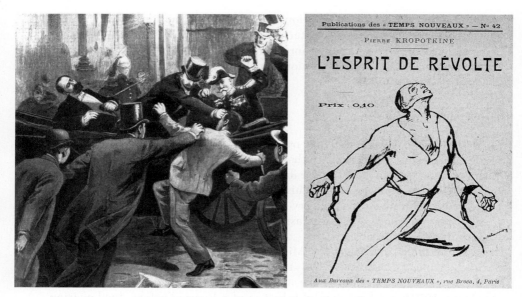

(*Left*) The assassination of French President Sadi Carnot by an Italian anarchist, 1894. (*Right*) Peter Kropotkins's publication *The Spirit of Revolt*.

southern Spanish province of Andalusia, anarchism took on a millenarian character stripped of most of the trappings of religion. Andalusian anarchists told the story of one of their own who, as he lay dying, whispered to one of his religious relatives to summon a priest and a lawyer. Relieved that the anarchist seemed at the last moment to be accepting the conventions of religion by accepting the last rites of the Church and drawing up a will, relatives sent for both. When they arrived, the anarchist beckoned them to stand on either side of his deathbed. As they leaned forward, one to hear his confession, the other to write down his will, the anarchist proclaimed, "Now, like Christ, I can die between two thieves."

In the 1880s and 1890s, a wave of anarchist assassinations and bombings shook Europe. To violent anarchists, the goal of "propaganda by the deed" was to spark a revolution. Bakunin's Italian disciple Enrico Maletesta (1853–1932), who had a following in Italy, Spain, and Argentina, expressed the bitter frustration of anarchists who had virtually nothing: "Do you not know that every bit of bread they [the wealthy] eat is taken from your children, every fine present they give to their wives means the poverty, hunger, cold and even perhaps the prostitution of yours?" Bakunin had believed that a single violent act might shock people into a chain-reaction revolution. "A single deed," Kropotkin once said, "is better propaganda than a thousand pamphlets." Barcelona became the "capital of bombs" in the 1890s. Anarchists killed six heads of states beginning in 1881, when members of

People's Will assassinated Tsar Alexander II. Other victims included King Umberto I of Italy, who was killed in 1900 (not long after saying that assassination was "a professional risk"), and President William McKinley of the United States, gunned down the following year.

From 1892 to 1894, a wave of bombings terrified Paris. "One does not kill an innocent person in striking the first bourgeois one sees," an anarchist told a shocked judge. François Claudius Ravachol, an impoverished worker, threw one of the bombs. "See this hand," Ravachol told the horrified judge and jurors, "it has killed as many bourgeois as it has fingers!" More attacks followed. In March 1893, an unemployed worker unable to feed his family threw a small bomb into the Chamber of Deputies, slightly injuring several members. He wanted to call attention to the plight of the poor. French President Sadi Carnot (1837–1894) turned down an appeal for mercy for the perpetrator. Next, Émile Henry, a young intellectual, tossed a bomb into a café near the Saint-Lazare railroad station, killing one man and injuring about twenty other people. In June 1894, an Italian anarchist assassinated Carnot. The wave of anarchist attacks subsided in France, but continued in Spain, where the government tortured and executed militant anarchists. In France, Italy, and Spain, harsh government repression itself brought a reaction against such policies, and soon the state gave anarchists fewer martyrs to avenge. With the rise of mass socialist parties and unions, anarchism faded further into the fringes of popular protest, except in Italy and, above all, Spain.

Syndicalists

At the turn of the century, syndicalism emerged as an ideology that held that union organization could provide a means for workers to seize control of their industries. Reflecting some anarchist influence, free associations of producers would eventually replace the state. Like revolutionary socialists and anarchists, syndicalists rejected participation in political life. Syndicalism, which was centered in France, Spain, and Italy, was sometimes called anarcho-syndicalism, because of its opposition to the existence of the state.

A retired engineer who proudly wore the prestigious legion of honor awarded by the French state, Georges Sorel (1847–1922) seemed an unlikely candidate to plan any revolution. But Sorel's *Reflections on Violence* (1908) encouraged direct syndicalist action against capitalism and the state, until a "general strike" by workers would bring both to their knees. By the general strike, Sorel meant a series of simultaneous walkouts that would shut down factories and lead to revolution.

The period 1895–1907 is sometimes referred to as "the heroic age of syndicalism" in France because so many strikes spread through so many industries there, as elsewhere in Europe. More than 1,000 strikes in France occurred in 1904 alone. During the "revolt of the south" in 1907, vineyard owners and vine-tenders aggressively protested the state tax on drink. In

Italy, Italian anarchists participated in the waves of strikes and insurrections in Sicily in 1893–1894. In Milan in 1898, fighting pitted the industrial suburbs against soldiers, and nearly 200 workers were killed and hundreds were wounded. Violent disturbances during "Red Week" shook the Italian Adriatic town of Ancona in June 1914 after police shot two people to death while preventing a crowd leaving an anti-militarist demonstration from marching into the downtown area. Even the normally peaceful Swedish capital of Stockholm was stirred by a general strike in 1909. It failed.

Anarcho-syndicalists dominated the labor movement in Barcelona, particularly among dockworkers, who confronted brutal police repression orchestrated from Madrid. Waves of strikes took place in Catalonia in 1902, 1906, and 1909, the latter followed by a bloody insurrection ("Tragic Week"). But gradually, revolutionary rhetoric gave way to the pursuit of concrete economic gains, particularly in Italy and France. In the end, at least in Western Europe, reformism won out.

The Quest for Women's Rights

Everywhere in Europe, women remained subordinate to men in legal rights. They were excluded from most universities, could not vote (in contrast, several U.S. states gave women the vote before 1914), and had limited or no control over family financial resources. Women made very little progress entering the professions because some men feared the advent of the "new woman," who demanded the same access to education and opportunity as men. The term "new woman" came from the title of a lecture given by the Italian feminist Maria Montessori (1870–1952), a doctor and originator of innovative schools (which still exist) that stress the encouragement of creativity in children. Still, the beginnings were difficult. When a female Greek scientist gave her inaugural lecture at the University of Athens, male students disrupted her lecture with shouts of "Back to the kitchen!" Women demanding equal rights faced daunting opposition. Queen Victoria of England called demands by women for equal rights "on which her poor feeble sex is bent . . . a mad, wicked folly . . . forgetting every sense of womanly feeling and propriety." The biologist T. H. Huxley (1825–1895) insisted that women were less intelligent than men. The claims of such bad science bolstered opposition to the women's movement.

Right-wing political parties opposed women's suffrage on principle. Moderate republicans claimed that women could not understand political issues. Socialists in Catholic countries feared that if women had the right to vote, they would support clerical candidates, although socialist parties and unions threw their support to women workers laboring for better wages and conditions. However, some women contended that social reforms would be inadequate as long as women were without the right to enter universities or vote.

The feminist movement (a name that only gradually took hold in Europe and the United States) developed very slowly in Europe. It was most active in Britain. There the first women's political organizations were created in the 1860s, and women gained the right to vote in municipal elections in 1864 and for county and parish councils six years later. Women also gained the right to enter university and made headway in achieving property rights for married women, child custody, and the right to initiate divorce. The movement for women's rights in Britain coincided with the "new imperialism" that began in the 1880s (see Chapter 21). Concern among feminists with the condition of indigenous women in the empire, particularly in India, where British women had more occasion to meet their counterparts and viewed them as backward victims of barbaric religious and cultural practices, helped shape British feminism. British feminists came to see themselves as the saviors of women in the colonies, while identifying themselves with the good of their empire, a special place in the "civilizing mission." As one put it, "We are struggling not just for English women alone, but for all the women, degraded, miserable, unheard of, for whose life and happiness England has daily to answer to God."

In 1889, the first International Congresses on Women's Rights and Feminine Institutions took place in Paris. By 1900, more than 850 German associations were working for women's rights, including improved educational and employment opportunities and equal wages. Near the end of the nineteenth century, British women's groups presented to Parliament a peti-

In 1913, the suffragette Emily Davison throws herself before the king's horse at the Derby at Epsom Downs and is killed.

tion with more than a quarter of a million signatures calling for reform. As more occupations opened up to women, the campaign for women's suffrage widened. The International Women's Suffrage Alliance encouraged organizations in a number of countries. A more militant group of feminists undertook a campaign of direct action. Emmeline Pankhurst (1858–1928) founded the Women's Social and Political Union in 1903. Members protested the lack of female suffrage by breaking shop windows on London's fashionable Oxford Street, tossing acid on golf putting greens (a sport then identified with aristocratic British males), and bombing the house of Liberal Party leader David Lloyd George (1863–1945). Other "suffragettes," as they were called, went on hunger strikes upon being arrested. In 1907, British women gained the right to serve in local government. In the most dramatic incident, a suffragette carrying a banner proclaiming "Votes for Women" hurled herself in front of a horse owned by King George V at the 1913 Derby at Epsom Downs and was killed.

CULTURAL FERMENT

Europeans had many reasons to be optimistic at the turn of the century. Since the fall of Napoleon in 1815, Europe had enjoyed a relatively long period of peace broken only by short wars with limited goals, including the bloody Franco-Prussian War (1870–1871). Literacy had risen rapidly, particularly in western and northern Europe. Nation-states, increasingly secular in character, commanded the loyalty of their populations. Advances in science and technology were transforming the way people lived. The standard of living had generally risen, and, at least in most of Europe, white-collar jobs provided hope of better things for more people. Furthermore, somewhat shorter working hours for employees, including many workers, left more time for leisure activities.

During the 1850s and 1860s, scientific progress and social change was reflected in the emergence of realism as the dominant cultural style for artists and writers. Then, beginning in the last decade of the nineteenth century, more technological advances and the emergence of a more urban world brought both a cultural crisis of previously unparalleled dimensions and remarkable achievements in the arts. More scientific discoveries and new theories about the functioning of the universe continued to tear away some of the old certainties. Social scientists tried to find explanations for the working of society and the inner world of the individual. At the same time, some writers and artists began to turn away from rationalism, materialism, and positivism. In France, Henri Bergson (1859–1941) emerged as the philosopher of irrationality. Challenging materialism and positivism, Bergson popularized the idea that each individual and each nation had a creative "dynamic energy," or vital force (*élan vital*), waiting for release. The "modernist" culture of the avant-garde turned against the century-old acceptance of rationality as one of the dominant values of Western culture. The notion of an avant-garde, a term taken from military tactics, implies a small group of people who see themselves in the forefront of artistic expression and achievement. Intellectuals and artists began to insist on the irrational basis of human nature, their work reflecting both uncertainty and cultural rebellion.

Realism

Influenced by the widening interest in science and the quickening pace of social change, some writers had in the middle decades of the century broken with literary traditions. Realism had emerged as the dominant European cultural style during the 1850s and 1860s. Charles Baudelaire (1821–1867) once described himself as the poet of modern life. Best known for his volume of poems *Les Fleurs du Mal* (1857; *The Flowers of Evil*), Baudelaire believed that art had to be the product of an exchange between the individual artist and contemporary society. The artist's own experience and self-discovery became critical in the emergence of modern literature. Baudelaire was fined in 1857 for "obscene and immoral passages or expressions." *Les Fleurs du Mal* became even more popular as his decadence and overt eroticism—he died of syphilis in 1867—angered officials and critics alike. Baudelaire was the consummate dandy and *"flâneur,"* the observer of modern urban life. Dressed in what modest elegance his small inheritance permitted, the flâneur strolled through Paris, finding beauty in its modern boulevards but also gazing at its hideous, even frightening aspects with objective detachment, both

reacting to and reflecting modern urban life. Baudelaire rebelled against bourgeois culture and conventional assumptions about artistic subjects and style. Rejecting the notion that absolute aesthetic values exist, Baudelaire was a crucial figure in the emergence of modern culture in the middle of the century.

In the 1850s, the Barbizon painters—so called because they gathered in a village of that name southeast of Paris—emphasized the painting of peasants, harvests, animals, and other symbols of village life. In doing so, they broke sharply with many of the long-accepted styles of painting, including romanticism. The development of photography during the 1840s may have contributed to the inter-

Charles Baudelaire, "the poet of modern life," in a photograph by Félix Nadar.

Jean-François Millet's *The Gleaners* (1857).

est in portraying artistic subjects with a vivid sense of actuality. Jean-
François Millet (1814–1875), a Barbizon painter, painted peasants at work
in such pieces as *The Gleaners* (1857) and *The Angelus* (1859), giving
peasants a dignity that repelled many middle-class viewers who thought
them unworthy of being painted.

Artistic style evolved far more rapidly than did official views of what constituted good art. Gustave Courbet (1819–1877) abandoned the idealiza-
tion that still characterized painting. "Show me an angel," he scoffed at his
critics, "and I will paint one." Taking as a compliment the assessment that
he was "a democratic painter," he startled viewers by choosing ordinary
workers as his subjects. Like Millet, Courbet shocked with his realism.
Burial at Ornans (1849) portrays a family of some means looking rather
unattractive, bored, or even indifferent as the body of a relative is being
lowered into a grave in Courbet's hometown. *The Bather* (1853) shows a
stout naked woman rising from a forest pool. Nudity did not bother many
viewers—it was, after all, a staple of classical painting. Rather, viewers
were upset by the fact that Courbet portrayed an ordinary-looking woman
holding herself up very awkwardly. The artist seemed to be mocking the
kind of classical scene painters had been expected to treat with reverence.
When Napoleon III saw the exhibited painting, he struck the canvas with a
riding-crop. Courbet, a political radical, believed that art should have a
social purpose. He exacted some revenge in a later painting by depicting
the emperor as a shabby poacher.

Realists continued to ruffle official feathers. The French police hauled the novelist Gustave Flaubert (1821–1880) into court, charging him with obscenity. His novel *Madame Bovary* (1857) evokes with flawless attention to detail the affair of a bored bourgeois housewife living in a small, dreary Norman town. Flaubert revealed the bohemian underside of bourgeois life. But like most writers and artists at the time, he also depended upon middle-class patronage for his work.

Gustave Courbet's *The Bather* (1853) in which the subject strikes an awkward pose.

The escapist science fiction fantasies of the French author Jules Verne (1828–1905) reflected contemporary fascination with developing sciences like geography, science, astronomy, and physics, as well as improvements in transportation and communication. Verne's *Around the World in Eighty Days,* first published in 1873, became a best seller. In Britain, Sir Arthur Conan Doyle's character of Sherlock Holmes emerged in the late 1880s as fiction's first truly scientific detective. The Norwegian playwright Henrik Ibsen (1828–1906) drew admiration and protest alike with works of unrelenting realism and concern with women's lives. His forceful dramas, such as *A Doll's House* and *Hedda Gabler,* offer realistic descriptions of the psychology and interaction of complex characters. Considered in some ways the father of modern drama, Ibsen privileged the themes of guilt and hypocrisy as he presented families in small-town life.

The French novelist Émile Zola (1840–1902) shocked critics with his evocation of working-class life, not only because the subject itself challenged traditional assumptions about literary worthiness but also because of his unabashed realism in depicting ordinary people as he saw them. Zola believed that naturalistic writing was a form of science. He went down into mine shafts in northern France so that he could offer a realistic depiction of the work there in his novel *Germinal* (1885).

Artists and writers who espoused the new realism confronted censorship in France. Napoleon III prohibited the historian Joseph Ernest Renan (1823–1892) from lecturing. Renan considered himself a proponent of "progressive ideas"—above all, a faith in science. His *Life of Jesus* (1863) offended the Catholic Church by presenting Christ as a historical figure, seemingly casting doubt upon his divinity. More than this, Renan argued that the Scriptures had to be studied like any other historical document.

Impressionism

During the French Second Empire, a group of artists developed impressionism, a remarkable artistic movement that lasted until the end of the century. Like the realists of the Barbizon school, impressionist painters rejected traditional religious and historical subjects and formal presentation. Instead, they depicted rural and urban landscapes, offering scenes from everyday existence, but generally integrated individual figures into landscapes. Embracing subjectivity, the impressionists preferred direct observation and the study of nature's effects to studio composition and imitation of classic styles. Édouard Manet (1832–1883), another dandy and flâneur, aspired to create what a contemporary called an art "born of today." The impressionists painted what they saw, and how they saw it at first glance, such as the way sunlight falls on inanimate objects (thus reflecting their interest in science). They put lighter and brighter colors on large canvases (which previously had usually been reserved for historical themes), applying many small dabs of paint to convey an impression of spontaneity, energy, and movement.

Although the impressionists did not begin to exhibit their paintings with the self-consciousness of an artistic group until 1874, their movement was shaped by official rejection. The Salon was a state-sponsored exhibition upon which artists depended in order to attract purchasers. In 1863, the jury for the official Salon turned down several canvases by Manet. After certain complaints reached the emperor, he allowed some of the paintings to be shown in other rooms. The "Salon of the Refused" included works by Manet, Auguste Renoir, and Paul Cézanne. Some critics raged against what they saw, but at least the public could now make up its own mind. Manet's *Olympia* (1863) generated a chorus of complaint. This study of a nude shocked public opinion—the outraged Empress Eugénie, not to be outdone by her husband, Napoleon III, who had attacked a Courbet canvas with a riding-crop, struck Manet's painting with her fan. Manet's *Déjeuner sur l'herbe* (1863) drew scathing commentary because it showed a nude female sharing a picnic with two fully dressed, upper-class males. Here, Manet, even more than the realists, challenged the hierarchy of subjects imposed by classicism.

Manet chose provocatively contemporary subjects, including very ordinary people, clients, and café waitresses enjoying themselves. He and his younger friend Claude Monet (1840–1926) painted the Gare Saint-Lazare, the point of entry each day for thousands of commuters, vacationers, and other visitors. Berthe Morisot (1841–1895), Manet's sister-in-law, placed her subjects, most of whom were women, in private gardens, in the Bois de Boulogne, boating on the Seine, and at the resorts of the Norman coast, which had been "discovered" by wealthy Parisians.

Édouard Manet's *Déjeuner sur l'herbe* (1863).

The rebuilding of Paris opened up new possibilities for the understanding of modernity. Impressionists found the great boulevards fitting subjects for their portrayal of modern life. The early impressionists were also influenced by the growing commercialization of leisure in Paris. Edgar Degas (1834–1917) followed wealthy Parisians to theaters, racetracks, cafés, and café-concerts, which offered entertainment that included vaudeville acts, poetry readings, comedians, and singers renowned for bawdy lyrics. Degas frequently chose female entertainers, most of whom were drawn from the popular classes, as his subjects. In the shadows of his ballet paintings lurk wealthy gentlemen awaiting their prey, like Napoleon III himself, who occupy the loges closest to the stage at the opera or stand in the shadows of the dressing rooms of the dancers, ready to claim their prizes. Degas, whose banking family had lost its money early in an economic depression, presented unflattering, dark stereotypes of Parisian speculators in *At the Stock Exchange* (1879). The increasing anonymity of the burgeoning city was also a frequent impressionist theme. Degas's *L'Absinthe* (1876–1877) shows two disconnected figures in a café. Such encounters with strangers seemed an intrinsic part of modern life.

Monet also manifested an uneasy ambivalence toward large-scale industry. In the 1870s, he lived in the industrializing Paris suburb of Argenteuil.

His paintings of the town reflect a balance between leisure and industry (seen, for example, in a painting of sailboats on the Seine River with factory smokestacks in the background). Monet eventually tired of the hustle and bustle of urban life and moved down the Seine to the village of Giverny. There his garden and its pond and lily pads provided an ideal rural setting for his work. He never painted the railway tracks that ran through his property.

Social Theorists' Analyses of Industrial Society

Edgar Degas's *L'Absinthe* (1876–1877) shows a woman and her companion with a glass of absinthe. Note how the lack of a table support helps draw the viewer's attention to the glass of absinthe.

Scientific advances contributed to the diffusion of the belief that human progress was inevitable and that it moved in a linear manner. This optimistic view became known as positivism. Auguste Comte (1798–1857) had already spread faith in the promise of science. Believing that scientific discovery had passed through three stages of development—the theological, the metaphysical, and the "positive" (or scientific)—Comte concluded that what he called "the science of society" could do the same. Society itself, he reasoned, like nature could be studied in a scientific manner and its development charted. Comte's positivism called for the accumulation of useful knowledge that would help students of society to understand the laws of social development.

Positivists challenged some of the central tenets of the established churches, particularly those of the Catholic Church, whose theologians held fast to a view of humanity as essentially unchanging. Darwinism (see Chapter 18) denied the literal biblical description of God creating the world in seven days. Clergy of many denominations, and many other people as well, were aghast to think that humanity could have descended from apes.

Now, in the face of rapid social change, intellectuals attempted to understand the structure of the society they saw changing around them. They did so by adopting the model of natural science and undertaking objective systematic analysis of observable social data. They gradually developed sociology, the science of society, which asked: How do societies hold together when confronted by economic and social forces that tend to pull them apart? The question itself expressed the cultural crisis of the fin de siècle. In 1887, the German Ferdinand Tönnies (1855–1936) published a groundbreaking work, *Community and Society* (*Gemeinschaft und Gesellschaft*), which sought to synthesize and apply historical experience to understand the development of modern Western civilization.

Influenced by Tönnies and fascinated by the emergence of industrial society and the growth of the state, Max Weber (1864–1920), one of the fathers of modern social thought and sociology, sought to create an objective and thus "value-free" science of society that he thought held the key to guiding the future. Trained as a professor of law in Heidelberg, Weber became interested in the relationship between religion and society. *The Protestant Ethic and the Spirit of Capitalism* (1904–1905) defined the "spirit of capitalism" to be the assumption that whoever works hard in the pursuit of gain fulfills a moral obligation. He identified the origins of capitalism with Calvinist entrepreneurship in the sixteenth and seventeenth centuries. Weber observed the contemporary trend toward larger structures of government and the bureaucratization of state, business, and political structures, which he believed marked the victory of Enlightenment rationalism, as well as increased social stratification. But he worried that in the advancing impersonal age of bureaucracy, state officials would ignore political and social ideals. Weber's modern man seemed to be trapped in what he called "the iron cage of modern life." Theorist of a nervous age, Weber had a nervous breakdown before the turn of the century.

Doctors diagnosed more cases of hypochondria, "melancholy," and hysteria, paralyzing nervous disorders that many blamed on the complexities of modern life, which seemed to be overwhelming the nervous system. In particular, neurasthenia seemed to be a sign of the times, with its symptoms of extreme sensitivity to light and noise—two characteristics of urban life—fatigue, worry, and digestive disorders.

Alcoholism was ravaging many countries. In England, the "habitual soaking" of workers in beer worried reformers. A contemporary investigator claimed that it was not uncommon for some workers to spend a quarter of their earnings on drink. The dramatic increase in the production of wine in France (with the exception of the 1880s and 1890s, when the phylloxera disease ravaged vineyards), Italy, Spain, and Portugal flooded markets, greatly reducing its price. In parts of France, the average person (and thus the figure for adults would be even higher) consumed well more than sixty gallons of wine a year, in addition to beer, brandies, and absinthe, a licorice-tasting drink made from wormwood that is highly addictive. There were almost half a million establishments licensed to serve drink in France at the turn of the century—one for every 54 people, compared to one British "public house" for every 843 inhabitants.

French temperance movements were swept aside like tiny dikes by the torrent of drink. Nationalists, worried about the plunging birthrate, joined some doctors and reformers in claiming that France faced "racial degeneration" since its population might cease to reproduce itself because of the ravages of alcoholism. Some doctors blamed women for not doing their part to increase the French population, their attacks complementing surging resistance to the rise of feminism. For their part, some women began to put forward their role as republican mothers to bolster demands for more rights. Nationalists insisted that only by rallying around patriotic values could France avoid total collapse. In Britain, the temperance movement began earlier and was far stronger than in France. It was also much more closely tied to churches, as was the movement in Sweden, where in 1909 temperance societies had almost half a million members who signed pledges promising not to drink alcohol at all.

The use of opium and its derivatives—morphine (the popularity of which increased with its use as an anesthetic), laudanum (a mixture of wine and opium), and heroin—as well as cocaine and hashish, unfortunately became common among the artistic avant-garde, well before most people were aware of their devastating effects. These drugs arrived from Turkey, Persia, and India, with coca (from which cocaine is derived) brought from Peru and Bolivia. The painter Pablo Picasso (1881–1973) was for a period a hashish user, which may have influenced his dreamy rose-colored paintings of 1905–1908. Only in the latter years did the French government ban such drugs, in the wake of a number of drug-related suicides. Less dangerous, exoticism, mysticism, spiritism (including attempts to contact the souls of deceased people during séances), and a fascination with the occult became more popular than ever before, another sign of the rejection of science and the associated preoccupation with the irrational.

Modern life seemed to provide evidence that industrialization and urban growth had uprooted traditional values. Crimes seemed to be increasing. Seeking an explanation, the French social theorist Émile Durkheim (1858–1917) believed that the rapid, seemingly uncontrollable growth of large cities had destroyed the moral ties that had sustained the individual in traditional society. Durkheim believed that the waning of religious practice had undermined authority and therefore social cohesiveness. Durkheim's quantitative study of suicide led him to conclude that the stresses and strains of increasingly urban, industrial life were becoming more debilitating. He concluded that individuals lost in the faceless urban and

Two elegant morphine addicts, 1891.

industrial world suffered "alienation" (*anomie* in French). Yet he optimistically believed that social problems could be solved by studying them in a systematic, scientific manner.

Durkheim was hardly alone in thinking that urban growth, spurred on by the arrival of rural migrants, generated social pathology of which criminality was but one manifestation. In 1895, Gustave Le Bon (1841–1931) published *The Crowd,* in which he worried that modern life submerged the individual in the "crowd." Riots and strikes, he warned, were becoming part of the political process. He described crowds as lurching erratically, and sometimes dangerously, like drunks, at a time of a growing awareness of the ravages of alcoholism. Some nationalists now worried that their peoples were being undermined by "racial degeneration," which might compromise the natural process of evolution by hereditary debasement. Certain scientists claimed that significant racial differences could be identified within specific peoples, and that they accounted for soaring rates of crime, alcoholism, insanity, syphilis, and even popular political action. An Italian anthropologist believed that criminals showed inferior physical and mental development and contended that they could be identified by measuring their skulls.

Nietzsche's Embrace of the Irrational

Friedrich Nietzsche (1844–1900) emerged in this period as the most strident philosophical critic of Enlightenment rationalism. The son of a strict Protestant German minister who died when Nietzsche was young, he was raised by his domineering mother. He became a professor of classics in Basel, Switzerland. The tormented Nietzsche, forced by illness to leave the university, moved to the Swiss Alps and thereafter lived by his pen, but with little success. He suffered a mental collapse at the age of forty-five, after sending off telegrams to some of his friends signed "The Crucified." Nietzsche was briefly confined in an asylum toward the end of his life, leading one wag to comment, "At last, the right man in the right place."

Nietzsche hated all religions equally, believing that they had

Friedrich Nietzsche, philosopher of the irrational.

destroyed the individual's capacity for natural development and fulfillment by imposing uniformity. He became an atheist, proclaiming, "God is dead . . . and we have killed him." He claimed strenuously that religion was incapable of providing ethical guidance and that no single morality could be appropriate to all people.

Espousing "philosophy with the hammer," Nietzsche awaited the heroic superman who, as part of a natural nobility of "higher humanity," would rule through the "will to power." Although indirectly influenced by the contentions of Hegel and Darwin that mankind could continue to develop to a higher stage, Nietzsche's thought marked a total rejection of all previous philosophy. His "vital" force, which he believed could be found only in new philosophers like himself, would be morally ambivalent, idealizing power and struggle. The free man, wrote Nietzsche, "is a warrior." Yet for all of his talk about "master races" and "slave races" in a period marked by a growth of racism, he castigated the herd-like instincts of frenetic German nationalists and anti-Semites.

Freud and the Study of the Irrational

The Viennese doctor Sigmund Freud (1856–1939) stressed the power of the irrational, which he placed in the human unconscious. Freud was born in the small Moravian town of Freiberg (now in the Czech Republic) in the Habsburg monarchy, the son of a struggling Jewish wool merchant and his much younger wife. When Sigmund was three, his father's business affairs went from bad to worse, forcing the family to leave its tranquil, small-town existence for Vienna. The younger Freud never felt comfortable in the imposing imperial capital. But he benefited from the period of liberal ascendancy in Austria, where Jews had received full civil rights only in 1867. The Viennese middle class had helped make their city a cultural capital of Europe. That reassuring atmosphere changed with the stock-market crash in 1873, which began a period of economic depression and culminated in the election of an anti-Semite, Karl Lueger ("I decide who is a Jew," Lueger insisted), as mayor of Vienna in 1895.

After beginning his career as a research scientist in anatomy, Freud fell under the influence of the French neurologist Jean Charcot (1825–1893). From his scientific laboratory, Freud moved to the study of the irrational, or the "unconscious," convinced that it could be studied with the same systematic rigor as human anatomy. In the spring of 1886, he opened a small office in Vienna, treating patients with nervous disorders.

Freud developed the method of psychoanalysis, a term coined in 1896. It was based on the premises that the mind is orderly and that dreams offer codes that can unlock the unconscious. To Freud, a dream represented "the fulfillment of a [suppressed] wish"; it was the expression of an unconscious conflict. Freud encouraged patients to dream and to "free associate" in order to break down their defense mechanisms (the means by which

The Austrian psychoanalyst Sigmund Freud in his study.

individuals repress painful memories from childhood or even infancy). Sexuality, specifically the repression of sexual urges, formed the basis of Freud's theory of the unconscious. One of Freud's followers described the role of his mentor's "dream-work": "The mind is like a city which during the day busies itself with the peaceful tasks of legitimate commerce, but at night when all the good burghers sleep soundly in their beds, out come these disreputable creatures of the psychic underworld to disport themselves in a very unseemly fashion; decking themselves out in fantastic costumes, in order that they may not be recognized and apprehended." Psychoanalysis became both an investigative tool and a form of therapy, in which, very gradually—from several months to many years and at considerable financial cost—the patient could obtain self-awareness and control over his or her symptoms, such as hysteria.

Freud's theories of human development established the irrational as an intrinsic and sometimes even determining part of the human psyche. Psychoanalytic theory, which Freud claimed as a new science, emerged, along with Darwin's evolutionary theory and Marx's writings on capitalist development and revolution, as one of the foundations of twentieth-century thought.

Avant-Garde Artists and Writers and the Rapid Pace of Modern Life

Progress seemed to have a price. At the Paris Exhibition of 1900, which celebrated the dawn of a new century, an uneasy visitor noted, "Life seethes in this immense reservoir of energy . . . a too violent magnificence." In *The Wind in the Willows,* published in 1908 by Kenneth Grahame (1859–1932), the motor car threatens stability. Behind the wheel, Toad, the amphibian protagonist, turns into "the terror . . . before whom all must give way or be smitten into nothingness and everlasting night . . . fulfilling his instincts, living his hour, reckless of what might come to him." The airplane, rapidly rising and then swooping dangerously, seemed not only a soaring symbol of scientific advances but also of the uncertainty that unsettled some fin-de-siècle Europeans.

During the last ten years of the career of the French impressionist painter and anarchist Camille Pissarro (1830–1903), perhaps the preeminent painter of the countryside, he took up urban subjects, painting bridges, riverbanks, and boulevards, crowding myriad forms and figures into his panoramic views. Emphasizing the motion of transportation, walking, riding, loading, and unloading, he depicted the light, color, nervous movement, and energy of the city and its seemingly uncontrollable throngs, calling one series of paintings "Social Turpitudes."

Other painters also presented urban scenes in a harsh, jarring light that suggested chaos. The German expressionist painter Ludwig Meidner (1884–1966) insisted that painters ought to abandon the gentle, almost rural style that characterized impressionist urban scenes: "A street," he wrote, "is rather a bombardment of hissing rows of windows, of blustering cones of lights between vehicles of all kinds and thousands of leaping globes, human rags, advertising signboards and masses of threatening, formless colors."

Avant-garde writers and artists loathed the culture of the public, or what the English aesthete Oscar Wilde called the "profane masses." Popular culture seemed to be eroding the ability of high culture to survive the assault of mass manufacturing and teeming cities. Sharp reactions against the seeming uniformity of the machine age permeated the arts. The English craftsman and designer William Morris (1834–1896) believed that mass production was in the process of eliminating the aesthetic control craftsmen had maintained over production. Describing capitalism as a "defilement" and Victorian England as the "age of shoddy," Morris argued that the machine had become the master of both workers and design, instead of the other way around. Only a revolution in aesthetics could save art and architecture. Morris spearheaded the "arts and crafts movement" in Britain, espousing craft production that would create useful but artistic objects for the general public, thereby elevating taste to a new level.

The Avant-Garde's Break with Rationalism

Symbolism, which began as a literary movement in the early 1870s but had origins a decade earlier—the symbolists revered Baudelaire as a founding father—also reflected the discontent of writers with the materialism of the industrial age. Symbolists sought to discover and depict aesthetically the reality of human consciousness and identity. They believed that analogies existed between the human mind and the external world, and thus between the spiritual and natural worlds. They held that the links could be discovered through the exploitation of symbols, particularly through poetry. Thus some continuity existed between symbolism and the romanticism of the early nineteenth century, as symbolists sought to bring emotions to the surface through dreamlike states of consciousness.

In May 1913, the Russian aristocrat Sergey Diaghilev's ballet *The Rite of Spring* opened in Paris. For Diaghilev (1872–1929), who organized major art expositions and outraged conventional society by flaunting male lovers, art and life went hand in hand—they imitated each other. Diaghilev sought liberation in erotic ballets. Hitherto, ballet had retained absolute loyalty to classical subjects and presentation, immune to avant-garde challenge. Aesthetes in the audience hissed at the men and women of Parisian high society filing into the theater wearing tails and evening gowns. When the curtain went up, the dancers were jumping up and down, toeing inward in defiance of conventional ballet. The majority of the audience reacted with catcalls, hisses, and then screams of anger. An elderly countess scoffed that it was the first time that anyone—in this case, the dancers with their provocative performance—had ever made fun of her. The audience was shocked by the jarring, primitive music of the Russian composer Igor Stravinsky (1882–1971), who dispensed with the sentimental music that had invariably accompanied ballet. The avant-garde, however, cheered. Art and life had merged.

Thus, rejecting the idea that rationalism should underlie the arts and that objective standards could exist by which to assess literature, painting, and music, the writers, painters, and composers of the avant-garde rebelled against accepted cultural forms. They believed that these threatened to render the individual insignificant and powerless. Mass-circulation newspapers,

Scene from Sergey Diaghilev's *The Rite of Spring*, 1913.

the popular theater inevitably playing Gilbert and Sullivan in London or soapy popular operas in Paris, music halls, military band concerts in Hyde Park, and the cinema were the stuff of popular culture. The avant-garde wanted none of it.

Avant-garde artists accepted nothing as absolute, certainly not the traditional forms of cultural expression or morality. Showing Nietzsche's influence, some sought to transcend the limits of reason and moral purpose. Far more than even impressionist painters, the turn of the century avant-garde artists broke with the past. This was, to an extent, a revolt of the young— because of the rise in population, a larger percentage of the population was indeed young—and self-consciously so. In Austria, the avant-garde called themselves "The Young Ones." They were defiantly "modern," a term they embraced with passion. They paid less attention to their subjects than the response their work would elicit in their audiences. The French playwright Alfred Jarry (1873–1907) staged the play *King Ubu,* a mockery of an authority figure. The story of an avaricious oaf in desperate search of a crown, the farce ran one tumultuous night in December 1896; it began with one of the characters pretending to hurl human waste at the outraged audience.

The avant-garde did not write or paint for everybody. In Paris, a group of artists and writers called themselves "Bohemians"—gypsy wanderers. These avant-garde young men gloried in the condition of being outsiders, rebels against the dominant culture in the way that romanticism had been a revolt against the classical tastes of court and château, even rebels against the strictures of their own middle-class social origins. They sought to surprise with their spontaneity and creativity, and even to offend by creating a scandal. However, although the proponents of cultural modernism may have mocked bourgeois "respectability" and popular culture by sporting long hair, wearing strange clothes, and behaving erratically, they nonetheless sought public acceptance and patronage of their work.

Many, including a number who were homosexual, celebrated their individuality and tried to keep themselves in the public eye. The flamboyant Irish-born poet and dramatist Oscar Wilde (1854–1900), whose witty dialogues greatly improved British comedy, became a symbol of contemporary "decadence." When asked by a customs official if he had anything to declare on arriving in France, Wilde replied, "Only my genius." He faced prosecution in 1895 for his sexual orientation and was sentenced to two years' hard labor for "immoral conduct." He died a lonely, premature death in a small Parisian hotel in 1900.

New musical composition also reflected the contemporary discovery of the unconscious, as avant-garde composers moved defiantly away from traditional forms. Many abandoned the ordered hierarchical scale, in which certain tones held precedence. The composer Gustav Mahler (1860–1911) sought to release in his audience dreams and fantasies, which he believed could not be distinguished from real life, just as Freud sought to elicit them from the patients on his office couch. The French pianist and composer

Erik Satie (1866–1925) composed music by the dim light of lampposts as he returned in an alcoholic haze from his favorite cafés, where he would eat only foods white in color. Both Satie and his countryman Claude Debussy (1862–1918) set out to free music from all constraints. Satie's compositions, with fanciful titles like *Three Pieces in the Form of a Pear,* explored new relationships between chords that surprised listeners, outraging some while delighting others with their humor. The Austrian composer Arnold Schoenberg (1874–1951) began to break the patterns of traditional harmonies to write free atonal music, beginning with his String Quartet No. 2 (1908). He believed atonality realistically and subliminally followed the dictates, instincts, and sometimes suffering of his psyche: "What counts is the capacity to hear oneself, to look deep inside oneself. . . . Inside, where the man of instinct begins, there, fortunately, all theory breaks down." For Schoenberg, the self became a refuge from the outside world.

The artists, writers, and composers of the avant-garde believed that art could reveal what is hidden in the unconscious, and thus open up new vistas of experience that could be communicated to viewers and audiences. The poet Guillaume Apollinaire (1880–1918), whose work defied stylistic convention, wrote reviews of books that only existed in his mind. Master of ambiguity, he abandoned direct statement and even punctuation and conventional word order to encourage readers to find new meanings in his work. One contemporary, affirming the particularly close link between symbolism and music, urged writers to "drop a syllable into a state of pure consciousness and listen for the reverberations."

Postimpressionists painted subjects in ways that even more consciously than impressionism distanced the artist from the subject. Georges Seurat (1859–1891) claimed that painters could evoke emotions through the visual suggestions of discontinuous lines, colors, and tones. Symbolist writers, who believed that symbols would stimulate memory through free association, were intrigued by Seurat's paintings because they consisted of thousands of dots of color forming figures and landscapes. This bold style, called "pointillism," influenced by the development of photography, left Seurat's figures appearing strangely mechanical and separate from each other. This may suggest the alienation, social division, and isolation of modern urban life. Yet in *A Sunday on La Grande Jatte* (1884), Seurat may have sought to portray social cohesion through the social mix of bourgeois and workers enjoying a Sunday afternoon along the Seine River in Paris.

Expressionist painters used daring distortions, curious juxtaposition, and bold, unfamiliar color schemes to express what lay deep inside them and to obtain an emotional response in viewers. They were greatly influenced by the art of "primitive" societies. The French painter Paul Gauguin (1848–1903) abandoned a comfortable living as a stockbroker for the uncertainty of a career as a painter. His lengthy stay on the Pacific Ocean island of Tahiti shaped the appearance of his painting. Edvard Munch (1863–1944), a Norwegian artist who came to Paris in 1893, demon-

Georges Seurat's *A Sunday on La Grande Jatte* (1884).

strated Gauguin's influence. Munch's *The Scream* (1893) evokes the viewer's alarm and fear, because the subject's scream seems to fill the entire canvas. In Munich, which along with Dresden was the center of the German expressionist movement, the Russian painter Wassily Kandinsky (1866–1944) had by 1910 moved expressionism even farther away from surface reality, portraying the inner being in a simplified form with lines, dots, and intense colors.

Art Nouveau, a sinuous decorative style offering a synthesis between traditional and modern art, also reflected the anxiety and moodiness of the fin de siècle. Art Nouveau evinced contemporary fascination with psychiatry. Charcot, the French neurologist, had opened up the unconscious to investigation through hypnosis. The dreamlike flowing forms and shapes of Art Nouveau, then, complemented the growing awareness of the contours and fluidity of the mind and its dreams and fantasies.

Although drawing upon past decorative traditions in furniture, jewelry, glasswork, and ceramics, Art Nouveau also influenced architecture, seen in the houses and sweeping entrances to subway stations that Hector Guimard (1867–1942) designed in Paris, and in apartment buildings and the beginnings of a cathedral undertaken (and still unfinished) in Barcelona by Antonio Gaudí (1852–1926).

Leading cultural figures in France identified Art Nouveau's style with the republic, seeing in its highly crafted luxury products something that was very French. At the same time, it could be associated with the conservative republic because the style's rococo origins were rooted in an aristocratic

(*Left*) Antonio Gaudí's Casa Batlló in Barcelona. (*Right*) Gustav Klimt's *Judith II* (*Salome*) (1909).

tradition and, perhaps as well, seemed to affirm women's traditional role in household decoration at a time when more feminists were stepping forward to demand equal rights for women.

Vienna became a vital center of avant-garde cultural experimentation at the turn of the century. But after first enjoying state sponsorship of their art, the painters and writers of the avant-garde faced rejection in a climate of intolerance. Some intellectuals and painters then embraced aestheticism, which emphasized form and beauty as a way of surviving in an increasingly irrational, hostile world. The painter Gustav Klimt (1862–1918), among other Viennese artists, retreated into subjectivism, attaching primary value to individual experience. Yet in Vienna the aestheticism of the avant-garde was not a reaction against the resilient cultural values of the middle class. It was a reaction against political intolerance. Klimt and the "secessionists," like their counterparts in Munich, rebelled against what Klimt considered the unsatisfactory values and dangers of mass society. He sought to stimulate and shock viewers by using, for example, classical images in strange, unprecedented juxtapositions, presenting erotic fantasies and other representations of utopian escape.

In Paris, a disparate but supremely talented group of younger modern painters exhibited their work in 1905. A critic dismissed the show as "touches of crude colorings juxtaposed haphazardly; barbaric and naive games of a child who is playing with the 'box of colors.'" Another dubbed them the "fauvists," or wild beasts. The name stuck. The fauvists remained committed to experimentation with colors and lines on canvas in their quest for the liberation of both subject and painter. They also painted landscapes, including coastal resorts, with bright colors and open spaces. One hostile critic in 1905 described a fauvist's brush as having been "dipped in dynamite," affirming the perceived association between artistic and social, and even anarchist, rebellion in some minds.

Pablo Picasso (1881–1973) is widely considered to be the first painter of the modern movement. Influenced by his Spanish homeland, Picasso's work (especially the paintings of his "blue period") revealed the gloomy obsession with death that had characterized earlier Spanish painters. Picasso drew on his own intense subjectivity. His work was rarely shown in Paris, where he spent most of his career, in part because he mistrusted art dealers. His great influence came later.

(*Left*) The young Pablo Picasso in his studio. (*Right*) Picasso's *Les Demoiselles d'Avignon*.

Picasso's daring *Les Demoiselles d'Avignon* (1907), depicting five nudes, may mark the beginning of modernist art. Abstract painting is a subjective form of expression. "I paint objects as I think them, not as I see them," Picasso asserted. Above all, abstract art abandoned the artist's system of perspective that had endured since the Renaissance. In Picasso's work, one finds a fragmentation of perception and dismantling of realistic depiction in favor of products of the imagination—flat, distorted, and highly simplified geometric patterns of solid forms, and space divided by sharp angles.

Critics called the Spanish painter's style "cubism" because of his preoccupation with basic shapes, particularly the three-dimensional prism. Picasso considered the prism the fundamental component of reality. The influence of Georges Braque (1882–1963) on the cubist style contributed to the development of a second, "analytical" phase of cubism with an even greater emphasis on geometric shapes, now constructed from inanimate, pasted materials. The cubists became a more cohesive "school" than the fauvists, and relied more on light and shade than color to represent forms.

Futurist artists, most of them Italian, were inspired by technological change. In 1910, a futurist wrote, "All subjects previously used must be swept away in order to express our whirling life of steel, of pride, of fever and of speed." *Dynamism of a Cyclist* (1913) by Umberto Boccioni (1882–1916) depicts the frenetic energy of pedaling without actually showing the cyclist. The poet Filippo Tommaso Marinetti's "Manifesto of Futurism," which was published in 1909 in the aftermath of Wilbur Wright's triumphant airplane flights in France (following his first controlled airplane flight in Kitty Hawk, North Carolina, in 1903), proclaimed, "We want to sing the love of danger, the habit of energy and rashness. . . . Beauty exists only in struggle. There is no masterpiece that has not an aggressive character. . . . We want to glorify war—the only cure for the modern world."

CONCLUSION

Artists in the early twentieth century suffered the shrill denunciations of chauvinists. In France, the nationalist press denounced the cubists, several of whom, like Picasso, were not French, for artistic decadence, specifically for importing "foreign perversions" with the goal of weakening French morale. Insisting on eclecticism and experimentation, some Munich artists affronted German nationalists by insisting that art ought to be international in character and by bringing French and Russian artists—including Kandinsky—into their circle. The turn of the avant-garde toward irrationality came at a time when the rational structures that governed domestic political life and international relations seemed to be breaking down amid aggressive nationalism and militarism in Paris, Vienna, Berlin, and other European capitals.

Aggressive nationalism was closely linked to the "new European imperialism." Between the mid-1880s and 1914, the European powers raced each other to increase their domination of the globe. The European imperial powers included Great Britain and France, old rivals for colonies, as well as Germany and Italy, which also sought to extend what each considered its national interests. Imperial rivalries helped solidify international alliances, dividing Europe into two armed camps. The avant-garde had good reason, as it turned out, to be anxious.

CHAPTER 21

THE AGE OF EUROPEAN IMPERIALISM

In one of the odd twists in the long, bloody history of European imperialism, the vast Congo region in Central Africa was colonized by a monarch acting as a private citizen. When he was heir to the Belgian throne, Leopold II (ruled 1865–1909) had given one of his father's ministers a piece of granite with the inscription "Belgium needs colonies." And so when he was king of Belgium, Leopold organized the Congo Company to explore and develop Central Africa.

In 1879, Leopold sent the British-American journalist Henry Stanley (1841–1904) to the Congo. Stanley emerged with treaties signed with local rulers establishing Leopold's personal claim over the Congo. The Belgian king would now have his "piece of that great African cake."

An international conference of representatives of European states held in Berlin in 1884–1885 to discuss claims to African territory declared the Congo to be the "Congo Free State," with Leopold as its head. This "free state," recognized as the private possession of the Belgian king and as part of his business organization, received the status of a "mandate." The Berlin conference established this designation to signify that a European power accepted the "mandate" to govern a territory and to provide, in principle, for the welfare of its "backward people." The European powers agreed on ground rules governing the race for colonies. Henceforth no power could simply declare a region its colony unless it exercised effective control over the territory.

Despite Leopold's pledge that each colonial power would "undertake to watch over the preservation of the native races, and the amelioration of the moral and material conditions of their existence," the horrors perpetrated on the people of the Congo at Leopold's orders in his quest for ivory and rubber may have been unmatched in the annals of European imperialism. For the indigenous population, the colonial experience was hell on earth.

An American missionary reported a macabre way the Belgian soldiers had of trying to reduce the waste of bullets: "Each time the corporal goes

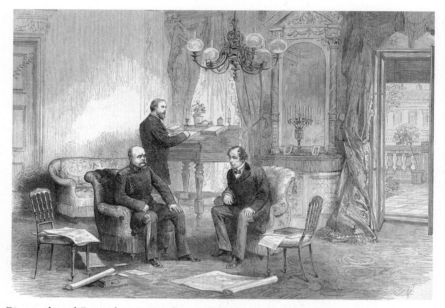

Bismarck and Disraeli meeting during the Congress of Berlin, 1878.

out to get rubber, cartridges are given to him. He must bring back all not used; and for every one used, he must bring back a right hand. . . . In six months, they had used 6,000 cartridges, which means that 6,000 people are killed or mutilated. It means more than 6,000, for the people have told me repeatedly that soldiers killed children with the butt of their guns."

The Belgian Parliament, stung by revelations of brutality uncovered by international investigations, demanded more humane standards. In 1908, it took the Congo away from Leopold and made it a colony of Belgium, a country one-eightieth the size of its colony.

From Colonialism to Imperialism

Imperialism is the process by which one state, with superior military strength and more advanced technology, imposes its control over the land, resources, and population of a less developed region. The repeated extension of Chinese control over the Vietnamese people of Indochina would fit most definitions of the term. At the same time, Japan emerged as an imperial power itself during the first decades of the twentieth century, as did the United States. Imperialism has above all characterized the relations of the European powers with Africa and Asia.

From the 1880s to 1914, the European powers expanded their direct control over much of the globe. Imperialism reflected and contributed to the development of a truly global economy: the manufacturing boom of the Second Industrial Revolution whetted the appetite of merchants seeking new markets and manufacturers seeking new sources of raw materials. The expansion of European empires during the period of the "new imperialism" generally included the exploitation of African and Asian lands with economic and strategic interests in mind.

Europeans had long visited, influenced, learned from, and conquered distant lands. Spain and Portugal began the first sustained European quest for colonies in the fifteenth century with excursions along the West African coast. During the sixteenth century, Spaniards built a vast colonial empire that stretched from what is now the southwestern United States to the southern tip of South America. In the seventeenth century, French traders, missionaries, and soldiers began small settlements in "New France" (present-day Quebec). The drive for colonies heightened the rivalry between Britain and France in the era of the American Revolution. After losing New France to Britain in the 1760s, France's modest empire included Algeria (conquered in 1830) and a few Caribbean islands, until the conquest of Indochina began during the Second Empire (1852–1870). During the early eighteenth and the nineteenth centuries, British merchants sought both raw materials and sizable markets for manufactured goods in Africa, India, and as far as Southeast Asia, China, and Japan.

In contrast to imperialism, colonialism from the last decade of the sixteenth century through the middle decades of the nineteenth century entailed economic exploitation and control, informal or formal, over territories. An essential element of colonialism was trade. Again, the British Empire provides the classic case. The British insisted on free trade, an open market that would allow English merchants to sell goods without tariff restrictions and return with luxury products—calicoes and spices from India, coffee, sugar, and rum from the Caribbean, and tobacco from Virginia—for the home market. European traders had established port facilities and made agreements with local rulers allowing them to trade freely (although Japan and China had only a few treaty ports providing trade access). North America, Australia, New Zealand, and parts of India, as well as some of the lands added to Russia's great inland empire in Siberia, Muslim Central Asia, and Northeast Asia, had become settlement colonies. However, relatively few Europeans had settled permanently in Africa or Southeast Asia, both of which had difficult tropical climates, or in China, which remained an independent state despite bullying by European powers. In these places the European presence remained generally peripheral, and staking out large chunks of territory as colonies seemed a daunting, expensive, and dangerous challenge. Despite their relative wealth and power, European imperial states lacked the resources for complete conquest and control.

Moreover, public opinion at home did not yet support massive colonial undertakings. In India, the British since the eighteenth century had drawn on a developed economic structure, credit networks, and, particularly in

Bengal, a full-fledged tax apparatus and local client armies to make possible conquest and absorption. With India as a base, Britain greatly increased its influence in the Persian Gulf, Arabia, and East Africa, after having forced China to open its ports following a quick military victory of 1842.

During the early nineteenth century, many of the original colonies of Spain and Portugal became independent. The Spanish Empire based on conquest, religious conversion, and the extraction of silver in the New World had largely disappeared by 1850. But Spain still held Cuba, Puerto Rico, and the Philippines. After Brazil, many times the size of Portugal, proclaimed its independence in 1822, Portugal was left with only toeholds in Africa, India, and East Asia.

The Dutch had established bases on the coast of West Africa (abandoned in 1872) and small island colonies scattered in the Caribbean, the Indian Ocean, and the Pacific. Dutch traders ended Portuguese control of Java, one of Indonesia's islands, and extended their own influence over the island in 1755. The Dutch gradually extended control over the rest of Indonesia. Britain and France had established bases on the west coast of Africa, despite its lack of natural harbors and estuaries. Both powers began to penetrate the giant continent during the nineteenth century—the British from the tip of South Africa, the French from Algeria and the coast of West Africa.

Yet only Britain, despite being only about the size of the island of Madagascar, still had a large empire by the middle of the nineteenth century. Despite the loss of thirteen of its American colonies, the British Empire still extended into so many corners of the world that it was tediously repeated that "the sun never sets on the British Empire." British imperialism rested in part on free trade, with the empire contributing to economic

A British colonial administrator settling a dispute between two indigenous chiefs on the Gambia River in West Africa.

domination. Britain's strength also rested on the pillars of its settlement colonies. In search of a more secure future or simply adventure, more than a million people emigrated from the British Isles in the 1850s alone, most of them to Australia, New Zealand, and Canada, as well as to the United States. Australia had become the world's largest exporter of wool by 1851, when the discovery of gold in New South Wales and Victoria brought another wave of immigrants dreaming of making their fortune, like those pouring into California at the same time. The Australian colonies and New Zealand received the right to maintain their own governments in the 1850s, under the watchful eye of the British Foreign Office, although Western Australia remained a convict colony until "transportation" to Australia ceased to be a punishment in England in 1865. Canada achieved Dominion status (that is, nominally autonomous within the empire) in 1867 with passage of the British North America Act by the British Parliament. The crown would grant Dominion status to Australia and New Zealand in 1907.

THE "NEW IMPERIALISM" AND THE SCRAMBLE FOR AFRICA

In the early 1880s, the hold of the European powers on the rest of the world was still relatively slight, as Map 21.1 demonstrates. Many leaders still could conclude that the cost of maintaining colonies outweighed the benefits. In 1852, British Prime Minister Benjamin Disraeli, later an outspoken advocate of imperialism, had referred to the colonies as "wretched" and "a millstone round our necks." William Gladstone, Disraeli's rival, reflected the prevailing liberal view when he pontificated, "The lust and love of territory have been among the greatest curses of mankind."

Distant, underdeveloped lands still seemed remote from urgent European interests. But this changed rapidly. Before the age of imperialism, Shaka, a renowned leader of the Zulus, who had established one of the two dominant African kingdoms in what is now South Africa, prophesied before his death in 1828 that his people would be conquered by the "swallows," white men who build mud houses. The prophecy came true.

The Second Industrial Revolution whetted the appetite of the powers for new sources of raw materials and markets for manufactured goods. The enormous resources generated by large-scale industrialization and the rapid spread of a contentious nationalism fueled the new imperialism. Despite rivalries between the powers, during this period they were not involved in wars with each other, allowing them to concentrate their energies and resources on imperial expansion, which new technological advances facilitated. Imperial powers Britain, France, Germany, and Italy no longer necessarily looked to preserve the balance of power on the continent, but rather to extend what each considered its national interests.

MAP 21.1 COLONIAL EMPIRES UNTIL 1880 Colonies of Britain, France, Russia, the Netherlands, Spain, Portugal, and the Ottoman Empire.

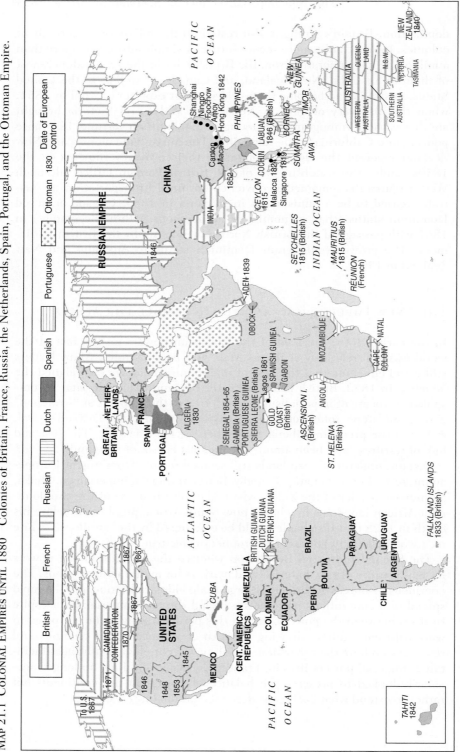

A British foreign minister recalled in 1891, "When I left the Foreign Office in 1880, nobody thought about Africa. When I returned to it in 1885, the nations of Europe were almost quarreling with each other as to the various portions of Africa which they should obtain." Another British foreign official would ask incredulously if his country sought to "take possession of every navigable river all over the world, and every avenue of commerce, for fear somebody else should take possession of it?" The colonial race extended even to the North Pole, first reached by the American Robert E. Peary (1856–1920) in 1909.

British and French Imperial Rivalry

A French colonial enthusiast assessed the "scramble for Africa"—the term was first used by a London newspaper as early as 1884—that began in the 1880s: "We are witnessing something that has never been seen in history: the veritable partition of an unknown continent by certain European countries. In this partition France is entitled to the largest share." Africa included about a fourth of the world's land area and a fifth of its population. Explorers plunged almost blindly into the uncharted and unmapped African interior. The source of the Nile River, the lifeline of Egypt, had been located in modern-day Uganda in 1862; most Western maps still showed blank spots for much of the continent's interior. Europeans discovered the bewildering complexity of a continent that included about 700 different autonomous societies with distinctive political structures.

France's imperial aspirations reveal some of the motives that fueled the new imperialism. After its humiliating defeat by Prussia during the Franco-Prussian War of 1870–1871, the gnawing loss of Alsace-Lorraine hung over France. German Chancellor Otto von Bismarck subtly encouraged the French government to pursue an interest in distant colonies, hoping it would forget about trying to retake Alsace-Lorraine. Indeed, French colonialism during the "new imperialism" was closely tied to a nationalist spirit that was linked with the idea of revenge against Germany.

At the Congress of Berlin in 1878, France agreed to abandon its claims to the island of Cyprus, while the British gave up claims to Tunisia. The French ambassador to Germany warned his own government in 1881 that if it failed to order bold action in Tunisia, France risked decline as a power, perhaps even "finding itself on a par with Spain." In March 1881, the French government claimed that raiders from Tunisia were harassing their troops in Algeria. French troops invaded Tunisia, which became a French protectorate two months later. Between 1895 and 1896, France also seized the island of Madagascar off the coast of East Africa and made it a colony (see Map 21.2).

French merchants and nationalists dreamed of an empire that would stretch across Africa. Railroads had begun to reach across continental Europe in the 1840s and 1850s. They became a symbol of modernity, but also

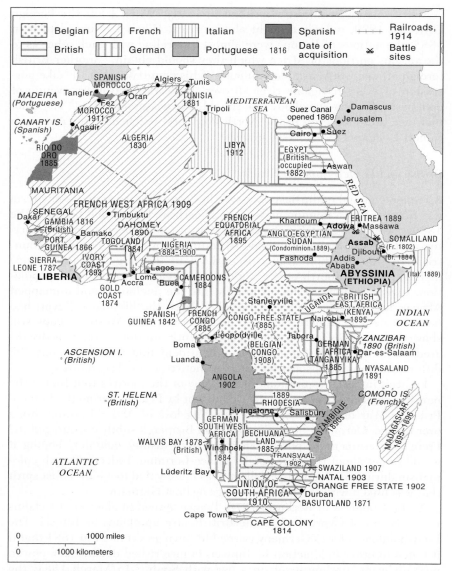

MAP 21.2 IMPERIALISM IN AFRICA BEFORE 1914   Belgian, British, French, German, Italian, Portuguese, and Spanish colonies in Africa and dates of European control.

of conquest, as in the case of the U.S. transcontinental railway. Not surprisingly, the railroad captured the imagination of imperialists. Cecil Rhodes (1853–1902), British entrepreneur and colonialist, reasoned that rails went farther and cost less than bullets. A French railway network was mapped out to connect Algeria and Senegal by crossing the Sahara Desert.

Most of the lines were never built, and, in any case, they could never have generated sufficient revenues to justify their enormous cost. France had little more than a series of forts to show for enormous expense. Yet British merchants on the coast of West Africa feared that French gains would lead to the loss of products such as palm oil and potential markets for their own goods in the African interior. The Franco-British rivalry in Africa heated up. Further French advances in western Sudan followed.

British and French rivalries in Egypt, a gateway to the markets and products of the Middle East, dated to the revolutionary years of the late 1790s. In 1869, a French engineer and entrepreneur, Ferdinand de Lesseps (1805–1894), completed a canal through the Isthmus of Suez, which connects the Red and Mediterranean Seas. The Suez Canal cut the distance of the steamship voyage from London to Bombay (now Mumbai) in half by avoiding the treacherous Cape of Good Hope at the southern tip of Africa. The severe financial difficulties of Ismail Pasha, the ruler (*khedive*) of Egypt, which was a part of the Ottoman Empire, brought Britain a stroke of incredibly good fortune. In 1875, Britain bailed out the bankrupt Ismail Pasha by purchasing a considerable portion of shares in the canal. Under British management, the number of ships passing through the canal rose from 486 in 1870 to 3,000 in 1882.

No power had a greater stake in the canal than Britain. The British government traditionally had sought to protect the land and sea routes to India by supporting the Islamic Middle Eastern states—above all, the Ottoman

British forces at rest around the Great Sphinx of Giza after defeating an Egyptian army at the Battle of Tel el-Kebir in 1882.

Empire—against Russian designs. With continuing social and political chaos in Egypt threatening the interests of British bondholders, in 1882 a British fleet shelled the Mediterranean port city of Alexandria. The British then established a protectorate over Egypt, still nominally part of the Ottoman Empire. The Egyptian *khedive* henceforth accepted British "advice." Over the next forty years, the British government repeatedly assured the other powers that its protectorate over Egypt would only be temporary. The French, who had loaned the *khedive* as much money as had Britain, were particularly aggrieved at the continued British occupation.

Central Africa became the next major focus of European expansion. In 1869, the *New York Herald* hired Henry Stanley to find the missionary and explorer David Livingstone (1813–1873), from whom there had been no word in almost four years. After a trip of fifteen months, he found the missionary in January 1871 on the shores of Lake Tanganyika and greeted him with that most understated Victorian salutation, "Dr. Livingstone, I presume?" Henry Stanley's subsequent long journey up the Congo River in 1879 to gain treaties for Belgian King Leopold II opened up interior Africa to great-power rivalry. In 1880, Savorgnan de Brazza (1852–1905), a French naval officer, reached Stanley Pool, a large lake Stanley had "discovered" in 1877. ("Stanley didn't discover us," one "native" put it reasonably, "we were here all the time.") Brazza returned with a piece of paper signed with an "X" by a king, which Brazza claimed granted France a protectorate over the territory beyond the right bank of the Congo River.

Although the French government first showed little interest, French nationalists made ratification of Brazza's "treaty" a major issue. Portugal then declared that it controlled the mouth of the Congo River. The British government demanded trade rights in the region. Leopold of Belgium voiced opposition to any French moves near his personal Congo territory. Amid continued resentment over British control of Egypt, the French Chamber of Deputies eagerly ratified Brazza's treaty. French colonial activity in West Africa continued unabated. Between 1880 and 1914, France's empire increased in size by twelve times, from 350,000 square miles to 4.6 million.

Germany and Italy Join the Race

Germany was the next power to enter the race for colonies. It did so despite the fact that Chancellor Otto von Bismarck at first viewed colonization as an expensive sideshow that distracted attention from the essential questions of power politics in European diplomacy. He once curtly rejected a German colonial explorer's plea for a more aggressive colonial policy: "Your map of Africa is very nice, but my map of Africa is in Europe. Here is Russia, and here is France, and we are in the middle. That is my map of Africa!"

The chancellor had routinely rejected pleas that Germany intervene in Africa on behalf of merchants, missionaries, and nationalistic adventurers.

The Germans in Africa. Cartoons originally appearing in the German journal *Jugend* in 1916 show an officer arriving to find chaos (*left*) and imposing military order (*right*).

The Colonial League, established in 1882, and the Society for German Colonization, a lobby of businessmen and other nationalists formed in 1884, pressured the government to pursue colonies. The German adventurer Karl Peters (1856–1918) sought an outlet for his financial interests and nationalist fervor through his East Africa Company. Peters's chartered company signed commercial agreements, built settlements, and assumed sovereignty over East African territories. These aggressive moves aroused the ire of British nationalists, exactly what Bismarck had hoped to avoid but, given the sudden intensity of nationalist and colonial fever at home, could not.

Bismarck gradually came to share the imperialist view that colonies might provide new markets for German products. But more than this, he realized that the establishment of colonies would solidify his political support within Germany. New markets could create jobs at home or abroad for unemployed German workers. Bismarck concluded that colonies could be administered indirectly at a relatively low cost.

The time also seemed right for the German government to appease its drooling colonial lobby, including merchants. The British Foreign Office was preoccupied with Islamic fundamentalist rebellions in the Sudan. France, with a new protectorate over Tunisia, was embroiled in debate over continued colonization in Indochina. In April 1884, Bismarck wired his consul in Cape Town, South Africa, ordering him to proclaim that the holdings of a German merchant north of the Orange River—the territorial limit of British colonial authority—would henceforth be the protectorate of German Southwest Africa. Britain acquiesced in exchange for Bismarck's acceptance of the British occupation of Egypt. That summer the German chancellor also decided to establish a protectorate over the Cameroons and Togoland in West Africa.

Bismarck, expertly playing off British and French interests against each other, called the Berlin Conference of 1884–1885 in response to a recent agreement signed between Britain and Portugal recognizing mutual interests. The Berlin Conference divided up the territory of the Congo basin between the Congo Free State (Leopold's private territory) and France (the French Congo), while declaring the Congo River open to all. French merchants penetrated Dahomey and the Ivory Coast, with French troops reaching the ancient trading town of Timbuktu (now in Mali) in 1894.

In 1885, Bismarck agreed to protect Peters's commercial enterprises in Tanganyika, which became German East Africa. Germany also established several coastal trading stations and the colony of Angra Pequena in German Southwest Africa, which merchants had portrayed with unerring inaccuracy as a territory of untapped wealth just waiting to be extracted.

To placate Britain, Germany recognized British interests in Kenya and Uganda and the protectorate status of Zanzibar in 1890. In exchange, Germany received a small but strategically important island naval station in the North Sea. The German colonial lobby was not happy: "We have exchanged three kingdoms for a bathtub!" moaned Peters. Nonetheless, by 1913, German colonies in Africa, including German East and Southwest Africa, Togoland, and the Cameroons, occupied over 1 million square miles, five times the size of Germany.

Italy was the last of the major European nations to enter the colonial fray. Its ravenous hunger for empire led Bismarck to note sarcastically that it proceeded "with a big appetite and bad teeth." In 1882, Italy established Assab, a small settlement on the Red Sea, and three years later it occupied Massawa, which in 1889 became the capital of the new Italian colony of Eritrea. Italian merchants hoped to force the adjacent African state of Abyssinia (now Ethiopia) to trade through Eritrea. In 1889, the Abyssinian emperor signed a treaty with Italy which the Italian government took to mean that Abyssinia was now an Italian protectorate. When the French began building a railroad that would link Abyssinia to French Somaliland and the Abyssinians attempted to cancel the treaty, Italian troops launched a war in 1894. The result was a disaster. In 1896, a general without adequate maps marched four badly organized columns of Italian troops into battle. The Abyssinians, some 70,000 strong, with Russian artillery advisers and French rifles, routed the Italian army in the hills near the coast at Adowa. Six thousand Italian soldiers were killed—many more than in the various wars that had led to Italy's unification—and several thousand were captured. The Italians became the first European army to be defeated in the field by Africans. Under the Treaty of Addis Ababa that same year, Italy was forced to renounce Abyssinia as a protectorate, although it kept the territory of Eritrea on the Red Sea.

Standoff in the Sudan: The Fashoda Affair

In 1898, the Anglo-French rivalry in Africa culminated in the standoff between French and British forces at Fashoda on the Nile River in the southern Sudan, nearly bringing the two powers to war. The French government resented the fact that Egypt served as a base for British initiatives in the hot, dry Sudan.

A fundamentalist Islamic and nationalist revolt led by a former Sudanese slave trader who declared himself to be the Mahdi (the Guided One) in the early 1880s challenged the nominal authority of the *khedive* of Egypt over Sudan. After the Mahdi and his followers (the Mahdists) began a holy war against Egypt and defeated Egyptian armies led by British officers, the British sent an expedition to the Sudanese capital of Khartoum to evacuate the Egyptian population. It was led by the dashing, eccentric British adventurer General Charles "Chinese" Gordon (1833–1885), so called because he had commanded troops that assisted the Chinese government in putting down the Taiping Rebellion in the 1860s. Besieged for ten months in Khartoum by the Mahdi's forces in 1884, Gordon was killed when the Mahdists stormed the garrison two days before a relief expedition from Britain arrived in January 1885.

Britain lost interest in Sudan until the French colonial lobby, still smarting from Britain's occupation of Egypt, sought a strategic foothold on the Nile River. In January 1895, Britain claimed the Sudan. The French government, in turn, announced that it considered Sudan open to all colonial powers. The British government responded that it would consider any French activity in Sudan "an unfriendly act."

In 1898, a British force commanded by Lord Horatio Kitchener (1850–1916) set out from Egypt for Sudan with the Upper Nile outpost of Fashoda

The charge of the dervishes (followers of the Mahdi) at the Battle of Omdurman in the Sudan, 1898.

as its goal. Kitchener and his army took revenge for Gordon's death, using machine guns to mow down 11,000 Mahdists at the Battle of Omdurman (September 1898) and retaking Khartoum. British troops desecrated the Mahdi's grave, playing soccer with his skull. At Fashoda, they encountered a French expeditionary force, which intended to establish a French colony on the Upper Nile. Kitchener handed his counterpart a mildly worded note of protest against the French presence, and the two commanders clinked drinking glasses, leaving their governments to fight it out diplomatically.

In both Britain and France, some nationalists demanded war. But the Dreyfus Affair (see Chapter 18) preoccupied French society; furthermore, as the French foreign minister lamented, "We have nothing but arguments and they have the troops." The Fashoda Affair ended peacefully when France recognized British and Egyptian claims to the Nile Basin and Britain recognized French holdings in West Africa. There seemed to be enough of Africa to go around. Only Abyssinia and Liberia, which had been settled in the 1820s by freed U.S. slaves, were independent African states.

The British in South Africa and the Boer War

In South Africa, Britain had to overcome resistance to its presence, first from indigenous peoples and then from Dutch settlers. The British had taken the Cape of Good Hope at the tip of South Africa from the Dutch in 1795. British settlers moved in, fighting nine separate wars against the Bantu people in the 1850s and 1860s. In 1872, the Cape Colony emerged from under the wing of the British Foreign Office, forming its own government, but remaining within the British Empire.

Known as the Boers, the Dutch settlers (Afrikaners) in South Africa were a farming people of strict Calvinist belief. The Boers resented the British abolition of slavery and the fact that the British allowed blacks to move about freely and to own property. In the "Great Trek" from the Cape Colony, which began in 1836 and lasted almost a decade, many Boers began to move inland to carve out states that would be independent of British rule (see Map 21.3). Overcoming Zulu resistance, Boers established the Natal Republic, a strip along South Africa's east coast. When the British intervened in support of the Zulus, the Boers left Natal, which became a British colony in 1843. The Boers crossed the Vaal River in search of new land. Slaughtering Zulus as they went, the Boers founded the Republic of Transvaal (later the South African Republic) and the Orange Free State, which the British recognized as independent in 1854.

The discovery of diamonds in the late 1860s, first in the Cape Colony and then west of the Orange Free State, attracted a flow of treasure seekers—at least 10,000 people—raising the stakes for control of South Africa. After annexing the Republic of Transvaal against the wishes of the Boers in 1877, the British gradually extended their colonial frontier northward, convinced that more diamonds and gold would be found beyond the Vaal River.

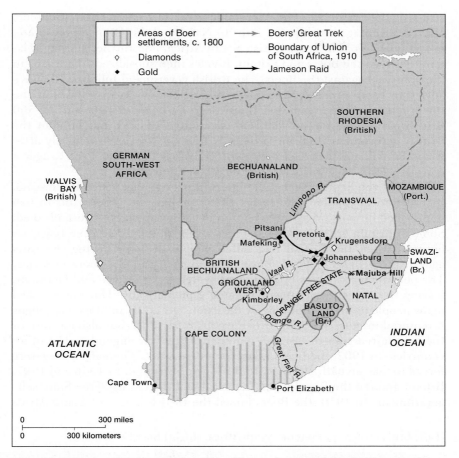

MAP 21.3 SOUTH AFRICA, 1800–1910   The settlement of South Africa by the Boers and English, including the Boers' Great Trek and the 1910 boundaries of the Union of South Africa.

Cecil Rhodes orchestrated British expansion in South Africa, leading to conflict with the Boers, who still bitterly resented annexation into the British Empire. In 1880, the Boers rose up in revolt, their sharpshooters picking off British troops at Majuba Hill a year later. Unwilling to risk further trouble, William Gladstone's Liberal government recognized the political independence of the South African Republic. But, at the same time, the British tried to force the Boers to trade through the port of Cape Town by denying them access to the sea, reflecting the primacy of commerce in the British grand scheme.

The Boers in Transvaal were given a boost by the discovery in the mid-1880s of more gold deposits, which enabled them to buy weapons. Constructing their railway to Port Mozambique on the eastern coast, the Boers offered advantageous shipping rates to Natal and the Orange Free State, taking business away from British South Africa, and further souring relations between the Boers and Britain. Rhodes then subsidized an uprising in the Transvaal against the Boers. The British government followed Rhodes's advice to send a military excursion against the Boers in 1895, but the Boers fought off the "Jameson Raid" (lead by Leander Jameson) by 500 British cavalry with ease. The raid discredited Rhodes, but brought the British government even more directly into the crisis, particularly after Emperor William II of Germany sent Transvaal President Paul Kruger a congratulatory telegram after the failed Jameson Raid.

In 1899, the British goaded the Boers into a war that lasted three years. In order to depopulate the farms that supplied the rebels, the British imprisoned farmers' wives and children in camps in which thousands died. Some in Britain criticized these camps, although there had been few such outcries when the British had killed people of color during the wars against the peoples of India, Burma (Myanmar), and elsewhere in Africa. The outnumbered Boers evoked great sympathy in France and Germany, leaving the British government isolated diplomatically. The war shocked many people in Britain not only by the extensive, costly military campaigns it required (almost 400,000 British troops were sent), but also because of the hostile reaction the British conduct of the war engendered in other countries. In 1902, the Boers asked for an armistice. Thereafter, they were forced to take an oath of loyalty to the king of England. In 1906 and 1907, Britain granted the Republic of Transvaal and the Orange Free State self-government. In 1910, the Boers joined the British Union of South Africa

(*Left*) British troops in Pretoria, South Africa. (*Right*) Boer Commandos.

(which now included the Cape Colony, the Orange Free State, Transvaal, and Natal, and which was given Dominion status by the British at that time).

The new Boer government immediately proclaimed that it would "permit no equality between colored people and the white inhabitants either in church or state." Apartheid—the unequal separation of whites and blacks by law—was the result of the Boer policy of racial domination. It proved to be the most extreme consequence of the "scramble for Africa."

THE EUROPEAN POWERS IN ASIA

The European powers and the United States divided up much of the entire Pacific region in their quest for raw materials, markets, strategic advantage, and prestige. From the populous Indian subcontinent, Britain expanded its interests into and beyond Burma, accentuating a rivalry with Russia for influence in the region. In the meantime, the Dutch extended their authority in Indonesia, while the French turned much of Indochina into their protectorate. The Russian Empire had expanded well into Central Asia and to the Pacific Ocean. By 1900, only Japan, the emerging power in Asia, maintained real independence against European incursion, having accepted western modernization following the Meiji Restoration in 1868. Siam (Thailand) stood as a buffer state between British and French colonial interests, and the Western powers dominated China, forcing trade and territorial concessions on that weakening empire.

India, Southeast Asia, and China

Europe's quest for colonies and domination in Asia had begun even earlier than in Africa. During the Seven Years' War (1756–1763), British troops defeated the French in India. The British East India Company, responsible to the British Parliament, administered India. The Company ruled with the assistance of various Indian princes. The British recognized their local prerogatives in exchange for their obedience and assistance. Britain later expanded east from India into Burma, overcoming Burmese resistance in a war from 1824 to 1826, and then expanded south into Malaya (see Map 21.4).

Using India as a base, British merchants, backed by British naval power, worked to overcome barriers to trade with East Asia. In the 1830s, British traders had begun to pay for silks, teas, and other Chinese luxury goods with opium grown in India. In 1833, the East India Company lost its monopoly on trade with the east, and other English traders appeared in China selling opium. With opium addiction rampant in southern China, in 1839 the emperor tried to limit trade with foreigners, insisting that all such trade pass through Canton (now Guangzhou). The Royal Navy sent gunboats—hence the origin of the term "gunboat diplomacy"—to Canton to force Chinese capitulation in the short, one-sided Opium War (1840–1842). British

MAP 21.4 INDIA AND THE FAR EAST BEFORE 1914   Areas controlled by the British, French, Dutch, Portuguese, Germans, and Americans in Asia.

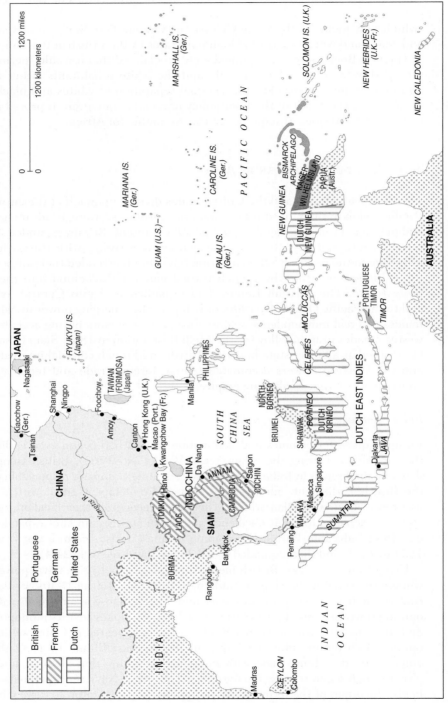

forces occupied Shanghai. By the Treaty of Nanking that followed in 1842, the first of the "unequal treaties," China was forced to establish a number of "treaty ports" open to British trade, including Canton and Shanghai, and it was required to grant Britain formal authority "in perpetuity" over Hong Kong (authority that lasted until 1997). British residents and European visitors received the rights of extraterritoriality, which meant that they were not subject to Chinese law. Britain and France together occupied Canton. Following hostilities in 1857 (see

Chinese men smoking opium.

Chapter 18), a combined British and French army forced China to open six more ports to British and French trade, including on the Yangtze River. The British trade route now ran from British ports to Bombay, Columbo in Ceylon (now Sri Lanka), Rangoon, and Singapore, dramatically assisted by the Suez Canal beginning in 1869.

In 1857, a revolt shook British rule in India, revealing some of the tensions between the colonialists and the colonized. Long-term causes of the mutiny of the Sepoys—Indian troops in the British army—included anger at the British policy of taking direct control over Indian states whose princes died without heirs. The immediate cause was the continued use of animal fat to grease rifle cartridges, a religious affront to both Hindu and Muslim soldiers. Other causes included low pay and resentment of British officers. Confronted with British intransigence, the Sepoys rebelled over a wide area, beginning near Delhi. In one place insurgents killed 200 British women and children. The rebels promised a return to Mughal power, as the emperor had been a mere figurehead since 1803. They found some support among local elites, particularly those who saw increased British authority to be a threat to Islam in areas of that religion. An extensive military campaign followed, involving almost 200,000 British and Indian soldiers. British authorities hanged rebels and burned a number of villages.

Following the mutiny, administration of India passed in 1858 from the East India Company to the British crown. Queen Victoria became "Empress of India" and British rule became more direct. Indian princes were guaranteed their lands if they signed agreements accepting British rule. The governor-general of India added the honorific title of "viceroy," as the

(*Left*) Ruins after the Sepoy Mutiny, 1857. (*Right*) Lord and Lady Curzon in Delhi, 1903.

monarch's personal representative, serving under the secretary of state for India. Lord George Curzon (1859–1925), who could trace his aristocratic family line back to the Norman Conquest of 1066, was one of the most forceful proponents of British imperialism. Viceroy of India before the age of forty, Curzon was determined to solidify British rule in India. He strengthened the northwestern frontier defenses against Russia, reduced the cost of government, and took credit for a modest increase in the Indian standard of living. The British government enacted educational reforms, initiated irrigation projects, reformed the police and judicial systems, and encouraged the cotton industry. Frightened by the Sepoy Mutiny, the British government also expedited railway construction in India in order to be able to move troops rapidly. From less than 300 miles of track in 1857, a network of 25,000 miles was established by 1900. By connecting much of the Indian interior with ports, railway development also encouraged production of Indian cotton, rice, oil, jute, indigo, and tea, which could now reach ports by train and then be exported to Britain. Railroads reduced the ravages of famine in India. So did the planting of new crops, such as potatoes and corn. The greater availability of food contributed to rapid population growth. The Indian subcontinent in the twentieth century would become one of the most populous places on earth.

But while some Indian merchants and manufacturers made money from expanded trading opportunities, others lost out. To assure a lucrative market in India, a country of almost 300 million people in 1900, the British at first banned some Indian manufactures that would compete with British goods produced at home, thereby destroying Indian village handicrafts such as textile weaving. Raw Indian cotton was shipped to England to be made into cloth there, and then re-exported to India. British tax collectors increased the indebtedness of Indian peasants in a vast nation beset by rising population, small holdings, and the increasing subdivision of land.

France made its first move to colonize Southeast Asia in the late 1850s. French and Spanish forces had bombarded the towns of Da Nang and Saigon (in present-day Vietnam) in joint retaliation for the execution of a Spanish missionary. When the Vietnamese counterattacked, a French admiral annexed three provinces. France attempted unsuccessfully to form a protectorate over northern Annam (the central part of Vietnam). In the early 1880s, the Emperor of Annam sought Chinese assistance against the French, invoking China's ancient claims to the region. An anti-foreign movement known as the "Black Flags," which included Vietnamese and Chinese brigands, harassed foreigners, aided by Chinese soldiers. In 1883, a French expedition captured the city of Hanoi in Tonkin in northern Vietnam. French troops sent from Cochin (the southern part of Vietnam) forced the Vietnamese to accept a protectorate that included all of Annam. In 1887, France created the Union of Indochina, which included Tonkin, Annam, Cochin, and Cambodia, and, in 1893, it unilaterally added Laos to French Indochina.

The colonial race extended to the islands of the South Seas. France claimed Tahiti and New Caledonia. Britain held the Fiji Islands, some of which served as refueling ports, but little else. Germany hoisted its flag over the Marshall Islands and Samoa. Smaller islands were sometimes bartered and traded as trinkets by the European powers in the various agreements signed to settle major disputes over the larger colonies.

Japan and China: Contrasting Experiences

In contrast to other Asian countries, Japan maintained real independence and gradually emerged as a power in Asia. Japan built up its army and navy after being opened to Western contact in the 1850s. The 1868 Meiji Restoration, ending a period of chaos, facilitated a remarkable Westernization of economic life in Japan. The new centralized state structure encouraged the development of international commerce and industry. Military conscription and the implementation of Western technology, assisted by Western technical experts, made it possible for Japan, with a modern army and navy, to emerge as a world power at the dawn of the twentieth century. Japan, too, then began to seek colonies in Asia.

In China, the Ch'ing (Qing) dynasty continued to be beset by internal division, as well as by the demands of the imperialist powers, and the government only slowly began to adopt Western technology. In the late 1860s, a few Chinese reformers had begun to favor building railways as a way of modernizing the Chinese state. Yet conservative opposition to modernization continued within the imperial court. Some Chinese scholars believed that railways damaged "the dragon's vein" across the landscape, threatening the earth's harmony. Imperial officials feared that in case of war China's enemies would quickly seize the rail lines.

With colonial rivalries reaching a fever pitch in the late 1890s, the European powers sought to impose further trade and territorial concessions on China. The Chinese government attempted to shore up the ability of China to resist demands and incursions by Western powers by making use of European and American science in a program of "self-strengthening." Internal uprisings, notably the Taiping Rebellion in South China in the 1850s and 1860s, further encouraged such reforms. However, military weakness made China an easy target for expansion of European influence. The Sino-Japanese War of 1894–1895 led to an independent Korea (which Japan made a protectorate and then annexed in 1910) and China's loss of the island of Formosa (Taiwan) and part of Manchuria to Japan. Needing loans to pay off a war indemnity to Japan, China was forced to make further trading concessions and disadvantageous railroad leases to Germany and Russia.

Following the murder of two German missionaries in 1897, the German government forced China in 1898 to grant a ninety-nine-year lease on the north Chinese port of Tsingtao (Qingdao) on Kwangchow (Jiaozhou) Bay and to grant two concessions to build railways in Shandong Province. Russia was eager to complete its own line to Vladivostok through Chinese territories, permitting it to open up the Chinese province of Manchuria, rich in soybeans and cotton. Russia seized and fortified Port Arthur (Lüshun) on the pretext of protecting China from Germany and compelled the Chinese government to lease Port Arthur and Dalian (Lüda) for twenty-five years. The Chinese gave France a lease on Canton Bay and recognized France's trading "sphere of influence" over several southern provinces.

The U.S. government now claimed to seek what it referred to as "an open door" in China, in accordance with the principle of free trade. The powers agreed not to interfere with any treaty port or with the interests of any other power. China agreed to lease Britain some of the Shandong peninsula and several ports, and to guarantee a British trade monopoly on the Yangtze River, the entry to much of central China. These forced concessions further weakened the ruling Ch'ing dynasty.

In northern China, many Chinese resented the foreigners, whom some blamed for floods and a drought, events that also were taken to mean that the "mandate of Heaven" of the ruling dynasty was at an end. The "Righteous and Harmonious Fists" was a secret anti-foreign society better known as the Boxers, after the training practices of its members. Many of the Boxers believed they were immune to foreign bullets. The targets of their wrath were missionaries who sought to convert the Chinese, railroads that took work away from Chinese transporters, foreign merchants who flooded the Chinese market with cheap textiles, bringing unemployment to the local population, and foreign soldiers, who often mistreated the Chinese.

In 1900, the Boxers attacked Europeans, Americans, and Chinese Christians in Shandong Province, cutting the railway line between Peking (Beijing) and Tientsin (Tianjin). These attacks spread quickly to the imperial capital and other parts of northern China. After the Boxers killed several hundred "foreign devils," British, Russian, German, French, Japanese, and American troops put down the rebellion. Their governments assessed the Chinese government a crushing indemnity of 67.5 million pounds.

The "scramble for concessions" went on. Russia's competition with Japan for Manchuria in northeastern China led to its shocking

A member of the "Righteous and Harmonious Fists" secret society that rose up against foreign influence in the Boxer rebellion in China in 1900.

defeat in the Russo-Japanese War of 1904–1905 (see Chapter 18). Following its victory, Japan took over and expanded the Manchurian railways. This humiliation, and the subsequent disadvantageous railway concessions granted to the European powers and Japan, intensified Chinese nationalist sentiment and contributed to the overthrow of the Ch'ing dynasty in 1911. In the meantime, Japan's aggressive imperialism in East Asia was well under way.

The United States in Asia

The United States, too, took colonies, believing that this was its right as an emerging world power. However, the American imperial venture in the Philippine Islands, an archipelago in the Pacific Ocean, was not all smooth sailing. During the Spanish-American War of 1898, fought largely over the Caribbean island of Cuba, the American admiral George Dewey (1837–1917) sailed into Manila Bay and defeated the Spanish fleet, capturing Manila. The United States had been helped by a Filipino nationalist,

Emilio Aguinaldo (1869–1964). But once the peace treaty ending the Spanish-American War was signed, President William McKinley announced that it would be "cowardly and discreditable" to leave the Philippines. In 1899, the Filipinos began a war of independence. U.S. troops defeated Aguinaldo's guerrilla forces after three years of fighting. American soldiers herded Filipinos into prison camps, torturing and executing some of those they captured. Aguinaldo himself was taken prisoner in 1901, and the insurrection, in which perhaps as many as 200,000 Filipinos died, ended the following year. The Philippines became a territory of the United States.

At the same time, the U.S. government did not want to be left out of the scramble for Chinese concessions. In 1899, Secretary of State John Hay announced his country's "Open Door Policy" with regard to China, and tried to convince the other powers to leave China open to all trade. Only the British government publicly expressed its agreement with this principle, but the scramble for advantage in China went on.

Map 21.4 demonstrates the remarkable impact of the scramble for colonies in Asia. Only Japan and Siam (Thailand) succeeded in really keeping their independence. The government of China was virtually helpless in the face of the imperial powers.

Domination of Indigenous Peoples

The eagerness with which many Europeans embarked on or applauded imperial ventures can be partially explained by their assumptions that non-Western peoples were culturally inferior. These were not new views, nor were they the only ones held. However, in early modern Europe, non-Western peoples—particularly Islamic peoples—had been viewed as enemies by virtue of their religions: Islam, Hinduism, and Buddhism, among others. The colonial powers assumed the right to exploit conquered "inferior" peoples and decide what was "best" for the colonized. British imperialists spoke of "the white man's burden," a phrase unfortunately immortalized by Rudyard Kipling's 1899 poem of the same name: "Take up the White Man's burden— / And reap his old reward: / The blame of those ye better, / The hate of those ye guard."

Nineteenth- and twentieth-century Western attempts to understand dominated or conquered peoples also reflected the intellectual and cultural processes of imperialism. What has become known as "Orientalism" began with the assumption that not only were Asian, African, and other colonized peoples different, but they were inferior as well. This was reflected by the Egyptian exhibit at an international exposition in Paris in 1900. There visitors could view what were presented as African and Asian villages, complete with "natives" on exhibit. An Egyptian visitor was outraged by the image that the hosts wanted to present of Cairo, his native city, as horribly old and run-down, such that "even the paint on the building was made dirty."

The competition for colonies also coincided with the emergence of pseudo-scientific studies that purported to prove the superiority of Western peoples (through, for example, measures of cranium size). Material progress represented by steamboats, railroads, and machine guns was assumed to follow logically from what was considered moral superiority. Thus a French prime minister insisted that "the superior races have rights over the inferior races." Imperial territories became a testing ground or laboratory for European science and technology.

Social Darwinism

In the eighteenth century, some of the philosophes of the Enlightenment had

The British image of themselves in Africa, from *The Kipling Reader*, 1908: "A Young man . . . walking slowly at the head of his flocks, while at his knee ran small naked cupids."

come to view cultural differences of non-Western peoples with interest, believing that they could learn from people who seemed in some ways different from themselves. In writing about the "propensity to war, slaughter, and destruction, which has always depopulated the face of the earth," Voltaire had noted that "this rage has taken much less possession of the minds of the people of India and China than of ours." Not all of the philosophes, to be sure, had been so enlightened in this respect: David Hume wrote in 1742, "I am apt to suspect the negroes and in general all the other species of men . . . to be naturally inferior to the whites." Likewise, social Darwinists in the nineteenth century did not believe that they could learn anything from non-Western peoples. Social Darwinists argued that what they regarded as the natural superiority of whites justified the conquest of the "backward" peoples of Africa and Asia. They misapplied theories of biological evolution to the history of states, utilizing the principle of "natural selection" developed by Charles Darwin, in which the stronger prevail over the weak. Another British scientist, Herbert Spencer (1820–1903), popularized these theories, uttering the chilling phrase "survival of the fittest." Nations, according to this view, must struggle, like species, to survive. Success in the international battle for colonies would develop and measure national mettle.

Cultural stereotypes of the peoples of the "mysterious" East or the "dark continent" of Africa held sway. These ranged from "childlike" (and therefore in need of being led) to "barbaric," "depraved," "sneaky," and "dangerous" (and therefore in need of constant surveillance). Lord Curzon called the Indian princes "a set of unruly and ignorant and rather undisciplined school-boys." British doctors contributed to a prevailing juxtaposition of the "African jungle," seen as a "hotbed of disease" (including stigmatized diseases like leprosy) by virtue of a lack of civilization, with the healthier "civilized" colonizers.

Even well-meaning critics of colonial brutality and other reformers assumed the inferiority of those they were trying to help. Josephine Butler, a feminist reformer, believed that Indian women stood lower on a scale of human development than did her British "sisters." Yet, at the beginning of the twentieth century, some feminist activists did begin to learn about and respect Indian culture and work closely with Indian women.

Imperial officials adopted racist ideology to justify colonialism and the brutalization of indigenous peoples. Colonial businessmen, as well as administrators, paid little attention to the damaging effects of colonialism on indigenous peoples, while simultaneously justifying their presence by claiming to "civilize" the people they dominated.

The experience of the Herero people in what had become German Southwest Africa provides perhaps the most egregious example of frightening Western attitudes toward indigenous peoples who stood in their way. A German official stated the goal of the colonial administration: "Our task is to strip the Herero of his heritage and national characteristics and gradually to submerge him, along with the other natives, into a single colored working class." In 1903, the Herero people, after losing their land to German cattle raisers and angered by the unwillingness of colonial courts to punish cases of murder and manslaughter against them, rose up in rebellion. The Germans killed about 55,000 men, women, and children, two-thirds of the Herero people, chasing survivors into the desert and sealing waterholes. The German official report stated: "Like a wounded beast the enemy was tracked down from one water-hole to the next until finally he became the victim of his own environment. . . . [This] was to complete what the German army had begun: extermination of the Herero nation."

Social Darwinism had other implications for the home countries. At the turn of the century, the U.S. historian Frederick Jackson Turner held that the westward expansion of the American frontier helped reduce discontent by providing land and opportunity to the surplus population of the East Coast. A French military administrator, Marshal Hubert Lyautey (1854–1934), once referred to Algeria and Morocco as the "French Far West." Some prominent Europeans began to believe that the powers could "export" their more economically marginal or politically troublesome population to the colonies. By "social imperialism," colonies would help countries easily dispose of their "least fit," such as unemployed or underemployed workers. Social tensions and conflict would be reduced, the ambitions of the working class for political power thus defused. Cecil Rhodes, as usual, put it most baldly: "If you want to avoid civil war, you must become imperialists." The British colonial armies alone absorbed thousands of "surplus" Scots and Irish, the latter making up about 40 percent of the non-Indian troops in India. By this view, then, colonies could serve as a social safety valve.

Technological Domination and Indigenous Subversion

Europeans employed technological advances in travel and weaponry in their subjugation of indigenous peoples. Railways aided imperial armies in their conquest and defense of colonial frontiers, although horses, mules, and camels still hauled men and supplies across African deserts and bush country. The steamship, like the train, lessened the time of travel to distant places. By the end of the century, thanks to the completion of the Suez Canal in 1869, linking the Mediterranean and Red Seas, British bureaucrats, soldiers, merchants, and tourists could reach India in about twenty days. The heliograph, which sent messages by means of a movable mirror that reflected sunlight, and then the telegraph speeded up communications and led to better coordination of troop movements. Observation balloons and, later, power searchlights aided European armies.

Advanced military technology invariably overcame open colonial rebellions. Along the South African frontier, Zulu warriors resisted the British advance in the late 1870s, earning several victories with surprise attacks. But by the 1890s, they were no match for cannon. The gunboat was the prototypical instrument of European power and enforcement, as it had proven to be in China during the Opium War in the early 1840s. The Gatling, or machine, gun and the single-barreled Maxim gun, which could fire rapidly without being reloaded, proved devastating. A contemporary quip described relations between colonists and the colonized: "Whatever happens we have got the Maxim gun, and they have not." A single gunner or two could fend off a large-scale attack, and British casualties were reduced to almost none. To soldiers, colonial battles now seemed "more like hunting than fighting."

The colonial powers tested new, lighter artillery that could be moved quickly and new, more powerful shells. The British developed the "dum-dum" bullet, which exploded upon impact, with the shooting of attacking "natives" in mind. (It took its name from the arsenal in Calcutta where it was developed.) For the most part, there was little to stop the European onslaught other than malaria and yellow fever carried by mosquitoes, and sleeping sickness carried by the tsetse fly.

Yet indigenous peoples could express resistance to powerful outsiders in other ways besides risking annihilation in open rebellion. The "weapons of the weak" ranged from riots and individual subversion to foot-dragging and gentle but determined defiance. The latter included pretending not to understand, or sometimes what Chinese called "that secret smile" that suggested not compliance but rather defiance in the guise of deference. Such play-acting in daily life offered only glimpses of the ridicule of Europeans that could be hinted at in theatrical productions, songs, dances, or other public expressions. Symbols, gestures, double meanings, and images were easily understood by the subordinate population, but sufficiently disguised from Europeans. These were small victories of political dissent, but victories nonetheless.

Imperial Economies

Once they had a foothold, the European powers established command, or "plunder," economies in three ways: they expropriated the land of the indigenous people; they used the soil and subsoil for their own profit; and they exploited the population for labor. The European powers imposed commercial controls over natural resources. Imperial powers routinely blocked long-standing trade routes that led to other colonies, preventing commercial exchanges from which their own merchants did not profit. European merchants, protected at home by high tariffs against foreign imports, maintained a monopoly on the sale of their manufactured goods in the colonies. Colonialists forced or, in the best circumstances, encouraged local populations to produce for the European market, discouraging or even forbidding the extraction of raw materials or production that would compete with that of the mother country. In Indonesia, for example, the Dutch employed the "culture" or "cultivation" system until 1870. They imposed production quotas on the indigenous population, organized forced labor, and ordered people in West Java to grow coffee when its price rose and to cut down spice-bearing

Trading ships in Calcutta at the end of the nineteenth century.

trees and plants when the price of spices fell. Local populations were forced over time to abandon traditional agricultural practices, ending up in a wage economy as poorly paid laborers. They also lost traditional rights to hunt, graze animals, and gather firewood on land they did not own, a process that had also characterized the early stages of capitalist agriculture in Western Europe.

In British Ceylon (Sri Lanka, captured from the Dutch during the Napoleonic Wars), Dutch Java, and German East Africa, indigenous people who could not produce formal, Western-style deeds or titles to their land lost it to the colonial power. In North Africa, the French government promoted the economic interests of French settlers, giving them the finest Algerian land. The government also ordered land owned collectively by Arabs to be sold as individual plots that only the French could afford to purchase. In Morocco and Tunisia, the French claimed "unexploited" land, such as that belonging to nomad peoples. In Algeria, the French government favored the Kabyles because their monogamous, sedentary, and mostly secular society with private property seemed to be more like republican France than did that of the nomadic Arabs. Above all, French colonial administrators sought to maintain order and collect taxes. One visitor found that "the head tax is above all a very effective agent of civilization," so that in one district "when a village could not or would not pay its taxes in full, the custom was to seize a child and place him in a village named 'Liberty' until the tax was paid." In some regions, taxes were collected through forced labor.

Portuguese colonists imposed conditions of virtual slavery in their African colonies in the nineteenth century. They kidnapped people from their colony of Angola, shipped them to the coastal island of São Tomé, and forced them to work on the cacao plantations for a "contract" period of five years, which few workers survived. In Angola, villagers who could not pay their taxes were required to work for the government for 100 days a year. Forced labor on mine and construction sites by colonial merchants and administrators alike was common; in the German Cameroons, about 80,000 Africans hauled goods for Germans on a single road in one year. Forced labor, which might be considered slavery in disguise, was widely practiced throughout most of the French colonies until 1946.

Colonial Administrations

European notions of the organization of states clashed with the way indigenous people lived. Almost all Africans lacked the European obsession with fixing exact boundaries, one that intensified in the age of nation-states and aggressive nationalism. For most Africans living in tribal societies, European notions of "boundaries" and "borders" established by colonial powers left many societies arbitrarily separated and sometimes interfered with the movements of migratory peoples. Colonial powers exploited tensions between peoples and tribes, purchasing the allegiance of temporary allies.

The British mastered the policy of "divide and rule," favoring and choosing officials from dominant ethnic groups to ensure cooperation. In India, the British effectively manipulated age-old tensions between Hindus, Muslims, and Sikhs to keep the Indian component of its army under control, ruthlessly repressing dissent.

How the European powers maintained control over colonies varied. Historians have distinguished between "formal" and "informal" imperialism, although the distinction is mainly one of degree, not kind. Britain, above all, took the path of informal imperialism by maintaining control through economic and military domination, without necessarily taking over political functions, as with indirect rule in India. But a "resident," or representative of Britain, retained ultimate authority. In formal imperialism, the European power assumed "protectorate" status over a territory, administering the colony directly.

The nature of a colonial "protectorate" changed during the scramble for Africa. Originally, the establishment of a protectorate meant that a colonial power defended its interests by controlling the foreign relations of a territory, leaving it to each ruler or chieftain to control his people. British colonial administration, headed by the Colonial Office in London with a relatively small staff, remained decentralized, like the home government itself. Colonial governors implemented policies. But gradually the colonial powers extended their authority over the local population through indigenous officials. In 1886, Britain assumed full sovereignty over most of its colonies. Local rulers found earlier agreements broken, and were increasingly treated as little more than intermediaries between the imperialists and their own people. Local systems of justice were left intact wherever possible—this, too, cost less money—but whites were subject only to the courts of the colonial power—a privilege called "extraterritoriality."

The British government wanted colonies to pay for themselves, with chartered commercial companies—which had launched British rule in Nigeria, Uganda, and what became Rhodesia—bearing the bulk of expenses in exchange for the right to extract profit. The British colonial administration directed railways and private capital toward regions where raw materials could be extracted or markets found. Imperial policy forced indigenous populations as well as colonists to produce revenues to pay for railroads, roads, and administrative officials.

The fate of the Ashanti kingdom in West Africa, which dated to the early eighteenth century, illustrates how informal control was transformed into more direct authority. In the early 1860s, British forces skirmished with the Ashanti people on the northern frontier of the Gold Coast, over which Britain had established a protectorate. After defeating the Ashanti in 1873–1874, Britain made the Gold Coast a crown colony, imposing more direct control. In 1891, the British proposed that the Ashanti kingdom itself become a protectorate. The king replied "my kingdom of Ashanti will never commit itself to any such policy; Ashanti must remain independent as of

British forces receiving supplies in 1874 during the Ashanti War, which led to the establishment of Ghana as a colony that same year.

old, at the same time to be friendly with all white men." Five years later, British troops occupied the Ashanti capital and deported the king when he could not come up with a huge sum in gold to buy continued independence. In a bloody sequel in 1900–1901, British troops crushed an uprising when the Ashanti refused to surrender the golden stool they treasured as the symbol of their people. In 1901, the Ashanti kingdom became a British colony.

African imperial ventures often began with the directors and principal shareholders of trading companies forging out territories from the underbrush and jungle. Following frenetic lobbying, the Royal Niger Company, with a charter from Parliament conveying administrative powers in 1886, began to develop what became Nigeria. To counter French moves in East Africa, the British government had authorized the Royal Niger Company to launch an expedition through the rain forests to reach Sudan. When German merchants, newcomers to Africa, began to establish trading posts to the east in the future Cameroons, the British government declared a protectorate over the Niger Delta.

The French government and the Royal Niger Company settled their respective claims through conventions. But when the Royal Niger Company went bankrupt in 1899, the British government took over administration of the territories. This scenario was common to the colonial experiences of France, the Netherlands, and Germany: merchant companies that had been granted state monopolies established trading interests in a new colony and then ran into financial difficulties, if not bankruptcy, necessitating the intervention of the imperial government itself.

Given the size of the British Empire, the number of colonial officials seems surprisingly small. Near the end of the nineteenth century, about 6,000 British civil servants governed India's 300 million inhabitants. The British colonial administration provided a career outlet for the sons of aristocrats, who became high-ranking administrators or officers in the navy and army. Eleven of the fourteen viceroys who served in India from 1858 to 1918 were peers by birth.

British officials recruited subordinates selectively from the colonial population, training, for example, upper-caste Indians to work in the administration of the subcontinent. In Nigeria, favored tribal chiefs assumed administrative functions. In the first decade of the twentieth century, at least partially in response to the first stirrings of Egyptian nationalism, the British government expanded the participation of Egyptians in running their country. In Malaya, the British "resident" was responsible for putting down disturbances that might threaten British control, while the local rulers were placed in paid administrative positions but had authority only in dealing with religious matters.

Many indigenous men who rose to positions of relative responsibility under the British managed to look and sound as much as possible like British gentlemen. But many Victorians disdained the Westernized Indian; they ridiculed the "babu," not because he seemed to be rejecting his own culture, but because they thought he could never be good enough to be British. At the same time, the British government often left intact the hierarchy of indigenous ruling elites, because this seemed more natural and made administrating the colonies easier.

French colonial rule differed from that of the British in ways that revealed contrasts between the British and French states. French colonial administration reflected the state centralization that had characterized France's development over the past century and more. Military control, more than commercial relations, formed the basis of its empire. The French colonial administration employed relatively more French officials and relied less on indigenous peoples than did its British rival.

The French colonial ministry then took a much greater role in economic decision making than its counterpart in the British Empire. The ministries of the navy and of commerce administered French colonies until the establishment of the colonial ministry in 1894. The French colonial civilian administration was staffed by bureaucrats, some trained at the Colonial School created in the 1880s. Africans and Vietnamese worked for the French governors-general as virtual civil servants. Like their British rivals, French colonial administrators also exploited pre-existing ethnic and cultural rivalries, using dominant groups to control their enemies. Thus, the French government used Vietnamese officials in key posts in Cambodia and Laos, and in Madagascar highland officials dominated the administration of their coastal rivals.

The French government directly ruled Algeria. Algerians could become French citizens, but with only limited rights. The sultan of Morocco and the bey of Tunisia still ruled their subjects, at least in name, although government and the exercise of justice remained in the hands of the French colonial administration. In Southeast Asia, the French government created the Union of Indochina between 1887 and 1893, which included Cochin, Tonkin, Annam, Cambodia, and Laos under a single governor-general, although France left pre-existing monarchies intact. The French government also centralized the administration of West Africa in 1895 by forming the federation of French West Africa, and in 1910 it established the federation of French Equatorial Africa, made up of its Central African colonies. Governors-general, based in Dakar and Brazzaville, served as the highest local administrative authority.

In the colonies, the British lived in isolation from the indigenous population. The upper class tried to replicate the world of the common rooms of Cambridge and Oxford Universities (more than a quarter of all graduates of Oxford's Balliol College at the turn of the century served in the empire) and of London gentlemen's clubs, served by Indian, African, or Asian waiters. British colonial women served only English recipes to their guests. In India, British "hill stations," which had begun as isolated sanitaria where the British could recuperate from tropical heat and illness, also provided commanding heights useful for surveillance. They became part of the imperial system, both as centers of power and closed British communities, "islands of white" that replicated the architecture and lifestyle of an English village. Indeed, in Kenya and Rhodesia, settler communities were organized around the sense of being "white" in unsettling and even dangerous surroundings; newcomers were discouraged from crossing racial lines because of the fear that such contact could undermine settler cohesion. In German African colonies, German women imagined themselves as cultural ambassadors, while colonial officials viewed them as representatives and even guarantors of German culture who would give birth and raise their children in the colonies as Germans.

Colonial urban architecture reflected the attempt to represent Western domination. In what became Vietnam in Indochina, the opera house built in Hanoi copied that in Paris. The French architects who planned the high Gothic vaulting of the cathedral in Saigon did not consider obvious differences in climate between France and Southeast Asia, providing insufficient ventilation. Outsized public buildings and long boulevards extended French authority in the form of architectural modernism into the daily life of French settlers and the local colonial population. In Madagascar, the medical school reflected design more appropriate to Lyon than a tropical island.

Yet one must also nuance the view that imperialists and indigenous peoples lived entirely in two different, necessarily antagonistic worlds. Some imperialists negotiated new cultural identities across East and West, for example by collecting (or accepting or extorting as gifts from princes or merchants) Hindu sculptures in India or various artifacts in Egypt, which to them represented the East. In doing so, they at least in some ways became part of two worlds. At the same time, Bengali patricians collected items that represented to them the European "other." Cross-cultural interaction revealed more fluid boundaries between imperialists and the colonized, a process of negotiation, learning, and exchange. In acquiring objects that represented the colonized, imperialists helped transform their own identities. Some of what they collected, of course, now fills museums in London and Paris. Objects from the colonies became part of the material culture of imperialism, increasingly common in middle-class homes.

ASSESSING THE GOALS OF EUROPEAN IMPERIALISM

Someone once summed up the reasons for which the European powers expanded their horizons as "God, gold, and glory," or as the geographer, missionary, and explorer David Livingstone put it, "Christianity, Commerce, and Civilization." Which, if any, can be singled out as the dominant impulse behind the "new imperialism"?

The "Civilizing Mission"

Most colonists insisted that God was on their side. Lord Curzon once gushed that the British Empire was "under Providence, the greatest instrument for good that the world has seen." A South African offered a more realistic perspective when he commented, "When you came here we owned the land and you had the Bible; now we have the Bible and you own the land." The "civilizing" impulse still animated some European missionaries during the age of the "new imperialism." Thousands of Catholic and Protestant missionaries went to Africa, India, and Asia in the name of God to win converts. In 1900, about 18,000 Protestant missionaries lived in colonial settlements around the world. French missionaries, both Catholic and Protestant, increasingly saw themselves as bringing the benefits of the French "civilizing mission" to indigenous people. Despite several decades of hostile relations with officials representing the secularized French Republic, French missionaries gradually accommodated themselves to the imperial project their work helped sustain. Some British officials considered Anglican and Methodist missionaries to be nuisances. Most Dutch, Belgian, and Italian clergy made little pretense of bringing indigenous peoples "civilization," tending primarily to the spiritual needs of their troops and settlers.

One aspect of the "civilizing mission" continued to be the attempt of some reformers to limit or end abuses of indigenous peoples. In some places, the clergy helped force Europeans to end or at least temper abuses

Queen Victoria giving a Bible to a man wearing Central African garb.

carried out against local populations. Missionary societies may have been the "conscience" of European colonization, and a small conscience was better than none at all. For British reformers, the primary goal of the "civilizing mission" in the early part of the century had been to abolish slavery in the British Empire, which was achieved in 1833. In the 1880s, pressure from the British Liberal Party helped end the transport of Chinese laborers to work as indentured workers in South African mines. The British government was embarrassed by the treatment of Indian workers in Natal, a province of South Africa, which was brought to light by, among others, the young and future Indian leader Mohandas (Mahatma) Gandhi (1869–1948). French religious leaders launched a campaign against the remaining Arab slave trade in Africa. British officials protested the brutal labor practices of Portuguese and Belgian entrepreneurs. Yet the British government declined to press a campaign to reduce or eliminate the sale of arms and liquor to Africans, because both commodities were extremely lucrative to British merchants. Similarly, it had refused to stop the sale of Indian opium by British traders in China.

Lord Frederick Lugard (1858–1945), a British colonial official, came up with the term "Dual Mandate" to describe what he considered the "moral" and "material" imperatives of colonial powers. The European powers, he believed, had an obligation to "civilize" native populations and also to "open the door" to the material improvements brought by Western technology. They were establishing "trusteeships." In exchange, the Europeans would extract raw materials and other products. While imperialism became associated with conservative nationalism in Western Europe, a few socialists believed that empires could improve conditions of life for colonial peoples. In general, however, European socialists did not view the question of imperialism as one of their central concerns.

Earlier in the century, the French had seen their "civilizing" mission as the assimilation of colonial peoples into French culture: they would, it was commonly thought, become French. By the end of the century, however, the goal of assimilation had given way to a theory of "association," similar to Lugard's British Dual Mandate. This theory of association held that although colonial peoples were not capable of absorbing French culture, French colonialists would help them develop their economic resources, to the benefit of both. Only in urban settlements in Senegal in West Africa did newborn children automatically become French citizens; in 1914, Senegalese voters elected the first black representative to the French Chamber of Deputies.

The Economic Rationale

When missionaries arrived on the shores of Africa or Asia, they usually found that merchants and adventurers were already there looking for gold, ivory, and rubber. Indeed, Cecil Rhodes once stated that in the business of running colonies "philanthropy is good, but philanthropy at five percent is better." The discovery of new markets seemed absolutely necessary in the 1880s, particularly to British manufacturers, as one continental country after another adopted high protectionist tariffs. "If you were not such persistent protectionists, you would not find us so keen to annex territories," the British prime minister told France's ambassador to London in 1897. In the rather far-fetched opinion of Cecil Rhodes' brother, "The Waganda [of Uganda] are clamoring for shoes, stockings and opera glasses and are daily developing fresh wants," which would enrich British manufacturers and merchants peddling the products of the Second Industrial Revolution.

Writing in 1902 and influenced by the Boer War in South Africa, the radical British economist J. A. Hobson (1858–1940) called imperialism "the most powerful factor in the current politics of the Western world." He agreed that the great powers sought colonies because their economies required outlets for domestically produced manufactured goods and for capital investment. In Hobson's view, businessmen, particularly the finance sector based in London, virtually determined British imperial policy. Missionaries and soldiers helped them accomplish their goals. Hobson believed that the quest for colonies simply deferred the resolution of the central economic problem in Britain, because money that went into empire resulted in the underconsumption of industrial goods at home. If governments took action to raise wages and impose progressive taxation on wealth, a more equitable redistribution of wealth would allow ordinary people to purchase more goods. Imperialism would be unnecessary and China and other countries in Asia and Africa would be free to develop on their own. Hobson's views on imperialism anticipated critiques in our day of the economic and social consequences of globalization.

Hobson was not a Marxist, but his views in some ways echoed those of Karl Marx. In *Capital*, Marx, who never used the word imperialism, postulated that the bourgeoisie required "a constantly expanding market for its products." Subsequent Marxists therefore agreed with Hobson's linking of industrial capitalism and imperialism. Lenin, the Russian revolutionary leader, took Hobson's analysis a step further. He argued that the incessant expansion of capital inevitably brought with it colonial rivalries and war; in this final stage of capitalist development, "international trusts" would divide up the globe.

If Hobson, Rhodes, and Lenin had ever sat at the same dinner table, they would have disagreed about a good many things. But they would have agreed that there was a close connection between the great age of European imperialism and the quest for economic gain. The drive for colonies took on urgency in a period of mounting economic tariffs: there might not be, many thought, enough raw materials and markets to go around.

Merchant traders, like their seventeenth- and eighteenth-century predecessors, counted on finding rich mineral deposits and untapped markets in Africa and Asia. Gold and diamond discoveries in South Africa in the 1860s and again in the 1880s unleashed a stampede of prospectors and inspired colonists' dreams. Coastal traders generated further colonial expansion in West Africa. Trade in palm oil, used in large quantities for making soap and glycerin, replaced the slave trade.

Was the hope of economic gain the most significant factor in the frenetic European rush for colonies during the last decades of the nineteenth century? Did the colonial powers actually realize great wealth through their exploration and conquest?

To be sure, colonies provided some valued products for European markets. Ivory and rubber from Congo, palm oil from Nigeria, Dahomey, and the Ivory Coast, peanuts from French Senegal, diamonds and gold from South Africa, coffee from British Ceylon, and sugar from Malaya proved to be lucrative commodities. The rubber trade of French Indochina, Dutch Indonesia, the Congo, and British Malaya expanded rapidly with the popularity of the bicycle and particularly when automobiles took to the road. The British colonies of Nigeria and the Gold Coast produced 4 percent of the world's cocao in 1905 and 24 percent ten years later. The consumption of tea, most of it from China and Ceylon, increased by almost four times between 1840 and 1900.

Colonies provided an inviting market for manufactured goods from the mother country. Henry Stanley described the Congo not in terms of square kilometers but as "square yards of cotton to be exported." In the 1890s, about a third of all British exports and about a quarter of all investment went

Ivory from Africa became a valuable item on the European markets.

to its colonies, above all India, which imported cotton cloth and other textiles, iron, hardware, and shoes from Britain. Yet British capital investment abroad was still principally directed toward its lost colony, the United States, as well as toward other independent states such as Ottoman Turkey. British subjects also invested in the settlement colonies— Australia, New Zealand, and Canada, as well as India. The African colonies attracted very little British investment. There was more British trade with Belgium in the 1890s than with all of Africa.

Because colonial investments were risky, only a very small percentage of French and German investment was directed into their respective colonies. French investment abroad was overwhelmingly directed toward other parts of Europe, particularly Russia. Only about 5 percent of French investment reached its colonies in 1900; in 1914, France bought more goods from its colonies than it sold them in return. Less than 1 percent of German trade was with its colonies. By 1907, German investment in all German colonies fell slightly below the value of investments in a single large bank at home.

Imperial governments, which had to foot the bill for troops, supplies, guns, and administrative and other expenses, therefore became increasingly suspicious of the confident assurances of adventurers that incredible riches lay just a little farther up a barely explored African river or beyond the next oasis. In 1899, a French politician whose ardor for imperialism had waned defined the two stages of colonization as "the joy of conquest," followed inevitably, as after a fine restaurant meal, by "the arrival of the bill." The French colonial lobby, including provincial chambers of commerce in manufacturing cities and ports and geographic societies, pictured western Sudan as teeming with lucrative commercial opportunities. It turned out that this vast region of desert offered merchants little more than rubber, a little gold, some peanuts, and an occasional elephant tusk. The French government spent vast sums to administer and police an increasingly unwieldy empire. In the meantime, the exploitation of natural resources by the imperialists contributed to the economic and political underdevelopment of these regions once they became independent nations in the twentieth century.

Overall, however, the economic interpretation of the imperial race for colonies cannot be discounted. Key economic sectors did benefit substantially from raw materials and markets provided by the new colonies, as did individual businessmen. Nonetheless, an economic explanation for colonialism was only one factor—often a minor one—and is difficult to detach from a more dominant motivation.

Imperialism and Nationalism

The new imperialism was, above all, an extension of the search for security and power on the European continent in a period characterized by aggressive nationalism and bitter international rivalries. Even in the case of Great Britain, the imperialist power with the greatest economic investment in colonies, the international rivalry of the European powers was the strongest impulse for imperialism. Britain expanded its domination into new regions, not only in search of new markets, but to keep the French, Germans, or Russians from establishing bases and colonies that might threaten British interests. Britain's definition of its interests in Egypt, the pursuit of which helped launch the landgrab in Africa, had far more to do with fear of competition from its rivals than with economic motives.

Burma, absorbed by Britain after wars in 1824 and 1852 to protect India's eastern frontier against possible colonial rivals, is a case in point. When France declared its economic interest in Burma in the late 1870s, the British expanded their control over Upper Burma, fighting a third war with Burma in 1885. They packed off the reigning king to India, shipped his throne to a museum in Calcutta, turned his palace into a British club, and annexed Burma to the administration of India. Likewise, the establishment of a British protectorate over Afghanistan in 1880 can best be explained by a desire to place a buffer state between India and expanding Russian interests in the region. Britain's immediate goal in what contemporary diplomats called "the great game" between Britain and Russia in the Near East and Asia was to prevent Russian troops from occupying the high range of mountains in and adjacent to Afghanistan. Lord Curzon put the issues at stake for Britain succinctly: "Turkistan, Afghanistan, Transcaspia, Persia—to many these names breathe only a sense of utter remoteness. . . . To me, I confess, they are the pieces on a chessboard upon which is being played out a game for the domination of the world."

The nationalism that surged through all the European powers in the 1880s and 1890s fueled the "new imperialism." In 1876, when Britain opposed Russian moves toward the Turkish capital of Constantinople, a popular British song went: "We don't want to fight, / But, by Jingo, if we do, / We've got the men, / We've got the ships, / We've got the money too." The term "jingoism" came into use in English to mean fervent nationalism. Generations of British schoolchildren gawked at maps of the world that displayed colony after colony, however varied the structure and effectiveness of British control, colored red, the map color of Great Britain.

In Britain, the colonial experience became an important part of British national consciousness, pervasive in literature and in material culture. The same was true within each of the imperial powers. Newspapers, magazines, popular literature, and the publication of soldiers' diaries and letters carried home news from the colonies and made imperialism seem a romantic adventure. In 1880, the annual Naval and Military Tournament in London began to present reenactments of colonial skirmishes and battles. One play, *Siege of Delhi*, ended with an Irish officer falling in love and dancing a jig as the curtain falls on Indians about to be shot out of a cannon. In 1911, an Italian writer's enthusiasm for the feats of the Italian army in Libya included descriptions of the "lustrous" eyes of the Sicilian horses, which seemed, by their neighing, to be attempting to pronounce the word "Italy." A general's daughter exclaims in a novel about Egypt, "Let the peace-people croak as they please, it is war that brings out the truly heroic virtues."

From the drawing rooms of country estates to the wretched pubs of Liverpool and Birmingham, the British howled for revenge for the death of General Charles "Chinese" Gordon, killed in Sudan by the forces of the Mahdi in 1885. Few Europeans wept at the destruction of entire cultures and the deaths of hundreds of thousands of people at the hands of European armies. "Special artists" and then photographers began to travel with British colonial forces; movie cameras recorded Horatio Kitchener's 1899 campaign against the Boers in South Africa. At a time of rising political opposition in Great Britain to costly colonial commitments, the romanticization of British expeditionary forces helped win support for spending even more, and kept the Conservatives in power in 1900.

Voluntary associations pressured the colonial powers to devote more resources to the building of empire. In Great Britain, Germany, and France, geographic societies, associations that met periodically to listen to talks about exploration in Africa and Asia, sponsored voyages that charted unexplored—at least by Europeans—territories. In Germany and Britain, naval leagues whipped up enthusiasm for imperialism. The Pan-German League (founded in 1891) demanded more expenditures for warships. The champion of colonial lobbying groups, the Primrose League in Britain (founded in 1884), had 1.7 million members by 1906, drawn primarily from business, finance, the military, and government, the groups with the greatest stake in imperialism. The lengthy economic depression that gripped Europe between the mid-1870s and the mid-1890s, bringing low prices for commodities, accentuated such lobbying for aggressive imperialism.

To be sure, strident critics of imperialism could be found. In Britain, anti-imperialists were to be found among Liberal or Labour Party intellectuals, such as members of the "Ethical Union," formed in 1896. Like Hobson, who frequently addressed their meetings, they disparaged jingoism with passion. But with British victory in the Boer War, anti-imperialist voices grew fainter in Britain.

In France, anti-imperialists focused on the financial burden of expansion. A member of the Chamber of Deputies complained, "We are being drawn along in an irresistible process, like that of Time, by the mere force of a colonial expansionism which has got out of control." In the United States, the American Anti-Imperialist League joined together groups opposing the annexation of the Philippines as a territory. But everywhere the strident imperialist roar drowned out dissident voices. It contributed to the aggressive nationalism that fueled the increasingly bitter rivalries between the European great powers and further destabilized the continent.

CONCLUSION

In 1500, the European powers controlled about 7 percent of the globe's land; by 1800, they controlled 35 percent; in 1914, they controlled 84 percent. Between 1871 and 1900, the British Empire, which came to include one-quarter of the world's land mass and population, expanded to include 66 million people and 4.5 million square miles, the French Empire to 3.5 million square miles, and Germany, Belgium, and Italy to about 1 million square miles each. In Spain, with little left from its once mighty empire, the shock of losing the Philippines and Cuba to the United States in 1898 led to an intense period of introspection by intellectuals known as the "generation of 1898" who wanted to "regenerate" Spain. The Spanish government took new colonies in Morocco and the Western Sahara.

Aggressive nationalism shaped the contours of the new European imperialism from the early 1880s to 1914. Imperialism sharpened the rivalries of the great powers, while solidifying international alliances. Competing colonial interests brought France and Britain to the verge of war after the Fashoda Affair of 1898. Subsequent crises assumed even more dramatic dimensions. Infused with the same sense of struggle that seemed to engulf Europe, these crises would defy peaceful resolution.

PART SIX

CATACLYSM

The Great War began in August 1914. Germany and Austria-Hungary fought Great Britain, France, and Russia. Although most statesmen, military leaders, and ordinary soldiers and civilians believed that the war would be over quickly, it raged on for more than four years. A military stalemate, bogged down in grisly trench warfare on the western front, took the lives of millions of soldiers. In the war's wake, four empires fell. In 1917, a revolution overthrew the tsar of Russia, and then the Bolsheviks overthrew the provisional government, withdrew from the world conflict, and imposed Communist rule. The German Empire collapsed in November 1918 upon the victory of Britain, France, and their allies (including the United States since 1917). The multinational Austro-Hungarian and Turkish Ottoman Empires (which had joined Germany on the losing side) also collapsed.

The Versailles Peace Treaty, signed by the new German Republic in 1919, carved up the fallen empires, creating successor states in Central Europe—Poland, Czechoslovakia, and Yugoslavia. The treaties signed between the victors and the vanquished left a legacy of nationalist hatred in Europe that poisoned international relations during the subsequent two decades. Out of the economic, social, and political turmoil of the 1920s and 1930s emerged authoritarian movements that were swept to power in many European countries, beginning with Mussolini's Italian fascists in 1922. In Germany, Hitler's National Socialist Party—the Nazis—grew in strength with the advent of the Great Depression in 1929. The Nazis drew on extreme right-wing nationalism that viewed the Treaty of Versailles as an unfair humiliation to Germany. In the Soviet Union, Joseph Stalin became head of the Communist Party following Lenin's death in 1924; he purged rivals within the party, launched a campaign of rapid industrialization, forced millions of peasants into collective farms, and ordered the slaughter or imprisonment of those who resisted. Britain and France retained their parliamentary forms of government, despite economic, social, and political tensions.

In this Europe of extremes, the search for political stability after World War I proved elusive. After coming to power in 1933, Hitler rearmed Germany and disdainfully violated the Treaty of Versailles by reoccupying the Rhineland in 1936 and forging a union with Austria. The same year, Hitler and Mussolini supported a right-wing nationalist insurrection in Spain against the Spanish Republic. They sent planes, advisers, and war materiel to aid General Francisco Franco's military forces, which were victorious three years later. After Hitler's initial aggressive moves against Czechoslovakia were unopposed by Britain and France, the German dictator brazenly sent German troops to occupy all of Czechoslovakia in 1938.

Just weeks after shocking the world by signing a nonaggression pact with Stalin's Soviet Union, Hitler began his long-planned invasion of Poland, which quickly fell. And after a brief "phony war" of inaction in the West, in the spring of 1940 Hitler invaded France, the Netherlands, and Belgium. Japan's sudden attack on the U.S. military bases at Pearl Harbor, Hawaii, on December 7, 1941, brought the United States into World War II. Over 17 million people were killed in the fighting, and another 20 million civilians perished, including more than 6 million Jews systematically exterminated by the Nazis during the Holocaust. The war finally ended in 1945, after the defeat of Germany, Italy, and Japan. Europe and the entire world entered a new and potentially even more dangerous period, one in which nuclear arms made the threat of another world war even more horrible.

CHAPTER 22

THE GREAT WAR

"The lamps are going out all over Europe. They will not be lit again in our lifetime." So spoke Sir Edward Grey, the British foreign secretary, in early August 1914, as the Great War began. His last-ditch diplomatic efforts to prevent war having failed, Grey was one of the few to share an apocalyptic vision of a conflict that most people thought would be over by Christmas. Few observers anticipated that this war would be more destructive than any ever fought. International peace conferences held in The Hague in 1899 and 1907 had considered ways of reducing atrocities in war, but they failed to take into account that future wars might be different from those of the past. Not even Grey could have foreseen the 38.2 million casualties, the downfall of four empires, and the shifts in Europe's economic, social, cultural, and political life after the war that made the period before the war seem like "the good old days."

The Great War was the first large-scale international conflict since the Napoleonic era. It involved all the great powers, with Italy entering the war in 1915, albeit without much popular enthusiasm, and the United States entering in 1917. Before the war ended, it would also draw a host of minor states into the monstrous struggle. The catastrophic conflagration was set off by a spark—the assassination of Austro-Hungarian Archduke Francis Ferdinand in Sarajevo, the capital of Bosnia, on June 28, 1914, by a Serb nationalist. In little more than a month, war engulfed the powers of Europe through the decades-old system of entangling alliances that interwove their fates. And while these alliances did not make a general war in Europe inevitable—in fact, the situation in Europe seemed much more precarious in 1905 and 1911 than it did in 1914 before the assassination—most heads of state, diplomats, and military planners expected a major war in their lifetimes. Some were relieved, and others delighted, when it began. Few were surprised.

Entangling Alliances

Among the national rivalries in Europe, none seemed more irreparable than that between Germany and France. However, none was potentially as

LE NEZ DE LA TRIPLICE
imité du « Laocoon » antique

Cartoon satirizing the alliance between Germany, Austria-Hungary, and the Turkish Ottoman Empire (1896).

dangerous as that between Russia and Austria-Hungary, which was focused on the Balkans. It was accentuated by the presence within the Habsburg Empire of South Slav peoples who looked to Russia as the protector of all Slavs. In the meantime, Russia, with its long-standing goal of increasing its influence in the Balkans, fanned the flames of Pan-Slavism. Germany and Austria-Hungary became firm allies, with their alliance directed, above all, against Russia. In 1882, Italy joined the two Central European powers to form the Triple Alliance, which was revived in 1891 and 1902. By 1905, growing German and British economic and military rivalry helped drive together France and Britain, the oldest rivals in Europe. Russia, France, and Britain formed the Triple Entente. Entangling alliances left the great powers of Europe divided into two armed camps. Because of this alliance system, the outbreak of war between any two rivals threatened to bring all of the powers into the conflict.

Irreconcilable Hatreds

The German Empire, proclaimed at Versailles in the wake of the French defeat in the Franco-Prussian War of 1870–1871, had absorbed Alsace and most of Lorraine. The French never reconciled themselves to the loss of two of their wealthiest provinces. Although most Alsatians spoke a German dialect, Alsace had been an integral and strategically important part of France since the seventeenth century. Most people living in the parts of Lorraine annexed by Germany spoke and considered themselves French. The growing rivalry between France and Germany over colonial interests added to mutual mistrust.

Francis Joseph (1830–1916), the elderly emperor of Austria-Hungary, was a plodding man of integrity who had assumed the throne in 1848 and who had once told Theodore Roosevelt, the president of the United States, "You see in me the last monarch of the old school." Respected by his people, he remained a largely ceremonial figure identified with the survival of the polyglot Habsburg state in an age of nationalism. Francis Joseph bore a series of family tragedies with dignity: the execution in 1867 of his brother Maximilian in Mexico, where he was briefly emperor, his son's suicide in 1889, and his wife's madness, separation, and assassination. Throughout his reign, fifteen years longer than even that of Queen Victoria of England, the Habsburg emperor had been determined that the imperial army be strong and that his dynasty maintain international prestige.

(*Left*) An Alsatian woman learning to goose-step in a caricature from the German satirical review *Simplicimus*. (*Right*) The aging Emperor Francis Joseph of the Habsburg monarchy.

Irreconcilable hatreds existed in the Austro-Hungarian Empire, which was made up of a great many different nationalities. The Austrians and the Hungarians, who dominated the other nationalities of their territories (see Chapter 17), were satisfied, but other peoples were not. Thus Czechs, Slovaks, Poles, and others resented Austrian and Hungarian domination. And Romanians were unhappy with Hungary's vigorous campaign to "Magyarize" public life at the expense of non-Hungarian minorities.

The South Slavs were the most dissatisfied peoples within the Austro-Hungarian monarchy. The southern territories of Austria-Hungary included South Slav peoples—majorities in some regions—who resented subservience to the monarchy. These included Slovenes, Croats, and Serbs (see Map 17.3).

During the mid-nineteenth-century revolutions, the Russian army had bailed out the then-youthful Emperor Francis Joseph, invading Hungary in 1849 and defeating its rebellious army (see Chapter 16). But by the turn of the century, the Russian government was eagerly fanning Pan-Slav fervor in the Balkans, stirring ethnic tension in the southern regions of the Habsburg domains. In the mountainous Habsburg Balkan territories of Bosnia and Herzegovina, which included Orthodox Serbs, Muslims, and Catholic Croats, many Serbs were committed to joining Bosnia to Serbia. The implication of Pan-Slav nationalism, that Slavs sharing a common culture ought also to share a common government, threatened the very existence of the Habsburg monarchy. The threat of Russian-oriented Pan-Slavism made Austria-Hungary even more dependent on Germany, as it contemplated the possibility of one day being drawn into a war against Russia.

For centuries Russia had coveted the strategically crucial Dardanelles strait, as well as the narrow Bosporus strait of Constantinople, controlled by the Turkish Ottoman Empire. Russian mastery over the straits that separate Europe and Asia would allow it to control entry to the Black Sea and afford it easy access to the Mediterranean. Russia's defeat in the Crimean War (1853–1856) by Britain, France, and the Ottoman Empire had only temporarily diminished Russian interest in the region. British policy in the Balkans had long been predicated on keeping the straits from Russian control.

The Alliance System

The alliance system of late-nineteenth-century Europe, then, hinged on German and French enmity, the competing interests of Austria-Hungary and Russia in the Balkans, and Germany's fear of being attacked from both east and west by Russia and France (see Map 22.1). Great Britain stood independent of any alliance until undertaking an Entente with France in 1904. Colonial rival of both Germany and France and the opponent of Russian expansion, Britain ultimately came to fear the expanding German navy more than French colonial competition or Russia.

MAP 22.1 EUROPE IN 1914 Highlighting Alsace and the part of Lorraine occupied by Germany before the outbreak of the Great War.

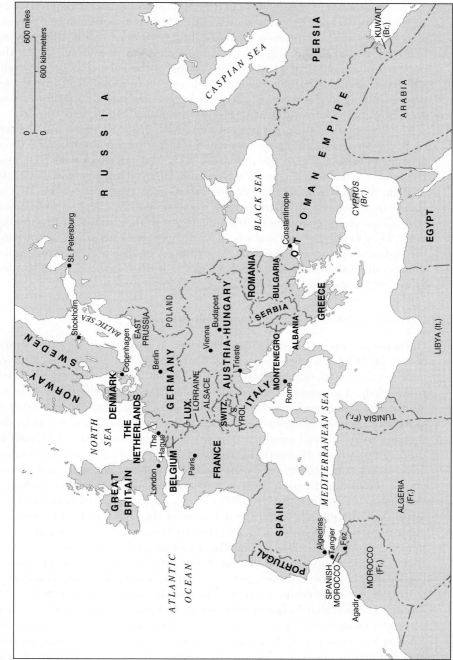

The foundation of nineteenth-century diplomacy lay in the assumption by each continental power that alliances with other great powers would protect it by forcing any nation considering war to face at least two hostile powers. Bismarck captured the urgency the European great powers felt about the necessity of alliances, and the delicate nature of the balance of power itself: "All [international] politics reduces itself to this formula: Try to be *à trois* (three) as long as the world is governed by the unstable equilibrium of five great powers"—Germany, Austria-Hungary, Russia, Britain, and France.

The diplomats of the great powers were the heirs of Klemens von Metternich, the Austrian leader who dominated international relations in the three decades following Napoleon's defeat in 1815. Many of them were conservative nobles determined, at least in Germany, Austria-Hungary, and Russia, to hold the line against forces of democratization in their own states. War to some extent became an instrument of domestic politics. Diplomats believed that the great powers ought to make decisions in the interest of the smaller ones. They embraced nationalism as a principle, but only when considering the rights of the great powers. If they allowed smaller powers some rights, they ascribed the non-European peoples (with the exception of the United States and Japan, the only non-European powers) none at all.

Germany and Austria-Hungary against Russia

Germany at first enjoyed good relations with Russia, another autocratic power. In 1873, Bismarck forged the Three Emperors' League, an alliance between Germany, Austria-Hungary, and Russia; by the alliance, the three rulers pledged to consult each other in order to maintain the peace "against all disturbances from whatever side they might come." But it was difficult to gloss over tensions between Austro-Hungarian and Russian interests in the Balkans. When Russia sought and found occasions to extend its influence in that region, Austria-Hungary reacted with concern. In 1875, a revolt against Turkish rule had broken out in the Balkan provinces of Bosnia and Herzegovina. Following Russian intervention against and victory over Turkey in the bloody Russo-Turkish War (1877–1878), the Congress of Berlin in 1878 left Bulgaria nominally under the authority of the Ottoman Empire but also subject to Russian influence. The Austro-Hungarian government would henceforth administer Bosnia and Herzegovina, although they would remain within the Ottoman Empire. But this had the effect of potentially antagonizing Russia, because both territories had populations of Serbs, who looked to Russia for leadership. Moreover, in part because Britain and Austria-Hungary feared that Bulgaria might serve Russian interests, the Congress of Berlin recognized the creation of the independent states of Serbia and Romania (consisting of Walachia and Moldavia) as buffers against further Russian ambitions in the Balkans. Montenegro also gained independence, and the Ottoman Empire ceded the Mediterranean island of Cyprus to British occupation. The Ottoman Empire not only lost considerable territory in the Balkans (including much of the empire's Christian population) but now faced two new small but hostile states. Moreover, hundreds of thousands of Muslim refugees fled Serbia, Bulgaria, and Bosnia and Herzegovina, pouring into the diminished Ottoman territories. By 1879, about half of the 1.5 million Muslims who had lived in Bulgaria were no longer there; 200,000 had died, and the others had taken refuge in Turkey.

In 1879, fearing Russian expansionism, Bismarck forged the Dual Alliance, the cornerstone alliance between Germany and Austria-Hungary, predicated on German support for Habsburg opposition to an expansion of Russian interests in the Balkans. Although the details of the alliance remained secret, its general outlines were well known. The alliance became one of the central factors of European diplomacy for the next thirty-five years. When Italy allied with Germany and Austria-Hungary in 1882, the Triple Alliance was formed. Italy was not a great power, but it wanted to be one. The Italian government also wanted support for its aggressive imperial ambitions, which were directed toward the Mediterranean region, particularly North Africa. There France stood in the way, having occupied Tunisia in 1881 before the Italians could get there (see Chapter 21), and Italy now sought support against France.

Germany's alliance with Austria-Hungary made the Three Emperors' League virtually meaningless. Germany and Austria-Hungary each agreed to come to the aid of the other in the event of a Russian attack. Bismarck had intended Germany's alliance with Austria-Hungary to force Russia to seek better relations with Germany. But it had the effect of driving Russia further away. Moreover, Austria-Hungary's alliance with Germany had the potential to make instability in the Balkans a threat to European peace by putting Russia at odds not only with Austria-Hungary, but with Germany as well.

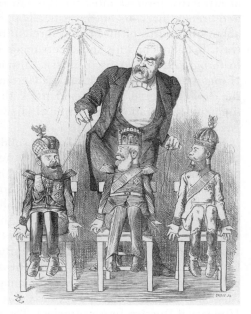

Germany Encircled: Russia and France Ally

The last thing Bismarck wanted was for his alliance with Austria-Hungary to drive Russia and France together. Such an eventuality might one day leave

In a caricature of the alliance system, Otto von Bismarck is depicted as a puppet-master controlling the emperors of Russia, Austria-Hungary, and Germany.

Germany confronting the necessity of fighting a war on two fronts, Bismarck's nightmare. In 1881, he resurrected the Three Emperors' League,
which again allied the tsar of Russia with the emperors of Germany and
Austria-Hungary. Despite considerable points of tension with the Habsburg
monarchy, the Russian government entered this alliance as a hedge against
Austro-Hungarian expansion in the Balkans toward the straits of Constantinople. The result was that Bismarck's resourceful diplomacy left Germany
allied, in one way or another, with all of its potential enemies except France.
As on the eve of the Franco-Prussian War of 1870–1871, France stood without allies.

Yet several factors seemed to draw Russia and France together, despite
great differences in their political systems. Both France and Russia stood
outside the Triple Alliance, which joined the powers of Central Europe with
Italy. Russia, too, faced diplomatic isolation, despite the Three Emperors'
League, because its Balkan interests clashed with those of Austria-Hungary.
Russia hoped that an alliance with France would limit German support for
the ambitions of the Habsburgs in southeastern Europe. Cultural ties
between the Russian aristocracy and France remained strong; many Russian nobles still preferred to speak French.

French investment in Russia increased dramatically in the late 1880s
and early 1890s. French bankers seized the opportunity to provide capital
at attractive interest rates for Russian railway and mining development,
and French investors enthusiastically purchased Russian bonds. By 1914,
about one-fourth of all French foreign investment was in Russia. In contrast, Bismarck and his successors made it a policy to discourage and even
to forbid German loans to Russia, although they invested in the Austro-
Hungarian and Ottoman Empires. German private investors usually lacked
the capital to undertake such loans. At the same time, German and French
financial cooperation was extremely limited. French and German capitalists saw each other as rivals.

Franco-Russian ties were further solidified by Tsar Alexander III's visit
to Paris during the Exposition of 1889. Yet the French left was outraged by
government overtures to the autocratic and often brutal tsarist regime. For
their part, Russian Tsar Alexander III and his successor Nicholas II were
uncomfortable with close ties to a republic.

As the Russian government blamed Austria-Hungary for opposing what
they considered its natural influence in the Balkans, the Three Emperors'
League lapsed. In 1887, Germany and Russia signed a Reinsurance Treaty,
by which each pledged to remain neutral if the other went to war, but it
did not cover the most likely contingency of all—war between Russia and
Austria-Hungary—because Germany was already committed to aid Austria-
Hungary if Russian forces attacked. The young, headstrong Kaiser William
II dismissed Bismarck as chancellor in 1890. Bismarck's successors were
increasingly anti-Russian and failed to prevent Russia's alliance with
France.

In 1892, Russia and France signed a military treaty by which each pledged a military response if the other were attacked by Germany or by one or more of its allies. A secret formal alliance followed in 1894. The alliance was essentially defensive in nature: the French no more encouraged Russian moves in the direction of the Balkans than the Russians wanted to see France embark on a war of revenge to recapture Alsace-Lorraine from Germany. But the Dual Alliance, as it was called, countered the Triple Alliance. It defeated the most essential thrust of Bismarck's foreign policy by ending France's diplomatic isolation.

Anglo-German Rivalry

During the 1890s, the possibility of Britain joining the Dual Alliance of France and Russia seemed remote. Whereas Germany and Britain had some competing colonial interests—for example, in Africa—the interests of France and Britain clashed in West Africa and Indochina, and France was jealous of British influence in Egypt. When a French force encountered a British army unit in 1898 on the upper Nile at Fashoda, war between the two seemed a distinct possibility (see Chapter 21) before the French government backed down. Furthermore, Afghanistan, lying strategically between British India and Russia, was a particular point of tension between those two powers.

The British government had long made it clear that it sought no alliance with anyone and that it would stand alone, its empire protected by the great British navy. But the British government signed the Entente Cordiale ("Friendly Agreement") with France in 1904. Britain did so for several reasons. The hostile reaction from every power in Europe to the Boer War (1899–1902; see Chapter 21) fought by British troops in South Africa demonstrated that it was one thing to stand in proud isolation from the continent, but another to have no friends at all. Furthermore, Britain's relations with Germany soured markedly. Germany's pointed criticism of Britain's war with the Boers strained relations between the two powers. In 1895, Kaiser William II, in his inimitably clumsy way, had sent a telegram congratulating the president of the Boer Republic of Transvaal in southern Africa on the Boers' successful stand against a British attacking force. This unleashed a storm of nationalistic fury in Britain and Germany.

Neither Anglo-German cooperation in the suppression of the Boxer Rebellion in China in 1900, nor a joint operation to force Venezuela to pay some of its foreign debts in 1902, significantly improved Anglo-German relations. Gradually, the British began to realize the growing extent of German influence in the Turkish Ottoman Empire. British military planners feared that Germany might be able to move troops more quickly overland into the Middle East than the Royal Navy could by ship.

German economic growth and the doubling of its foreign trade during the last three decades of the nineteenth century had begun to make some in Britain anxious, although Britain still accounted for about 45 percent of world investment. It also inspired a campaign to establish an empire-wide tariff barrier that would encourage trade within the British Commonwealth, while keeping foreign goods out.

Above all, it was the Anglo-German naval rivalry that pushed Britain toward a rapprochement with France. German military spending had already quadrupled between 1874 and 1890 (in a period of little inflation). In 1897 the Reichstag allocated funds for the accelerated expansion of the German navy over six years. William II's uncontrolled enthusiasm provided no small degree of impetus—the vain kaiser loved breaking bottles over the bows of brand new ships of war. Admiral Alfred von Tirpitz (1849–1930) belligerently cited the strength of the British navy as the *raison d'être* for the passage of the bill to build up the German navy. The nationalistic Pan-German League and the Naval League whipped up popular enthusiasm for the navy. The new German fleet began to include some of the biggest, fastest, and widest-ranging warships ever built.

Britain reacted quickly when confronted with the sudden and almost unexpected naval competition. In 1906, the fastest and most powerful battleship in the world, the *Dreadnought,* took to the sea. Germany began to build comparable ships of war, and wild British estimates had the Germans turning out even more, leading to a brief panic in 1909 that a German invasion of Britain was near.

British-French Rapprochement

The British government took a hesitant step toward ending its diplomatic isolation by signing a treaty in 1901 with the United States, which permitted the latter to construct the Panama Canal. By undertaking an alliance with Japan in 1902, Britain sought to counter Russian ambitions in East Asia. The Russo-Japanese War of 1904–1905 helped push Britain toward France (see Chapter 18). The Russian Baltic fleet, embarking on a disastrous voyage around the world to confront the Japanese navy in the Yellow Sea, sank several British fishing trawlers in the North Sea, somehow mistaking them for Japanese ships. Germany expected that France would immediately support Russia, with whom it was allied. Yet, to almost everyone's surprise, French Foreign Minister Théophile Delcassé (1852–1923) helped mediate between Russia and Britain. Russia's defeat in East Asia confirmed that Britain had far more to fear from Germany than from Russia.

The Entente Cordiale reached between Britain and France in 1904 had the immediate goal of eliminating points of tension between the two powers: Britain recognized French interests in Morocco in exchange for the French recognition of British control over Egypt; both sides accepted the existence of neutral Siam in Indochina standing between French Indochina and British-controlled Burma; and they settled a centuries-old dispute over fishing rights off the coast of Newfoundland.

The First Moroccan Crisis (1905)

The First Moroccan Crisis solidified the rapprochement between Britain and France, while highlighting the role of imperial rivalries in international politics. Germany had only modest commercial interests in Morocco, but German Chancellor Bernhard von Bülow (1849–1929) convinced William II to test the recently concluded Anglo-French agreement and perhaps force the British government to leave France to its own devices while casting Germany as defender of Moroccan sovereignty. In March 1905, the German kaiser arrived in Tangier aboard a yacht. William II demanded that Germany receive from Morocco the same commercial benefits as any other trading partner.

The French government reacted with fury, but backed down when British support for war seemed highly unlikely. Germany also pulled away from possible conflict, seeing that only Austria-Hungary took its side. The crisis ended with an international conference in the Spanish town of Algeciras in January 1906. Germany recognized the primacy of French interests in Morocco. This left the German government determined that another humiliation must not be suffered. The incident also seemed to confirm the bellicose and bullying nature of German foreign policy to both France and Britain. Anti-German feeling intensified in France among political moderates as well as those on the nationalist right. French and British generals and admirals began to draw up joint contingency plans for combined warfare against Germany.

The Algeciras Conference, and particularly the policies of Russian Foreign Minister Alexander Izvolsky (1856–1919), also brought Russia and Britain closer together. For Izvolsky, Russian interests were in the Balkans, where they competed with those of Austria-Hungary, not in Asia, where British interests lay. Set on the road to recovery from the disastrous Russo-Japanese War by British loans, the Russian government was now eager for better relations with Britain. The British government had long viewed Russian economic influence in Persia (Iran) and Afghanistan as threatening to its interests because a strong Russian presence in Persia might one day compromise the sea route to East Asia, and because Afghanistan served as a buffer between Russia and British India. In 1907, taking

France and Germany quarrel over Morocco (1905).

advantage of the collapse of the shah's authority, the two powers divided Persia (Iran) into three zones—a Russian zone, a British zone, and a neutral zone—and agreed to respect each other's zone of influence. The Russians accepted British influence in Afghanistan, and both powers agreed to stay out of Tibet. Russia hoped that Britain might support, or at least tolerate, its interests in the Balkans, and its ultimate desire of controlling Constantinople. The elimination of some of the tensions between Britain and Russia strengthened the Franco-British Entente Cordiale.

The Europe of Two Armed Camps, 1905–1914

The inclusion of Russia in what was increasingly known as the Triple Entente moved Europe toward a clear division into two camps. Cordial relations, however, continued between Tsar Nicholas II and his cousin, German Kaiser William II. The German emperor was also the grandson of Queen Victoria of England—a standing joke in Berlin went that William feared no one except God and his English grandmother. But in the Europe of entangling alliances, blood relations were subordinate to the logic of great-power interests and alliances.

The German government could find little reassurance in Italy's nominal alliance with Germany and Austria-Hungary. Improved relations between Italy and France confronted Germany with the prospect that Austria-Hungary would be its only dependable ally.

Should Austria-Hungary cease to be a power or, in the worst-case scenario, completely collapse because of national movements from within, Germany might be left alone, encircled by enemies. The German high command prepared for a possible war against both France and Russia, a war that would have to be fought on two fronts. This left the German government in the position of having to support its troubled Habsburg ally unconditionally in the Balkans.

Moreover, the German government, like the other great powers, began to see military strength in a different way in 1904–1905. German military planners, concerned that Russia was rapidly reconstituting its army in the years following its humiliating defeat in the Russo-Japanese War of 1904–1905, continued to build their forces, as did Austria-Hungary. The powers increased ranks of soldiers and sailors, and almost frantically improved weapons, aided by technological advances in warfare, including artillery that could be fired more rapidly, machine guns, telephones, and even airplanes, at first intended essentially for reconnaissance. Moreover, the German government demonstrated that it was increasingly willing to use the threat of war as a tool of diplomacy. This new approach reflected a growing sense that it would be better to fight a war sooner rather than later, while Germany still had what appeared to be a favorable military balance of power. In the meantime, the public in every major power followed international politics with increasing care and were attentive to the capacity of their armed forces. Thus, perceptions of the balance of military power came into play in the international crises that led to war in 1914.

The Balkan Tinderbox

The Balkans increasingly became the key to maintaining peace in Europe (see Map 22.2). In 1897, Russia and Austria-Hungary had agreed informally to respect the *status quo* in the region. However, cultural and political nationalism continued to grow among the South Slavs living within the Austro-Hungarian Empire, in Serbia, or under Ottoman rule. In the Balkans, the vast majority of peoples had remained indifferent or ignorant of nationalist identities until at least the beginning of the twentieth century. Religious identities—Greek, Russian, or Bulgarian Orthodox, Muslim, Catholic, or Jewish—had always defined a sense of community, along with regional and village identities. Then, encouraged by the new states carved out of what had been Ottoman territory, national identities began to take hold. This made southeastern Europe ever more the focus of the rivalry between Austria-Hungary and Russia.

When a bloody revolution led to the assassination of the king and queen of Serbia in 1903, Russia quickly recognized the new king, Peter, hoping that Pan-Slav elements would dominate. Fearing any delay would push Serbia closer to Russia, Austria-Hungary recognized the *fait accompli*. The Serb parliament voiced its unqualified support for Russian ambitions in East Asia and its disastrous 1904–1905 war against Japan. Serb nationalists began to call for union with Serbs in Macedonia, which was still part of the Ottoman Empire and was peopled by Macedonians, Serbs, Bulgarians, Sephardic Jews, and Greeks, who had largely gotten along in the past. As Greek and Bulgarian Orthodox churches battled for the allegiance of peasants, the strident, aggressive calls of various nationalist groups helped create a nationalism that had previously existed on only a superficial level among elites. Now Greek, Bulgarian, and Macedonian armed groups operated inside Macedonia, as did Bulgarian and Macedonian nationalists. Provocative addresses to minorities worsened ethnic tensions in the region. Religion became much more identified with emerging national identities.

Relations between Serbia and Austria-Hungary further deteriorated. When Serbia tried to lessen its economic dependence on Austria-Hungary (the destination of almost all Serb exports) by signing a commercial treaty with Bulgaria, Vienna responded by forbidding the importation of Serb livestock. Thus began an economic battle in 1906 that became known in much of Europe as the "Pig War," as the humble pig formed a basis of Serbia's fragile agricultural economy. The Serbs resourcefully found new markets for their pigs. The Habsburg government, despite the lack of Hungarian support for economic retaliation, responded in 1908 by announcing the construction of a new railroad that would further isolate Serbia economically. Serb

MAP 22.2 THE BALKANS, 1914   The Austro-Hungarian Empire and the Balkan states, including territory acquired in the Balkan Wars of 1912–1913.

nationalists viewed Bosnia and Herzegovina as South Slav states that should, with Russian encouragement, become part of Serbia.

Instability in Turkey

Political instability in Turkey in the early 1870s had further whetted the appetites of both Russia and Austria-Hungary for the Balkans, amid financial crisis, poor harvests, and the opposition of religious conservatives to secularization. Following the Crimean War (see Chapter 18), Britain and France had condescendingly invited the sultan "to participate in the advantages of public law and the system of Europe," while insisting on further Western reforms. The Ottoman default on foreign loans in 1875 led six years later to the administration of the Ottoman public debt being placed under the control of European administrators. The Ottoman governor of Egypt was constrained to sell his shares of the Suez Canal to the British government for a quarter of their real value, leading Egypt to bankruptcy.

Turkish Sultan Abdülhamid II (ruled 1876–1909) agreed to a constitution upon his ascension to the throne in 1876, consolidating some of the reforms of the past several decades. The constitution established parliamentary rule and guaranteed personal freedom and equality before the law. The sultan hoped to discourage the powers from intervening in Ottoman affairs on the pretext of forcing political reform. But in 1878 he suspended the constitution and dissolved the parliament it had established. The secret police rooted out potential opposition. During Abdülhamid's rule, foreign trade increased, agriculture developed, railway lines and paved roads more than doubled, and public schools increased in number. But his reign was also marked by the brutal repression of non-Muslim peoples of the Ottoman Empire. About 200,000 Armenians (who made up about 6 percent of the empire's population) were slaughtered in 1894–1895 in eastern Anatolia in response to Turkish fears of Armenian nationalism, encouraged by Russia. Moreover, the empire continued to be beset by financial problems, above all, high-interest debt owed to foreign bondholders. Influenced by Western political ideas and reflecting the emergence of a generation of Turkish intellectuals, a group of nationalists in 1889 founded the Committee of

Union and Progress, finding support in the bureaucracy and army. In July 1908, these "Young Turks," as they were called, revolted in the name of "order and progress" and forced the sultan to restore the constitution of 1876. One of their leaders was Mustafa Kemal (later known as Atatürk, 1881–1938). The Young Turks wanted to unify and modernize the Ottoman lands, while preventing Western intervention on behalf of the Armenians. Abdülhamid II was deposed in 1909 when he tried to plot a counter-revolution, and gradually a Western-like bureaucracy was put in place.

The chaos within the Ottoman Empire seemed to promise the realization of the Russian dream of opening the

The Young Turks, 1908.

straits of Constantinople to Russian ships, and perhaps only Russian ships. The Austro-Hungarian government faced the possibility that lands still held by the Ottoman Empire might be added to Serbia and Romania, further destabilizing the Balkans. This pushed Russian and Austro-Hungarian relations toward a breaking point.

The Bosnian Crisis of 1908

Turkish instability led to the Bosnian Crisis of 1908. In 1878, the Congress of Berlin had authorized Austria-Hungary to occupy Bosnia and Herzegovina, although both territories technically were still part of the Ottoman Empire. Austria-Hungary had done so, at the risk of bringing more Slavs into the empire, not only to solidify its position in the Balkans but to prevent Serbia from absorbing them. The Russian government had been secretly negotiating with Austria-Hungary to trade Russian acceptance of the absorption of Bosnia and Herzegovina for Austria-Hungary's support for the opening of the Bosporus and the Dardanelles straits to the Russian fleet. In October 1908, a day after Bulgaria, nominally under Ottoman sovereignty, declared its independence, the Austro-Hungarian government suddenly announced that it would directly annex Bosnia and Herzegovina, fearing the influence of the Young Turks there. The annexation was a clear violation of the agreements reached at the Congress of Berlin in 1878. The Russians reacted with rage. Serbia, furious that two territories in which many South Slavs lived were to be incorporated into the Habsburg Empire, mobilized its army with Russian support. Austria-Hungary responded in kind. The annexation also considerably strained relations between Austria-Hungary and Italy, nominal allies, because of Italian strategic and economic interests on the Adriatic coast. Pressured by Germany, Turkey received financial compensation in exchange for accepting the *fait accompli*.

The resolute opposition to war by Hungarian leaders within Austria-Hungary, as well as the opposition of the heir to the Habsburg throne, Archduke Francis Ferdinand (1863–1914), helped defuse the crisis. Not only would war be expensive, victory might well add a considerable South Slav population (from Serbia) to Hungarian territories. Furthermore, despite diplomatic bluster, Russia was not ready to fight, and its ally France was unwilling to go to war over the Balkans, where it had no interests. Lacking French or British support, the Russian government backed down, forcing Serbia to recognize the Austro-Hungarian annexation of Bosnia and Herzegovina.

War had been avoided, but the European powers had drawn significant conclusions from the Bosnian Crisis. Italy remained allied with both Central European powers, but both Berlin and Vienna viewed Italy's commitment to the alliance as uncertain. Italy's problematic status as an ally thus further firmed up Germany's alliance with Austria-Hungary. German and Austro-Hungarian military commanders met to plan for hostilities with Russia,

France, Serbia, and possibly—given its announced interests in Tyrolean Austria and Dalmatia—Italy. The German government demanded that Russia recognize Austria-Hungary's annexation of Bosnia and Herzegovina. The Russian government, viewing itself as a victim of German bullying, now sought a closer relationship with Britain. With German shipyards rapidly producing the most modern and heavily armed fighting ships at a frightening pace, British officials quickly gave up their reservations about the Entente Cordiale with France.

The Bosnian Crisis left deep scars on Russian relations with Austria-Hungary. Serb relations with Vienna worsened. The Habsburg government presented poorly forged documents to support claims that Serb authorities were trying to stir up the Slav populations within the empire. However, in fact, several groups of devoted Serb nationalists, including "The People's Defense" and "The Black Hand," received tacit support from the Serb state, as well as Russian encouragement.

The Second Moroccan Crisis (1911)

Germany also provoked the Second Moroccan Crisis. France had established a virtual protectorate in Morocco, which violated the Algeciras agreements of 1906. Using a local rebellion against the new Moroccan sultan as an excuse, a French army marched on the town of Fez, allegedly to protect French settlers. When the French government did not offer to compensate Germany because France had added another protectorate to its empire, the German emperor sent a small gunboat, the *Panther,* to the port of Agadir. It arrived on July 1, 1911, with demands that Germany receive the French Congo as compensation for France's claiming Morocco as a protectorate. France refused, bolstered by its closer relations with Britain, Russia's increased stability, and a wave of nationalist sentiment at home. Even German moderates seemed angered at what appeared to be a British commitment to preventing Germany from finding its "place in the sun."

The Second Moroccan Crisis, like the first, passed without war. In November 1911, Germany agreed to recognize Morocco as a French protectorate in exchange for 100,000 square miles of the French Congo. But the crisis further solidified Europe's competing alliances. Britain and France now formalized the agreement by which each pledged to aid the other in case of an attack by Germany. In April 1912, the British and French admiralties established zones of responsibility for their fleets—the French in the Mediterranean and the British in the English Channel and the North Sea. The arms race intensified.

The Balkan Wars

The Bosnian Crisis of 1908 had demonstrated that events in the Balkans could carry Europe to war. In 1911, the Turkish Ottoman Empire provided the kindling for another international flare-up. Late in the year, Italy invaded Libya, part of the Ottoman Empire, in what became known as the Tripoli War, overcoming resistance in October 1912. France acquiesced to the Italian seizure of Libya in exchange for Italian recognition of Morocco's status as a French protectorate. Another piece of the Ottoman Empire had been swallowed up.

Serbia, Bulgaria, Montenegro, and Greece had formed the Balkan League with the intention of freeing the Balkans from Ottoman rule. Encouraged by the difficulty the Turkish army had in putting down an insurrection in Albania in 1910 and by the Turkish defeat in Libya, they declared war on Turkey in 1912. The First Balkan War lasted less than a month, with the Balkan League emerging victorious. However, the success of the Balkan states worried the Austro-Hungarian government. Russia and the Austro-Hungarian monarchy seemed on a collision course in the Balkans. Serbia, Bulgaria, and Greece each annexed Ottoman territory (for Greece, which increased its territory by 70 percent, this new territory included the prize port of Salonika). Only one small chunk of the once enormous Ottoman Empire now remained on the European side of the straits (see Map 22.2).

Yet Russia and Austria-Hungary had avoided war. New foreign ministers, Sergei Sazonov (1861–1927) of Russia and Leopold Berchtold (1863–1942) of Austria-Hungary, helped defuse the crisis. Austria-Hungary's goals were to see that no Balkan state became so strong that it could generate nationalist agitation within its territories, and to prevent Serbia, Russia's friend, from gaining a port on the Adriatic. In the interest of peace, Britain and France supported Austria-Hungary's call for the creation of the independent state of Albania on the Adriatic, which would prevent Serbia from having its port. The German government viewed these issues as sufficiently grave to warrant its unconditional support for Austria-Hungary. The Treaty of London of May 1913 divided up most of the remaining Ottoman holdings in southeastern Europe among the Balkan states.

However, Bulgaria felt aggrieved by the fact that Serbia and Greece had ended up with large parts of Macedonia and attacked both states. Serbia and Greece, with the assistance of Romania and the Turks, quickly defeated Bulgaria in 1913 in the Second Balkan War. With the Peace of Bucharest, Serbia received the parts of what had been Ottoman Macedonia, which Bulgaria was to have received; Greece gained more territory on the Aegean coast as well as Crete, where Greeks had risen up against Turkish rule on two previous occasions and which Greece tried to occupy in 1897 before being easily defeated by Ottoman forces. The small Muslim state of Albania came into existence. Serbia emerged from the Balkan Wars larger, stronger, more ambitious, and angry that Austria-Hungary had frustrated its quest for an Adriatic port. It also may have emerged with the impression that there were limits to Germany's support for Austria-Hungary, since the German government had at least appeared to restrain the Habsburg government's aggressive response to Serbia's demand for a port.

"The Vortex—Will the powers be drawn in?" This image of the Balkan Wars, 1912–1913, had a ring of prophetic accuracy.

South Slav nationalism gained more adherents in the Balkans. After backing down against Austria-Hungary for the second time (the first having been the Bosnian Crisis in 1908), Sazonov irresponsibly placated the Serbs by telling them that their promised land lay inside the frontiers of Hungary. Some Serb political leaders sympathized with the young fanatics of "The People's Will" and "The Black Hand" nationalist organizations. In 1910, a boy who had been taught to shoot a gun by a Serb officer attempted to use it on the Austrian governor of Bosnia; the youth committed suicide after failing, becoming a martyr in Serbia. A few Habsburg personages, possibly including the Archduke Francis Ferdinand, may have been willing to consider the South Slavs as partners in a tripartite empire—the mere suggestion of which infuriated almost all Magyars and most Austrians. But the Austro-Hungarian government considered the South Slav nationalists to be threats who would ultimately have to be crushed. Because of the Balkan situation, the German military command once again turned its attention to readying its army, reacting to Russian measures of military preparedness. But in 1914 Europe seemed far less close to war than it had been in 1905 and 1911, the years of the two Moroccan Crises.

THE FINAL CRISIS

The powers of Europe were poised for conflict, divided into two armed camps by two rival alliances. While the outbreak of war was probably not inevitable—although many nationalists and military planners believed it to be—it was likely. Furthermore, once two powers seemed on the verge of war, the entangling alliances that pitted the Triple Alliance against the Triple Entente seemed likely to bring all of the European powers into the conflict. The crisis that precipitated World War I occurred in the Balkans, when Serb nationalists assassinated the Archduke Francis Ferdinand of Austria. Europe's diplomatic house of cards collapsed and the Great War began.

Assassination in Sarajevo

Archduke Francis Ferdinand was heir to the Habsburg throne. His first love was his commoner wife, Sophie; his second, hunting—he bragged of having killed 6,000 stags in his lifetime and of having bagged 2,763 seagulls on a single day. The archduke was not considered particularly pro-German, and probably had more sympathy for the problems of the South Slavs than any member of the royal family. Hungarians disliked him, fearing that when he came to the throne, he might eventually grant the South Slavs the same status as the Austrians and Hungarians. But many Serb nationalists would accept nothing less than an expanded independent Slavic state, or what they called Greater Serbia.

On June 28, 1914, Francis Ferdinand and his wife were on an inspection tour of the army in Sarajevo, the capital of Bosnia. As the archduke's motorcade approached the center of the city, a small bomb exploded under the archduke's car. The motorcade continued to the town hall, where the archduke expressed his indignation at the attempt on his life. When the motorcade departed, the drivers had not been informed of a change in route chosen to avoid the tangle of streets in central Sarajevo. When the first several vehicles began to turn into a narrow street, the military governor ran ahead, ordering their drivers to back up. Gavrilo Princip (1895–1918), a young member of the Black Hand Serb nationalist group, saw his chance, as

On an inspection tour of the army in Sarajevo, capital of Bosnia, Archduke Francis Ferdinand and his wife bathe in a warm welcome. They were assassinated a few hours later.

he happened to be only a few feet from the archduke's car. He opened fire, killing Francis Ferdinand and his wife.

Although the Serb government had been aware of the Black Hand nationalist organization and some individual officials had supported it, the Austrian description of the youthful killers as puppets whose strings were pulled in Belgrade was incorrect. Nonetheless, Serb newspapers virtually celebrated the death of the Habsburg heir. In Vienna, even those who had disliked the archduke for having married a commoner now mourned the couple fervently.

The Ultimatum

Within the Habsburg imperial administration, many officials immediately took the view that the chance to crush Serbia had arrived, and that, unlike 1908 and 1912, this time the opportunity would not be missed. The usually indecisive Austrian foreign minister, Leopold Berchtold, who had opposed war during the Balkan Crisis of 1912, now took a hard line.

From Berlin, William II urged retaliation, blaming Serbia for the assassination. German Chancellor Theobald von Bethmann-Hollweg (1856–1921) stubbornly held the view that Germany's strength must be paramount. ("Necessity knows no law," he once said.) Bethmann-Hollweg was now determined to stay the course with a numbing fatalism undoubtedly accentuated by the recent death of his wife. He advised his son not to plant his estate with trees that would take a long time to grow, because they would please only the Russians, whom by then he expected to have occupied northeastern Germany. He expected a war and wanted Russia to appear the aggressor. In Berlin, the German government gave an Austrian official a "blank check" to act with knowledge of full German support, that Germany would, if necessary, fight both France and Russia if those two powers intervened once Austria had declared war on Serbia. In this case, Bethmann-Hollweg expected Britain to remain neutral.

But for the moment, Austria-Hungary waited. Berchtold convinced the Hungarian leaders to support war against Serbia, promising that no Slavs from territories taken from defeated Serbia would be incorporated into Austria-Hungary. The Hungarian Social Democrats ended their opposition to the war. On July 21, 1914, Russian Foreign Minister Sazonov, encouraged by Maurice Paléologue, the French ambassador, warned Austria-Hungary against taking any military measures against Serbia.

On July 23, 1914, almost a month after the assassination, the Austrian ambassador in Belgrade presented a lengthy ultimatum to Serb officials. It denounced what it claimed was Serb activity aiming to "detach part of the territories of Austria-Hungary from the Monarchy." Austro-Hungarian demands included the end of all anti-Habsburg publications, the dissolution of all Serb nationalist organizations, and a purge of officials and army officers to be named by Austria-Hungary. The Serb reply was expected

within forty-eight hours. Grey, the British foreign secretary, called the ultimatum "the most formidable document ever presented by one independent
state to another."

The Serb government was in a no-win situation. Serbia's small army was
no match for that of Austria-Hungary. Its options were either to capitulate
completely to the ultimatum and suffer a humiliating diplomatic defeat,
or, as one official put it, to die fighting. This made Serbia almost totally
dependent upon Russian intervention.

The ultimatum sent shock waves through the capitals of Europe. Upon
learning its contents, Sazonov exclaimed, "It's the European War!" He
blamed Germany, claiming that the ultimatum was part of a German plan
to keep Russia from reaching Constantinople. Some of Tsar Nicholas II's
advisers saw war as a means of rallying the support of the Russian Empire
behind the tsar. Yet others remembered Russia's disastrous defeat in the
Russo-Japanese War, which had contributed to the outbreak of the Revolution of 1905 (see Chapter 18). Sazonov's first concern was to mobilize
French support against Austria-Hungary, believing that a united show of
strength would force the Central European allies to back down. From the
Russian point of view, if Austro-Hungarian influence expanded in the
Balkans, German influence would soon be manifest in the straits, because
a coup in Turkey in 1913 had brought the Ottoman Empire even closer to
Germany. French President Raymond Poincaré's state visit to Saint Peters-
burg from July 20 to July 23 seemed to indicate that France would stand by
Russia, and Sazonov received quick assurance from the French ambas-
sador of full French support.

On July 25, 1914, two days after the Austro-Hungarian ultimatum, the
tsar placed the Russian army on alert, a stage that would normally precede
mobilization. Such a step was fraught with consequences for the military
planners of each power. Mobilization meant preparing an army for war, calling up reserves, declaring martial law in frontier areas, readying the railways
for hauling troops and supplies, and accelerating the production of munitions. In these circumstances, a Russian decision to mobilize would be tan-
tamount to an act of war in the eyes of German military planners.

The Schlieffen Plan

Germany's plan for war against France had been drawn up in 1905 by
Count Alfred von Schlieffen (1833–1913), a former chief of the German
general staff. Based on the assumption that it would take Russia, France's
ally, several weeks to prepare its armies to fight, the Schlieffen Plan called
for the German armies to use a lightning attack to knock the French out of
the war. Then the German forces would be able to confront the Russian
army attacking in the east. The German attack on France would require its
forces to violate Belgian neutrality in order to bypass the sturdy fortifications the French had constructed on their eastern frontier after the

Franco-Prussian War of 1870–1871. German troops would march through the flat terrain of Belgium and the Netherlands, and turn south once the last soldier on the northern flank had brushed his sleeve against the English Channel. A pincer movement southward would encircle Paris from the northwest, and then turn to trap the French armies that had moved into Alsace-Lorraine. France would surrender. Schlieffen and his successors recognized that the plan would probably bring Great Britain into the war because that nation would never accept the violation of Belgian neutrality and the possible presence of an enemy power just across the Channel. But German commanders believed that the war on the continent would be over before the superior British navy could make a difference and that the small, volunteer British army posed little immediate threat. Then there would still be time to ship enough of the victorious army to the east to defeat the Russians as they rolled slowly toward Germany. This was the solution to Bismarck's nightmare, a simultaneous war on two fronts.

The French high command had its own plan for war. "Plan XVII" called for a rapid attack by two French armies into Alsace-Lorraine, as the Germans expected. With the bulk of the German army tied up by French and British troops in Belgium, and, at worst, northern France, the way to Berlin would be open. The French army was itching to redeem itself. Unlike Germany, which had to contemplate fighting a war on two fronts, the French army enjoyed the advantage of being able to focus its full attention on Germany. Marshal Joseph Joffre (1852–1931) had overseen French plans for the war. (When asked in 1911 if he thought about war, he replied, "Yes, I think about it all the time. We shall have a war, I will make it, and I will win it.") To the French high command, *élan,* or patriotic energy, was expected to bring victory: "The French army . . . no longer knows any other law than the offense," announced one of Joffre's disciples; "[we need only] to charge the enemy to destroy him." The French plan counted on the Russian army attacking Germany from the east by the sixteenth day of mobilization.

The British government suggested that, following Russian mobilization, the other powers help arrange a peaceful solution. Britain was unwilling to back Russia, a move that at this point might have made both Austria-Hungary and Germany consider backing down. The German government still assumed that the British would remain neutral in a war between France and Russia against Germany and Austria-Hungary.

The Russian government continued to believe that its resolute support for Serbia might well be enough to force Austria-Hungary to reconsider. Austria-Hungary and Germany were laboring under the same kind of illusion about Russia. Both believed that a show of unconditional support— Germany's "blank check" to Austria-Hungary—would force Russia to pull back. Yet Germany's aggressive support for its ally, combined with the bellicose prodding of the Russian government by the French ambassador, had just the opposite effect.

The Serb government therefore ordered military mobilization on July 25, 1914, confident of full Russian support. It then presented a formal reply to the Austro-Hungarian ultimatum just before the forty-eight hours had elapsed. It was surprisingly conciliatory. The Serbs accepted five of the demands without reservation; four others they would accept pending discussion and some further explanation. They rejected only one outright—that Austro-Hungarian representatives collaborate in the investigation of the Serb "plot" against the Habsburg Empire.

The Austro-Hungarian government viewed anything less than total compliance as unsatisfactory. It ordered military mobilization against Serbia, but stopped short of declaring war. The British again proposed a meeting of the powers in the hope of avoiding conflict in the Balkans, or at least keeping it limited to the Balkans. This the German government rejected, believing that Britain would not go to war unless it appeared that Germany was intending to conquer and absorb France.

"A Jolly Little War"

Austria-Hungary declared war on Serbia on July 28, 1914, exactly one month after the archduke's assassination. The declaration claimed an unsatisfactory Serb response to the Austro-Hungarian ultimatum, as well as an attack on Austro-Hungarian troops along the Bosnian frontier, an event that never took place. In a final attempt to avert war, British Foreign Secretary Edward Grey asked if Germany would participate in a last-ditch attempt to negotiate a settlement to the crisis. Germany accepted, but at the same time did nothing to try to forestall an Austro-Hungarian invasion of Serbia. If anything, Bethmann-Hollweg egged his ally on. In Saint Petersburg, the Austro-Hungarian declaration of war generated popular support for Serbia. An American diplomat reported tersely, "Whole country, all classes, unanimous for war."

On July 28, the same day as the Austro-Hungarian declaration of war, Bethmann-Hollweg sent a telegram to Vienna suggesting that its ally find a way to make it appear that, if a European war followed, it would be Russia's fault. And finally he warned that if Russia continued to support Serbia, Austria must stay the course, even if it led to war, or else forever renounce its status as a great power.

By the time the British cabinet discussed the Serb crisis on July 24, it was clear that Germany would not restrain Austria-Hungary. The Liberals, who had come to power in 1905, had long opposed entangling international alliances and large military expenditures, and they were divided over British intervention. Many Liberals and most Labourites disliked the idea of fighting alongside tsarist Russia. The government was beset by a number of pressing political issues, including the Home Rule Bill for Ireland—on July 16, British troops had fired on rioters in Dublin. The Royal Navy was placed on alert.

Bethmann-Hollweg now sent a sealed envelope to the German ambassador in Brussels, which was to be presented to the Belgian government when the order came. It contained a demand that German troops be allowed to march through Belgium. But, for the moment, there still seemed to be hope. William II sent a telegram to the tsar expressing his desire for peace. He signed it, "your very sincere and devoted friend and cousin, Willy."

Russian ministers and generals had debated since July 28 whether the crisis called for a limited mobilization of a million soldiers on the Polish and Galician frontiers, or a full mobilization. On July 29, word reached Saint Petersburg that the Austrians had bombarded Belgrade from the Danube. After twice changing his mind, Nicholas II ordered a full mobilization on July 30 for the following day. The tsar's diary entry for that day read: "After lunch, I received Sazonov. . . . I went for a walk by myself. The weather was hot. . . . I had a delightful bath in the sea." The Russian mobilization put an end to any hope for a negotiated settlement to the crisis. In Vienna, Francis Joseph declared general mobilization against Russia and Serbia.

A mood of anxious excitement prevailed in Paris. The army had already readied France's frontier defenses, but French troops were pulled back several kilometers from the frontier to avoid any incident with German units. In France, only the Socialist Party spoke out against the imminent outbreak of the international war. Many socialists still hoped that French and German workers would lay down their weapons and refuse to fire on fellow proletarians. Anti-militarism ran deep in some of France, not only because the army took sons away from farms, industrial work, and families, but also because the French government used the army to break strikes. The government maintained a list of socialists and other leaders of the left to be arrested in the event that war was declared.

In the meantime, the Russian and French ambassadors demanded assurance of British military support. The French ambassador even asked if the word "honor" would be stricken from British dictionaries if Britain refused to join France and Russia. Britain asked both Germany and France for a guarantee that Belgian neutrality (which had been accepted by Britain, France, Austria, Prussia, and Russia in 1839) would not be violated. Germany did not reply, Bethmann-Hollweg having earlier referred to the old guarantee as "a scrap of paper."

In Berlin, even the Social Democratic newspapers now accepted war as inevitable. Helmuth von Moltke (1848–1916), chief of the German general staff, pushed for an immediate attack on France, fearing that should Russian mobilization proceed any further, the Schlieffen Plan might fail. On July 31, 1914, Germany warned Russia to suspend mobilization at once. Germany demanded that France guarantee its neutrality in the event of a Russo-German war, and that German troops be allowed to occupy a number of French frontier forts as a show of French good faith. This no French government could accept. When no response was heard from either Russia or France, on August 1 the German army mobilized.

The relentless logic of the entangling alliances and military plans propelled Europe to war, as if the great powers were being pitched forward on an enormous wave. In Britain, Grey's frantic attempts to arrange a direct negotiation between Russia and Austria failed. The struggle of socialists in many countries to rally opposition against the war fell far short. On July 31, a rightist assassinated the popular French socialist leader Jean Jaurès. But Jaurès, too, had apparently just come to the conclusion that he should support the war against autocratic Germany. The Austrian socialist leader Victor Adler predicted: "Jaurès's murder is just the beginning. War unchains instincts, all forms of madness."

Of the powers, only Italy was not committed by alliance to fight, unless its allies in the Triple Alliance were attacked, and Italy could now reasonably claim that Austria-Hungary and Germany were launching hostilities. France ordered mobilization after receiving the impossible German demands. Germany declared war on Russia that same day, August 1. This obliged France, by virtue of its alliance with Russia, to fight Germany. German troops invaded Luxembourg, claiming falsely that a French attack on them was imminent and that they needed to seize the small duchy's railroads to defend themselves. On August 2, the German ambassador in Brussels handed the Belgian government the letter requesting permission to march armies through its territory. The negative reply came the next morning. Britain assured France that the Royal Navy would defend its Channel ports. On August 3, Germany declared war on France, falsely claiming that French planes had attacked Nuremberg. When Moltke's army marched into eastern Belgium and the German government ignored the British government's formal demand that they withdraw, Britain declared war on Germany on August 4, 1914. Enthusiastic crowds toasted departing soldiers in Paris and Berlin. The German crown prince anticipated "a jolly little war."

THE OUTBREAK OF WAR

When war was declared, eager commanders put long-standing military plans into effect. The German general staff counted on a rapid victory against France in the west before the giant Russian army could effectively be brought into action in the east. German troops outflanked French defenses by invading Belgium. However, this violation of Belgian neutrality brought Britain into the war on the side of France and Russia. Thus, the Great War pitted the Triple Alliance (Germany and Austria-Hungary, minus Italy, which for the moment remained neutral) against the Triple Entente (France, Great Britain, and Russia). These alignments had been shaped by the international tensions of the past decades.

(*Left*) French soldiers depart for war. (*Right*) British men surge toward a recruiting office.

Opening Hostilities

The Schlieffen Plan dictated the course of the opening hostilities. It was as if Schlieffen's "dead hand automatically pulled the trigger." However, Moltke had eliminated the Netherlands from the invasion plan and reduced the strength of the attacking force in order to bolster German defenses in Alsace-Lorraine. The French high command, which had known the basics of the Schlieffen Plan for years, did not believe the German army could move rapidly through Belgium, in part because the attacking forces would have to overcome the imposing fortress at Liège. The French also doubted that reserves incorporated into the German army could quickly become an able fighting force. In any case, the French command expected a frontal attack between the Meuse River and the hills of the Ardennes in northeastern France. The French generals also underestimated the speed with which their enemy could attack.

Although the Belgian army fought bravely against vastly superior strength, Liège fell on August 16 after a massive bombardment, followed by the fall of Namur. The Belgian army retreated north to Antwerp. Moltke then deployed seven divisions to prevent the Belgian army from escaping, further weakening the attacking forces that Schlieffen had anticipated would move as rapidly as possible toward the English Channel.

General Alexander von Kluck, commander of the First German Army, turned his troops toward the Belgian town of Mons. He hoped to force the French to surrender before they could bring up more troops from the Paris region. French advances in Alsace now convinced Moltke to divert troops to that border region from the primary attacking force, which intended to

Old and new combat in World War I.

encircle the French capital. Both the French and German high commands still considered success in Alsace critical to their strategies and to morale at home.

The British Expeditionary Force of 100,000 troops arrived to take its place on the French flank on August 20. One British soldier who went off to war in the summer of 1914 reassured his family, "At least the thing will be over in three weeks." But by August 24, the Allied (Entente) armies were rapidly retreating. At Mons and then Le Cateau, the British army fought its biggest battles since Waterloo in 1815. Yet retreat did not yet spell defeat. The Germans, fatigued by the pace of their march, also suffered from Moltke's indecision and inadequate communications. Kluck's army was already spread too thinly across a wide front. Now Moltke, surprised by the relatively rapid Russian mobilization and told of an early Russian victory on the eastern front, ordered four divisions to confront the surprisingly rapid Russian advance.

Nonetheless, the German armies managed to fight to within thirty-five miles of Paris (see Map 22.3). The French government provisionally withdrew to the safety of Bordeaux, just as they had been forced to do during the Franco-Prussian War. But despite heavy losses, Joffre was able to reinforce his defensive positions around Paris. This was in part possible because the French had concluded a secret treaty by which Italy, whose commitment to Germany and Austria-Hungary was defensive in nature, agreed to remain neutral if Germany attacked France. The German government, unaware of the treaty, still hoped Italy would join Germany and Austria-Hungary. Joffre

MAP 22.3 THE GERMAN ADVANCE, 1914   The Germans moved quickly into Belgium and France, largely following the Schlieffen Plan of 1905.

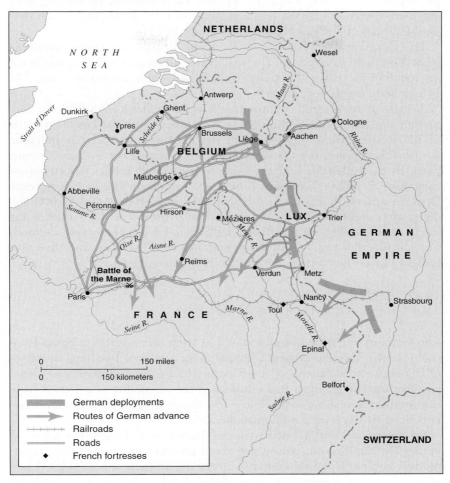

could thus count on troops that otherwise would have been needed in southeastern France to halt a possible Italian invasion.

At the dawn of air warfare, a French reconnaissance pilot noticed Kluck's army changing direction as it swept toward a point southeast of Paris, leaving its flank open. The French army rushed every available soldier into action, some arriving at the front in requisitioned Parisian taxis. When the Germans crossed the Marne River on September 5, the French counterattacked. Two German armies retreated, fearing that the French might take advantage of a sizable gap between their forces. It was the end of the Schlieffen Plan, and of the offensive war that the German generals had planned. The British poured through another gap between German armies, forcing the Germans to retreat forty miles to the Aisne River. There, on September 14, the Germans fortified their position by digging deep defensive trenches. Like the Battle of Valmy in 1792 during the French Revolution, the Battle of the Marne saved France in 1914.

The Germans then tried to outflank the British and French forces in what amounted to a race for the sea, as the Allied armies kept pace, holding much of Picardy and Flanders, before both sides ran out of space. The British and French, too, dug in.

A series of attacks and counterattacks in the fall took frightful tolls, with neither side able to break through. In November 1914, the last open battle of the western front was fought in the mud around Ypres in Belgium; British forces prevented the Germans from reaching the French Channel ports. By the end of the year, the German and French armies had combined casualties of 300,000 killed and 600,000 wounded. The British Seventh Division arrived in France in October with 400 officers and 12,000 soldiers; after eighteen days of fighting around Ypres, it had 44 officers and 2,336 men left. In a special British battalion of football players, originally brought together to play exhibition matches near the front and then sent to fight like everybody else, only 30 of 200 men survived.

THE CHANGING NATURE OF WAR

The German and Allied armies stared at each other across a broad front that reached from the English Channel to Switzerland. Two long, thin lines of trenches ended dreams of rapid victory based upon a mastery of offensive tactics. Few analysts had considered the possibility of a frozen front that would rarely move more than a few hundred yards in either direction and along which several million soldiers would die.

Besides trench warfare, new weapons dramatically changed the nature of battle. During the war, poison gas, hand grenades, flamethrowers, tanks, military airplanes, and submarines entered the arsenals of both sides. A new scale of warfare required an unparalleled, total mobilization of the home front to sustain the war effort.

Trench Warfare

Spades for digging trenches and rows of tangled barbed wire became more important than the rifle and bayonet, weapons of attack. Soldiers on both sides dug about 6,250 miles of trench in France. The front-line trenches were six to eight feet deep and about fifty yards to a mile apart. They were supplemented by support trenches several hundred yards to the rear and linked by communications trenches. Small fortress-like "strong points" held the line together even if part of the system was overrun. Sandbags and rows of barbed wire protected the trenches from attack. As the months passed in sectors where the front lines were immobile, the trenches became more elaborate, offering electricity and a certain minimal level of comfort. When there was no fighting, the soldiers confronted boredom. The French theater star Sarah Bernhardt, who had herself lost one leg to amputation (because of several bad falls) was carried on a stretcher near the front so she could entertain soldiers by reciting poetry. Some soldiers read voraciously to pass the time; the British poet Siegfried Sassoon was only half kidding when he remembered, "I didn't want to die, not before I'd finished reading *The Return of the Native* anyway." Since they were below ground, trenches offered soldiers some protection from rifle or pistol fire, but not from direct artillery hits. The periscope, sticking up from the trench below, provided the only safe way of looking across at the enemy lines without being shot by enemy snipers.

The front-line soldier lived amidst the thunder of barrages and the scream of falling shells. Persistent lice, mice, and enormous rats were his constant companions in the stagnant water of the trenches. So, for many, was venereal disease, contracted in the brothels near the front. A British soldier described a night in the trenches in January 1916:

> Lights out. Now the rats and the lice are the masters of the house. You can hear the rats nibbling, running, jumping, rushing from plank to plank, emitting their little squeals behind the dugout's corrugated metal. It's a noisy swarming activity that just won't stop. At any moment I expect one to land on my nose. And then it's the lice and fleas that begin to devour me. Absolutely impossible to get any shut-eye. Toward midnight I begin to doze off. A terrible racket makes me jump. Artillery fire, the cracking of rifle and machine-gun fire. The Boches [Germans] must be attacking. . . . Everything shakes. Our artillery thunders away without pause. . . . I doze off so as to get up at six. The rats and the lice get up too; waking to life is also waking to misery.

The cold and wind tore into the troops, especially in winter. "Before you can have a drink," one soldier wrote home, "you have to chip away the ice. The meat is frozen solid, the potatoes are bonded by ice, and even the hand grenades are welded together in their cases." The German army had been so sure of an easy victory that it had not equipped its men with high lace-up boots or adequate coats. German troops prized the British soldiers' sheepskin coats and removed them from enemy corpses when they had the chance. After battle, the screams of the wounded and dying filled the air; groans in German, French, and English from no-man's-land grew increasingly faint, but sometimes lasted for days.

Death was everywhere. It numbed. An Austrian soldier, a violinist, wrote: "A certain fierceness arises in you, an absolute indifference to anything the world holds except your duty of fighting. You are eating a crust of bread,

Paul Nash's *We Are Making a New World*, a tormented painting evoking the pockmarked landscape around Ypres in Flanders.

and a man is shot dead in the trench next to you. You look calmly at him for a moment, and then go on eating your bread. Why not? There is nothing to be done. In the end you talk of your own death with as little excitement as you would of a luncheon engagement." Hundreds of thousands of soldiers suffered shell shock, psychologically devastated by the battle raging around them.

On the western front, as both sides believed that a breakthrough was possible, massive attacks were preceded by an intensive bombardment of enemy positions. Such bombardments, lasting hours and even days, clearly indicated where the next attack could be expected, allowing the enemy to bring up sufficient reserves to prevent a breakthrough. Both sides adopted the use of "creeping barrages," which moved just ahead of the attacking army to soften resistance. The shelling mangled the terrain, leaving huge craters, thereby creating unanticipated obstacles to the attacking troops. The attackers then faced the most effective weapon of trench warfare, the machine gun—a defensive weapon that mowed down line after line of advancing soldiers carrying rifles, bayonets, and pistols that they often never had a chance to use.

Piles of the dead filled shell craters left by the first barrages. If attacking Allied troops managed to reach, take, and hold the first line of trenches, they confronted fresh reinforcements as well as an even more solid second line of defense. The defensive lines could bend, but then snap back against attacking forces that soon outran their cover. Joffre's second offensive in Champagne in 1915 illustrated this situation well. The French offensive ran right into the second line of defense, took enormous casualties, and

(*Left*) French soldiers wearing gas masks prepare to attack. (*Right*) Victims of a German gas attack lining up at a field hospital.

then faced a vigorous counterattack. The Germans lost 75,000 killed and wounded, the French 145,000, for not more than a few miles of ravaged land. Still, Joffre ordered another attack. The result was the same.

Soldiers also faced new, frightening perils. German attacks against British positions around Ypres featured a horrifying new weapon, mustard gas, which, carried by the wind, burned out the lungs of the British soldiers. A member of the British medical corps wrote, "I shall never forget the sights I saw by Ypres after the first gas attacks. Men lying all along the side of the road . . . exhausted, gasping, frothing yellow mucus from their mouths, their faces blue and distressed. It was dreadful, and so little could be done for them." The gas mask soon offered imperfect protection—"this pig snout which represented the war's true face," as one combatant put it.

War in the Air and on the Seas

Airplanes became weapons of combat. In the first months of the war, airplanes were only used for reconnaissance in good weather; in 1915, techniques evolved and pilots began to photograph enemy trenches. Some pilots kept carrier pigeons in a cage, so that, if they had to ditch their planes, they could scribble their approximate location on a paper and send the information back to headquarters with the bird. Pilots fired pistols and hurled hand grenades and even bricks at enemy planes and troops before both sides discovered that machine guns could be mounted and timed to fire between the blades of the plane's propellers.

By the end of 1916, dashing and brave "aces," such as the German Red Baron, Manfred von Richthofen, and beginning in 1917 the American Eddie Rickenbacker, chased each other around the skies in fighter planes, cheered on by the trench soldiers below. When Richthofen was shot down behind British lines in April 1918, he was buried by his enemies with full military honors. Although the "dogfights" of combat in the skies had a romantic dimension, the airplane soon began to terrorize civilians. Paris and London were bombed several times during the war, as the speed and capacity of the first warplanes increased; the Rhineland German cities suffered heavy bombardments later in the conflict. By the war's end, Germany had produced more than 47,000 aircraft, France more than 51,000, and Britain more than 55,000 planes.

With the European powers fighting a land war unlike any ever seen, and conflict having taken to the skies, the seas remained relatively quiet. The British navy retained control, and the famed and feared German dreadnoughts stayed in port. The British navy won a series of initial encounters as far afield as the coast of Chile, the Falkland Islands near Argentina, and the Indian Ocean. German battleships trapped in the Mediterranean at the beginning of the war took refuge in Constantinople and were turned over to the Turks. The German navy took them back when Turkey entered the war in November 1914 on the side of the Central Powers (Germany and Austria-Hungary). Turkey was again pitted against its old enemy, Russia. The Austro-Hungarian navy, based in Trieste, was small and its influence was limited to the Mediterranean. The British admiralty, which possessed the German code book—plucked from the Baltic Sea by Russian sailors—

German and British planes in a dogfight high above the trenches.

awaited a major confrontation. Certain that the German fleet was going to sail from Wilhelmshaven, the British Grand Fleet lay in wait. At Dogger Bank on January 24, 1915, the Royal Navy sunk a German battleship. The British blockaded the principal German ports, neutralizing the kaiser's proud fleet.

Late in the 1880s, several countries had experimented with underwater warfare. At the turn of the century, the U.S. Navy was the first to commission a submarine. Although all of the powers had submarines by the time of the Great War, those of Germany made the greatest impact. The German navy believed that its fleet of submarines, which brought another fearful dimension to warfare, could force Britain to pull out of the war by sinking its warships and by preventing supplies from reaching the British Isles from the United States. In September 1914, a German submarine, or "U-boat," sank three large British armored cruisers off the coast of Belgium. U-boats, 188 feet long and with a range of 2,400 miles, could slip in and out of ports undetected. Yet ships carrying supplies to Britain continued to get through.

The Home Front

The waging of war on such an unprecedented scale required the full support of the "home front," the very concept of which emerged during the war. Sustaining the massive war effort depended first on mobilizing enough soldiers and food to supply the front, and then on producing enough guns and shells. It also depended on maintaining morale at home. Popular enthusiasm increasingly fed on a deep hatred of the enemy. German propagandists portrayed the war as a fight for German culture, besieged by Russian barbarians and the dishonorable French. A German soldier wrote, "We know full well that we are fighting for the German idea in the world, that we are defending German feeling against Asiatic barbarism and Latin indifference." British propagandists depicted the Allies as defending law, liberty, and progress against German violations of national sovereignty and international law. French propagandists had the easiest case to make: Germany had, after all, invaded France.

Such propaganda mixed elements of myth and truth. By the end of 1914, false tales of Germans impaling children and raping nuns were horrifying British and French readers. The German high command had instructed officers to ignore provisions of the Hague Conventions that sought the humane treatment of soldiers and civilians during war, which Germany had signed. Rumors had spread that civilians had killed German soldiers. The German army executed 5,500 Belgian civilians in two months, including in Louvain, where troops panicked when they heard shots fired in the distance by French troops and mistook them for action by Belgian citizens. The Germans then burned the library of the University of Louvain, which included rare manuscripts, for good measure. Austrian soldiers massacred, mutilated, and raped villagers in Serbia, as did Russian troops in East Prussia and Galicia. These actions, reflecting the brutalization of war and the banalization of death, foreshadowed a new kind of war—a total war in which civilians were not spared.

At the outbreak of hostilities in Britain and France, shops owned by people with German-sounding names were pillaged (in the latter case, some victims were French Alsatians for whom the war, at least in part, was supposedly being fought). A publication for French schoolchildren told this story: "Your little brother in your presence has lied to your mother. You take him aside and tell him, 'Do you want to behave like the Krauts?'" The younger boy confesses, now understanding that "the French don't lie." A publication for girls informed them that "pillage is a German word." German propaganda similarly smeared their enemies, particularly the British, who supposedly used dum-dum bullets that exploded upon impact and gouged out the eyes of German prisoners.

The outbreak of the war pushed aside bitter political divisions at home. In France, competing parties proclaimed a "sacred union," and the socialist Jules Guesde became minister of commerce. There was little public criticism of the way the war was being run until later in the conflict when casualties mounted. In Germany, too, socialist opposition to militarism based on class solidarity quickly turned to patriotic support. In Russia, at least in the first few years, only the tsar's will seemed to matter. In Austria-Hungary, the ability of the imperial bureaucracy to supply its multinational army, the prestige of which had helped keep the Habsburg Empire together, seemed almost miraculous. Tensions between the empire's nationalities remained beneath the surface, at least in the war's early years.

A poster showing support from the home front.

In Britain, the angry quarrels over strategy among the generals, as well as between them and the cabinet, were well hidden from the public. A volunteer army was raised with remarkable enthusiasm and speed, aided by an effective recruitment poster sporting the face of Lord Horatio Kitchener, the secretary of war. On a single day in September 1914, 33,000 men joined up. By the end of the year, the British had 2 million men in uniform. The volunteer force that German Kaiser William II had called "a contemptible little army" fought very well. In 1916, Britain began military conscription.

David Lloyd George (1863–1945), the Liberal politician who headed the wartime Ministry of Munitions, skillfully oversaw the transition from peacetime to wartime industrial production, using the powers specified by the Munitions of War Act of May 1915. The act forbade strikes and provided for the requisition of skilled workers for labor in factories, which were converted to the production of war materiel. Supplying the front with shells alone was a monumental task. In the opening months of the war, 500 German trains crossed the Rhine every day to supply troops. The nineteen-day artillery barrage at the third Battle of Ypres in 1917 expended all shells carried to the front by 321 trains, the output of a year's work for 55,000 armament workers.

The war spurred other changes in daily life at home. As heavy drinking became more widespread, legislation restricted the operating hours of British pubs. Some complained that the war had brought Britain a loosening of morals, frivolous dress and dancing, and an increase in juvenile delinquency. Daylight savings time was introduced for the first time to conserve fuel. A successful campaign for voluntary rationing of essential commodities such as sugar allowed the British to avoid mandatory rationing until early 1917, when hoarding contributed to shortages. The government instituted a coupon system, but price controls on essential commodities served to ration food.

Suffragette leaders, who had put aside their campaign for women's right to vote, threw their support behind the war. Millicent Garrett Fawcett (1847–1929), a leading British feminist, appealed to the readers of a suffrage magazine: "Women, your country needs you. . . . Let us show ourselves worthy of Citizenship," proclaiming that she considered pacifism almost the equivalent of treason.

THE WAR RAGES ON

Early in 1915, the French general staff predicted that its army would break through the German lines. However French attacks in the spring in Champagne and then in Artois further north brought enormous casualties but little progress (see Map 22.4). A British assault at Neuve Chapelle on March 10 gained 1,000 yards at a cost of 13,000 casualties. The British lost almost 300,000 men in 1915 alone; the Germans, who had a much larger army, suffered at least 610,000 casualties. Both nations' casualties, however daunting, paled alongside those of the French, who suffered 1,292,000 killed and wounded in 1915. French infantrymen were not helped by the fact that their uniform pants were, at least in the early stages of the war, bright red, which could be more easily seen through the morning mists than the German gray.

Italy had remained neutral at the outbreak of the war but gave in to street demonstrations and entered the war on the Allied side through the secret Treaty of London, signed in April 1915. Britain and France held out as bait territories many Italian nationalists claimed as part of "Italian Irredenta" ("unredeemed lands"), including the Tyrol in the Alps and Istria along the

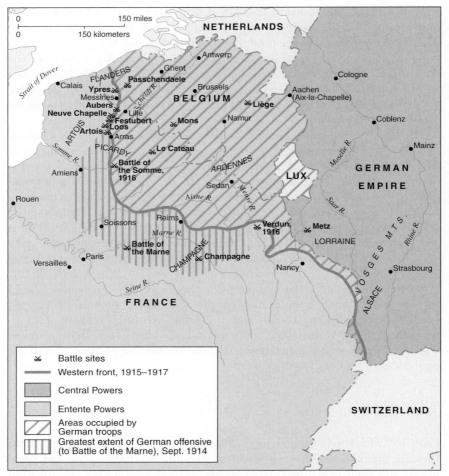

MAP 22.4 THE WESTERN FRONT, 1914–1917   Major battles from 1914–1917, and location of trenches at the end of 1915 and at the end of 1917.

northern Adriatic coast. Italian nationalism, as well as the desire of powerful Italian businessmen to find new markets in the Balkans, had proved stronger than Italy's pre-war commitment to its former allies. Austria-Hungary now found itself, like Germany, fighting a war on two fronts. The Italians attacked with the port of Trieste as their goal. The struggle between Britain and Turkey—which was also allied with the Central Powers—carried the war into the Middle East. Japan, coveting several German islands in the Pacific and the German naval base at Kiao-chao, and seeking sanction for its interest in northeastern China, entered the war on the Allied side in 1914. What began as a European war became a world war.

The Eastern Front

In the wide-open spaces of the eastern front, the Russian armies had advanced into eastern Prussia despite the incompetence of the Russian general staff, intense animosity among commanders, hopelessly archaic equipment, and communications so inadequate that the Germans could easily listen to Russian officers discussing tactics on the telephone. In late August 1914, German forces trapped a Russian army almost 200,000 strong at Tannenberg in East Prussia, killing, wounding, or capturing 125,000 soldiers. Two subsequent military victories ensured that Russian forces would remain outside of German territory for the duration of the war. On the more confident German side, sixty-seven-year-old General Paul von Hindenburg (1847–1934), a stolid Prussian who had been called out of retirement, and the determined General Erich Ludendorff (1865–1937) embellished their reputations in these battles.

The Austro-Hungarian army, which had no joint plan of military coordination with its German ally, found the huge Russian army an imposing foe. Too many divisions had been diverted to the punitive invasion of strategically unimportant Serbia. In September 1914, the Russians captured the fortress of Lemberg in Galicia from the Austro-Hungarian armies and took 100,000 prisoners (see Map 22.5). Many of these were conscripted Slavs who felt more allegiance to Russians, their fellow Slavs, than to their German-speaking officers.

In January 1915, the Habsburg forces launched an offensive against the Russian army in the Carpathian Mountains. Although the offensive looked good on a map, the reality was otherwise. Snow-covered mountains posed a daunting obstacle: supplies had to be moved over ice or freezing marsh; low clouds obscured artillery targets; and soldiers had to warm their rifles over fires before they could use them. When the Russians counterattacked, the Germans had to send troops to support their ally in the Carpathians, and as a result they lost over 350,000 men. With the stalemate in the west, the Germans wanted to defeat the Russians before the latter could vanquish the Habsburg army. In May 1915, a massive German attack drove the Russian army back almost 100 miles. The Russian retreat, which had been orderly in the beginning, turned into chaos. A million civilians moved eastward with the Russian armies. An observer remembered that "while thousands of people trudge along the railway lines they are passed by speeding trains loaded with couches from officers' clubs, and carrying quartermasters' bird cages." The Russian retreat from the Carpathian Mountains gave the Austro-Hungarian forces some badly needed breathing room. German forces reached Brest-Litovsk in August 1915, ending 100 years of Russian control of Poland.

MAP 22.5 THE EASTERN, ITALIAN, AND BALKAN FRONTS   Russian and Austro-German advances and battles along the eastern front; Austro-Hungarian and Italian armies face off along the Italian front; and Turkish and Allied armies clash on the Balkan front.

The War in the Middle East, Africa, and the Far East

British military and political leaders were divided between those who believed that victory would have to be won in the west, and others who pushed for a series of dramatic strikes against Germany or its allies on Europe's periphery. The latter included Winston Churchill (1874–1965), the First Lord of the Admiralty, and Lloyd George. Such victories might also even expand the British Empire, thus such a campaign would please the colonial lobby at home. This strategy angered the French government, which bitterly opposed any reduction of British support on the western front.

Churchill and Lord Kitchener planned an attack on Germany's ally, Turkey. When the Turks entered the war on the side of Germany and Austria-Hungary in November 1914, they closed off the Dardanelles strait, which separates the Aegean Sea from the Sea of Marmara. This cut off an important route for supplies to Russia through the Black Sea. Turkish forces also tied up Russian troops in the Caucasus Mountains. Turkey posed a potential threat to the Suez Canal. The British high command planned an assault on the Dardanelles strait. If everything went well, a British success might bring an end to the power of the pro-German faction in the Turkish government. Moreover, a successful campaign could open up a route to Russia through the Black Sea. With Turkey out of the war, Churchill reasoned, the German effort in the Balkans could be undermined, and Bulgaria would stay out of the conflict.

In April 1915, British ships sailed through the Dardanelles, destroyed several Turkish ships, and disembarked five divisions of troops on the beach of Gallipoli (see Map 22.5). British soldiers hurled themselves against the well-defended heights held by the Turks. British troops managed to dig in,

British troops massing during the ill-fated Gallipoli campaign.

and in August launched an assault that failed miserably. In the meantime, British, French, and German submarines were active during the campaign, forcing both sides to adapt supply tactics to the new threat. After committing more than 400,000 men, half of whom were killed or wounded, the British were fortunate to evacuate their remaining forces in January 1916. Amid harsh criticism of the campaign's humiliating failure, Churchill and Kitchener lost influence. To this day, the Gallipoli Campaign remains controversial. Some historians consider it an imaginative, even brilliant stroke that might have won the war. Others agree with most contemporaries who believed that it was a needless diversion dictated by British colonial interests in the Middle East and for which Australian and New Zealander troops paid a disproportionate price.

Still hoping to knock Turkey out of the war, the Allies tried to coax Bulgaria into the war on their side. But in October 1915 Bulgaria joined the Central Powers, who promised Bulgaria all of Macedonia, which the Allies could not because of Serb claims there, as well as much of Thrace. Austro-Hungarian and Bulgarian forces thus controlled an important part of the Balkans. A month later, a Franco-British force landed in Salonika, Greece, to try to aid Serb troops. But within two months, the German, Austro-Hungarian, and Bulgarian armies had crushed the Serb army, which by 1916 had suffered 100,000 deaths of the 450,000 men serving in 1914. The Germans called Salonika their "largest internment camp," since that campaign tied up half a million Allied troops fighting the Bulgarians. In the meantime, British troops fought a desert war against the Turks in Palestine and Mesopotamia.

Smaller British forces were occupied fighting for the German colonies in Africa (see Map 22.6). German Togoland fell in August 1914, German Southwest Africa in 1915, and the German Cameroons in 1916. In German East Africa (Tanganyika), combat continued for the duration of the war, pitting German troops against British and South African soldiers, and both sides against mosquitoes and disease. In Asia, Japanese forces captured the fortress and port of Tsingtao (Qingdao) from a German garrison, and seized the undefended German islands of the Marianas, Carolines, and Marshalls in the North Pacific.

The Western Front

Following Gallipoli, the British again focused on the western front. Southern England was so close to this front that officers who had lunch in private railroad cars before leaving Victoria Station could be at the front—and perhaps dead—by dinner. When British miners managed to blow up a previously unconquerable ridge near Messines in western Belgium, it was said that the explosion could be heard in Kent.

General Douglas Haig (1861–1928) was named commander in chief of the British army in France in December 1915. He agreed with Joffre's plan

MAP 22.6 THE WORLD WAR The expansion of the war beyond Europe to the German colonies in Africa and the Far East.

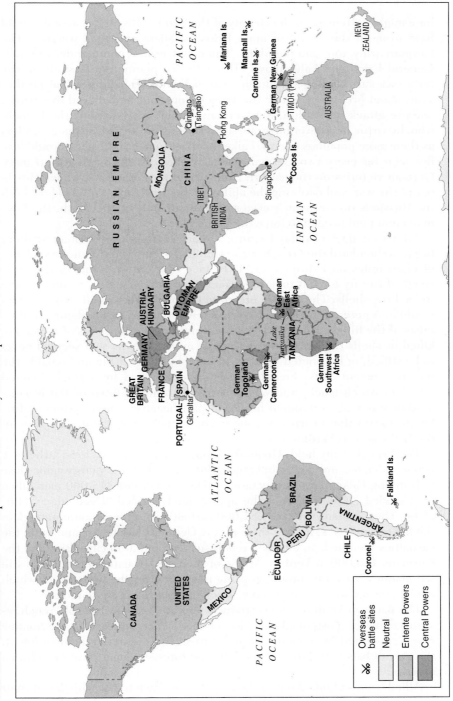

Legend:
- ⚔ Overseas battle sites
- Neutral
- Entente Powers
- Central Powers

Labels on map:
PACIFIC OCEAN
NEW ZEALAND
AUSTRALIA
Mariana Is.
Marshall Is.
Caroline Is.
German New Guinea
TIMOR (Port.)
Cocos Is.
Singapore
INDIAN OCEAN
Qingdao (Tsingtao)
Hong Kong
CHINA
MONGOLIA
TIBET
BRITISH INDIA
RUSSIAN EMPIRE
AUSTRIA-HUNGARY
BULGARIA
OTTOMAN EMPIRE
GERMANY
FRANCE
GREAT BRITAIN
PORTUGAL SPAIN
Gibraltar
German Togoland
German Cameroons
German East Africa
Lake Tanganyika
TANZANIA
German Southwest Africa
ATLANTIC OCEAN
BRAZIL
BOLIVIA
ARGENTINA
PERU
ECUADOR
CHILE
Coronel
Falkland Is.
CANADA
UNITED STATES
MEXICO
PACIFIC OCEAN

for a mighty offensive in the vicinity of the Somme River. The assault would have to await the arrival of more British soldiers and good weather. The German army, too, had big plans. The new German commander in chief, General Erich von Falkenhayn (1861–1922), planned an assault on the fortresses surrounding Verdun in eastern France. Falkenhayn had no illusions about breaking through the French lines, but he believed that with a massive attack on Verdun, the Germans could "out-attrition" the French, who, by virtue of a lower birthrate, could not afford to lose as many soldiers as their more populous enemy. Falkenhayn assumed that France would lose five men for every two German soldiers killed. Realizing that even more German victories on the eastern front would not necessarily knock Russia out of the war, and doubting the ability of Austria-Hungary to hold off both the Russians on Germany's eastern front and Italy in the south, the German command needed to force the French to sue for peace.

After nine days of delay because of bad weather, the German artillery began to bombard the French forts stretched around Verdun across a front of eight miles on February 21, 1916 (see Map 22.4). Some of the guns weighed twenty tons; it took nine tractors to move each piece and a crane to load the shells. The French prepared to hold Verdun at all costs. Its loss would be a potentially mortal blow to French morale. In the damp, chilling mists of the hills northeast of Verdun, hundreds of thousands of men died, killed by shells that rained from the sky, machine guns that seemed never to be stilled, or bayoneted in hand-to-hand fighting within and outside the massive cement forts. French troops were supplied by a single "sacred road" on which trucks and wagons arrived from the town of Bar-le-Duc. Verdun was truly a national battle, in part because a new system of furloughs meant that nearly everyone in the French army spent some time in the hell that was Verdun.

The French army held. General Philippe Pétain (1856–1951), the new commander, became a hero in France. But the cost of this victory came close to fulfilling Falkenhayn's expectations. The French lost 315,000 men killed or wounded; 90,000 died at the appropriately named "Dead Man's Hill" alone. The Germans suffered 281,000 casualties. A French counterattack in the fall recaptured several of the forts the Germans had taken, and again the casualties mounted. In all, the French suffered 540,000 casualties and the Germans 430,000 at Verdun. At one of the forts, Douaumont, one can still see plaques put up by proud, grieving relatives after the war, one of which reads, "For my son. Since his eyes closed mine have not ceased to cry."

The Battle of Verdun, while extremely important as a symbol of French resistance, merely postponed plans for a huge British offensive on the Somme River, supported by a similar French thrust. After a week's bombardment, the assault began on July 1 in the hills and forests along a front of eighteen miles.

Allied troops climbed out of the trenches at dawn to the whistles of their officers and moved into no-man's-land. Artillery barrages had chopped up the terrain over which the attackers had to struggle but left intact most of the German barbed wire, too strong for British wire cutters. German machine gun emplacements had also survived the barrage. Many British soldiers managed only a few yards before being hit, falling with the sixty-six pounds of equipment they were carrying. A captain sought to inspire his men by jumping out of the trench and leading the attack by dribbling a soccer ball across no-man's-land. He was shot dead far from the goal. The Germans moved up reserves to wherever their lines were bending. The British commanders sent wave after wave of infantrymen "over the top" to their death; corpses piled up on top of those who had died seconds, minutes, or hours before. Of 752 men in the First Newfoundland Regiment, all 26 officers and 658 men were killed or wounded within forty minutes. Sixty percent of the Tenth Battalion of the West Yorkshires died in the initial assault. At the end of the first day of the Battle of the Somme, about 60,000 soldiers of the 110,000 British soldiers had become casualties, including 19,000 killed. (There were more British soldiers killed and wounded in the first three days of the Battle of the Somme than Americans killed in World War I, the Korean War, and the Vietnam War combined, and three times more killed than in fifteen years of war against Napoleon.)

When the disastrous offensive finally ended in mid-November 1916, Britain had lost 420,000 men killed and wounded. The French lost 200,000 men in what was primarily a British offensive. It cost the Germans 650,000 soldiers to hold on. This was almost 200,000 casualties more than at Verdun. Such losses helped convince the German high command that only a campaign of unrestricted submarine warfare against ships supplying Britain might bring victory. Yet the maximum German retreat was a few kilometers; in most places, Allied gains were measured in yards. A sign left over one mass grave said, "The Devonshires held this trench, the Devonshires hold it still." The British poet Edmund Blunden, who survived the Battle of the Somme, tried to answer the question of who had won: "By the end of the [first] day both sides had seen, in a sad scrawl of broken earth and murdered men, the answer to the question. No road. No thoroughfare. Neither race had won, nor could win, the War. The War had won, and would go on winning."

Futility and Stalemate

Futility and stalemate also prevailed on the mountainous Austro-Italian front, where in 1916 there were *twelve* different Battles of the Isonzo River, where the Habsburg armies had well-developed defensive positions. The Italian army considered one of these, the sixth, a great victory because it moved three miles forward. After half a million casualties, the Italians were still only halfway to Trieste. In the twelfth Battle of Isonzo in 1917—more widely known as that of Caporetto 1917—Austro-Hungarian and German forces broke through the Italian lines, capturing more than 250,000 troops.

British soldiers wearing gas masks firing a machine gun during the Battle of the Somme, 1916.

On the eastern front, General Paul von Hindenburg claimed that there was no way of gauging the number of Russians killed with any accuracy: "All we do know is that, at times, fighting the Russians, we had to remove the piles of enemy bodies from before our trenches, so as to get a clear field of fire against new waves of assault." In June 1916, the Russian offensive pushed back the Austrians by combining smaller surprise attacks by specially trained troops, without the preliminary barrages, against carefully chosen targets. But the arrival of more German troops minimized Russian gains. Each side lost more than 1 million men in these encounters.

In 1916, the British poet Isaac Rosenberg, who would later be killed in the war, wrote "Break of Day in the Trenches," one of the most haunting poems to come out of the war.

The darkness crumbles away.
It is the same old druid Time as ever,
Only a live thing leaps my hand,
A queer sardonic rat,
As I pull the parapet's poppy
To stick behind my ear.
Droll rat, they would shoot you if they knew
Your cosmopolitan sympathies.
Now you have touched this English hand
You will do the same to a German
Soon, no doubt, if it be your pleasure

To cross the sleeping green between.
It seems you inwardly grin as you pass
Strong eyes, fine limbs, haughty athletes,
Less chance than you for life,
Bonds to the whims of murder,
Sprawled in the bowels of the earth,
The torn fields of France.
What do you see in our eyes
At the shrieking iron and flame
Hurled through still heavens?
What quaver—what heart aghast?
Poppies whose roots are in man's veins
Drop, and are ever dropping;
But mine in my ear is safe—
Just a little white with the dust.

The winter of 1916–1917 was bleak. There seemed few families on either side who had not lost a relative or friend at the front. On the Allied side, there was some cheer when Romania joined the war in exchange for the promise of some Hungarian territory with a significant Romanian population once the Central Powers had been defeated. But Falkenhayn, removed from the western front in disgrace after Verdun, quickly defeated the Romanian army. The war eroded the resources and morale of Bulgaria and Turkey. In December 1916, both states issued declarations expressing willingness to discuss terms for peace. The following March, Emperor Charles I (ruled 1916–1918) of the Austro-Hungarian Empire, who assumed the throne after Francis Joseph's death in November 1916, sent the Allies a peace proposal, without having consulted Germany. It included a willingness to recognize French claims to Alsace-Lorraine. But talk of a compromise peace was hushed and, at least in Vienna, deemed unpatriotic.

Unlike the French and British, the Germans realized that victory by breakthrough was extremely unlikely, if not impossible. To the Allies, a compromise peace seemed out of the question given that enemy troops were occupying much of the north of France. The complete withdrawal of German troops required a total victory that would guarantee France's future security. Increasingly criticized for the staggering casualty rate, Joffre was replaced by General Robert Nivelle (1856–1924) as commander in chief of the French forces in 1916. Nivelle insisted that a breakthrough on the western front could be achieved.

In Britain, Lloyd George became prime minister in December 1916. Even after staggering losses on the Somme, he agreed with British commanders that military victory was possible if the Allies cooperated more closely. The British government thus rejected a peace note sent by Germany on December 12, the aim of which was to force an end to the war by splitting apart Britain and France.

Soldiers and Civilians

In some ways, life in Britain and in the other combatant powers seemed to go on as before, which increasingly outraged soldiers returning from the front. Elegantly dressed people of means dining in the finest restaurants or watching the races at Derby and Ascot contrasted dramatically with the returning trainloads of badly wounded soldiers, and with the rationing of coal and food. A newspaper headline in 1917 gave equal emphasis to its two lead stories: "Battle Raging At Ypres. Gatwick Racing—Late Wire." Some big businessmen found the war very profitable, amassing fortunes on war supplies: Anglo-Persian Oil, which had lost money in 1914, enjoyed profits of 85 million pounds in 1916, 344 million in 1917, and over 1 billion in 1918. Profits of rubber companies increased fourfold.

In every belligerent country, women made contributions to the war. Nurses served courageously at the front and were acclaimed as heroines. Women took over many of the jobs of men who left to fight, or who had been wounded or killed. These included the enormous, back-breaking tasks of working the land. Over 1 million British women stepped into jobs from which they had previously been excluded, ranging from skilled and semi-skilled jobs in munitions factories ("Shells made by a wife may save a husband's life" went one poster in Britain) to positions as tram conductors and

Russian sharpshooters in a trench on the eastern front.

gas-meter readers. A visitor to Berlin in March 1916 reported "no men any-where, women are doing everything."

But women workers, as in the past, received lower wages than their male counterparts, allowing many employers to reduce expenses and increase their profits. In France and Austria, women workers struck in 1917 and 1918 to protest working conditions. Everywhere, shortages and economic hardship made women's tasks of managing the household economy that much more difficult, including standing in line for hours at stores. Crowds of women demonstrated against high prices in Italy in 1917.

Censorship, particularly in the first year, prevented the population from knowing about the staggering death tolls, or about the strategic blunders of the generals. "The war, for all its devastating appearances, only seems to be destructive," one Parisian newspaper assured its readers in November 1914, and in July 1915 it asserted that "at least [those killed by German bayonets] will have died a beautiful death, in noble battle . . . with cold steel, we shall rediscover poetry . . . epic and chivalrous jousting." Other papers emphati-cally related that "half the German shells are made of cardboard, they don't even burst," and that "Boche corpses smell worse than [those of the] French."

The British poet Robert Graves wrote that "England looked strange to us soldiers. We could not understand the war-madness that ran wild every-where. . . . The civilians talked a foreign language; and it was newspaper lan-guage." Lord Northcliffe, the press baron named by the British government to provide the public with reports of the war, described the trenches, "where health is so good and indigestion hardly ever heard of. The open-air life, the regular and plenteous feeding, the exercise, and the freedom from care and responsibility, keep the soldiers extraordinarily fit and contented." A French newspaper headline in December 1916 read, preposterously enough, "Among the many victims of gas, there is hardly a single death." A French captain wrote to protest newspaper accounts of heroic fighting and glorious death on the battlefield: "How does [the civilian] picture us combatants? Does he really believe we spend our time brandishing great swords with heroic ges-tures and yelling 'Long live France!' at the top of our lungs? When will these ladies and gentlemen in civilian life spare us their fantasies?"

The men in the trenches forged close bonds with those with whom they served. They bitterly resented senior officers who barked out deadly orders from the safety of requisitioned châteaux behind the front lines, and they detested government propagandists and censors. On leave, soldiers headed together to music halls, cabarets, and bars, hoping to forget a war they felt uncomfortable trying to describe to civilians who knew so little about it.

More than this, embittered soldiers occasionally felt more sympathy for those in the opposite trenches than for the politicians and generals at home. On Christmas Day, 1914, on the western front in France, German and British soldiers spontaneously declared their own one-day truce, some meeting in no-man's-land to exchange greetings, souvenirs, and even home addresses. In one or two places, soldiers from both sides played soccer.

A year later, a British soldier was executed for ignoring orders that such an event was not to recur. There were even occasional informal arrangements between units that had been facing each other across no-man's-land for several months, agreeing not to fire during mealtimes, or entertaining each other in verse or song. A British writer later recalled calmly discussing Nietzsche with a German he had captured just minutes after almost killing him. One prevalent rumor in both trenches had an entire regiment of German, French, and British deserters living under no-man's-land in tunnels, coming out only at night to rob corpses and steal food and drink from both sides. They, many soldiers said, were the lucky ones.

It was impossible to hide the effects of the war. In all combatant countries, women in mourning clothes were an increasingly frequent sight, clutching telegrams that began, "Be proud of X, who has just died like a brave man. . . ." Illegitimate births rose rapidly. In Germany, state governments, except for that of Prussia, for the first time allowed "illegitimate" birth certificates and gave unmarried or widowed women the right to call themselves *Frau* (Mrs.) instead of *Fraulein* (Miss).

As casualties mounted and the fighting ground on, opposition to the war emerged, particularly in Britain. Elsewhere in Britain, a relatively small number of pacifists and conscientious objectors protested against the war. Some of them were prosecuted and imprisoned. In 1916, when Britain adopted military conscription, pacifists became more vocal. In *No Conscription Leaflet No. 3,* the writer Lytton Strachey (1880–1932) warned, "The Cat kept saying to the Mouse that she was a high-minded person, and if the Mouse would only come a little nearer they could both get the cheese. The Mouse said, Thank you, Pussy, it's not the cheese you want, it's my skin."

Irish Republicans opposed Britain in order to gain Ireland's independence. The Germans encouraged Irish Republican preparations for an insurrection in Dublin set for Easter Sunday, 1916. Sir Roger Casement (1864–1916), an Irish nationalist who had denounced the brutal conditions under which indigenous laborers worked in imperial colonies, tried to form an Irish Legion and urged the Germans to send military assistance to those working for independence in Ireland. But seeing that the Germans had no plans to offer substantial help, he landed on the Irish coast with the help of a German submarine with the goal of convincing Irish Republicans to call off the insurrection, but was arrested immediately. The Easter Rising went ahead, but ended in dismal failure after five days of bloody fighting with 450 insurgents killed. Casement was among those executed, traitor to the British, hero to many Irish.

In Germany, Clara Zetkin (1857–1933), a militant socialist, went to jail because she refused to stop denouncing the war and tried to mobilize working-class women against a struggle between capitalist states that pitted worker against worker. Rosa Luxemburg, a Polish socialist living in Germany, also went to prison for her efforts to turn more members of her party against the war.

When Dutch socialists initiated a peace conference in Stockholm in December 1917, Britain prohibited British citizens from attending. The poet Siegfried Sassoon, wounded at the front, returned to England and publicly declared, "I believe the War is being deliberately prolonged by those who have the power to end it. I am a soldier, convinced that I am acting on behalf of soldiers." After being incarcerated in a mental asylum, he returned to the front because of his allegiance to his comrades. There he was wounded again.

In the meantime, the French government faced different problems on the home front than those confronting Britain. The German armies occupied some of France's richest agricultural land and industrial centers of the north and northeast. Refugees from the war zone arrived in Paris and, increasingly, the south carrying their remaining possessions. But the French home front held together, despite ebbs and flows in morale as the war went on and on. Although there was grumbling about peasants who profited from price rises for commodities, or about specialist workers exempt from conscription because munitions factories required their skills, and about other "shirkers" who escaped service, there were relatively few signs of opposition to the war in France, particularly early on. The government's decision in the war's first month to provide some financial assistance to families with husbands, brothers, and sons in uniform was popular. The French gradually adapted to the war. With the German army deep inside France, close to Paris, capitulation was unthinkable, as was even a negotiated settlement.

The German home front also held together. Posters showed an ogre-like British "John Bull" with the caption "This man is responsible for your hunger." However, in 1917 signs of war weariness increased as casualties reached astronomic levels and rumors spread that the campaign of unrestricted submarine warfare against the Allies was failing. Open criticism of

Berliners hunt for food.

officials became more common. In July, the Reichstag passed a resolution by a large majority asking the government to repudiate a policy of annexation and commit itself to seeking a peace of reconciliation. But the Reichstag had little influence in what amounted to a military government. In Germany, when William III dismissed Chancellor Bethmann-Hollweg in 1917, he gave Generals Hindenburg and Ludendorff even more power.

THE FINAL STAGES OF THE WAR

In 1917, two events of great consequence changed the course of the war. Reacting in part to the German campaign of unrestricted submarine warfare against Allied shipping, the United States entered the war in April on the Allied side. And Russia, where the February Revolution toppled the tsar (see Chapter 23), withdrew from the war after the Bolsheviks seized power in October. Meanwhile, the French armies seemed on the verge of collapse. Widespread mutinies occurred. And a massive German offensive that began in March 1918 pushed Allied forces back farther than they had been since 1914, before grinding to a halt in the face of stiff resistance. The stage was set for the final phase of the war.

The United States Enters the War

In 1916, Woodrow Wilson had been re-elected president of the United States on the platform "He kept us out of war." The U.S. government had adopted a declaration of neutrality, but American popular sympathy generally lay with the Allies, even though the German government tried to capitalize on American resentment of the British blockade, which entailed searches of American ships. U.S. bankers made profitable loans to both sides, but far more funds went to the Allies than to the Central Powers.

On May 7, 1915, a German submarine sank the British cruise liner *Lusitania* off the coast of Ireland. The ship was, despite U.S. denials, carrying American-made ammunition to Britain; 128 U.S. citizens were among the almost 1,200 killed. The United States, already outraged by the recent German introduction of mustard gas into combat, protested vigorously, and on September 1 the German government accepted the American demand that it abandon the unrestricted submarine warfare. Germany, wanting to keep the United States neutral, adopted a policy of warning liners before sinking them, providing for the safety of the passengers.

The fact remained that only with submarines could Germany prevent Britain from maintaining total control of the high seas. In 1916, the German fleet left port to challenge the British Royal Navy. The German admiralty hoped to entice part of the main British fleet into a trap by offering a smaller fleet as a target off the Norwegian coast. German submarines lay in wait, along with a sizeable surface fleet. The British, who had broken the German code, hoped to have the last laugh when the entire Grand Fleet suddenly appeared. The German and British fleets stumbled into each other off the coast of Denmark, in the Battle of Jutland, May 31–June 1, 1916. In a heavy exchange of gunfire, the British lost fourteen ships and about 6,000 men; eleven German ships were sunk and about 1,500 men were killed. Both sides claimed victory, but British losses were heavier, surprising and embarrassing British naval leaders (such that one admiral turned to a junior officer and stammered, "Chatfield, there seems to be something wrong with our bloody ships today!"). Yet in the end, it was the German fleet that fled, leaving the Royal Navy in control of the seas for the duration of the war.

The continuing success of the British blockade led Germany to announce on February 1, 1917, that its submarines would attack any ship in "war zones." In March 1916, the U.S. government had forcefully protested the sinking of the British ship *Sussex* in the English Channel, with the loss of American lives. Germany agreed to the "*Sussex* pledge," reaffirming the agreement to give up unrestricted submarine warfare. But pressure came from the German high command to turn loose the submarine fleet, now 120 strong, as the only hope for knocking Britain out of the war. This was a calculated risk, like the invasion of Belgium in 1914, because it would surely entail American intervention. Two weeks earlier, the United States had intercepted a coded telegram from the German foreign secretary, Arthur

(*Left*) Allied tanks stuck in the mud. (*Right*) A German U-boat surfaces.

Zimmermann, to his ambassador to Mexico. The "Zimmermann telegram" brazenly offered Mexico German help in taking back the states of Texas, Arizona, and New Mexico if it would go to war against its powerful northern neighbor. With more Americans killed in submarine attacks, Wilson used the telegram to bolster support for a declaration of war on April 6, 1917. Wilson promised a war that would "make the world safe for democracy." The United States turned its industrial might toward wartime production and drafted and trained an army that reached 4 million, of which half was in France by November 1918. The entry of the United States into the war tipped the balance fatally against Germany.

During 1917, German submarines sank one-fourth of all ships sailing to Britain. Half a million tons of shipping were sunk in February, three-quarters of a million in March, and nearly 1 million tons in April, when 350 British ships were sunk. But in the midst of despair, the British admiralty discovered that heavily escorted convoys could get through. Submerged mines at the entrances to the Channel also helped reduce the German U-boat threat. Within a few months, the first American troops reached the continent, along with a steady stream of military supplies.

Russia Withdraws from the War

The second remarkable event of 1917 was the Russian Revolution. The eastern front had stabilized following the Russian offensive at the end of 1916, as the Russian and Austro-Hungarian armies were depleted and exhausted. The Russian home front seemed on the verge of collapse. In February 1917, amid a chorus of demands for political reform, strikes and bread riots in Petrograd spread rapidly. Tsar Nicholas II abdicated on March 15. The head of the provisional government, Alexander Kerensky (1881–1970), had no intention of abandoning the war effort, and he ordered the commander in chief to launch another offensive on July 1. But "peace, land, and bread" became the motto of the soldiers. Many deserted or refused to obey their officers. Within a matter of weeks, a German counterattack pushed the Russians back nearly 100 miles.

As the Russian provisional government faced opposition from many sides, the Bolsheviks aimed to seize power and then take Russia out of the war as quickly as possible. They expected revolutions to break out in other countries as well, beginning with Germany. The German government desperately wanted to force the Russian provisional government to make peace as soon as possible, so that the German high command could turn its full attention to the western front before the American entry into the war could turn the tide. With this in mind, they allowed exiled Bolshevik leader Vladimir Lenin (1870–1924) to return to Russia from neutral Switzerland through Germany and Finland.

On November 6 (October 24 by the Old Russian calendar), the Bolsheviks overthrew the provisional government. The German army, facing little opposition, had captured Riga, the fortified capital of Latvia, and was advancing along the Baltic coast. The Germans were happy to comply with Lenin's request for an immediate armistice. In return, the German government wanted the revolutionary government to agree to the independence of Finland, Poland, Galicia, Moldavia, and the Baltic states of Estonia, Latvia, and Lithuania. Their goal was to create a series of small buffer states between Germany and Russia that they could dominate. The Allies understandably worried that such a peace between Germany and Russia would make it difficult to obtain peace in the west, as the German army could devote all its attention to that front.

The French and British governments feared the effect Russia's withdrawal from the war, in the wake of a revolution, might have on workers and socialists at home, as well as on the war's outcome. French Prime Minister Georges Clemenceau and British Prime Minister Lloyd George denounced the Bolsheviks, but relatively few people in Russia wanted the war to continue. In December, the Bolsheviks unilaterally declared the war over and signed a temporary armistice with Germany. When the revolutionary Russian government did not agree to the German terms for a formal armistice, the German armies marched into the Russian heartland. They reached the Gulf of Finland—only 150 miles from Petrograd—as well as the Crimean peninsula in the south, and advanced far into Ukraine. The Germans then offered a cessation of hostilities in return for virtually all Russian war materiel they could carry with them. They also again demanded the independence of the border states of the Russian Empire. The Bolsheviks abandoned Russian claims on Poland, Ukraine, and what would become Estonia, Latvia, and Lithuania. In March 1918, the Treaty of Brest-Litovsk officially ended Russian participation in the war.

Offensives and Mutinies

The year 1917 brought another major Allied offensive in the west. General Nivelle of France convinced his British counterpart in February that the long-awaited knockout punch was at last possible if a British attack would divert German forces along the Aisne River. But the British attack ran headlong into the impenetrable German second line of defense, the "Hindenburg Line." On April 16, Nivelle sent 1.2 million soldiers into battle along the Aisne River in miserable weather. Allied tanks, which had been introduced into battle for the first time in 1916, became stuck in the mud or in shell craters. Ten days later, French losses totaled 34,000 dead, 90,000 wounded, and 20,000 missing. Soldiers sang, "If you want to find the old battalion, I know where they are, I know where they are—They're hanging on the old barbed wire. I've seen 'em, I've seen 'em, Hanging on the old barbed wire." Nivelle again promised the increasingly anxious government in Paris that the breakthrough was just around the corner. More troops were sent into the meat grinder.

For the first time, soldiers resisted. Some French regiments were heard "baaing" like sheep led to the slaughterhouse as they marched past their commanding officers. On May 3, mutinies broke out. By the end of the month, they had spread to other regiments, even though soldiers who refused to go over the top knew they could be summarily shot. They reasoned that they were going to die anyway. Some regiments elected spokesmen, who declared that they would defend the trenches against German attacks, but would not participate in any more foolish assaults. The mutinies affected half of the French divisions along the western front, and at the beginning of June, only two of twelve divisions holding the line in Champagne had been unaffected. More than 21,000 French soldiers deserted in 1917.

Some soldiers were summarily shot where the officers retained the upper hand; 23,000 others were court-martialed, 432 sentenced to death, and 55 executed. Some generals blamed socialist "agitators" and peace propaganda. General Pétain, the hero of Verdun, knew otherwise, and at least tried to improve the conditions of daily life for the soldiers. The Nivelle offensive ground to a halt.

In the meantime, Haig planned another British offensive around Ypres, the "fields of Flanders." The goal was to push the Germans back from the coast to Ghent. Haig had not bothered to inspect the front himself, nor did he pay attention to the pessimistic reports of his intelligence staff. He had not reported estimates of German troop strength to the war cabinet in London. The battle began in heavy rain; the preliminary barrage turned the chalky soil into something like the consistency of quicksand. In the Battle of Passchendaele ("They died in hell, they called it Passchendaele"), named after a devastated village, the British gained four miles in exchange for 300,000 dead or wounded. One soldier determined that, in view of such gains, it would take 180 years to get to the Rhine River. The offensive ended. Haig kept his command.

Morale plunged during the winter in Germany and France. A writer was surprised to see a soldier who had lost an arm drunkenly begging on a Parisian boulevard, muttering, "Peace, Peace." Shortages became worse, rationing more vexing. Occasionally, in the south of France were heard sarcastic references to "Paris's war," or to the blond refugees from the embattled northern departments known as "the Krauts (*boches*) of the North." The French armaments minister faced shouts of "Down with the War!" when he visited a factory. There were waves of strikes in 1917. But Georges Clemenceau rallied the war effort after again becoming prime minister. He used troops against strikers, as he had before the war. He ordered the arrest of those calling for peace without victory, including his minister of the interior. A cartoon in Britain—unthinkable until 1917—pictured the encounter of two enlisted soldiers at the front. One said, " 'Ow long you up for, Bill?" "Seven years," was the reply, to which the first soldier said, "You're lucky—I'm duration."

Compounding this bleak picture for the Allies was a combined Austrian and German offensive in Italy, strengthened by the arrival of German troops from the Russian front. They pushed the Italian army back seventy-five miles in the Battle of Caporetto on the Isonzo River in October 1917, taking three-quarters of a million prisoners. Despite 200,000 casualties and twice that many desertions, the Italians held along the Piave River, just twenty miles from Venice. The Allies coordinated their war efforts. In October 1917, they established a Supreme War Council, which held regular meetings of the prime ministers of France, Britain, and Italy, as well as a representative sent by President Wilson.

Better news for the Allies came from the Middle East. The discovery of oil there prior to the war had dramatically increased the stakes for influence in the region. During the war, the British took advantage of Arab resentment—particularly by Muslim fundamentalists—of the Turks, who had ruled much of the Middle East for centuries. They stirred up revolts beginning in June 1916. The writer T. E. Lawrence (1888–1935), a British colonel, coordinated attacks against the strategically important Turkish railway that led from the sacred city of Medina to Damascus.

In the last decades of the nineteenth century, more Jews in Europe had begun to long for a homeland in Palestine, which was part of the Turkish Ottoman Empire. By 1914, 85,000 Jews had moved there. The British government in principle supported the Zionist movement for a Jewish state. On November 2, 1917, the Balfour Declaration expressed British willingness to support the future creation of a "national home" for the Jews in Palestine, once the Turks had been defeated, provided that such a state would recognize the rights of the Arab populations who already lived there. This declaration partially contradicted the Sykes-Picot Agreement of 1916, which had secretly divided Syria and other parts of the Middle East into British and French zones of influence. The British government hoped that the eventual creation of a Jewish state in Palestine could serve as a buffer between the Suez Canal and Syria, the latter controlled by France. In December 1917, a British force captured Jerusalem. The Central Powers' ally Turkey seemed on the verge of collapse.

The German Spring Offensive

In the spring of 1918, the Germans launched their "victory drive," their first major offensive since 1914. But Austria-Hungary showed signs of virtually dissolving, with major national groups openly calling for independence. The United States now had 325,000 troops in Europe. They were commanded by General John Pershing (1860–1948), who had won early fame for leading a "punitive expedition" (which turned out to be a wild-goose chase) against the Mexican bandit Pancho Villa. He had also served in campaigns against the Sioux in the American West, and had fought in the Philippines and Cuba. Pershing, a tall, tough, stubborn commander, insisted that his troops remain independent, fearing that French and British generals would lead them to slaughter.

Emboldened by the withdrawal of revolutionary Russia from the war, Ludendorff decided on a massive German assault along the Somme River, thereby avoiding the mud of Flanders and the hills and forts of eastern France around Verdun. On March 21, 1918, after a brief bombardment of five hours to maintain some element of surprise, 1.6 million men attacked the Allied defenses in five separate offensives over a front of forty miles (see Map 22.7). When the weather cleared at noon, British pilots observed that the Germans had succeeded in breaking through the Allied lines. Five days later, some German units had pushed forward thirty-six miles. The Germans now advanced in Flanders, moving forward with relative ease against troops from Portugal, which had recently entered the war on the

MAP 22.7 THE GERMAN OFFENSIVE, 1918   The spring offensive of 1918 in which the Germans attacked the Allies in five separate offensives along the western front.

Allied side. Ludendorff hurled all available reserves into the battle. It looked as though the Germans would take the Channel ports. The Germans bombarded the French capital with their giant gun, "Big Bertha," which could lob shells, each weighing up to a ton, twenty-four miles through the air before they fell to earth with deadly impact. Late in May 1918, the offensive pushed French troops back to Reims, and then as close to Paris as the Marne River in early June. The French stopped the German advance short of Paris. In the gloom of the Allied headquarters, French Marshal Ferdinand Foch (1851–1929) assumed command of the combined French, British, and American armies.

However, the Germans had outrun their cover and supplies, and faced fresh Allied reserves. On July 15, 1918, another major German attack was repulsed. Ludendorff's offensive, which he viewed as the last chance to win the war, had failed. France was not about to negotiate for an armistice. Morale plunged in Germany, amid extreme shortages of food, gas, and electricity. Rationing became more stringent and black markets spread. Inflation was rampant, pushed by the circulation of more paper money, as gold and silver were withdrawn to prevent hoarding. In January 1918, 400,000 workers in Berlin went on strike, demanding a democratization of the government and peace. Carefully couched criticism of the war and of Kaiser William II began to appear in the press. Socialists became bolder. Demonstrations took place in several cities, including Berlin.

The Allies counterattacked in July 1918. The British used their tanks with increasing effectiveness to go over craters and barbed wire and to protect the advancing infantry. Coordinated attacks on the German lines began on August 8, 1918, when the British moved forward eight miles north of the Somme River. A month later, the Germans had been pushed back to the positions they had held at the start of the Ludendorff spring offensive.

The Allies were now confident that they would win the war, probably in 1919 if all went well. Ludendorff advised the kaiser to press for an armistice before it was too late. With the Allies gaining ground, on October 4, 1918, Germany's new chancellor, Prince Max von Baden (1867–1929), a liberal monarchist, asked President Wilson for an armistice based on the American president's call for "peace without victory." The Reichstag passed laws making ministers responsible to it and not to the kaiser. It was a revolution of sorts. Given the circumstances, Kaiser William II could do virtually nothing.

The situation for the Central Powers worsened on the Italian front. His armies in retreat, Austro-Hungarian Emperor Charles I seemed little inclined nor able to continue the war as desertions mounted. There was now little doubt that the defeat of Germany and Austria-Hungary was near.

The Fourteen Points and Peace

On January 8, 1918, in an address to a joint session of the U.S. Senate and House of Representatives, President Wilson set out a blueprint for permanent peace. His "Fourteen Points" were based upon his understanding of how the Great War had begun and how future wars could be avoided. The first point called for "open covenants, openly arrived at," in place of the secret treaties whose obligations had pulled Europe into war. Wilson also called for freedom of the seas and of trade and the impartial settlement of colonial rivalries. Other points included the principle of nonintervention in Russia; the return of full sovereignty to Belgium and of Alsace-Lorraine to France; autonomy—without mentioning independence—for the national groups within the Austro-Hungarian Empire; and the independence of Romania, Serbia, Montenegro, and Poland. The last of the Fourteen Points called for the establishment of an organization or association of nations to settle other national conflicts as they arose. If the desire of the European peoples to live in states defined by national boundaries had been one—if not the principal—cause of the war, then a peace that recognized these claims would be a lasting one. Or so thought Wilson, and many other people as well.

Germany now appeared willing to accept Wilson's Fourteen Points as grounds for an armistice, hoping to circumvent the British and French governments, which clearly would demand unconditional surrender and were not terribly interested in Wilson's idealism. The British, for example, opposed the point calling for freedom of the seas. As Wilson considered what to do with the German proposal for an armistice, a number of U.S. citizens were killed when a U-boat again sank a British ship off the Irish coast. An angry Wilson then replied to Prince Max that the German military authorities would have to arrange an armistice with the British and French high command, and not with him. Germany called off unrestricted submarine warfare and tried to convince Wilson that recent changes in the civilian leadership in Berlin amounted to a democratization of the empire. Foch and Clemenceau demanded unconditional surrender of the German fleet and occupation of the Rhineland by France.

The collapse of the Central Powers accelerated. When French and British troops moved into Bulgaria in September 1918, Bulgaria left the war, as did Turkey the next month. British forces occupied Damascus and Constantinople. When the Austro-Hungarian Empire also tried to get Wilson to negotiate an armistice based on the Fourteen Points, which trumpeted the sanctity of the nation-state, Czechs in Prague proclaimed an independent Czechoslovakia. Croats and Slovenes announced that they would join the Serbs in the establishment of a South Slav state of Yugoslavia. Hungary, too, proclaimed its independence, as if the Great War had been something forced on it by the Austrians. Facing no opposition, the Italian army finally managed to advance into Habsburg territory. Austria-Hungary signed an armistice on November 3, 1918. German sailors mutinied in the Baltic port of Kiel and riots rocked Berlin. An insurrection in Munich led to the declaration of a Bavarian Republic.

On November 7, 1918, an ad hoc German Armistice Commission asked the Allies for an end to hostilities. Two days later, a crowd proclaimed the

German Republic in Berlin. William II blamed socialists and Jews for the overthrow of the empire and then fled across the Dutch border. On November 11, 1918, a representative of the provisional German government and General Foch signed an armistice in a railroad car in the middle of the forest near Compiègne, north of Paris. Celebrations in London, Paris, and New York lasted for days. The mother of the poet Wilfred Owen received news that he had been killed as the church bells of her village were ringing for victory. A French veteran, tiring of the street festivities in his town, went at dusk to a cemetery. There he came upon a woman crying next to the tomb of her husband. Their small boy was with her, playing with a tricolor flag. Suddenly the boy cried out, "Papa, we've won!"

THE IMPACT OF THE WAR

There had been nothing like the Great War in history. About 6,000 people had been killed each day for more than 1,500 days. On average, more than 900 French and 1,300 German soldiers were killed each day during the more than four years of war. Nearly 74 million soldiers were mobilized. Of the 48 million men who served in the Allied armies, at least 18 million were casualties, not including the hundreds of thousands listed as missing. The Central Powers mobilized 25.5 million men and had 12.4 million casualties, again not counting the missing. In all, approximately 9.4 million men were killed or "disappeared," 21.2 million wounded (of whom an estimated 7 million may have been left permanently disabled), and 7.6 million prisoners of war. Many—perhaps millions—of civilians died from war-related causes, principally related to not having enough to eat. As Table 22.1 shows, the Austro-Hungarian, Russian, and French armies suffered proportionally more than the other major combatants. Of all French troops mobilized during the war, 16.8 percent were killed (compared to 15.4 percent of German soldiers). Furthermore, about 50 million people died in a worldwide influenza epidemic in 1918–1919 that killed more people in Europe than did the war.

But sheer numbers, however daunting, do not tell the whole story. Of the wounded who survived, many were condemned to spend the rest of their lives—shortened lives, in many cases—in veterans' hospitals. Soldiers who had lost limbs or who were mutilated in other ways became a common sight in European cities, towns, and villages after the war. Europe seemed a continent of widows and spinsters; so many men were killed in the prime of life that the birthrate fell markedly after the war. Support for families of the dead soldiers and invalids unable to work strained national budgets. War cemeteries stretched across northern France and Belgium. Warfare had changed. The Battle of Verdun had lasted ten months, that of Gallipoli more than eight months, and the Battle of Somme in 1916 more than five

TABLE 22.1. CASUALTIES IN THE GREAT WAR

ALLIED POWERS

Country	Mobilized	Dead	Wounded	POW/ Missing	Total	% Casualties
Russia	18,100,000	1,800,000	4,950,000	2,500,000	9,250,000	51.10
France	7,891,000	1,375,800	4,266,000	537,000	6,178,800	78.30
G.B., Emp. and Dom.	8,904,467	908,371	2,090,212	191,652	3,190,235	35.83
Italy	5,615,000	578,000	947,000	600,000	2,125,000	37.85
U.S.	4,273,000	114,000	234,000	4,526	352,526	8.25
Japan	800,000	300	907	3	1,210	0.15
Romania	1,000,000	250,706	120,000	80,000	450,706	45.07
Serbia	750,000	278,000	133,148	15,958	427,106	56.95
Belgium	365,000	38,716	44,686	34,659	118,061	32.35
Greece	353,000	26,000	21,000	1,000	48,000	13.60
Portugal	100,000	7,222	13,751	12,318	33,291	33.29
Montenegro	50,000	3,000	10,000	7,000	20,000	40.00
Total	48,201,467	5,380,115	12,830,704	3,984,116	22,194,935	46.05

CENTRAL POWERS

Country	Mobilized	Dead	Wounded	POW/ Missing	Total	% Casualties
Germany	13,200,000	2,033,700	4,216,058	1,152,800	7,402,558	56.08
Austria- Hungary	9,000,000	1,100,000	3,620,000	2,200,000	6,920,000	76.89
Turkey	2,998,000	804,000	400,000	250,000	1,454,000	48.50
Bulgaria	400,000	87,500	152,390	27,029	266,919	66.73
Total	25,598,000	4,025,200	8,388,448	3,629,829	16,043,477	62.67
Grand Total	73,799,467	9,405,315	21,219,152	7,613,945	38,238,412	51.81

Source: J. M. Winter, *The Great War and the British People* (London, Macmillan, 1985), p. 75.

months (in which 4 million soldiers fought, of whom more than a quarter were killed, captured, or "disappeared"). The carnage was not limited to the European continent. In response to Armenian demands for an independent state, in 1915 the Turks forced 1.75 million Armenians to leave their homes in Turkey; more than a third of them perished without water in the desert sun on the way to Syria.

The flower of European youth—or much of it—had perished in the war. There were other costs as well. The economic structure of northern France and part of Belgium had been chewed up in the fighting. The German economy, which was devastated by the war, would be further crippled by the terms of the peace treaty (see Chapter 24). The Carnegie Endowment for International Peace made a brave attempt to calculate the war's actual

A widow in mourning before her husband's grave at the
end of World War I.

cost, coming up with a figure of $338 billion dollars after establishing a
rough value for property and even lives lost.

No one could begin to measure other dimensions of the war's impact.
The psychological damage to the generation of survivors can hardly be
measured. "Never such innocence again," observed the British writer Philip
Larkin, referring to the period before the war. The post-war period, rampant
with hard times and disappointments, caused many people to look back even
more on the pre-war period as the "Belle Époque," the good old days.

Woodrow Wilson was not alone in thinking that the Great War was the
war to end all wars. Many people reasoned that no one could ever again
wish such a catastrophe on humanity. The American writer F. Scott
Fitzgerald took a friend to a battlefield in the north of France: "See that little stream—we could walk to it in two minutes. It took the British a month
to walk to it—a whole empire walking very slowly, dying in front and pushing forward behind. And another empire walked very slowly backward a
few inches a day, leaving the dead like a million bloody rags. No European
will ever do that again in this generation." He was wrong.

CONCLUSION

The Great War had several causes, with none alone standing as a sufficient cause. To be sure, the entangling alliances of the European great powers were undeniably a principal factor in the outbreak of hostilities. Aggressive nationalism spilled out of the opposing alliances during this period. Schoolchildren throughout much of Europe were taught that their country was the greatest nation in history, and that their rivals and enemies were craven reptiles. The imperial rivalries of the great powers—above all, in Africa—helped make the alliance system more rigid, sharpening rivalries between Germany and Britain and France. Nationalists strongly believed that having colonies helped define status as a great power: by such reasoning, states had to expand their military forces and be prepared to defend their empires as they would their own borders.

Military planners (who were, after all, nationalists themselves) in Germany, Austria-Hungary, France, and, to a lesser extent, Russia, all considered war not only inevitable but desirable. To one British writer, "War . . . is the sovereign disinfectant, and its red stream of blood . . . cleans out the stagnant pools and clotted channels of the intellect." In Germany, an official in the chancellery wrote that "the hostility that we observe everywhere [is] the essence of the world and the source of life itself." War would be the ultimate test by which the fit—individuals and nations—would be measured. "Give me combat!" rang out from the dueling fraternities in Heidelberg to the gymnastic and shooting clubs of Paris.

For those who had been lucky enough to survive, how much greater the disappointment, disillusionment, and bitterness that would follow. One contemporary observer did not mince words: "The World War of 1914–1918 was the greatest moral, spiritual and physical catastrophe in the entire history of the English people—a catastrophe whose consequences, all wholly evil, are still with us." Soldiers returned home to find skyrocketing prices and unemployment awaiting them. In Britain, parents whose sons had died as foot soldiers in France or Belgium learned that families of aristocratic officers had complained that their sons had been buried alongside ordinary people. Politicians who had put aside their differences during the war in a common effort for victory—such as the "Sacred Union" in France—reverted to bitter disagreements that were compounded by the dilemmas posed in the peace settlement. The problems of making peace and putting Europe back together again, as well as paying for the war, would not be easily resolved. U.S. participation in the war and, particularly, the Russian Revolution, which we will examine in the next chapter, would each have a profound impact on Europe's future. War became the continuing experience of the twentieth century.

CHAPTER 23

REVOLUTIONARY RUSSIA AND THE SOVIET UNION

~~~∞~~~

When Nicholas II (1868–1918) was crowned tsar of Russia upon the death of Alexander III in 1894, he decided to hold a great public festival on a huge field outside of Moscow, considered the sacred center of the empire. Convinced that it was his duty to uphold the principles of autocracy, Nicholas was sensitive to the tsar's traditional role as the Holy Father of all his people. He wanted to reaffirm the ties that bound his subjects to him, and he to them. The festival attracted enthusiastic crowds numbering in the hundreds of thousands. It featured rides, fortune telling, and other staples of Russian popular festivals. But in the stampede to get free beer and coronation souvenirs, more than 1,200 people were crushed to death and between 9,000 and 20,000 injured. Celebration had turned to tragedy. And during the coronation itself, the heavy chain of the Order of Saint Andrew dropped from Nicholas's shoulders to the ground. Many people—perhaps even the superstitious tsar himself—saw these events as bad omens for the tsar's reign.

Not bad omens, however, but rather the failure to implement meaningful political reform brought down Nicholas II and the Russian autocracy in 1917. First, the Revolution of 1905 led to reforms but did not alter the autocratic nature of the regime. This revolution forced Tsar Nicholas II to grant increased freedom of the press and to create an elected Duma (assembly). These reforms had disappeared, for all intents and purposes, when the tsar regained the upper hand in the counter-revolution that began in 1906, yet the Revolution of 1905 demonstrated the vulnerability of even a police state to popular mobilization. In August 1914, the Russian Empire went to war, and the conflict itself encouraged those who demanded political reform. In February 1917, the tsar abdicated. Then, after six months of uncertainty and political division, the Bolshevik (October) Revolution overthrew the provisional government. Russia withdrew from the Great War. The "dictatorship of the proletariat" became that of Vladimir Lenin's Communist Party. Upon Lenin's death in 1924, Joseph Stalin consolidated his personal authority in the Soviet Union, ruthlessly establishing state socialism (see Chapter 25).

The Russian Revolution of 1917, like that of 1905, was not the kind of revolution that the Russian populists or anarchists had predicted—massive uprisings of the peasant masses against lords and imperial officials—although peasant rebellion was an essential ingredient in both revolutions. Nor did it correspond to Karl Marx's prediction that a successful bourgeois revolution would be followed by a revolution undertaken by an industrial proletariat. War played a catalytic role in the Russian Revolution of 1917: Russia's shocking defeat in the Russo-Japanese War (1904–1905) and, above all, the horror of the Great War created hardships that increasingly undermined the legitimacy of the tsarist regime.

WAR AND REVOLUTION

Reformers were still biding their time when Russia went to war in 1914. However, Lenin (see Chapter 18) was dumbfounded when most socialists in other countries supported their nation's mobilization for war. Among Russian socialists, "defensists" (Mensheviks and most Socialist Revolutionaries) argued that Russian workers should defend their country against German attack. "Internationalists" (including Bolsheviks) opposed the war, viewing it as a struggle between capitalist powers in which workers were but pawns.

Lenin took the war as a sign that capitalism might be ripe for what he thought was its inevitable fall. "Imperialism is the last stage," he wrote, "in the development of capitalism when it has reached the point of dividing up the whole world, and two gigantic groups have fallen into mortal struggle." He believed that if revolution were to break out in several countries, the fall of Russian autocracy and capitalism could be near, even without the true "bourgeois revolution" Marx had predicted. Even if the Russian working class was less developed than those of Western nations, the corresponding weakness of the Russian bourgeoisie could facilitate a successful revolution. This revolution would be followed by the establishment of a dictatorship of the proletariat, that is, by a mobilized working class led by its most dedicated elements, his party, the Bolsheviks. The revolution would then spread to other countries, where the working classes would follow the example of the first successful socialist revolution.

Russia at War

The Great War became a catalyst for demands for reform within Russia, first in the management of the war itself, and then in Russian political life.

The war had begun with an upsurge of patriotism and political unity, with the tsar blessing icons and the faithful kneeling before him. A Bolshevik noted bitterly that amid shouts of "'God Save the Tsar!' our class struggle went down the drain." Within a year, however, the war had shattered the "sacred union" that represented a patriotic consensus in 1914. Liberals renewed demands for political reform. Workers agitated for higher wages and better working conditions. By 1917, 15 million men had been drafted into the army, the vast majority of whom were poor peasants. It proved difficult to transform peasants who were more used to holding rakes than rifles into soldiers. Sent by high command into battle ill equipped, Russian losses were staggering.

In the interest of the war effort, the government allowed national organizations to exist that earlier had been forbidden. These groups became the organizational base for the liberal opposition. Liberal *zemstvo* representatives established a committee, the Union of *Zemstvos,* to organize relief for the sick and wounded; an organization of municipal governments, the Union of Towns, was also created.

In the spring of 1915, liberal Duma members began to express open dissatisfaction with the way the war was being run. Russia's factories experienced difficulties in meeting military needs; the army lacked sufficient rifles and artillery shells. The tsar permitted industrialists to form a War Industries Committee, to which delegations of workers were added, in order to expedite wartime production.

The war gradually transformed Petrograd (the new name given to Saint Petersburg, because it sounded more Russian), accentuating social polarization. By 1916, most of Petrograd's workers, who made up 35 percent of

Tsar Nicholas II, holding an icon, blesses his troops.

the population, were producing war materiel, swelling the ranks of metal, textile, and chemical workers. More peasants flocked to the capital, as did waves of refugees from the war zones of Russian Poland and the Baltic states.

As Russian society strained under the pressures of war, liberals demanded that the Duma be allowed to meet and that Tsar Nicholas dismiss a number of reactionary ministers. With military defeats—none more disastrous than that at Tannenberg (August 1914), where 100,000 Russian troops were captured—followed by humiliating retreats weighing on him, the tsar established a Council for National Defense. He summoned the Duma to meet in July 1915 and replaced four ministers. In August, some liberal members of the Duma formed a "Progressive Bloc" committed to working with the tsar in the hope of encouraging reform.

The melancholy, ineffectual tsar remained extremely superstitious. Seventeen was his unlucky number: on January 17, 1895, the day of his first speech as tsar, an elderly noble had dropped a traditional gift of bread and salt, a bad omen, and on October 17, 1905, he had been constrained to sign a constitution. But he retained the respect and distant affection of most of the Russian people. Tsarina Alexandra, in contrast, was loathed by many of her subjects. Born in Germany, she was the granddaughter of Queen Victoria and had been raised in England before marrying Tsar Nicholas in 1894. She had converted from Anglicanism to the Russian Orthodox Church. The illness of their only son, Alexei (1904–1918), a hemophiliac and the heir to the throne, increasingly weighed on the royal couple.

As she became ever more conservative, Alexandra extended her influence over her weak-willed husband. Nicholas dismissed ministers on the whims of the tsarina. ("Lovey, don't dawdle!" she wrote her husband, urging him to fire one of them.) When he met in an emergency session with his Council of Ministers, the tsar followed Alexandra's instructions to clutch a religious icon. Nicholas then dismissed his liberal ministers. Many Russians wrongly believed that Alexandra was actively working for the interests of Germany, although no German agent could have served Germany as well. In the meantime, Nicholas had assumed command of the army. Liberals feared this could lead to more military disasters, and would also take the tsar away from Petrograd, leaving imperial decision making even more subject to the influence of Tsarina Alexandra.

Tsarina Alexandra with Grigory Rasputin (center).

Alexandra's great favorite was Grigory Rasputin (1872–1916), a debauched "holy man." Claiming occult power and the ability to heal Alexei's hemophilia, Rasputin had moved gradually into the inner circle of court life. On one occasion, he predicted that one of Alexei's spells would shortly subside, and it did. To the consternation of the tsar's ministers, the influence enjoyed by the man the tsarina called "our friend" became a matter of state. In December 1916, noble conspirators, who feared Rasputin's influence on military operations, put what they thought was enough poison into his many drinks to kill a cow. When Rasputin seemed almost unfazed, they shot him repeatedly and smashed his skull in a protracted struggle.

Food shortages eroded the revival of the workers' patriotism that had accompanied the beginning stages of the war. The growth of public organizations, which opened up a larger public sphere for discussion and debate, helped mobilize opposition to autocracy. Cooperative associations formed by workers to resist high prices had 50,000 members by the end of 1916. Some workers on the War Industries Committee pushed for greater militancy. The Bolsheviks found support among industrial workers. Attacks on the management of the war rang out in the Duma, as well as in the Union of Towns and the Union of the *Zemstvos*. In December 1916 the latter passed a resolution calling on the Duma to stop cooperating with the tsar and demanded ministerial responsibility. Liberals remained paralyzed, however, cowed by tsarist repression amid increased worker militancy.

For the moment, the tsar and the liberals needed each other. Outright revolution or violent repression seemed equally dangerous to both. The state needed the continued participation of voluntary committees and agencies of local self-government in order to keep the state from collapsing into shortage-induced anarchy. Liberal-dominated committees and agencies required the centralized apparatus of the state to carry out their work.

Food shortages reached a peak during the harsh winter of 1916–1917. Peasants hoarded their grain. Police repression of strikes helped close the ranks of workers against the government. In Lithuania, nationalists demanded autonomy within the empire, and some nationalist agitation occurred in other Russian borderlands as well. In 1916 Muslims in Turkistan in Central Asia rose up in arms against Russian rule after the government attempted to move a quarter of a million people to factories near the front. Increasing anger at the continued arrival of Russian settlers in Turkistan also played a role in the unrest. These occurrences revealed the complexity of the problem of nationalism in the Russian Empire.

Alexander Kerensky, (1881–1970), a lawyer, and leader of the Socialist Revolutionaries (see Chapter 18), denounced the war in a speech whose daring rhetoric had never been heard in the Duma. Some loyal nobles now urged reforms. But Nicholas replaced members of the Progressive Bloc with uncompromising reactionaries. He and his family withdrew into retreat, leaving the government floundering like a rudderless boat in high seas.

The February Revolution

The Russian Revolution that took place in Petrograd in February 1917 grew out of the massive discontent with hunger and deprivation, and amid mounting frustration at tsarist intransigence against reform. Like most large European cities, Petrograd's neighborhoods reflected social segregation. The upper- and middle-class residential districts and the palatial buildings of imperial government lay on and near a long street called the Nevsky Prospect. This central artery was lined with banks, hotels, restaurants, cafés, a giant department store, and offices. The streetcars did not run as far as the muddy streets of the workers' districts, nor in many cases did the city's water mains or electric power lines. Epidemics were still frequent in Petrograd, as in Moscow and other Russian cities, which were characterized by acute overcrowding and inadequate sanitation.

Revolutionary organizations prepared a massive general strike in early 1917, the anniversary of Bloody Sunday in 1905. During January and February, almost half of the capital's 400,000 workers went out on strike, including munitions workers at the Putilov factory—the largest factory in Europe with 30,000 workers. Yet the Petrograd garrison of about 160,000 soldiers still seemed adequate to the task of maintaining order, even though most were raw recruits. Demonstrators demanded that a provisional government be appointed with the power to enact major reforms. Food lines stretched longer in Petrograd, Moscow, and other cities in temperatures that reached forty below zero. Bread riots, in which many women and young people participated, became a daily occurrence.

On February 23 (all subsequent dates in this chapter refer to the Old Russian calendar, which was thirteen days behind the Western calendar), more determined demonstrators took to the streets. Workers in the Putilov munitions factory tore up factory rule books and created committees to represent their interests to the company. Female textile workers led the way out of the factories.

On February 25, a general strike closed down Petrograd. While Petrograd's Duma debated ways of dealing with severe food shortages, crowds of ordinary people poured into Petrograd's center. Military attention was focused on the front. Tsar Nicholas then ordered the commander of the garrison to suppress demonstrations. Street fighting began and spread in the city. The attitude of soldiers, most of whom were peasants or workers, now became crucial. Many were shocked when ordered to fire on insurgents. When a commanding officer tried to restore order by reading a telegram from the tsar, he was shot while trying to flee the barracks. Thousands of soldiers and some officers went over to the insurgent side, and a number of officers and soldiers who continued to resist were summarily executed after being captured.

Miserable conditions of war, the unpopularity of the officers (who addressed the rank and file as masters had spoken to serfs), awful food,

Bolshevik soldiers marching at the Kremlin in Moscow, 1917.

and empathy with the demands of the workers for "bread and peace" explain the massive defection of soldiers. Sailors mutinied on ships of the Baltic fleet. The capture of the Petrograd arsenal put thousands of rifles as well as ammunition into the hands of workers. The insurgents controlled Petrograd, the capital of Russia.

Nicholas, who was away at his seaside resort with his family, now ordered the Duma to dissolve. Some of its members drawn from privileged society obeyed, but the majority simply moved to a new meeting place. They voted to remain in Petrograd—a move not unlike the Tennis Court Oath of the third estate during the first period of the French Revolution, a precedent of which they were keenly aware. The Duma then elected a provisional committee, whose mandate was to restore order. In the meantime, the liberals, who tried to walk a tightrope between a desire for reform and a fear of the masses, now were in the position of trying to contain the revolution they had helped set in motion.

The Russian Revolution of February 1917 was unplanned and its outcome uncertain. But the soil was fertile. Experienced in strikes, Socialist Revolutionary, Menshevik, and Bolshevik activists helped impart a sense of direction to the movement. Their goal, unlike that of the liberals, who wanted only reform, was the overthrow of the tsarist regime. Amid the turmoil of sudden change effected by groups who did not necessarily agree on what should happen next, the provisional committee began to function as a provisional government, organizing a food supply commission and a military commission to try to bring the soldiers roaming through the city under some control.

On February 27, in response to calls in the streets, the Petrograd Soviet of Workers' and Soldiers' Deputies was created—*soviets* were councils that had been established during the Revolution of 1905. Members of the organization included several hundred workers, some of whom the demonstrators had freed from jail (where they had been placed for their political or trade union activities), as well as soldiers. They elected officers, discussed ways to defend Petrograd against a possible German attack, and sent representatives to encourage the formation of soviets in other cities. Menshevik leaders took the lead in the Petrograd Soviet's creation as Bolshevik leaders held back, fearing that a large and effective soviet might make it more difficult for their party to direct worker militancy.

Hoping to overwhelm the rebellion with his presence, the tsar now decided to return to Petrograd. He spent almost two full days aboard his private train, critical moments in the February Revolution. On the train, the tsar received an erroneous report that insurgent troops held the next stations and that they would refuse to let his train through. Nicholas then went to the northern military front, hoping to find a loyal army ready to march on Petrograd. In disbelief, he learned that Moscow, too, had fallen almost overnight to insurgents. His generals made no effort to save the

Workers at the giant Putilov factory in Petrograd vote during a meeting of the Petrograd Soviet.

regime. They believed the tsar's cause lost and that only his abdication could prevent civil war, and perhaps military defeat at the hands of Germany as well.

Nicholas II abdicated on March 2, 1917, leaving the throne to his brother, Prince Michael. He did so with characteristic calm and fatalism—scribbling in his diary that day, "All around me—treason and cowardice and deceit." A few hours in revolutionary Petrograd convinced Prince Michael to refuse to succeed his brother. The Soviet placed the tsar and his family under house arrest until the summer, when they were taken by train to a small Siberian town. The Russian autocracy had fallen in a matter of days, with only about a thousand people killed. No legions of faithful peasants had risen up from the land of the black earth to save the "Holy Father."

The Provisional Government and the Soviet

The provisional government and the Petrograd Soviet were left in the awkward position of serving as dual or parallel governments. The provisional government included Constitutional Democrats, liberals who had demanded only that the tsar initiate political reforms. The Petrograd Soviet, in contrast, consisted largely of workers and soldiers who had helped overthrow the tsar. The relationship between the moderate provisional government and the radical Soviet would ultimately affect the course of the Russian Revolution itself. For the moment, the Petrograd Soviet promised to accept the provisional committee's authority. Both the provisional government and the Soviet met in the same palace, with Kerensky, named minister of justice but also a member of the Soviet, running back and forth between the two bodies, trying to smooth relations between them.

On March 8, the provisional government granted civil liberties, including the right to strike, democratized local government, announced that it would convene a constituent assembly to establish a constitution, and amnestied political prisoners. The Petrograd Soviet, now with 3,000 members and an executive committee meeting virtually around the clock, demanded immediate economic and social reforms. The provisional government and the Soviet quickly became the focus of attention of competing political groups—Liberals, Socialist Revolutionaries, Mensheviks, and Bolsheviks—all of whom wanted to shape Russia's future.

The Army

In the meantime, the army was the last functioning imperial institution. On March 1, the Petrograd Soviet issued Order Number One, which claimed for the Soviet the authority to countermand orders of the provisional government on military matters and called for the election of soldiers' committees in every unit. In fact, such elections had already widely occurred, a remarkable attempt to democratize army life. In some places on the front, soldiers had refused to obey officers and, in a few cases, beat them up or even shot them. The soldiers wanted peace. Yet the danger that the military front might collapse against German pressure seemed quite real. Desertions increased in the first month of the Revolution. For the moment, however, the Bolshevik promise of "land and peace" seemed a distant prospect. As soldiers put it, "What good is land to me if I'm dead?"

The United States, first, and then Great Britain, France, and Italy quickly gave diplomatic recognition to the provisional government, hoping that the Revolution would not drastically affect the Russian military commitment to hold the eastern front. But in a few places on the front, Russian troops fraternized with astonished German and Austro-Hungarian soldiers.

The Revolution Spreads

As news of the Revolution and the abdication of Tsar Nicholas II spread, ordinary people in the vast reaches of what had been the Russian Empire attacked and disarmed police stations, freed political prisoners, and created provisional governing bodies. Yet it sometimes took weeks for "commissars of the revolution" to arrive. In some industrial regions, workers had already occupied factories, demanding higher wages, an eight-hour day, and control over production. But in most places, the situation remained unclear. One Russian reflected: "We feel that we have escaped from a dark cave into bright sunlight. And here we stand, not knowing where to go or what to do."

With Petrograd and much of European Russia caught between war and revolution, some of the minority peoples of the empire began to demand more favorable status. Their demands were as myriad and complicated as the old Russian Empire itself. Among the nationalities, some nationalists sought only cultural autonomy; others wanted some degree of political freedom within the context of a federal structure; still others demanded outright independence. Such demands soured relations in regions where ethnic and religious tensions had persisted, sometimes for centuries. In the steppes of Central Asia and in the northern Caucasus, fighting broke out between Russian settlers and the Cossacks (who had begun to settle the regions in large numbers following the emancipation of the serfs in 1861), the Kazakh-Kirghiz, the Bashkirs, and other Turkish peoples. Thousands of people perished in these struggles. In the Baltic states of Lithuania, Latvia, and Estonia, nationalist movements grew rapidly.

The provisional government's goal was to hold the empire together until a constituent assembly could be elected to establish the political basis of the new state. Its declaration of civil rights for all peoples had made each nationality in principle equal. In some places, representatives of the new regime immediately turned over administrative responsibility to local committees or individuals. But elsewhere, local peoples set up their own institutions of self-rule in the hope of maintaining order. In some places,

Alexander Kerensky (front center) head of the provisional government, with troops in Petrograd, 1917.

nationalist movements competed with Socialist Revolutionaries, Mensheviks, and Bolsheviks for allegiance.

Kerensky's provisional government announced that Poland, which had been an independent state until the Third Partition by Russia, Prussia, and Austria in 1795, would again become independent, in the hope of undermining German and Austro-Hungarian troops who occupied most of Poland. In neighboring Belarus—like Poland, a battleground—a national committee led by Socialist Revolutionaries demanded autonomy and established a Rada (council).

The situation in Ukraine was particularly complicated. The provisional government feared that if it granted Ukrainian autonomy, other nationalities would demand similar treatment. Shortly after the tsar's abdication, Ukrainian socialists had formed a soviet. On March 4, 1917, nationalists and socialists established the Ukrainian Central Council. Centuries-old resentment of Russia, based on cultural and linguistic differences, rose to the surface. As more radical nationalists gathered in Kiev, the Rada convoked a Ukrainian National Congress, which began to draft a statute for autonomy. Ukrainian soldiers formed their own military units. Serving as a *de facto* provisional government in Ukraine, the Rada broadened its social and national base by including non-Ukrainian residents. In the meantime, nationalism began to grip Ukrainian peasants, and many of them occupied lands owned by Russian or Polish landlords.

In regions with sizable Muslim populations, national movements were divided between religious conservatives, Western-looking liberals, and leftist Socialist Revolutionaries. The first All-Russian Muslim Congress, which began on May 1, 1917, reflected these divisions. Islamic conservatives attempted to shout down speakers advocating rights for women, but

Westernizers predominated, passing the measure. The congress announced the future formation of a religious administration that would be separate from the state.

Besides the enormous challenge of assuring the food supply—by ordering the army to curtail the unpopular requisitioning of grain—the provisional government had to make sure that the military front held. At the same time, the provisional government faced increasing pressure from the Soviet for economic and social reforms, above all, land reform. The provisional government authorized the formation of local food supply committees and "land committees," which were charged with gathering information in order to draft a land reform measure for the Constituent Assembly. Liberals also wanted land reform, but insisted that it be carried out in a deliberate, legal manner. Peasants, however, wanted action, not committees.

An All-Russian Congress of Soviets began at the end of March 1917 in Petrograd. Bringing together representatives of other soviets that had sprung up after the Revolution, this congress transformed the Petrograd Soviet into a national body, establishing a central executive committee dominated by members of the Petrograd Soviet.

A groundswell of opposition to Russia's continued participation in the war gradually drove a wedge between workers and soldiers and the provisional government. Nonetheless, at the All-Russian Congress of Soviets, the Bolsheviks' call for an immediate end to the war was easily defeated. Mensheviks and the Socialist Revolutionaries were willing to continue the war, but on the condition that the provisional government work for peace without annexations of land from Russia's enemies.

The issue of the war led to the provisional government's "April Crisis." The minister of foreign affairs, a leader of the Kadets (Constitutional Democratic Party), added a personal note to an official communication to the Allies that called for "war to decisive victory," evoking Russia's "historic right" to take Constantinople. Protests by the Petrograd Soviet and demonstrations against the war led to his resignation from the government at the beginning of May. The April Crisis led to the formation of the first coalition government, which reflected the push to the left. The provisional government now accepted the Petrograd Soviet's demand that "peace without annexations" be henceforth the basis of Russian foreign policy.

Worsening material conditions radicalized many workers, particularly in trade unions that had sprung up since February 1917. Workers organized factory committees and strikes. In the countryside, the poorer peasants operated on the simplest principle of all: those who work the land ought to own it. Many children or grandchildren of former serfs began to occupy the land of the lords for whom they had worked, sometimes killing landlords or former imperial officials in the process. Indeed, the percentage of landless peasants may have fallen by half during the 1917–1920 period. Soviets sprung up in the countryside as civil authority disappeared. In some villages, the Orthodox Church could no longer compel obedience. A priest reported, "My parishioners will nowadays only go to meetings of the soviet, and when I remind them about the church, they tell me they have no time."

Lenin's Return

The German government expedited Lenin's return to Russia from Switzerland, where he had been in exile since 1900. The Bolshevik leader's return might exert further pressure on the provisional government to sue for peace, allowing the German army to concentrate its efforts on the western front. After passing through German territory in a sealed railway car to assure that he had no contact with the German population, Lenin arrived in Petrograd in early April 1917.

Lenin gradually rallied the Bolshevik Party around his leadership, based on the following propositions: (1) Russian withdrawal from the war, the continuation of which he viewed as a serious obstacle to a Bolshevik victory; (2) no support for the provisional government; (3) a call for revolution in the other countries of Europe; and (4) the seizure of large estates by the peasantry.

In his "April Theses," Lenin argued that wartime chaos had allowed the bourgeois and proletarian revolutions to merge in a dramatically short period of time. The overthrow of the autocracy had suddenly and unexpectedly handed power to a weak bourgeoisie. The bourgeoisie, holding power through the provisional government, could be in turn overthrown by the proletariat, supported by the poorest peasants. Local power would be held by workers, soldiers, and peasants through the soviets, but under Bolshevik Party guidance. The soviets would provide the basis on which a new state could be constructed through the "dictatorship of the proletariat and peasantry." It sounded so simple.

Aided by the provisional government's division and growing unpopularity, Bolshevik support grew among the factory committees, Red Guards (newly created factory workers' militias), sailors at the naval base of Kronstadt, and soldiers within the Petrograd garrison. The failure of the existing provisional government to provide either peace or land undermined its support among peasants. It was powerless to resolve industrial disputes or to put an end to land seizures. In the meantime, Menshevik leaders warned that continued Bolshevik radicalism might push conservatives toward launching a coup d'état.

The July Days

Although neither troop morale nor the military situation boded well, in mid-June Kerensky announced a Russian offensive in Galicia. This was to reassure conservatives and moderates that military discipline had been restored, and to convince the Allies that Russia remained committed to winning the war.

On July 3, 1917, the Bolsheviks rose in insurrection. They had been encouraged by their increasing popularity among workers, the ongoing agrarian revolution, and widespread dissatisfaction with the war. Nearly 100,000 soldiers who feared being sent to the front joined the chaotic uprising. However, sensing defeat, the Bolshevik Central Committee tried to call off the insurrection the next day. Most troops remained loyal to the provisional government, and the insurrection failed.

These "July Days" hardened political lines in Russia. The provisional government ordered the arrest of Bolshevik leaders, and troops closed down party headquarters and the offices of the Bolshevik Party's newspaper, *Pravda* (Truth). Kerensky became prime minister of the second coalition government, depending even more on support from the liberal Kadets. Lenin fled to Finland.

The provisional government now believed that the Bolsheviks were finished. Kerensky tried to portray Lenin as a German agent, noting that the Bolsheviks in exile had received some German money. Kerensky's government disarmed army regiments it considered disloyal, reinstated the death penalty for military disobedience, and staged a state funeral, replete with national and religious symbolism, in honor of soldiers killed at the front.

But the repressive measures undertaken against the Bolsheviks were relatively ineffective because of the disorganization of the judicial apparatus, the rapid turnover of government officials, and the support the Bolsheviks enjoyed in the working-class districts of Petrograd. Many Bolshevik leaders escaped arrest and others were soon released from jail. The repressive measures further discredited the provisional government, which seemed to be using the July Days as an excuse to undertake a counter-revolution.

Doubting the revolutionary potential of the soviets, many of whose members and leaders remained Mensheviks and Socialist Revolutionaries, the Bolsheviks turned to the factory committees to consolidate their support. Bolshevik newspapers and brochures in factories denounced the provisional government and accused moderate socialists of counter-revolution.

The Kornilov Affair

Disillusioned by Kerensky's indecision, frustrated by the ineffectiveness of the repression against the Bolsheviks, and frightened by peasant land seizures, Russian conservatives, including some military officers and Kadets, began to think in terms of a coup d'état.

General Lavr Kornilov (1870–1918), newly appointed commander in chief of the army and a tough Cossack, seemed the obvious candidate to overthrow the provisional government. Prelates of the Orthodox Church sent him icons in the hope that the military could restore religious principles to Russia. In early August 1917, a "Conference of Public Figures," including influential leaders drawn from industry, commerce, banking, and the military, pledged Kornilov their support.

Kerensky organized a Moscow State Conference, which he hoped would mobilize support for his second coalition government. Most of the delegates (some of whom were leaders of trade unions, as well as bankers, representatives from the state dumas, military leaders, and professional people) now believed only a military dictatorship could save Russia from the soviets and from having to pull out of the war. German troops had captured Riga, a major Baltic seaport, posing a direct threat to Petrograd.

Kerensky wanted Kornilov to form a military government that could restore order, but he believed that the general would remain loyal to him and to the idea of establishing a democratic republic. Kornilov probably wanted to seize power and impose a right-wing military regime. A confusing exchange led each leader to misconstrue what the other meant. Kerensky demanded Kornilov's resignation as commander in chief and, when the latter refused, called on the army to remain loyal to the provisional government. On August 27, Kornilov issued an ultimatum to the provisional government declaring that "the heavy sense of the inevitable ruin of the country commands me in this ominous moment to call upon all Russian people to come to the aid of the dying motherland."

Bolsheviks, Mensheviks, and Socialist Revolutionaries formed a committee against counter-revolution. Workers reinforced security around their factories. Bolsheviks were among those receiving arms at the arsenals in anticipation of a stand against a military coup. But no coup d'état took place, and probably nothing specific had actually been planned. However, by raising the specter of counter-revolution, the Kornilov Affair aided the Bolsheviks, who portrayed themselves as the only possible saviors of the Revolution.

THE OCTOBER REVOLUTION

The provisional government seemed both incapable of solving the worsening economic crisis and unwilling to take Russia out of the war. The workers of Petrograd were organized and armed, their demands increasing. Only the Bolsheviks promised in their program to turn over to the soviets some degree of political power. The radicalized All-Russian Executive Committee of the Soviets now approved the Bolshevik demand that a "democratic" republic be declared by a government "of representatives of the revolutionary proletariat and peasantry" from which Kadets, moderate constitutional democrats, would be excluded.

The Bolsheviks Seize Power

After returning to Petrograd in disguise, on October 10 Lenin convinced the Bolshevik Central Committee that a second insurrection could succeed. Kerensky believed a Bolshevik insurrection imminent, but he vastly underestimated the party's influence with the Petrograd workers, the soviets,

and some army units. Bolshevik propaganda hammered away at the theme
that their party was untainted by support for the provisional government.
Even if a majority of soldiers or of the population of Petrograd or of Russia
did not necessarily favor the Bolsheviks, Lenin's assessment that they
would not oppose their seizure of power proved correct.

Late on October 24, 1917, Kerensky shut down Bolshevik newspapers
and sent troops to hold the bridges over the Neva River. About 12,000 Red
Guards launched the insurrection, supported by factory committees in
Petrograd's industrial districts. Leon Trotsky (Lev Davidovich Bronstein,
1879–1940) coordinated the uprising. Trotsky, the revolutionary son of a
wealthy Jewish farmer, had borrowed his alias from one of his prison guards.
Bolsheviks repelled an attack by army cadets loyal to the provisional government, the only serious fighting of the October Revolution. The regiments
upon which Kerensky had counted remained in their barracks, their neutrality striking a blow for the insurrection.

The provisional government collapsed. Kerensky left Petrograd the same
day in a car borrowed from the U.S. embassy, hoping in vain to rally military support at the front. That night, the battleship *Aurora,* under the control of revolutionaries, lobbed a couple of shells toward the Winter Palace,
where the last ministers of the provisional government were holding out.
The provisional government surrendered after eight months of existence.
The Bolsheviks held power in Petrograd.

The October Revolution had occurred as if in slow motion. There were
fewer people killed than in the February Revolution or even the July Days.

The Bolsheviks seize the Winter Palace, October 1917.

Life went on in many districts of the city as if nothing unusual was occurring. Restaurants, casinos, theaters, and the ballet remained open, although banks closed and streetcars were hard to find. Shares on the stock market, which had risen in anticipation of a military coup d'état during the Kornilov crisis, declined. John Reed, an American sympathetic to the Bolshevik takeover, recalled that in Petrograd's fancy quarters "the ladies of the minor bureaucratic set took tea with each other in the afternoon, [each] carrying her little gold or silver or jeweled sugar-box, and half a loaf of bread in her muff, and wishing that the tsar were back, or that the Germans would come, or anything that would solve the servant problem . . . the daughter of a friend of mine came home one afternoon in hysterics because the woman streetcar conductor had called her 'Comrade.'"

Most Mensheviks and many Socialist Revolutionaries walked out of the All-Russian Congress of Soviets to protest the Bolshevik insurrection. On October 26, the remaining members approved the Bolshevik proposal that "all local authority be transferred to the soviets." The Central Committee of the Congress of Soviets, all Bolshevik except for some leftist Socialist Revolutionaries, now ran the government.

In Moscow, Russia's second city, the insurrection began after the first reports from Petrograd arrived. There, too, the Bolsheviks found support in workers' neighborhoods. After a week of fighting, the forces of the provisional government surrendered. In the vast reaches of the former Russian Empire, a "revolution by telegraph" took place. Commissars representing the Bolsheviks went into the provinces (see Map 23.1). In industrial regions, where the Bolsheviks already dominated some soviets, it was easy enough to establish a military revolutionary committee to assume local power. In the countryside, the Bolsheviks cultivated support among the poorest peasants. Socialist Revolutionaries, with considerable influence among peasants, believed that they could coexist with the new Bolshevik-dominated government. But the Bolsheviks manipulated ethnic, social, and political tensions, purging the soviets of non-Bolsheviks and pushing aside not only the local institutions of self-rule that had spontaneously sprung up after the February Revolution but also their nominal allies, the Socialist Revolutionaries.

In Ukraine, the situation remained calm at least partially because the Bolsheviks had early in the Revolution made an agreement with Ukrainian nationalists. In the distant borderlands where ethnic Russians were a minority, however, strong anti-Russian national feeling often made it extremely difficult for the Bolsheviks to take control.

The Bolsheviks were a small minority in Russia at the time of the October Revolution. "We shall not enter into the kingdom of socialism in white gloves on a polished floor," Trotsky had warned shortly before the October Revolution. The revolutionary government, under Lenin's leadership, seized banks, closed down newspapers, and banned the liberal Constitutional Democratic Party. In December, a new centralized police authority, the

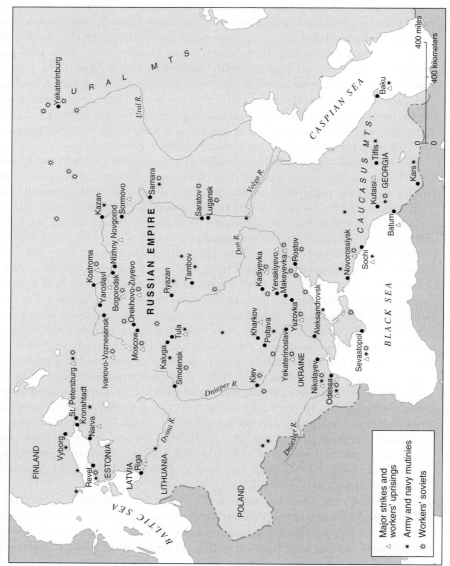

Map 23.1 The Russian Revolution Sites of strikes, uprisings, and army and navy mutinies during the Russian Revolution, as well as the cities in which soviets were established by the revolutionaries.

Cheka, began to arrest those who disagreed with the Bolsheviks. It rapidly proliferated into a large organization with virtually unlimited power. Arbitrary arrests led the eminent writer Maxim Gorky to ask, "Does not Lenin's government, as did the Romanov government, seize and drag off to prison all those who think differently?"

In elections for the Constituent Assembly, the Bolsheviks were supported only by the left wing of the Socialist Revolutionaries. The Bolsheviks won just 29 percent of the vote, compared with 58 percent for the Socialist Revolutionaries. When the elected deputies arrived early in January 1918, the Bolsheviks forced the assembly to adjourn the next day. It never met again. Red Guards fired on protesters.

That month, Lenin proclaimed the "Declaration of the Rights of the Toiling and Exploited People," which stated that the goal of the revolutionary government was "the socialist organization of society and the victory of socialism in all countries." The third All-Russian Congress of Soviets established the Russian Socialist Soviet Republic, a federation of "soviet republics." But, as in the Russian Empire, Russia's interests, even under Bolshevik communism, remained paramount.

The Peace of Brest-Litovsk

After the Bolsheviks took power, Trotsky, now "People's Commissar for Foreign Affairs," offered Germany an armistice, signed early in December 1917. However, Trotsky broke off negotiations for a permanent peace agreement because of draconian German demands. In mid-February, German troops captured Kiev and much of Ukraine and Crimea, as well as some of the Caucasus region. On March 3, 1918, the Bolshevik government signed the Treaty of Brest-Litovsk with Germany, giving up one-fourth of the area of what had been imperial European Russia, containing some of its most fertile land and most of its iron and steel production. The Bolsheviks also agreed to German occupation of Estonia, Lithuania, and Latvia and agreed to pull Russian troops out of Ukraine and Finland. Angered by the treaty and demanding rapid attention to the agrarian question, the leftist Socialist Revolutionaries ended their cooperation with the Bolsheviks. The Germans then occupied all of Finland and Ukraine, setting up puppet regimes in both states.

Civil War

The Russian Civil War began in 1918 when Kornilov and other generals raised armies to fight the Bolsheviks (see Map 23.2). The anti-Bolshevik forces became known as the "Whites" because they shared a common hatred of the Bolsheviks, the "Reds." The White armies held Central Asia and Siberia, territory east of Moscow, and the Caucasus Mountains. A

legion of 50,000 Czechoslovak troops, which had surrendered earlier in
the war, operated as an anti-Bolshevik force along an extensive stretch of
territory into Siberia, holding the crucial trans-Siberian railway. The White
army played upon anti-Semitism by denouncing Trotsky and other Bolshevik leaders because they were Jews. A wave of pogroms spread through
Ukraine and parts of Russia. More than 2 million people fled abroad to
escape the Russian Revolution and the ensuing Civil War.

MAP 23.2 THE RUSSIAN CIVIL WAR   Boundaries of areas controlled by the Whites
and the Reds during the Russian Civil War, including advances by the White and
foreign armies.

Ukraine passed back and forth between Bolshevik and nationalist control in bloody fighting, falling again briefly into the hands of the Germans. A huge peasant army led by the anarchist Nestor Makhno (1889–1934) allied with the Bolsheviks and controlled parts of Ukraine after the Germans had fallen back. In Siberia, General Alexander Kolchak (1874–1920), backed by Britain and France, established a dictatorship that claimed to be the new government of Russia.

In February 1918, the Soviet government proclaimed the nationalization of all land. Food shortages and famine spread that summer. The Bolsheviks reacted to the crisis by implementing "War Communism." The state appropriated heavy industries and gradually put an end to private trade. The Bolsheviks forcibly requisitioned food and raw materials, turning poor peasants against more prosperous ones, known as "kulaks." Peasants from whom grain was being taken sometimes reacted with shock—after all, before the October Revolution the Bolsheviks had loudly proclaimed their support for immediate land reform. Now soldiers were confiscating their grain. Many peasants resisted. War Communism may have saved the Revolution, but it took a terrible toll, leading to a dramatic decline in industrial production.

Bolshevik guards moved Nicholas II and his family to Ekaterinburg, a town in the Ural Mountains, as rumors spread that the Czech legion or monarchist generals were planning to rescue them. On July 17, 1918, they

Lenin addressing the troops leaving for the front during the Civil War, 1920. Trotsky is in uniform standing to the right of the podium, and was later removed from this famous photo on Stalin's order after he was purged.

were brutally executed on the orders of the local soviet, an act evidently approved by Bolshevik leaders.

The Allies, particularly Britain, provided supplies to the White armies. In August, British, American, and Canadian soldiers landed in the northern port of Murmansk, claiming that such measures were necessary to prevent Russia's northern ports from falling to the Germans. Allied suspicion of the new Bolshevik government strengthened their decision to intervene. British troops attacked Soviet forces, and American troops landed at the icy northern port of Archangel. Japanese troops moved into Siberia, where the Bolsheviks had little effective control, remaining there until 1922.

Allied intervention helped rally popular opinion against the Whites, whose wanton brutality, including routine rape and murder (some victims were forced to kneel and kiss portraits of the tsar before being killed), exceeded that of the Bolsheviks. Whites filled three freight cars with bodies of Red Guards, sending them along to the Bolsheviks, who were starving, with the wagons labeled "fresh meat, destination Petrograd." However, the Whites had no monopoly on savagery, as in some places Red forces massacred peasants and Cossacks. In Finland, after a bitter civil war between local Reds and Whites, the "White Terror" took 80,000 victims among those who had supported the Revolution. Moreover, the Russian nationalist calls of White leaders for an "indivisible" Russia alienated other national groups, aiding the Bolsheviks, who falsely promised to respect the rights of non-Russian nationalities.

Following attempts on the lives of several Bolshevik leaders, including Lenin, the "Red Terror" began in September 1918. Government decrees gave the Cheka almost unlimited authority and set up forced labor camps to incarcerate those considered enemies. While many victims were indeed working for the overthrow of the regime, many others were simply Mensheviks, Socialist Revolutionaries, or others who held political beliefs that displeased the Bolsheviks.

Fighting the Whites required the mobilization of 5 million men. The Red Army defeated the largest White army in Ukraine during the summer of 1919 and turned back a final march on Moscow in October. General Alexander Kolchak's White army held out until late that year. The Civil War continued in 1920, and in the Pacific region fighting lasted into 1922.

In 1920, Józef Pilsudski, commander of the Polish army, sought to take advantage of apparent Soviet weakness in the wake of the Civil War by creating a federation of independent states, including Lithuania, Ukraine, and Belarus, under Polish leadership. Having defeated the White armies, Lenin planned a Soviet attack on Poland. But the Polish army invaded Ukraine, until the Red Army repelled the attack and pushed Polish forces back into Poland. However, Polish peasants and workers refused to join the Red Army. Pilsudski's forces surrounded the Soviet army on the edge of Warsaw in August 1920—the "miracle of the Vistula" River. This put an end to the possibility of the Soviet army pushing toward Berlin and linking up with a revo-

The White army executes suspected Bolsheviks during the Civil War.

lution in Germany. The Treaty of Riga in March 1921 ended the hostilities between Poland and the new Soviet government, which had been largely at the expense of Ukraine. While much of Ukraine was left within the Soviet Union, 5 million Ukrainians now found themselves living in Poland.

THE SOVIET UNION

The Revolution seemed to offer peasants in Russia hope. After destroying the authority of the imperial regime in the countryside, they then broke the power of the landlords. Many peasants feared the Whites, and they therefore went along with the demands of the Soviet regime, hoping that "peace and land" would follow. The Bolsheviks were able to install a centralized state authority to mobilize the countryside against the counter-revolution. Like the old imperial elites, the Bolsheviks mistrusted the peasants, their notions of family and village ownership of land, their sense of collective responsibility, and their eagerness to market what they produced. The Civil War established a precedent for the use of mass terror to enforce the party's will in rural areas. Gradually, Bolshevik commissars reestablished Bolshevik authority over Ukraine and border lands such as Georgia and Turkistan.

A constitution promulgated in July 1918 promised freedom of speech and assembly, as well as the separation of church and state. The "dictatorship of the proletariat" became that of the Bolsheviks. Marxist theory promised the "withering of the state" once socialism had been constructed, and Lenin himself warned against the growing power of the bureaucracy, which he had helped create. But the Soviet state did anything but wither.

MAP 23.3 THE SOVIET REPUBLICS, 1922–1939 Soviet Socialist Republics (SSRs) and their capitals in the Union of Soviet Socialist Republics.

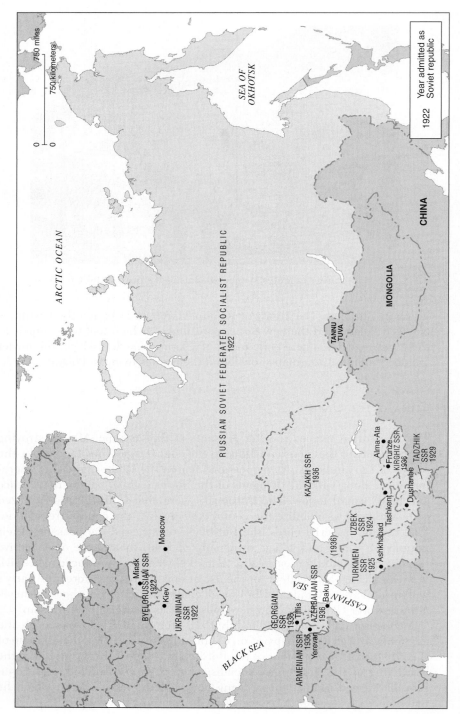

The Union of Soviet Socialist Republics was created in 1922. It included Russia, Belarus, Ukraine, and Transcaucasia (Georgia, Armenia, and Azerbaijan, which all became separate republics in 1936), to which Uzbek (Uzbekistan) was added in 1924, Turkmen (Turkistan) in 1925, Tadzhik in 1929, and Kazakh (Kazakhstan) and Kirghiz in 1936 (see Map 23.3).

Democratic Centralism

For Lenin, "democratic centralism," which had referred to decisions taken by the Bolshevik Party, was also a goal in itself in the organization of the socialist state. In the summer of 1918, the Bolsheviks took the name of the Communist Party, a name Lenin had favored during the war as a way of more clearly differentiating the more radical Bolsheviks from the Mensheviks, their socialist rivals. Lenin's concept originally called for open and free discussion and debate on policy issues, but once party leaders made a decision all dissent had to end and all party members were to unite around the party line. Major decisions and discipline would thus come from the top. The structure suffocated the democratic apparatus on the local level, which henceforth received orders that flowed downward and outward from the central party apparatus in the name of the state.

The Communist government did not tolerate workers' self-management, a goal of many people who had helped overthrow the tsarist autocracy. A group called the Left Communists had opposed signing the Treaty of Brest-Litovsk with Germany, arguing that Russia should lead a revolutionary war against the capitalist powers. Furthermore, they denounced the growing centralization of power. In response, Lenin acidly denounced "Left Infantilism and the Petty Bourgeois Spirit" in the summer of 1918, referring to those who criticized the abandonment of the principles of workers' self-management. Now "workers' control" meant state control.

In June 1919, the Bolsheviks nationalized most of the large-scale industries. In early 1921, at the end of the Civil War, worker discontent erupted in strikes and demonstrations in some industrial centers. In March 1921, the Red Army crushed a revolt at the Kronstadt naval base, where sailors demanded freely elected soviets. Massive strikes rocked Petrograd after Bolshevik authorities rebuffed workers' demands for better working conditions and more control over their shops and factories. Party officials pushed the soviets out of the way as the state turned against the idea of workers' self-management. In 1922, someone asked Trotsky, "Do you remember the days when you promised us that the Bolsheviks would respect democratic liberties?" Trotsky replied, "Yes, that was in the old days." That same year, when protests occurred in one region against the confiscation of Orthodox Church treasures, Lenin himself suggested that demonstrators be shot: "The more [of them] we manage to shoot, the better. Right now we have to teach this public a lesson, so that for several decades they won't even dare to think of resisting."

The New Economic Policy

Lenin and the other Bolshevik leaders debated how socialism could be implemented in a vast, poor country of many nationalities. The new Soviet government had to repair the massive disruption done to the economy by the Great War and subsequent Civil War. More than 7 million people died of starvation and sickness during a famine in 1921–1922. Moreover, the war against Poland and the loss of territory also accentuated the gravity of the economic situation. With the economy in near total collapse, Lenin recognized that communist ideology, which called for the abolition of private ownership, for the moment would have to be sacrificed. Market incentives would have to be tolerated, perhaps for some time.

Furthermore, War Communism had collapsed because of the resistance, active and passive, of peasants and workers. The cities and army had only been fed because the state had been able to requisition or commandeer supplies in the vast countryside. At a time of severe famine, the government needed to feed the population and build up a surplus of raw materials and food supplies. After the threat from the White armies had ended, peasants had violently resisted grain requisitioning. Against this background, in March 1921, Lenin announced a "New Economic Policy" (NEP). Although the state maintained its centralized control over the economy, the NEP permitted peasants to use the land as if it were their own and allowed trade of produce at market prices, although the state retained control of heavy industries. The goal was, above all, to encourage peasants to bring their crops to market. Lenin called this a temporary "retreat" on the road to socialism. Some merchants whose stores had been nationalized during the Civil War were now allowed to manage them again, and the government permitted small-scale, privately owned manufacturing. Lenin even invited foreign investment in mining and other development projects.

The NEP revived the economy. The amount of land under cultivation and industrial production gradually began to reach pre-war levels. In towns, small businesses run by "nepmen" prospered, and kulaks gained. But if the NEP brought economic concessions, there were virtually none in the political realm. The Bolsheviks further consolidated their hold over most government functions, claiming to be serving the interests of the working class by protecting them against the Western Allies. They declared all other political parties illegal, although Lenin claimed that this ban would be only a temporary measure, like the NEP itself. The Bolsheviks continued the campaign against Socialist Revolutionaries, as well as Mensheviks. In 1924, the state limited the entrepreneurship of "nepmen" and, three years later, of kulaks.

In the meantime, Joseph Stalin (1879–1953) emerged as an important figure in the Soviet hierarchy. Stalin—an alias taken from the Russian word for "steel"—was born Joseph (Soso) Dzhugashvili in Georgia, beyond the Caucasus Mountains in the southern reaches of the Russian Empire. His father was a tough cobbler who may have been killed in a tavern brawl, his mother a religious woman who worked as hard as her husband drank. The young Stalin entered an Orthodox seminary in 1894 in the Georgian capital of Tbilisi. Stalin rebelled against the conservatism of the Orthodox Church. In the seminary, Stalin learned Russian, secretly read Marxist tracts, and joined a radical study circle, for which he was expelled. Arrested in 1902 and exiled to Siberia the next year, Stalin escaped and returned to Georgia. There he sided with the Bolsheviks against the Mensheviks (see Chapter 18). The Bolsheviks' hardened secrecy appealed to the young Georgian's acerbic personality. More arrests, jail terms, exile to Siberia, and escapes followed in rapid succession over the next seven years. In 1912, Vladimir Lenin appointed Stalin to the Bolshevik Central Committee, and, after yet another escape from prison, he became editor of *Pravda*.

At the time of the February Revolution, Stalin was a prisoner in Siberia, 600 miles from even the trans-Siberian railway. He managed to return to Petrograd and, after the October Revolution, helped Lenin draft the "Declaration of the Rights of the Peoples of Russia," which promised the peoples of the former Russian Empire self-determination. During the Civil War, he served on the military revolutionary council and quarreled with Trotsky over military strategy.

Trotsky had surprisingly little talent for the ruthless political infighting that was as natural to Stalin as breathing. An intense intellectual and powerful orator, Trotsky considered Stalin a "mediocrity." Stalin remained suspicious of "cosmopolitan"—often an anti-Semitic code word for Jewish—intellectuals such as Trotsky. Espousing "permanent revolution," Trotsky believed that socialism in the Soviet Union could only be victorious following world revolution and that the capitalist nations of the West were ripe to be overthrown by proletarian revolutions. The Communist International had been founded in 1919 to help organize and assist revolutionary Communist parties in other countries. Lenin had believed that workers would overthrow one Western state after another. But this had not happened. The German Revolution of 1919 and the revolutionary government of Béla Kun in Hungary had been crushed (see Chapter 24). The International also promised to help colonial people win independence from imperialist domination.

The problem of the status of the 180 nationalities in the Soviet Union became ever more pressing. Lenin's support for national self-determination had been principally intended to undermine the provisional government and win the support of non-Russian nationalities. Furthermore, concerned with the Soviet Union's image in the colonial world, he wanted to give the impression that the various peoples enjoyed a degree of sovereignty. He still believed that national differences posed a threat to the revolution and that they would become irrelevant in the communist state. Stalin, who served as commissar for nationalities (1917–1923), wanted the peoples of the old imperial state incorporated into the existing Russian state. During the Civil War, he had crushed what he called "the hydra of nationalism" in his native Georgia. Russian interests prevailed within the party, and thus within the government. The

Vladimir Lenin (*left*) with Joseph Stalin (*right*) in a photo doctored by Stalin, who was eager to exaggerate his close association with Lenin.

republics created within the Soviet Union in 1922 and thereafter enjoyed virtually no autonomy. The official line was that communism had brought stability by eliminating ethnic tensions and that nationalism would disappear in the new socialist world. If Soviet policies encouraged the survival of some local languages, one reason was to ensure that state bureaucratic directives could be read by Soviet citizens. The Constitution of 1924 would declare the states of the Soviet Union equal, but the reality was completely otherwise.

In May 1922, Lenin suffered a stroke. His illness set off a struggle of succession infused with personal as well as ideological rivalries. Stalin had demonstrated forceful independence while remaining loyal to the party, and a capacity for organization. The previous month, the Central Committee had named Stalin to the recently created post of general secretary, which allowed him to appoint allies to various important posts and to repress dissent within the party. Stalin kept Lenin isolated as much as possible from visitors. In December, a day after suffering a second stroke, Lenin dictated his doubts about Stalin: "Comrade Stalin, on becoming general secretary, concentrated boundless power in his hands, and I am not sure whether he will always know how to use this power with sufficient caution." Lenin also warned against the expansion of the bureaucracies of both the Communist Party and the state.

Lenin's death in January 1924 consolidated Stalin's position. He placed his own men on the Central Committee and made party appointments throughout the Soviet state. He took every occasion to leave the impression that Lenin had handpicked him to be the next Communist Party leader, later doctoring photos so that he appeared to have been constantly at Lenin's side. Under Stalin, the Soviet Union became even more of a totalitarian regime. The promised "dictatorship of the proletariat" became that of the Communist Party and that of Joseph Stalin.

CHAPTER 24

THE ELUSIVE SEARCH FOR STABILITY IN THE 1920S

In the preface to his novel *The Magic Mountain* (1924), Thomas Mann (1875–1955) wrote that it took place "in the long ago, in the old days, the days of the world before the Great War." Mann sets up a parallel between a Swiss sanatorium and European civilization. In the sanatorium, rationality (Enlightenment thought and democracy) confronts irrationality (the aggressive nationalism of the right-wing dictatorships). In *The Magic Mountain,* which was an allegory for the post-war era, Mann expressed the mood of despair prevalent among European intellectuals in the 1920s: "For us in old Europe, everything has died that was good and unique to us. Our admirable rationality has become madness, our gold is paper, our machines can only shoot and explode, our art is suicide; we are going under, friends."

The Great War swept away the empires of Germany, Austria-Hungary, Turkey, and even before the end of the war, Russia. The Treaty of Versailles, signed in 1919 by a frail new German Republic, and the accompanying treaties signed by the victorious Allies and Germany's wartime partners, did not resolve national rivalries in Europe. Dark clouds of economic turmoil, political instability, and international tension descended on Europe in the two decades that followed the war. The specter of revolution frightened Europe's business and political leaders. Communist parties sprung up in one country after another, even though outside of the Soviet Union Bolshevism only triumphed briefly in Hungary and Bavaria. Although Europe experienced a brief return to relative prosperity and political calm after 1924, the Wall Street Crash of 1929 ended that short period of hope. The search for what U.S. senator and future president Warren G. Harding called "normalcy" proved elusive, if not impossible, in the 1920s.

The Great War helped unleash the demons of the twentieth century, as parties of the political extremes sprang up to threaten parliamentary

955

The Big Four deciding the future of Europe, 1919. Left to right: Vittorio Orlando of Italy, David Lloyd George of Great Britain, Georges Clemenceau of France, and Woodrow Wilson of the United States.

governments. Fascist and other extreme nationalist groups (see Chapter 25), intolerant of those considered outsiders and committed to aggressive territorial expansion, carried their violence into the streets. Many members of these organizations were former soldiers who vowed to replace democracies and republics with dictatorships. In Eastern Europe and the Balkans, parliamentary rule survived only in Czechoslovakia. Moreover, ethnic rivalries within nations, many inflamed by the Treaty of Versailles, intensified social and political conflict. The post-war treaties could not create new states that satisfied all nationalities.

THE END OF THE WAR

Even before the representatives of the victorious Allies (along with those representing a host of smaller states) met in Versailles in 1919 for a peace conference, the German and Austro-Hungarian Empires had collapsed, rocked by revolutions. Amid social and political turmoil, the leaders of the great powers set out to reestablish peace in Europe. But the Treaty of Versailles reflected the determination of Great Britain and France to punish Germany for its role in unleashing the conflict. Representatives of the new German Republic were forced to sign a clause essentially accepting full blame for the outbreak of the war, and to agree to pay an enormous sum in war reparations to the Allies, but the amount and schedule of German payments was established only in 1921.

Despite the idealistic belief of U.S. President Woodrow Wilson that the Great War had been the "war to end all wars" and that an era of collective security had begun that would prevent future wars of a similar magnitude, the Paris Peace Conference left a legacy of bitterness and hatred that made it even more difficult for the German Republic to find stability because of massive dissatisfaction with the terms of the treaty. Furthermore, the individual treaties between the Allies and Germany's former wartime partners left several nationalities, notably Hungarians, dissatisfied with the establishment of new states constituted out of the old empires; the newly drawn borders often left them on what they considered the wrong side of frontiers. Nationalists in Germany, above all, but also those in some other countries, were determined to revise or abrogate the post-war peace settlements.

Revolution in Germany and Hungary

The end of the war brought political crises in Germany and Hungary. In the face of defeat, the German Empire came apart at the seams. In late October 1918, German sailors mutinied at two Baltic naval bases, demanding peace and the kaiser's abdication. In southern Germany, socialists led by Kurt Eisner (1867–1919) proclaimed a Bavarian socialist republic in early November. The new chancellor, Prince Max von Baden, called on William II to abdicate, as the socialists threatened to leave the emergency coalition cabinet if he did not do so. William abdicated on November 9. Von Baden then named Friedrich Ebert (1871–1925), a member of the left-wing Social Democratic Party, to succeed him as chancellor.

That same day, a German commission met with Allied representatives to begin drawing up terms for an armistice. On November 9, 1918, another Social Democrat, Philip Scheidemann (1865–1939), fearing that radical revolutionaries would declare a socialist state, proclaimed the German Republic. That night, William II fled into the Netherlands. On November 11, 1918, Germany signed the armistice with the Allies, ending the war. Chancellor Ebert named a provisional government, which was dominated by Social Democrats but with members of the more radical Independent Social Democratic Party also represented.

From its very beginning, the new German Republic was under siege from left and right. Inspired by the success of the Bolshevik Revolution in Russia, workers began to set up "workers' and soldiers' councils" and demanded higher wages and better working conditions. Workers also angered the army by calling for the dismissal of the right-wing General Paul von Hindenburg from the military high command on which he had served since 1916, and by demanding the abolition of the special military schools for officers that for generations had sustained Prussian militarism.

The right posed a more serious threat to the fledgling republic, a threat the Treaty of Versailles would strengthen. Germany had very weak democratic traditions. Monarchism and militarism ran deep, particularly in Prussia.

Furthermore, demobilized soldiers, many of whom were anti-republican, still held their weapons. Ominously, a veteran wrote that he believed the Great War of 1914–1918 was "not the end, but the chord that heralds new power. It is the anvil on which the world will be hammered into new boundaries and new communities. New forms will be filled with blood."

The head of Germany's Supreme Army Command offered the chancellor the army's support, but on condition that the new government not only order the army to maintain order but also to fight "Bolshevism." Ebert accepted and, in doing so, made the new republic virtually a prisoner of the army. Some generals had already begun to enlist demobilized soldiers into right-wing paramilitary units known as the "Free Corps."

Within the new government itself, a rift developed between the Social Democrats and the Independent Social Democrats, who demanded immediate assistance for workers and wanted the government to organize a militia loyal to the republic. When Ebert refused, the Independent Socialist Democrats left the governing coalition, weakening the shaky government. The new minister of defense turned over security operations to the army, and continued to encourage the Free Corps. To the left, this seemed like leaving the fox to guard the hen house.

Workers in Berlin mounted huge demonstrations against the security police. In January 1919, police and soldiers put down an uprising by the Spartacists, a group of far-left revolutionaries who took their name from the leader of a revolt by Roman slaves in the first century B.C. Military units hunted down the Spartacists, murdering Karl Liebknecht and the Polish Marxist Rosa Luxemburg, two of their leaders, who had just founded the German Communist Party.

The German Republic's first elections in January 1919 provided a workable center-left coalition of Social Democrats (who held the most seats in the Reichstag), the Catholic Center Party, and the German Democratic Party. The Reichstag elected Ebert president, and he in turn appointed Scheidemann to be the first premier of the Weimar Republic. The Reichstag met in Weimar, a small, centrally located town, chosen to counter the Prussian aristocratic and militaristic traditions identified with the old imperial capital of Berlin.

Hungary also soon became a battleground between the competing ideologies of the post-war period. Demobilized soldiers and former imperial officials were among those stirring up trouble. Hungarian nationalists feared, with good reason, that the victorious Allies would award disputed territories from pre-war Hungary to Czechoslovakia, Romania, and Yugoslavia. With the collapse of the Austro-Hungarian Empire in the autumn of 1918, Count Mihály Károlyi (1875–1955) led an unopposed revolution of liberals and socialists that proclaimed Hungarian independence. Károlyi favored a republic and initiated a program of land reform by turning over his own estate to peasants. Other wealthy landowners, however, prepared to defend their vast estates against land-hungry peasants. In March 1919, Béla Kun (1886–c. 1937), a Communist journalist, took advantage of the post-war chaos, seized

Karl Liebknecht addresses his supporters in January 1919, shortly before his assassination. (*Right*) Leaders of the Hungarian Communist movement, including Béla Kun, on the right, after they were overthrown.

power, and tried to impose a Soviet regime by means of a "Red terror." He announced a more extensive land-reform policy, established collective farms and labor camps, and nationalized banks, insurance companies, and large industries. Inflation and food rationing soared and the Hungarian currency lost 90 percent of its value. In July 1919, Kun attacked Romania, with the goal of retaking territory with a large Hungarian population. His forces also invaded Slovakia and proclaimed a brief Soviet republic there.

The Romanian army drove Kun's forces back, invading Hungary and marching to Budapest to help overthrow him. Admiral Miklós Horthy (1868–1957), a former Habsburg naval officer (with not much to do, as Hungary would lose its access to the sea), seized power in 1920, with the title of regent and head of state. He encouraged attacks against Jews—Kun was Jewish as was the head of his secret police—claiming that they were Bolsheviks, and he ordered the execution of thousands of workers and Communists. Backed by the Hungarian upper classes, he declared his determination to see Hungary maintain its previous borders.

The Treaty of Versailles

In this volatile atmosphere, delegates from twenty-seven nations and the four British Dominions (Canada, South Africa, Australia, and New Zealand) gathered for the Paris Peace Conference in the château of Versailles. As they convened in January 1919, the representatives of the "Big Four"—Prime Minister David Lloyd George of Britain, Prime Minister Georges Clemenceau of France, President Woodrow Wilson of the United States, and Prime Minister Vittorio Orlando of Italy—agreed that Germany, the nation they believed responsible for the war, should assume the financial burden of putting Europe back together again.

Beyond this area of agreement, the "Big Four" powers went to Versailles with different demands and expectations. France, which had suffered far greater losses than Britain, Italy, or the United States, demanded a harsh settlement that would eliminate Germany as a potential military threat. The diminutive, elderly, and thoroughly vindictive Clemenceau, a combative loner nicknamed "the Tiger," realized the dangers of a punitive peace settlement. But he was also mindful that the quest for security against Germany dominated French foreign relations and weighed heavily upon domestic politics. Defeated Germany was still potentially a stronger state because of its economic capacity and larger population.

France's victory had been Pyrrhic. More than 1.3 million Frenchmen were killed in the Great War. France seemed a country of crippled or traumatized veterans, widows dressed in mourning black, and hundreds of thousands of children left without fathers, for whom pensions would have to be paid. Much of the north and northeast of the country lay in ruins; factories and railways had been destroyed in a region that contained 70 percent of the country's coal. The state had to borrow money from its wartime allies and from its citizens at high interest rates to pay off those who had purchased war bonds.

Clemenceau demanded that Germany's military arsenal be drastically reduced and that French troops occupy the Rhineland until Germany had paid its reparations to the Allies. These payments would be based on a rough estimate of damages caused to the victorious powers by the war. Many in France wanted to go further, demanding annexation of the left bank of the Rhine River, or the creation of an independent Rhineland state that would serve as a buffer against further German aggression.

The British, represented by the Liberal Lloyd George, came to Versailles with more flexible views than the French. Britain had been spared almost all the physical devastation suffered by its cross-Channel allies. Still, the British had suffered horrific loss of life, and they had borne more than their share of the war's financial costs. The British government thus supported France's position that Germany had to be contained in the future. The slogan "Squeeze the German lemon 'til the pip squeaks" was current. However, Lloyd George now concluded that it was in Europe's interest to restore the fledgling German Republic to reasonable economic strength. Moreover, Britian also was wary of a possible increase in French power that could upset the future balance of power in Europe. In view of the perceived threat posed by the Russian Revolution, Lloyd George reasoned that Germany could emerge as a force for European stability.

Italian Prime Minister Vittorio Orlando (1860–1952) came to Versailles assuming that his country would receive territories of the former Austro-Hungarian Empire promised by the Allies in 1915, when Italy had entered the war on their side—namely, the port of Trieste; the strategically important Alpine region around Trent (the South Tyrol), which would give Italy a natural boundary; and Istria and northern Dalmatia on the Adriatic coast (see Map 24.1). Italy had entered the war in part with the goal of generating Italian nationalism, and its allies arguably considered Italy's war effort to have been lamentable. President Wilson found acceptable Italian annexation of the first two, which had sizable—although, except in the case of Trieste, not majority—Italian populations. As a result, Italy extended its frontiers to the Brenner Pass and to Trieste. But Wilson staunchly opposed Italian demands for Istria, northern Dalmatia, and the strategically important Adriatic port of Rijeka (known to its Italian minority as Fiume), which Italy had omitted from its demands in 1915, but now claimed. Italian nationalists denounced the "mutilated peace" of Saint-Germain that had not allowed annexation of all of the territories the Italian government had anticipated receiving.

Wilson's position on Italy's territorial demands reflected one of the broad principles this high-minded son of a Presbyterian minister brought with him to Versailles as representative of the United States. Wilson stood for national self-determination, the principle that ethnicity should determine national boundaries, and went to Versailles hoping to "make the world safe for democracy." This was manifest in his Fourteen Points (see Chapter 22). The U.S. president hoped that diplomacy would henceforth be carried out through "open covenants of peace," not the secret treaties that he held responsible for the Great War. Wilson believed that if the victorious powers applied "the principle of justice to all peoples and nationalities . . . whether they be strong or weak," Europe would enter an era of enduring stability.

The U.S. president's main concern at Versailles was with the creation of a League of Nations, which began in 1920, to arbitrate subsequent international disputes. He was less concerned with forcing a punitive settlement on Germany. In Wilson's opinion, the Great War had been fought largely over the competing claims of national groups, thus it was not right to separate Rhineland Germans from Germany.

Wilson believed that the outbreak of the Great War had demonstrated that the diplomatic concept of a "balance of power," by which the predominant strength of one power was balanced by alliances between several other powers, was unequal to the task of maintaining peace. Henceforth, Wilson wanted the United States to assume an international role, joining Great Britain, France, Italy, and Japan as permanent members of the League of Nation's Council. The League would stand for collective security against any power that would threaten the peace.

Yet idealism and reality were at odds at Versailles. Among the leaders of the three main victorious powers, Wilson's idealism contrasted with the determined realism of Lloyd George and Clemenceau. During four

Legend:

Territory lost by:
- Germany (Plebiscite areas remaining in country)
- Bulgaria (Demilitarized zone)
- Austria-Hungary
- Russia

MAP 24.1 TERRITORIAL SETTLEMENTS AFTER WORLD WAR I Territories lost by Germany, Bulgaria, Austria-Hungary, and Russia as a result of the treaties ending the Great War.

months, the British and French leaders wrestled with public pressure at home for a harsh peace, which they had to balance against the possibility that a draconian settlement might push defeated Germany, Austria, and Hungary in the direction of the Soviet Union. The French and British views prevailed in what was called the "victor's peace." Moreover, both Lloyd George and Clemenceau, unlike Wilson, enjoyed the full support of their constituents.

By the "war guilt clause," Article 231 of the treaty, Germany accepted full responsibility for "the loss and damage" caused the Allies "as a consequence of the war imposed upon them by the aggression of Germany and her allies." Many Germans were outraged in April 1919 when they learned of the treaty that Germany had been forced to accept. The Allies seemed to be punishing the new German Republic for the acts of the old imperial regime, which arguably had, with Austria-Hungary, done more to start the war than the other powers. Premier Scheidemann resigned rather than sign the treaty. The next Social Democratic government signed it a week later, on June 28, 1919, but only after the Allies had threatened to invade Germany. The Treaty of Versailles returned to France Alsace and the parts of Lorraine that had been annexed by Germany after the Franco-Prussian War of 1870–1871 (see Map 24.2). French troops would occupy the parts of Germany that stood on the left, or western, bank of the Rhine River, as well as occupy for fifteen years a strategically critical strip of land along its right bank. These territories were to remain permanently demilitarized. France would retain economic control over the rich coal and iron mines of the Saar border region (which would be administered by the League of Nations) for fifteen years, at which time the region's population would express by plebiscite whether it wished to become part of France or remain German (the latter was the result in 1935). Germany also had to cede small pieces of long-contested frontier territory to Belgium (Eupen and Malmédy). Moreover, Germany lost its colonies.

In the east, Germany lost territory to Poland, which became independent for the first time since 1795. Poles had been forced to fight in the armies of the German, Austro-Hungarian, and Russian Empires during the war, and thus had been pitted against each other. During the war, both Russia and Germany had promised Poland independence. Indeed, in November 1916 the Central Powers had reestablished the Polish kingdom viewing it as a potential buffer against Russia. In September 1917 they appointed a "Regency Council" with no real power but with the goal of representing Polish Society, with an eye toward Polish autonomy, in the quest for Polish support. In the meantime, Polish nationalists campaigned for support for Polish independence in Britain, France, and the United States. During the war, Józef Pilsudski (1867–1935), one of the leaders of the Polish independence movement during the last decade of the Russian Empire and a leading member of the Polish Socialist Party, commanded a "Polish Legion." Allied with the Central Powers for tactical reasons, it fought against Russian forces in

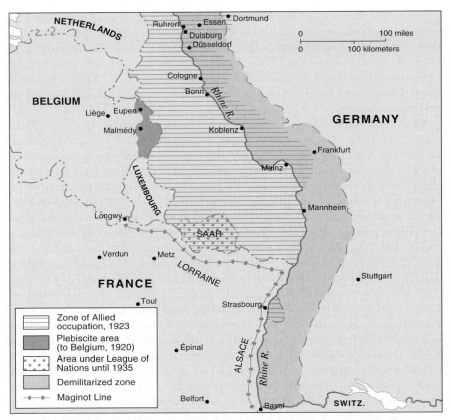

MAP 24.2 AREAS OF FRENCH AND GERMAN DISPUTES, 1920s   Border areas, including the Rhineland and the Saar Basin, that were occupied by Allied troops or were part of a demilitarized zone after the Great War.

the hope of winning independence. In January 1918, one of Wilson's Fourteen Points was an independent Poland. On Armistice Day, November 11, 1918, Poland became independent. The Treaty of Versailles awarded Poland much of Pomerania, constituting what the Germans would call the "Polish Corridor" (Eastern Pomerania, which had been annexed by Prussia during the late-eighteenth-century partitions of Poland) that led to the Baltic Sea and divided East Prussia, which remained German, from the rest of Germany. The port city of Danzig (Gdańsk) became a free city under the protection of the League of Nations. Poland's new frontiers were settled in 1921 and accepted by the League of Nations two years later.

The German army was to be reduced to 100,000 volunteer soldiers. The German navy, now blockaded by the British fleet, would be limited to twelve warships, with no submarines. Germany would be allowed no air force.

Furthermore, Germany was to pay a huge sum—132 billion gold marks, the estimated cost of the war to the victorious Allies—in war reparations. (There was a precedent: France had been required to pay an indemnity to the German Empire following defeat in the Franco-Prussian war of 1870–1871). The Weimar Republic would be required to turn over to the Allies much of its merchant fleet and part of its fishing fleet and railroad stocks, among other payments. The German Baltic shipyards were to build ships at no cost to the Allies. Each year, Germany was to give the Allies more than one-fourth of its extracted coal as further compensation.

But how was the new Weimar Republic to raise the remainder of the reparations? Tax revenues were low because the economy was so weak, and powerful German industrialists opposed any new taxes on capital or business. The outflow of reparations payments in gold fueled inflation. Government

A German woman using worthless paper money to light her stove during the runaway inflation of 1923.

expenses far outweighed income, exports rapidly declined, and prices began to rise far faster than in other countries, destabilizing the new Weimar government.

The English economist John Maynard Keynes (1883–1946) left the British delegation to Versailles in protest of what seemed to be the draconian treatment afforded Germany. He warned, "If we aim deliberately at the impoverishment of Central Europe, vengeance, I dare predict, will not limp." In particular he denounced the reparations payments in his book *The Economic Consequences of the Peace* (1919), prophesying accurately the failure of the Versailles settlement. The reparations issue poisoned international relations in the 1920s.

The Allies counted on German payments to help them remedy their own daunting economic problems. The promise of German reparations enabled the British and French governments to accede to conservative demands that taxes not be raised or levies imposed on capital. But, in fact, Germany paid only a small portion of the reparations and received more in loans from the other powers than it ever returned in reparations. Germany received three times as much in loans from the Allies than it paid out. Reparations did not ruin the German economy, but their psychological impact in Germany damaged the very republic the Allies wanted to stabilize. The bitter resentment harbored by German right-wing parties toward the reparations compromised the ability of the Weimar Republic to survive.

France wanted the League of Nations to enforce the Treaty of Versailles and to ensure German payment of reparations. (Germany was not permitted to join the League of Nations.) But without an army, the League had no way of enforcing its decisions against member—or, for that matter, non-member—states that chose to ignore its principles or decisions.

After his six-month stay at Versailles, President Wilson returned to the United States to fight for Senate ratification of the treaty. But the elections of November 1918 had given Wilson's Republican opponents control of the Senate. A mood of isolationism swept the country. A majority of senators opposed U.S. membership in the League of Nations, fearing that the treaty would commit the nation to entanglements in Europe. Influenced by the large numbers of German, Italian, and Irish American constituents, some senators believed the treaty to be too harsh on Germany, insufficiently generous to Italy, and irrelevant to Irish demands for independence from Britain. The U.S. government refused to participate in the various international organizations set up to enforce the treaty and to air economic and security concerns. In November 1919, the U.S. Senate refused to ratify the Treaty of Versailles.

The absence of both the United States and the Soviet Union from the League doomed it to failure. The new Soviet government had not even been invited to Versailles. There were two reasons for this: (1) the Bolsheviks had simply declared an end to the war in 1917 and withdrawn troops from the front; and (2) Great Britain, France, and the United States had sent troops and military supplies to support the anti-Bolshevik forces in the Civil War in Russia.

Even among the victorious powers, the treaty generated some apprehension. It seemed a precarious peace. Keynes recalled, "Paris was a nightmare, and every one there was morbid. A sense of impending catastrophe overhung the frivolous scene; the futility and smallness of man before the great events confronting him; the mingled significance and unreality of the decisions." When Marshal Ferdinand Foch of France read the treaty, he exclaimed, "This isn't a peace, it's a twenty year truce!" He was right.

Settlements in Eastern Europe

A series of individual treaties, each named after a suburb of Paris, sought to recognize the claims of ethnic minorities of each country, in some cases redrawing national boundaries (see Map 24.1). But each also left the defeated country feeling aggrieved. "Revisionist" or "irredentist" states wanted the revision of the agreements in order to regain territory they believed should be theirs.

Bulgaria, allied in the war with Germany and Austria-Hungary, lost territory on the Aegean coast, ceded to Greece by virtue of the Treaty of Neuilly (November 1919), as well as small pieces of land to Romania and parts of Thrace that had been won in the Balkan Wars. By the Treaty of Saint-Germain (which specifically forbade Austrian union with Germany), Vienna was reduced to being the oversized capital of a small country, Austria. By the Treaty of Trianon (June 1920), Hungary lost two-thirds of its territory, 60 percent of its total population, and 25 percent of its ethnic Hungarians. Romania received more Hungarian territory than was left to Hungary, and one-third of its population now consisted of Hungarians, Germans, Ukrainians, and Jews. The treaty left 3.4 million Hungarians living beyond the borders of Hungary, hardly Wilsonianism in action. The Hungarian response to the treaty that ended the war is best summed up by the contemporary slogan "No, no, never." Moreover, 1 million Bulgarians—16 percent of the population—now lived outside of Bulgaria.

The Treaty of Sèvres (August 1920), the most harsh of the treaties with Germany's wartime allies, dismembered the Turkish Ottoman Empire. Britain, France, Italy, and Greece all coveted—as had the Russian and Habsburg empires in previous centuries—parts of the old Ottoman Empire that had stretched through much of the Middle East. Now the treaty awarded Smyrna, the region around present-day Izmir on the Anatolian peninsula, and much of Thrace to Greece; the island of Rhodes to Italy; Syria (then including Lebanon) to France, under a mandate from the League of Nations; Iraq and Palestine to Britain, also under mandate from the League of Nations; and Saudi Arabia to Britain as a protectorate (see Map 24.3). Italian troops occupied Turkish territory even as the peace conference was proceeding; Greek forces moved into Smyrna and into Thrace.

In Turkey, the Italian and Greek occupations generated a wave of nationalist sentiment. Mustafa Kemal Pasha (1881–1938)—known as Atatürk—organized armed resistance against the foreign incursions. Turkish forces pushed Greek units out of Smyrna in 1922 and threatened a neutral zone occupied by British troops. When the British government prepared to intervene, an exchange of populations was arranged. The Treaty of Lausanne of 1923 recognized Turkey's independence, ending the European role in administering the country's international debts. Turkey was left with a little territory on the European side of the Bosporus, as well as the Sea of Marmara and the Dardanelles strait, which themselves were declared open to all nations. The treaty called for the exchange of Turkish and Greek populations. Greece had to withdraw from the Anatolian peninsula, and at least 1 million Greek refugees moved from Turkey to Greece. Almost 400,000 Muslims were forced out of Greece, ending up in Turkey. Turks now comprised about 1 percent of the population of Greece; only about 3,000 Greeks remained in Turkey in a population of 70 million people. The Kurds, an ethnic minority within Turkey and Iraq, were still without an independent state. Atatürk became president of the Republic of Turkey, establishing his capital at Ankara in the interior of the Anatolian peninsula. The last Ottoman ruler left Turkey for the French Riviera. Seeking to Westernize and secularize his country, Atatürk promulgated legal codes separating church and state, implemented compulsory education and the Latin alphabet, required Turkish families to take Western-style names, and prohibited Turks from wearing the fez (a traditional brimless hat).

National and Ethnic Challenges

President Wilson's espousal of ethnicity as the chief determinant of national boundaries had unleashed hope among almost all the Eastern European peoples for independent states based on ethnic identities. The Treaty of Versailles accentuated the role of nationalism as a factor for political instability in Europe after the Great War. At the same time, the failure of the peacemakers at Versailles to address the demands of peoples colonized by the European powers left a legacy of mistrust.

The National Question and the Successor States

The Treaty of Versailles acknowledged the existence of "successor" states out of the ruins of the Austro-Hungarian Empire, as well as out of the territories that had belonged to defeated Germany and the defunct Russian Empire. The creation of these new states by the Treaty of Versailles in theory followed the principle of nationalism—that ethnicity should be the chief determinant of national boundaries—which had helped cause the Great War. However, the principle of nationalism was not applied to the former Russian

Empire, as the Treaty of Versailles did not concern itself with the nationalities of Russia, ostensibly a victorious power, although now transformed into a Communist state. In the north, Finland finally gained its independence after having been for centuries subject to Swedish and, since the beginning of the nineteenth century, to Russian rule. The three Baltic states of Latvia, Estonia, and Lithuania also became independent of Russia (see Map 24.1). The largest of these successor states were Yugoslavia in the Balkans and Czechoslovakia and Poland in Central Europe. Referring to the new states and redrawn boundaries, Winston Churchill complained, "The maps are out of date! The charts don't work any more!" The creation of smaller national states (which Lloyd George referred to as "five-foot-five nations"), whose boundaries were largely determined by ethnicity, added to the number of independent states in Europe. This number had decreased since 1500 as absolute monarchies had expanded their territories, and with German and Italian unification in the nineteenth century. But after the war, that trend was suddenly reversed. In 1914, there had been fourteen currencies in Europe; in 1919, there were twenty-seven.

The signatories at Versailles also had the strategic containment of communism in mind when they recognized the existence of the new nation-states as buffers—or what Clemenceau called a "cordon sanitaire" that would help contain the spread of Bolshevism from the Soviet Union. After the armistice, the Allies allowed German armies to remain inside Russia, Ukraine, and Poland to prevent the Red Army from carrying the Russian Revolution into Central Europe. German troops held railway lines in the Baltic states in order to thwart any attempted Bolshevik takeover there.

Seeking collective security against Hungary, which demanded revision of the Treaty of Versailles in order to win back territory lost to its unwanted new neighbors, as well as against Germany, the three nations of Czechoslovakia, Romania, and Yugoslavia formed the Little Entente by signing alliances in 1920 and 1921. (Poland sometimes worked with these states to achieve mutually beneficial goals but did not formally join the alliance.) Moreover, all three states depended on a series of defensive alliances that each had signed with France—Czechoslovakia in 1924, Romania in 1926, and Yugoslavia the following year. (Poland had signed a treaty with France in 1921.) The French government viewed such alliances with the Eastern European states as a means of countering a revival of German power, as well as a check on the Soviet Union. In 1934, Romania, Yugoslavia, Greece, and Turkey signed a Balkan Entente, intended to counter any revisionist territorial claims by Bulgaria.

The Allies applied Wilson's idealized formula of "one people, one nation" unequally when it came to those states that had fought against them in the war. The "Polish Corridor" dividing East Prussia from the rest of Germany contained a sizable—but not majority—German population. Mineral-rich Upper Silesia, claimed by Poland and with a large Polish population, was divided between Germany and Poland after a plebiscite. But in parts of Austria, where German-speaking majorities might have wanted to join Germany, the Allies specifically disallowed plebiscites. The Allies also refused Hungarian demands for plebiscites, which they accorded to Germany in East Prussia (which voted overwhelmingly to remain in Germany) and Schleswig (which was divided between Denmark and Germany).

Including part of the old Habsburg Balkan domains as well as the kingdoms of Serbia and Montenegro, Yugoslavia (called the Kingdom of Serbs, Croats and Slovenes until 1929) was the most ambitious attempt to resolve the national question through the creation of a multinational state in which the rights of several nationalities would be recognized. After complicated negotiations in 1917, the Serb government and a Yugoslav Committee made up of Croat and Slovene leaders in exile had agreed to form a new South Slav state when the war was concluded. They set up a provisional government even before an armistice had been signed. The new parliamentary monarchy would include Serbia, Montenegro, Croatia, and Slovenia (which lies between northern Italy and Austria), as well as Bosnia-Herzegovina and the smaller territory of Kosovo, two regions in which a majority of the population had converted to Islam during centuries of Turkish rule. Yugoslavia also absorbed part of Macedonia, which was populated by Bulgarians, Greeks, and Macedonians.

From its beginning, Yugoslavia was caught in a conflict between the "Greater Serb" vision of Yugoslavia, in which Serbia would dominate, and a federalist structure in which all nationalities and religions would play equal, or at least proportional, roles. Serbs, who are Orthodox Christians, were the largest ethnic group in Yugoslavia, but they still only made up 43 percent of the total Yugoslav population, with the Catholic Croats accounting for about 23 percent. Belgrade became the capital of Yugoslavia, as it had been of Serbia. Middle-class Serbs held almost all of the key administrative, judicial, and military positions. Concentrations of Serbs lived in Croatia, and Croats in Serbia, further complicating the rivalry between the two major peoples of the new state, who spoke essentially the same language, although the Serbs use the Cyrillic alphabet. Other major ethnic groups within Yugoslavia included Hungarians, Romanians, Bulgarians, Greeks, Germans, and gypsies.

Beginning in 1919, the League of Nations signed so-called national minority treaties with Poland, Czechoslovakia, and Yugoslavia (and later Greece and Romania), which agreed in principle to assure the protection of ethnic minorities. However, these treaties could not really be enforced. Moreover, ethnic rivalries were compounded by religious differences. For example, Poland included about 1.5 million Belorussians and 4 million Ukrainians, who, unlike the Catholic Poles, were largely Orthodox Christians. Poland also had the largest population of Jews in Europe—3 million. Moreover, about 1 million Germans, overwhelmingly Protestant, now lived in Poland.

The case of Czechoslovakia illustrates the complexity of the national question. In 1916, a National Council, made up of both Czechs and Slovaks, became a provisional government. The Slovak philosopher Tomáš Masaryk (1850–1937), who had spent the war years making contacts in London in the hope of advancing the cause of an independent Czechoslovakia, became the president of the new state in 1918. He was extremely popular among both Czechs and Slovaks. But Czechs and Slovaks together made up only 65 percent of the population of the new country. Three million Germans living in the Sudetenland found themselves included within the borders of Czechoslovakia, as did 750,000 Hungarians. Furthermore, Slovaks complained that promises of administrative and cultural autonomy within the Czechoslovak state were never implemented.

Facing similar economic, social, and political tensions, Poland became a dictatorship. Pilsudski became head of state in 1918. He commanded the Polish army that defeated in August 1920 the Soviet force that had reached the suburbs of Warsaw. "The miracle of the Vistula" River saved the independence of Poland, as well as that of the Baltic countries. Pilsudski pursued the policy of building a Federation of Poland and Ukraine, as well as Belarus and the Baltic states, regions that had been conquered by the Russian Empire and would form a bloc. But the Polish economy lay in ruins. No rail links between Warsaw and other major cities survived the war; tracks from Germany and Austria simply stopped at the Polish border. Inflation was rampant: a dollar was worth 9 Polish marks at the end of the war, and 10 million at the peak of the hyperinflation of 1923! (The zloty was introduced as the currency of Poland in 1924.)

The new Polish government faced the challenge of unifying the three parts of the country that had been part of three different empires. Deep divisions endured between nobles, who although many were greatly in debt owned most of the land and had subverted central authority in virtually every period of Polish history, and the peasants, who demanded land reform and were well represented in parliament. There were two main political blocs (and many smaller parties): National Democracy, the largest party of the right, which cooperated with a centrist Polish Peasant Party, and the Socialists and other parties on the left. In the 1922 parliament, there were eighteen different political parties. As no party ever enjoyed a solid parliamentary majority, governments fell on an average of almost two a year. Yet many peasants did receive land after World War I, although the process went increasingly slowly. Legislation limited the holdings of land that could be held by a single landowner to about 100 acres (three times that in the eastern regions), and about a third of Polish land changed hands. Pilsudski refused to stand for election for president in 1922 on the grounds that the constitution would not grant him sufficient executive authority. Although not by instinct a man of the right, he saw himself above political parties. However, he allied with leading conservatives and criticized the parliamentary regime, calling for a "moral regeneration" of Polish life.

Many Poles held the parliament responsible for the economic disaster of the post-war years and considered Marshal Pilsudski a hero. In 1926, Pilsudski, backed by the army and supported by Socialists fed up with the weak government and its policies, overthrew Poland's parliamentary government. After saying that he would have to wait to see whether Poland could be governed "without a whip," he imposed authoritarian rule, although political parties in principle continued to function and the press was relatively free. In 1930 Pilsudski arrested leaders of a center-left opposition group who demanded his resignation and the restoration of parliamentary government, and a new constitution followed in 1935, providing for stronger executive authority. After Pilsudski's death a month after the promulgation of the constitution, authority passed to a group of army officers who had been with him from the beginning.

The post-war period brought considerable instability to Greece and the Balkans. In Greece, which had only come into the war in 1917 on the side of Britain, France, and Russia, King Alexander died in 1920, after being bitten by his pet monkey. When parliament deposed his successor, Greek political life lurched into uncertainty accentuated by the arrival of 1.5 million Greeks expelled from Turkey and Bulgaria. In Greek Macedonia, refugees now made up half of the population. In the small, isolated Muslim state of Albania on the coast of the Adriatic Sea, moderate reformers battled proponents of the old ways against a backdrop of Italian territorial claims and bullying. The Prime Minister, Harvard-educated Ahmed Zogu, fearing for his life, fled to Yugoslavia in 1924. The next year, backed by Yugoslavia, he invaded his own country with an army, assumed the presidency of the Albanian Republic, and set up a dictatorial monarchy in 1928 (ruled 1928–1939).

In Bulgaria, King Boris III (ruled 1918–1943) was head of the country in name only. Alexander Stamboliski (1879–1923), leader of the Agrarian Union Party, elbowed opponents aside to become premier in 1919. He signed the Treaty of Neuilly, agreeing to try to prevent Macedonian nationalists from using Bulgarian territory to organize attacks inside Greece. Stamboliski assumed dictatorial powers in 1920. Army officers helped engineer a coup d'état in 1923, with the support of the king. Stamboliski fell into the hands of Macedonian nationalists, who cut off his right arm, which had signed the Treaty of Neuilly, then stabbed him sixty times, decapitating him for good measure. The army killed about 20,000 peasants and workers who wanted reform. It was a sign of the times in the Balkans.

Colonial and National Questions

The peace treaties failed to address the rights—or lack of them—of people living in the colonies of the European powers. Some of these peoples demanded national independence. Representatives of ethnic, religious, and national groups—including the Irish, Persians, Jews, Arabs, Indians from the subcontinent, Vietnamese, Armenians, and American blacks—went to Versailles in the hope of attaining recognition of their national rights. Lloyd George belittled these outsiders as "wild men screaming through the keyholes." The Allies refused to allow Ho Chi Minh (1890–1969), a young Vietnamese, to read a petition that asked that the Rights of Man and Citizen be applied to the French colonies. Only the representatives of Zionist groups—Jews who wanted the creation of a Jewish national state in Palestine—and their anti-Zionist Jewish rivals ever made it into the conference halls, and then only briefly. Women's groups, too, in vain sent representatives who hoped to be heard at Versailles.

Britain, still the world's largest colonial power, refused to accept President Wilson's plan that the League of Nations or some other international board arbitrate the future of colonies. The British government refused to recognize the right of self-determination. Still, the war had altered the relationship between Britain and its colonies, as well as that between France and its empire. The dramatic contraction of world trade during the postwar era, and above all during the Great Depression that began in 1929 (see Chapter 25), provided impetus to emerging independence movements. Imperial governments had long and loudly proclaimed that empire brought economic benefits to colonial peoples. Now such benefits were hard to find, as Britain, in particular, abandoned a cornerstone of the construction of its empire: free trade. The Dominions (Britain's original "settlement colonies" of Canada, South Africa, Australia, and New Zealand) had borne a great financial and material burden in the Great War, and a considerable loss of life as well. While they were not fully independent, a delegation from each had signed the Treaty of Versailles, and each had a government responsible to its own citizens and had become a member of the League of Nations. The "British Commonwealth" was created in 1926 and formalized in 1931. In this union of Britain and the Dominions, each state would be independent and not subordinate to Britain but united by common allegiance to the crown.

The powers created the "mandate system" to deal with Germany's colonies. The colonies were placed under the nominal authority of the League of Nations but were actually administered by Allied powers. Through this system, Britain increased the size of its empire by a million square miles, for example, by adding the former German colony of Tanganyika and parts of Togoland and the Cameroons as "mandate" colonies (see Map 24.3).

In Palestine, both Arabs and Jews had reason to be disappointed by the settlement. In 1915, in order to encourage Arab resistance against Turkey, the British government had promised some Arab leaders that after the war Britain would support an independent Arab state. But a year later, the British and French governments had secretly drawn up plans to divide the Middle East into two spheres of influence. Moreover, in the 1917 Balfour Declaration (see Chapter 22), Britain had promised to help Jews create a "national home" in Palestine, without necessarily promising to establish a

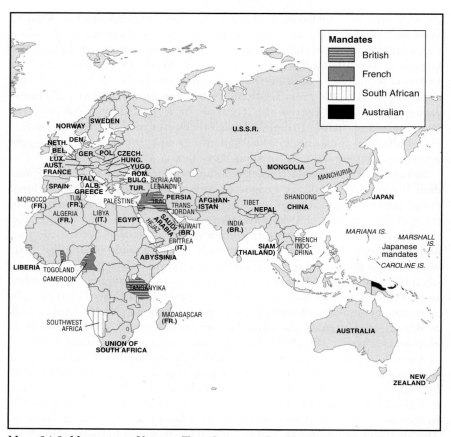

MAP 24.3 MANDATES UNDER THE LEAGUE OF NATIONS   German colonies became mandates of the League of Nations and administered by Allied powers after the Great War.

Jewish state. Once the war ended, the promises disappeared at Versailles. Britain established mandates over Trans-Jordan (which would later become Jordan), as well as over Iraq (which became nominally independent in 1932) and Palestine, each of which was ruled by a viceroy responsible to the colonial office in London. Britain maintained informal control over Egypt through the sultan and Egyptian ministers and the Suez Canal even after nominal Egyptian independence in 1922. Following an agreement made in 1916 between Britain and France, the French also established a mandate over Lebanon and Syria, where troops put down a revolt in 1925–1927.

But the British government could no longer put aside the challenge of the Irish movement for independence. The imposition of military conscription in Ireland in 1918 had angered Irish who felt no allegiance to the empire. The Irish Republican Army, which was organized from remnants of the rebel units disbanded after an ill-fated Easter Sunday insurrection in 1916, gained adherents amid high unemployment, strikes, and sectarian violence between Catholics and Protestants in largely Protestant Ulster (the six counties of northeastern Ireland). In a mood of mounting crisis, British Liberals wanted to begin negotiations as soon as possible with Irish political leaders. Conservatives, in contrast, wanted to crush the Irish Republicans. In the 1918 elections to the House of Commons, Irish voters elected a majority of members of Sinn Féin ("We Ourselves" in Irish Gaelic), the Irish Republican political organization. Sinn Féin members refused to take their seats in Parliament and then unilaterally declared a republic. Parliament finally passed the Government of Ireland Act in 1920, dividing Ireland into two districts. The Catholic district in the south—most of the island—was to become a crown colony. Largely Protestant Ulster remained part of Britain.

Most Catholic Irish, however, wanted nothing less than complete independence. The British government kept about 50,000 troops and 10,000 police in Ireland, including the "Black and Tans," a special police force that terrorized the Irish population supporting the Irish Republicans. More than a thousand people were killed in fighting during 1921, half of whom were British policemen or soldiers ambushed by the Irish Republican Army. In January 1922, the British Parliament went a step further, creating the Irish Free State, a Dominion within the British Commonwealth, although many Irish Republicans demanded the severance of all formal ties to Britain and the creation of the Irish Republic (which would come in 1948). Ulster, or Northern Ireland, remained within the United Kingdom. Continuing sporadic sectarian violence in Ulster proved that tensions between the Protestant majority and Catholic minority, which did not accept British rule, would not subside.

The Great War accentuated other nationalist movements for independence. Total war had brought the mobilization of men and resources from the colonies. This led to considerable resentment among indigenous peoples. In Egypt, following the arrest of an Egyptian nationalist, more than a thousand people were killed in the repression that followed an uprising. In India, which the British viewed as the key to sustaining the Empire (providing a vast reservoir of soldiers for the army), a growing Indian national movement developed. It was led by Mahatma Gandhi, who merged Hindu religion and culture with peaceful political resistance. Gandhi adapted Western-style propaganda techniques to the Indian struggle. Unlike the Indian National Congress, which had since the 1880s sought greater autonomy for India within the British Empire, Gandhi and his followers, who included many Indian Muslims, sought outright independence. Following riots in 1919, Indians held a protest in Amritsar in Punjab against the Rowlatt Acts, which allowed the government to forgo juries in political trials. The British army

Houses set ablaze in Ireland by the Black and Tans of the Royal Irish Constabulary, about 1920, during the fight for Ireland's independence from Great Britain.

retaliated by massacring 400 Indian civilians. Like the Sepoy Mutiny of 1857 (see Chapter 21), the incident exacerbated the mutual suspicion and mistrust that had existed between the Indians and British for decades. Bengali groups undertook terrorist attacks against British residents.

France also confronted and repressed revolutionary nationalist movements in its colonies of Indochina, Tunisia, Morocco, and the African island of Madagascar, as it did moderate groups asking only for the extension of political rights. During and following World War I (until the 1930s), most of the nationalist movements in the French colonies sought reform from within the colonial framework, not outright independence through revolution.

Japan strengthened its position as the only Asian great power and growing empire. Japanese armies were already taking advantage of the turmoil that followed the Russian Revolution to grab land from the old Russian Empire in Asia. Furthermore, Great Britain, France, and Italy had secretly agreed in 1917, in exchange for active Japanese support against the German navy, to back Japanese demands for concessions China had been forced to grant Germany in 1898 and 1899 (see Chapter 21). The members of the Chinese delegation to Versailles in 1919 had not been aware of the 1917 agreement; nor did the Chinese delegates know that their warlord premier had secretly agreed, in return for loans, to grant Japan a full concession to build railways in the northeast province of Shandong (Shantung). When the Allies publicly agreed to Japanese claims, demonstrations and riots erupted in China. The May 4 (1919) movement in China, named for the day of the first major demonstrations in Beijing against the Treaty of Versailles, accentuated the development of Chinese nationalism and resentment against foreign domination.

The United States, eager to protect its interests in Asia and wary of the alliance between Japan and Britain, which was determined to maintain its empire, agreed to join the Washington treaties of 1921–1922. These called for "consultations" between the three powers, as well as France, when events in Asia required them. A subsequent Nine-Power Treaty that included Belgium, the Netherlands, Portugal, and Italy, as well as China, guaranteed China's independence and territorial integrity.

ECONOMIC AND SOCIAL INSTABILITY

Because of the relief and—for the victors—exhilaration with which many Europeans greeted the end of the Great War, the 1920s has often been described as "the roaring twenties." Europeans thrilled to quests for record speeds or landmark travel by air and automobile. They gathered around radios, lined up to attend movies, dressed in more casual clothing styles than ever before, crowded into cabarets and clubs, and danced late into the night.

However, the two decades following the Great War were above all marked by tremendous economic and social instability. The continent was wracked by inflation and unemployment, factors that exacerbated international tensions and rivalries and poisoned domestic political life—particularly in Germany, but also in a number of other states reeling from the impact of the war. In Western Europe, after the long, bloody war finally ended and with the Russian Revolution fresh in mind, workers (and some women's groups as well) put forward demands for better living conditions. At the same time, economic and social elites were determined to overcome the challenge to their power launched by organized labor and the political parties of the left. But one of the results of the long ordeal of a war that had necessitated the mobilization of virtually all of the economic resources of the combatant powers was a growing determination among the parties of the political left that states ought to increase the services they provided their citizens. The origins of the welfare state may in part be traced to the immediate post-war period.

Social Turmoil

The staggering economic disruption caused by the war contributed to the international disorder that ensued at its end. Soaring inflation and unemployment destabilized European political life. The conflict cost more than six times the national debts of all countries in the entire world from the end of the eighteenth century until 1914.

Manufacturing and agricultural productivity fell dramatically during the conflict. Only countries far from the battlefields, such as the United States, Canada, India, and Australia, experienced economic growth. But they, too, could not escape high inflation and unemployment when the war ended. European states had borrowed vast sums of money to pay for the war; governments now began to print money to pay it back. This accelerated inflation (See Table 24.1). Prices were three times higher in 1920 in Britain than before the war, five times higher in Germany, and, in an ominous sign of things to come, 14,000 times higher in Austria and 23,000 times higher in Hungary. Workers resented the widening gap between themselves and the wealthy.

The British press carried stories about well-placed entrepreneurs who had amassed fortunes selling war materials to the government, living it up while others died for their country and everyone else tightened their belts. The Conservative politician Stanley Baldwin referred to businessmen elected to Parliament in the first post-war election as "hard-faced men who looked as if they had done well out of the war."

French steel magnates and German arms producers, among others, had emerged from the war with huge profits. These were enhanced by cartel arrangements within their industries that allowed them to monopolize production and set prices. War production had benefited large companies more than small ones, as in Germany, where the War Raw Materials Corporations provided essential materials to large enterprises. The chemical giant I. G. Farben had been formed in Germany by joining together a number of smaller firms. Industrialists enjoyed greater prestige and political influence than ever before. With governments playing the leading role in establishing economic priorities, allocating resources, and recruiting labor during the war, fewer people now embraced the old classic liberal principle of laissez-faire. Some businessmen and state officials, particularly in Germany, Italy,

TABLE 24.1. INDEX OF WHOLESALE PRICES (1913 = 10)

	1914	1915	1916	1917	1918	1919
Germany	106	142	153	179	217	415
France	102	140	189	262	340	357
Great Britain	100	127	160	206	227	242
Italy	96	133	201	299	409	364
Canada	100	109	134	175	205	216
United States	98	101	127	177	194	206

Source: Gerd Hardoch, *The First World War 1914–1918* (Berkeley: University of California Press, 1977), p. 172.

and France, had been impressed by the degree of wartime cooperation between state, business, and labor. They now believed these arrangements should be permanent. They hoped that corporate entities could be established in each major industry to coordinate production, ending competition between companies. They called themselves "corporatists" and their ideas "corporatism." Corporatists in Germany, France, and Italy believed that by creating cartel-like corporations that joined all people dependent on one industry, ruinous competition between companies and conflict between bosses and workers could be eliminated in the interest and prosperity of the "national economic community." Such cartel arrangements might well reduce or even eliminate the social and political tensions inherent in capitalist economies by forging an organized alliance of interests, including those of the state, big business, and labor.

However, Europe's business elite greeted the post-war era with some anxiety. For more than a half century, European economic elites had worked to preserve their power against the mounting challenge of organized labor and the political parties of the left. They did so, for example, by trying to maintain the elite character of higher education, pressuring governments to maintain high tariff barriers at the expense of consumers, seeking to limit government intervention in factory conditions, or trying to maintain legislation that restricted the right to strike. Above all, many people of means had wanted to keep their countries from adopting universal male suffrage or becoming democracies. Despite their efforts, however, the role of parliamentary bodies had expanded in every Western country during the last decades before the war, as universal male suffrage had come to France, Italy, Belgium, Norway, Sweden, and even imperial Germany.

Women's movements were one of the forces for democratization that gained considerably during the war. Having suspended their suffrage campaigns for the duration of the conflict, women's groups now demanded recognition for their wartime contributions—when they had taken the place of conscripts in factories and fields. After the war, women won the right to vote in Germany, Sweden, and several other countries in Western Europe, as well as in the newly created Eastern European states of Czechoslovakia, Poland, and Hungary. The legal position of women was probably strongest in Britain. Women voted for the first time in the British elections of December 1918, and the first woman was elected to the House of Commons soon after. The Sex Disqualification Act of 1919 opened the way for women to enter professions from which they had previously been excluded. However, women who had taken men's jobs during the war gradually lost or abandoned their employment, many returning to domestic service. During the 1920s, the percentage of British working women declined for the first time in many decades. Nonetheless, a greater variety of jobs became available to women. During the next two decades, many women found work in textile factories, commerce, transport, and in new jobs within the service sector (as hairdressers, department store clerks, or telephone operators). For many women, such jobs represented an advance in opportunity and working conditions.

The labor movement gained strength in the immediate post-war period. In France, the General Confederation of Labor, which had recruited hundreds of thousands of new members after the war, reached 2 million members in 1920, although the proportion of unionized workers remained small when compared to the proportion in Britain. In Italy, more than 3 million workers joined unions in the first two years of peace. Unions mounted massive campaigns to make the economy more democratic, a goal that was more rev-olutionary than bread-and-butter issues like hours, wages, and working conditions. Strikes spread in all Western countries. Some Britons began to think that their nation, which, unlike its continental rivals, had avoided insurgency and revolution in the nineteenth century, might now be vulnera-ble to an uprising by dissatisfied workers influenced by the Bolsheviks. In Glasgow, workers demanding a forty-hour workweek raised the Communist red flag on the town hall.

If anything, the mobilization of workers in defense of their interests con-tributed to conservative victories in the post-war elections. Britain's Conser-vative Party had swept to victory in the "khaki" elections (so called because of the color of British army uniforms) in December 1918. The influence of business interests also helped bring conservatives to power in Germany, Italy, and France in post-war elections. The French Employers Association printed thousands of posters showing a Bolshevik with a blood-stained knife between his teeth. The "National Block," drawing upon a wave of patriotism following the victory of the blue-clad French soldiers, in 1919 brought a strongly nationalist majority to the "horizon blue" Chamber of Deputies. Many French conservatives, who before the war dreamed of a monarchical restoration or the overthrow of the republic by a military man, now supported the republic, as long as it was a conservative republic. A general strike failed completely in May 1920. Union efforts failed to obtain the nationalization of key indus-tries, such as French railroads, or German and British coal mines. Factory councils, which workers hoped would meet with employers to set production targets, wages, and conditions, had within a few years been eliminated in Germany, never got off the ground in France, and were quickly banned in Italy. In Britain, an attempt to call a general strike, organized by the "triple alliance" of railway workers, miners, and dockworkers—the three largest unions—fizzled completely on April 15, 1921, "Black Friday" for British workers. Rates of unionization fell. "Corporatist" rhetoric about how bosses and workers within the same industries shared the same goals grad-ually disappeared in Germany and France. Employers still called the shots with the notable exception of those in the Soviet Union, where the state exercised increasing control.

The Left and the Origins of the Welfare State

The Great War was a devastating experience for the international socialist movement, which had in 1914 split into pro- and anti-war factions. The German Social Democrats and the socialist parties of France, Italy, and Belgium had rallied to the war effort of their respective countries despite opposition to what they saw as a war between capitalists. The Russian Revolution of 1917, too, divided socialists. The unexpected victory of the Bolsheviks in Russia suggested to some that socialists could come to power through a tightly organized, hierarchical party structure. In France, at the Congress of the French Socialist Party in Tours in December 1920, three-fourths of the delegates supported joining the Third Communist International, which had been founded in Moscow

The French reaction to the Russian Revolution is illustrated by this anti-Bolshevik poster: "How to vote against Bolshevism."

in 1919 to encourage the organization of Communist parties in all countries. They founded the French Communist Party. Those remaining loyal to the French Socialist Party continued to accept reformism and thus loyalty to the republic, as well as to the democratic organization of their party.

Léon Blum (1872–1950) led the French Socialist Party. A Jew born into comfortable circumstances in Paris, Blum was a literary critic and intellectual who took a law degree and became a civil servant. Like his hero Jean Jaurès, the French socialist leader assassinated in 1914 on the eve of the war, Blum was an idealist for whom socialism followed philosophically from what he considered the humanism of the French Revolution. Blum remained convinced that socialism would be achieved through the electoral process.

For Communists, the economic malaise of the 1920s seemed proof that capitalism's defeat was near. Within two years, the French Communist Party grew as large as the Socialist Party. In 1922, on orders from Moscow, the party purged intellectuals from its membership. The Communist Party attracted many followers in the grim industrial suburbs of Paris, the "red belt" around the capital. Communist-dominated municipalities provided social services, such as unemployment relief, as well as light and drinking water for residents living in hastily constructed, insalubrious dwellings. In contrast, the British Communist Party, founded in 1920 and repudiated by the Labour Party, never attracted more than a few thousand followers.

Reformism dominated the parties of the left in post-war Europe. The German Social Democratic Party and the French Socialist Party participated in parliamentary alliances that underlay, respectively, the Weimar Republic and French moderate center-left governments. The British Labour Party, closely allied with the trade unions, emerged as the second largest party in Britain after the war. All three parties depended, to a large extent, on the support of the reformist labor movements in their respective countries. In some ways, unions had become interest groups like any other, bargaining with governments and employers. To this extent, the Communist critics of union reformism may have been correct when they warned that reformism served to integrate workers into the structure of the capitalist state.

The emerging outlines of the welfare state in the 1920s reflected the pressure of the parties of the left and of trade unions. At the same time, the origins of the welfare state must be seen in the context of earlier programs of social reform adopted in most countries in the decades before the Great War (see Chapter 20). While the Communist parties of Europe espoused, at least in principle, working-class revolution, socialists and most union members demanded that states provide certain minimum protection for workers. Scandinavia, Denmark, Sweden, and Norway evolved into social democracies, implementing pathbreaking social services. The socialist municipal government of Vienna constructed an attractive working-class apartment complex that provided communal facilities such as laundries, bathhouses, and kindergartens.

In Britain, Prime Minister Lloyd George had promised demobilized soldiers "a country fit for heroes to live in." The reality was considerably less grand. However, pressured by the Labour Party, which now held the second largest number of seats in the House of Commons, the Housing and Town Planning Act of 1919 provided town councils with subsidies to encourage the construction of cheap row houses. This eliminated some slum overcrowding and provided many working-class families with centralized heating and bathrooms. Within old city limits, "council" flats paid for by town councils provided more modest lodgings for some of the poorest workers. In 1920, the British government expanded unemployment insurance coverage to include most industrial workers, and in 1925, Parliament granted pensions to war widows and orphans, major steps in the emergence of the British welfare state. In France, the Chamber of Deputies in 1930 provided insurance for 10 million workers.

Political Instability

In October 1919, Italian Prime Minister Orlando reflected the uncertainty prevalent in the immediate post-war period when he stated that the growing disillusionment threatened Europe "like a blind whirlwind of destruction and disordered violence." The economic crisis that followed the war and the political instability it helped engender were nowhere clearer and ultimately more damaging than in Germany, where the new Weimar Republic sought to steer an even course between threats from the left and the right. Moreover, in Britain and France, states with established parliamentary governments, the subsequent division between left and right was also bitter.

Germany's Fragile Weimar Republic

The newly elected German Reichstag adopted the red, gold, and black flag of the ill-fated 1848 Frankfurt Parliament (see Chapter 16). The civil strife in which the Weimar Republic made its start influenced its constitution, approved by the Reichstag in July 1919. The constitution left the German president, who was to be popularly elected, considerable powers. Serving a term of seven years, he could dissolve the Reichstag and call for new elections. Although ministers would be responsible to the Reichstag, the president retained the power to suspend the constitution to restore order and to rule by decree, leaving the republic vulnerable to the president's authority.

Challenges to the republic came from the left and the right. In Bavaria, Kurt Eisner's rebel socialist republic collapsed. Following Eisner's murder by a rightist gunman in February 1919, Bavarian leftists rose up again in Munich in April to proclaim a Soviet-style republic. When a general strike paralyzed Berlin in early March, members of the Free Corps and regular German soldiers from Prussia gunned down several thousand workers and socialists.

The new German Republic desperately needed political stability. But many members of several key social groups, including bureaucrats and university professors who had received their posts under the empire, were against the republic from the beginning. Magistrates handed down absurdly light sentences to members of the Free Corps arrested for murder.

Groups of army officers began to plot against the republic during the summer of 1919. Conservative politicians and businessmen attempted a coup d'état, or "putsch," led by Wolfgang Kapp, a former Prussian imperial bureaucrat, with the goal of overthrowing the republic. On March 20, 1920, the rebels took over Berlin. The conservative parties proclaimed their support for the new government. In Bavaria, right-wingers seized power after forcing the resignation of the socialist government that had come to power the previous April. Chancellor Ebert appealed to the workers to defend the republic. They responded by launching a general strike that shut down much of the country. When some Berlin army units wavered, the Kapp Putsch collapsed.

But the threat to the republic was not over. The center and center-left parties of the Weimar coalition all suffered substantial losses in subsequent elections, while the conservative parties and radicals gained. When the Social Democrats withdrew from the government, the republic depended on a shaky coalition of Center Party politicians and moderate right-wing parties less committed than the Social Democrats to the republic they now governed. As Germany's economy floundered in ruinous inflation, political instability and violence mounted. Right-wing groups and parties sprang up, among them the National Socialists (Nazis), led by Adolph Hitler (see Chapter 25).

Walther Rathenau (1867–1922), the new foreign minister, was determined to negotiate the reparations issue with the British and French governments. Rathenau then shocked Britain and France by signing a statement of mutual friendship with the Soviet Union, the Rapallo Treaty (April 1922), in the hope of countering Western pressure. The Soviet Union received German technical assistance, which it paid for by helping Germany evade some of the military stipulations of the Treaty of Versailles. Subsequently, German officers provided technical assistance to the Soviet army. The Soviets, winning diplomatic recognition and German acquiescence to its repudiation of debts contracted under tsarist rule, renounced any future war reparations from Germany. Two months later, right-wing nationalists murdered Rathenau.

The German mark plunged dramatically in value. The Weimar government informed the Allies that it could not meet the schedule of reparations payments in gold or cash, but that it would continue payments of coal and other natural resources. With the United States pressuring Britain and France to repay their war debts, the Allies grew all the more determined that Germany pay up. France's new prime minister, Raymond Poincaré (1860–1934), threatened a military occupation of the Ruhr Valley industrial district if Germany failed to meet the reparations schedule. He accused Germany of deliberately withholding payments and trying to force the Allies to make concessions by ruining its own currency.

Britain and France, however, could not agree on a common policy. The French refused a German request for a moratorium on reparations payments so that the German currency (the mark) could be stabilized. The resentful German government, backed by virtually all political parties except the Communist Party, called on the miners of the Ruhr region to stop working for the Allies. This seemed to confirm Poincaré's contention that Germany was sabotaging repayment of its war debts.

On January 11, 1923, against the advice of the British government, French and Belgian troops occupied the Ruhr. When the German government began to finance the passive resistance in the Ruhr by simply printing more money with which to pay its miners not to work, inflation in Germany spiraled completely out of control, as Table 24.2 luridly demonstrates.

In 1923, Germans wheeled shopping carts filled with literally trillions of marks down the street to pay for a single loaf of bread. A half pound of

TABLE 24.2. THE MARK AND THE DOLLAR, 1914–1923

Date	Rate: 1 dollar =
July 1914	4.2 marks
January 1919	8.9
July 1919	14.0
January 1920	64.8
July 1920	39.5
January 1921	64.9
July 1921	76.7
January 1922	191.8
July 1922	493.2
January 1923	17,972.0
July 1923	353,412.0
August 1923	4,620,455.0
September 1923	98,860,000.0
October 1923	25,260,208,000.0
November 15, 1923	4,200,000,000,000.0

Source: Gordon Craig, *Germany 1866–1945* (New York: Oxford University Press, 1978), p. 450.

apples went for 300 billion marks. Employees asked to be paid their wages each morning so that they could shop at noon before merchants posted the afternoon price rises. Spiraling inflation wiped out people with fixed incomes and small savings they had put aside for retirement. Many of those who believed that they had done their patriotic duty by buying war bonds during the war now blamed the Weimar Republic when those bonds became worthless. The poor found staples and other goods not only ridiculously expensive but often unavailable at the market as farmers hoarded produce. Nonetheless, those people who were able to pay off bank loans with wildly inflated currency or to invest in property did well. The rich got richer. In such an atmosphere, the German Communist Party attracted bitter, discouraged workers in great numbers, undercutting the Social Democrats.

In August 1923, Ebert turned to Gustav Stresemann (1878–1929) to form a government. Stresemann, a former monarchist converted by right-wing violence to the republic, governed by decree with the support of the Social Democrats. He convinced miners to go back to work and to cease their passive resistance in the Ruhr Valley. France and Belgium ended the occupation after a nine-month period that had been as financially damaging to those nations as it was ruinous to Germany. Government printing presses stopped cranking out billion-mark notes and issued a new mark. The hyperinflation in Germany ended.

Stresemann hoped to meet the Allied demands as much as possible, and in doing so, open the way for Germany's return to respectability as a European

power. He hoped that this might clear the way for future Allied concessions, namely on Germany's disputed eastern frontier with Poland. Stresemann convinced both Britain and France to provide loans to help Germany
emerge from the economic crisis.

In 1924, a League of Nations commission, chaired by an American
banker, Charles G. Dawes (1865–1951), extended the schedule for payment of German reparations. The Dawes Plan left the Reichsbank partially
under the direction of an American commissioner who was to oversee German payments, but it did not lower the amount Germany was expected to
pay. Meanwhile, the United States had reduced the debt the Allies owed it
by percentages ranging from 30 percent (Britain) to 80 percent (Italy).
Still, the Dawes Plan improved relations between the Allies and Germany
and, with the revival of the European economy beginning in 1924, the
reparations issue receded in importance. The Weimar Republic seemed to
find stability as the economy finally began to improve. German industries
became more competitive, and unemployment began to decline.

Stresemann's discreet and effective diplomacy, now as foreign minister,
paid off. By the The Treaty of Locarno (really five separate treaties), signed
in 1925 between Great Britain, France, Belgium, Italy, and Germany, the
signatories pledged to settle all future controversies peacefully and guaranteed Germany's western borders as settled at the end of the war. At Locarno,
France also signed security treaties with Czechoslovakia and Poland to offset
to some extent the fact that Germany's eastern borders were not guaranteed,
which the German government refused to include in the agreement. European leaders and newspapers now began to use the phrase "the spirit of
Locarno" to refer to a mood of increasing international cooperation. The following year, Germany became a council member of the League of Nations in
return for agreeing that it would not seek to alter its western boundaries
with France and Belgium.

Nonetheless, German right-wing parties could never forgive Stresemann
for collaborating with the socialists. The opponents of the republic seemed
almost more vehement in their denunciations of Weimar when it succeeded
than when it failed, for success might generate stability and survival. Even
after what appeared to be a diplomatic victory for Weimar, German elections reflected the renewed strength of the right; the old Prussian warrior
General Hindenburg was elected president upon Ebert's death in 1925.

The Established Democracies: Britain and France

Britain and France were, to be sure, not immune from the political tensions
of the post-war period. Britain, in particular, remained a class-segregated
society. Nowhere in Europe was the concentration of wealth so marked as
in Britain. The top 1 percent of the population possessed two-thirds of the
national wealth, and one-tenth of 1 percent owned a third of the land in
England. Education, occupation, dress, accent, the newspapers one read,

and leisure activities all defined and revealed the social class to which one belonged. The distance between the elegant country gentleman and the Yorkshire factory worker, or the top-hatted London banker and the cloth-capped East End docker, remained as great as in the eighteenth century.

The Labour Party benefited from the decline of the Liberal Party, whose major nineteenth-century issue, free trade, now appealed to relatively few voters. Labour gained the support of most new voters. In 1924, James Ramsay MacDonald (1866–1937), a skilled orator who moved in the most elegant social circles, formed the first Labour government. However, the fall of MacDonald's government after several months demonstrated the resilience of British Conservatives, assisted by a widespread fear in Britain of communism. Conservatives had denounced MacDonald after his government became the first to accord official recognition to the Soviet Union. The press fanned the flames of a "red scare," similar to one then sweeping the United States. A newspaper published a letter it claimed had been written by Grigory Zinoviev, the head of the Communist International, detailing for British Communists ways of destabilizing the government. In fact, the letter was a forgery, the work of a Polish anti-Bolshevik. Returned to power, the Conservatives were determined to restore financial stability and to reject working-class demands. The government put Britain back on the gold standard in 1925, which meant that pounds sterling could be exchanged for gold according to a fixed rate of exchange. But this depleted the amount of gold reserves available to back the British currency and led to the pound's overvaluation. British products became more expensive on the international market, particularly when the other European powers stabilized their own currencies at lower rates. British manufacturing, the key to prosperity for more than a century, remained sluggish, its markets increasingly challenged by goods from the United States and Japan. The United States had become the world's leading creditor nation. New York City was now the new center of international finance.

In Britain, tensions between industrialists and workers came to the fore in 1926. The mines still employed over 1 million workers. After the war, the mining companies had reduced wages and lengthened the workday. A government commission in March 1926 recommended that firms implement safer working conditions, but that the miners accept lower wages. The miners rejected these conclusions with the slogan, "Not a minute on the day, not a penny off the pay." The Trade Union Council launched a general strike of miners in defense of the unions in May 1926. The vast majority of unionized workers in Britain went out in solidarity. The strike enraged the upper and middle classes, inconvenienced by the shutdown of all public transportation. Conservative Winston Churchill castigated the strikers as "the enemy," demanding their "unconditional surrender" as if he were talking about a German bunker in the war. The Labour Party was sympathetic to the plight of the workers, who truly suffered during the strike for defending their principles, but it maintained a safe political distance. Businessmen and students from Oxford and Cambridge Universities drove buses and trucks carrying people in and out of London while troops hauled food. After two weeks, most workers returned to their jobs, although the miners remained on strike for seven months. The strike was broken. A year later, Parliament passed the Trade Disputes Act, which forbade "sympathy strikes," walkouts in support of striking workers by those in other industries. This amounted to a crushing defeat for British workers.

When the French franc, long considered invulnerable to economic shocks, collapsed in value in a financial panic in 1924, the rightist government in France collapsed with it. A coalition of Radicals and Socialists, sharing little more than anticlericalism, formed a left-center government. But this alliance broke apart when the Socialists suggested a sizable tax on capital as a solution to the economic crisis. Ministries came and went with bewildering regularity.

In 1926, the conservative Poincaré returned as premier. He raised taxes on consumption, which the wealthy preferred to levies on capital, because the burden did not fall on them. The franc stabilized, as wealthy Frenchmen brought assets back from abroad and began to buy francs, which then rose rapidly in value. Poincaré became known as the savior of the French currency. But his idea that political consensus existed in France was, like the belief that France was the most powerful country in Europe, only an illusion. Many ordinary French men and women believed that a "wall of money" still held the country hostage and, along with an entrenched bureaucracy, prevented social reform. With an institutionally weak presidency, the Chamber of Deputies increasingly came to be seen as a debating

A barricade during the London General Strike, 1926.

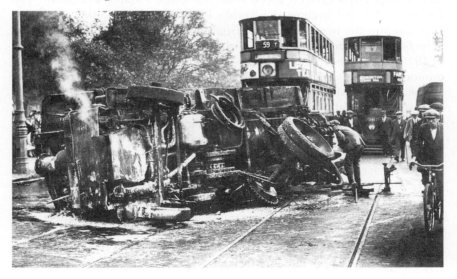

society incapable of responding effectively to domestic and international crises. Political and social tensions encouraged the disillusionment with democracy felt by parties of the political extremes such as the French Communist Party on the one hand, and the fledgling right-wing fascist movements intrigued by Benito Mussolini's seizure of power in Italy on the other (see Chapter 25).

ARTISTS AND INTELLECTUALS IN THE WASTE LAND

The effects of the Great War could also be clearly seen in European intellectual and artistic life, as writers and painters wrestled with the consequences of a devastating struggle that stood as a great divide between the present and a world that was no more. A veteran of the trenches described the war's cataclysmic destruction as "a cyclopean dividing wall in time: a thousand miles high and a thousand miles thick, a great barrier laid across our life." The resulting cultural uncertainty reflected the economic, social, and political chaos of the period.

The defiant modernism of artists and intellectuals in the wake of the war was part of a revolt against traditional cultural conventions within the arts but also against the strictures of bourgeois society. In Britain, for example, people still read Victorian novels and romantic poetry, but such texts seemed to offer no explanation for what had gone wrong in Europe. Horrified by the war, many artists and writers now rejected the social conventions that had inculcated the values of nationalism and blind obedience. In the wake of the war, the "outsiders" of the Belle Époque had become, at least in the realm of the arts, "insiders." To be sure, most of the dramatic changes in artistic expression that followed the war had their origins in the pre-war years—for example, the adoption of psychological, subjective themes and approaches to painting and writing (see Chapter 20). The war had destroyed not only millions of lives but many of the signposts by which artists and writers defined reality. The American writer Gertrude Stein (1874–1946), who bounced back and forth between her artist and writer friends in London and Paris, called the war's survivors "a lost generation." In a 1922 lecture, the French poet Paul Valéry (1871–1945) said, "The storm has died away and still we are restless, uneasy, as if the storm were about to break . . . among all these injured things is the mind. The mind has indeed been cruelly wounded. . . . It doubts itself profoundly."

The bleak 1922 poem *The Waste Land,* by American-born poet and critic T. S. Eliot (1888–1965), reflected the disintegrating impact that the war had on Europe.

A heap of broken images, where the sun beats,
And the dead tree gives no shelter, the cricket no relief,
And the dry stone no sound of water. . . .

Hooded hordes swarming . . .
Falling towers
Jerusalem Athens Alexandria
Vienna London
Unreal

The Dadaists, a group of artists and writers who had gathered in Zurich in 1916, were the first to rebel against the absurdity of the slaughter of 1914–1918 by rejecting all artistic convention. They penned and painted nonsense; some wrote poems that consisted of words gathered from newspapers. It was all nonsense, but no more, they argued, than the war itself.

The artists and writers of the post-war generation stressed the primacy of subjectivism. Like soldiers emerging from the ghastly trenches, they looked into themselves in their quest to comprehend what seemed incomprehensible. Their subjectivism unleashed an imaginativeness that defined much of the new art.

The painters Piet Mondrian (1872–1944), Paul Klee (1870–1940), and Max Beckmann (1884–1950), among others, thumbed their noses at classical rules about painting, and even about what constituted art. Mondrian, a

French Dadaist painter Francis Picabia sitting on his "Dada"—or horse—among friends.

Dutch modernist painter, offered two-dimensional abstractions and straight lines forming grids. Klee's fantasies assumed unexpected shapes and distortions on the canvas; "the artist must distort," he contended, "for therein is nature reborn."

The expressionist movement, too, had its origins before the war. Beckmann rejected the label, but he defined the movement when discussing his own work: "What I want to show in my work is the idea which hides itself behind so-called reality. I am seeking the bridge which leads from the visible to the invisible." Expressionist poets rejected linguistic conventions in an attempt to communicate the emotion buried beneath the human exterior. Expressionist playwrights ignored long-established conventions of plot, character, and dialogue to represent what they considered to be unseen reality. In his modernist epic *Ulysses* (1922), the Irish writer James Joyce (1882–1941) abandoned long-accepted stylistic and narrative conventions to present the chaotic and seemingly unconnected—at least at first glance—"stream of consciousness" dialogue of three main characters, through which he revealed all their sensations and feelings. The novel's eroticism led it to be banned in Britain (but not in traditionally prudish Ireland) and in the United States until 1934.

In 1924, a group of nineteen painters and writers, led by the French artist and poet André Breton (1896–1966), published a "Surrealist Manifesto." In it they rejected "traditional humanism" and the respect for reason that seemed to have so manifestly betrayed mankind. They were not interested in rationality, which seemed defunct, but in what lay beneath it. The surrealists were obsessed with the crater-pocked landscape of churned-up earth, tree stumps, and twisted rubble in northern France and Belgium. They sought to shock audiences and viewers by expressing themselves in a way that was spontaneous and deeply personal, but still realistic. Breton's work sometimes defies interpretation because none was intended.

After four years in the trenches, the German surrealist Max Ernst (1891–1976) wrote that he had "died on the first of August 1914 and returned to life on the 11th of November 1918." Ernst joined a circle of Dadaists in Cologne. His 1933 painting *Europe after the Rain (I)* depicts with oil and plaster what appears to be a distorted, disfigured, and unsettling aerial relief map of Europe. It suggests the mutilation of the continent, which appears to be slowly swallowing itself. The surrealists were militant leftists, and they were also among the minority of Europeans who opposed colonial domination.

For his part, the Viennese doctor Sigmund Freud, founding father of psychoanalysis, believed that the war demonstrated the irrational nature of mankind. Freud's scientific analysis of the unconscious, translated into many languages during the 1920s, had begun to influence sociologists, political scientists, and cultural anthropologists. They applied ideas drawn from psychoanalysis to try to understand group behavior and social conflict. The war lent a sense of urgency to this enterprise. Freud also greatly influenced surrealists such as Breton, who drew images and words from his dreams.

Max Ernst's *Europe after the Rain (I)* (1933).

Some of Freud's early ruminations about the role of the unconscious in art were based on the haunting experience of seeing shell-shocked soldiers.

In 1928, Erich Maria Remarque (1898–1970), who had fought in the war, published *All Quiet on the Western Front,* the powerful pacifist novel about the trenches that quickly became a classic. In 1929, the British writer Robert Graves published his memoirs, focused on his experiences in the Great War. He called his book *Goodbye to All That.* The problem was that Europe could not say "goodbye to all that" and put the war behind it. Amid economic chaos and social and political turmoil in the two decades following the end of the war, one European dictator after another ended parliamentary democracy, imposed authoritarian rule, and suppressed political opposition. Fascist states, particularly Nazi Germany, poisoned international relations with nationalist bullying, making grandiose claims on the territories of other states. At the same time, in the Communist Soviet Union, Joseph Stalin consolidated his power. In what has been called the "Europe of Extremes," Europe entered an even more dangerous period in which it became increasingly clear that Woodrow Wilson's description of the Great War as the "war to end all wars" was meaningless in the Europe of economic Depression and dictatorship.

CHAPTER 25

THE EUROPE OF ECONOMIC DEPRESSION AND DICTATORSHIP

$\sim$

In 1922, Benito Mussolini became the first dictator to take power in Europe. By the end of 1925, fascist parties demanding the imposition of dictatorships had sprung up in many other nations. Other more traditional right-wing authoritarian movements, too, were on the rise. In Portugal, where junior army officers had overthrown the monarchy in 1910 and declared a republic, right-wing military officers staged a coup d'état in 1926. General Józef Pilsudski overthrew the Polish Republic the same year. All of the Eastern European and Balkan states became dictatorships in the 1920s and 1930s, with the exception of Czechoslovakia. In the meantime, Joseph Stalin transformed the Soviet Union into a totalitarian state. Amid the ravages of the Great Depression that began in 1929, Europe entered an even more dangerous period of instability. In 1933, a right-wing government came to power in Austria, and Adolf Hitler, leader of the National Socialist (Nazi) Party, became chancellor of Germany. The right-wing nationalist revolt against the republic of Spain began in 1936, starting a civil war that ended in 1939 with the victory of General Francisco Franco's right-wing nationalist forces. Britain and France were the only major powers in which parliamentary government was strong enough to resist the authoritarian tide. Democracy also survived in the smaller states of Belgium, the Netherlands, Switzerland, Denmark, Sweden, and Norway, despite the existence of small fascist movements in each.

ECONOMIES IN CRISIS

The global economic Depression that began in October 1929 had dramatic political consequences in Europe. Economic insecurity and accompanying social unrest undermined parliamentary rule. More and more people sought scapegoats who could be blamed for hard times: Jews, Socialists, Communists, ethnic minorities and other nationalities, big business. Under such circumstances, many people could be convinced that parliamentary government itself was to blame and that nationalistic dictatorships were the solution. Amid plunging confidence and general bewilderment, international cooperation became more difficult, particularly as the powers began to blame each other for adopting policies that adversely affected them. Germans castigated their wartime enemies for assessing massive, seemingly unjust reparations; people in Britain and France blamed Germany for not paying all the reparations; many Americans blamed their own former allies for not paying back loans. The vicious cycle of mistrust grew.

The Great Depression

By 1924, prosperity seemed to have returned to much of post-war Europe, at least in the Western states. But beneath the surface, the increasingly interdependent world economy had not recovered from the war. The wartime inflation greatly increased during the years that followed the armistice. At the same time, steel and iron prices fell sharply after the war when demand plunged for tanks, artillery pieces, and munitions. Overproduction and the increasing use of hydroelectricity and oil caused the price of coal to fall rapidly. Slowly some industrial jobs began to disappear.

European agriculture, particularly in Eastern Europe, was in a depressed state well before the Crash of 1929. More grain, meats, and other food sup-

(*Left*) The Wall Street Crash, October 1929. (*Right*) An unemployed Briton seeks work, 1930.

I KNOW 3 TRADES
I SPEAK 3 LANGUAGES
FOUGHT FOR 3 YEARS
HAVE 3 CHILDREN
AND NO WORK FOR
3 MONTHS
BUT I ONLY WANT
ONE JOB

plies arrived on the continent from Australia, Argentina, Canada, and the United States. The price of locally produced agricultural goods fell. Lower farm incomes, aggravated by the burden of taxation, in turn reduced demand for manufactured goods.

European states reacted by erecting tariff barriers to try to protect their internal markets for domestic agricultural products. Countries like Bulgaria that depended on agricultural exports saw their foreign markets dry up, or they received less for what they sold. With less income and less Western investment, Eastern European and Balkan nations could not repay their wartime debts. Germany's defeat, the dismemberment of the Austro-Hungarian Empire, and the Russian Revolution significantly weakened the region's three largest pre-war trading partners.

The contraction of demand and price deflation probably would not have been enough to generate full-fledged economic disaster. But unrestrained financial speculation also undercut the world economy. In Germany, high interest rates attracted considerable foreign investment following the 1924 economic recovery. Credit was easily available, and companies issued huge amounts of stock shares based upon insufficient real assets. In the United States, a sizable reduction in demand for goods was already apparent by 1927. Wealthy people began to invest in highly speculative stocks.

Wartime loans and post-war debts made the finances of the larger powers more interdependent and helped destabilize the international economy. German reparations also adversely affected the world economy because, ironically, they accentuated the flow of capital into Germany. Following the Dawes Plan, which in 1924 extended the schedule of reparations, Germany borrowed $110 million from U.S. banks to meet its reduced reparations payments to the Allies, rather than paying them out of current income through higher taxes. German railroads served as collateral for the loans, which were immediately oversubscribed in New York. Like bonds and speculative investments, reparation loans diverted investment away from industry and ignited further foreign lending. Besides loans to pay reparations, other loans also poured into Germany. Most of this debt was short term rather than long term, which made Germany even more vulnerable to a sudden calling in of those loans. In 1928, U.S. banks refused to issue more loans to Germany, investing available funds instead in the Wall Street stock market, further undercutting German banks.

By early 1929, the U.S. economy was in recession. In late October, the New York stock market crashed. Thousands of large and small investors were ruined as stocks lost most of their value. American and British investors with assets still tied up in Germany now began to pull their money out as quickly as possible. German gold reserves were depleted, as banks owed far more money to creditors than they had assets. Table 25.1 shows the importance of the U.S.-German financial connection, which contributed to the fact that the Depression began earlier and production fell more in those two countries than in the other major powers.

TABLE 25.1. INDICES OF INDUSTRIAL PRODUCTION

Year	Germany	United States	France	Britain
1925	79.3	93.7	85.0	94.8*
1927	97.2	95.5	86.6	101.2
1929	101.4	107.2	109.4	106.0
1930	83.6	86.5	110.2	97.9
1931				
August	71.9	74.8	99.2	84.6
December	59.4	66.7	87.4	84.7
1932				
January	55.2	64.9	82.7	90.1
August	54.7	53.2	73.2	89.2

*For Great Britain, 1924.
Source: David E. Sumler, *A History of Europe in the Twentieth Century* (Homewood, IL: Dorsey Press, 1973), p. 145.

As unemployment mounted to unprecedented levels, the "roaring twenties" became the "threadbare thirties." Jobs disappeared and families were compelled to spend the savings they had so painstakingly amassed over the previous five years, even as manufacturing and agricultural prices continued to fall because of the dramatic contraction of demand. Manufactured goods piled up on the docks.

Confronted by a catastrophic fall in production and prices, as well as unemployment approaching 20 percent of the workforce, British government officials and economists debated strategies that might revive their floundering economies. There were no easy answers. The economic orthodoxy of the day held that the way out of the crisis was to reduce public expenditures. The inflation of the immediate post-war period, particularly the hyperinflation that had ravaged Germany in 1922 and 1923, frightened statesmen and economists away from even limited financial or fiscal expansion.

National policy options, too, were further constrained by the interdependence of the international economy, especially under the gold standard. For example, James Ramsay MacDonald's British Labour government first reacted to the Wall Street crash by increasing unemployment benefits and funding more public works, while raising taxes. These expenditures further increased the government deficit, already soaring because of reduced tax revenue. But the British government was then forced to reduce unemployment benefits in order to be deemed creditworthy by New York and Parisian bankers, in the hope of stabilizing the pound and maintaining the gold standard.

The international monetary system collapsed as the world economy plunged into dark Depression. Banks and private interests that had loaned money to Germany began to call in debts. Already reeling from agricultural Depression in Eastern Europe, the failure of the largest Austrian bank in May 1931 immediately brought the collapse of several German banks to which it owed money. A general financial panic ensued. U.S. President Herbert Hoover (1874–1964) suggested a moratorium on the repayment of all reparations and war debts, hoping that confidence and the end of the cycle of defaults would follow. The other powers accepted the moratorium in August 1931.

As the British economy floundered because of the decline in world trade, European bankers intensified the run on the pound. They exchanged their holdings of British pounds sterling for gold, 2.5 million pounds' worth per day during the summer of 1930, dangerously reducing Britain's gold reserves. As investors panicked, sterling quickly lost a third of its value.

With Labour not having a majority in the House of Commons, McDonald was forced to negotiate with the other parties, but the latter insisted on reducing the budget, including cutting unemployment benefits. This McDonald's Labour colleagues could not accept. But instead of resigning as everyone expected, McDonald formed a "National Government" of members from the three parties, although most Labour leaders declined to join him. He thus stayed on as prime minister. Worsening conditions forced the National Government to take Britain off the gold standard in September 1931. This meant that the Bank of England would no longer remit gold in exchange for pounds. This seemed like a step into the economic unknown. Wild fluctuations in the values of other currencies followed. This further discouraged business, and international trade declined even more steeply, but it did permit some domestic recovery. In April 1933, the United States, too, went off the gold standard.

In Britain, the Conservatives' deflationary measures, which sought to reduce expenditures, seemed to British voters to be the only way out of the crisis. In the elections of October 1931, the Tories won an overwhelming majority of seats in the House of Commons. Neville Chamberlain (1869–1940) now became chancellor of the Exchequer. His aloof manner, inveterate dullness, rasping voice, and whiny disposition did little to inspire confidence—one critic suggested that he had been "weaned on a pickle." Chamberlain promised a "doctor's mandate" to extract Britain from the economic crisis. The government imposed higher tariffs, further reducing consumer spending. Many members of the Labour Party called MacDonald a traitor for going along with deflationary measures because they included reducing unemployment benefits, and they proposed the nationalization of mining, the railways, and other essential industries as first steps toward the implementation of a more planned economy. But Labour's campaign ran headlong into traditional Conservative opposition and middle-class fear of socialism, as well as the orthodoxy of deflationary economic policies.

Across the English Channel, smaller-scale industries, artisans, and family farmers in France at first were sheltered from the Depression because they depended, above all, on local markets. France also had considerable gold reserves, which helped maintain business and consumer confidence and keep consumer spending at a relatively high level. The run on the British pound and the German mark, too, at first aided France, as gold exchanged by investors ended up in Paris. The franc initially remained stable, and undervalued, encouraging the purchase of French goods. But gradually French prices also fell and unemployment rose, again revealing the interdependence of the global economy. The Depression hit France only in 1932. French exports declined with the contraction of the world market, particularly because the franc, which had not plunged like the pound, was now overvalued, making French goods expensive abroad. But most French leaders considered devaluation to be anathema. "Who touches the franc," cautioned one newspaper, "touches France!" The French government, like that of Britain, stuck to classical economic remedies, ignoring demands for active state intervention to stimulate the economy both from right-wing corporatists who sought support for cartels and from left-wing socialists who called for the nationalization of crucial industries and more unemployment benefits.

Gradual European Economic Revival

In the rest of Europe, government leaders debated strategies that they hoped would pull their countries out of the Depression. The major powers acted in their own interests—establishing high tariffs and devaluing their currencies—without prior consultation with other governments. The U.S. government, like that of Britain, followed contemporary economic orthodoxy. Both sharply reduced government spending, cutting unemployment benefits and restricting credit. However, John Maynard Keynes (1883–1946), the English economist, insisted that recovery would depend upon just the opposite strategy: an increase in government expenditures, including deficit spending—for example, on public works—to stimulate consumer spending by reducing unemployment. Keynes argued that deflationary measures, such as cutting government spending, reducing unemployment benefits, or encouraging companies to limit production and thus keep prices artificially high, were counterproductive. They could prolong the Depression by reducing the demand for goods. With one-quarter of the labor force out of work early in 1933 and wages falling, there was insufficient demand to generate a manufacturing upswing in Great Britain, the United States, or anywhere else. But Keynes stood virtually alone, and most of what he had written was then still largely unknown.

Only very gradually did the Depression begin to recede in the industrialized countries. A modest recovery began in Britain in 1932. But it was not due to the dramatic improvement of British international trade upon which the Conservatives had counted. Rather, it followed a slow increase in consumer spending. Keynes had been right. Increases in 1934 and 1935

Reflecting the enormity of class divisions in Britain during the Depression, these working-class boys look in amazement at two Eton students outside a cricket ground.

of unemployment benefits and the restoration of government salaries to their pre-Depression levels helped. The subsidized construction of more houses pumped money into the economy, helping to increase consumer confidence. While some inefficient steel and textile manufacturers went under, others consolidated and became more efficient, perhaps benefiting from the imposition of higher tariffs on industrial imports. Real wages slowly rose. The imposition of quotas on agricultural imports aided farmers. As industry and agriculture gradually returned to prosperity, unemployment began to fall.

The German economy also slowly improved, at least in part because, after Hitler came to power in 1933, rearmament created many jobs. Business confidence slowly returned. In 1930, the Young Plan, named after its American originator, had extended the date by which Germany was to have paid all reparations to 1988. Then the Lausanne Conference of 1932 simply declared the end of reparations payments. In France, the Depression lingered longer than in any other European industrialized power. The government, constrained by weak executive authority, failed to act decisively until 1935, when it lowered taxes to encourage consumption, after trying to protect France with a wall of protectionism and productions quotas. When other countries devalued their currencies, France's comparative advantage disappeared, and demand for exports trailed off. Moreover, France's low birthrate, combined with the horrific loss of life during the war, reduced demand.

In the United States, where the Depression hit hardest, recovery came even more slowly. Franklin D. Roosevelt (1882–1945), elected president in 1932, implemented his "New Deal." It facilitated loans that saved banks, provided relief for the unemployed through public works programs, and provided assistance to farmers and to businesses. When Keynes learned of Roosevelt's plans, his assessment was that "Roosevelt was magnificently right" (though as someone noted Keynes might have said that he was "magnificently left"). Gradually, a return of consumer confidence, boosted by the president's low-key "fireside chats" by radio to the American people, improved the economy. But only with the entry of the United States into the Second World War in 1941, with its massive mobilization of economic resources in the production of war materials, did the Depression finally end its grip on the United States.

The Dynamics of Fascism

It is against the background of hard times that followed the Great War that the rise of fascism and other authoritarian movements must be seen both in the industrialized countries of Western Europe and in the largely agrarian states of Eastern Europe and the Balkans (see Map 25.1). Fascist parties developed in the 1920s as political movements seeking mass mobilization— but not political participation. There was nothing democratic about fascist organizations: they were hierarchically structured and, rejecting parliamentary rule, sought to bring dictators to power.

Several factors contributed to the rise of the extreme right, with none serving as a single explanation. If in the nineteenth century the middle class had stood as a bulwark of liberal values in Europe, this was no longer the case in the post-war climate. In Germany, Italy, and Austria, fascists found disproportionate support among the middle class, which had been ravaged by years of economic crisis. Middle-class families watched in horror as their pensions and modest savings disappeared. They feared union leaders, Socialists, and Communists, who all demanded an extension of public programs to aid unemployed workers. Many in the middle class feared such reforms would come at their expense. Big business in Italy and Germany, in particular, turned against parliamentary rule. But middle-class frustrations do not provide a sufficient explanation for the rise of authoritarian movements in Eastern Europe and the Balkans, where the middle classes were extremely small. Moreover, the middle classes in Britain and France endured many of the same economic frustrations, but only in France did a minority turn to authoritarian political movements.

Fascists, Nazis, and other authoritarian right-wing groups blamed parliamentary government itself for the weaknesses and failures of their states in the post-war years. They believed parliamentary regimes to be unstable and weak by their very nature, undercut by factionalism and class divi-

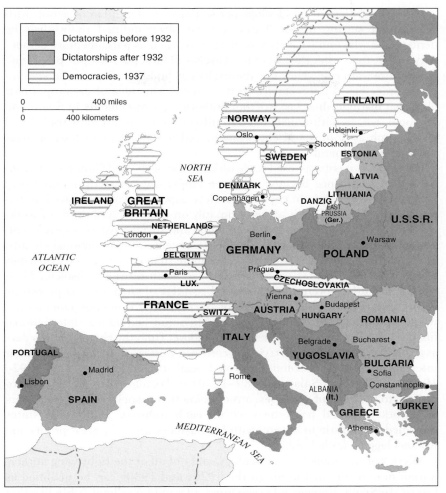

MAP 25.1 DICTATORSHIPS IN EUROPE, 1932–1937   States ruled by dictators before 1932; states that became dictatorships after 1932; remaining democracies in 1937.

sions. The states in which authoritarian dictators came to power lacked strong traditions of parliamentary democracy. Moreover, the seeming instability of parliamentary regimes in times of crisis during the 1920s contributed to the attractiveness of the idea of a strong leader—a dictator who would restore order and embody nationalist aspirations, fulfilling what some considered their nation's "historic destiny." Frenzied crowds, with arms raised in fascist salutes, greeted their authoritarian leaders as heroes. The irony was, of course, that fascist gangs themselves were largely responsible for creating the political turmoil that ultimately led to the destruction of parliamentary governments.

Fascism was less of an ideology per se than a violent plan of action with the aim of seizing power. Fascists most often defined themselves by denouncing who and what they were against, such as parliamentary democracy, rather than what they were for. Fascists did not put forward "programs" for authoritarian rule. They saw themselves as building a new social and political order based upon service to the nation. This idea of creating a new elite also distinguished fascist from authoritarian movements in Spain and Portugal, where nationalists tried to affirm the domination of traditional elites, such as nobles and churchmen, and remained suspicious of mass movements in general.

Fascist movements opposed trade unions, Socialists, and Communists with particular vehemence because all three emphasized class differences they believed were endemic in capitalist society, espoused working-class internationalism, and based their appeal primarily on the perceived needs of workers. Fascists, by contrast, viewed economic and social tensions as irrelevant, arguing that it was enough that all people shared a common national identity, and that this national community meant more than did economic disparities between social classes. Fascism would make such divisions obsolete. Mussolini and Hitler covered up the brutal realities of their rule by promising with vague rhetoric that the needs of the "national economic community" would be fulfilled. In the early 1920s, Mussolini had added "international finance capital" to his list of enemies, a holdover from the rhetoric of his days as a socialist before the war, trying to convince workers that he spoke for their interests, too. Like Mussolini, dictators Engelbert Dollfuss in Austria (1892–1934) and Antonio Salazar (1889–1970) in Portugal also added "corporatism" to their list of promises, announcing that associations of employers and workers would be formed within each industry. But fascist states remained capitalistic in nature, with big business accruing great profits and workers lagging far behind.

There was no single fascist ideology, and not all of the right-wing authoritarian movements in Europe in the 1920s and 1930s can be qualified as fascist. In Spain, Francisco Franco imposed a military dictatorship like that of Salazar in neighboring Portugal; both were predicated upon the influence of traditional elites, the Catholic Church, and the army. Yet, while sharing the anti-Bolshevism of fascist Italy and Nazi Germany, neither the Spanish nor the Portuguese dictatorship shared the expansionist ideology of those regimes, and both distrusted the kind of mass movement that helped sweep the Italian fascists and German Nazis to power. The agrarian populist authoritarian regimes of Eastern Europe may also be described as fascist states, or at least "para-fascist" dictatorships. Some of these also were aggressive, nationalist mass movements built upon anti-communism, anti-Semitism, and fierce opposition to parliamentary rule. Yet although inspired in some ways by Italian fascism and German National Socialism, they had no illusions about expanding their states beyond what each claimed as the "historic" limits of their nationality. Moreover, Stalin's Soviet Union, too,

An enthusiastic crowd, which includes many youths, greets Hitler at a rally at the Nuremberg stadium in 1937.

had become a state dictatorship, like the fascist regimes, but one organized at least on Communist rhetoric about creating a workers' paradise. Stalin, casting aside the claims of the many non-Russian nationalities, and for that matter, of the workers themselves, tolerated no opposition to or within the Communist Party. The Soviet Union was also a totalitarian state, with centralized control of all political functions by a dictator ruling through terror in the name of a single party.

Hatred of parliamentary and democratic rule, Socialists, Communists, and Jews helped give fascism an international character. In 1935, there was even a short-lived attempt to create a fascist international, similar to the Communist International (Comintern) on the other end of the political spectrum. Mussolini contributed funds to the Belgian, Austrian, and British fascist movements. But the stridently nationalist aspect of fascism worked against fascist internationalism. Yet fascist and right-wing authoritarian states found ready allies among similar regimes, as joint German and Italian assistance to the nationalist rebellion during the Spanish Civil War (1936–1939) solidified the alliance between Hitler and Mussolini.

Middle-class economic frustration, anti-parliamentarianism, upper-class fears of socialism, anti-Semitism, aggressive nationalism, and the belief that a dictator could bring order and national fulfillment were all present in European society before the Great War. But the cataclysmic experience of the war channeled them all in new and frightening directions, contributing to the proliferation of aggressive nationalism. For many veterans of the trenches, the experience of the war had made them increasingly indifferent to brutality and human suffering. To an extent, nationalism represented a continuation of the Great War—and the camaraderie of the trenches—now transformed into a race war against those considered internal or external enemies. In Germany, in particular, right-wing movements attracted demobilized soldiers, who had returned home with weapons, habits of military order, and experience with violence. Fortunate enough to have returned home from the war at all, demobilized troops found not a significantly better life to repay them for their sacrifices, but hard times driven by inflation. They kept right on marching. Paramilitary squads of war veterans destabilized political life in France and Italy, in victorious states, but above all in revisionist states that did not accept The Versailles Settlement (see Chapter 24). The Free Corps in Germany, the Home Guard in Austria, and the Cross of Fire in France denounced the "decadence" and "softness" of parliamentary regimes. They wanted continuation of war, the dominant experience in their lives, not peace.

Aggressive nationalism easily became racism. From the beginning, Hitler's National Socialism espoused German racial supremacy. Nazism manifested an unparalleled capacity for violence and destruction based upon the assumption that Nazis could assume the authority to determine who could live and who could die. Their principal target was Jews. This carried Nazi ideology and practice beyond other violent nationalist right-wing regimes. Germans were not alone in believing spurious literature proclaiming the superiority of their race and the degeneration of other races. Eastern European dictators denounced other ethnic groups and nations, which could be blamed for practically anything. Anti-Semitism also characterized authoritarian movements in Austria, Poland, Romania, and Yugoslavia, as well as in France and Belgium. Inspired by Hitler, Mussolini also added anti-Semitism to his nationalist ravings in 1938.

Fascism borrowed some symbols and rites that represented spiritual revolution (for example, "blood" and "martyrdom") from Christianity, replacing the latter with nationalism. Fascism became something of an all-embracing civic religion that sought to build a "national community." In a totalitarian way, fascism sought to eliminate the distinction between private and public life. Fascists sought to create the "new man" who would serve the nation (women were to remain at home) and a new elite defined by service to the state. Fascists emphasized youth and youthful energy, contrasting the "new men" with what they considered the old, failed political systems. Lining up behind authoritarian dictators whom they believed to be natural, aggressive leaders who incarnated their national destiny, fascists trumpeted the historical rights of, and duties to, the nation, which they believed outweighed any other rights. In their view this gave them the right to exclude from the national community—and, for some fascists, to kill—those they considered outsiders in the interest of racial "purity." They believed that this also gave them the right to expand their national frontiers toward what they considered their proper "historical" limits. They placed such struggles in the context of what they conceived of as a Darwinian struggle of the fittest that they would win, and celebrated what they considered to be the beauty of violence. When the film version of Erich Maria Remarque's *All Quiet on The Western Front* appeared in 1930, Nazis marched in protest and shut down some theaters.

Fascists did more than rule through terror—their dictatorships were also built upon popular consensus. Fascism created what has been called a "magnetic field" in Europe in the 1920s. Extreme right-wing movements won widespread support among millions of ordinary people in many corners of Europe, beginning in Italy.

Mussolini and Fascism in Italy

The economic and social tensions of the immediate post-war period destabilized Italy's liberal government. The dissatisfaction of Italian nationalists with the Treaty of Versailles accentuated a political crisis. This made Italy vulnerable to a growing threat from the far right.

Gabriele D'Annunzio (1863–1938), a bombastic, decadent poet, had in 1914 described war as perfect hygiene for the modern world. Having proclaimed, "I am not, and do not wish to be, a mere poet," he took matters into his own hands. In September 1919, the decorated war veteran who had lost an eye in combat swept into the Adriatic city of Fiume (Rijeka). He led a force of 2,000 men, many of whom were demobilized soldiers. D'Annunzio planted the Italian flag, forcing the Italian government to begin negotiations with the new Yugoslav state, which also claimed the Adriatic port. Both countries agreed that Fiume would be independent, but that most of Istria and northern Dalmatia would remain in Yugoslavia, as the Treaty of Versailles had specified. D'Annunzio's little republic lasted sixteen months, until Italian ships lobbed a few shells in the general direction of the city and sent the poet and his small force packing.

D'Annunzio had briefly stolen the thunder of another fervent Italian nationalist, Benito Mussolini (1883–1945). Mussolini was born to a family of modest means in northern Italy. His father, a blacksmith, was something of a revolutionary; he had taught himself to read from socialist tracts and named his son after the Mexican revolutionary Benito Juarez. The young Mussolini was a schoolyard bully quick to raise his fists and pull a knife, once stabbing a girlfriend. He had no close friends and was proud of it—"Keep your heart a desert," he once advised.

Mussolini read Karl Marx, and Friedrich Nietzsche, whose espousal of daring revolt and the "will to power" intrigued him. After a stint in the army, Mussolini proclaimed himself a socialist and anti-militarist and became a political journalist. He took to the streets to denounce Italy's

Italian dictator Benito Mussolini and his fascists, 1935.

colonial war against Libya (see Chapter 21). Late in 1912, Mussolini became editor of the Italian Socialist Party's newspaper, *Avanti!* At the outbreak of war in 1914, Mussolini led a chorus of socialists demanding that Italy remain neutral.

In October 1914, a small number of members broke away from the Socialist Party, demanding that Italy join the war. They took the name "fascists" from the Latin word *fascio,* meaning "a bundle of sticks," or, by extension, an association. When Italy entered the war in 1915, Mussolini joined the army. His views toward war were already changing. "Only blood," he wrote, "makes the wheels of history turn." The influence of Nietzsche was overwhelming that of Marx in his mind. Lightly wounded in 1917, he returned to journalism. At the war's end, Mussolini led the chorus of nationalist demands for a peace settlement favorable to Italian interests. In March 1919, he founded the National Fascist Party.

The post-war crisis of Italy's liberal state aided the fascists. The major parties of Italy—the Liberals, the Socialists, and the new Catholic Popular Party—struggled in vain to find consensus. While governments formed and fell in quick succession, severe economic difficulties followed the armistice. Hundreds of thousands of demobilized troops joined the ranks of the unemployed. Inflation soared, eroding middle-class savings and undercutting the already low standard of living of workers and landless peasants. Agricultural Depression compounded high unemployment.

As in Britain, France, and Germany, workers flocked to organized labor in Italy, and waves of strikes spread in 1919 and 1920. Peasant laborers demanded land and formed unions called "red leagues." In the south, thousands of poor families had begun to occupy some of the vast, often uncultivated holdings belonging to wealthy landowners. Banditry exploded in the south and Sicily.

During these "red years" of 1920–1922, many landowners and businessmen turned against parliamentary rule. The Liberal government had alienated the wealthy by proposing a progressive tax on income and a high imposition on war profits and outraged them by legalizing peasant land seizures. Wealthy industrialists helped bring the Italian fascists to power. In the north, ship owners and iron and mining magnates, as well as wealthy landowners, provided funds for Mussolini's fascists. Uniformed squads of fascists wearing black shirts intervened on behalf of big landowners and businessmen, attacking Socialists, Communists, and union members. Laborers and sharecroppers fought back against the fascists, but had little chance because the landowners supplied the *squadri* with weapons. The left was divided and hesitant.

Mussolini, now boasting a private army and a sizable claque, or "applause squad," of paid supporters, praised the "bath of blood" that swept parts of Italy. He reveled in rumors of a coup d'état associated with his name, cranking out violent articles denouncing parliamentary government.

In 1921, the Liberals, hoping to find a parliamentary mandate to impose order, offered the fascists qualified support and accepted them as electoral allies. Mussolini and several dozen other fascists were elected to the Italian Parliament. The fascist leader now had an ideal soapbox for his flamboyant oratory, as well as immunity from prosecution. The Liberal government of Giovanni Giolitti (see Chapter 17) resigned, succeeded by another coalition government.

The fascists were now a powerful political movement with prominent allies, money, newspapers, and hundreds of thousands of party members. Fascist thugs had carved out territories in which their word was law. They disrupted local political life, shattering the organization and support for the traditional parties. Mussolini, who took the title of the Duce, or "the leader," presented himself as a defender of law and order, blaming Socialists and the newly formed Communist Party for the turmoil for which the fascists were largely responsible. Fascists enjoyed the tacit support of many state and police officials, and fascist violence went unpunished.

For Mussolini, fascism was an ideology of violent confrontation, a means of winning and maintaining political power, more than a coherent doctrine of political philosophy. Italian fascists, as with their counterparts who would soon emerge elsewhere, advocated a strong, virulently nationalist, militarized state. Italy would fulfill its "historic destiny" by transforming the Mediterranean into "a Roman lake."

In October 1922, Mussolini made his move. He pressured indecisive King Victor Emmanuel III (ruled 1900–1946), a shy man who loved to hunt, wear military uniforms, and collect coins, to name him and several other fascists to cabinet posts. The king remained out of Rome for weeks at a time as the crisis built, hoping that it would simply go away. Even as he planned a coup d'état, Mussolini charmed members of the royal family. He told 40,000 fascists in Naples, "Either we are allowed to govern, or we will seize power by marching on Rome." The prime minister asked the king to declare martial law and to use the army to restore order by suppressing the fascists, who had seized control of several towns.

The king declared a state of emergency and then changed his mind even as thousands of black-shirted fascists surged toward Rome on the night of

October 27, 1922. Mussolini took a comfortable night train to the capital. When one politician refused the king's request to form a government, Victor Emmanuel turned to Mussolini. On October 29, the Duce became prime minister. Fascists celebrated in the streets by beating up political enemies and shutting down left-wing newspapers.

Despite the fact that his party held a small proportion of the seats in the chamber and could not claim the party allegiance of a single senator, Mussolini convinced both bodies to grant him full powers to rule by decree for a year. Many mainstream politicians endorsed him because the fascists promised to restore social order. They also assumed that Mussolini could not long survive once brought into respectable political life.

Mussolini's shrewd management of fascist newspapers and his ability to plant favorable articles in other papers through cajoling and bribery helped win further support. Aided by the intimidating tactics of the fascist militia, the National Fascist Party won enough votes in the 1923 elections to emerge as the majority party, at least with the support of the Catholic Popular Party.

Despite a major political crisis in 1924 that followed his implication in the murder of a Socialist deputy, Mussolini developed an almost cult-like following. The Duce encouraged the phrase "Mussolini is always right" and managed to convince millions of people that this was indeed the case. He was the first politician of the twentieth century to make use of modern communication techniques. Mussolini subsidized several films about his accomplishments; his rambling speeches, voluminous tomes, an autobiography, and several authorized biographies were sold in glossy editions. By the early 1930s, Italian journalists were required to capitalize He, Him, and His when referring to the Duce, as they did when mentioning God or Jesus Christ. All Italians at age eighteen had to take an oath to obey Mussolini. Italian press agents worked to enhance his image abroad. In Vienna, Sigmund Freud at first praised him; the American poet Ezra Pound remained an admirer. The U.S. ambassador saluted "a fine young revolution," and *Time* magazine put him on its cover eight times. To some foreign visitors, Mussolini's fascism seemed to offer a third way—namely, corporatism—that lay between unchecked capitalism and the contentious challenge of socialism and communism. The Duce became known abroad as the genius who managed to make Italian trains run on time, although, in fact, such a description applied only to those carrying tourists to the ski resorts in the Italian Alps.

Not long after Mussolini took power, however, French newspapers began to describe him as a Carnival Caesar. The tag stuck. The Duce strutted about, boasting egregiously, his eyes rolling and his chin jutting out as he piled falsehood upon exaggeration. He insisted that officials and assistants sprint to his desk, and ordered photographers to take pictures of him fencing, playing tennis, or jogging by troops he was reviewing. Mussolini obnoxiously boasted of his sexual energy and prowess. But despite his insistence that he be portrayed as dynamic, he was rather lazy. To some extent, the

Italian dictator was an actor, and the balconies from which he thundered speeches were his stage.

Mussolini planned an army of "eight million bayonets" and an air force that would "blot out the sun." But despite the dictator's attempt to project an image of fascism that emphasized youthful physical vigor, relatively little military training actually took place in Italy. The Italian army remained beset by inadequate command structures and poor training.

The Duce took over the most important operations of the state and was like an orchestra conductor trying to play all of the instruments at once. He warned ministers not to disagree with him because they might divert him "from what I know to be the right path—my own animal instincts are always right." Officials reported only what they thought Mussolini wanted to hear. The gap between Mussolini's assessment of Italy's military strength and reality widened.

Mussolini treated domestic policy as an afterthought, once claiming that "to govern [Italy], you need only two things, policemen, and bands playing in the streets." Yet while it is easy to emphasize the farcical aspects of Mussolini's rule, in Italy, as in other fascist states, there was nothing comical about the brutality of the police or about his provocative foreign policy, which made Europe an increasingly dangerous place.

In order to placate a potentially powerful source of opposition, Mussolini made peace with the Catholic Church, which had previously denounced the regime after fascist squads smashed Catholic workers' cooperatives along with similar Socialist organizations. In 1929, the Duce signed the Lateran Pacts with the Church, a concordat that left the Vatican an independent papal enclave within Rome. In exchange, the papacy for the first time officially recognized Italy's existence. The Italian dictator returned religious instruction to all schools, and banned freemasonry, literature that the Church considered obscene, the sale of contraceptives, and swearing in public. Mussolini won further Church support with his pro-natal campaign (which included a tax on "unjustified celibacy"), vague statements about the importance of the family, measures limiting Protestant publications, and fulminations against women participating in sports. The Duce now had his grown children baptized and his marriage recognized by the Church, ten years after his civil marriage to a wife with whom he no longer lived. Pope Pius XI called Mussolini "the man sent by Providence."

Like Hitler and Stalin, Mussolini sought to eliminate the boundary between private and public life. He wanted the "new Italian woman" to espouse the values of, and serve, the nationalist state. With the fascist motto, "Everything within the State, nothing outside the State," he viewed the family as an essential component of fascism. "The Nation is served even by keeping the house swept. Civic discipline begins with family discipline," advised an Italian children's book. But fascism could never overcome the inevitable tensions between family obligations and what fascists considered national duties. Mussolini and the fascists believed they were restoring old values. But the idea of women serving the nation-state was very new—for example, the attempt to create mass fascist organizations of women ranging from after-work recreational clubs to female paramilitary squads. The Duce disliked the fact that women had obtained the right to vote in Great Britain, Germany, and several other countries, and that more Italian women were going to work. In Italy's fascist state—as in Hitler's Germany—the place of women was, in principle, in the home, obeying their husbands and having babies.

Mussolini viewed corporatism (see Chapter 24) as a possible remedy to the economic problems that beset Italy. The Duce created twenty-two corporations, or assemblies, overseen, at least in theory, by a National Council of Corporations. Each corporation was based on a council of employers and employees. But Italian fascist corporatism had very little impact in Italy. Its chief practical consequence, at least until the early 1930s, was to swell the number of state bureaucrats hired to supervise creaky, inefficient, and largely superfluous organizations.

The Duce wanted to make Italy economically independent. State agencies invested in industries Mussolini considered crucial to the colonial and European wars he was planning. By 1935, no other European state, except Stalin's Soviet Union, controlled such a large portion of industry, with major shares in industries like steelworks and shipbuilding. Hydroelectricity and automobile manufacturing developed, but Italian industry still depended on raw materials imported from abroad, including copper, rubber, and coal.

Mussolini dubbed his most ambitious agricultural program the "battle for grain." But wheat production was uneconomical in many regions; by converting from labor-intensive crops to wheat, the Duce's pet program generated unemployment and reduced pasture and fruit-growing lands and the number of farm animals. High tariffs on grain imports raised food prices. Land reclamation and irrigation projects also failed. While Mussolini's speeches celebrated "blood and soil" (a constant refrain on the fascist and authoritarian right in inter-war Europe), the number of Italian peasant proprietors declined.

The failures of Mussolini's economic policies were compounded by the demands of military spending, which absorbed a full third of Italian income by the mid-1930s. While the state spent heavily on planes and submarines, Italy's per capita income remained about that of Britain and the United States in the early nineteenth century. Illiteracy remained high, particularly in the south. Under fascism, the gap between the more industrialized north and the poor south continued to grow.

The paradox of Italian corporatism was revealed in Mussolini's rhetoric that there were no social classes in Italy, only Italians. The Duce cheerily proclaimed the end of class struggle and bragged that he had done more for workers than any other leader. But employers and workers were certainly not on an equal footing. Their trade unions destroyed (replaced by fascist trade unions), their conditions of life basically unimproved, and strikes now

Italian women with gas masks line up for the Duce as part of a parade of 70,000 fascist women and girls in celebration of the twentieth anniversary of fascism in 1939.

illegal, most workers remained skeptical about Mussolini. The fascist government did limit the workday in 1923, and in 1935 it introduced a five-day workweek. But employers broke contracts with impunity. The conditions of life for sharecroppers and other landless laborers worsened.

In other respects, some things went on as before. In the south, where peasants particularly resented and resisted the state, the Mafia provided an alternative allegiance, a parallel underworld government. Mussolini failed to destroy the power of the Neapolitan and Sicilian Mafias, even though the number of Mafia-related killings fell dramatically. The Church also remained at least an alternative source of influence to fascism. A Catholic revival, which included a rapid rise in the number of priests and nuns, was independent of fascism. Pope Pius XI lost some of his enthusiasm for Mussolini's fascism, denouncing in the early 1930s "the pagan worship of the state." Few Italians paid attention to the Duce's attempts to convince Italians to stop singing in the streets, or his insistence that they dress babies in fascist black shirts. That not all Italians listened to Mussolini's bombastic rhetoric (nor to the Catholic Church) was demonstrated by the continuing fall of the birthrate (from 147.5 births per 1,000 in 1911 to 102.2 in 1936), despite the call of the Duce for more baby soldiers and the ban on the sale of birth-control devices. Massive emigration out of Italy continued throughout the 1920s and 1930s. However, overall, most Italians still supported Mussolini, if only passively.

Hitler and the Rise of the Nazis in Germany

Like Italian fascism, the rise of the Nazis became closely identified with the rise to power of a charismatic leader, Adolf Hitler (1889–1945). Hitler was born in the small Austrian town of Braunau, on the border with Bavaria. His father was a customs official of modest means. As a boy, the young Hitler lacked discipline and was, as a teacher remembered, "notoriously cantankerous, willful, arrogant, and bad-tempered. He had obvious difficulty in fitting in at school."

Hitler quit school in 1905. Turned down for admission to the School of Painting at the Academy of Fine Arts in Vienna, he nonetheless moved to the imperial capital where he lived in a hostel with little money and few friends. In the 1914 city directory, Hitler had himself listed as "painter and architect," although his painting amounted to earning a little money painting postcards for tourists.

Hitler was of average height with a large head, dark hair, broad cheekbones, and an unusually high forehead. Wearing baggy clothes and sporting his characteristic trimmed mustache, he was not an impressive-looking man. He had bad teeth and poor eyesight. Hitler was compulsive about daily routines, did not drink coffee or smoke, was a vegetarian, and took only an occasional drink. He enjoyed the company of women but may, in fact, have been impotent.

During this time in Vienna, Hitler expressed great hatred for the Social Democrats, not Jews, despite Vienna's rampant anti-Semitism. He moved to Munich and, as a German nationalist, cheered the proclamation of war. He joined the German army and was wounded in the leg in 1916, gassed in a British attack just before the end of the war, and decorated on three occasions for bravery. But his superiors found Hitler unfit for promotion to the officer corps, believing that he lacked leadership qualities.

Hitler would later recall "the stupendous impression produced on me by the war—the greatest of all experiences . . . the heroic struggle of our people." He claimed to have warned fellow soldiers that "in spite of our big guns victory would be denied" to Germany because of "the invisible foes of the German people," Marxists and Jews. The war accentuated Hitler's fanatical German nationalism and transformed him into a raging anti-Semite.

In 1918, Oswald Spengler (1880–1936) published the first volume of *The Decline of the West*. He blamed Germany's defeat on the decay of Western civilization. "We no longer believe," he wrote, "in the power of reason over life. We feel that life rules over reason." He anticipated that new, powerful leaders would emerge out of the maelstrom to destroy "impotent democracies." Spengler believed that the German race would emerge victorious in a biological struggle against its competitors. German culture would be embodied in a new state in which the individual would be subsumed in the racial nation.

By 1919, Hitler had constructed a view of the world that was strikingly similar to that of Spengler. Moreover, it was increasingly shared by many Germans. It was composed of racism, anti-Semitism, anti-communism, and aggressive nationalism. He believed that Germans were "Aryans," descended from a superior Caucasian people. That year, Hitler joined the German Workers' Party, a newly formed right-wing nationalist organization. The following year, when Hitler became the head of the organization, he renamed it the National Socialist German Workers' Party, or Nazi Party. Some Nazis now referred to Hitler as the "Führer," or "leader," as Mussolini was the Duce in Italy.

Nazis organized a paramilitary organization, the "storm troopers," known after 1921 as the S.A. (*Stürmabteilung*), led by the hard-drinking Bavarian Ernst Röhm (1887–1934). Like the Free Corps, the S.A. offered comradeship and an outlet for violence to frustrated right-wing war veterans. To its members, Hitler appeared to be a man of action, a survivor of the trenches—one of them.

Emboldened by their success at attracting adherents, the Nazis marched out of a Munich beer hall on November 9, 1923, planning to seize power and then march on Berlin. Troops loyal to the government put an end to the "Beer Hall Putsch." An anti-republican judge sentenced Hitler to five years in prison. He served only one year and emerged from prison a national figure. Hitler then built up the Nazi Party.

Some of the first Nazi storm troopers in 1922, with swastikas on their arms and flag.

In 1925, Hitler published *Mein Kampf* (*My Struggle*), which he had written in his comfortable jail quarters. Here he reiterated the claim, originally that of General Paul von Hindenburg and believed by many Germans, that Germany had been stabbed in the back by Jews and Communists during the war. It was easy to forget that the military front had collapsed before the home front, a convenient collective amnesia. "If, at the beginning and during the war," Hitler wrote, "someone had only subjected about twelve or fifteen thousand of these Hebrew destroyers of the people to poison gas—as was suffered on the battlefield by hundreds of thousands of our best workers from all social classes and all walks of life—then the sacrifice of millions at the front would not have been in vain." His identification of communism with Jews intensified his obsessive anti-Semitism. Hitler never strayed from the most salient themes of his appeal, believing that people could only absorb a few ideas, which must be hammered in over and over again. Germany would rearm and then conquer "living space" at the expense of the "inferior" Slavic peoples. Many Germans now believed that the problem was not that Germany had fought the war, but only that victory had been stolen from them.

In these early days, the Nazis, like Mussolini's fascists, drew much of their support from the middle class, which had been devastated by the hyperinflation of the early 1920s and turned against the Weimar Republic itself. Pensioners struggled to make ends meet; many small businessmen, shopkeepers, craftsmen, and clerks had to sell or pawn silver or other items of value that had been passed down in their families for generations. Many big businessmen were at first suspicious of Nazism's mass appeal. They preferred more traditional kinds of authoritarian ideas that appealed to their sense of social exclusiveness, such as a monarchy backed by the armed forces in the Prussian tradition. Middle-class businessmen of more modest means early on were more likely to back the Nazis. They looked to Hitler to protect them from "Bolsheviks" and did not care how he did so.

Slowly the Nazis built their party. They won less than 3 percent of the vote in the 1928 elections. But German political life was moving to the right, led by the powerful National People's Party, most of whose members were increasingly anti-republican but not yet necessarily attracted to the Nazis. They preferred a monarchy or military dictatorship. The death in October 1929 of Gustav Stresemann, Germany's able and respected foreign minister, removed a powerful voice of support for the republic, gravely weakening the Weimar coalition in the Reichstag. Socialists, too, were divided, despite considerable popularity—indeed the largest veterans' organization was that of the Socialist (SPD) Party. The political center disappeared as support for Weimar crumbled. The American Wall Street Crash in October 1929 compounded social and political instability. The economic hardship of the Great Depression swelled the ranks of parties committed to overthrowing parliamentary rule in Germany and other states.

Right-Wing Authoritarian Movements in Eastern Europe

In Eastern and Central Europe, parliamentary governments did not survive the instability wrought by the economic dislocation of the 1920s and 1930s, nor the bitter ethnic rivalries within these nations, which included states that already existed at the outbreak of the war (Romania, Bulgaria, and Greece, as well as Poland, once again independent) and the new state of Yugoslavia. Except for the kingdom of Yugoslavia, each of these multinational states had some sort of liberal constitution in the 1920s. But by the end of the 1930s, only Czechoslovakia had not become a dictatorship.

With the exception of Czechoslovakia, which included industrialized Bohemia, all of these countries were heavily agricultural, poor, and had high percentages of illiteracy. When compared with the countries of Western Europe, the countries of Eastern Europe had very small middle classes, except Czech Bohemia, parts of Serbia, and major cities like Budapest.

A daunting variety of conflicting economic interests could be found among the people of Eastern Europe, ranging from those of wealthy Hungarian landowners to Bosnian mountain dwellers scratching out a meager living from thankless land. In Eastern Europe, most peasants were not interested in politics and associated states with taxes. But they wanted land reform, and this demand brought them into the political process. After the war, the governments of the Eastern European states did implement ambitious land reform programs that reduced the number and size of the large estates, adding to the ranks of small landholding farmers. But populist agrarian parties, such as the Smallholders in Hungary and the Romanian National Peasant Party, were essentially single-interest parties that fell under the sway of fascist demagogues. Such agrarian parties vilified Jews as ethnic outsiders, mobilizing resentment against their economic roles as bankers, small businessmen, and shopkeepers. In Hungary, Romania, and Bulgaria, wealthy landowners, desperate to protect their estates against further land reform and frightened by the rise of small Communist parties, turned toward authoritarian rule. As political parties and ultimately parliamentary rule failed amid agricultural Depression, nationalism filled the gap, becoming ever more strident and aggressive.

Poland was the first Eastern European state to become a dictatorship. General Józef Pilsudski seized power in 1926, imposing a military dictatorship that survived his death in 1935 (see Chapter 24). The Yugoslav experiment in parliamentary rule ended abruptly in 1929, when King Alexander I (ruled 1921–1934) dissolved the assembly and banned political parties. That year, Croats established the Ustaša (Insurrection) Party, a right-wing nationalist party that demanded an independent Croatia. In 1934, King Alexander was assassinated, with the help of Ustaša members. Five years later, Croatia won status as an "autonomous" region with its own assembly, but this did not reduce Serb domination of the multinational state. In Yugoslavia, then, the principal battle was not between partisans of dictatorship

King Alexander I of Yugoslavia and French Foreign Minister Jean-Louis Barthou were assassinated while driving through Marseilles in 1934; the assassin was later lynched by onlookers.

and those of parliamentarian government, as in Germany, but between the authoritarian Serb government and a right-wing Croat organization.

In Hungary, Admiral Miklós Horthy (1868–1957), the head of state since 1920, appointed a fascist prime minister in 1932 but repressed the extreme right-wing parties when they threatened to seize power for themselves. Bulgarian political life was marked by assassinations and coups d'état followed by dictatorship in 1935. In Greece, republicans, monarchists, and military officers battled it out. In 1936, Greek King George II (1890–1947) gave his blessing to the dictatorship of General Ioannis Metaxas (1871–1941), who, in the fascist style, took the title of "leader." In 1938, Romanian King Carol II (1893–1953) established a dictatorship by suspending the constitution. He did so to protect his rule against a challenge from the fascist "Legion of the Archangel Michael" and particularly its murderous shock troops, the "Iron Guard," a fanatically Orthodox religious group with strong anti-Semitic prejudices. Romanian fascists drew upon peasant discontent created by agricultural deflation. The king's bloody suppression of the Legion and the Iron Guard only postponed the victory of fascism in Romania.

In Eastern Europe, only Czechoslovakia managed to achieve political stability as a parliamentary democracy, despite differences between Czechs and Slovaks. The two largest political parties, the Agrarian Party and the

Social Democratic Party, drew members from both peoples. By the late 1930s, it was apparent that the greatest threat to parliamentary rule in Czechoslovakia would come from Nazi Germany, as Hitler seized upon ethnic tensions in the Czech Sudetenland between the German-speaking population and the Czechs. Consequently, even Central and Eastern Europe's most stable country was not immune from destabilizing ethnic rivalries.

Fascism in Austria

In Austria, the undersized, German-speaking remnant of the Habsburg Empire, fascism was closely tied to German nationalism and anti-Semitism. Moreover, lying between Germany and Italy, Austria almost inevitably came under the influence of those states. During the 1930s, Mussolini wanted to absorb the Austrian Tyrol, although only the southern part was Italian speaking, and Hitler wanted Germany to annex all of Austria. The Nazi Party of Austria was eager to assist Hitler by destabilizing political life.

The split between right and left in Austria led to "Bloody Friday," July 15, 1927, when police killed a hundred striking workers during demonstrations in Vienna by Socialists protesting right-wing violence. Yet in Vienna social democracy was rooted in areas of public housing on the edge of the city. The contrast between the stately inner city, where some of the old Habsburg nobles still lived, and its political "red belt" of working-class housing could not be missed. Much of the tax burden fell on the Viennese middle classes, which were for the most part socially conservative, fervently Catholic, and overwhelmingly supportive of the conservative ruling Christian Social Party. Anti-Semitism had deep roots in Vienna as well as in provincial Austria. As everywhere, the Depression accentuated existing social and political tensions and violence.

The violent anti-parliamentary groups in neighboring Bavaria, where Hitler had got his start, served as a point of attraction for the Austrian Nazis. Members of the Austrian right-wing Home Guard wore traditional green woolen coats, lederhosen, and Alpine hats, but carried quite modern machine guns. The Social Democrats formed their own guard, determined to protect their members.

In 1933, Chancellor Dollfuss, a diminutive, awkward man who wore traditional Austrian peasant garb because he was proud of his provincial origins, dissolved the Austrian Parliament because it stood in the way of an authoritarian state. In February 1934, after Home Guard raids on workers' organizations and newspapers, the workers of Vienna, led by the Social Democrats, undertook a general strike. Fighting erupted when Dollfuss unleashed the Home Guard and army against the left. Army units attacked the industrial suburbs with artillery fire, killing several hundred workers during four days of fighting. Police closed down all Social Democratic organizations, and tried and executed some of their leaders. Dollfuss then banned all political parties except the fascist Fatherland Front.

The Popular Front in France against the Far Right

Fascist parties in France had their origins in the anti-republican nationalism of the late nineteenth century. The Great War and the economic and
social frustrations of the post-armistice period, as elsewhere, contributed
to the rise of the far right. War veterans were prominent in the Faisceau
movement, which was founded in 1919 and emulated the newly created
Italian fascist organization, and in the Cross of Fire, established in 1929.
French fascist leaders included two renowned producers of luxury products, the perfume magnate François Coty and the champagne baron Pierre
Taittinger. The latter's Patriotic Youth movement, founded in 1924, counted
more than 100,000 members by the end of the decade.

The rise in immigration to France increased xenophobia and racism.
Beginning in 1935, more people died in France each year than were born
there, and its population grew only because of the arrival of immigrants—
Italians, Poles, Spaniards, and Belgians, as well as Jews from Eastern
Europe. About 7.5 percent of the French population in the late 1930s con-
sisted of immigrants—the highest percentage in Europe.

French fascists decried the existence of the Third Republic, which seemed
to them an anomaly in a continent of dictators. Political power in France lay
not with a strong executive authority but with the Chamber of Deputies.
Governments came and went in turn, increasing rightist dissatisfaction. In
1934, a seamy political scandal offered the extreme right an opening for
action. The appearance of government complicity in a fraudulent bond-
selling scheme engineered by Serge Stavisky (1886–1934), a Ukrainian-
born Jew, led to violent rightist demonstrations against the republic. On
February 6, 1934, right-wing groups rioted, charging across the Seine River
in Paris toward the Chamber of Deputies before being dispersed by troops,
with casualties on both sides. But, unlike the right in Germany, Italy, or
Spain, the French right did not have a dominating figure capable of uniting
opposition to parliamentary rule. On February 12, millions of French men
and women marched in support of the republic.

The formation of the Popular Front in France, an alliance between the
Radical, Socialist, and Communist parties, must be seen in the context of
the threat posed by the right not only in France but throughout Europe.
Socialists and Communists had been at odds since the Congress of Tours in
1920. The split became policy when the Communist International (Comintern) of 1927 adopted the tactic of "class against class," which tolerated
no concessions to "bourgeois" parties, including the Socialist Party. But in
the 1930s, the reality of the threat of the right to France overcame ideology.
Stalin's fear of German rearmament led the Comintern to repudiate the
"class versus class" strategy in June 1934. The French Communist Party was
now free to join forces with the Socialist and Radical parties in a Popular
Front to defend the republic against fascism. The three parties prepared
a compromise program incorporating tax reform, a shorter workweek,

increased unemployment benefits, support for the League of Nations and international disarmament, and the dissolution of the fascist leagues.

The Popular Front won a clear victory in the subsequent elections of May 1936. But the Communists refused to participate in the ensuing government, on orders from Moscow. Léon Blum (1872–1950) became prime minister of the Popular Front government. That the Socialist leader was Jewish intensified the rage of the extreme right. Shouts of "Better Hitler than Blum!" echoed in Paris.

As unions, encouraged by the Popular Front's pre-election promises, put forward demands for better work conditions, the largest strike wave in French history broke out across the country. For the first time, workers occupied plants, singing, putting on theatrical productions, and staging mock trials of bosses. The strikes, many by non-unionized workers, took both French labor organizations and the Communist Party by surprise. The Communists tried to bring the strikes to a speedy conclusion, fearful that defeat might hurt their influence with workers or help the Socialists. The Communist Party newspaper *L'Humanité* answered the workers' optimistic slogan "Everything is possible" with the headline "Everything is not possible!"

Blum convinced employers and union representatives to sign the "Matignon Agreements," establishing a forty-hour workweek, pay raises, and paid vacations. The strikes gradually ended. But the economy continued to falter in the face of intransigent opposition from employers and wealthy families shipping assets out of France. Moreover, the reduced workweek undercut production. Blum declared a "pause" in his reform program, and cut back social benefits and other state expenditures.

The Popular Front began to unravel. In March 1937, police fired on workers demonstrating against the rightist Cross of Fire group. The Communists denounced the government, which they had helped bring to power but never joined. The government had to devalue the franc several times because of the flow of gold abroad. Blum asked the Senate to grant him power to rule by decree. When the conservative-dominated Senate refused, he resigned in June 1937. For all intents and purposes, the Popular Front was over. A centrist government lurched on in France as the international situation worsened.

Fascism in the Low Countries and Britain

Fascism threatened even Belgium and the Netherlands, as well. In Belgium, the fascist party "Rex" (from the Latin for "Christ the King"), led by Léon Degrelle (1906–1994), drew on the frustrations of white-collar workers and shopkeepers, victims of the Depression who blamed competition from department stores and socialist consumer cooperatives for their plight. Economic malaise compounded tensions generated by the linguistic division between French-speaking Walloons and the Flemish speakers of Flanders, some of whom demanded Flemish autonomy. A wave of strikes tore through

Belgium in 1936, similar to the one in France at the same time. However, Belgian fascists never won more than 12 percent of the vote. The majority of the middle class remained loyal to parliamentary government. Banks and the Socialist and Catholic parties successfully pressured the government for action to assist the lower middle class by increasing credit available to small retailers and extending union rights to white-collar employees. The Catholic Church's condemnation of Rex in 1937 led many of the group's members to return to moderate Catholic parties.

Similarly, in the Netherlands, the Dutch National Socialist League, which emulated the Nazis, was condemned by both the Calvinist Reform Church and the Catholic Church. It won the support of only 8 percent of Dutch voters in 1937.

In the depths of the Depression, a fascist movement developed even in Britain, the home of parliamentary government. That there were considerably fewer immigrants in Britain than, for example, France, probably limited the appeal of the nationalistic far-right parties. However, Oswald Mosley (1896–1980) started a small fascist party in Britain. Born into a wealthy aristocratic family, Mosley left the Conservative Party in 1924 over his concerns about unemployment in Britain. The philandering Mosley proclaimed his new motto "Vote Labour, Sleep Tory." In 1931, he founded a small party with disastrous electoral results. Then, infatuated with Mussolini and the idea of corporatism, he attacked "international finance capital," as well as the Labour Party, and formed the British Union of Fascists in 1932, delivering violent speeches attacking Jews. Mussolini provided funds, as did Hitler, who served as best man at his second wedding. Mosley surrounded himself with black-shirted toughs, but he attracted more attention than followers (they never numbered more than 20,000). The British people once again avoided political extremes.

THE THIRD REICH

In Germany, the Depression helped swell the ranks of not only the Nazi Party but also other parties and groups (including powerful army officers and big businessmen) committed to the end of parliamentary government. Political parties, labor unions, and voluntary associations crumbled before the Nazi onslaught. Nazi organizations enrolled millions of Germans.

The Collapse of the Weimar Republic

The Depression increased opposition to the Weimar Republic, particularly among the middle classes. The Nazis in 1929 were but one of a number of extreme right-wing groups determined to overthrow the republic. The Depression also further eroded the centrist coalition within the Reichstag upon which the republic had depended from the beginning. In March

1930, the last remnants of the Weimar coalition came apart under the pressure of the economic turmoil; the government, led by the Social Democrats, resigned. Social and political compromise seemed impossible. President Hindenburg began to rule by decree.

The new elections held in September 1930 confirmed the erosion of the parliamentary center. The Nazis received five times more votes than in the last elections, obtaining 18 percent of the popular vote and 107 seats in the Reichstag. The Communist Party, too, gained seats, while the Social Democratic Party remained the largest party with 143 deputies, although it lost seats, as did the moderate conservative parties. Bolstered by rising numbers of supporters, in 1932 Hitler ran for president against Hindenburg, winning 13.5 million votes to the general's 19 million and the Communist candidate's 4 million. The Nazi Party now had more than 800,000 members.

Traditional conservatives, including military men, not the least of whom was Hindenburg, turned against the republic. Franz von Papen (1879–1969), power broker of the traditional anti-parliamentarian right, became chancellor in June 1932. After elections for the Reichstag in November 1932, the Nazis became the largest party in the Reichstag (with 196 seats against 121 held by Social Democrats, 100 by Communists, and 90 by the Catholic Center Party). Although support for the Nazis had fallen by 2 million votes, the Nazis and Communists, both of whom rejected the Weimar Republic, had won more than half the votes cast.

Papen resigned as chancellor in December 1932. His successor, General Kurt von Schleicher (1882–1934), an enemy of Papen's who had arranged his fall, wanted to form a parliamentary majority by wooing some Nazis—but excluding Hitler—and even trade unionists, an improbable idea. When Schleicher's government resigned the next month, Papen, intriguing with Hitler, proposed a coalition government that would include the Nazis, with Hitler as chancellor. Hoping to transform Germany from a republic into a military authoritarian regime (perhaps through a monarchical restoration), Papen believed that Hitler could serve his purposes if the Nazis received only three of twelve cabinet posts. Once Hitler and the Nazis had helped assure the end of the Weimar Republic, they could be tossed aside. In Italy, Giolitti's Liberals had made the same fatal miscalculation in 1922 in their dealings with Mussolini.

Now joined by members of Hindenburg's family and staff, Papen convinced the president to appoint Hitler as chancellor, believing that he could control Hitler in his capacity as vice-chancellor. On January 30, 1933, Adolf Hitler formed the seventeenth—and last—Weimar government. "We've boxed Hitler in," was the way Papen memorably put it, "We have hired him."

Many Prussian nobles and generals still mistrusted Hitler. To the former, he seemed a vulgar commoner; to the latter, a mere foot soldier who made boastful claims of military expertise. But the generals had been taught, above all, to obey orders. Furthermore, Hitler's denunciations of Bolshevism appealed to their dislike of Russia, their enemy on the eastern front during the Great War.

Most wealthy businessmen still preferred more traditional nationalists like Hindenburg and Papen and worried about Hitler's unpredictability and his early denunciations of capitalists and promises to create a new elite. The Nazi Party found only one major donor among big businessmen; a group of industrialists even tried to convince Hindenburg to leave Hitler out of the cabinet. Although some big businessmen shared the Nazis' virulent anti-Semitism, they were uneasy with the foreign condemnation it brought, and concerned that it might one day undercut their markets abroad.

But big business nonetheless contributed to the fall of Weimar. Most Rhineland industrialists were no more in favor of parliamentary government than were Prussian Junkers. Hitler flattered business leaders and promised public order, which was good for business, even if achieved at gunpoint.

The Nazi State

Hitler's appointment as chancellor sparked a wave of systematic and brutal Nazi attacks on union members, Socialists, Communists, Jews, and some Catholics who opposed Nazism. Mussolini had consolidated his power over the Italian state in about three years. It took Hitler less than three months. During the night of February 27, 1933, a fire caused considerable damage to the Reichstag building in Berlin. The police arrested a deranged, homeless Dutch Communist, charging him with arson.

Citing an imaginary Communist plot, Hindenburg issued an emergency decree suspending virtually all individual rights. Penalties of imprisonment and even death could be imposed without due legal process as police arrested thousands of Communists. Hermann Göring (1893–1946), one of Hitler's long-time disciples and now minister of the interior in Prussia, authorized a new auxiliary police force made up of members of the S.A. and other paramilitary groups.

But the parliamentary elections of March 5, 1933, which Hitler promised would be the last held in Nazi Germany and which took place amid enormous Nazi intimidation, did not give Hitler the overwhelming majority he had anticipated—the Nazis emerged with 44 percent of the vote. Nonetheless, Hitler proceeded as if the vote had been unanimous. On March 23, the cowed Reichstag approved an Enabling Act, which extended the unlimited "emergency" powers of the Nazis. The liberal political parties of the Weimar Republic simply disbanded. In July 1933, Hitler banned all political parties except the Nazi Party. It tripled in size, with 2.5 million members by the end of 1933, adding so many people that the "old fighters" who had joined early in the 1920s began to grumble that the party was losing its so-called elite character.

The Nazis implemented a dictatorial state. In May 1933, they organized the state-controlled German Labor Front to replace the unions they had

Communists under arrest after the Reichstag fire of 1933.

decimated. Strikes were illegal. Hitler dissolved the state parliaments and took away the remaining autonomy of the individual German states, appointing Nazis to take over state governments. A new law empowered officials to dismiss subordinates whom they considered potentially disloyal to the Nazis, or who could not prove that they were of pure "Aryan" racial stock. In October, the first concentration camp began operation at Dachau near Munich for the incarceration of political prisoners.

Despite Nazi rhetoric about a racially pure community of Germans, Hitler was far from envisioning social equality, which he associated with socialism and communism. Still, for some Germans, the Nazi Party, and particularly the S.S. (*Schutzstaffel*, security units that guarded Hitler), provided a means of social mobility; military trappings conveyed the respectability many Germans associated with a uniform. Although the Nazis drew support from all social classes (although proportionately less support from workers), the Depression in particular drove desperate middle-class Germans into the Nazi fold.

Hitler needed the loyalty of Germany's army. But many German officers were becoming increasingly wary of the S.A., which was now almost 3 million strong and which seemed out of control. Its members openly competed with Nazi officials for appointments and influence. Röhm announced that henceforth members of his force could not be tried by courts and that they were not subject to police authority. Believing that Hitler would betray the party's radicalism, he foolishly bragged that he would free Hitler from his "stupid and dangerous" advisers.

The S.S. and the Gestapo (the Nazi secret police) crushed the S.A. on June 30, 1934. They killed at least eighty people, including Röhm. The "night of the long knives" also swept up some conservatives and military officers, as Hitler had feared trouble from the old right as well as from the S.A. Hitler convinced President Hindenburg that the gory purge had saved the German Third Reich (Third Empire) from a plot.

Hindenburg's death in August 1934 allowed Hitler to combine the titles of chancellor and *Führer* ("leader"), which replaced that of "president," a title that smacked of a republic. The army agreed to take an oath of personal allegiance to "the executor of the whole people's will." Ninety percent of those voting in a plebiscite approved Hitler's assumption of both functions.

The Nazi program of "coordination" was applied to most aspects of civil society, such as organized groups and activities outside the family. The Nazis had already gradually taken over voluntary associations, such as professional associations and sports clubs. Depoliticized, closely monitored voluntary associations and churches could remain centers of local public life without threatening Nazi domination. The Nazis worked to convert schools into mouthpieces for Hitler's state, providing new textbooks with instructions for teachers as to what should be taught, including "racial theory" and "Teutonic prehistory." Instead of students fearing their teachers, as had often been the case in German schools, non-Nazi teachers now had reason to fear their students; members of the Hitler Youth organization were quick to report to Nazi Party members teachers who did not seem enthusiastic about Nazism. New university chairs in "racial hygiene," military history, and German prehistory reflected Nazi interests. Pictures of Hitler went up in every classroom and radios broadcast his speeches.

The Nazis brought hundreds of thousands of active Germans into carefully controlled Nazi organizations, the goal of each being to "reach toward Hitler"—that is, to share the racist, nationalist goals of the Führer. By 1936 the Hitler Youth included almost half of all German boys between ten and fourteen years of age; a League of German Girls also flourished. The Nazis reduced social life to its most basic component, the family. (At

Hitler paying homage to Hindenburg shortly before the latter's death.

the same time, the Nazis encouraged children to denounce their parents for being disloyal to the fatherland, and the party sponsored "Aryan breeding" programs outside the family.) Vicarious participation in Nazi ceremonies and rituals also helped augment a sense of national identity.

Hitler implemented the Nazi "leadership principle," which he defined as a "doctrine of conflict." He applied a strategy of "divide and rule" to the higher echelons of government, such as the three chancelleries that replaced the cabinet. He tolerated and even encouraged open competition between his most trusted subordinates and between branches of government. Those who enjoyed Hitler's confidence ruthlessly and aggressively carved out personal fiefdoms. Unlike Stalin, who watched over even the most minor details with obsessive care, the Führer provided little supervision to government agencies. Occasionally something would catch Hitler's attention and brief, frenzied activity would follow. But he missed meetings, worked irregular hours, and was often disorganized. Hitler valued personal loyalty far more than efficiency.

The "doctrine of conflict" adversely affected the economic goals Hitler set for the state. The army and the air force quarreled over resources, the S.S. and the police over jurisdiction. The Four-Year Plan launched in 1936 under Göring's direction illustrated the functioning of the Nazi state. Hitler wanted to stimulate economic development, above all in industries necessary for rearmament: steel, iron, and synthetic fuel and rubber. Göring spent much time warring with other branches of government. Furthermore, industrialists resisted state intervention in their businesses. The Four-Year Plan failed to achieve its lofty goals.

Hitler had to confront the daunting challenge of unemployment. Although he knew or cared very little about economics, Hitler correctly determined that the rapid rearmament of Germany would help create jobs. Food shortages remained severe until 1936, but public works projects helped reduce unemployment and inflation. Big industrial concerns prospered, particularly those manufacturing war materials. The German gross national product rose by 81 percent, in part because of state direction of the economy. Hitler bragged that he had wrought an economic miracle. Millions of Germans believed him. An ordinary German woman wrote in her diary, "One feels absolutely insignificant in the face of the greatness, the truthfulness and the openness of such a man."

More consumer goods, such as radios, reached the consumer market, contributing to a sense of optimism about material conditions of life. The Labor Front organized cut-rate Nazi vacations. Some families of modest means who had never had the opportunity to travel took cruises in the Baltic Sea or even in the Mediterranean Sea. Hitler named this program "Strength Through Joy," taking the idea from Mussolini's after-work program of recreational trips in Italy. However, production of Hitler's planned low-cost "Volkswagen," or "people's car," was postponed because factories were needed for military production.

Yet sectors of the German economy remained weak. German industry depended on imports of iron ore, copper, oil, rubber, and bauxite. Many Germans found that their share in the "national community" was small. And although Hitler liked to identify the German people with what he considered rural virtues—"blood and soil"—the number of small farms continued to decline. There was no marked return to the soil as Germany continued to urbanize.

Like Mussolini, the Führer preached that a woman's place was in the kitchen or in the delivery room. A Nazi book for children announced, "The German resurrection is a male event." The state offered attractive financial benefits to families with children, and the German birthrate continued to rise, bolstered by an improving economy. Just months after becoming chancellor, Hitler forced women to give up industrial jobs and excluded them from public service and teaching. Fewer women went on to university. Certain occupations were classified as "women's work," primarily those involving traditional textile or handicraft production or farm work. But, despite the slogan "Women at home," the reality in Nazi Germany, as in Mussolini's Italy, was increasingly otherwise. The campaign to remove women from paid employment ended in the late 1930s, as women were needed to replace men conscripted into the army. The number of women working in German industry rose by a third between 1933 and 1939.

Hitler and the Nazis did not rule by sheer terror alone. Hitler also sought and won overwhelming popular approval. After defeat in the Great War, humiliation by the Treaty of Versailles, and years of Weimar instability in which the Nazis and other right-wing groups played a major part, Germans applauded as he dismantled the treaty piece by piece. But most ordinary Germans also approved of police action undertaken by the well-organized apparatus of the Nazi state. Regular police units drawn from every walk of German life assisted. The Nazi state won approval with a harsh campaign against crime, which had increased during the Depression. Most ordinary Germans approved of and indeed many collaborated in the arrest and imprisonment of common criminals. The Gestapo and the "Kripo," or criminal police, who became ever more aggressive, also arrested people considered "work shy," or others like gays who did not seem to them to fit in. Doctors used sterilization as a form of punishment and social control, part of Nazi "racial hygiene." Germans looked the other way or were indifferent to the rounding up of political dissidents and Jews. A contemporary described a Gestapo office:

> Grimy corridors, offices furnished with Spartan simplicity, threats, kicks, troops chasing chained men up and down the reaches of the building, shouting, rows of girls and women standing with their noses and toes against the walls, overflowing ashtrays, portraits of Hitler and his aides, the smell of coffee, smartly dressed girls working at high speed

behind typewriters—girls seemingly indifferent to the squalor and agony about them . . . and Gestapo agents asleep on tables.

Moreover, thousands of Germans denounced neighbors to the Gestapo for being Jewish, Socialist, or Communist, and did so well aware of the consequences of their acts. Certainly by 1939, most Germans were fully aware of the existence of concentration camps. Indeed the Nazi government eagerly publicized the "trials" and sentences that sent people to them.

Some intellectuals and artists jumped on the Nazi bandwagon. Very few members—though the novelist Thomas Mann, who had moved from being an angry conservative to a supporter of the republic by 1922, was one—resigned from the prestigious Prussian Academy of Arts when called upon to pledge allegiance to Hitler. The philosopher Martin Heidegger (1889–1976) saluted the Führer as "guided by the inexorability of that spiritual mission that the destiny of the German people forcibly impresses upon its history." Hitler hauled out Heidegger on formal occasions to claim that Germany's finest scholars had become Nazis. In fact, some of the finest German minds were already leaving Germany.

The Nazis burned books that espoused ideas of which they disapproved. In May 1933 storm troopers coordinated the burning of books by Jews, Communists, Socialists, and other disapproved authors. In 1937, posters in the municipal library of Essen boasted that in the four years that had elapsed since the book burnings, there had been a "healthy" decline in books borrowed and in the use of the reading room.

Hitler railed against what he called "decadent" art and its new experimental forms, ordering many works removed from museums. During the Weimar period, Berlin, a city with 40 theaters and 120 newspapers, had become a center of daring and successful experimentation by artists, writers, and composers, as well as scholars. In 1919, the architect Walter Gropius (1883–1969) had begun a school that combined art and applied arts in the town of Weimar. The Bauhaus—"House of Building"—set the architectural and decorative style of Weimar, stressing simplicity and beauty, expressing function through form, combining art and craft. By using the most modern materials available in the quest for "total architecture," Gropius hoped to reconcile art and industry. The Bauhaus's modernism and the presence of foreign architects, artists, and designers made it suspect to Nazis. Hitler, the former aspiring artist, detested modernism. He closed the Bauhaus as a symbol of "cultural Bolshevism."

In 1937, the Nazis in Munich staged an "Exhibition of Degenerate Art," including expressionist and dadaist paintings, among other modernist works. A Great German Art Show opened at the same time, putting on view officially approved painting. While Stalin's preferred style of "socialist realism" emphasized work, Nazi art celebrated being German. Nazi artists offered sentimental portraits of German families tilling the land, blond

Adolf Hitler visiting the "Exhibition of Disgrace" in 1935, which anticipated the so-called "Exhibition of Degenerate Art" of 1937.

youths hiking in the Pomeranian forests, and square-jaw soldiers portrayed as medieval Teutonic knights.

In their attacks upon modernist composers, the Nazis reserved particular vehemence for the works of Jewish composers, while the late-nineteenth-century compositions of the anti-Semitic Richard Wagner delighted Hitler. The theater, too, suffered from censorship, as well as from the departure of a number of Germany's leading playwrights. Hitler himself preferred light plays, such as a rustic comedy that earned the Critic's Prize in Berlin in 1934, in which the leading character was a pig. Anti-modernism could be seen in Nazi attacks on the supposed hedonism of the "roaring twenties," which Nazis associated with licentiousness, homosexuality, neon lights, jazz, and modern dances. Nazis did not do the Charleston.

Joseph Goebbels (1897–1945), Hitler's minister of propaganda, orchestrated the cult of Hitler. The Führer commissioned the popular filmmaker Leni Riefenstahl (1902–2003) to produce *Triumph of the Will*. This imposing propaganda film, which depicts the carefully orchestrated Nuremberg rally of 1934 where 250,000 regimented, uniformed Germans with Nazi banners and flags saluted Hitler, contributed to the cult of the Führer. The Nazis encouraged the production of a number of virulently anti-Semitic films, above all *The Jew Suess* (1940), the story of an eighteenth-century

Jewish financier who betrays a German state and is executed, to the cheers of Nazi audiences.

Hitler's New Reich and the Jews

Hitler made anti-Semitism a cornerstone of Nazi ideology and state policy. In 1935, the Nuremberg Laws, which made the swastika the official symbol of Nazi Germany, deprived Jews (defined by having had at least one Jewish grandparent) of citizenship. Jews were forced to wear a yellow Star of David prominently on their clothing when they left their homes. In the quest for racial "purity," the laws also forbade marriage or sex between non-Jewish Germans and Jews. Signs in restaurants, movie houses, and parks warned that Jews were not allowed, such as one proclaiming "Jews enter this locality at their own peril!" Yet some Jewish businesses, including banks, at first continued to operate, if only because Hitler feared the economic consequences if they were closed. Some of these were "Aryanized" by removing Jewish owners and managers. By July 1938, only 9,000 of the 50,000 businesses owned by Jews were still open. Shortly thereafter, the German state forced Jewish families to list the value of what they owned and to turn over their assets to Gentile trustees, who could dispose of these estates as they wished. Decrees established a list of professions and occupations from which Jews were to be excluded.

When Hitler came to power, some Jews emigrated immediately, or made plans to do so. With Jews unable to teach in universities after early 1933 or to attend university as of 1937, many distinguished Jewish scholars and artists left for Britain or the United States, including the brilliant physicist Albert Einstein (1879–1955). More than 1,600 scholars and scientists had lost, resigned, or left their positions. Other intellectual exiles from Hitler's Germany were not Jewish, among them the poet Stefan George, the writer Thomas Mann, and the painter Max Beckmann. But one had to have some

Nazis post placards in a Jewish shop window. The notice reads "It is forbidden to buy from this Jewish shop."

place to go. The borders of Hungary and Yugoslavia were closed to refugees. One by one, countries that had accepted Jewish refugees refused to do so. In 1938, the French government greatly tightened restrictions on the admission of refugees. Britain made it harder for Jews to get in, or to go to Palestine, which Britain controlled. Switzerland, which had been known as a haven for political exiles, also in 1938 closed the door on Jews fleeing Germany or Austria. Moreover, the Swiss government suggested that German passport officials stamp "non-Aryan" on passports of Jews so that they could be easily identified and turned back at the frontier. The Swiss police hunted down refugees living in Switzerland whom they deemed illegal residents, putting them across the German border, or other frontiers.

On the evening of November 9, 1938, following the assassination of a German embassy official in Paris by a Polish Jew, S.S. and other Nazi activists launched planned attacks on specific Jewish businesses and homes throughout Germany. They destroyed stores, killed several hundred Jews, and beat up thousands of others. Thirty thousand Jews were imprisoned in camps. The terrifying night became known as *Kristallnacht,* because the sound of shattering glass windows resounded in German cities that night. Few Germans protested.

Hitler's Foreign Policy

Hitler had never concealed his goal of shattering the Treaty of Versailles. German foreign policy came to dominate European international affairs. Hitler planned to rearm Germany, and he demanded the return of the Saar Basin, whose rich mines the French held north of their border, and of German parts of Upper Silesia on the border of Poland, the remilitarization of the Rhineland, and the absorption of the Polish (or Danzig) Corridor, which divided Prussia from East Prussia. But Hitler's long-term goals, which were far greater, were inseparable from his megalomaniacal determination to expand Germany by armed conquest.

Hitler's foreign policy was predicated upon the German conquest of "living space" (*Lebensraum*) and his theory that the Aryan race was superior to any other and therefore had the right, indeed the obligation, to assert its will on the "inferior" Slav peoples. A week after becoming chancellor in January 1933, Hitler told German generals of his plans to rearm Germany, to conquer land for agricultural production, and to establish German settlements in Central and Eastern Europe and the Balkans. The Slavic peoples of the Soviet Union, Poland, and Czechoslovakia would serve the German "master race" as slaves.

Once Hitler came to power, he was less open about his previously stated goals because Germany was then vulnerable to invasion, but these goals did not change. Hitler had to move with particular caution to avoid confrontation with Britain and, particularly, France. For the moment, Poland and Czechoslovakia each had a stronger army than Germany. Hitler had to carry out his foreign policy with patience. He left in place the foreign minister and much of the old diplomatic corps, although he viewed them as weak and suspected their loyalty. Four months after coming to power, he declared that he had no intention of rearming Germany and that he wanted only peace. That October, in a typical switch, Hitler announced that Germany would walk out of the Geneva Disarmament Conference, which had begun the previous year, and that it would leave the League of Nations, to which it had been admitted in 1926. He insisted that Germany wanted peace and respect and would take only legal steps to "break the chains of Versailles."

In the meantime, Germany worked to extend its influence in Eastern Europe. During the Depression, as France pulled back credits, German officials signed a series of economic agreements with Eastern European states, bringing them into Germany's economic orbit and increasing their economic dependency. Hitler's policy of deficit spending—particularly to rebuild Germany's armed forces despite the Treaty of Versailles—was perceived in Eastern Europe as successful.

Hitler signed a nonaggression agreement with Poland in January 1934 (the Soviet Union had done the same two years earlier), while assuring his generals that he had no intention of respecting the agreement. The German-Polish pact was a blow to France's plans to maintain Germany's diplomatic isolation by a collective treaty system directed against Hitler. French military alliances with the Eastern European states of Poland, Czechoslovakia, Romania, and Yugoslavia would have left Germany surrounded by potential enemies, albeit relatively small ones. The Polish dictator Józef Piłsudski did not trust Hitler, but Piłsudski believed that he might be able to balance Poland's strategic position between Germany and the Soviet Union and could take advantage of a possible German attack on either Austria or Czechoslovakia to annex disputed territories. The Soviet Union, which had joined the League of Nations in 1934, signed a defense treaty with France a year later and another with Czechoslovakia soon after, which bound the Soviets to defend Czechoslovakia in case of a German attack, but only if France fulfilled its treaty obligations.

The Führer and the Duce

While France scurried to find allies, Germany for the moment had none. Hitler had long admired Benito Mussolini. Both had taken advantage of economic and social crisis to put themselves in a position of unchallenged authority. Both intended to overturn the Treaty of Versailles. Hitler's territorial ambitions in Eastern Europe did not conflict with Mussolini's goal of empire-building in the Balkans and North Africa. But because of possible conflicting interests, notably Hitler's long-range intention to annex Austria and Mussolini's claim of the Austrian Tyrol for Italy, some possible tension existed. Yet fascist Italy and Nazi Germany seemed natural allies, sharing an ideology as well as France as an enemy. The Duce had proclaimed in 1933, the year Hitler came to power, "Hitler's victory is also our victory."

Mussolini had reduced Albania, the small, impoverished nation across the Adriatic, to a virtual Italian protectorate, although it had almost no Italian population. In the South Tyrol, absorbed by Italy under the terms of the post-war settlement, Mussolini ordered a policy of Italianization, forbidding the use of the German and Slovene languages in schools. Somalia, the country at the horn of Africa that Italy had conquered before the war, turned into a military base from which new conquests could be launched. Italian troops burned villages and slaughtered their inhabitants. In Libya, Italian forces routinely ordered the use of mustard gas and public hangings to solidify their control.

Mussolini worked to increase international tensions in the hope of taking advantage of instability. The Duce had signed the Kellogg-Briand Pact in 1928, in which the major powers renounced war as an instrument of national policy, not because he believed in its principles, but because he wanted Britain and France to treat Italy as a great power. Meanwhile, Italy funneled secret arms to Germany and trained German pilots in violation of post-war treaties. In the Balkans, Italian agents provided financial support to right-wing terrorist groups, including ethnic Hungarians and Croats plotting against the Yugoslav government.

Hitler's plan to absorb Austria required Italian support, or at least neutrality, until Germany had been fully rearmed. But for the moment, Germany was still in no position to antagonize France. However, the German dictator took a calculated risk in 1934. Dictator Dollfuss shared much with the Nazis, but intended to maintain Austrian independence and had banned the Austrian Nazi Party, which was funded by German Nazis. He had also signed alliances with Italy and Hungary. Austrian Nazis, backed by Hitler, assassinated Dollfuss during their badly organized coup attempt. The steely Kurt von Schuschnigg (1897–1977) replaced Dollfuss as leader of an authoritarian government. Schuschnigg, like his predecessor, believed he could maintain right-wing rule in Austria without German help. The dual allegiances to Austrian independence and to an institutional role for the Catholic Church separated Austria's authoritarian regime from its German counterpart.

Hitler correctly assessed that it was unlikely that Britain, France, and Italy—Mussolini was absorbed by planning an invasion of Ethiopia in East Africa—would mount an effective, concerted response to blatant German moves to overthrow the Austrian government. Each government limited itself to a protest against German meddling in Austrian internal politics, asserting its interest in Austria's independence. The British government was convinced that conciliatory moves toward Germany might keep Hitler in line, particularly if, as a good many British conservatives believed, Hitler wanted no more than to be recognized as a power and to be able to defend Germany's borders. The French government did no more than express irritation, as it was confronting a fascist threat at home.

In 1935, Hitler's foreign policy entered a new and more aggressive phase. He defied the Versailles Treaty in March by announcing that Germany's army would be increased to half a million men, that military service would become compulsory, and that the German air force had already been rebuilt, despite the prohibition of the peace agreement. British, French, and Italian representatives met in Stresa, Italy, in April 1935 to discuss Germany's violation of the Treaty of Versailles—as did the League of Nations itself—and to reaffirm the Treaty of Locarno of 1925, in which the German government had joined Britain, France, and Italy in pledging to resolve future international disputes peacefully. Hitler then made the usual reassuring noises, stating that he would sign bilateral agreements with any of the powers (as opposed to the collective security agreements he had already helped shred), uphold the Treaty of Locarno, and recognize the territorial integrity of Austria.

Great Britain expressed wariness by signing a naval agreement with Germany in June 1935 that established a ratio of 100 to 35 between the two navies. This agreement, however, enraged the French government, which had not even been informed by Britain of the hasty negotiations that led to the agreement. France then signed a secret treaty with Italy, the goal of which was to assure Austrian independence.

In October 1935, Mussolini's armies invaded Ethiopia, where Italian forces had suffered humiliating defeat in 1896. Determined to expand Italy's fledgling empire, a quarter of a million Italian women, including the

Ethiopian soldiers use donkeys to carry machine guns to confront the Italian invasion, 1935.

queen, pawned their wedding rings (women who turned in their gold rings received in exchange tin ones blessed by the pope) to help raise money for the war of conquest. The Duce correctly assessed that Britain and France would do little more than denounce the invasion because they still desired Mussolini's support against Hitler. Realizing this, Hitler had encouraged Italy to attack Ethiopia.

Ethiopian Emperor Haile Selassie (1892–1975) appealed to the League of Nations for help for his country, which had been a member nation since 1923. The League imposed economic sanctions against Italy, but left them weak by excluding oil from the list of products affected, and it did not try to prevent passage of Italian ships through the Suez Canal on the way to Ethiopia. The British government made it clear that it considered the appeasement of Italy the only way to end the crisis and placed an embargo against the sale of arms to Ethiopia. U.S. President Franklin Roosevelt even offered Italy American loans in order to develop Ethiopia.

Italian troops took the Ethiopian capital of Addis Ababa in May 1936. Over 500,000 Ethiopians were killed in the one-sided fighting. Italy lost only 5,000 soldiers, a number Mussolini decried as so small that it seemed to cheapen his victory. On July 15, 1936, the League of Nations formally lifted all sanctions against Italy. The Stresa agreement, which had been made with the goal of containing Hitler, collapsed. The Duce now began referring to himself as the "invincible Duce."

Remilitarization and Rearmament

On March 7, 1936, German troops moved into the Rhineland, which had been declared by the Treaty of Versailles to be a demilitarized zone. Hitler had secretly promised his anxious generals that he would order German forces to pull back if the French army intervened. Whether or not an armed British and French response might have stopped Hitler at this point has long been debated.

German ambassadors in the European capitals then claimed that the move had been necessitated by the destruction of the Locarno agreements by France's pact with the Soviet Union. The German ambassador to Britain, Joachim von Ribbentrop (1893–1946, who had simply added the aristocratic "von" to his name), failed to browbeat the British into an alliance with Germany. France pushed the British government to react sharply against Hitler's brazen move, but would not act alone. In Germany, Hitler's prestige soared. He had delivered as promised, facing down the powers that had imposed the Treaty of Versailles and destroying the Locarno Treaty.

Hitler now speeded up the pace of German rearmament, particularly of the air force. By 1938, armament production absorbed 52 percent of state expenses and 17 percent of Germany's gross national product. Prodded by the Labour Party, British military expenses more than doubled between 1934 and 1937; however, the total amount was far less than what Germany spent

TABLE 25.2. DEFENSE EXPENDITURES OF THE GREAT POWERS, 1930–1938 (IN MILLIONS OF 1989 DOLLARS)

Year	Japan	Italy	Germany	U.S.S.R.	U.K.	France	U.S.
1930	218	266	162	772	512	498	699
1933	183	351	452	707	333	524	570
1934	292	455	709	3,479	540	707	803
1935	300	966	1,607	5,517	646	867	806
1936	313	1,149	2,332	2,933	892	995	932
1937	940	1,235	3,298	3,446	1,245	890	1,032
1938	1,740	746	7,415	5,429	1,863	919	1,131

Source: Paul Kennedy, *The Rise and Fall of the Great Powers* (New York: Vintage, 1989), p. 296.

at the same time (see Table 25.2). Germany also had the advantage of rearming with the most up-to-date war materials, including glistening fighter planes of steel and bombers with four engines that increased their range.

THE SOVIET UNION UNDER STALIN

In the meantime, under Joseph Stalin (1879–1953), the Soviet Union was transformed into a totalitarian Communist state. Stalin assured his dictatorship by purging dissident groups within the Soviet Leadership. The Left Opposition to Stalin was led by Leon Trotsky (1879–1940) and Gregory Zinoviev (1883–1936), the humorless but scrupulous curly-haired party secretary of Leningrad (Petrograd's name after Lenin's death) and a former ally of Stalin. The Left Opposition believed that the Soviet Union ought to support independent—that is, non-Communist—working-class organizations, and criticized Stalin for abandoning Communist internationalism. Stalin, in contrast, argued that the Bolsheviks first had to build "socialism in one country"—that is, the Soviet Union. Between 1925 and 1927, Stalin isolated leaders of the left by assigning their allies to inconsequential posts in distant places.

Against the backdrop of a severe shortage of grain that lasted two years, in 1927 the Left Opposition demanded an immediate accelerated industrialization in the state sector and worker mobilization against "bourgeois" bureaucrats. It feared the effects of Lenin's New Economic Policy (NEP), which it viewed as having been an unnecessary ideological compromise that risked bringing back capitalism (see Chapter 23). Wealthier peasant proprietors, the Left Opposition argued, could be forced to provide the surplus that would sustain gradual industrialization. If the state, which controlled heavy industries, kept the prices of manufactured goods high, state revenue would increase, permitting further industrial development. In

1927, the Central Committee, with Stalin completely in charge, voted to expel Trotsky and Zinoviev from the Communist Party and refused to publish Lenin's "Political Testament," which had suggested that Stalin be replaced as general secretary.

Five-Year Plans

Stalin believed that socialism could not be fully implemented until the Soviet Union had a stronger industrial base. Then an expanded proletariat would provide a larger base for Soviet Communism. After purging the Left Opposition, he then openly favored their plan of accelerated industrialization. This would be paid for by extracting more resources from the peasantry. In 1928 and 1929, Stalin resumed the forced requisitioning of "surpluses" and expropriated the land of wealthier peasants, the "kulaks." When this led to growing peasant opposition, he took the next step in 1930: the forced collectivization of agriculture—the elimination of private ownership of land and animals. The Five-Year Plan marked a complete abandonment of Lenin's New Economic Policy.

Nikolai Bukharin (1888–1938) objected to a policy of renewed requisitioning and immediate collectivization on the grounds that it would greatly undermine peasant support for the regime. The result would ultimately be to slow down rather than speed up industrialization. In 1928, he became the leader of the Right Opposition, which also disagreed with Stalin's complete abandonment of the principle of collective leadership, thus fortifying Stalin's personal authority. Stalin accused Bukharin of trying to surrender to "capitalist elements." By the end of 1930, Stalin had purged the Right Opposition from the party. With both the Left Opposition and the Right Opposition out of the way, the long dictatorship of Joseph Stalin really began. Bukharin was executed in 1938.

In formulating his Five-Year Plan, Stalin sought to take advantage of social tensions in Soviet society. He knew that workers believed that material progress was not coming fast enough and that they blamed peasants and smug bureaucrats. Stalin wanted to inspire workers to storm the "fortress" of remaining inequalities in Soviet society. He used the rhetoric of class struggle as a means of mobilizing effort, trying to turn workers against kulaks and "bourgeois" managers and technical specialists.

The first Five-Year Plan (1928–1933) led to a bloodbath in the countryside. Hundreds of thousands of peasants who refused to turn over their harvests, animals, or farms were killed. An officer in the secret police told a foreign journalist: "I am an old Bolshevik. I worked in the underground against the tsar and then I fought in the Civil War. Did I do all that in order that I should now surround villages with machine guns and order my men to fire indiscriminately into crowds of peasants?" Peasants, often led by women, resisted with determination and resourcefulness the establishment of collective farms, the redistribution of land, or the introduction of new

The deportation of prosperous peasants (kulaks) from a Russian village during land collectivization, 1930.

crop systems. In 1929, 30,000 fires were reported set in Russia. Peasants slaughtered livestock rather than allowing them to be taken by the collective farm. The number of horses fell from 36 million in 1929 to 15 million four years later, cattle from 67 million to 34 million.

Small plots were forcibly consolidated into collective farms. Peasants had to work a certain number of days each year for the collective farm; the state supplied machinery, seed, and clothing. The free market disappeared and the state set production quotas and prices. One of the primary goals of the collectivization of agriculture was to force peasants into industrial labor. During the first Five-Year Plan, the Soviet Union's industrial and urban populations doubled, as 9 million peasants were conscripted to work in factories.

In March 1930, Stalin signed an article in *Pravda* entitled "Dizzy with Success." He announced that his Five-Year Plan was succeeding beyond his wildest expectations and that the time had come for a pause. In fact, forced collectivization had catastrophically reduced Soviet agricultural production. Indeed, Stalin ordered officials to return expropriated animals to their owners. But he viewed this as a lull, not a change in theory.

When the Five-Year Plan ended in 1932 after four years and three months (in part because of the effects of peasant resistance), 62 percent of peasants now worked for the state on collective farms. Peasants were allowed to retain small private plots; the vegetables and fruits that they grew provided almost half of the produce reaching markets.

Overall, however, living conditions deteriorated in the Soviet Union during the Five-Year Plan. Shortages of fuel and machine parts became severe. Hundreds of thousands of peasants had been killed, and perhaps 2 million exiled to Siberia or other distant places under the sentence of hard labor. Around 7 million people died of hunger between 1930 and 1933, and 4 to 5 million people starved during 1932 and 1933, most in Ukraine. In Kazakhstan in Central Asia, about 2 million people (one-tenth of the population) died or were killed between 1926 and 1933.

The campaign for heavy industrialization was successful, but only if the human cost is conveniently forgotten. Despite inaccurate and sometimes misleading Soviet data, the state did meet some ambitious production targets in heavy industry (iron and steel), fuel production (oil and electricity), new industries (especially chemicals), and in the manufacture of tractors. While the Depression devastated Western economies, between 1929 and 1934 the Soviet economy may have had an annual growth rate of a remarkable 27 percent. These successes occurred despite inefficiency due to inadequate planning, chaotic reporting of figures (compounded by the mounting sense of urgency to report successes), and the replacement of many of the most able technicians (because of their social class) by dedicated but semiliterate workers or peasants who sometimes mistook mud for oil.

Giant show projects such as the Dnieper Dam and the new industrial city of Magnitogorsk in the Ural Mountains attracted international attention. Foreign visitors found many workers who seemed enthusiastic. Party officials selected "heroes of labor," praised for surpassing their production targets by record amounts. A certain Andrei Stakhanov, a Don Basin miner, was credited in August 1935 with cutting 102 tons of coal during a single shift. A "Stakhanovite" became the idealized Soviet worker, working as fast as he or she could, and ready to step forward to denounce "Trotskyite wreckers and saboteurs."

The second Five-Year Plan (1933–1937) relied less on the shrill rhetoric of class warfare, despite ongoing collectivization. By 1936, 93 percent of peasants labored on collective farms. Stalin relaxed the ideologically charged campaign against "experts" of bourgeois origins, and technocrats again appeared in factories. But the quality of Soviet life did not significantly improve. Centralized planning had its bizarre aspects: the sudden arrival of women's red stockings or of ketchup in stores, or of bathtubs, even if someone had forgotten to order the production of plugs for them. The promised "radiant" future always seemed to be far away.

In the meantime, Stalin reinforced his hold on power. Even with most consumer goods still wanting, 4.5 million radios in the Soviet Union broadcast Stalin's speeches in the 1930s. The grandson of a Soviet minister recalled, "Stalin was like a God for us. Somebody told me that Stalin could be the best surgeon. He could perform a brain operation better than anyone else, and I believed it." A poem from the 1930s entitled "There Is a Man in Moscow" reflects this bizarre, troubling adulation:

Who is that man who appears to the toilers,
Spreading happiness and joy all around?
It is Stalin, I shout, so the whole world will hear,
It is Stalin, our Leader and Friend.

Soviet Culture

Many artists and writers were originally enthusiastic about the Russian Revolution, and a spirit of utopianism survived into the early 1920s. The Communists wanted to build a unique culture based upon mass mobilization and commitment that would both reflect and accentuate the collectivization of life in the Soviet Union, helping forge consensus. The culture of utopianism would be defiantly proletarian and egalitarian.

In view of Stalin's determination that the Soviet Union rapidly industrialize, the machine was a common motif in Soviet imagery in the inter-war period. Soviet artists and writers believed that mechanization in the service of capitalists had further enslaved the masses but that technology could be potentially liberating. The state created art schools and provided assistance to struggling artists, hoping to enroll them in the service of the Revolution. In its first years, the Soviet state patronized futurists (see Chapter 20) as revolutionary artists who had embraced technological change and who would provide a new aesthetic for socialism in the construction of an ideal society. Soviet futurists issued a manifesto in which they promised to "re-examine the theory and practice of Leftist art, to free it from individualist distortions, and develop its Communist aspects." Artists collaborated with designers in producing models for standardized clothing and household items.

As the Soviet state subsumed most aspects of public life, the initial mini-explosion of cultural forms that had occurred during the first years of the Soviet state gave way to repressive orthodoxy. Rejecting traditional and avant-garde art as bourgeois escapism, Stalin believed that art and literature should assume a social function, depicting what he called "socialist realism." Stalin preferred monumental murals that presented smiling workers toiling for the state. Artists who did not conform stood accused of pandering to "bourgeois values," an increasingly dangerous denunciation. The Union of Communist Youth (*Komsomol*) sent out members to preach cultural uniformity, disrupting plays considered "bourgeois."

Stalin charmed and deceived many foreign statesmen and visitors, impressing them with the fact that millions of working-class children were now entering school for the first time. Some workers attended night classes, or even university. Women obtained training and positions in fields from which they previously had been excluded, such as medicine. Soviet guides whisked foreign visitors around on Moscow's new subway to see the Soviet capital's improved housing, water supply, and sewage facilities. "Potemkin village" was a series of gleaming facades that impressed visitors who did not realize that virtually nothing stood behind them. Although church and state had been officially separated in 1918, religious life went on as before, at least in rural areas, both in Orthodox regions and in the Islamic republics. Moreover, despite promoting atheism Stalin nonetheless discouraged unmarried couples from living together, banned abortion, and forbade homosexuality. Gradually in the 1930s, Stalin's early enthusiasm for equal opportunity for women waned; the state-approved image of the female as mother of committed Soviet children prevailed.

"Darkness at Noon": Stalin's Purges

By 1934, Stalin was no longer content merely to expel from the party those who did not share his views. He promulgated a state decree that expedited the punishment of those deemed to be "terrorists." As arrests mounted in number, executions replaced sentences of hard labor. The charges became more and more outrageous—accusations of secretly plotting to overthrow the state, of "wrecking" Soviet industries, of trying to restore capitalism, or of simply being "bourgeois" or the wife of an "enemy of the people." Lead-

The first Stalinist "show trial," 1930: an accused bureaucrat "confesses" to industrial sabotage.

ers of the Polish Communist Party were liquidated in Moscow in 1938 after having been invited there by Stalin.

The first of the great show trials—staged before audiences and cameras—took place in 1936, the last in March 1938, when Bukharin and the remainder of the Right Opposition faced judges who sometimes appeared to be more nervous than they. Those on trial were forced to sign confessions in court, where sympathetic foreign observers sometimes nodded in agreement to absurd accusations. Children—who could be executed at age twelve—were encouraged to denounce their parents for crimes against the state. At least 680,000 people were sentenced to death in 1937–1938 and probably about 1 million people were executed in the camps (in addition to those who died of harsh conditions).

The poet Osip Mandelstam (1889–1938) mocked Stalin with a poem that he read to friends in 1933. He noted the rumor about Stalin's origins in Ossetia, in the mountains of Georgia, and, as dictator, related the enormous weight of his words:

> We live, deaf to the land beneath us,
> Ten steps away no one hears our speeches,
> But where there's so much as half a conversation
> The Kremlin's mountaineer will get his mention
> His cockroach whiskers leer
> And his boot tops gleam.
> Around him a rabble of thin-necked leaders—
> Fawning half-men for him to play with.
> They whinny, purr or whine
> As he prates and points a finger,
> One by one forging his laws, to be flung,
> Like horseshoes at the head, the eye or the groin.
> And every killing is a treat
> For the broad-chested Ossete.

Mandelstam was arrested in 1934, sent to a camp for three years, and, after returning to Moscow, arrested again and sentenced to five years hard labor in another camp. There, in 1938, he died or was executed.

Estimates of the number of prisoners in labor camps, colonies, and prisons have ranged from about 1.5 million to 7 million. These included an elderly woman sentenced to camp terms for having said "if people prayed they would work better." Increasingly paranoid, Stalin's long arm reached far beyond the boundaries of the Soviet Union to force Communist parties in Spain, France, and other nations to purge those who disagreed with his policies. Stalin's agents caught up with Trotsky, who had gone into exile in 1929 and lived outside Mexico City, and stabbed him to death with an ice pick as he sat in a garden in August 1940.

The purge of the "national deviationists," accused of nationalist sentiments, for example in the Muslim lands of Central Asia, was an economic blow to the Soviet Union. It eliminated many engineers and other people with badly needed technical expertise. Furthermore, at a time when the rise of Hitler to power in Germany was increasing international tensions, the purge weakened the Soviet armed forces. Behind Stalin's move against military commanders was his fear that they might one day oppose his conduct of foreign policy. Among the 30,000 to 40,000 officers who perished, all 8 Soviet admirals were executed, as were 75 out of 80 members of the Supreme Military Council.

A journalist recalled that one of the most striking things about the Russian Revolution of 1917 "was the speed with which the masses, after the overthrow of tsarism, created new forms of organization," including soviets of workers and soldiers, factory committees, military organizations at the front, peasant soviets that supplemented township committees, and rural land committees. But once the Bolsheviks seized power on behalf of the working class and poor peasants, they never relinquished it. They destroyed these popular organizations that had embodied the aspirations of millions of people. The Russian Revolution, which had begun as a quest for economic and social justice by intellectuals, workers, middle-class and lower-middle-class radicals, peasants, and non-Russian nationalists, turned into the dictatorship of the Communist Party. Under the rule of Joseph Stalin, the Soviet Union took on some of the murderous characteristics of the fascist regimes its leaders so bitterly denounced. This was the tragedy of the Russian Revolution.

THE SPANISH CIVIL WAR

Spain became the battlefield of European ideologies during the bloody civil war that began in 1936. The world's attention turned to Spain for the first time since the time of Napoleon. Indeed, there was relatively little to distinguish the Spain of 1920 from that of more than a century earlier. The days of empire and glory had long since passed. With the exception of relatively industrialized Catalonia and the Basque provinces in the northwestern corner of the country, Spain remained an overwhelmingly agricultural society. Coalitions between the nobility, the Catholic Church, and the army determined political power in Madrid.

Social and Political Instability

The ineffectual King Alfonso XIII (ruled 1886–1931) confronted social and political problems that defied solution. Catalonian and Basque regional separatism challenged the Spanish government in Madrid. Chronic political and social instability helped push the army into the role of chief arbiter of political life. Labor strife, assassinations, street battles, and police violence became the order of the day in the early 1920s. Spain had declared a protectorate over northern Morocco in 1912 and used poison gas against

Moroccan insurgents who wanted independence. In 1921 Moroccans inflicted a shocking defeat on Spanish forces, costing the lives of 10,000 Spanish soldiers. This increased pressure from socialists and republicans on the monarchy.

In 1923, General Miguel Primo de Rivera (1870–1930) seized power with the support of the army and even the king. Four years later, espousing "nation, church and king," Primo de Rivera set out to "modernize" Spain, ordering the construction of dams, sewers, roads, and prisons. He became a familiar sight in the cafés and bars of Madrid, and such evenings occasionally were followed by gushing, incoherent bulletins to the Spanish people drafted on his return home. Primo de Rivera antagonized the left by promulgating a constitution in 1927 that left ministers no longer responsible to the Cortes and upset army officers (so numerous that they made up one-sixth of the army) by intervening in promotions. The weak Spanish economy eroded middle-class support for his regime. Primo de Rivera resigned in 1930.

The following year, Alfonso XIII left the country after elections returned an anti-monarchist majority to the Cortes. The army refused to save the monarchy, because most officers now hoped to impose authoritarian rule. The nobles, upon whose support the kings of Spain had for centuries depended, sat back and watched the monarchy fall.

A coalition of republicans and moderate Socialists established the Second Spanish Republic in 1931. The government of Manuel Azaña (1880–1940) enacted anticlerical measures, including the formal separation of church and state, imposed new taxes, passed labor reforms, and enacted land reform, including the outright expropriation of some of the largest estates. Strikes, land seizures by peasants, and attacks on churches and convents drove wealthy landowners and churchmen farther toward the anti-parliamentary right. The Spanish Republic could not count on the support of the unions, which wanted even more far-reaching social reforms, or of anarchists, who wanted the abolition of the state itself. Azaña fell from power in September 1933.

Thus began the republic's two "black years," marked by increasing social and political violence. The inclusion of the right in a more conservative republican government angered the left. During the "October Revolution" of 1934, leftists in Madrid, Catalan autonomists, and miners in the northern province of Asturias rose up, quickly setting up local "soviets" throughout their region. They held out for two weeks before being brutally crushed by Moroccan troops commanded by General Francisco Franco (1892–1975).

In 1935, Radicals, Socialists, Communists, and some anarchists formed a "Popular Front" in defense of the republic against the right. It barely won a majority in elections held at the beginning of the next year, and then quickly fell apart because of ideological differences amid high unemployment and political violence. The Falange, a small paramilitary fascist movement begun in 1933, further destabilized the republic, emulating the Italian fascist

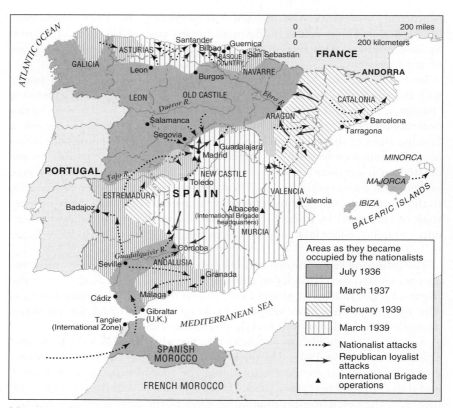

MAP 25.2 THE SPANISH CIVIL WAR, 1936–1939   The growing domination of Spain by the nationalists; arrows show nationalist and republican loyalist attacks during the Spanish Civil War.

"black shirts." In response to a wave of violence against republicans, the government declared the Falange illegal and arrested its leader in March 1936.

A military insurrection against the republic began in Morocco on July 17, 1936. It was quickly followed by planned garrison uprisings in most of Spain's major cities (see Map 25.2). German and Italian planes carried insurgents to the Spanish mainland. Right-wing nationalist rebels overwhelmed loyalist troops and soon held the traditionally conservative regions of Castile, Galicia, and Navarre.

The fragility of the loyalist alliance compromised the loyalist defense of the Spanish Republic. In Madrid, socialist trade unions held the upper hand. In Catalonia and Andalusia, anarchist workers and peasants were a majority. They took the outbreak of the war as a signal to begin a social revolution, expropriating land, occupying factories, and establishing cooperatives. Workers' committees, holding power in some regions, unleashed terror against the upper classes. The Socialists now were in the awkward position of trying to rein in the social revolution for which they had originally called. Communists feared that an attempted social revolution from below would compromise the attempt to save the republic and, furthermore, that it might undercut support for their party. The Communist Party grew six-fold in less than a year, adopting the centralized, hierarchical structure upon which Stalin in Moscow insisted. It purged members who had joined the Workers' Party of Marxist Unification (POUM), which supported Trotsky against Stalin. The Communists withheld supplies and ammunition from anarchist and Socialist units.

Whereas the loyalists suffered the consequences of disunity, the nationalists benefited from increasing unity. General Franco, who believed that freemasons had undermined Catholic Spain, considered himself a warrior king struggling against infidels who deserved no mercy.

The Struggle between Loyalists and Nationalists

The Spanish Civil War was fought with a savagery unseen in Western Europe since the seventeenth-century wars of religion. At least 580,000 people, and probably many more, died as a result of the war. Of these, only about a sixth died on the battlefield. Ten thousand died in (largely nationalist) air raids on civilians, and thousands more died from disease and malnutrition. During the war, nationalists executed at least 200,000 loyalists, and about that same number died at the hands of the loyalist forces or from disease in prison. Throughout the first two months of the war, in areas controlled by the loyalists, social and political tensions exploded in violence and death. Members of the Falange and monarchists were taken from their cells in the Madrid prison and shot; in the province of Catalonia alone, more than 1,000 clergy and nuns perished. The nationalists made effective propaganda use of loyalist atrocities, real or imaginary—the pro-nationalist London *Daily Mail* proclaimed "Reds Crucify Nuns." The nationalists organized "fiestas of death" in bull rings, machine-gunning loyalists, including prominent intellectuals and Basque priests.

The Spanish Civil War polarized Europe because it pitted against each other the political extremes that had emerged in Europe since the Great War. For the political right, religion and social hierarchy were at stake in a pitched battle against socialism and communism, as well as anarchism. Those supporting the Spanish Republic saw the civil war as a struggle against international fascism. Foreign volunteers, including 20,000 Britons and Irish and many refugees from Nazi Germany, joined the loyalist forces. The volunteers of the Abraham Lincoln Brigade from the United States fought with idealism and determination—but with only occasional effectiveness. However, these "International Brigades" were largely responsible for the heroic defense of Madrid that began in November 1936. The writers who fought in the Spanish Civil War, virtually all on the loyalist side, produced some of the most remarkable literature about war written in the twentieth century, including the American novelist Ernest Hemingway's *For Whom the Bell Tolls* (1940). The British writer George Orwell's *Homage to Catalonia* (1938) memorably related an account of his service on the loyalist side and of the damaging divisions between the major political factions, above all, the role of the Communists.

The nationalists enjoyed a significant military advantage over the loyalists because their forces included the bulk of the Spanish armed forces. The loyalists lacked such necessities as reliable maps. Orwell recalled his amazement at being issued an 1896 model German Mauser rifle and at the difficulties of forging an able fighting force out of a motley crew of illiterate peasants, anarchist workers, shop clerks, and foreign volunteers, many of whom did not speak Spanish and for whom the only word known in common was "comrade."

The republican loyalists counted on receiving arms, munitions, and other supplies from the Western democracies. But the British government wanted to maintain peace at all costs, and many of its prominent political figures admired Franco. In France, Premier Léon Blum's Popular Front government hesitated to take any steps that would widen the Spanish conflict and further polarize his own country. Moreover, he did not want to alienate the British government, as he was counting on its assistance in any eventual war against Germany. Without tanks, airplanes, and other supplies from the Soviet Union, the Spanish Republic probably would have almost immediately collapsed in the face of the nationalist forces.

German and Italian assistance to the nationalists proved decisive. While Britain, France, and the United States abided by nonintervention agreements, Italy sent 100,000 soldiers to Spain. However, the loyalists easily defeated the ill-equipped Italian forces, which relied on Michelin tourist

Pablo Picasso's *Guernica* (1937), mourning a German and Italian air attack on the Basque village.

maps in a spring 1937 ground battle. The Italians fared somewhat better in the air, where they faced virtually no opposition. Mussolini's pilots helped destroy loyalist supply lines. Hitler used the Spanish Civil War as a military training ground, sending planes, guns, munitions, and other supplies through Portugal. German advisers trained nationalist pilots and military personnel. The pilots of the German Condor Legion flew bombing runs against loyalist forces, as well as against civilians. On April 26, 1937, German and Italian planes bombed and strafed the small town of Guernica, killing more than 100 residents. Within a month, the Spanish-born painter Pablo Picasso had immortalized the martyrdom of Guernica on his canvas depicting the horrors of modern warfare.

When the nationalists attacked Madrid at the end of August 1937, the Communist militant Dolores Ibarruri, known as "La Pasionaria" (1895–1989), rallied loyalists with her defiant shout, "They shall not pass!" However, in the north, the nationalists reached the Atlantic coast, cutting off the loyalist Basque region from France. The loyalists struggled along an imposing front that stretched from the Mediterranean south of Granada to the Pyrenees. When Franco's army reached the Mediterranean Sea, it isolated Catalonia from remaining loyalist territory. Barcelona fell in January 1939. Britain and France (where the Popular Front had fallen from power) quickly recognized the Franco regime. Republican refugees carried what they could through the mountains and snows of the Pyrenees to France. Those who fled into Portugal, where the republic had been overthrown in 1926, were returned to Spain by the dictatorship of Salazar to be killed or

(*Left*) Communist leader Dolores Ibarruri, "La Pasionaria." (*Right*) General Francisco Franco.

imprisoned. Bloody reprisals against loyalists in Spain began immediately, and 150,000 more Spaniards were executed.

Franco, now known as "Caudillo," or "leader"—like the Italian Duce and the German Führer—established authoritarian rule based on the support of the army, the Church, and wealthy landowners, three forces that had opposed the republic. But recognizing Spain's weakness, Franco did not pursue a policy of expansion that characterized Italian fascism or German National Socialism. The Catholic Church's institutional role in Franco's Spain or Salazar's Portugal would have been unthinkable in Nazi Germany, and was less significant in Italy.

CONCLUSION

The collapse of the political center in Europe in the aftermath of the Treaty of Versailles and the Depression helped create the Europe of dictatorships. When Germany invaded Poland on September 1, 1939, World War II began. In retrospect, given the deterioration of the political climate, the rise of dictatorships, and the violence of the inter-war period of economic, social, and political crisis in the Europe of extremes, one can view the entire period between 1914, when World War I began, and 1945, when World War II finally ended, as a war of thirty years.

CHAPTER **26**

WORLD WAR II

~~~

For the second time in just twenty-five years, a European conflict became a world war. It would be even more devastating than World War I, wreaking destruction on a global scale. Germany's invasion of Poland on September 1, 1939, like its invasion of Belgium in 1914, started a chain reaction that brought the world powers into the conflict. The Soviet Union occupied eastern Poland, Finland, and the Baltic states of Lithuania, Latvia, and Estonia. Japan joined Germany and Italy, and the United States entered the war on the side of Great Britain and the free French government exiled in London. Following Germany's invasion of the Soviet Union in June 1941, the Communist state became an ally of Britain and the United States.

The Second World War was the first in which civilian populations became systematic, strategic targets. Beginning with the invasion of Poland, Germany used genocide both as an instrument of war and as an end in itself. More than 6 million Jews perished in Europe during World War II, most in German death camps. The technology of warfare developed rapidly; existing weapons were perfected, and by the end of the war, the atomic bomb, a terrible new weapon, had taken a terrible toll on human life. When the war ended in 1945, Europe seemed to be entering an even more threatening era. Unlike at the end of World War I in 1918, few people imagined that World War II would be the "war to end all wars."

THE COMING OF WORLD WAR II

Determined to achieve his territorial goals and willing to go to war if necessary to do so, Adolph Hitler in 1936 allied with Italy and Japan. He sent German troops into Austria in 1938 and then Czechoslovakia a year later, believing that Great Britain and France would not resist, but prepared to go to war if they did so. Finally, Germany and the Soviet Union astonished the world in August 1939 by signing a mutual nonaggression pact. This cleared the way for Hitler to launch a murderous attack on Poland. That pact included a secret agreement by which Germany and the Soviet Union would divide Eastern Europe between them. Attempting to avoid war at all costs, Britain and France accepted the occupation of Austria and Czechoslovakia but drew the line at Poland. The Second World War began.

The Axis

Benito Mussolini had already signed a pact with Hitler in October 1936, forming what the Italian dictator called an "Axis." Hitler made clear that Germany's interests lay to the east; Mussolini could have the Mediterranean and a free hand in Yugoslavia, Albania, and Greece. Joint participation in support of the Spanish nationalists during the Spanish War (1936–1939; see Chapter 25) brought Nazi Germany and fascist Italy closer together. Mussolini accepted Austria's loss of independence in exchange for a closer relationship with Germany. Concluding that German military strength could further Italian aims, the Duce ordered his soldiers to goose-step like the Germans, claiming that it was the military stride of ancient Rome. This led to considerable embarrassment for the elderly King Victor Emmanuel III, who tried it but fell down. Mussolini also ordered his countrymen to stop shaking hands and take up the ancient Roman military salute of an outstretched arm at a 45-degree angle.

Racial theories had hitherto never played more than a minor part in Mussolini's rise to power or his daily bombast. The Duce, who had a Jewish mistress, had mocked Hitler's "delirium of race." Mussolini had at first enjoyed widespread support among Italian Jews—about one of every three had first joined the Fascist Party. But in 1938 Mussolini began a campaign against Italian Jews, who numbered no more than 50,000 in a country of 40 million people. These measures managed only to irritate many Italians in a country in which Jews seemed perfectly well assimilated.

Germany found another authoritarian partner in Japan. Over the last half of the nineteenth century following the Meiji Restoration of 1868, Japan had made itself an industrial and military power. In need of raw materials such as oil and rubber, the Japanese government sought to build an empire in Southeast Asia. By the late 1930s, the Japanese army had reached 1 million men, with reserves of twice that number. The Japanese air force had 2,000 fighter planes, including the new "Zero" fighter, as fast as any in the world. In 1931, Japan embarked on a piecemeal conquest of Manchuria at the expense of China. Since Japan has virtually no natural resources, its goal was to create a resource base, which would be necessary for fighting the total war that many young Japanese generals eagerly anticipated. A year later, the Japanese government created the client state of Manchukuo, declaring the last emperor of China, Henry Pu-Yi, to be its emperor.

Fearing that the Soviet Union might try to hinder its military expansion, Japan late in 1936 signed a formal friendship treaty with Germany, the "Anti-Comintern Pact" (anti–Communist International), hoping also to discourage possible British and American intervention in Asia. In 1937, Japa-

Prisoners of the war between China and Japan over the Japanese invasion of Manchuria, 1931.

nese forces began to conquer chunks of northern China to establish a buffer zone between Manchukuo and the Soviet Union. Japan then embarked on a major naval expansion program, exceeding both in number and size the limits stipulated by the Washington Naval Conference (1921–1922) to which Japan, among the other powers, had agreed. The United States was entrenched in isolationism and still suffering the Depression. Angered by Japanese aggression and Japan's alliance with Nazi Germany, Britain joined the United States in imposing an embargo on the sale of oil and other vital raw materials to Japan.

German Aggression and British and French Appeasement

In November 1937, Hitler unveiled to his generals plans to absorb Austria and Czechoslovakia, perhaps as early as the next year. Hitler's confidence derived partly from information he had received that Neville Chamberlain, the new Conservative British prime minister, who in a speech had once called Hitler's National Socialism "a great social experiment," might accept Germany's annexation of Austria and the Czech Sudetenland as inevitable. Chamberlain was concerned only that the annexation occur without strife. The British prime minister feared that if Britain went to war against Germany, Hitler's allies Italy and Japan would strike British imperial interests in the Middle and Far East—for example, in Egypt and Burma. Furthermore, he viewed German ambitions toward the German-speaking parts of Austria and Czechoslovakia, as well as toward the Polish Corridor, as in keeping with the principle of nationalism. He believed that Germany had been treated too harshly by the Treaty of Versailles.

Convinced that Britain would not act, Hitler bullied Austrian Chancellor Kurt von Schuschnigg to legalize the Austrian Nazi Party. When Schuschnigg announced that a plebiscite on the question of his nation's independence would be held, Hitler ordered German troops into Austria, justifying the invasion with the absurd claim that German citizens were being mistreated there and that Austria was plotting with Czechoslovakia against Germany. On March 12, 1938, most of the Austrian population greeted German troops not as conquerors, but as liberators. Hitler thus effected the unification (*Anschluss*) of Germany and Austria that had been specifically forbidden by the Versailles Peace Settlement. The Nazis arrested more than 70,000 people and frenzied Viennese crowds beat up Jews. Britain and France sent official protests, but the British government permitted the German Reichsbank to confiscate funds that the Austrian National Bank had deposited in the Bank of England. This provided the Nazis with valuable gold and foreign currency reserves.

Czechoslovakia was next on Hitler's list. During the summer of 1938, he orchestrated a campaign against the Czech government. At issue was the status of the 3 million Germans living in Czechoslovakia, most in Sudetenland. However, Hitler was also furious that some anti-Nazi Germans had found refuge in Prague. President Edvard Beneš (1884–1948), with Poland casting a covetous eye on the long-disputed coal-mining region of Teschen, now desperately sought reassurance from France and the Soviet Union. Both were obligated by separate treaties to defend Czechoslovakia against

Austrians salute Germany's annexation of Austria, March 1938.

attack. But the Soviets refused to act unless joined by France, and France refused to act without considerable British assistance, which Chamberlain had already ruled out. In any case, France could really only help its Eastern European allies by attacking Germany, which the French government viewed as out of the question. In May, German troops massed along the Czechoslovak border.

On September 15, 1938, Chamberlain flew to the Führer's mountain retreat in southern Germany. When Hitler informed him that he would risk world war to unite the Sudeten Germans to their fatherland, Chamberlain agreed to try to convince the French and Czech governments that Germany's absorption of the Sudetenland was the best hope for peace. Hitler promised Chamberlain that this would be the last territorial revision of the Treaty of Versailles that Germany would demand. On September 19, 1938, Britain and France virtually ordered the Prague government to cede to Germany territories where the 3 million ethnic Germans formed a majority. Chamberlain returned to Germany to see Hitler again on September 22. He asked only that the new borders of Czechoslovakia be protected by a joint agreement.

Faced with the kind of collective security agreement he loathed, Hitler now threatened that Germany would occupy the Sudetenland by October 1 and would recognize Polish and Hungarian claims on territory ceded to Czechoslovakia in 1918 (he was already encouraging Slovaks to push for autonomy). This would have dismembered Czechoslovakia for all practical purposes (see Map 26.1). The French government balked, demanding Hitler's original terms as presented to Chamberlain. Hitler then seemed to draw back, agreeing to meet with Mussolini, French Prime Minister Édouard Daladier, and Chamberlain to settle everything once and for all. In London, Chamberlain confronted mounting skepticism. The British government ordered preliminary measures for civil defense in case of war. Chamberlain tried to rally British public opinion with a speech on September 27: "How horrible, fantastic, incredible it is that we should be digging trenches and trying on gas masks here because of a quarrel in a faraway country between people of whom we know nothing. It seems still more impossible that a quarrel which has already been settled in principle should be the subject of war."

At the multilateral conference at Munich in September 1938, Hitler refused to allow representatives of the Soviet Union to attend. Czech officials were not even permitted to assist at the dismemberment of their own country. Chamberlain and Daladier agreed to immediate German occupation of the Sudetenland (the most industrialized part of the country), Poland's annexation of Teschen, and the transfer of parts of Slovakia to Hungary, all in exchange for Hitler's personal guarantee of the redrawn borders of the partitioned nation. Chamberlain stepped off the plane in London announcing to cheering crowds that he had brought his country "peace in our time."

MAP 26.1 GERMAN AND ITALIAN EXPANSION, 1935–1939   Aggression by Germany and Italy against their neighbors.

In France, popular opinion did not want another war, and the military expressed apprehension about taking on the refurbished and expanded German armed forces. The French government felt abandoned by Britain, and by neighboring Belgium, which three years earlier had abrogated its 1920 military agreement with France and proclaimed its neutrality. France,

Neville Chamberlain promises "peace in our time" after his return from Munich in September 1938.

which had completed a line of bunker-like fortifications—the Maginot Line—to the Belgian frontier and counted on Belgium's ability to defend against a German attack, was now more exposed to a German onslaught. The French government also feared that Hitler might convince Franco of Spain to join Germany in a war against republican France from the other side of the Pyrenees.

The appeasement of Hitler at Munich provided the German army with more time to prepare for the conquest of what remained of Czechoslovakia. Appeasement—the term would subsequently take on a negative sense—had already characterized both British and French foreign policy in dealing with Mussolini (as the Ethiopian invasion demonstrated). Appeasement as foreign policy was influenced by the sheer horror of the Great War and many Europeans' unwillingness to contemplate a new conflict. Appeasement did not mean peace at any price, but rather the belief that if Germany could be appeased on one or two demands, then Hitler would be satisfied, or so the reasoning went, and Europe would be safe from war. It was pure delusion.

On March 16, 1939, Hitler shattered the Munich agreements. German troops marched across the Czech border and occupied Prague. Again, as in the case of Austria, the British government helped Hitler out by allowing the transfer of 6 million pounds of Czech gold deposits from London banks to the German-occupied state. Germany strengthened its forces with the addition of the Czech air force and army, and it no longer had to maintain strong defenses on its southern border. Hitler's brazen move shocked Mussolini, who complained, "Each time Hitler occupies a country, he sends me a message." In April 1939, Italian troops invaded and annexed Albania. British factories began turning out fighter planes as quickly as possible.

Looking east, the euphoric Hitler now demanded that Lithuania relinquish the Baltic port of Memel, which had been given to Lithuania by the Treaty of Versailles. Lithuania did so. He then insisted that Poland relinquish the port of Gdańsk (Danzig) and international access to the Polish Corridor that had by virtue of the Treaty of Versailles separated East Prussia from the rest of Germany. As always, Hitler offered a concession that would prove empty as soon as it had served its purpose: this time it was support against the Soviet Union's claim to parts of Poland that bordered Ukraine.

The Polish government, which had been in a state of crisis since the death of Józef Piłsudski, its authoritarian ruler, in 1935, readied its military defenses. The British government, which had refused to consider any alliances with the small states of Central Europe, now hurriedly signed a pact with Poland on April 6, 1939, guaranteeing Polish independence and assistance in case of German aggression. On April 26, Chamberlain—even he had now lost his illusions—announced to the House of Commons that conscription of men twenty and twenty-one years of age would begin. France (which was now also committed to Poland by alliance) and Britain then signed pacts with Romania and Greece and offered military support to Turkey. Hitler probably hoped that rapid Polish capitulation in the face of a German invasion might present its Western allies with a *fait accompli* that could discourage a military response. But Hitler accepted the strong possibility that war would follow any German move against Poland, even though he knew that the German economy could not reach full capacity for war production until 1943.

Few statesmen in France or Great Britain still harbored any illusions about what was next. British public opinion rapidly turned against appeasement. Winston Churchill (1874–1965), one of the few British leaders who had been convinced since 1936 that war against Hitler was inevitable, called for an alliance with the Soviet Union against Germany. Discussions with Soviet diplomats dragged on, stumbling on the refusal of either Poland or Romania to accept Soviet troops on their territory, necessary to any effective defense against a German attack. Chamberlain then heard rumors that Stalin and Hitler were conducting diplomatic discussions, but laughed them off.

Undeterred by Britain's reaffirmation of its commitment to defend Polish independence, or by doubts expressed by some of his confidants in April 1939, Hitler ordered the German army to prepare for an invasion of Poland on the following September 1. He signed in May the "Pact of Steel," a formal military alliance with Italy. Mussolini, who called the pact "absolute dynamite," nonetheless thought that he could continue to play off Germany, Britain, and France against each other. He had believed Hitler when he said that he would not begin a war with Poland for several more years. But knowing that doctored statistics could not hide the fact that Italy was unprepared for war, and now tied by a formal alliance to Hitler, the Duce had painted his country into a corner.

The Unholy Alliance

Stalin himself no longer had doubts about Hitler's ultimate intentions toward the Soviet Union. But the Russian army needed time to prepare for war. Stalin had decimated the officer corps during the purges of the past three years. In the short run, Hitler wished to avoid war with the Soviet Union while he was fighting in Poland; in the longer run, anticipating war with the Western powers, he sought, like Bismarck in different circumstances before him, to avoid fighting a war on two fronts. Stalin did not trust the Western Allies to maintain their commitment to resist Hitler and did not think that even a Soviet pact with Britain and France would prevent Hitler from attacking Poland.

In one of the most astonishing diplomatic turnarounds in history, Hitler announced on August 23, 1939, that Germany had signed the Molotov-Ribbentrop Nonaggression Pact with the Soviet Union, which was named for the two foreign ministers who negotiated it. The man Stalin had called "the bloody assassin of the workers" signed an agreement with the Communist leader Hitler had referred to as "the scum of the earth" and who dominated a state that Hitler planned to conquer. Hitler believed that a German pact with the Soviet Union would smash the will of Britain and France to defend Poland.

Stalin had reasons not to trust Britain or France, which had not bothered to consult the Soviet Union while appeasing at Munich. Hitler and Stalin divided up eastern Central Europe into "spheres of influence." The German dictator assured Stalin that "in the event of a territorial and political rearrangement," the independent states of Latvia and Estonia, coveted by Russia, as well as Finland and eastern Poland, would be fair game for the Soviet Union. Stalin still assumed that the imperialist powers ultimately would destroy each other in a protracted war.

In the meantime, most Germans seemed prepared to follow Hitler into a new war. A popular German magazine in April 1939 had cheerfully run the headline, "Gas Masks for German Children Now Ready."

THE WAR IN EUROPE BEGINS

The war for which Hitler had prepared for so long began with a rapid, brutal German attack on Poland. Stalin's Soviet Union then occupied eastern Poland. As Nazi troops overran Poland, the latter's Western allies, Great Britain and France, protested, but took no military action. Soviet troops soon invaded Finland, and German forces occupied Denmark and then

Norway. Hitler next turned his attention to the west, invading France, the Netherlands, and Belgium, and launching massive bombing attacks against Britain.

The German Invasion of Poland

On September 1, 1939, about 1.5 million German troops, led by an armored division, poured into Poland. Fighters and light bombers thundered overhead, carefully coordinating their attacks to protect the infantry. Britain and France responded two days later by declaring war on Germany.

Hitler wanted Polish resistance crushed quickly enough that Britain, and possibly France as well, would limit their reaction to a declaration of war. But he was prepared to fight the Western allies if necessary.

Poland had a large and well-trained army of more than 1 million soldiers. The German air force destroyed half of Poland's planes in the first attacks on its bases. Bombers battered Warsaw. Poland's frontier defenses collapsed before the onslaught of motorized columns of the German *Blitzkrieg* ("lightning war"). After moving east as German forces advanced, suffering heavy losses in the process, the Polish government moved to Paris on September 17. Warsaw fell ten days later. The German armies immediately implemented a policy of terror, killing prisoners of war, burning hundreds of towns and villages, and systematically massacring the Polish elite, while preparing the way for the settlement of the conquered lands by Germans.

German tanks move into Poland, September 1939.

From the east, Soviet armies invaded Poland on September 17. They did so with Hitler's blessing, under a secret agreement made between Stalin and Hitler as part of the Molotov-Ribbentrop Nonaggression Pact. Poland, partitioned three times late in the eighteenth century, was once again divided up. On Stalin's orders, more than 14,000 Polish officers and intellectuals were executed in the forest of Katyn about 200 miles southwest of Moscow. The Soviet dictator ordered the transfer of Poles in cattle wagons as "special settlers" to the eastern reaches of the Soviet Union.

The "Phony War"

As Hitler had hoped, Britain and France took no military action. Few people seemed willing to "die for Danzig (Gdańsk)," the Polish port Germany had lost by the Treaty of Versailles. British and French military experts, shocked by the speed of the German victory over Poland, overestimated the strength of Hitler's armies. An immediate French and British attack on Germany from the west might have been successful while the Germans were tied up in Poland, where the German army and air force had seriously depleted available munitions. Britain and France had more than twice as many divisions ready, and the German air force had few planes available to fight in the west. French troops made one brief, unopposed excursion fourteen miles into Germany, and then fell back. The British Royal Air Force flew over Germany, but dropped only leaflets calling for peace. Both the British and French governments believed that an attack on Germany would fail. They had been stunned by Hitler's pact with Stalin; unlike in World War I, it now appeared that Germany would only have to fight a war on one front.

Hitler confidently announced to his generals that he planned to order an invasion of France in the near future. The German army and air force were readied, while the French army dug in behind the supposedly impregnable fortifications of the Maginot Line, that line of bunkers stretching from Switzerland to the Belgian border (see Map 26.2).

The winter months that followed the Polish invasion became immediately known as the "phony war." Planned first for November and then for January, the German invasion of Western Europe was postponed until the spring of 1940. French troops stared into the rain, mist, and fog from their bunkers. Fearing German bombing attacks, the British government issued Londoners gas masks and imposed a nighttime blackout. In Rome, Mussolini had developed cold feet just before Hitler's invasion of Poland, because he knew that Italy lacked enough coal, oil, iron, and steel to wage a lengthy war. But he believed a German invasion of France inevitable. Mussolini announced that Italy's status would be one of "non-belligerence," a term he selected to avoid comparisons with the "neutrality" against which he had vociferously campaigned before Italy entered World War I in 1915.

MAP 26.2 THE GERMAN AND ITALIAN ADVANCE, 1939–1942   The opening of the war included advances by the Germans into Poland, the U.S.S.R., the Scandinavian countries, the Balkans, and North Africa. The Italians sent troops into Albania, and from there into Greece. The British unsuccessfully attempted to take a stand against the Germans in Norway, and British and French troops were evacuated from the continent at Dunkirk.

The War in the Frozen North

While the "phony war" continued in the west, fighting began in northern Europe. The Russian border with Finland, independent since the Russian Revolution, lay only fourteen miles from Leningrad. Stalin demanded that the Finnish government cede strategically important territories to the Soviets. When the Finnish government refused in November 1939, the Red

Army invaded. Badly outnumbered Finnish soldiers fought bravely in sub-zero temperatures, sometimes on skis, carrying light machine guns against Russian tanks and temporarily holding back the Soviet forces. Finland harbored no illusions about winning the "Winter War," but, like Poland, hoped to be saved by British and French diplomatic or military intervention. France now favored, at least in principle, armed intervention on behalf of Finland. So did Britain's Winston Churchill, who had angered his Conservative Party by opposing appeasement of Hitler at Munich. But Finnish resistance soon was broken. By the Peace of Moscow, signed March 12, 1940, the Soviet Union annexed about 10 percent of Finnish territory.

With the goal of stopping Swedish iron ore from being shipped to Germany, in April British ships mined the Norwegian harbor of Narvik, despite the objections of the government of Norway. On November 9 German troops occupied Denmark, which surrendered without a fight (see Map 26.2). German paratroopers landed at Oslo and other Norwegian port cities, followed by troops put ashore by ships. German soldiers repelled Allied troops, who arrived at the end of April with sketchy orders and inadequate weapons.

Prime Minister Chamberlain had assured the British House of Commons that Germany "had missed the bus" by waiting so long to attack in the west. But Germany's lightning occupation of Denmark and victory in Norway brought down the Chamberlain government. Churchill, who had been a member of Parliament on and off since 1900, became prime minister on May 10, 1940. The outspoken Churchill was an unpopular choice among even some Conservatives, who held an overwhelming majority in Parliament. Many remembered his impulsive attachment to far-fetched military operations during the First World War, which had led to the catastrophic defeat of British troops at Gallipoli in 1915. Even one of his trusted advisers said that Churchill had ten new ideas each day, but that nine of them were bad. Still, his resilience, determination, and dedication made Churchill an extraordinary wartime leader.

The Fall of France

German troops stared confidently across the Rhine River at their French opponents. The German army could simply sidestep the French Maginot Line, which stopped at the Belgian frontier. Germany enjoyed vast superiority over France in the air (France had only about 500 first-line fighter planes, Germany 4,000). Furthermore, the German army and air force were already well-practiced, having conquered Poland.

French soldiers had become demoralized by the winter months in the damp bunkers along the Maginot Line. The plan of the French high command to engage the enemy forces as they moved into the Low Countries was undermined by the Belgian and Dutch governments; both, hoping to remain neutral, had been unwilling to coordinate defense planning with the French army. The French generals lacked confidence in the strength of their forces and—at least some—in the Third Republic itself. French tanks were as good as those of Germany but lacked sufficient fuel and were dispersed among infantry divisions, instead of concentrated in tank divisions as in the German army. French communications networks along the front were inadequate. After eight months of "phony war," many people in France were uncertain as to why they might be once again fighting Germany.

Compounding serious military problems, the British and French governments were already sniping at each other. The French resented the fact that their ally sent a relatively small British Expeditionary Force to France; the British government seemed willing to defend France down to the last Frenchman. On the other hand, the French had irritated their British counterparts by opposing Allied bombing of Germany, fearing that the expected swift reprisals would strike them, not Britain.

On May 10, 1940, the "phony war" in the west suddenly ended. In a carefully rehearsed attack, German gliders landed troops who captured a massive Belgian fortress. Airborne divisions took the airport and central bridges of the Dutch port of Rotterdam; German bombers then destroyed ships, docks, and the heart of the old city, killing 40,000 people. The German assault on France began through the Ardennes Forest on the Belgian border; ten tank divisions pushed seventy miles into France. German planes, controlling the air, swept down on French troops and destroyed half the planes of the British Royal Air Force in three days. Mussolini, a portly vulture circling above the wounded French prey, declared war on France on May 10, but an Italian army managed to advance only about a hundred yards across the border toward Nice.

French commanders then foolishly sent most of their armored reserves into the Netherlands while German tanks, having reached the Meuse River in eastern France, now turned west and moved toward the English Channel. They were vulnerable to an Allied counterattack, but only a minor challenge by a tank column commanded by French General Charles de Gaulle (1890–1970) slowed the German drive to the Channel. Instead of attacking, British troops retreated from Belgium into France, heading toward the Channel. German columns reached the Channel on May 21, 1940, cutting the Allied forces in half. The Netherlands surrendered on May 15, Belgium on May 28. By now the roads of northern France were choked, not only with retreating British and French troops, but with Belgian and French refugees fleeing the battle zones, strafed by German planes.

France's defeat was now only a matter of time. British troops, joined by remnants of the French forces, managed to hold off the German army, making possible the evacuation of 340,000 British and French troops at the end of May and early June 1940 from Dunkirk by every available British vessel, including fishing trawlers and pleasure craft. The German army wheeled to confront the French troops still uselessly defending the Maginot Line. The French government left Paris for Bordeaux, as it had in 1870. The German

Hitler takes a triumphant stroll through Paris in June 1940.

army occupied the capital on June 14. On June 16, Marshal Philippe Pétain, hero of the Battle of Verdun in 1916, became premier. The next day, he asked Germany for an armistice. France and Britain had several months earlier agreed that neither ally would ask for an armistice without the approval of the other. The British government wanted the French armies to move to North Africa and continue the war from there. However, on June 22, the gleeful Hitler accepted the French surrender in a railway car in the spot where Germany had signed a similar document in November 1918. Hitler then set out to tour Paris. On July 3, the British navy sunk a battleship, a cruiser, and several destroyers of the French fleet as they lay in port at Mers el-Kébir in Algeria, killing 1,300 French sailors. The British command feared that the ships might fall into German hands.

The Battle of Britain

Britain would fight on. Addressing the House of Commons, Churchill declared, "I have nothing to offer but blood, toil, tears, and sweat. . . . You ask, what is our policy? I will say: it is to wage war, by sea, land, and air, with all our might and with all the strength that God can give us."

Hitler now considered whether an invasion of Britain could succeed. Germany held the French and Belgian Channel ports, a position it had never achieved during World War I. Furthermore, with Ireland having proclaimed its neutrality, the Royal Navy no longer had use of southern Irish ports.

Fearing a German attack, the British government interned German subjects, including some of the 50,000 Jewish refugees from Nazism. In some places, officials took down road signs and place names, and shopkeepers shredded local maps to disorient any German invading army. For an invasion of Britain to succeed, the German air force (the Luftwaffe) had to control the skies. The ensuing Battle of Britain, fought over the Channel and above southern England, lasted four dramatic months, from the very end of July through October 31, 1940, although most of the climactic duels in the sky took place in August and September. The German bombing "blitz" of London began on September 7. Londoners took to the subway stations and underground air-raid shelters for protection. The British used radar, first developed in 1935, to detect German attacks. Recently built British Spitfires and Hurricanes reached greater speeds than the German Messerschmitt fighters and could break through fighter escorts to get to the cumbersome German bombers. Hitler ordered the bombing of key industries and aircraft factories in England even as British bombers appeared over Berlin in August, demonstrating that Britain was far from defeated.

Britain lost 650 fighter planes, but factories were producing replacements and new pilots were being trained. As German air losses mounted, the Luftwaffe turned to less accurate night bombing to keep the British fighters out of the air. At the end of September 1940, Hitler was forced to abandon his plan to invade England. Churchill called the Battle of Britain his country's "finest hour."

(*Left*) Evacuating children from London during the German bombing "blitz," 1940. (*Right*) British Prime Minister Winston Churchill amid the rubble in London, 1940.

A GLOBAL WAR

World War II rapidly spread to almost all corners of the globe. Total war absorbed national resources on an unprecedented scale, as factories began to turn out weapons, munitions, and war materiel. Governments assumed considerable control over economies, coordinating production, raising taxes, and imposing rationing. Scientists were put to work in the war effort.

In June 1941, Germany launched an air and ground attack on the Soviet Union. However, Hitler failed to reckon with determined Russian resistance, as well as with the harsh Russian winter. The largest invading army in history ground to a halt in the frozen snow. Finally, on December 7, 1941, Japanese planes carried out a surprise attack on the U.S. naval and air force base at Pearl Harbor, Hawaii. The raid inflicted great damage on the U.S. Pacific Fleet and brought the United States into what had become a global conflict fought on an unprecedented scale.

Total War

Britain was the first combatant in World War II to find itself engaged in a total war. As the war expanded, other states confronted similar challenges. German military planners counted on Hitler's confident assertion that the United States would stay out of the war and that Germany could bring the British to their knees. But the United States, where British resistance won sympathy and admiration, could help Britain in other ways. On December 29, 1940, President Franklin D. Roosevelt announced that the United States would be "the arsenal of democracy," despite official neutrality. Since direct loans might recall for many Americans the defaults by those countries in debt to the United States after World War I, Congress passed the Lend-Lease Act in March 1941. It authorized the president to lend destroyers, trucks, and other equipment, and to send food to Great Britain, which in exchange would lease naval bases in the Caribbean to the United States.

Unlike Germany, which had been preparing for war virtually since Hitler came to power, Britain had to start almost from scratch. The British government succeeded in rallying the king's subjects to wartime sacrifices. Because very few people had any doubts about the extent of the Nazi threat to Britain itself, military conscription at the beginning of the war was quickly accepted. Before the war began, the British armed forces comprised 500,000 people; at the end of the war, 5 million. Women took the places in industry vacated by departing troops, accounting for 80 percent of the increase in the labor force between 1939 and 1943. In 1939, 7,000 women worked in ordnance factories in Britain; in October 1944, there were 260,000.

The British War Cabinet imposed governmental controls on the economy and by 1942 had achieved a high degree of coordination in wartime production. The government imposed higher taxes, implemented rent control, established rationing, and called for voluntary restraints on wage raises.

Pants came without cuffs or zippers; a suspicious gray "utility loaf" replaced white bread. British farmers augmented agricultural production by increasing the amount of land under cultivation by a full third.

In October 1940, Churchill established a scientific advisory committee to put some of Britain's most eminent scientists to work designing more powerful and reliable weapons. One of the most significant breakthroughs of the war was not a technological innovation but the solving of the complex puzzle of a secret code. British intelligence officers, aided by mathematicians, deciphered communications between Hitler and his high command during the Battle of Britain. This subsequently allowed the Allies to know many German military moves in advance. British intelligence officers then broke the German communications code, facilitating, among other things, the identification of spies. By the end of 1943, the code breakers, some using the "Enigma" machine developed after World War I to decipher secret messages, were intercepting more than 90,000 messages a month. The British Psychological Warfare Division, along with their U.S. counterpart, also put the science of psychology into the service of modern warfare, waging radio and leaflet campaigns in an attempt to weaken the enemy's will to continue fighting.

Hitler's Allies

Hitler sought other allies in an attempt to win the war quickly. Seeking to discourage the United States, Japan's rival in the Pacific, from entering the war on the Allied side against Germany and Italy, the two Axis powers signed the Tripartite Pact with Japan in September 1940. Germany and Italy recognized Japan's interests in Asia, while Japan acknowledged those of Germany and Italy in Europe. The treaty specified that each power agreed to cooperate should any one of them be attacked by "a Power at present not involved in the European war or in the Chinese-Japanese conflict." Hitler then tried to convince Francisco Franco, whose victory in the Spanish Civil War Hitler had helped make possible, to join the war of the Axis powers against Britain. The German dictator envisioned a Spanish seizure of Gibraltar and German use of naval bases in the Spanish Canary Islands. The Spanish dictator pleaded the poverty of his country and, as if to emphasize the point, arrived at the meeting with Hitler hours late on a plodding train. After spending eight hours cajoling Franco, Hitler said, "I would prefer to have three or four teeth extracted rather than go through that again." Franco's Spain, however much ideologically in tune with Hitler's Germany, remained officially neutral.

In Romania, King Carol II was powerless in the face of his greedy neighbors, who were encouraged by Germany. He surrendered to Hungary a part of Transylvania that had been awarded to Romania by the Treaty of Versailles and that included a considerable Hungarian population. Stalin forced Romania to hand over to the Soviet Union northern Bukovina and Bessarabia, which had once been part of the Russian Empire. Bulgaria also helped itself to Romanian territory. As a result, the Romanian fascist Iron Guard rebelled and forced King Carol to abdicate in favor of his son Michael in September 1940.

Now convinced it was facing a long war, Germany hurried to secure a supply of raw materials by occupying Romania and its rich oil fields in October 1940. A right-wing general, Ion Antonescu (1882–1946), ran the country with the help of the Iron Guard, which served German interests and unleashed its fury against Romania's Jews and Communists. Both Romania and Hungary formally joined the Axis in November 1940.

From the beginning, it appeared that Italy's contributions to the German war effort would be minimal at best. Mussolini aimed to take as much territory in North Africa as possible before the British surrender upon which he counted. After having failed to launch air attacks, as Hitler had wanted, on British bases on the Mediterranean island of Malta, Mussolini invaded Egypt in September 1940, refusing a German offer to supply tanks because he wanted Italy to claim victory on its own. Unable to provide troops with air cover, Italian forces suffered a series of defeats at the hands of British forces.

Desperate for victory somewhere, on October 28, 1940, the Duce surprised Hitler—as well as his own generals—by ordering his army to invade Greece from Albania. Having paid large bribes to Greek generals and officials not to resist, Mussolini anticipated an easy victory. But a Greek patriot army drove the Italians back into Albania, where resistance movements made life difficult for Mussolini's troops. The Italian army took out its frustrations against the Croatian population of Dalmatia on the Adriatic coast. In the meantime, the British navy battered the Italian fleet.

Italy's imperial holdings in East Africa rapidly crumbled in the spring of 1941. A British and French force took Addis Ababa, Ethiopia's capital, in April. Hitler sent General Erwin Rommel (1891–1944), commander of a tank division, to North Africa to bail out the Italian troops. Mussolini vowed to continue the war "until the last Italian is killed."

The German Invasion of Russia

Hitler always intended to invade and defeat the Soviet Union, despite the Molotov-Ribbentrop Nonaggression Pact of August 1939. After occupying eastern Poland following the German invasion of Poland, Soviet troops had occupied the Baltic republics of Estonia, Latvia, and Lithuania during the summer of 1940, claiming that they had been illegitimately detached from Russia after World War I, when they had become independent. German interest in Finland and moves in Romania now made Soviet Foreign Minister Vyacheslav Molotov (1890–1986) anxious. The Soviets sought reassurance in a new pact, one that Mussolini would sign as well. Molotov went to Berlin. Assured personally by Hitler that Britain lay defeated,

Molotov replied, "Then whose bombers are those overhead, and why are we in this bomb shelter?"

Hitler intended "Operation Barbarossa," the invasion of Russia, to be a "quick campaign" of no more than ten weeks' duration. He hoped that Japan would attack Siberia, thereby forcing Stalin to divert troops there. Some German generals held the Russian army in such contempt that they ordered no serious assessment of Russia's existing or potential military strength. If the Finns on skis had been able to hold off Russian divisions with seemingly little more than snowballs, how could German fighters and tanks fail to break through with relative ease?

The opening of a Balkan front delayed Hitler's invasion of the Soviet Union, which had been planned for May 1941. Britain had sent forces to Greece following the Italian invasion, which made German bases in Yugo-slavia even more crucial. An anti-German faction had overthrown the Yugoslav government in March and refused to join the Axis or to allow German troops into the country. Hitler ordered an invasion of Yugoslavia in April. German armies then pushed into Greece. As in World War I, Bulgaria in March cast its fate with Germany. Bulgarian troops occupied parts of Greek Macedonia and Thrace. The German army forced a British withdrawal from the Greek mainland to the Aegean island of Crete, which soon itself fell to German paratroopers. Greece was occupied by German, Italian, and Bulgarian troops. Five percent of the Greek population died of starvation, along with hundreds of thousands killed in the fighting or executed. By the end of May 1941, Hitler's armies held all of the Balkans.

Hitler could now concentrate on an invasion of the Soviet Union. Stalin, however, failed to heed warnings from Britain and the United States that Russia was Germany's next target. Believing these warnings, including some of his own army's military reports, to be part of a conspiracy to turn him against his German ally, Stalin ordered the execution of some of his intelligence officers.

On June 22, 1941, German planes, tanks, and more than 3 million troops attacked the Soviet Union. The German generals were convinced that the Soviet forces could be easily defeated. However, the Soviets had many more men, field artillery, tanks, and aircraft than Germany, and for the most part their weapons were of quality equal to or even superior to that of the Germans. But German forces quickly devastated Soviet defenses and communication and transportation networks. One army pushed toward Leningrad in July 1941, laying siege to the city. But Leningrad held. The battleship *Aurora,* which had served the Bolshevik cause in the Revolution of 1917, was pressed into service, its guns commandeered from a museum. A second German army captured more than 250,000 prisoners near Minsk (now in Belarus), 250 miles northeast of Warsaw; a third, finding support from anti-Russian Ukrainians, took Kiev in September 1941. Hitler rejected his generals' suggestion that the attack on Moscow be given priority. Instead, armored units were transferred to the northern army besieging Leningrad.

Peasants watching the effects of the German invasion of Ukraine, August 1941.

The German advance left Russian towns and villages in ruins, and hundreds of thousands of civilians dead. But despite enormous battlefield casualties, as well as half a million captured prisoners dying of hunger and cold in German camps, Russian resistance stiffened. News of Nazi atrocities helped rally virtually the entire population. German armies bogged down in the face of determined resistance around Smolensk. Soviet state-run factories were converted to wartime production, soon turning out great numbers of tanks of good quality. The United States, still officially neutral in the conflict, extended the Lend-Lease policy to the Soviet Union.

Their drive to victory stalled, despite having captured more than a million square miles of Soviet territory, the German troops, like Napoleon's armies in 1812, found that a frozen winter, the coldest in a century, followed the chilly Russian fall. "Hitler no more resembles Napoleon than a kitten resembles a lion," Stalin taunted. Oil for tanks and guns froze. So did soldiers. The German high command, so certain of a quick victory, had not bothered to provide them with warm clothing and blankets for temperatures reaching far below zero.

After ordering a halt in the push toward Moscow, Hitler, fearing the consequences of retreat on German morale, ignored the advice of his generals to pull back and await spring weather. Early in December 1941, a desperate German attack stalled twenty miles from Moscow. The German army never got closer. During the first year of the Russian campaign, German casualties reached 1.3 million, or 40 percent of the original invading force, the greatest losses of any single military operation in history.

Japan's Attack on the United States

Four years of aggression in Asia brought Japan to the point of confrontation with the United States. Since invading Manchuria in 1931 and proclaiming it the puppet state of Manchukuo a year later, Japan had sought to expand its influence and territory in the Pacific region. Southeast Asian oil was one Japanese target, particularly after the United States, Great Britain, and the Netherlands imposed an economic boycott following the Manchurian invasion. The Japanese quest for rubber, tin, and other raw materials threatened British economic interests in Burma and Malaya, as well as those of the Dutch in Java and of the United States in the Philippine Islands.

In 1937, Japan had joined the Anti-Comintern Pact that Germany and Italy had signed the previous year. Also in 1937, the Japanese army moved further into China and occupied the main ports, moves that the American government viewed with alarm. The Molotov-Ribbentrop Nonaggression Pact, signed between the Soviet Union and Germany in August 1939, had voided the Anti-Comintern Pact, as the Soviet Union was a Communist state. After Japanese troops entered Indochina, in September 1940, Japan concluded the Tripartite Pact with Germany and Italy, thus becoming part of the Axis. In an effort to stop the flow of Allied supplies to Chinese forces over the railway from Hanoi and a long dirt road from Burma, Japan had assumed a "protective" occupation of French Indochina in July 1941. A nonaggression

Japanese dive bombers preparing to take off from an aircraft carrier before attacking Pearl Harbor, December 7, 1941.

pact with the Soviet Union, signed in April 1941, two months before the German invasion of Russia, bolstered Japanese confidence that it could attack and inflict a stinging defeat on the United States and force the Americans to a negotiated settlement.

On Sunday morning, December 7, 1941, a Japanese force of fighters and dive-bombers surprised the American naval and air force base at Pearl Harbor, Hawaii. Three U.S. battleships were sunk, and five were severely damaged; ten other vessels were destroyed or disabled and 188 planes destroyed. The attack killed 2,403 naval and other military personnel, and more than 1,000 were wounded. However, three aircraft carriers were at sea and could still be readied to take on the Japanese fleet in the Pacific Ocean. Vast stocks of oil, too, survived. Japan quickly followed with successful invasions of Malaya, the Philippines, Singapore (where almost 60,000 British soldiers surrendered), and Pacific islands as far distant as the Aleutians near Alaska (see Map 26.3).

Because American intelligence officers had deciphered Japan's coded messages, President Roosevelt had known that Japan was planning to launch a war against the United States. Yet the attack on Pearl Harbor came as a surprise, in part because U.S. intelligence services were swamped with messages suggesting attacks at other locations. Calling December 7, 1941, "a day that will live in infamy," Roosevelt declared war on Japan.

Hitler, bound by treaty to Japan, then declared war against the United States. He believed that public opinion in the United States was against American involvement in another European war. In fact, he knew amazingly little about the United States.

Upon hearing the news of Pearl Harbor, Churchill exclaimed, "We have won the war!" The entry of the United States into the war against Germany provided, as in 1917, a crucial material advantage to the Allies. Despite its slow recovery from the Depression, which hit it harder than any other nation, the United States had become the largest industrial power in the world, producing more than the next six powers combined. American factories were quickly converted to military production. In response to wartime demand, industrial production in the United States doubled by the end of 1943, finally pulling the United States out of the Depression.

Despite the patronizing attitude of the self-assured British prime minister, a warm personal relationship gradually developed between Churchill and Roosevelt. Their rapport helped overcome the tension that had developed between the two powers because of the original unwillingness of the United States to join Britain in the war. The Japanese attack on Pearl Harbor ended U.S. isolationism. American citizens rallied to the war effort, particularly against the Japanese. "Remember Pearl Harbor!" struck a chord in the United States that "Remember Belgium" or "Remember France" could not have.

The fact that an Asian power had attacked the United States galled Americans, many of whom believed that Asians were inferior. Amid rumors

MAP 26.3 THE JAPANESE ADVANCE AND ALLIED COUNTEROFFENSIVE, 1941–1945 After launching a surprise attack against the U.S. naval and air force base at Pearl Harbor, Hawaii, the Japanese successfully invaded most of the Southeast Asian countries and many of the Pacific islands.

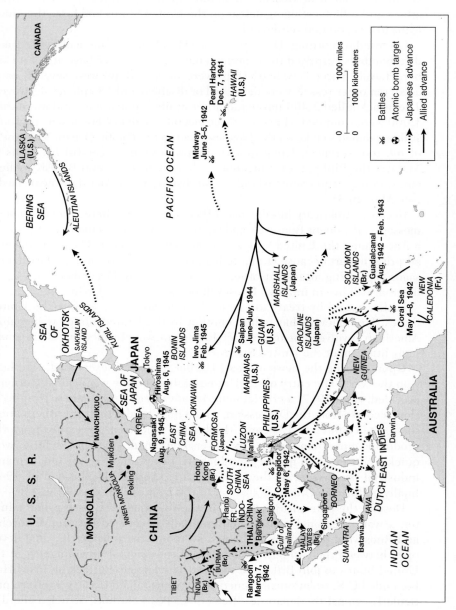

that Japanese citizens and Japanese Americans were preparing to carry out acts of sabotage in the United States, the U.S. government interned in "relocation centers" about 40,000 Japanese citizens residing in the United States and 70,000 Japanese Americans, most living on the West Coast. American citizens of German descent, in contrast, were not interned.

The first of several meetings between the British and American military chiefs of staff took place in Washington, D.C., in January 1942. The Allied commanders decided to give the European theater of war the highest priority. An immediate concentration of attacks against Japanese forces seemed less urgent. In any case, it would take considerable time to dislodge the Japanese from the Southeast Asian countries and Pacific islands they had conquered.

HITLER'S EUROPE

Whether or not each conquered state retained some autonomy, German policies were first directed at extracting useful raw materials needed to wage an extended war. The exact nature of the relationship between Germany and each occupied state varied from country to country. Yet in all of these states the Nazis carried out Hitler's policy of genocide against Jews and others belonging to what he considered to be inferior races, often aided by local collaborators.

In every country overrun by German troops, people could be found who were eager or willing to collaborate with the Nazis. These ranged from leaders willing to serve German interests to ordinary people whose political biases or hope for gain or even just survival led them to help the Nazis. Yet, in many countries, resistance movements bravely opposed the rule of the Nazis or their allies. The largest and most successful resistance was in mountainous Yugoslavia, where resisters were able to take on entire German divisions, and, to a lesser extent, in France, where groups of guerrilla fighters undertook hit-and-run attacks against the Germans and the collaborationist government. In Germany, resistance to Hitler and the Nazis barely existed, notwithstanding a courageous attempt by disenchanted army officers to assassinate Hitler in July 1944. To the end, most Germans remained loyal to the Führer, or at least could not or did not resist.

The Nazi "New European Order"

Hitler sought to exploit the economic resources of the countries his armies had conquered and to assure that no effective opposition could emerge in any of them. Germany annexed the disputed Polish territories it had claimed, including Poznan, Upper Silesia, and the Polish Corridor; Hitler considered them German in the first place. Direct German administration was extended to Ukraine and Belarus. Germans who lived in Poland,

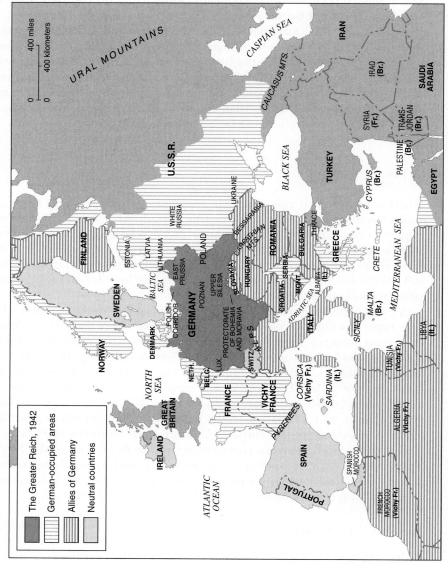

MAP 26.4 HITLER'S EUROPE, 1942 Hitler's expansion to the east and west, showing the greatest extent of the German occupation of Europe.

The Greater Reich, 1942

German-occupied areas

Allies of Germany

Neutral countries

ATLANTIC OCEAN

IRELAND

GREAT BRITAIN

NORTH SEA

NORWAY

SWEDEN

FINLAND

DENMARK

NETH.

BELG.

LUX.

FRANCE

VICHY FRANCE

PYRENEES

SPAIN

PORTUGAL

SPANISH MOROCCO

FRENCH MOROCCO (Vichy Fr.)

ALGERIA (Vichy Fr.)

TUNISIA (Vichy Fr.)

CORSICA (Vichy Fr.)

SARDINIA (It.)

ALPS

SWITZ.

GERMANY

POLISH CORRIDOR

EAST PRUSSIA

POZNAN

UPPER SILESIA

PROTECTORATE OF BOHEMIA AND MORAVIA

SLOVAKIA

HUNGARY

CROATIA

SERBIA

MONT.

ITALY

SICILY

MALTA (Br.)

ALBANIA

ADRIATIC SEA

MEDITERRANEAN SEA

LIBYA (It.)

BALTIC SEA

ESTONIA

LATVIA

LITHUANIA

WHITE RUSSIA

POLAND

UKRAINE

BESSARABIA

CARPATHIAN MTS.

ROMANIA

BULGARIA

THRACE

GREECE

CRETE

U.S.S.R.

URAL MOUNTAINS

CASPIAN SEA

CAUCASUS MTS.

BLACK SEA

TURKEY

CYPRUS (Br.)

SYRIA (Fr.)

IRAQ (Br.)

IRAN

TRANS-JORDAN (Br.)

PALESTINE (Br.)

SAUDI ARABIA

EGYPT

0   400 miles

0   400 kilometers

Lithuania, or those parts of the Soviet Union that were behind German lines were "repatriated" to Germany, or settled in the newly conquered territories (see Map 26.4).

German policies were different in Poland and Russia, whose peoples Hitler considered to be racially inferior. Following the fall of Warsaw, Hitler had sent five special "action" squads to Poland with orders to wipe out the Polish upper class. All over the country, businessmen, political leaders, intellectuals, and teachers were executed or sent to extermination camps.

Norway and Denmark, deemed by Hitler to be sufficiently "Nordic" or "Aryan" to be "Germanized," were allowed relative autonomy. In Denmark, where the only elections in any country under a Nazi regime took place, the Danish Nazi Party won a paltry 2 percent of the vote. Hitler left Germany's central and southern European "independent" allies with some autonomy, depending on the extent to which they followed his wishes. Admiral Miklós Horthy ruled Hungary under increasingly close German supervision, particularly after Hitler learned that he tried to play both sides by getting in touch with the Allies in 1942. Slovakia, which had been denied independence by the Versailles settlements, had become autonomous when Germany marched into Czechoslovakia in 1938, splitting the country into two parts. Pro-German nationalist fascists held power in Slovakia. In wartime Romania, the fascist Ion Antonescu ruled. Hitler divided Yugoslavia into the states of Serbia, Montenegro, and Croatia. Placing Serbia under direct German administration, he put Croatia and Montenegro under the rule of an authoritarian leader informally responsible to Mussolini.

The Germans imposed crushing obligations on conquered lands, including enormous financial indemnities and exchange rates that strongly favored the German currency. Germans operated factories and shipping companies in occupied countries. In France, the Germans first took movable raw materials and equipment useful for war production. As the war went on, German demands became greater; the occupation authorities closely regulated the armament, aircraft, mining, and metal industries. Some French businesses made the best of the situation, eagerly working with German firms. A few quietly subverted German demands and expectations for cooperation.

The "Final Solution"

Hitler's obsessive racial theories had become official policy in Nazi Germany before the war (see Chapter 25). For the Nazis, the process of forging the "national community" meant the elimination of groups they considered to be "outsiders." They made a temporary exception of foreign laborers, upon whom the economy depended during the war. In 1939, Hitler had ordered the killing, often by injection, of Germans who were mentally deficient and handicapped. At least 70,000 mentally retarded people perished, including children, before public objections that the victims were German halted this practice in August 1941. In addition, the Nazis sterilized between

320,000 and 350,000 German "outcasts" between 1934 and 1945; these included people determined by Nazi doctors to manifest "hereditary simple-mindedness," alcoholism, homosexuality, chronic depression, schizophrenia, or those who were deemed "work shy." Hitler mandated experiments to determine how thousands of people could be killed "efficiently" in assembly-line fashion.

In 1939, Hitler told Heinrich Himmler (1900–1945), the leader of the S.S., to plan for the occupation of Poland and the Soviet Union. The short, stout Himmler was obsessed with the pagan Germans of prehistory, establishing several spurious academic institutes to study his crackpot theories. Himmler welcomed Hitler's order to "eliminate the harmful influence of such alien parts of the population." Hitler announced to the Reichstag on January 30, 1939, that the result of the anticipated war would be "the annihilation of the Jewish race in Europe," the "final solution."

Nazi plans to exterminate Jews took shape as German military defeats mounted in Russia. There the massacre of Russians had already begun. In January 1941, Himmler announced to S.S. leaders a change in policy. Hitler no longer wanted to transform Slavs into a slave labor force, but rather wanted to destroy at least 30 million of them. Germans eventually would occupy their lands. German troops and death squads executed Russian prisoners and civilians. Before the war ended, at least 3.3 million Soviet prisoners of war—of 5.7 million captured—were executed or died in German prisoner-of-war camps.

A Gestapo directive on July 17, 1941, ordered commanders of prison camps in the east to liquidate "all the Jews." In October 1941, the Nazis began to prepare for the Holocaust, the genocide of European Jews. Hermann Göring ordered Reinhard Heydrich (1904–1942), the chief of the secret police, to prepare "a total solution of the Jewish question." By the end of 1941, 1 million Jews had been massacred. Heydrich and other Nazi officials met in Wannsee, a Berlin suburb, in January 1942. There they drew up even more systematic plans for genocide.

The assembly-line-like murders of Jews began, first in mobile vans, using carbon monoxide gas, then in the extermination camp of Auschwitz-Birkenau near Krakow in southern Poland. By 1942, the Nazis had built other extermination camps, surrounded by barbed-wire, electrified fences, and watchtowers (see Map 26.5). Gallows stood in an open space near the prisoners' wooden huts. But most victims were exterminated in airtight gas chambers with Zyklon B gas, chosen because it killed with efficiency. The victims' eyeglasses, gold from their teeth, and all other valuables became the property of the Reich.

Inmates of the camps wore tattered striped uniforms, and they were identified by numbers tattooed on their arms. They were ordered to file past an officer, who selected those deemed "unfit" for hard labor, which at Auschwitz was about 70 to 75 percent. He sent them toward a building marked "shower" or "bath," and some were given, in the ultimate cynical

MAP 26.5 NAZI DEATH CAMPS   Sites of the death camps in Europe.

gesture, a small piece of soap. A recent, unknowing arrival at Auschwitz inquired of another prisoner as to the whereabouts of his friend. " 'Was he sent to the left side?' . . . 'Yes,' I replied. 'Then you can see him there,' I was told. 'Where?' A hand pointed to the chimney a few hundred yards off, which was sending a column of flame up into the gray sky of Poland. It dissolved into a sinister cloud of smoke." Those people sent to the right— mostly the young in relatively good health—would continue to live until they dropped dead of fatigue or were subsequently sent to the left side in another "selection." Almost all children were killed right away, because they were too young to work as slave laborers in the I.G. Farben chemical factory near the camp. At Auschwitz, the daily death count reached as high as 15,000 victims. Overall, Hungarian Jews perished in the largest numbers, followed closely by Poles. One of the granddaughters of Alfred Dreyfus, the Jewish French army officer falsely accused of treason in the 1890s (see Chapter 18), perished there in 1944.

Jews being massacred in Lithuania, 1942.

The fascist states of Croatia and Romania, both Germany's allies, carried out the mass murder of Jews themselves. The Romanian government killed 300,000 Jews in the provinces that the Soviets had occupied in 1940, but few in what the Romanians considered the heartland of the country. In Lithuania, Ukraine, and, to a lesser extent, Poland, there were many cases of local populations massacring Jews.

Some people protected the Jews. A small French town took in Jewish children, producing identity cards for them that made them family members. In Marseille, Varian Fry, an American editor, journalist, and member of the American Refugee Committee, relentlessly planned escape routes, purchased tickets, and, where possible, obtained transit and other visas and found sponsors for about 1,000 Jews early in the war, including the painter Marc Chagall and the poet André Breton. A Warsaw woman rescued 2,500 children from the city's Jewish ghetto. In Amsterdam, Christians brought food and other supplies to a German Jewish family, hidden in a secret annex apartment in the father's office building for several years. In her resolutely cheerful diary, the young Anne Frank described her family's hiding place as "a paradise compared with how other Jews who are not in hiding must be living." It frightened her to think of her friends who had fallen into the clutches of "the cruelest brutes that walk the earth." Several months after her fourteenth birthday, Nazi soldiers discovered Frank's family. She and her family were deported to Auschwitz. Frank died in the death camp of Bergen-Belsen in the spring of 1945.

In Denmark, most of the Jewish population was saved in October 1943. When word came that the German occupying forces were preparing to

Dutch Jews on their way to the trains for transport from Amsterdam to a concentration camp.

deport Danish Jews, Danes ferried Jews across the straits to nearby neutral Sweden. There a courageous German cultural attaché had helped prepare the way. Perhaps fearing that mass deportations might spark Danish resistance, in this case the German authorities looked the other way. In Bulgaria, King Boris and his government, although allied with Nazi Germany, simply abandoned plans to deport the country's 50,000 Bulgarian Jews. (yet Bulgaria willingly handed over to the Nazis and thus to certain death Greek and Yugoslav Jews). In Hungary, Horthy resisted for three years German demands that the Jews of Hungary be sent to death camps. After German occupation in 1944, he ordered the deportations of Jews that had begun to be stopped. Yet Hungarian police killed tens of thousands of Jews in Hungary. In Croatia, where Italy had established an occupation zone, some Italian army officers protected Jews (and Serbs as well) from Croatian death squads. But when, in August 1942, Germany requested that the Italians turn the Croatian Jews over to the Nazis, Mussolini wrote "No objection" across the letter. Italian authorities had little interest in rounding up Italian Jews. They ignored German directives, or they could be bribed to look the other way. Some non-Jewish Romans contributed their jewelry to help raise a ransom demanded by the Germans from Jews under threat of deportation. Others helped Jews hide. They did so at great risk; German troops executed entire families of those who hid or even gave food to Jews.

Nazi doctors performed barbaric experiments on prisoners. These included experiments in the sterilization of Slavic women; measuring the pain a patient could survive when being operated on without anesthesia;

how long one could live in subfreezing temperatures; or whether prisoners would allow themselves to be killed if they thought their children might be spared. Gypsies were also Nazi targets, viewed as "biological outsiders" who were both "alien" by virtue of not being "Aryan" and "asocial," because they were nomadic. A half million gypsies perished. Communists, socialists, and repeat criminal offenders were also considered "asocial." Many of them perished as well. The Nazis persecuted homosexuals ruthlessly, identifying them in the death camps with pink stars.

One of the most haunting questions of World War II is at what point the leaders of the Allies and of neutral states actually learned that the Nazis were undertaking the extermination of an entire people. Rumors of mass exterminations had begun to reach Britain and the United States in 1942, although the details were not known. Even after confirmation provided by four young Jews who escaped from Auschwitz in the summer of 1942, and by information arriving via the Polish underground and diffused by the Polish government in London, many people—including even some leaders of the Jewish communities in Britain, Palestine, and the United States—refused to believe "the terrible secret." ("Who, after all, speaks today of the annihilation of the Armenians [by the Turks in 1915]?" Hitler exclaimed just before the war.) Articles in British, Swiss, and U.S. newspapers began to relate the mass killings of Jews. Pope Pius XII (pope 1939–1958), who had served as the Vatican's representative in Berlin before his election as pope and who issued no papal encyclicals condemning anti-Semitism, knew of the death camps by the end of 1943. Yet the pope did no more than offer reminders of the necessity of "justice and charity" in the world.

The U.S. and British governments had no official reactions to the terrifying news. A head of the British intelligence service claimed that Poles and Jews were exaggerating "in order to stoke us up." President Roosevelt certainly knew by the summer of 1942, but he rejected the idea of retaliatory bombing of German civilians. He believed that only a sustained military effort could defeat the Nazis. With Hitler's invasion of Russia having gone awry, it looked as though the tide was beginning to turn against Germany. The Allied governments feared that if too much publicity was given to the disappearance of hundreds of thousands of Jews—millions seemed simply too many to believe—it might generate calls to aid them directly. This, they worried, might undercut the united war effort. The Holocaust continued until the very end of the war; by then 6.2 million Jews had been murdered.

Collaboration

In Western Europe, the Nazis found leaders willing to follow German directives obediently and often enthusiastically. In Norway, Vidkun Quisling (1887–1945), organizer of a fascist party in the 1930s, became the puppet head of state in Norway, his name entering the dictionary as synonymous with traitor. In Belgium, principally Flanders, the Dutch-speaking part of the country, the German occupation gave the fascist leagues influence they had not had before the war. France had been divided by Germany in June 1940 into an occupied zone and a smaller southern zone that retained independence through collaboration with the Nazis. The free zone had its capital in the spa town of Vichy in central France, although in November 1942 German troops occupied all of France. The xenophobia and anti-Semitism of the right-wing French politicians and writers of the 1930s came to fruition in Vichy. Traditional conservatives dissatisfied with the Third Republic for religious and political reasons also lent their support to the Vichy regime.

The elderly Marshal Pétain served as the head of state of the Vichy government, which the United States officially recognized. He remained popular, at least until late 1942, because some people shared his anti-Marxism and anti-Semitism. He presented himself as having saved the French state from extinction at the hands of the German invaders.

But although Vichy may have temporarily saved the French state, Pétain and other collaborators sacrificed the French nation. In the "new order," "country, family, work" replaced "liberty, fraternity, equality" on French coins. Vichy proclaimed a "spiritual revival" against "decadence." Pétain dissolved the Chamber of Deputies and favored the Catholic Church by banning Masonic lodges and divorce. As in Mussolini's Italy, Vichy attempted to impose a structure of "corporatism" on the French economy and society, but with little success. These vertical economic structures were intended to replace unions, which, as in Germany and Italy, became illegal.

The Vichy *milice* (police) raiding a French farmhouse looking for *maquis* (resisters).

Vichy enacted restrictions on Jews similar to those in force in Germany. Beginning in October 1940, a series of laws forbade Jews from holding jobs in public service, education, or cultural affairs, or in professions such as medicine and law. A law in July 1941 sought "to eliminate all Jewish influence in the national economy"; the state appointed a trustee who could sell any property or liquidate any business owned by Jews.

These exclusions were only the beginning. French police cooperated with German soldiers after Hitler's May 1941 order to round up 3,600 Polish Jews in France. In December, the Vichy government proclaimed that it would collaborate with the Nazis with "acts, not words," and did just that. In July 1942, the French police seized 13,000 Jews, most of them foreign-born, in Paris, sending them to death camps in the east. Premier Pierre Laval (1883–1945) insisted that children be sent along with their parents. A Parisian woman later recalled, "I saw a train pass. In front, a car containing French police and German soldiers. Then came cattle cars, sealed. The thin arms of children clasped the grating. A hand waved outside like a leaf in a storm. When the train slowed down, voices cried, 'Mama!' And nothing answered except the squeaking of the springs of the train." Vichy France was the only territory in Europe in which local authorities deported Jews without the presence of German occupying forces, at least in the so-called free zone until November 1942. A militia of determined collaborators created in January 1943 continued to round up Jews, seeking to crush all resistance.

Resistance

Everyone in German-occupied territories knew the potential cost of resistance. In Czechoslovakia, the assassination in May 1942 of Reinhard Heydrich brought the destruction of the entire village of Lidice and most of its inhabitants. When partisans killed ten Germans in a Yugoslav town in October 1941, the Nazis retaliated by massacring 7,000 men, women, and children.

Yet people did resist. On April 19, 1943, the Jewish ghetto in Warsaw, from which already about 300,000 Jews had been sent to the death camps after German troops had concentrated Jews there from other places, rose up against the Nazis. They were crushed almost a month later with the loss of at least 12,000 lives. Thousands of those who had survived perished in the camps. Poland had what amounted to a secret underground state linked to the government in exile, many clandestine publications, and a "Home Army" about 300,000 strong, whose members fought with Allied troops in Europe and Africa, On August 1, 1944, the Warsaw Uprising began. After two months of intense fighting, German military strength again won out, with 200,000 Poles perishing in the fighting or executed afterwards.

Resistance movements were most effective where hills and mountains offered protection from German troops, as in central and southern France, Greece, and Yugoslavia. Active and effective resistance was least possible in the flatlands of Holland, western Belgium, Moravia, and northern France, areas in which it was difficult to hide and where there were heavy concentrations of German troops, and many collaborators as well. Wherever possible, the Allies dropped supplies to resistance groups. But only in Yugoslavia and, to some extent, France, did the resistance movements help bring about Germany's defeat.

In Yugoslavia, the tenacious Croatian Communist Josip Broz (1892–1980), who became known by his code name of Tito, formed the first army of partisans able to engage the Germans effectively in combat. Tito had served in the Austro-Hungarian army during World War I and was badly wounded and captured. Returning in 1920 to newly independent Yugoslavia, he became an active trade unionist and in 1923 joined the Yugoslav Communist Party. Tito spent six years in prison for his political activities. In 1937 he was named general secretary of the Communist Party.

Tito's partisans fought courageously against the collaborationist Yugoslav puppet states. The Croatian minister of education voiced the opinion that a third of the Serbs should be forced to convert, a third expelled from Croatia, and a third killed. Croatian forces killed 300,000 Serbs. The Cyrillic alphabet used by Serbs became illegal. When asked if he did not fear the punishment of God for what he had done, a fascist (Ustaša) guard retorted,

Marshal Tito (Josip Broz), pictured on the right, Communist head of the Yugoslav Resistance, with his wartime staff in the mountains of Yugoslavia, 1944.

"Don't talk to me about that. . . . For my past, present and future deeds I shall burn in hell, but at least I shall burn for Croatia." At the same time, members of the conservative Serb resistance (Chetniks), who remained loyal to the Yugoslav king, killed thousands of Croats and other non-Serbs.

Tito insisted on cooperation between Serb and Croat resisters, and maintained contacts with non-Communist groups. Protected by the rugged mountains of Croatia, Tito commanded 20,000 men by 1943. Despite being hounded by German, Italian, and Bulgarian troops, and both Croatian fascists and Serb Chetniks, he managed to carve out entire zones under his control. Late in the war, the British government ended support for the Chetniks and began to supply Tito's forces with heavy equipment. Yugoslav partisans tied up entire Italian and German divisions. Tito established local Communist committees to serve as governing authorities in each region liberated.

On June 18, 1940, General Charles de Gaulle, broadcasting from London, called on the French people to resist German rule. The next month, Churchill established an agency in London to provide material assistance to resistance groups. Churchill grudgingly respected de Gaulle for his uncompromising will to oppose the Nazis and the Vichy collaborators, but he also detested him personally. The same room could not hold the two domineering personalities. Roosevelt believed the towering Frenchman dangerously ambitious, a potential thorn in the Allied side. In December 1941, de Gaulle surprised the Allies by sending a small force to capture the French islands of Saint Pierre and Miquelon off the coast of Newfoundland, which were controlled by Vichy France.

Roosevelt believed that there was nothing to be gained from recognizing de Gaulle's London-based "Free French" movement as the legitimate French government. The U.S. government hoped that Vichy might be convinced to try to keep French North Africa out of German hands. The British and U.S. governments worried that recognizing de Gaulle's movement might alienate many people in France. In the meantime, Vichy propaganda repeatedly reminded the public that the British navy had sunk French ships in July 1940, with a huge loss of life.

Several resistance movements in France were united only by a hatred of Nazi occupation and Vichy collaboration. Communists, despite not officially turning against Vichy until Germany attacked the Soviet Union in June 1941, formed a well-organized and effective resistance force, building on pre-war organizational networks. Jean Moulin (1899–1943), a former departmental prefect during the Third Republic, led de Gaulle's Free French resistance in France. Moulin managed early in May 1943 to unify the resistance groups within the National Council of Resistance. He was betrayed by a collaborator and died under torture in July 1943 without revealing the names of others in the resistance network.

Resistance spread when the Germans in 1943 began to force France to provide workers for factories in Germany. Many of those refusing to go to

Germany fled into the hills and mountains of France. These resistance bands came to be called the *maquis,* a name for rugged brush in the south of France that could conceal them.

Better armed by airplane drops of guns, the *maquis* grew bolder. By 1944, they controlled some areas in southern France, at least at night, vulnerable only to the arrival of German military columns, diversions that the German army could by then ill afford. General Dwight Eisenhower (1890–1969), commander of Allied forces in the European theater of operations, later claimed that the resistance in France was the equivalent of fifteen military divisions.

Against Hitler in Germany

The vast majority of Germans remained loyal to their Führer, even as defeats mounted and Allied bombers frequently droned overhead and news of horrendous losses on the Russian front became known. Disgruntlement and bitter jokes were common, but they did not threaten the regime. Those who had never approved of Hitler retreated into family life and the daily struggle to get by. When wartime deprivation left people grumbling, Germans tended to blame Hitler's subordinates, not the Führer.

German resistance against Hitler was fragmented and ineffective. Courts sentenced 15,000 Germans to death for crimes against the state, under an expanded definition of capital crimes, which included listening to BBC radio broadcasts from London. Trade union and Communist groups, earlier smashed by the S.S., emerged again as economic conditions worsened in 1942 and 1943. Some students in Munich and Communists in Berlin bravely distributed anti-Nazi propaganda, but such courageous acts were not widespread. About 250,000 people in Germany were imprisoned or forced to emigrate because of their political opposition and at least 150,000 German Communists were executed. The active connivance of ordinary Germans aided the S.S. and Gestapo in rooting out potential sources of opposition. Even humane gestures toward Jews or foreign workers were dangerous. Here and there, young people responded to Nazism by adopting a counterculture of nonconformity, refusing to join the Hitler Youth, listening to American music deemed decadent by Hitler, and scrawling anti-Nazi graffiti on walls. The Nazis publicly hanged several sixteen-year-old boys for such actions.

The only serious plot against Hitler came among traditional conservatives within the army. On July 20, 1944, Colonel Claus von Stauffenberg (1907–1944) carried a bomb in his briefcase to a staff meeting with Hitler near the Russian front. Stauffenberg, who had been badly maimed in battle, was a conservative aristocrat appalled by the Nazi murder of Jews and Soviets and by what he considered Hitler's amateur management of the war. He hoped that Hitler's assassination would allow the army to impose its rule. He placed the bomb under the table beneath Hitler, who instinctively shoved the briefcase out of his way, moving it to the other side of a heavy table support.

The bomb exploded, wounding Hitler slightly. Those implicated in the plot were quickly arrested and slowly strangled by nooses of piano wire as they writhed on meat hooks. Movie cameras recorded their agonizing death for the later amusement of Hitler, his mistress, and friends. Hitler also ordered the execution of about 5,000 other Germans in positions of authority whose loyalty seemed suspect, including family members of conspirators. Thousands of Germans poured into the streets in major cities to celebrate their Führer's escape from death.

The Tide Turns

By the end of 1942, the Germans were on the defensive on the high seas, in the Soviet Union, and in North Africa, where Italian forces were routed and German forces pushed back (see Map 26.6). The entry of the United States into the war in December 1941 helped turn the tide against Germany. American war supplies and then armed forces strengthened the Allied cause as they had in World War I. The German war machine was chaotically managed and German resources increasingly inadequate to fighting a war on so many fronts.

Hitler's invasion of Russia turned into a full-fledged military disaster, culminating in the crushing defeat and surrender of German forces at Stalingrad in February 1943. As Hitler's Balkan allies one by one pulled out of the war, the Allies launched an invasion of Italy from North Africa, forcing the king of Italy to agree to a secret armistice and pushing German troops to retreat to the north. On June 6, 1944, Western Allied forces launched a massive invasion of France, landing on the beaches of Normandy, and forcing the German army to pull back, fighting all the way. The Allies first reached the Rhine River in March 1945.

Now confident of victory over Hitler, the Big Three (Churchill, Roosevelt, and Stalin) began to plan for the end of the war. As the Soviet army began to push the Germans back across a broad front in July 1943, it became clear that when the war ended, the Red Army could control large parts of Eastern and Central Europe. This probability brought dissension to the Big Three, particularly as Churchill feared that the Red Army might never leave the Eastern European nations it liberated from German occupation.

Germany on the Defensive

With the majority of German men between the ages of eighteen and fifty in the army, Germany's war machine required more workers. By late 1941, there were already 4 million foreigners working in Germany, including prisoners of war (in violation of international agreements), and in May 1944, almost twice that number, the majority of whom were Soviet citizens. More German women now worked in the factories.

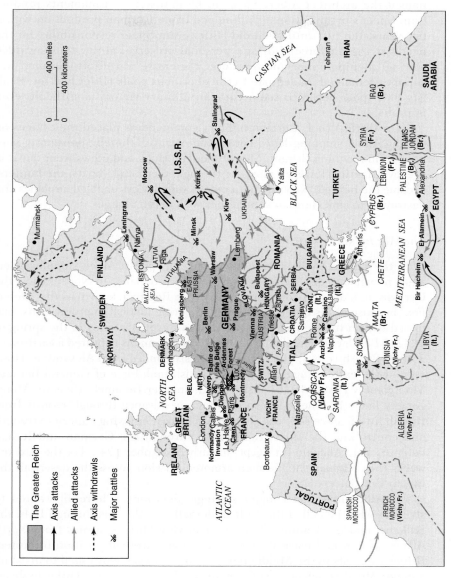

The Greater Reich

Axis attacks

Allied attacks

Axis withdrawls

Major battles

400 miles

400 kilometers

0

0

CASPIAN SEA

IRAN

Teheran

Murmansk

Moscow

U.S.S.R.

Stalingrad

Kursk

Leningrad

Narva

Kiev

UKRAINE

Yalta

BLACK SEA

SAUDI ARABIA

IRAQ (Br.)

SYRIA (Fr.)

TURKEY

CYPRUS (Br.)

LEBANON (Fr.)

PALESTINE (Br.)

TRANS-JORDAN (Br.)

Alexandria

EGYPT

El Alamein

Bir Hacheim

MEDITERRANEAN SEA

CRETE

Athens

GREECE

ALBANIA (It.)

MONT.

BULGARIA

ROMANIA

SERBIA

Budapest

Sarajevo

Zagreb

CROATIA

HUNGARY

AUSTRIA

SLOVAKIA

Vienna

Trieste

Cassino

Anzio

Rome

Naples

ITALY

Milan

SWITZ.

GERMANY

Prague

Berlin

EAST PRUSSIA

Königsberg

Warsaw

Lemberg

Minsk

Riga

LITHUANIA

LATVIA

ESTONIA

BALTIC SEA

FINLAND

SWEDEN

NORWAY

DENMARK

Copenhagen

NORTH SEA

NETH.

BELG.

LUX.

Antwerp

Ardennes Forest

Battle of the Bulge

Rhine R.

Po R.

Metz

Paris

Dieppe

Calais

Le Havre

Caen

Normandy Invasion

London

GREAT BRITAIN

IRELAND

ATLANTIC OCEAN

Bordeaux

FRANCE

VICHY FRANCE

Marseille

CORSICA (Vichy Fr.)

SARDINIA (It.)

SICILY

MALTA (Br.)

Tunis

TUNISIA (Vichy Fr.)

LIBYA (It.)

ALGERIA (Vichy Fr.)

SPAIN

PORTUGAL

SPANISH MOROCCO

FRENCH MOROCCO (Vichy Fr.)

In the meantime, Germany's day-to-day operation of the war effort remained chaotic, as ministries, military branches, and Hitler's favored henchmen competed against each other. In the spring of 1942, Hitler named the architect Albert Speer to be minister of armaments production. Speer's organizational skill helped triple German production within two years. But not until 1944 did Hitler grant Speer responsibility for the needs of the air force, Göring's personal preserve. Hitler then awarded Göring "plenipotentiary powers" over the entire war effort. German war supplies remained inadequate to the enormous goals Hitler had set. Realists like Speer began to see a German military victory as difficult, even improbable.

As in World War I, German military commanders placed their hopes on closing Allied shipping lanes across the Atlantic, thereby preventing supplies from reaching Britain. Many American ships and crews went down in the icy Atlantic. However, most got through. German U-boats, the hunters, became the hunted. New submarine-detecting devices enabled airplanes and destroyers to sink German submarines with depth charges.

The War in North Africa

With the failure of the submarine campaign against Allied shipping, Germany now had to depend on its army's success on land. In North Africa, the German tank division commanded by Erwin Rommel, known as the "Desert Fox" because of his quick judgment and daring tactical improvisations, had forced British troops back from Libya into Egypt. Victories in the spring of 1942 at Bir Hacheim and Tobruk, where the Germans captured a garrison of 35,000 British troops, put Rommel only sixty miles from Alexandria. However, at the end of August 1942, the British tank force of General Bernard Montgomery (1887–1976) pushed back another Rommel offensive. Montgomery knew his enemy's plan of attack in advance through reports from British intelligence services. The Allied forces, enjoying superior strength and controlling the skies, then broke through the German and Italian defenses at El Alamein (in Egypt) in early November 1942. For the next ten weeks they pursued the German armored division across the desert all the way to Tunisia.

The Allies now faced major strategic decisions. Churchill wanted to strike at what he called the "soft underbelly" of the axis through Italy, the Balkans, and the Danube Basin after driving Hitler's armies from North Africa. This would leave British forces in an excellent position to protect British interests in the Middle East. Stalin, however, continued to insist on a major Allied attack against Germany in the west to force Hitler to divert resources from the Russian campaign. Stalin pointed out that the Red Army had borne the brunt of the war against Hitler, inflicting 90 percent of the losses the German armed forces had suffered in battle since June 1941. Churchill, however, feared that a direct confrontation with the

Free French troops attacking in the North African desert, 1942.

largest concentration of German troops might be disastrous and wanted to postpone a cross-Channel invasion of France as long as possible.

With the Axis reeling in North Africa and British troops now controlling Egypt and Libya, the Allied commanders now decided first to drive all German and Italian troops out of North Africa before contemplating an invasion of France from Britain. They had been sobered by a disastrous cross-Channel raid by Canadian troops against the French port of Dieppe in August 1942.

In November 1942, the Allies launched "Operation Torch." A British and American force commanded by American General Eisenhower landed on the coast of French Algeria and Morocco, easily overcoming Vichy French resistance. To his consternation, de Gaulle now learned that the Allies were negotiating with the Vichy commander in North Africa, Admiral Jean Darlan (1881–1942). Despite Pétain's order that Vichy forces in North Africa continue to oppose the Allied invasion, Darlan ordered his troops to accept a cease-fire after three days of fighting. Hitler used Darlan's capitulation in North Africa as an excuse in November 1942 for German forces to occupy the "free" zone of Vichy France. Little now remained of Vichy's illusion of independence. French naval commanders scuttled their own ships to prevent them from being used by the German navy.

The Allies named Darlan as "the head of the French state" in return for his promise that French troops in North Africa would now join the Allies. De Gaulle demanded that Britain and the United States recognize his

French Committee of National Liberation as France's legitimate government. But Churchill, an old imperialist, viewed with concern de Gaulle's pressing determination to maintain France's empire, in the context of the two powers' long-standing imperial rivalry. Churchill feared that if the British government recognized de Gaulle as the head of the French state, it would be committing itself to supporting a new France, the direction of which could not yet be seen. A French monarchist solved part of the Allied dilemma by assassinating Darlan. The Allies forced de Gaulle to share leadership of Free France with another general, a slap in the face that de Gaulle neither forgot nor forgave. After the defeat of a vigorous German counterattack, by the end of May 1943, no German or Italian troops remained in North Africa.

The Allies' strategic bombing campaign, the goal of which was to sap German morale as much as to hamper the production of planes and guns, began to take its toll in 1943. The American poet Randall Jarrell remembered, "In bombers named for girls, we burned / the cities we had learned about in school." The Royal Air Force could now strike at night with reasonable accuracy, and the ability to scramble German radar reduced losses. British bombers dumped tons of bombs during night raids over the industrial Ruhr Valley and major cities. Many American bombers were lost despite fighter escorts because the U.S. Air Force preferred daytime attacks, when pilots could more easily find their targets. However, the impact of the strategic bombing campaign on German wartime industrial production was far below Allied expectations.

Hitler's Russian Disaster

On the eastern front, Hitler's invasion of the Soviet Union turned into a military disaster. Defeats in Russia during the last months of 1942 and in 1943 sent the German invaders reeling. The Red Army was now receiving better and more plentiful supplies from the Allies through the icy northern port of Murmansk and from Iran in the south. By now Soviet factories were turning out a steady supply of tanks and trucks equipped to fight in the snow and ice. German tanks faced not only improved Soviet tanks but also handmade incendiary bombs consisting of bottles, gasoline, and cloth fuses known derisively as "Molotov cocktails," after the Soviet foreign minister, which had first been used by Finnish partisans against Soviet troops.

Improvements in the organization and discipline of the Red Army also made their mark. Stalin held back on the ideological indoctrination and murderous purges that had characterized the 1930s. The Soviet army that Hitler had once mocked, now larger and more effectively deployed than his own, wore down German forces.

In the north, Leningrad, first reached by German troops in July 1941, held on against a German siege that lasted 506 days, the longest in modern history. More than 300,000 Soviet troops were killed; more than a million Russian civilians starved to death. Hitler's printed invitations to celebrate

Leningrad's fall could never be sent out. Further defeats in the north made Germany's drive to the Soviet oil fields of the Caucasus Mountains, and the Donets Basin industrial region in the south, all the more critical. In the south, the Red Army slowed the German advance toward Stalingrad, a strategically located industrial city on the Volga River.

The battle of Stalingrad, which began in November 1942, was a great turning point in the European war. The Soviets had begun concentrating a huge force around the city, even as early German successes deluded Hitler into thinking Stalingrad's fall was inevitable. As Soviet troops held off the German assault in house-to-house fighting, Hitler confidently began to transfer some of his exhausted troops to the north. The Soviet army counterattacked on November 19, trapping the weakened German armies as Soviet tanks moved easily across the frozen ground. From Berlin, Hitler ordered his troops to hold out until the last man. By the time German survivors surrendered on February 2, 1943, the German army had lost more than 300,000 soldiers.

Soviet troops fought their way into Leningrad. In July 1943, in a battle involving more than 9,000 tanks, the Red Army lost many times more men and tanks in a decisive battle in and around the city of Kursk, 500 miles south of Moscow. In the greatest tank battle ever fought, the Soviets managed to repell a massive German attack against an exposed Soviet line of defense and then pushed the Germans back, with a huge loss of life, a Pyrrhic victory. This further depleted the German armored divisions that had once seemed invincible. The Soviets were now battering the enemy on three fronts, even as Hitler was forced to divert troops to Italy and the

Red Army soldiers pick their way through the rubble of Stalingrad.

Devastation in Hamburg (*left*) and Stuttgart (*right*) after Allied bombing of Germany.

Balkans. The Red Army recaptured all of the Crimea in the south by May 1943, pushing the Germans back to Ukraine in the summer.

In February 1944, Soviet troops reached what had been the eastern Polish border before the German invasion. In the meantime, waves of British and American bombers continued to devastate German cities; over 40,000 people perished in attacks on Hamburg in July 1943, during which more than 9,000 tons of bombs rained down on the port city.

One by one, Germany's Balkan allies bailed out. Romanian troops had greatly aided the Nazi campaign in Odessa and the Crimea; Romanian oil and wheat had fueled the German war effort. Now, in March 1944, seeing the writing on the wall, the Romanian government approached the Allies, hoping to arrange a separate peace. In August, King Michael finally ended Ion Antonescu's military dictatorship, and the new Romanian government declared war on Germany.

Hitler intended Bulgaria to serve as a buffer against a possible Allied invasion from Turkey. Bulgaria enjoyed the most autonomy of any Nazi-held Eastern European state because it provided Germany with badly needed grain, permitted German military bases on its territory, and had declared war on Britain and the United States back in 1941. Hitler had allowed Bulgaria to annex Thrace from Greece (where Bulgarian forces had executed thousands of Greeks and banned the Greek language) and to take Greek and Yugoslav Macedonia. Now, as Germany's defeat appeared increasingly likely, the Bulgarian government brazenly announced its war against the Allies had ended. The Soviet Union declared war on Bulgaria in

September 1944. Following a popular insurrection, the Soviet Union controlled the resulting coalition government, as in the case of Romania. Soviet domination began to take shape.

The Allied Invasion of Italy

With North Africa and its airfields secure, the Allies decided to invade Sicily as a first step in an invasion of southern Italy. The plunging morale and material conditions of the Italian population, who had been promised an empire by Mussolini but had received only hardship, contributed to the Allied decision.

In July 1943, Palermo and Messina quickly fell to Allied troops. The fascist Grand Council asked King Victor Emmanuel III to end Mussolini's dictatorship. The king, eager to save his throne and fearing a complete German takeover, dismissed the stunned Mussolini as prime minister and ordered his arrest. The new government, while announcing that Italy would continue to fight alongside Germany, began secret negotiations with the Allies. When Hitler learned this in September 1943, he ordered his troops to occupy Italian airfields.

At a minimum, an Allied invasion of the Italian mainland would tie up considerable numbers of German troops and probably knock Italy completely out of the war. Romanian oil fields would be within reach of bombers taking off in Italy. The Italian resistance had gained momentum. Socialists, Catholic groups, and above all, Communists began to print clandestine newspapers and organize scattered attacks against fascists. The United States, still pushing for a full-scale landing in France, reluctantly agreed to the Italian invasion. In the meantime, the Italian king, fearing Hitler's wrath, reassured Germany of Italy's loyal participation in the war as an ally. However, the Italian government signed an armistice with the Allies on September 3, 1943. Victor Emmanuel naively hoped that Italy could make peace with both Germany and the Allies, and that his monarchy would survive the end of the war.

On the same day that the armistice was signed between Italy and the Allies, British and Canadian troops crossed the Strait of Messina, beginning the invasion of the Italian peninsula. The king and his family fled Rome with the new prime minister, leaving a million Italian soldiers with the choice of being interned by the Germans or deserting their units. Most deserted and 80,000 Allied prisoners of war escaped from camps in Italy.

The Allies set up a new government in the south, its members drawn from the resistance groups. In the meantime, on September 12, 1943, a daring German commando raid freed Mussolini from a mountaintop prison. In Berlin, Hitler proclaimed the Duce head of the "Italian Social Republic," a puppet regime. Mussolini ordered the execution of the members of the Grand Council who had opposed him and denounced the Italian people for having betrayed him.

The Germans slowly retreated behind one river after the next, with both sides taking large losses. The new front settled on a series of fortifications a hundred miles south of Rome, over which stood the old monastery of Monte Cassino. In January 1944, two Allied divisions landed behind the German lines at Anzio. Only in the spring, after terrible losses, were Allied troops able to break through the German defenses to free their armies still trapped near Anzio. The Allies took Rome on June 4, 1944. The German armies fell back to establish a new defensive perimeter south of the Po River between Pisa and Florence.

The Big Three

Soviet advances against German forces increasingly focused Western attention on the future of Central and Eastern Europe and the Balkans once Hitler's Germany had been defeated. At a meeting in Casablanca, Morocco, in January 1943, Churchill and Roosevelt had concerned themselves only with military strategy and not with the future of Europe. With Stalin absent, the British and American governments agreed to put off discussions of the territorial settlements that would follow Germany's defeat. Churchill and Stalin had already informally agreed to Soviet absorption of the Baltic states after the war. They did so despite the opposition of Roosevelt, who argued that Stalin had joined the war against the Nazis only after Hitler had attacked the Soviet Union.

Stalin's insistence that the United States and Britain open another front in the west by invading France in part stemmed from his fear that his allies wanted to see the Red Army slowed in its drive westward. As deliveries of Allied supplies to Russia through Murmansk trickled to a halt, Stalin seemed confirmed in his suspicions.

Meeting at Moscow in October 1943, the British, American, and Soviet foreign ministers reaffirmed an agreement that the Allies would accept nothing less than Germany's unconditional surrender. The Allies also reaffirmed their intention, originally stated in the Atlantic Charter of August 1941 signed by Roosevelt and Churchill, that a United Nations organization replace the ineffective, moribund League of Nations. But again they left open the thorny question of the political future of Central and Eastern Europe and the Balkans after the war.

Stalin finally met Churchill and Roosevelt in Teheran in November 1943. The leaders formulated harsh plans for post-war Germany. Stalin stated that the Soviet Union was not about to contemplate any change in its border with Poland as it existed in June 1941, the result of the Soviet invasion and absorption of much of eastern Poland in 1939. Yet, despite the occasional flurry of improvisational map-making—using knives, forks, and matchboxes on the tablecloths—the Big Three still left the essential specifics of the proposed outlines of post-war Europe for the future.

The D-Day Invasion of France

At Teheran, Stalin and Roosevelt convinced Churchill to accept a plan for the invasion of France. General Dwight Eisenhower coordinated the "D-Day" landing in France, "Operation Overlord." Born in a small town in Kansas, Eisenhower was a forthright man of integrity. Beneath his sparkling blue eyes, folksy manner, and smile lay shrewdness, cunning, and a remarkable ability for organization. The plan was for 150,000 troops to attack the English Channel beaches of Normandy in western France, followed in the next days and weeks by almost 500,000 more. About 4 million tons of support materiel would have to be landed as well. Floating caissons and old ships sunk off the coast would provide three makeshift harbors. In the meantime, German commanders believed that the most likely place for an all-out assault was near Calais to the north, which offered the closest crossing points from England.

The first hours of Operation Overlord would be crucial. The Allies needed to take and protect a beachhead that would allow the bulk of their troops to get ashore quickly. Planes would drop squadrons of parachutists behind German lines. Hitler had assigned Rommel to organize the German defense against the Allied invasion. Defenders would depend on the rapid arrival of armored units to back up the coastal batteries and infantry units trying to hold their positions against attacking Allied troops.

After a one-day postponement because of a gale, at dawn on the morning of June 6, 1944, Allied troops struggled ashore in shallow water from landing craft and established beachheads on the coast of Normandy. They confronted murderous fire from the cliffs above, taking heavy losses. But the landing succeeded, at least in part because the German air force was outnumbered by 20 to 1. As more men, tanks, trucks, and materiel came ashore, German troops gradually fell back. By the end of July 1944, despite fierce resistance, the Allies held most of Normandy. After seven weeks, the Allies had landed 1.3 million troops and sustained over 120,000 casualties. The Germans lost 500,000 men trying to defend Normandy. Hitler allowed Rommel, discovered to have known about the plot against the Führer's life, to escape execution by committing suicide.

On August 15, 1944, another Allied army landed on the French Mediterranean coast and moved up the Rhône Valley with little opposition. In the meantime, the main Allied army pushed from Normandy toward Paris. Encouraged by the proximity of Allied troops, on August 19, an uprising began in Paris. Because de Gaulle demanded that a French unit be the first to reach the capital, French forces reached Paris on August 22, 1944. In October the British government recognized de Gaulle's administration as the legitimate government of France.

German resistance stiffened at the Rhine River, and the first Allied attempts to cross into Germany failed. Hitler, whose moods varied between wild optimism and resigned depression, had aged rapidly through recurring

U.S. troops wading ashore at Utah Beach, Normandy, June 6, 1944 after the first bloody assault.

bouts with illness. Now, although Germany's collapse seemed imminent, he again seemed confident, telling Albert Speer in November 1944, "I haven't the slightest intention of surrendering. Besides, November has always been my lucky month." In December, Hitler ordered a massive counterattack in the hills and forests of the Ardennes in Belgium and Luxembourg, with the goal of pushing rapidly toward the Belgian river port of Antwerp. After retreating forty-five miles, the U.S. army pushed the Germans back in the Battle of the Bulge.

As the Nazi army retreated in northern Italy, the Red Army approached Germany from the east. On every front, Allied troops increasingly found that their enemies turned out to be boys and older men who had been rushed to the front with virtually no training. German cities burned, notably Dresden, which American planes fire-bombed early in 1945. About 50,000 residents of Berlin died in Allied air attacks. In 1993, about one unexploded World War II bomb was still being discovered every day in Berlin.

Hitler, expressing confidence that the Big Three alliance would break up, held out hope for Germany's newly developed weapons, in which he had earlier expressed no interest: the deadly V-1 jet-propelled "flying bomb" could strike targets from 3,000 feet at speeds of 470 miles per hour; the terrifying V-2 rocket could fly faster than the speed of sound. Launched from France, the first V-1 struck London on June 12, 1944, doing considerable damage. The first jet- and rocket-propelled fighter planes, the former reaching speeds of 500 miles per hour, arrived in time to join the Battle of the Bulge, but without significant effect. Many ordinary Germans, too, clung to the hope that such a new weapon would turn things around, or that the Western democracies would join Germany in a war against the Soviets. However, with defeat ever closer, Hitler accepted, even desired, the total destruction of Germany, considering it better than the shame of surrender.

ALLIED VICTORY

Romania and Bulgaria had surrendered in August and September 1944, respectively. With the Red Army in control of much of the Balkans, the question was not if Berlin would be taken, but when, and by whom. Though worried that the Soviets sought a preponderant role in Central Europe, as well as in Poland and the Balkans, Eisenhower was prepared to allow the Red Army the prestige of capturing Berlin. The much greater problem still remained: the future of Germany and Eastern Europe. As the Red Army moved closer to Berlin, the meetings of the Big Three in the waning months of the year proved exceptionally important for the future of Europe. Churchill and Stalin met in Moscow in October 1944 and worked out a rough division of post-war Western and Soviet interests in Central and Eastern Europe. By the time the Big Three came together at Yalta in Crimea in February 1945, German armies were falling back rapidly on every front and the Red Army was closing in on Berlin. The American army crossed the Rhine River on March 8, and on April 25, 1945, met up with Soviet troops at the Elbe River just sixty miles south of Berlin.

Victory in Europe

Churchill was determined to work out an informal agreement with the Soviets as to the respective spheres of influence in the Balkans when the war ended. In October 1944, he met with Stalin in Moscow. This time Roosevelt, who suspected Churchill of trying to maintain the British Empire at all costs, did not participate. Churchill later described the conference with Stalin: "I said, 'Let us settle about our affairs in the Balkans. How would it do for you to have ninety percent of the say in Romania, for us to have ninety percent of the say in Greece, and go fifty-fifty about Yugoslavia?'" After adding 75 percent for the Soviet Union in Bulgaria and fifty-fifty for Hungary, the British prime minister pushed the paper across to Stalin. "There was a slight pause. Then he took his blue pencil and made a large tick upon it, and passed it back to us. It was all settled in no more time than it takes to sit down."

When the Big Three met in the Soviet Black Sea resort of Yalta in February 1945, the Red Army had drawn within 100 miles of Berlin. Some soldiers in the Red Army enacted terrible revenge against the Germans, encouraged by Soviet propaganda that emphasized the necessity of humiliating the defeated German population, as well as by the impersonal nature of the war. Soviet soldiers, some of whom had come upon the ghastly death camps in Poland, gunned down German soldiers who had surrendered, and pillaged villages. Soviet soldiers sometimes systematically raped all German females who were more than about twelve years old. Hungarian and Romanian women also were attacked—in Hungary, Soviet soldiers entered a mental hospital, where they raped and killed. Soviet officers tried to bring the situation under control but incidents of rape occurred for several years in Germany after the Nazi defeat. For some Soviets the occupation seemed to represent a continuation of the war and the exacting of revenge.

Soviet military might in Eastern and Central Europe hung over Yalta, where the Allies considered the post-war fate of Germany. Churchill agreed to the post-war division of Germany into British, American, French, and Soviet zones of military occupation. The Soviet zone would be eastern Germany. In Eastern Europe, Communist Party members were working feverishly to expand Soviet influence. Stalin feared that his wartime allies might lead a post-war campaign against communism, which had been the case after World War I. He secretly agreed to Roosevelt's demand that the Soviet Union declare war on Japan three months after Germany's defeat, which the U.S. president believed would expedite Japan's defeat in Asia. But, in exchange, Stalin asked for and received Allied promises that the Soviet Union would control Outer Mongolia, the Kurile Islands, the southern half of Sakhalin Island, and its former naval base at Port Arthur.

Outlines of the Cold War began to take shape at Yalta. Stalin insisted that the new government of Poland be based on the provisional Polish Communist government (to which would be added representatives from the non-Communist Polish government, which had been functioning in London

Joseph Stalin, Franklin Roosevelt, Winston Churchill, and Vyacheslav Molotov at the Yalta Conference, 1945.

during the war). Churchill and Roosevelt also went along with Stalin's insistence that the Soviet Union keep the parts of eastern Poland that had been absorbed by the Soviet invasion in 1939. Poland's western frontier with Germany was to be left to a future conference, one that was never held. The Big Three all agreed that free elections would be held in Eastern Europe. Yet Stalin defied the Atlantic Charter of 1941, when the Allies had agreed that free elections would lead to democratic governments in the nations freed from German occupation, by setting up an unelected puppet government in Romania, as well as Poland.

At Yalta, the Allies remembered that the League of Nations had been doomed in its attempts to keep the peace by the nonparticipation of the then-isolationist United States and by the exclusion of the Soviet Union from the League. Roosevelt wanted to avoid committing the United States to an active role in post-war Europe. He counted instead on the United Nations to resolve future problems by facilitating collective security. In the meantime, with the Red Army occupying Eastern Europe, Stalin held all the cards. Eastern European peoples subsequently had reason to view Yalta as a betrayal and a victory for Stalin.

The awful world conflict moved toward an end. The Red Army launched a final attack on Berlin in April 1945. Italian partisans captured Mussolini near the Swiss frontier. They executed him and his mistress, hanging their bodies upside down at a gas station. Himmler, von Ribbentrop, and Göring

Soldiers from the Red Army hoist the Soviet flag over the German Reichstag in Berlin.

now agreed that Germany must end the war. As Soviet tanks drew near on the night of April 28–29, 1945, Hitler married his longtime mistress, Eva Braun, in the depths of a fortified bunker in central Berlin. Then they committed suicide on April 30 as the rumble of Russian tanks could be heard above. Joseph Goebbels poisoned his six children, shot his wife, and killed himself. Admiral Karl Dönitz, to whom Hitler had delegated authority, surrendered to the Allies on May 8, 1945. The Reich that Hitler had once bragged would last for a thousand years lay in ruins twelve years after its creation.

The Defeat of Japan

The German collapse in North Africa, Russia, and Eastern Europe now allowed the Allies to turn their attention more fully to the war in the Pacific. The sheer scope of Japanese military operations, spread from the Aleutian Islands southwest of Alaska to the South Pacific, put Japan on the defensive. Troops and supplies poured into the Pacific from the United States, which had speedily reconstituted its fleet after the Pearl Harbor disaster. Victory in the Battle of the Coral Sea (May 1942), which turned back Japanese ships carrying troops to the southern coast of New Guinea, protected Australia from possible invasion. A month later, the American fleet and torpedo bombers inflicted a major defeat on the Japanese navy at the Battle of Midway, an island almost a thousand miles northwest of Hawaii (see Map 26.3), sinking four Japanese aircraft carriers.

In August 1942, an American offensive had begun against Guadalcanal, one of the South Pacific Solomon Islands. Guadalcanal fell on February 8, 1943, the first of the Japanese wartime conquests to be recaptured. American assaults in New Guinea and far north in the Aleutian Islands also succeeded. General MacArthur's forces began driving the Japanese from New Guinea in January 1943, completing the task early in 1944. The Americans then adopted the strategy of driving Japanese forces from one island to another, "leapfrogging" through the Pacific. Gradually, the U.S. navy gained control of the seas, its submarines picking off Japanese supply ships. Hard-earned summer victories brought U.S. troops within 1,400 miles of Tokyo. In October 1944, MacArthur's forces attacked the Philippines, defeating the Japanese fleet and the demoralized Japanese troops. There, the Japanese first used kamikaze tactics, suicide missions flown by pilots who crashed their planes into American ships.

The American capture of the island of Iwo Jima on March 27, 1945, brought U.S. planes to within 700 miles of Japan. On Okinawa, the next stop, piles of bleached human bones could still be seen on the beaches a decade after the war's end. Saipan and Guam provided bases from which American long-range bombers could reach Japan. American "super fortress" bombers showered Japanese cities with incendiary bombs that turned wooden buildings into fiery death traps. One attack destroyed 40 percent of Tokyo within three hours. American forces prepared to invade the southern islands of Japan itself. With the American fleet off Okinawa confronting suicide missions by Japanese pilots, it was clear that such an invasion would cost many lives.

Meanwhile, the United States was readying a new weapon hitherto unimaginable. The development of the atomic bomb (and its more lethal successor, the hydrogen bomb, first tested by the U.S. in 1954) had its origins in theories developed by Albert Einstein (see Chapter 19). In 1938, a German scientist in Berlin had achieved nuclear fission, splitting the atom and releasing tremendous energy. This meant that if a means could be found to split the nucleus of the atom, setting off a nuclear chain reaction, a bomb of enormous destructive power could be built. During the first years of the war, British and American scientists had worked separately on the project. German scientists, too, were working in the same direction. In the United States, German scientists who had fled the Nazis first discovered that an isotope of uranium could set off the anticipated chain reaction. At the same time, Soviet scientists were frantically trying to come up with the atomic bomb, but they were several crucial years behind American scientists.

In 1945, nuclear theory became reality, and the United States exploded the first atomic bomb in a desert in New Mexico on July 16. President Harry Truman (1884–1972; Roosevelt had died in April 1945) learned of this the day before the opening of the Potsdam Conference in the Berlin suburb in July 1945. He informed Stalin of the new weapon the United States now had at its disposal. The Potsdam Proclamation of July 26, 1945, warned Japan that it risked "prompt and utter destruction" if it did not agree to unconditional surrender. When Japanese resistance continued, a U.S. plane dropped an atomic bomb on the Japanese port city of Hiroshima on August 6, 1945, engulfing the city in a mushroom cloud of fire and radiation that killed 80,000 people. The Soviet Union then declared war on Japan and Soviet troops moved into Manchuria. On August 9, a U.S. plane dropped a second atomic bomb that destroyed much of Nagasaki, killing 36,000 people in a storm of fire. Thousands more would die of radiation sickness in the days, months, and years to follow.

On September 2, 1945, Japanese representatives signed documents of unconditional surrender on the battleship *Missouri*. The Second World War was over. But a new and potentially even more dangerous atomic age had begun.

CONCLUSION

The first Soviet troops arriving at the Nazi death camps discovered nightmarish horrors. Technology harnessed to the task of genocide had created factories of death. They came upon piles of corpses and of children's shoes; and the few lucky survivors—the living dead—barefoot human skeletons fortunate enough to have been liberated before their turn to be exterminated

(*Left*) A mushroom cloud envelops Nagasaki after the U.S. Army's deployment of an atomic bomb. (*Right*) The destruction after the atomic blast at Hiroshima.

had come. The death camps became perhaps the most awful symbol of the total war that was World War II, during which 6.2 million Jews perished, including 2.7 million Polish Jews. At the end of the war, only about 40,000 to 50,000 Polish Jews had survived the Holocaust.

World War II brought mass military mobilization and mass death. At least 17 million people were killed in the fighting and another 20 million civilians perished, half in the Soviet Union, not including those who died in Stalin's gulags. About 30 million people in China perished in the war begun by Japan in Manchuria in 1937. Germany lost more than 6 million people, Japan 2 million, and Britain and France lost about 250,000 and 300,000 respectively. Part of the horror of the period is that we will never really know the full extent of human loss. Millions had been wounded, many crippled for life. Millions of survivors had been carried far from home. Husbands, wives, children, and other relatives were often lost forever. Europe became a continent of "displaced persons," as they were called.

The psychological damage to those who lived through night bombing in shelters, those who spent years waiting for definitive news about missing loved ones, or those who had somehow survived the death camps, cannot be calculated. Europe seemed haunted by the sad memories of last conversations and letters. One survivor recalled his determination to hold on against all odds "to tell the story, to bear witness; and that to survive, we must force ourselves to save at least the skeleton, the scaffolding, the form of civilization."

After World War II, in contrast to the end of World War I, there seemed little optimism that such a total war could not occur again. Two factors, in particular, contributed to this new feeling of angst. The first was the rising tension even before the war ended between the Soviet Union and the Western Allies. The second was the development of rockets, the jet plane, and above all, the atomic bomb, a terrifying weapon for a new age.

The cataclysmic experience of the Second World War weighed heavily on the social, political, and cultural climate of the post-war era. In every country, those who resisted Nazi rule played a major part in the reconstitution of their nations after the war. Politicians, intellectuals, and virtually everyone else would try to come to grips with what had happened to Europe, to assess blame, and to find hope. For the moment, however, for many, it seemed enough to have survived.

PART SEVEN

EUROPE IN THE POST-WAR ERA

Following the devastation of World War II, Europe rebuilt under the growing shadow of the Cold War between the Western powers, led by the United States, and the Soviet Union. The dawn of the nuclear age added to rising tensions. The Soviet Red Army, which had liberated Eastern Europe from the Nazis, became an occupying force. In Poland, Czechoslovakia, Bulgaria, and the other states of Eastern Europe, Soviet-backed Communists pushed other political parties aside until they held unchallenged authority in each state. They nationalized industries and undertook massive forced collectivization of agriculture. Germany, devastated by total defeat, was divided into a western zone, which became the German Federal Republic (West Germany), and an eastern zone, which became the Communist German Democratic Republic (East Germany). Berlin, lying within East Germany, remained divided between East and West, and quickly became a particular focus of Cold War rivalry. Soviet intervention in 1956 to crush a revolt against Communist rule in Hungary further strained relations between East and West. The Cuban Missile Crisis of 1962 brought the United States and the Soviet Union to the brink of nuclear war. The United Nations became a battleground for the Cold War (see Chapter 28). Yet it was an arena for verbal battles—hostile words and strident denunciations were better than war.

Signs of gnawing poverty were not hard to find in every country in the post-war period. Only half of the houses in France had running water, and only a third of those in Austria, Spain, and Italy. Providing decent housing became a goal of governments in most countries. However, Western Europe did slowly recover from the ordeal of total war, and the relative peace and new prosperity engendered a "baby boom" (1946–1964), as in the United States. More and more people lived in cities, with fewer working the land, and a burgeoning culture of consumption took hold, increasingly influenced by America. The status of and opportunities for women gradually improved. Women finally achieved the right to vote in France and Italy. In Britain, the Labour government laid the foundations for the modern welfare state, with governments assuming increased responsibility for their citizens. The welfare state emerged in part out of the experience of state planning and social solidarity during World War II, as many countries began wide-ranging social services to aid and protect their people. Other Western states, too, increased the number of social services provided by their governments, as did their Communist counterparts.

The period between 1950 and 1973 was a period of dynamic economic growth in Western Europe. The number of people working in manufacturing or the service sector increased dramatically, as the percentage of people working the land fell. Reflecting the wartime experience, economic and social planning played an important part in the recovery of the European economy and its rapid expansion.

In the post-war period, movements for independence in the Asian and African colonies of the European powers led to rapid decolonization and further loss of European authority. The age of empire ended with decolonization. Britain granted independence to its former colonies. France, the Netherlands, Belgium, and Portugal also lost their empires, but after nationalist insurrections and bloody fighting.

Political change in Europe came rapidly in the 1970s and 1980s. In Greece, Spain, and Portugal, repressive dictatorships gave way to parliamentary regimes. Parties concerned with the environment—the "Greens"—made sizable political inroads in West Germany. But, at the same time, terrorism brought a new, unsettling dimension to political life. Terrorist groups threatened security in such areas as Northern Ireland and the Basque region of Spain, where nationalists were demanding independence, and in the Middle East, where militant Arab organizations opposed the policies of Israel (which became independent in 1948) toward the Palestinian people.

In the Soviet Union, following his rise to head of state in 1985, Soviet leader Mikhail Gorbachev initiated a bold series of economic and political reforms, hoping to maintain communism by eliminating its authoritarian nature, encouraging greater political participation, and bringing economic prosperity. When movements for reform arose in the countries of the Eastern European bloc, beginning in Poland and Hungary, Gorbachev made clear that the Soviet Union would not intervene. Communism collapsed in one Eastern European state after another in 1989. Throngs of East Germans pouring through the Berlin Wall in November 1989 symbolized the fall of communism in Eastern Europe. Germany became a unified state once again. The Soviet Union itself then broke apart, as one former Soviet republic after another declared independence. The Cold War ended, after having largely defined international relations since the end of World War II. The collapse of what has been called the Soviet Union's empire left the United States as the world's only superpower, with an informal empire of its own.

In the former Communist states, the challenges of achieving democratic rule with little or no democratic traditions or a successful market economy were daunting. The ethnic and religious complexity of these states compounded the difficulties. In the former Yugoslavia, a bloody civil war began in Bosnia in 1992. The war brought atrocities on a scale not seen since World War II, most of which were perpetuated by Serb forces against Muslims.

The post-war era also brought about European economic cooperation among Western states. European economic cooperation had begun in the years following World War II, with the founding of the Organization for European Economic Cooperation in 1948, the creation of the Common Market in 1959, and the European Community in 1967. The Treaty of Maastricht, signed in 1992 by the twelve members of the European Community, created the European Union, which had as a base a partnership between France and Germany. The single market that began for member states in 1993 led to the implementation of a common currency—the "euro"—in 2002 (although three states have retained their former currencies). Twenty-seven states are now members of the European Union. Romania and Bulgaria were admitted in 2007, with the candidacies of Croatia, Macedonia, and Turkey still pending.

The globalization of the world economy, reflecting remarkable improvements in transportation and communication, has brought the continents of the world closer together, facilitating the movement of people, ideas, and products across the globe. Migrants from Africa and Asia began to arrive in Europe in ever greater numbers, attracted by the possibility of jobs and a better life. Many fled political turmoil at home, arriving as political refugees or simply crossing borders without detection. Hundreds of thousands of immigrants from the Balkans also headed west. Periods of economic downturn have left immigrants unwanted by many in their adopted countries, which have been subject to xenophobia. Even as Europe now enjoys peace, the question of immigration remains a challenge, particularly in Western Europe. And so does the specter of increased terrorism across the globe, in the wake of the attacks in New York City and Washington, D.C., on September 11, 2001.

CHAPTER 27

REBUILDING DIVIDED EUROPE

～～～

The Second World War ended with little of the optimism that had followed the conclusion of the First World War. Winston Churchill, for one, was pessimistic: "What is Europe now? A rubble heap, a charnel house, a breeding ground of pestilence and hate." Four times more people had been killed in World War II (as a direct or indirect result of the fighting) than had died in World War I, which had been "the war to end all wars." As the smoke of war cleared, Europeans struggled to comprehend the devastation around them: flattened cities, crippled industry, and millions of refugees. The world soon learned that more than 6 million Jews had been exterminated by the Nazis. Countries that the German armies had occupied or that had been Nazi allies had to determine how to deal with collaborators, and they also faced the challenge of establishing democratic political institutions. In the meantime, intellectuals wrestled with the horrendous catastrophe that had occurred.

The shift from a wartime to a peacetime economy would pose a great challenge. The economies of the Western nations recovered from the war with remarkable speed and entered a period of spectacular economic growth. Economic growth came even as superpower competition between the United States and the Soviet Union made the other European powers less important in the world, as did the growing prodigious economic might of Japan and the rise of China as a great power.

The European population grew from 548 million in 1950 to 727 million in 2000. The post-war period brought a "baby boom." Life expectancy increased as people lived longer due to improvements in medicine and diet. Mechanization and commercialization augmented agricultural production. Because of what became known as a "Green Revolution," more and more rural people left the land for cities, which grew rapidly. Over the decades that followed, greater opportunities for women became available. At the same time, simultaneous revolutions in transportation, communications, and consumerism transformed the way Europeans lived.

IN THE WAKE OF DEVASTATION

Putting Europe back together proved a daunting task. By the time World War II ended in 1945, as many as 60 million people had been killed as a result of the war. Although fewer people from France and Great Britain were killed in the Second World War than the First World War, death tolls in Central and Eastern Europe during the Second World War were almost beyond comprehension. In the Soviet Union, deaths due to the war can only be estimated at between 15 and 25 million people—even more, if one includes the millions who were victims of Joseph Stalin's purges. Moreover, 1,700 cities and towns and 70,000 villages were completely destroyed. About 6 million Germans died in Hitler's war. Poland lost 6 million people—a fifth of the population—including 3 million Jews, more than 90 percent of the Jewish population. Ten percent of the population of Yugoslavia had perished. Damage to property from air raids, ground warfare, and reprisals by retreating German forces was incalculable. German air raids in the first year of the war devastated sections of London and Coventry in Britain, Leningrad and Kiev in the Soviet Union, and the Dutch port of Rotterdam. The German army completely leveled Warsaw in retaliation for the 1944 uprising there. In turn, Allied bombing runs left Berlin, Dresden, and the industrial cities of the Rhineland in ruins, and key French industrial and port cities were severely damaged as well.

Only recently have historians become aware of the tragedies stemming from what would in the 1990s be known as "ethnic cleansing" during and immediately after the war. For example, between April 1943 and August 1947 in the territories that would become Communist Poland and the Soviet republic of Ukraine, about 100,000 civilian Poles and Ukrainians were killed and another 1.4 million were forced from their lands by the invading Red Army. During the period of Nazi and then Soviet occupation (for the second time, as the Soviets had occupied these territories during 1939–1941), first Ukrainians and then Poles themselves undertook "ethnic cleansing." Ukrainian nationalists killed Poles in Volhynia and Galicia in 1943, and the Poles committed atrocities when civil war between the two ethnic groups followed the liberation of Poland.

The Potsdam Conference

Decisions taken by the Allies toward the end of the war brought a radical restructuring of the national boundaries of Central and Eastern Europe. The restructuring was largely determined by the Soviet military advance. By the time of the German surrender in May 1945, the Red Army had occupied all of the states of Eastern Europe except Yugoslavia and Greece. In Germany, Soviet troops controlled what became the eastern zone; the British held the industrial Rhineland and Ruhr Basin, as well as much of the north; American and French armies held southern Germany; and the four powers divided Berlin.

At the Potsdam Conference of July 1945, Stalin, Churchill, and Truman considered the fate of defeated Germany. The defeat of Churchill's Conservative Party in the election that took place at the same time as the conference brought Clement Attlee (1883–1967) to Potsdam as British prime minister, leading one diplomat to conclude that the meeting of the "Big Three" had become a meeting of "the Big 2 and a half." The Allies had already decided to divide defeated Germany into a British, French, Russian, and American zone of occupation. They created a new border between Germany and Poland, which would be the Oder and Niesse Rivers. The port of Gdańsk was restored to Poland. The Allied leaders agreed that Germany should be reunified, despite the original opposition of de Gaulle, and that German populations living in Poland, Czechoslovakia, and Hungary should be forcibly resettled in Germany, as the new governments of those states demanded. The Four Power Allied Control Council (France had joined the Potsdam powers) planned a new, disarmed, and de-Nazified Germany.

The growing mistrust between the Western Allies and the Soviet Union affected the Potsdam Conference. Stalin's territorial demands included

Winston Churchill, Harry Truman, and Joseph Stalin at the Potsdam Conference in 1945.

strategically crucial parts of Turkey. The Western Allies refused, because such a move would have given the Soviet Union virtual control of the straits of Constantinople—which Russian tsars had sought since the eighteenth century. The Soviet Union had already occupied in 1940 the Baltic states of Estonia, Latvia, and Lithuania, a large chunk of East Prussia, and parts of Finland, Czechoslovakia, and Romania (Bessarabia and some of Bukovina). Poland, which lost much of its eastern territory to the Soviet Union, gained in the west at Germany's expense (see Map 27.1).

Other territorial adjustments came at the expense of Germany's wartime allies, such as Italy, from which Yugoslavia acquired a small border region. As the Allies dictated the new alignments, little attention was paid to the fact that the new borders, as after World War I, left various nationalities dissatisfied. Hungarians living in Transylvania did not want to be left within the redrawn borders of Romania; the many fewer Romanians who found themselves inside Hungary resented what they considered to be punishment for having been forced by the Nazis and their wartime dictators to fight on the side of Germany. Austria, which Hitler had annexed to his Reich in 1938, had its independence restored. Military occupation of Austria by the victorious World War II powers ended in 1955 with the withdrawal of Soviet troops in exchange for Austria's declaration of neutrality. In northern Europe, Finland retained its independence and the Soviet Union accepted Finnish neutrality.

As after the end of World War I, the Western Allies disagreed on the question of war reparations. The Soviet Union, which had suffered far more than Great Britain and the United States, demanded that Germany be forced to pay for the costs of the war. Specifically, Stalin wanted the equivalent of $20 billion in reparations, as well as German industrial equipment. The Soviet Union eventually received half the amount of money demanded (although in greatly inflated currency), as well as about 25 percent of industrial equipment from the German zones occupied by Britain, France, and the United States. In the meantime, Soviet trains and trucks began to haul German machinery and other industrial materials from the eastern zone back to Russia. By now fully suspicious of Soviet intentions in Eastern Europe, Truman eliminated the Soviet Union from the list of nations eligible for U.S. loans to help with rebuilding their economies.

The Western Allies concurred that the victors should negotiate peace treaties with Germany's former allies (Italy, Hungary, Romania, and Bulgaria), which were to be represented by "recognized democratic governments." But it was soon clear that the governments of the last three nations were anything but democratically elected.

The United Nations and Cold War Alliances

In November 1944, the Dumbarton Oaks Conference in Washington, D.C., planned the United Nations, which would replace the League of Nations.

MAP 27.1 POST-WAR TERRITORIAL SETTLEMENTS   Territorial changes as of 1947, including American, British, French, and Soviet zones in Germany, as well as boundaries of the Soviet Union, Poland, Bulgaria, and Yugoslavia after the war.

The League, which did not include the United States, Germany, Japan, or Italy as members, had stood by when Italy invaded Ethiopia and Germany re-occupied the Rhineland and then absorbed Czechoslovakia. Now, the Allies desired a system of international security that would protect the freedom and self-determination of member nations. An international conference in San Francisco in 1945 drew up the UN Charter. The UN headquarters was placed in New York, where a secretary-general would coordinate its activities. The United Nations would consist of a General Assembly of member nations (fifty-one at the organization's inception), each of which would have one vote, and a Security Council of eleven members (fifteen after 1965). The United States and Britain agreed to Stalin's demand that the Soviet Union would have one of the five permanent seats—and thus veto power—on the Security Council once the proposed United Nations had been established. The United States, Great Britain, the U.S.S.R., France, and the Republic of China (Taiwan) were designated as "permanent members of the Security Council," each with a veto over deliberations, and the other five seats (ten after 1965) would be filled on a revolving basis by states chosen by the General Assembly. When China was admitted to the UN in 1971, it received the Republic of China's permanent seat on the Security Council.

The United Nations helped the European state system reemerge after the war. Furthermore, in some cases the UN provided necessary mediation in disputes between nations. However limited its powers, the United Nations, unlike the defunct League of Nations, could send peacekeeping forces to various hot spots on the globe, although the accomplishments of these efforts would vary considerably. Moreover, the UN provided emergency relief funds in the immediate post-war period to Czechoslovakia, Poland, Italy, and Greece.

In 1941, the Atlantic Charter (see Chapter 26), which had defined Allied war aims, had led to agreement that trials for war crimes would follow the war, once national sovereignty had been restored when Germany had been defeated. At the Saint James Conference in January 1942 the Allies declared their intention to punish war criminals. Gradually, consensus had emerged that an international order had to be constructed that went beyond state sovereignty. In 1944, the Permanent Court of Justice in The Hague organized a commission to consider definitions of war crimes, with the assumption that the United Nations would bring such criminals to justice.

The concept of war crimes that had developed during the war led in 1948 to the UN General Assembly adopting the Universal Declaration of Human Rights. This document has subsequently served as the basis for efforts to protect the rights of individuals. Building in part on the Bill of Rights of the United States and the Declaration of the Rights of Man and of Citizen of the French Revolution, the Universal Declaration proclaimed civil and political rights; the right to a fair trial; the freedoms of assembly, belief, and speech; and the rights to education, an adequate standard of living, and to participation in cultural life. Moreover, slavery and torture were acknowledged as violations of human rights. The Genocide Convention of 1949 made genocide a crime under international law.

Besides joining the United Nations to mediate disputes, the states of Europe also hedged their bets by establishing military alliances, whereby they pledged to come to the defense of their allies in case any one of them was attacked. Thus, in March 1948, Great Britain, France, Belgium, the Netherlands, and Luxembourg signed the Pact of Brussels. It served as the military component of the subsequent Council of Europe to which most of the nations of Western Europe adhered. The United States joined members of the Pact of Brussels in the North Atlantic Treaty Organization (NATO) in 1949, which subsequently added Italy, Denmark, Norway, Iceland, Portugal, Canada, Greece, and Turkey (see Map 27.2). Directed against the Soviet Union, the treaty bound all of the member countries to defend jointly any of the signatories who were attacked, creating a unified command for a common army and placing NATO's headquarters in Paris. NATO became the cornerstone of the alliance between the United States and Western Europe.

Confronting Turmoil and Collaborators

Europe became a continent of "displaced persons" (DP's) as well as of widows and orphans. Now national minorities within newly redrawn boundaries were forced into boxcars and moved—displaced—to new locations so as to correspond more or less to newly drawn national frontiers. In all, there were about 50 million refugees in the immediate post-war period. Furthermore, millions of prisoners of war, such as Germans incarcerated in the Soviet Union, had to be repatriated. Germans living in Lithuania, which in 1940 had been incorporated against its will into the Soviet Union, were returned to Germany. In the spring of 1945, about 20 million people were on the move. In addition, tens of thousands of Germans were forcibly expelled from Czechoslovakia during the period from May to August of 1945 and during the organized transfers of January through November 1946. Thousands died during this hard time. In all, about 12 million Germans were forced to leave their homes. Almost 4 million returned to Germany, most arriving from the U.S.S.R. and Poland with virtually nothing. In Germany, one of every six persons was a refugee and 1.5 million Germans still lived in camps for displaced persons in 1947.

Although drab and carefully regulated along military lines by the American, British, and French occupiers, with barbed wire, the careful distribution of food and clothing, and curfews, DP camps brought some normalcy to the lives of their occupants, many of whom had been slave laborers for Germany, including Polish and Ukrainian Jews, as well as Jews from the Baltic states, and some fortunate survivors of the death camps.

Stalin repopulated East Prussia with about 1 million people hauled from Russia, Belarus, Ukraine, and even distant Kazakhstan. Poles whose homeland had become part of the Soviet Union now moved into western Poland. At the same time, almost 500,000 Ukrainians were forced by Poland to head eastward to the Soviet Union. Several hundred thousand Jews from Eastern Europe who had survived the Holocaust now headed west, some fleeing new pogroms in Poland in 1946. In all, about 7 million members of

MAP 27.2 EASTERN AND WESTERN BLOCS, 1955 NATO and the Warsaw Pact were the military alliances that defined the post-war world.

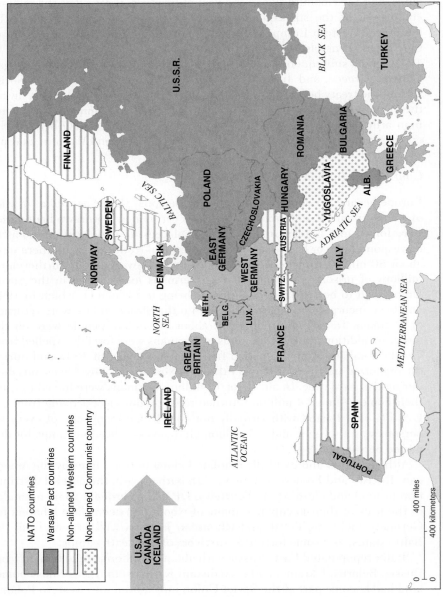

Refugees waiting for food in a Displaced Persons Camp in Germany.

Eastern European ethnic groups faced resettlement. The result was a dramatic decrease in the percentage of ethnic minorities living in Poland, Czechoslovakia, and Romania, declining from 32 percent to 3 percent in the first case. Churches, synagogues, and even a few mosques were razed, depending on the location; towns and streets received new names to reflect the brutal transfer of ethnic minorities.

The punishment of those who had collaborated with the Nazis began as soon as the occupied territories were liberated (and, in some cases, had begun during the war itself). In France, resistance forces summarily executed (sometimes after quick trials) about 10,000 accused collaborators. Courts sentenced about 2,000 people to death (of whom about 800 were executed) and more than 40,000 to prison. Vichy Prime Minister Pierre Laval was executed. Marshal Philippe Pétain was found guilty of treason, but because of his age and stature as the "hero of Verdun" during the First World War, he was imprisoned on a small island off the western coast of France, where he died in 1951. Women who had slept with German soldiers had their heads shaved and were paraded through their towns in shame.

In countries that had been occupied by Hitler's armies, people struggled to determine degrees of guilt. In Belgium, courts prosecuted 634,000 people for their part in the German occupation—a staggering figure in a country of only 8 million people. In Norway, 55,000 members of the Norwegian Nazi Party were put on trial after the war, and although many drew jail terms, only 25 were executed. On the other hand, in Austria, where much

A French collaborator whose head has been shaved is paraded, with her baby, through a village near Cherbourg following liberation of the region by Allied troops, 1944.

of the population had seemed to welcome union with Hitler's Germany with frenzied enthusiasm, only 9,000 people were tried and only 35 collaborators executed. In Italy, where reprisals against Nazi collaborators at the war's end had been carried out with speed and efficiency (about 15,000 executions between 1943 and 1946), there were few trials of fascists after the war. This was in part because the Italian fascists had been, at least when compared to the Nazis, relatively mild in their treatment of their enemies. Furthermore, millions of people had joined fascist organizations or unions because they felt obliged to do so. In Eastern Europe, purges of former Nazi collaborators took on a high profile, such as in Yugoslavia, where Tito's victorious forces executed thousands of Serbs, Croats, and Slovenes who had collaborated, many of them murderously.

The most dramatic post-war trial occurred in Nuremberg in August 1945 when the Allies put twenty-four high-ranking German officials on trial before an international tribunal. The court found twenty-one of the defendants guilty of war crimes, and ten were executed. Hermann Göring committed suicide in his cell shortly before he was to be executed. Less spectacular trials of more minor Nazi figures went on in Germany for years.

Many war criminals, however, escaped or were let free after the war. Doctor Josef Mengele, who had carried out brutal experiments on living patients, including children, managed to escape to Paraguay. A good many Nazis found a warm welcome from right-wing dictatorships. The U.S. government facilitated the escape of a number of Nazi war criminals in exchange for information about Communists in Germany and elsewhere in Europe. Indeed, growing anti-communism put a brake on purges of wartime collaborators in Western Europe. Other war criminals managed to fade into the chaos of post-war Europe, some with new names and identities. Some did not even bother to change their names, and more than a few eventually served in the West German government. In 1959, Israeli agents in South America kidnapped Adolph Eichmann, who had participated in the murder of thousands of Jews. He was put on trial in Israel, where he was convicted and put to death. In the mid-1980s, a French court convicted Klaus Barbie, a Nazi war criminal who had fled after the war, sentencing him to life in prison. Maurice Papon, an official who had signed away the lives of hundreds of Jews during Vichy and then gone on to a successful career as an official in several French governments, was finally tried and convicted in 1998, proud to the end that his superiors thought well of his work as a bureaucrat. The justice meted out to Nazis and collaborators may have been imperfect, and sometimes came quite late, but it was better than no justice at all.

ECONOMIC RECOVERY AND PROSPERITY, THE WELFARE STATE, AND EUROPEAN ECONOMIC COOPERATION

The European economy lay in ruins. Bombing on both sides had been systematic, destroying with increasing accuracy the industrial structure of Europe. Sunken ships blocked port harbors. Almost all bridges over the major rivers had been destroyed. Only fragments of Europe's transportation and communication networks remained in service. In Britain, gold and silver reserves had sunk dramatically, and the government had been forced to take out large loans, initiating a long period of virtual British dependence on the United States, which provided the bulk of these funds. Non-military manufacturing had plunged during the war. The markets for British manufactured goods, which had all but disappeared during the war, could not be quickly reconstituted.

Agricultural production in every war zone had fallen by about half, leaving millions of people without enough to eat. Inflation was rampant; the value of European currencies plunged. As after World War I, the German currency became virtually worthless. German housewives picked through the rubble of bombed-out buildings looking for objects of value, combing forests for mushrooms and berries for their families to eat. The black market supplied many necessities.

However, the European economy revived with impressive, unanticipated speed (see Table 27.1). As a response to growing Communist influence, in March 1947 President Truman announced the "Truman Doctrine," which proclaimed "the policy of the United States to support free people who are resisting attempted subjugation by armed minorities or by outside pressures."

TABLE 27.1. INDICES OF INDUSTRIAL PRODUCTION, 1946–1950
(1938 = 100)

	1946	1947	1948	1949	1950
Belgium	91	106	120	129	139
Britain	106	114	128	137	148
France	79	95	111	122	125
Italy	75	93	99	105	119
Netherlands	74	94	113	126	137
W. Germany	29	34	51	75	90

Source: William I. Hitchcock, *The Struggle for Europe: The Turbulent History of a Divided Continent, 1945–2002* (New York: Doubleday, 2003), p. 135.

Because great economic turmoil had contributed to social and political instability between the world wars, the United States undertook a program of massive economic aid to Western Europe. Through the Marshall Plan, named after the American secretary of state, George Marshall, who devised it, the United States contributed $13 billion between 1948 and 1951 toward the rebuilding of the Western Allies' economies. The Marshall Plan was intended to help Western Europe resist communism—as the United States pressured the governments of France and Italy not to name Communists to key ministries—and to make Europe a powerful trading partner for American industry.

The Marshall Plan contributed to the revival of Western Europe. However, the European economic recovery was already well under way by the time the Marshall Plan began in 1948. Britain and France had already matched their industrial production of the pre-war period, and Italy, the Netherlands, and Belgium followed within a year. Moreover, the monies provided by the Marshall Plan amounted to only 6.5 percent of France's gross national product, 2.5 percent of that of Britain, and 5.3 percent of that of Italy. The Marshall Plan did assist Western European states to purchase raw materials, fuel, and machinery for industry. In Britain, about a third of the aid went to the purchase of food. Funds from the Marshall Plan also allowed Western European governments some margin to pay for the beginnings of social programs emerging with the construction of welfare states (see p. 1126). The United States offered loans and credits to a number of European countries, with an eye toward encouraging anti-communism, while having excluded the Soviet Union from the provisions of the Lend-Lease Act.

The difficult years in the immediate post-war period gave way to a period of considerable economic growth from 1950 to 1973. European economies benefited from the globalization of trade, the availability of a labor supply, and the use of oil instead of coal as the principal source of fuel for industrial growth. This rapid rise in the demand for oil dramatically increased the strategic importance of the Middle East. Natural gas, much of which was imported from the Soviet Union, offered another source of energy.

Economic growth followed a combination of state involvement in the economy and the liberalization of trade, creating mixed economies. The most successful mix seemed to be a combination of state planning, timely nationalizations (notably of railroads, coal, and steel), and encouragement of private industry. Nationalized railroads aided the process of rebuilding and expansion in West Germany, France, Belgium, and Britain. The Italian government owned almost 30 percent of Italian industry. In Italy, the role of the state in orchestrating industry, encouraged by Mussolini, survived the war. The Institute for Industrial Reconstruction, which had been founded in 1933, controlled an increasing number of enterprises. The National Agency for Hydrocarbons emerged as a veritable cartel in itself, drawing huge profits from a variety of activities, including construction, chemicals, and textile production. Government investment helped the emergence of the Italian steel industry, and a state-owned petroleum company provided industry with inexpensive fuel.

The British economy slowly revived following the war. Industrial production reached pre-war levels by 1946 and grew by a third by the end of the decade, despite increasingly obsolete factories and low rates of investment and savings. In France, the state assumed control of the largest banks, the Renault automobile plants (whose owner had collaborated with the Germans), natural resources (such as gas and coal), steel and electricity, and airlines. The brilliant French economist Jean Monnet (1888–1979) headed an Office of Planning, which encouraged and coordinated voluntary plans for modernizing business enterprises and agriculture, drawing on the capital and expertise of government technocrats. French industrial production in 1959 was twice that of 1938. Table 27.2 provides comparative rates of industrial productivity for the major nations of Europe, as well as for Japan and the United States. Italy also enjoyed a real boom. Real wages in Italy in 1954 were more than 50 percent higher than they had been before the war, as the Italian economy grew rapidly with the help of U.S. financial assistance. Smaller nations also thrived. Norway, Denmark, and Sweden all became more prosperous thanks largely to the development of fishing, agriculture, industry, and booming service sectors.

The Western Allies recognized that the economic recovery of West Germany was essential to achieving political stability in Central Europe and resisting communism. Aided by a stable political life, the German Federal Republic reformed its battered currency, the mark. Price controls and rationing ended. This helped restore confidence, which in turn helped fuel the economic resurgence. Black-marketeering gradually ceased as inflation and unemployment were brought under control.

An infusion of American aid—$1.5 billion between 1948 and 1952, primarily through the Marshall Plan—contributed to the rebuilding of key industries in West Germany, which contained most of the nation's natural

TABLE 27.2. INDEX OF INDUSTRIAL PRODUCTION

	1938	1948	1952	1959	1963	1967
United States	33	73	90	113	133	168
West Germany	53	27	61	107	137	158
France	52	55	70	101	129	155
Italy	43	44	64	112	166	212
Holland	47	53	72	110	141	182
Belgium	64	78	88	104	135	153
Britain	67	74	84	105	119	133
Austria	39	36	65	106	131	151
Spain				102	149	215
Sweden	52	74	81	106	140	176
Japan	58	22	50	120	212	347

Source: Walter Laqueur, *Europe Since Hitler* (New York: Penguin, 1982), p. 194.

resources. The German Federal Republic also had the advantage (one, to be sure, bought at horrific cost during the war) of starting from scratch and building new factories that utilized the most modern equipment. West Germany's other advantages included the presence of many engineers, a skilled labor force, and protection by the Western Allies—so it did not have to spend much for defense. The government of the German Federal Republic took a lesser role in economic planning, but imposed short-term tariffs and encouraged agricultural modernization. The influx of refugees from East Germany contributed to the remarkable growth of the West German economy. West Germany in the 1960s attracted streams of migrant workers from Spain, Italy, Greece, Yugoslavia, and above all, Turkey.

As a result of the German economic "miracle," West Germany's gross national product tripled between 1950 and 1964. West Germany's imports multiplied during the 1950s by four times and its exports by six times. German industrial production more than doubled between 1948 and 1951, and it increased by six times from 1948 to 1964. West Germany assumed pre-war Germany's role as a major producer of steel and machinery. The chemical industry, strong in Germany since the late nineteenth century, continued to develop. By 1960, the German Federal Republic was the world's second leading exporter of goods, including machinery, appliances, radios, chemicals, and automobiles, as Volkswagens now streamed off the assembly lines.

The continued concentration of industrial production in large companies characterized the post-war period. Western Europe entered the world of conglomerates. A single Belgian company controlled as much as 80 percent of Belgian bank deposits, 60 percent of insurance business, 40 percent of the iron and steel produced, 30 percent of coal, and 25 percent of electrical energy. This monopoly did not seem to slow the development of the Belgian economy, which expanded rapidly.

With the rapid development of the service sector of Western economies, the proliferation of white-collar jobs lifted the expectations, status, and income of hundreds of thousands of families. A more equitable distribution in taxation helped remove some of the tax burden from ordinary people. Still, in 1960, 5 percent of the British population owned about 75 percent of the nation's wealth.

Great economic disparities also remained between European nations. By the end of the 1960s, the German Federal Republic, Switzerland, and Sweden were the most prosperous European countries; Ireland, Portugal, Greece, and Spain were the poorest in Western Europe; and Romania and Albania were the poorest Communist states. In Table 27.2, Britain's relative decline clearly stands out.

Economic Cooperation

The post-war era also brought international economic cooperation among Western states. The Organization for European Economic Cooperation (OEEC) was founded in 1948 with seventeen member states, which the United States later joined. It was succeeded in 1961 by the Organization for Economic Cooperation and Development (OECD), which was expanded to include Australia, Canada, and New Zealand. The OEEC helped plan European economic reconstruction after World War II. Cooperation among the Western states also led to the creation in 1952 of the European Coal and Steel Community (ECSC). The inspiration of the French statesman Robert Schuman (1886–1963), the ECSC also reflected the influence of U.S. Secretary of State Dean Acheson and of French economist Jean Monnet. The ECSC, which overcame strenuous British opposition, coordinated production of French and German coal and steel in the interest of efficiency, but it also was intent on forging a new relationship that ultimately would place France and West Germany at the center of the new Europe. Despite inevitable problems stemming from sometimes competing interests, the ECSC first raised the possibility of serious European economic integration. Such economic cooperation between countries also contributed to economic growth in Western Europe.

The Treaty of Rome (1957) laid the groundwork for the European Atomic Energy Community and the European Economic Community (EEC, the European Common Market). The EEC began in 1958 with six member nations—France, Italy, the German Federal Republic, Belgium, Luxembourg, and the Netherlands. The EEC gradually eliminated trade barriers between member states in Western Europe, established common customs tariffs— thus reducing trade barriers and increasing trade between member states— and worked toward equalizing wages and social security arrangements among the member countries.

The Post-War Baby Boom

Following the war, a veritable "baby boom" occurred in Europe, as in the United States. Europe's population grew from 264 million in 1940 to 320 million by the early 1970s. The increase in the birthrate after the war more than made up for the loss of hundreds of thousands of emigrants to North America and Latin America, particularly from Italy. Europeans were also living longer, aided by improvements in diet and in medicine. The aging of the population presents major challenges for the twenty-first century. As the percentage of people no longer working rises, major strains on national budgets are a certainty because of increased costs for welfare and social security systems.

In the post-war period, increases in industrial and agricultural productivity, which opened up new jobs, encouraged families to have more children, as did government policies that aided families that had children. In France, where leaders had openly worried about the low birthrate, special incentives were offered to families that had more than two children. Medical advances (such as the virtual elimination of polio by the end of the 1950s) and an increase in the number of doctors further reduced infant mortality. The birthrate increased between 1950 and 1966 in every country in Western Europe, with Switzerland, the Netherlands, the German Federal Republic, and France leading the way. The Soviet Union and Poland, too, saw high annual natural increases. Nonetheless, because of virtually unchecked population growth in India, China, and other Third World nations, Europe's percentage of the world population fell to 16 percent in 1990.

The increase in the birthrate had far-reaching social and political implications. British, French, and German eighteen-year-olds received the right to vote in the early 1970s. Moreover, governments had to increase spending on education dramatically to prepare the young for jobs in an economy that was rapidly becoming more complex. The age until which school attendance was obligatory rose to fourteen or sixteen years old, depending on the country. Illiteracy became quite uncommon in Europe by the 1960s. As a result of the baby boom, more young people attended university. But despite the tripling of the number of university students in Britain, France, and Italy between 1938 and 1960, there was relatively little democratization of university enrollment, which remained the preserve of the upper classes. In 1967, fewer than 10 percent of French university students were the children of workers or peasants. In Great Britain, particularly, but also in the other countries of the West, working-class and farm families could not afford to send their children to university. Time away from earning a living represented an economic hardship. Still, in Eastern Europe and the Balkan countries, the number of students in higher education rose rapidly.

The Green Revolution

In the two decades that followed World War II, Western European agriculture was transformed by the "Green Revolution." Fewer farmers fed a much larger population. Large-scale, commercialized agriculture permitted most nations to produce most of the food consumed by their populations. Agricultural productivity rose by 30 percent between the end of the war and 1962. In the German Federal Republic, agricultural production increased by two-and-a-half times between 1950 and 1964.

There were several reasons for these changes in farming. First, mechanized agriculture was increasingly widespread, particularly use of the tractor. Second, fertilizers augmented farm yields in northern Europe, while pesticides—a mixed blessing because of the long-term ecological costs—prevented blight. Advances in types of seeds, animal husbandry (particularly artificial insemination), and irrigation also contributed to greater productivity. Third, the size of many farms increased as smaller and less productive plots were consolidated into larger units.

Government programs encouraged the cooperative use of tractors and provided agricultural information to farmers. In many countries, government assistance facilitated reforestation, electrification, irrigation projects, and road building that would have been beyond the means of private initiatives. Improvements in agriculture were spread unevenly across Europe. Agriculture became most efficient in Great Britain, the Netherlands, Belgium, West Germany, Denmark, and France. Agricultural surpluses helped some countries during the 1970s and 1980s become major exporters of food.

The continued commercialization of agriculture accentuated the exodus from the land to the rapidly growing cities of Europe. In Italy, the farming population fell from about 40 percent after the war to 24 percent in 1966. In Great Britain, the first European nation in which agriculture was substantially mechanized even before the war, less than 4 percent of the population worked the land by the early 1970s. Before World War I, about half the population of Europe worked in agriculture, a figure that included fishermen and foresters. In 1955, the percentage had fallen to about 24 percent, and it has continued to decline, although it remains higher in southern Europe. In every country, agriculture's share of the gross national product has fallen. At the same time, the increasing industrialization of agriculture and the use of synthetic fertilizers means that the old term "Green Revolution" in some ways no longer seems appropriate.

In the 1950s, Western European peasants started to join organizations to lobby for assistance and favorable tariffs. Peasants blocked traffic of capitals with tractors and farm animals to protest government policies. In France, wine producers have often attempted to block the arrival of cheaper products from Italy and Spain. Ironically, such protests have come at a time when peasants, because of the rural exodus in Western Europe, have lost most of their political voice.

Welfare States

The emergence of welfare states within the context of market capitalism was one of the most significant evolutions in the post-war period. State economic and military planning during World War II helped shape expectations of continued government assistance. In response to popular desire for social reforms, the British Parliament, spurred by the Labour Party, implemented new social benefits. These included the remarkable British National Health Service that began in 1948, funds for the unemployed, retirement pensions, and assistance for widows. It also enacted a series of bills nationalizing the Bank of England, airlines, railways, roads, canals, buses, London's subway, and the coal and steel industries. After the war, the shortage of homes was apparent and a quarter of all homes in Britain did not have their own lavatory. By 1951, a million new homes had been constructed in Britain. Economic growth and a low rate of unemployment made such programs, financed through taxation, easier than they would have been in a period of economic slowdown. The Conservatives, in power between 1951 and 1964, expanded the services of the British welfare state, even though Conservative policy had long been in principle against such strong government.

In other countries, too, the general appreciation of the sacrifices ordinary people had made during World War II led to a growing consensus that states should provide services to citizens. The welfare state also reflected the assumption that the monopoly of wealthy people over the economy had contributed to the rise of fascist movements in Europe between the wars.

Thus European states greatly expanded comprehensive welfare programs that provided social services for their citizens. "Welfare states" would provide cradle-to-grave social services. This was true in Western states, in which laissez-faire economic theory had long held the upper hand, as well as in Communist states, in which the role of centralized state economic planning was a major part of Communist ideology and practice. In many countries, social legislation provided government assistance to the sick and impoverished. Government insurance programs covered health care costs in Britain, Sweden, Denmark, France, Italy, and in the Soviet Union and other Communist states. Most countries in the West provided financial assistance to the unemployed; in Communist states, where there was not supposed to be any unemployment, menial jobs were found for almost everyone. In all, states expended four times more funds for social services in 1957 than in 1930. Progressive taxation helped raise funds to provide these services. In most European countries, education was made free, or fees were kept at modest rates. The prevalence of social programs in most European countries led to the characterization of welfare states as part of a "European" model of society, often contrasted with the United States. Between 1965 and 1981, the proportion of government expenditures in Britain that went to social welfare rose from 16 to 25 percent and in Sweden from 19 to 33 percent. Everywhere, the increase in government services added to the size of bureaucracies. Yet the advent of welfare states was predicated on economic growth. When economies do not grow, social-welfare costs become drains on national budgets. Great Britain, France, and Sweden would later find, for instance, that rising medical costs could outstrip the ability of government programs to pay for them.

POLITICS IN THE WEST IN THE POST-WAR ERA

With Germany, Italy, and Vichy France defeated, political continuity with pre-war governments could be found only in Britain among the major Western European powers. Yet, even in Britain, political change occurred as voters in the first post-war election turned against the Conservatives and brought the Labour Party to power in July 1945. Labour's victory was a repudiation of the Conservative government's pre-war economic policies and its inadequate reaction to Hitler's aggressive moves in Central Europe in the late 1930s. Clement Attlee (1883–1967), a hard-working but uninspiring man who lacked Churchill's charisma, became prime minister. Churchill allegedly remarked, "An empty cab pulled up to 10 Downing Street, and Attlee got out." Nonetheless, Attlee proved to be an effective leader.

Following the economic recovery after the war, Britain's share in international trade declined sharply during the 1950s, 1960s, and 1970s. West Germany and France passed Britain in most economic categories. Some conservatives blamed the welfare state and the strength of the unions for Britain's relative economic decline, arguing that both forced the government and private companies to pay higher wages. Yet British welfare costs were less than those of France, and British citizens paid proportionally fewer taxes than German or French citizens. Rather, the costs of maintaining the British Empire undercut the government's quest for austerity as it faced enormous trade deficits and debts to the United States. The Attlee government had to choose between financing domestic economic recovery and maintaining the British Empire. It chose the former (see Chapter 28).

Conservatives returned to power in Britain in 1951. Britain remained governed by an inter-connected elite of wealthy families—at one time during the government (1957–1963) of Conservative Prime Minister Harold Macmillan, thirty-five of his ministers, including seven members of his cabinet, were related to him by marriage. (Princess Margaret, sister of Queen Elizabeth, once suggested sarcastically that the traditional debutante balls no longer be held because "every little tart in London was getting in.") The Tories were committed to undoing the nationalizations undertaken by Labour after the war. But they found it difficult to privatize the iron and steel industries because they had become unprofitable and failed to attract private interest. Furthermore, the welfare system was generally popular. Labour

(*Left*) Winston Churchill giving his famous "V for Victory" sign. (*Right*) Charles de Gaulle returns to France after the German occupation and the Vichy years.

returned to power in 1964 with the support of the trade unions, and remained there until 1970.

In some ways, France emerged from World War II in better shape than it had from World War I. And although industrial cities and ports had been pounded by bombing raids—German in 1940 and Allied in the last years of the war—the systematic devastation that had taken place in northern and northeastern France during 1914–1918 had not been repeated, in part because the French armies had collapsed so rapidly in 1940.

In the eighteen months that followed his triumphant march down the Champs-Elysées to Paris's town hall in August 1944, Charles de Gaulle ruled virtually alone. In October 1945, the vast majority of French men and women voted against a return to the political institutions of the Third Republic, identified with France's defeat five years earlier. This referendum was the first election in which French women could vote after receiving the suffrage that year. In the subsequent elections for the Constituent Assembly, the Communist Party—whose contributions to the resistance had been essential—took the greatest percentage of seats. They were followed by the Popular Republican Movement (MRP), a new center-right party built on de Gaulle's reputation and Catholic support. However, frustrated that the new regime would have a weak executive authority, de Gaulle resigned from government in January 1946.

After voters overwhelmingly rejected the Constituent Assembly's proposed constitution in May, a second Constituent Assembly was then elected to write a new constitution. It was approved by a narrow majority of voters in October 1946. Like the Third Republic, the political institutions of the new Fourth Republic seemed conducive to governmental immobility and instability. Between 1946 and 1958, France had twenty-four different governments, most based on left-center coalitions of the MRP, the Socialists, and smaller parties. The president and the prime minister had influence, but little power. While de Gaulle cooled his heels in his village, awaiting a call for him to return to power, a new Gaullist party (the Rally of the French People, or RPF) became the opposition party of the right.

In Italy, a new regime had to be constructed after the war. The monarchy's passive capitulation to fascism had discredited King Victor Emmanuel III. In June 1946, more than half of those voting repudiated the monarchy, despite the abdication of the king in favor of his son and the pope's attempts to influence the election. Italy became a republic.

The new Italian constitution provided for the election of the president by the two houses of parliament, both of which were to be elected by popular vote, now including women for the first time. The president had little real authority. Many Italians feared a powerful centralized state, at least partially because it would seem a continuity of fascism, but also because it seemed antithetical to long-standing regional identities. Fearful of losing influence, the Church vigorously opposed state centralization.

The new Italy was to be built on values associated with the resistance, which had been active in the north. Some Italians now called this a "cleansing wind from the north." But the Italian south and Sicily had been liberated by the Allies with very little help from a resistance movement, which remained dominated not only by powerful landowners but also by the Mafia. Moreover, many fascist officials in the south retained their positions, weakening the republic's prestige.

The government of Italy remained rooted in the center-right. The Christian Democratic Party, a staunchly anti-Communist centrist force with close ties to the Catholic Church and powerful economic interests, controlled political life in post-war Italy, dispensing patronage and bribes. Like its counterparts in West Germany and France, the Italian Christian Democratic Party reflected the accommodation of most Catholics with democracy. At the same time, the Communist Party became the second-largest political party, claiming the allegiance of a quarter of the population. In the 1960s, Italian governments undertook modest social reforms, encouraged by the popular Pope John XXIII (pope 1958–1963). This pushed the Christian Democrats to form coalitions with the Socialists.

POLITICAL REALIGNMENTS

Backed by the Soviet Union and its secret police, Communist governments took power in every Eastern European state in the post-war period. After first declaring support for the constitution of parliamentary democracies, calling for a union of "anti-fascist" political groups, and participating in elections, in each case Communist parties gradually eliminated competing parties, beginning with underground resistance organizations that had been created where possible during the war. Arguably only a mass base of Communist support existed in Yugoslavia. At the same time, Communist parties grew in strength in several Western European states. Communists dominated the major trade-union organizations in Italy and France; they entered post-war governments in Belgium and Denmark. Communist wartime resistance against Nazi Germany helped swell the prestige of Communist parties, even as their close identification with the Soviet Union began to engender suspicion among political elites. France, Italy, and the German Federal Republic had right-center governments in which Catholic parties played a major role.

Divided Germany

The Allies oversaw the development of the political institutions of what became the German Federal Republic. Until 1951, all legislation passed by the Federal Republic had to be approved by the Western Allies. They carried out a process of de-Nazification, beginning with education, but did not undertake any major social reforms. This meant that the powerful industrial cartels remained in place, despite the Allies' agreement to the contrary at Potsdam. The devastation of the German economy seemed to necessitate leaving what was left of Germany's industrial base intact. The constitution of the German Federal Republic stated that parties obtaining a minimum of 5 percent of the popular vote in an election could be represented in the Federal Parliament (the Bundestag). This kept small parties, principally those of the extreme right, out of the parliament. (During the Weimar Republic, many small parties had contributed to political instability.) The Federal Constitutional Court banned neo-Nazi parties, and the Communist Party was outlawed as well. The Allies insisted that the German president's powers be limited to avoid the unrestricted executive power that had existed in Hitler's Germany. The president was elected for a term of five years by a federal assembly consisting of all members of the Bundestag and about the same number of delegates from each state. The chancellor, appointed by the president, became the effective head of state. The states of the Federal Republic elected representatives to an upper house (Bundesrat). Because the upper house could block legislation, this electoral process, too, strengthened the decentralization of political power in West Germany.

Konrad Adenauer (1876–1967), the Catholic mayor of Cologne, served as chancellor of the German Federal Republic until 1963. His wartime opposition to the Nazis, hostility to the Soviets and to East Germany, and his social conservatism reassured the Allies. Yet at the same time, Adenauer handed out positions to former Nazis and bent over backward to help Germans who had endured Allied reprisals for their service to the Nazi cause. In West Germany, the Allied program of "de-Nazification," intended to remove all former Nazis from positions of power and influence, overall had relatively little impact. It proved impossible to purge millions of people from government, industry, and education. The Allies concluded that Germany could not do without tens of thousands of experienced doctors, teachers, and engineers. Moreover, it would be difficult to distinguish between different degrees of Nazi commitment and action. Supported by smaller parties on the right, the Christian Democratic Union Party held power from 1949 until 1969, with the Social Democratic Party the chief opposition party. Adenauer forged a close alliance with France intended to serve as a bulwark against the Soviet Union.

In the meantime, the Cold War hastened the acceptance by the Western powers of the German Federal Republic and its rearmament in the Western alliance. In 1950 the Federal Republic became a nonvoting member of the Council of Europe. Moreover, bolstered by economic recovery and the total discrediting of the extreme political right wing, the German Federal Republic achieved full sovereignty and diplomatic respectability, joining NATO in 1955.

West Berliners looking across the mined "death strip," intended to discourage East Berliners from attempting to cross into the western zone, before the construction of the Berlin Wall, 1961.

The Soviet-occupied eastern zone of Germany became in 1949 the German Democratic Republic (GDR, or the DDR, also commonly known as East Germany). Walter Ulbricht (1893–1973), who had spent the war years in the Soviet Union, returned to Berlin with the Red Army and became secretary of the Communist Party. He remained, for all practical purposes, head of state until his forced retirement in 1971.

The GDR took over the administration of the eastern zone in 1955 from the Soviets, although its government continued to follow Soviet instructions. The Communist Party controlled most facets of cultural life. Many writers and artists left for West Germany, although the talented playwright Bertolt Brecht (1898–1956) remained.

Eastern Europe under the Soviet Shadow

As the Red Army stood near, the states of Eastern Europe fell under the domination of Soviet-backed Communist parties. The Bulgarian Communist Party had about 14,000 members in late 1944 and 422,000 in 1946; that of Poland 20,000 in mid-1944 and 300,000 a year later. Moreover, the Soviet Union at first went along with the tide of Eastern European nationalism, supporting, for example, the annexation of Transylvania by Romania, at the expense of Hungary. During 1945–1946, coalition governments (in which Communists participated) took over large estates and distributed land to peasants, transferring about half of the land of Poland and a third of that of Hungary.

From the beginning, parties that had collaborated with the Nazis and other right-wing groups were excluded from power. The Communists eliminated coalition partners, as in Czechoslovakia and Hungary, including socialist and peasant agrarian parties, or absorbed them. Thus, coalition governments elected or otherwise constituted at the end of the war disappeared one by one until the Communists controlled each state. In Hungary in 1947, two years after the Communist Party had been roundly defeated in elections, the Communists ousted the Smallholders, or Peasant Party, which had won 57 percent of the vote. In neighboring Romania, King Michael was forced out in similar circumstances. Bulgarian Communists won a contested victory in a plebiscite that established a "People's Republic," which quickly became a single-party state. After the first election in post-war Poland, where no party had collaborated with the Germans, Communists gradually pushed aside the Socialists, who constituted the other major party. The Soviets completely destroyed the Polish People's Party in Poland, as they did the Smallholders Party in Hungary. Thereafter, Communist governments controlled the bureaucracies that increased in size with state management of the economy—above all, the police—and implemented strict censorship. In what were rapidly becoming Soviet "satellite" states, the Communists benefited from the fact that the Nazis had decimated the political elites of Eastern Europe and the Balkans during the war.

Czechoslovakia alone in Central and Eastern Europe and the Balkans had not become a dictatorship between the wars. In the first post-war elections there in May 1946, Communists won more than a third of the vote. Two non-Communists, Eduard Beneš (1884–1948) and Jan Masaryk (1886–1948), served as president and foreign minister, respectively, in a coalition government. But in 1948 the Communists seized power, shutting down other political parties. Masaryk died after he jumped—or was pushed—from his office window.

From Moscow, Stalin engineered purges that swept away even loyal party members in the Eastern European nations. Political arrests in Hungary have been estimated at 200,000, at 180,000 in Romania, and 80,000 in tiny Albania. Widely publicized trials (including those of popular Catholic prelates in Hungary and Czechoslovakia), prison sentences, labor camps, and many executions followed. In six years, the Communists in Hungary executed perhaps a thousand political opponents among the more than 1.3 million people hauled before tribunals (from a population of 9.5 million). Purges included not only fascists but many Social Democrats and even Communists thought to oppose Stalinism. Stalin also tightened Moscow's grip on the fourteen non-Russian republics in the Soviet Union, purging "bourgeois nationalists" in several of them.

The Soviet Union and Its Satellites in the Post-War Era

Rebuilding the Soviet economy after World War II was a monumental task. After the Soviet Union's decidedly Pyrrhic victory, those who had managed to flee the war zones returned to devastated cities. Successive years of harvest failure from 1946 to 1947 compounded the extreme suffering. The highly centralized planning of the fourth Five-Year Plan, which began in 1945, allowed the Soviets to concentrate on key industries like coal and steel. Soviet planners benefited from the commandeering of industrial capital goods from Germany and Eastern Europe. Large-scale industrial production exceeded pre-war levels in 1950 by a comfortable margin, although such results were only modestly reflected in the quality of life of Soviet citizens.

Once they recovered from being forced to contribute resources to Soviet economic growth and from buying Soviet products at inflated prices, the Communist states of Eastern Europe benefited from Soviet technological assistance. Yet they were prevented from importing technology from the West and had to export raw materials and manufactured goods to the Soviet Union at below market prices. In 1949, the Soviet Union and its Eastern European allies formed the Council of Mutual Economic Assistance, which sought to coordinate economic planning. Industrial production rose most rapidly in Eastern Europe in the German Democratic Republic and Czechoslovakia. Bulgaria, Romania, and Yugoslavia also developed manufacturing bases.

The economic development of the German Democratic Republic, how-ever short on freedom, was at first impressive. Before Soviet occupation, the eastern zone of Germany had had a small industrial base, but this industrial infrastructure had suffered the Soviet extraction of raw materials and machinery. The collectivization of industrial production then proceeded rapidly, and by 1952 the state employed three of every four workers. Despite the loss of many skilled workers to the German Federal Republic, East Germany emerged with the strongest economy of the Soviet Union's Eastern bloc; only Hungary boasted a similar standard of living by the 1960s. Steel production and shipbuilding, particularly, expanded rapidly in the 1950s and 1960s, as the German Democratic Republic fulfilled its assigned role in the Soviet government's plan for economic development in the Communist states. Nonetheless, to many East Germans conditions of life seemed more attractive in West Germany. Hundreds of thousands of people voted with their feet and left for West Germany.

The planned economies of the Soviet Union and its Eastern European allies could count some accomplishments, although adequate attention to the desires of their citizens was not one of them. The Soviet gross national product, which had stood at 36 percent of that of the United States in 1957, rose to about 50 percent of that of its rival in 1962, and it edged closer in the subsequent two decades. Yet the Soviet economy remained haunted by daunting inefficiency. The housing shortage remained acute into the 1960s, and families still had long waits for better apartments.

While Stalin promoted economic growth in the Communist states of Eastern Europe, economic policies furthered a division of labor whereby some of the Soviet satellite states produced agricultural products and others manufactured particular goods. The Soviet Union used the Eastern European economies to further Soviet economic interests through unfavorable trade arrangements. One by one, beginning with Bulgaria and Czechoslovakia in 1949, the states of Eastern Europe launched five-year plans based on the Soviet model. However, consumer goods of all kinds were de-emphasized until the mid-1950s, sacrificed, as had been the case in the Soviet Union before the war, to the drive for heavy industrialization that gave birth to enormous plants that produced steel and iron.

The collectivization of agriculture began in earnest, but this at first sharply reduced productivity. Like peasants in the Soviet Union during the early 1930s, hundreds of thousands of peasants in Eastern Europe resisted by rebellion, arson, sabotage, and simply by dragging their feet. Yet gradually there were increases in productivity. By the mid-1960s, state farms accounted for more than 80 percent of the land in the German Democratic Republic, Bulgaria, Romania, and Czechoslovakia. In Poland, in sharp contrast, more than 85 percent of the land remained in private hands because the Polish Communist leadership feared open popular resistance to massive agricultural collectivization.

In Yugoslavia, Communist leader Tito refused to permit Soviet domination of his multinational country. In 1948, Tito broke with the Soviet Union. Over the next decades, Yugoslavia received millions of dollars in Western aid. The Yugoslav economy remained "mixed" in the sense that the private sector coexisted with state planning. Workers were permitted more self-administration through workers' councils or committees. In the 1950s, the collectivization of agriculture, which had begun after the war, was abandoned, with farmers retaking their old plots. Yugoslavia's economy improved, despite shortages and great inequalities among its six republics.

In the Soviet Union, Stalin had emerged from the war with his authority within the Communist Party unchallenged and with enormous prestige. But weakened by arteriosclerosis, Stalin's paranoia became virtually psychotic as he ordered more purges in the name of the Communist Party. The ruthless Lavrenty Beria (1899–1953), head of the omnipresent secret police, used a gold-plated phone to order arrests. Between 1948 and 1952, some prominent Jewish intellectuals and artists were tried and executed or simply disappeared, targeted because some were believed to have had contacts with the West. In 1953, Stalin died. Beria's subsequent arrest, trial, and execution signaled an end to the Stalinist period.

The Soviet Union entered a period of "collective leadership," a concept that had been abandoned during Stalin's personal dictatorship. Decisions were made by the fourteen members of the Presidium (a permanent executive committee) of the Communist Party, which included Georgy Malenkov (1902–1988), a pragmatist who had been trained as an engineer and who believed that Stalin's dictatorship had hampered the Soviet economy. Meanwhile, the coarse, rotund Nikita Khrushchev (1894–1971), the son of a miner in a family of peasants, advanced within the Communist Party. He was part of a "technocratic" faction, but he was also a successful party organizer. In 1955, Khrushchev, with support from within the Soviet bureaucracy, won the upper hand in his struggle with Malenkov for power. While maintaining an emphasis on heavy industry, Khrushchev also concentrated on planning and investing in Soviet agriculture, a sector that had never recovered from the effects of forced collectivization. He understood that the production of consumer goods would have to take a more prominent place in economic planning. The quality of life for most Soviet citizens began to improve gradually, although not as fast as that of highly placed Communist Party members, who sported cars and comfortable country houses.

The Soviet people were largely unaware of the power struggles fought in secrecy within the Kremlin. Like Western "sovietologists"—specialists who studied the Soviet Union—they could only chart the waxing and waning of party leaders' authority by their ranking or the omission of their names on official lists, or by their placement among the gray heads on the giant reviewing stand in Red Square during the annual May Day military parade.

In February 1956, Khrushchev denounced Stalin's "cult of personality" and his ruthless purges in an unpublished but widely cited speech delivered at the Twentieth Party Congress. Such direct criticism was unprecedented in the history of the Soviet Union. Khrushchev accepted the fact that different paths to socialism could exist in different countries. He allowed the national republics within the Soviet Union more authority over their own affairs and gave intellectuals and artists in the republics more freedom to develop non-Russian cultural interests. A brief relaxation of censorship permitted the publication of books that offered brutally frank critiques of the Stalin years.

However, the strict centralization of government and its domination by the Communist Party continued. The party's authority over the republics remained for the most part in the hands of ethnic Russians. The thaw in censorship soon ended. Censors banned *Doctor Zhivago* (completed in 1956 and translated in 1958) by Boris Pasternak (1890–1960). Published in Italy and winning the Nobel Prize for literature, it offered a nuanced picture of tsarist Russia and therefore implicitly stood as a criticism of the Soviet regime. Soviet artists and filmmakers, too, were reined in, although some remained daring and imaginative within the confines of official toleration.

As the Soviet Union's economic difficulties continued and the sixth Five-Year Plan floundered badly, Khrushchev blamed its failure on excessive centralization of planning and administration. His political rivals, however, blamed him. In 1957, Khrushchev ousted Malenkov, Vyacheslav Molotov, and the premier, Nikolai Bulganin (1895–1975), from key party positions.

Changing Contours of Life

Since World War II, the economic transformations in Europe have engendered several major social changes. Trade and technology led to an increasing interconnectedness and interdependence of global economies. The workforce changed as the percentage of population working the land fell sharply and more and more women began to work outside the home in careers that had traditionally been off-limits to them. Consumerism began to thrive, and goods that might have been considered luxury items just a few decades earlier became readily available.

Intellectual Currents in the Post-War Era

Outside of a sense of relief, there seemed little about which to be optimistic at the end of World War II. The British writer George Orwell summed up the general feeling when he wrote, "Since about 1930, the world had given no reason for optimism whatsoever. Nothing in sight except a welter of lies, cruelty, hatred, and ignorance." Unlike the period immediately following World War I, few people now believed that another total war was inconceivable. Many writers and artists seemed overwhelmed with pessimism, even hopelessness, in the face of the atomic age and the Cold War (see Chapter 28). Claiming "alienation" from the society they increasingly criticized, many Western intellectuals withdrew into introspection. However, for some, communism still seemed to offer a plan for the harmonious organization of society.

French existentialism became an influential cultural current during the first two decades following the war. The French philosopher Jean-Paul Sartre (1905–1980) believed that in the wake of the unparalleled destruction of World War II, the absurdity of life was the most basic discovery one could make. Denying the existence of God, existentialists like Sartre posited that life has no meaning. Their conclusion was that a person could only truly find any fulfillment while living "a suspended death" by becoming aware of his or her freedom to choose and to act. Sartre titled one of his plays *Huis clos* (*No Exit*), as he believed there was nothing beyond this life. Sartre's novels glorify the individual spirit seeking freedom, not through Enlightenment rationalism, but rather through a comprehension of life's irrationality. However, Sartre believed that violent revolution could free the individual from the human condition by allowing him or her to find truth by redefining reality. To this end, he joined the French Communist Party when the war was over. However, existentialism slowly lost its grip on French intellectual life, at least in part because of growing disillusionment with the Soviet Union among many leftist intellectuals.

The Algerian-born French writer Albert Camus (1913–1960) shared Sartre's view of mankind's tragic situation, but broke with Sartre in 1952 over the latter's enthusiasm for Stalin's Soviet Union. Camus's answer to the dark world of brutality reflected by the war (during which he participated in the resistance) and the frustrations of the post-war period was for the individual to search for meaning in life by choosing a path of action—even revolt—against absurdity, irrationality, and tyrannies of all kinds. The rebel should act, according to Camus, from a personal sense of responsibility and moral choice independent of belief in God or in a political system. Confronting the arrival of murderous disease in the Algerian city of Oran, Dr. Rieux, the central figure in Camus's *The Plague* (1947), does not believe in God or absolute standards of morality, but he nonetheless helps people respond to the epidemic.

The "theater of the absurd," which also reflected intellectuals' reaction to the horrors of the war, was centered in Paris from 1948 to about 1968. It offered highly unconventional and anti-rational plays. The Irish-born Samuel Beckett (1906–1989) and other playwrights sought to shock audiences with provocative themes and by stringing together seemingly unrelated events and dialogue to demonstrate that existence is without purpose—absurd. They rejected plots, conventional settings, and individual identities. Their clownish, mechanical characters are perpetual exiles alienated in a bizarre, nightmarish world that makes no sense. The lack of causality in these plays is a

A gathering of intellectuals after the war, including Jean-Paul Sartre (seated left), Albert Camus (seated center), Pablo Picasso (standing with arms folded), and Simone de Beauvoir (to the far right and standing next to some of Picasso's work).

commentary on life itself. Beckett's *Waiting for Godot* (begun in 1948 but not published in French until 1952 and in English two years later) tells a disconnected tale of two old derelicts, Vladimir and Estragon (although they call themselves by childish nicknames). They meet night after night in anticipation of the arrival of a certain Godot (perhaps intended to be a diminutive of God), though it is never clear what difference in their lives his arrival would ever make, if any. He never comes, so we never know.

Anti-Americanism emerged as a current among many European intellectuals in the post-war period. This reflected hostility to U.S. foreign and nuclear policy during the Cold War and fear of American domination of NATO. The U.S. placement of nuclear weapons in Western Europe, beginning in West Germany in 1955, generated both anti-nuclear organizations and protests. Intellectuals also criticized U.S. culture as reeking of vulgar materialism. There was an economic dimension to this struggle, as U.S. companies and products dramatically augmented their presence in Western Europe. None generated more controversy than Coca-Cola. During the early 1950s, the French government feared the competition that Coke could give the wine industry. Encouraged by the powerful wine lobby, the French government tried—ultimately without success—to keep Coke from the French market.

Yet Europe also continued to embrace some aspects of U.S. culture. World War II brought only a brief hiatus in the export to Europe of Hollywood films, which audiences flocked to see. American film stars became those of the continent (at the same time, some European actors and actresses, such as Richard Burton, Marlene Dietrich, Sophia Loren, Audrey Hepburn, and Elizabeth Taylor became stars in the United States). Yet Western European filmmakers made important contributions to cinema. While most American film producers emphasized light entertainment (such as westerns and war movies with special effects), Italy's Federico Fellini (*La Strada*, 1956, and *La Dolce Vita*, 1959) and Sweden's Ingmar Bergman (*The Seventh Seal*, 1956) turned out serious art films. French New Wave directors, including Jean-Luc Godard (*Breathless*, 1959) and François Truffaut (*400 Blows*, 1959), rebelled against traditional cinematographic techniques, using innovations such as jump cuts and disruptive editing to create a sense of dislocation. Their experimental films explored human relationships and often portrayed antiheroes. In contrast, the English producer and director Alfred Hitchcock (1899–1980) frightened and intrigued generations of audiences with riveting suspense films like *Psycho* (1960).

In France, some films took subjects from recent and sometimes painful history, notably Gilles Pontecorvo's *The Battle of Algiers* (1961), in which appeared some actual participants of the Algerian insurrection (see pp. 1169–1171), to which the film is sympathetic. Marcel Orphuls's documentary about collaboration and resistance in World War II France, *The Sorrow and the Pity* (1969), helped spur the rethinking of the extent of French collaboration with the Nazis during the Vichy years.

Intellectuals of the left were preoccupied by the possibilities of social liberation. Frantz Fanon (1925–1961), a black French social critic from Martinique, explored the revolutionary potential of the Third World, some of which were unaligned in the Cold War, in *The Wretched of the Earth* (1961). The French anthropologist Claude Lévi-Strauss (1908–) espoused cultural relativism, moving anthropology away from a Western-centered view of "peripheral" or "underdeveloped" regions with his work on Brazil and Southeast Asia. Lévi-Strauss's interest in how communities behave, too, led away from the emphasis on the individual that characterized both Freudianism and existentialism.

Intellectuals in the Soviet Union were stymied by the state. Writers, artists, and filmmakers confronted a state apparatus that made the costs of free expression so high that voluntary adherence to state-dictated norms followed. "Socialist realism" (art and literature of generally horrendous quality, intended to inspire the population by showing smiling Soviet citizens at work; see Chapter 25) was the only authorized form of artistic expression; the works of most Western artists were condemned as tools of capitalism. Art was intended to encourage devotion to and sacrifice for the state. Stalin gave official approval to the crackpot theories of the geneticist Trofim Lysenko (1898–1976), who insisted that knowledge or beliefs that were experienced by one generation could be genetically inherited. Stalin's particular interest in this theory was that it suggested that party members who learned official orthodoxy and experienced conformity in social behavior would pass on the same characteristics to their offspring.

Advances for Women

In the decades following World War II, the status of women gradually improved, although their situation varied across the continent. While women lost some skilled jobs to men returning from service after the war, economic expansion and the creation of more white-collar jobs provided new employment possibilities. Simone de Beauvoir's *The Second Sex* (1949) helped mobilize movements for the rights of women in the United States and, more slowly, in Europe. In Western countries, the important contribution of working women made it difficult to continue to deny half the population the right to vote. After the war, women received the suffrage in France, Italy, Belgium, and Portugal. Women probably were more equal in the countries of the Soviet bloc (where there were no free elections) in terms of employment opportunities, although in practice this often meant that they bore the dual burden of wage earning and domestic duties. In the Soviet Union and Sweden, women made up more than half of all employees, and more than a third in every European country. In Western Europe, more and more middle-class women began to work full-time. Beginning in 1977, French women no longer needed their husbands' permission to work. In Communist countries, women more easily entered the medical profession, but men dominated the state bureaucracies. Women were most successful in reaching rough equality in the Scandinavian countries, least so in the Mediterranean lands where traditional biases remained difficult to overcome.

At the same time, the number of female university students rose dramatically, and so did the number of women in the professions. Women received legal protection against job discrimination in England in the late 1960s, and in France the government created a Ministry for the Status of Women.

Feminism, reviving during the 1968 protests, helped the cause of women's rights. Gradually, the percentage of women serving in legislatures increased. Moreover, gays and lesbians gained more rights beginning in the 1970s, even if some countries retained laws permitting discrimination against them.

Catholicism in Modern Europe

Like the nations of Western Europe, the Catholic Church, for centuries a major force in European life, has been forced to confront pressure for change. Within the Catholic Church, a liberal current of thought and action developed in response to some of the social problems of modern life. "Worker priests" entered factories in the 1950s, trying to win back workers to the Church while supporting their demands for better working conditions, until the pope condemned the movement. The election in 1958 of the more liberal Pope John XXIII signaled a new direction, marked by the opening of dialogue with other religions. Pope John presided over a council (Vatican II) that undertook significant changes in Church practices, allowing the Mass to be said in local languages and appointing more cardinals from other places than Europe and North America, without altering dogma.

Pope John's successor Paul VI continued the move toward ecumenism, visiting Istanbul and Jerusalem to meet with leaders of the Eastern Orthodox churches. But several notable theologians who challenged Church doctrine drew the wrath of Rome. In 1978, Paul died, as did his successor, John Paul I, after only two months on the throne of Saint Peter. The puffs of white smoke rising from the Vatican chimney then announced the first non-Italian pope since the sixteenth century, the Polish-born Pope John Paul II (Karol Wojtyla, 1920–2005; succeeded by Benedict XVI). While remaining conservative on matters of faith and doctrine, the new pope traveled far and wide across the world, calling for social justice. He became a symbol of hope for millions of oppressed people. If the percentages of Catholics practicing their religion fell rapidly in France, Italy, and Spain, the Catholic Church retained particular allegiance in Poland, Croatia, Portugal, and Ireland. Yet even these solidly Catholic countries legalized divorce, despite ecclesiastical opposition.

An industrial chaplain speaks with a factory worker in Scotland, in an effort to liberalize the Catholic Church and bring it into modern life.

An Urban World

Europe rapidly urbanized following World War II. In the German industrial Rhineland, it became difficult to tell where one city ended and another began. Giant cities like London and Paris engulfed their surrounding regions. In Eastern Europe, the population living in cities increased from 37.5 million at the end of the 1940s to 58 million twenty years later.

The necessity of housing millions of new urban residents contributed to a uniformity of architectural style. Tall, drab, uniform towers filled with small apartments sprang up in and around major urban centers, providing adequate lodging, but not much more, in cramped quarters with thin walls. Commuting became a fact of urban life in much of Europe. By the 1980s, almost 20 percent of the French population resided in Paris and its surroundings. Of this 20 percent, only about 3 million lived in the City of Light itself, the rest inhabiting sprawling suburbs.

In the early 1960s, the Soviets began to build new suburbs and satellite towns to accommodate the population seeking to live in Moscow, which grew from 2 million in 1926 to more than 5 million in 1959. Leningrad's population increased from 1.7 million to 3.3 million during the same period.

Rapid urban growth, closely tied to the concentration of large-scale industries, posed problems of health and safety. Factories increasingly polluted the air of industrial regions. Moreover, the number of cars on the road increased from 5 million in 1948 to 44 million in 1965. The construction of new freeways and toll roads could not begin to keep up with the increase in traffic. The traffic jam in Europe began, as cities became increasingly clogged with automobiles, which also polluted the air. Nonetheless, projects of urban renewal enhanced the quality of life in cities and towns. West German, Belgian, French, and Dutch cities, among others, sported shining urban centers, with some streets reserved for beleaguered pedestrians tired of dodging onrushing cars and the aggressive chaos of honking horns.

Living Better

The transportation and communications revolutions made the world a much smaller place. With a gradual reduction in the workday and higher wages, families had more time and money for leisure. Travel became an essential part of life. Air travel gradually linked European cities to each other and to other continents. With the introduction of the passenger jet in the late 1950s, the airplane replaced the passenger ship for cross-Atlantic travel. The era of the shipboard romance was over.

The rapid rise of international tourism offers another example of economic globalization. Jumbo jets greatly increased the number of passengers who could be squeezed into a single plane, reducing the cost of tickets. The era of the charter flight began in the 1960s. Tourists from the United States and, beginning in the 1980s, from Japan, arrived in Europe in droves. North American, Asian, and African destinations became more common for Europeans.

The French and British governments collaborated on the development of the supersonic Concorde, which, in the late 1970s, began to fly a small number of extremely wealthy passengers from Paris and London to New York and Washington, D.C., in three hours and fifteen minutes, less than half the time of a regular jet. However, an aging fleet, a disastrous crash near a Paris airport, and years of financial losses ended supersonic travel by Concorde in 2003. Far more successful, the first high-speed trains (the TGVs) began service in France in 1981. They carry passengers in comfort at speeds well over 170 miles per hour. Other countries, too, developed fast trains. In 1994, the "Chunnel" opened, a thirty-mile tunnel linking France and Great Britain by trains running under the English Channel, putting London little more than two hours away from Paris and Brussels.

Beginning in the 1960s, millions of Europeans began to take to the road, above all in July and August, many heading toward the sunny beaches of southern Europe. Paid vacations became an expected part of the "good life." Tourism became essential to the economies of France, Spain, Italy, Portugal, and Greece.

American consumerism and popular culture found increasing favor in European societies. Supermarkets began to put many small grocery stores out of business. American words and terms crept into European languages. Tennis shoes and tee-shirts swept Europe, and so did American television shows. By the late 1970s, McDonald's had begun to dot European capitals and gradually smaller cities as well. In the 1980s, EuroDisney (now called Disneyland-Paris), opened its doors outside of Paris. One French theatrical director called it "a cultural Chernobyl" (referring to the nuclear accident in Ukraine in 1986). In the first decade of the new century, Starbuck's cafés began to arrive in Europe in increasing numbers.

Communications also underwent an amazing revolution in Europe as elsewhere. Household telephones became more common in the 1960s in most of Western Europe. Forty years later, cell phones had taken over, increasingly putting telephone booths out of business. (Reacting to the annoyance of people shouting into portable phones on trains and street corners and in restaurants, or while driving, one wag noted that he had had great faith in humanity until the arrival of the cell phone.) The cost of transatlantic phone calls fell rapidly with the advent of optical fiber in the 1980s. Then in the 1990s the computer revolution and the Internet put a world of information at the fingertips of Europeans, as well as people almost everywhere.

Television helped shape a mass consumer culture, catapulting entertainers to fame and making household names of politicians who could be heard instead of simply imagined. The first television sets had been viewed at the World's Fair in New York City in 1939. By the late 1960s, a majority of Western European households had a television, and by the mid-1970s, relatively

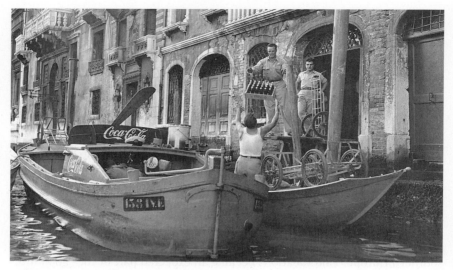

Delivering Coca-Cola in Venice.

few were without one. In the mid-1980s, the U.S.-based CNN network began to reach across the world. Just as television coverage of dramatic news events could be seen around the world, so sports took on an increasingly global dimension as well (above all, the World Cup and the Olympics, but also games of the National Basketball Association, with the globalization of that sport).

The era of television and radio ended the great age of the newspaper. During the first years after the war, Europeans read more—and arguably better—newspapers than ever before or since. As Europeans increasingly received their news and their entertainment from television and radio, however, newspapers merged and many folded. With the exception of the stately, serious dailies like *Le Monde* of Paris, the British *Manchester Guardian*, the German *Frankfurter Allgemeine*, and *La Stampa* of Milan, an increasing number of tabloid papers relied upon sensationalism, scandals, and the proclamation of juicy unsubstantiated rumor as truth to attract readers. In the Soviet Union, where the state was the only source of printed news, more than 7 million copies of *Pravda* were printed every day.

Credit cards and then personal computers transformed the way people make purchases. In the context of the ongoing revolution in communications, the advent of computer viruses demonstrated the extent to which the world has become increasingly interconnected. The apparent vulnerability of even the most sophisticated computer systems to knowledgeable hackers has led to fears for national security systems. In this way, too, Europe entered a new era.

Oil and the Global Economy

The Six-Day Arab-Israeli War of 1967 and the 1973 Yom Kippur War both resulted in easy Israeli victories over their Arab rivals. Israel now held all of Jerusalem, a holy city for Christians, Jews, and Arabs, and occupied the West Bank and the Gaza Strip. While the United States has almost always supported Israeli actions, the plight of the stateless Palestinian people has attracted the attention of Arab states, in particular. In 1973, following a short, unsuccessful war against Israel by its Arab neighbors, the oil-producing Arab states began an embargo of the supply of oil from the Middle East; it was undertaken by the Organization of Petroleum Exporting Countries (OPEC).

The Arab oil embargo led to a rapid rise in the price of oil and contributed to the high inflation that undermined Western economies for the rest of the 1970s. Dependency on oil led states to urge people to consume less gasoline (for example, by encouraging greater use of public transportation and, in the United States, by reducing speed limits). Britain and Norway each began to extract oil in the stormy North Sea. Some European countries, especially France, had already begun to develop nuclear installations to generate more energy.

The oil crisis helped bring an end to what had been a long period of relative prosperity and stability. The subsequent rising energy prices undermined

British motorists waiting for gasoline during the Arab oil embargo in 1973. The sign on the left indicates that French motorists are welcome to wait as well.

the ability of European states to support their extensive social services. The oil crisis also helped cause the economic recession that gripped Western Europe from the mid-1970s to the mid-1980s. Inflation, which had been at modest levels during the 1950s and 1960s but had been accentuated by the U.S. war in Vietnam, then began to soar. The oil embargo brought unemployment, which also strained European welfare budgets.

CONCLUSION

The end of World War II engendered two major changes that largely defined international politics for the next decades. First, the post-war division of Europe into zones of U.S. influence in the West and Soviet domination in the East brought a Cold War between the two superpowers, in which Western European states, Soviet Eastern European and Balkan satellites, and so-called Third World, or unaligned countries, most of them underdeveloped, became caught up. Second, sacrifices made by the colonies of the European great powers during the war—including military service and considerable loss of life—encouraged national liberation movements. These movements and the resistance they encountered from colonial powers led to a dramatic period of decolonization.

CHAPTER 28

THE COLD WAR AND THE END OF EUROPEAN EMPIRES

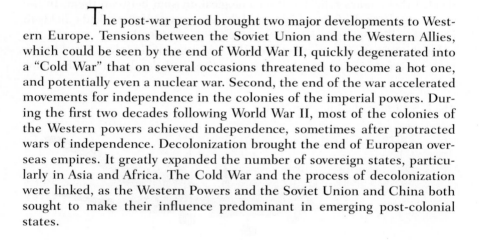

The post-war period brought two major developments to Western Europe. Tensions between the Soviet Union and the Western Allies, which could be seen by the end of World War II, quickly degenerated into a "Cold War" that on several occasions threatened to become a hot one, and potentially even a nuclear war. Second, the end of the war accelerated movements for independence in the colonies of the imperial powers. During the first two decades following World War II, most of the colonies of the Western powers achieved independence, sometimes after protracted wars of independence. Decolonization brought the end of European overseas empires. It greatly expanded the number of sovereign states, particularly in Asia and Africa. The Cold War and the process of decolonization were linked, as the Western Powers and the Soviet Union and China both sought to make their influence predominant in emerging post-colonial states.

COLD WAR

In a speech in March 1946, Churchill lamented that "an iron curtain is drawn down upon their front. We do not know what is going on behind." As Europe counted its millions of dead, hot war gave way to the Cold War between East and West. The Red Army's drive into Central Europe in the waning months of the war had left part of Central Europe and Eastern Europe and the Balkans under Soviet domination. The division of Europe into two camps—Communist, dominated by the Soviet Union, and Western democracies, under the influence of the United States—was formalized by the creation of corresponding military alliances after the war. The

Cold War helped prevent any possible return to the relative isolationism that had characterized the United States during the inter-war period. The United States, now by far the wealthiest state in the world, had 450 military bases in 36 countries in 1955. At the same time, the Soviet Union rapidly added to its military arsenal, soon having the second largest navy in the world.

Germany became the first focal point for Cold War tensions. The failure of the Soviet, British, French, and U.S. foreign ministers to agree on the nature of a peace treaty with Germany in the spring of 1947 began the Cold War. That year Stalin, who had in 1943 officially announced the end of the Comintern, which had been established with the goal of fomenting worldwide revolution, inaugurated its successor organization, the Cominform. It was intended to consolidate Soviet authority in the states of Eastern Europe (see Chapter 27). This, too, accentuated tensions with the Western powers. In 1949, the Soviet-occupied eastern zone of Germany became the German Democratic Republic; the American, British, and French occupation zones became the German Federal Republic. The barbed wire and minefields that divided these zones reflected the ideological division between them. In the meantime, both the Soviet Union and the Western powers worked quickly to create intelligence agencies of great size to spy on the other.

Each international crisis between the Soviet Union and the United States took on great significance because scientists had developed bombs many

The U.S. airlift to Berlin, 1948–1949.

times more destructive than those that had leveled Hiroshima and Nagasaki. During the 1950s, children in the United States participated in mock air raid drills, putting their heads between their knees to practice bracing for the shock of a nuclear explosion, as if such a position would make the slightest difference in the case of a nuclear attack. The United States and the Soviet Union drew up plans to evacuate American and Soviet leaders into elaborate shelters from which they could order the launching of more missiles and bombs. Britain exploded its first atomic bomb in 1952, France in 1960. China, too, before long had "the bomb." In the 1970s, Israel, India, and Pakistan gained nuclear capability.

The Cold War focused on a series of crises that, drawing world attention, exacerbated tensions between the United States and the Soviet Union. The Soviet Union claimed that the Western Allies had unilaterally broken agreements reached at the Potsdam Conference. In July 1948, Soviet troops blocked trains and truck routes through the Soviet zone of occupation in East Germany to prevent supplies from reaching the Allied half of Berlin. The Allies began a massive airlift of supplies to West Berlin; at times, planes landed in Berlin every three minutes, bringing much-needed food, medicine, and other necessities. After secret negotiations, Stalin backed down, allowing trucks to roll through the German Democratic Republic beginning in 1949, the year of that state's creation. Berlin remained divided into eastern and western zones.

A Greek soldier stands guard during the Civil War in 1947.

In Greece, the departure of German troops led to a bloody civil war that lasted until 1949, pitting Greek Communists against an alliance of forces that supported the monarchy. The Soviet Union held to an agreement made with Churchill in 1944 not to intervene militarily, but it provided the Communists with considerable material assistance. The United States and Britain aided the monarchist forces, who finally prevailed in 1949 and then banned the Communist Party.

The Cold War soon reached Asia. Japan's defeat left China divided between the nationalist government of Chiang Kai-shek (1887–1975), which held the south, and the forces of the Communist leader Mao Zedong (1893–1976). In the civil war that followed, Mao's Communist forces gradually pushed the nationalist forces out of China. In full retreat by 1949, Chiang Kai-shek's army occupied the large island of Formosa (Taiwan). There Chiang established a government that claimed to represent all of China. On the mainland, Mao proclaimed the People's Republic of China. The Soviet Union quickly recognized the new, giant Communist state, while the United States recognized the nationalist government of Taiwan as China's legitimate government. In the atmosphere of the Cold War, the United States and its allies worried they would be facing a unified Communist front that included China.

People in Beijing welcome Chinese Communist forces, 1949. Note the portrait of Mao Zedong in the center.

The Korean War (1950–1953)

Adjoining China, Korea had a Communist "people's republic" in the north, supported by the Soviet Union, and in the south, a republic created under the patronage of the United States. In June 1950, North Korean troops, upon Stalin's go-ahead, invaded the southern zone. General Douglas MacArthur took command of the U.S. forces defending South Korea, backed by small contingents sent by other members of the United Nations, which had passed a resolution condemning the Communist invasion. For the first time—with the exception of events in Greece—Communist and non-Communist forces engaged in open warfare, a conflict fought with conventional weapons, but with nuclear bombs lurking in the background.

Although Chinese troops were aiding the northern side, U.S. forces pushed back the Communist forces in 1951. In any case, neither side wanted to see the war expand beyond Korea. The armistice signed in July 1953 left the division between North and South Korea almost the same as before the war, but at the cost of 3 million casualties (including 140,000 U.S. troops killed or wounded).

The Korean War heightened Cold War tensions in Europe. To the Allies, the war raised the outside possibility of a Soviet-led invasion of the German Federal Republic, similar to that launched by North Korean troops against South Korea. In the United States, the war contributed to a mood

U.S. marines file past a burning building in North Korea during the Korean War, 1950.

of anti-communism and fear of "the enemy within" that bordered on mass hysteria, orchestrated by Senator Joseph McCarthy. "McCarthyism" entered the dictionary as a term for political name-calling and persecution.

Stirrings in Eastern Europe

Following Stalin's death in 1953, East German workers complained loudly about high quotas, low wages, and food shortages. On June 17, 1953, Berlin workers rioted. East German troops, backed by Soviet tanks, ended the disturbances. A wave of repression followed. That year alone, more than 330,000 East Germans fled to the West.

The East German Communist government realized that state planning had to provide more consumer goods. Ideology alone could not generate commitment. The Soviet Union sent material assistance to the German Democratic Republic and let it write off most of the war reparations owed from the eastern zone. Despite inadequate housing, few automobiles, and occasional food shortages, more consumer goods gradually became available in the 1960s. Long rows of drab apartments sprang up near the Brandenburg Gate that divided East and West Berlin. State-sponsored clubs for children provided recreation, as well as ideological indoctrination. Through intensive training and programming—and, in some cases, steroids—East Germany began in the late 1960s to produce athletes of great accomplishment in international sporting events, particularly in swimming and track and field.

Khrushchev's denunciation of Stalin and the "thaw" in foreign and domestic policies had repercussions in Eastern Europe in 1956. That year the Communist government of Poland reined in the secret police and gave amnesty to thousands of political prisoners. However, strikes soon brought military repression. In October 1956, Wladyslaw Gomulka (1905–1982), a moderate imprisoned during the Stalin era, returned from oblivion to head the government by the Polish Politburo. A reformer, Gomulka purged Stalinists and reached accommodation with the enormously influential Polish Catholic Church. Furthermore, Gomulka halted the collectivization of agriculture. Independent peasants held three-quarters of the nation's arable land, a far greater percentage of privately held farms than in any other country in the Eastern bloc. However, Gomulka also reassured the Soviet Union that Poland had no intention of abandoning the Warsaw Pact or turning its back on socialism.

Soviet concessions to Yugoslavia and Poland encouraged a movement for reform in Hungary, where liberal Communists were already eager to turn their backs on Stalinism. Imre Nagy (c. 1895–1958), a liberal, had risen to become prime minister of Hungary. He had sought to move Hungarian manufacturing away from heavy industry in order to increase production of consumer goods. Nagy also tolerated peasant resistance to the implementation of agricultural collectivization. At the same time, workers' councils sprung up spontaneously, espousing reform. In 1955, Nagy's policies drew opposition from Communist hard-liners, and he was ousted from office. A profound movement for reform now took root in Hungary. Intellectuals and students held meetings to discuss possible paths to liberalization. A defiant response from the new prime minister led to a demonstration of 50,000 people on October 23, 1956. Protesters smashed a statue of Stalin. Police opened fire on a crowd trying to storm a radio station. Hungarian troops sent to rout the demonstrators refused to fire, in some cases joining those now protesting communism itself. That night, the Hungarian Communist leadership requested Soviet assistance but also named Nagy as prime minister in the hope of ending the demonstrations. Western radio broadcasts heard in Hungary hinted that outside help might be forthcoming, firming popular resolve. Nagy named a new coalition government that included liberal Communists. He began to negotiate with the Soviet government, but he made clear that he intended to end the one-party system by adding several non-Communists to his government. Furthermore, he called for Hungarian withdrawal from the Warsaw Pact and asked that Soviet troops be removed from his country.

To the Soviet government, Hungary's defection was unthinkable because it might spark similar movements in other Eastern European nations and even destabilize the republics of the Soviet Union. On November 4, Nagy announced that Hungary would withdraw from the Warsaw Pact. While the French, British, and U.S. governments were preoccupied with the Suez Canal crisis (see pp. 1164–1167), the Soviet government sent tanks and soldiers into Budapest and other major Hungarian cities to crush resistance. Nagy was tried and executed, along with about 2400 other people, perhaps many more. From 1956 through 1961, almost 400,000 people were found guilty of political crimes. More than 200,000 Hungarians fled to Western Europe and the United States. Soviet intervention ended hope that Stalin's death might bring about change in Eastern Europe and end the Cold War. János Kádár (1912–1989) became Hungary's new leader, backed by the Soviet army. Over the long run, Kádár skillfully liberalized the Communist regime, while remaining careful not to antagonize unnecessarily the Soviet Union with any ideological justification for his policies. He relaxed government control if the interests of the Communist Party were not at stake. Hungary's "goulash communism" included market-oriented, decentralized reforms and toleration of some degree of entrepreneurship and profit. The result was a higher standard of living than existed elsewhere in the Communist world.

With their hands full with Hungary, the Soviets were in no position to move aggressively against Poland. In any case, Gomulka was careful to give them no excuse for military action. He gradually rescinded some of the relatively liberal policies, including toleration of free artistic and political expression, and put workers' councils that had sprung up in 1956 under party control.

In Yugoslavia, despite its determined independence from the Soviet Union, open political opposition was not tolerated. One of the distinguished founders of post-war Yugoslavia, the Montenegrin intellectual Milovan Djilas (1911–1995), was expelled from the party in 1954 for having contended in his book *The New Class: An Analysis of the Communist System* (1961) that privileged party officials had become a ruling caste, with little in common with ordinary people.

In the meantime, in the Soviet Union the liberal agitation in Poland and the Hungarian Revolution in 1956 threatened Khrushchev's authority. Stalinists claimed that Khrushchev's attack on Stalin at the Twentieth Party Congress in 1956 was to blame for agitation in those countries. Furthermore, Soviet aid to stabilize its Eastern European client states undermined economic development at home. But, at the same time, the failure of the Western powers to intervene on behalf of Hungary—because they feared nuclear war with the Soviet Union—seemed to the Soviets to legitimize the division of Europe into spheres of influence dominated by the United States and the Soviet Union.

Soviet–U.S. Tensions

Khrushchev was responsible for a mild thaw in the Cold War. The Soviet leader claimed that "peaceful coexistence" was possible between the two political worlds. In 1955, Khrushchev met with U.S. President Dwight Eisenhower (1890–1969) in Geneva, the first of the "summit" meetings between the two great powers. At the Twentieth Party Congress the following year, Khrushchev rejected Stalin's contention that Communist and capitalist powers would inevitably go to war. Soviet foreign policy became less contentious and somewhat more flexible. Looking to the Third World for allies, the Soviet leader courted India, Egypt, and Syria, as well as a number of smaller states, winning their friendship with technical and material assistance. Soviet foreign policy was carried out with the aim of detaching countries from the direct influence of the United States.

In 1955, the Soviet Union and its Eastern European allies countered NATO, the defense organization of the Western powers, by signing the Warsaw Pact, which offered its members similar guarantees to those of NATO against attack. It formalized and internationalized the individual pacts of mutual defense that the Soviet Union had signed with its client states during or immediately following World War II. The Warsaw Pact provided a new justification for the stationing of Soviet troops in Poland, Hungary, Czechoslovakia, and East Germany.

Soviet armed intervention in Hungary in 1956 increased mutual suspicion between East and West, and rapid advances in Soviet military science further augmented the rivalry with the West. Bilateral negotiations between the Soviet Union and the United States to reduce their respective nuclear capabilities failed in 1955 and again in 1958. In 1957, the Soviets launched the first satellite (*Sputnik*) after developing an intercontinental ballistic missile (ICBM). Space exploration became part of the Cold War. The United States won the race to the moon, when American astronauts landed on the lunar surface in July 1969, an event seen by millions on television.

In May 1960, the Soviets shot down an American U-2 plane taking spy photographs from high over the Soviet Union. The Soviets demanded an apology for this violation of Soviet air space and received none. Khrushchev then refused to participate in a Geneva summit meeting (probably also because Soviet relations with China were rapidly deteriorating).

Again Cold War tensions centered on Germany. In 1958, the hot-tempered Khrushchev threatened to hand over to East German authorities the administration of all of Berlin, but backed down in the face of Allied intransigence. In the meantime, streams of East Germans—about 2.6 million people between 1950 and 1962—left for the West, most to the German Federal Republic. The exodus included many doctors and other trained specialists vital to East Germany. Yet between 1950 and 1964, about 500,000 West Germans moved to the East, some fleeing the persecution of Communists in the German Federal Republic, and others simply wanting to be with their families.

On August 17, 1961, Berliners awoke to find East German workers building a wall to divide the eastern sector from the western one. Ground floor windows that permitted escape from East to West were boarded up. Telephone lines leading to West Berlin were cut.

The Berlin Wall became a symbol of the Cold War. U.S. President John F. Kennedy visited Berlin later that summer to view the wall, proclaiming in a speech that he, too, was a "Berliner" (not realizing that a Berliner was also a popular name for a local pastry). Enforcement was brutal, although a subsequent relaxation of East German controls allowed Germans on both sides to visit their relatives. Guards checked car trunks and even the bottoms of cars looking for hidden passengers trying to escape. Western tourists climbed stairs to have a look at East German guards staring back from watchtowers behind barbed wire on the other side. Still, people tried to escape and many succeeded: they sprinted across no-man's-land, defying a hail of bullets, swam across rivers, flew small planes or homemade balloons into West Germany, dug tunnels, and hid in trucks and cars. Some did not make it: hundreds were killed attempting to escape.

Because of the threat of nuclear war, the Cuban Missile Crisis of 1962 was the world's most dangerous moment since the end of World War II. The island of Cuba, which had been a virtual protectorate of the United States since the Spanish-American War in 1898, became a Communist state in 1959 after Fidel Castro (1926–) led a guerrilla force that ousted the corrupt American protégé, Fulgencio Batista (1901–1973). Batista's supporters, with the help of the U.S. military, then launched an ill-conceived invasion of

(*Left*) The Berlin Wall goes up in 1961. (*Right*) U.S. President John F. Kennedy addresses West Berliners, 1961.

Cuba at the "Bay of Pigs" in 1961. It failed miserably. In October 1962, American aerial photographs revealed that Soviet missiles capable of being armed with nuclear warheads were stationed on the island of Cuba. The U.S. government demanded the removal of the missiles and threatened to destroy them if this demand was not met. Some knowledgeable advisers to President John F. Kennedy estimated the chances of the outbreak of a nuclear war at between one-third and one-half, dangerous odds indeed. Debates in the United Nations helped buy time while negotiations proceeded. The world breathed a collective sigh of relief as Khrushchev ordered the missiles removed.

Despite the fact that the United States and Soviet Union both signed a 1963 treaty banning nuclear tests, the arms race had accelerated. Soviet and American naval vessels and submarines closely monitored each other's movements. The Soviet secret police (KGB) and the American Central Intelligence Agency (CIA) spread their well-financed spy networks worldwide. Periodic spy scandals occurred in the West, most notably in Britain, where several prominent intellectuals turned out to have been spying for the Soviet Union. The growing number of colonies receiving their independence from Britain and France fostered increased competition between the two systems in Africa and Asia.

By the mid-1960s, the rivalry between the United States and the Soviet Union spread to Southeast Asia. In 1964, the United States officially became involved in the civil war in Vietnam. When President Lyndon B.

Johnson (1908–1973) announced that an American naval vessel had been attacked off the coast of Vietnam—which in fact never occurred—the American Congress passed the Tonkin Gulf Resolution against the North Vietnamese government. The United States committed more and more men and material in support of the South Vietnamese government against the North Vietnamese Communist troops of Ho Chi Minh and their allies, the Vietcong guerrillas fighting in the south. The Soviets backed the Communist forces. The costly American role in the civil war came under increasing opposition at home and in Europe, beginning with university students. The Vietnam War badly divided public opinion in the United States and strained U.S. relations with its allies.

Soviet leader Nikita Khrushchev and Cuban leader Fidel Castro meet in Moscow, 1963.

Sino-Soviet Rivalry

The alliance between Mao's China and the Soviet Union, cemented by the Korean War, began to break apart. A common Communist ideology could not gloss over issues of power politics between the two giants. Not only did they share an immense frontier, but certain border regions—above all, Mongolia—had long been claimed by both states. Border clashes took place in 1969. In addition, growing Soviet influence in India threatened Chinese relations with the subcontinent. Khrushchev's turn away from Stalinism angered Mao, as did the Soviet leader's overtures for support among Asian political leaders. Khrushchev's policy of peaceful coexistence with the West—and particularly his visit to Washington, D.C., in 1959—irritated Mao, who used the perceived threat from the West as a means of pushing the Chinese to make more sacrifices to modernize the economy. In China, a "cult of personality" focused on Chairman Mao just as one in the Soviet Union had celebrated Stalin. Furthermore, attempts to modernize China's economy had been heavily influenced by Stalin's five-year plans, which had emphasized heavy industry. At the same time, China underwent rapid, ruthless collectivization of all industrial and agricultural production. Chinese economic growth made the Chinese less dependent on Soviet technical advisers and they were sent home.

The Chinese Communist government also grew increasingly uneasy about Russia's nuclear weapons. Mao believed Stalin's contention that war between capitalism and Communism was inevitable. He resented the unwillingness of the Soviets under Khrushchev, who had abandoned that particular tenet of Communist thought, to share their military secrets. In 1964, Mao accused the Soviet Union of itself being an "imperialist" power because it dominated the smaller states of Eastern Europe.

Chinese and Russian diplomats and advisers now competed as rivals for the ears of Third World leaders. The Chinese Communists received support from an unlikely place. Albania, the small, isolated, largely Muslim state squeezed between Yugoslavia and the Adriatic Sea, broke with the Soviet Union. The Soviet Union broke off diplomatic relations with Albania in 1961. This represented an embarrassing rejection of Soviet authority, particularly when put into the context of the ongoing Sino-Soviet split. However, Albanian Communist leader Enver Hoxha (1908–1985) then broke with the Chinese Communist leadership in 1978, criticizing China's improved relations with the United States.

The Brezhnev Era

Soviet economic stagnation and the humiliation of the Cuban Missile Crisis contributed to Khrushchev's sudden fall from power. Some military leaders had opposed Khrushchev's support of economic planning that emphasized consumer goods over heavy industry, although severe shortages still alienated many Soviet citizens. Old Stalinists surfaced again, resistant

Medium-range Soviet strategic missiles displayed in a military parade in Moscow on November 7, 1963, in a Soviet show of strength.

to any reform. Army commanders, wary of the Chinese situation, accused Khrushchev of having taken too great a risk by establishing missile sites in Cuba. In October 1964, Khrushchev returned to Moscow for a meeting called by his enemies only to find out that he was being retired into honorable obscurity.

Leonid Brezhnev (1906–1982), who had risen in the Communist Party with Khrushchev's assistance, became its general secretary. Brezhnev returned to Communist orthodoxy. He affirmed the authority and prestige of party bureaucrats and of the KGB, but he stopped well short of Stalinism. While building up Soviet military capability, the Soviet leader ordered an increase in the production of consumer goods. Nonetheless, centralized planning and agricultural collectivization remained the basis of the inefficient Soviet economy.

There was little talk of a "thaw" either inside or outside the Soviet Union during the Brezhnev era. Cynicism mounted within the Soviet Union, even among committed Communists who had long awaited the day when the corner would be turned and prosperity would arrive. That day never came.

Nuclear Weapons and Superpower Tensions

The phased U.S. withdrawal from Vietnam beginning in 1973 (followed two years later by the victory of the Communist North Vietnamese and their southern allies, the Vietcong) removed one thorny issue between the United States and the Soviet Union. Continued tension between the Soviet Union and China (accompanied by a concentration of Soviet forces along the disputed borders in Manchuria and Siberia) gradually eroded the old U.S. view of Communism as a monolithic force, engendering more realistic diplomatic assessments of international politics. Furthermore, both the United States and the Soviet Union faced daunting economic problems that partially shifted the focus of government to domestic concerns.

The period from 1969 to 1979 brought a period of détente between the Soviet Union and the United States, leading to serious negotiations between the two powers to reduce nuclear arms. In 1972, Soviet leader Leonid Brezhnev and U.S. President Richard Nixon (1913–1994) signed an arms-reduction agreement known as SALT I (Strategic Arms Limitation Talks), by which they agreed to maintain parity in nuclear offensive weapons systems. However, as military technology continued to advance rapidly, both sides began to defy the spirit of the agreement by developing new systems. Both the Soviet Union and the United States deployed new missiles in Europe. Nixon was forced to resign as U.S. president in 1974 because of the Watergate Affair: he had approved illegal operations against Democratic Party headquarters and then lied about what he knew. His successors sought to link further arms-reduction talks to issues of human rights in the Soviet Union. In 1979, U.S. President Jimmy Carter (1924–) and Brezhnev signed a new agreement, SALT II, by which the Soviets agreed to limit missile launchers and nuclear warheads and the United States agreed not to develop a new missile. Carter, however, had to withdraw the agreement from consideration by the Senate in January 1980 because of political opposition, primarily from conservatives who feared that the SALT II agreement would leave the Soviets with greater nuclear capability than that of the United States. As the number of nuclear weapons increased in Europe, anti-nuclear movements revived, particularly in Britain and Germany.

The Soviet invasion of Afghanistan in December 1979 put an end to détente. Soviet troops were sent in support of the pro-Soviet government, which was besieged by a variety of rebels, including Islamic fundamentalists, who received support from the United States. (One of the motives of the Soviet invasion of Afghanistan was to forestall fundamentalist movements in Soviet republics with sizable Muslim populations.) Reacting to the Soviet invasion, the United States limited grain sales to the Soviet Union and boycotted the Olympic Games in Moscow in 1980. The Soviet-American chill lasted into the mid-1980s.

Decolonization

The Second World War accelerated the independence movements that had developed after World War I. In the colonies in Africa, Asia, and Southeast Asia, the rise of nationalism led to movements demanding independence. Thus, beginning in the 1950s, European colonies became central actors in some of the dramas of international politics. The peacemakers at Versailles (particularly President Wilson) in 1919 had espoused nationalism as a principle for the territorial organization of states. But France and Britain, in particular, had been unwilling to grant freedom to their colonies, both viewing their empires as part of their national identities. During and after the war, the U.S. government had made clear its unwillingness to support the maintenance of the British and French colonial empires. The Soviet Union, too, was in principle against colonial empires, while, ironically, building something of an empire of its own by controlling states in Eastern Europe and the Balkans.

For his part, Winston Churchill had believed that if Britain was to remain a world power, it had to retain its empire, despite the opposition of Eisenhower to colonialism. "I have not become the king's first minister," Churchill thundered, "to preside over the liquidation of the British Empire." However, succeeding prime ministers realized that it would be better to grant colonies independence than to have to confront massive insurrections. With the economies of the Western European nations still suffering the effects of the war, the costs of resisting independence movements were high for the remaining imperial powers. Moreover, opposition to colonialism came not only from the colonized peoples but also from intellectuals, students, and political parties of the left at home.

The end of the colonial era reflected the relative decline of the European powers in international affairs. The sun finally set on the British Empire as its colonies became independent states. Britain and France left important traditions of government, culture, and language in Africa, Asia, and the Middle East (for example, French prestige in Lebanon). Britain's former colonies achieved independence peacefully for the most part. In contrast, France and Portugal battled to retain their colonies even in the face of popular insurgency. The Netherlands and Belgium both resisted nationalist movements briefly before recognizing the independence of their former colonies. In many colonies, educated and active groups stood ready to work for independence and, when that was achieved, to become leaders of new states. But during the 1960s and 1970s, the United States and the Soviet Union aggressively competed for influence in these young states. By 1980, more than half of the 154 members of the United Nations had been admitted to membership since 1956.

Decolonization in South and Southeast Asia

India, a densely populated, vastly complex subcontinent of many peoples, languages, cultures, and several major religions, was the largest colony in the world. Hindus formed the largest religion, but there were millions of Muslims as well, particularly in Bengal and Punjab in the north. Many Muslims wanted a partition of the subcontinent and the establishment of a Muslim state.

During the 1920s and 1930s, Indian nationalism developed among the Indian elite, some of whom had been educated in England (see Chapter 24). When World War II began, the British government asked the Congress Party, the largest Indian political organization, which included Sikhs and Muslims, for its support against the Japanese. The Hindu leaders of the Congress Party, Mahatmas Gandhi (1869–1948) and Jawaharlal Nehru (1889–1964), refused to offer unqualified support during the war, and the British government imprisoned them. In 1942, the British government promised them self-government following the war—and full status within the British Commonwealth—if India, which had provided thousands of soldiers for the fight (although Indian soldiers captured in Southeast Asia had joined the Japanese in 1943–1945), fully cooperated in the war against Japan. However, Nehru and Gandhi demanded complete independence for India. Gandhi, who dismissed the offer as "a post-dated check on a crashing bank," became a powerful symbol of Indian resolution to win independence by peaceful means. When he threatened a massive campaign of nonviolent resistance to British rule, the British government sent him to jail again. Political unrest swept through India following the war in 1945–1946.

Mahatmas Gandhi steps from a third-class train after Indian independence.

With the British Conservative Party out of government after the war, Labour Prime Minister Clement Attlee announced in 1946 that India would be granted full independence, which the Labour Party had long advocated. The last British viceroy, Lord Louis Mountbatten (1900–1979), oversaw the British departure in 1947. India became independent, but bitter fighting followed between Hindus and Muslims. The Muslim League, which represented Muslim interests, insisted on the creation of a separate Muslim nation; however, the Congress Party, dominated by Hindus, rejected this demand outright. Hindus and Muslims battled in much of India. Britain partitioned the Indian subcontinent: India would be largely Hindu, and Pakistan, which also obtained independence in 1947 and was divided into East Pakistan and West Pakistan on either side of India, would be Muslim. Since millions of Muslims lived in India and many Hindus lived in Pakistan, however, it proved impossible to draw state boundaries so that they exactly corresponded to ethnic and religious differences.

Fighting between Hindus and Muslims continued. Hindus drove millions of Muslims out of India. Many of them starved to death during forced marches to Pakistan. Likewise, about the same number of Hindus and Sikhs were expelled from Pakistan. A Hindu extremist assassinated Gandhi in 1948 because he had accepted the establishment of Pakistan.

India became the world's largest democracy (its population now is well over 1 billion people), but many daunting problems remained unsolved: poverty compounded by a phenomenally high birthrate, underdeveloped democratic institutions, and bitter religious rivalries. Pakistan faced similar challenges. The awkward division of Pakistan into East and West, separated by Hindu India, ended in 1971 when East Pakistan rebelled against

Pakistani authority. After Indian troops intervened against Pakistani forces, Bangladesh became an independent state, one of the poorest nations in the world. Meanwhile, the British government had also granted independence to other British colonies in Asia: the island of Ceylon (Sri Lanka) and Burma (Myanmar) in 1948, and Singapore in 1965.

In Southeast Asia, the end of Japanese occupation during World War II served as a catalyst for decolonization, leaving the way open for independence movements. The Japanese occupation had driven the British out of the Malay Peninsula and the Dutch colonists out of Indonesia. The states on the Malay Peninsula formed the Federation of Malaya after the war. Communists battled British troops off and on during the 1940s and 1950s, until Britain granted complete independence in 1957 to what became Malaysia in 1963. In Indonesia, the nationalist leader Sukarno (1901–1970) took advantage of the Dutch absence from the region to proclaim Indonesian independence. Negotiations arranged by the United Nations led the Netherlands to grant Indonesian independence in 1949. Sukarno called his government a "guided democracy," assuming the presidency for life in 1963. As the economy floundered, however, the Indonesian Communist Party grew in size. The Indonesian government accepted large sums of money from the Soviet Union and the United States. In 1965, Lieutenant General Suharto (1921–2008) seized power. Undertaking a bloody campaign of terror against Communists, he consolidated his dictatorship with the support of the armed forces. In 1998, riots in the capital of Jakarta led to his resignation.

Britain and the Middle East

British influence also declined in the Middle East. Growing dependence on oil as a source of energy made the Middle East increasingly important in international politics. Egypt had achieved independence after World War I. Britain still controlled Palestine as a Mandate. Zionists before World War I considered Palestine the promised land for Jews. In 1917, by the Balfour Declaration, the British government had supported the creation of a "national home for the Jewish people," with the understanding that "nothing shall be done which may prejudice the civil and religious rights of existing non-Jewish communities in Palestine." However, Palestine had an Arab majority. During the 1920s and 1930s, many Jews had emigrated there, hoping one day to construct a Jewish state. In the wake of World War II, they were joined by hundreds of thousands of Jews from Europe. For them, the Zionist revival and the creation of an independent Jewish state now seemed enormously more urgent, indeed becoming an important part of the collective identity of many Holocaust survivors. In 1947, the British government, already facing attacks from militant Jews committed to ending British occupation, asked the United Nations to resolve Palestine's future. In its first major international decision, the United Nations called for the division of Palestine into the Jewish state of Israel and an Arab state. That land intended for a new Arab state was incorporated into the neighboring states of Jordan and Egypt, as well as Israel. Israeli forces took over much of the British Mandate in 1948, achieving independence. Jerusalem, a holy city for Jews, Arabs, and Christians, was to remain temporarily under the control of the United Nations.

As in India, the policy of partition led to turmoil. Fighting between Palestinian Arabs and Jews began soon after the UN resolution. In May 1948, Arab forces from Egypt, Syria, Lebanon, and Jordan attacked the newly established state of Israel, but were defeated the following year. The victorious Israeli army expelled large numbers of Arabs from their lands, although about 150,000 Palestinian Arabs remained in Israel. At least 700,000 Palestinian refugees fled to Jordan, which had become independent in 1946. The seeds were sown for future conflicts. The Arab states refused to recognize the existence of Israel, as well as a separate Palestinian Arab identity. Palestinians retained some rights in Israel, such as being able to vote and to serve in the parliament. Yet those Palestinians remaining in Israel believed that they had been relegated to the status of second-class citizens, and they remained under military rule until 1965. After 1948, no new Arab towns were established in Israel, although the population of Palestinians increased five-fold, and until recently it remained Israeli policy that no land "redeemed" by Jews in Israel could be sold to non-Jews.

The Suez Canal Crisis

The Suez Canal had been the centerpiece of British interests and defenses in the Middle East since British troops first occupied Egypt in 1882. Although the British withdrawal from India in 1947 had somewhat reduced its strategic importance to Britain, about two-thirds of the oil from the Middle East on which Britain and Western Europe depended was transported through the canal. Egypt had been independent since 1922, but Britain maintained considerable influence there. Furthermore, the canal itself was owned by the British (more than 40 percent) and French governments, as well as by stockholders, primarily British.

In 1952, when Egyptian nationalist sentiment against Britain ran high (in part because the British government refused to allow Egypt to occupy Sudan), a group of young nationalist military officers overthrew Egyptian King Farouk in a bloodless coup. Gamal Abdel Nasser (1918–1970), the head of the new Egyptian government, emerged as one of the most influential figures in rising Pan-Arab nationalism. Nasser established Egyptian neutrality in the tug-of-war between East and West. He refused to sign a treaty with the United States, and he castigated Iran and Turkey for their pro-American policies.

As Egyptian nationalism mounted, the Egyptian government, which had renounced the Anglo-Egyptian alliance treaty of 1936, demanded British withdrawal from the narrow zone along the Suez Canal. In 1954, the Egypt-

(*Left*) A Russian cartoon salutes Nasser's seizure of the Suez Canal in July 1956. The banner reads "Shares of the Suez Canal Company Ltd." (*Right*) Sunken ships block the Suez Canal.

ian and British governments signed an agreement (vehemently opposed by some British Conservatives) by which British troops would begin a phased withdrawal that would be completed in June 1956. Britain would retain the right to send military forces back should the canal be attacked (presumably by the Soviet Union); the British and Egyptian governments would respect the freedom of navigation through the canal. Many Egyptians, particularly a radical organization, the Muslim Brotherhood, opposed this agreement, which seemed to maintain some degree of British control over the Suez Canal. They sought to end once and for all Egypt's semi-colonial status.

Egypt became a pawn in the struggle between the United States and the Soviet Union for the allegiance of non-aligned nations. Gradually, Nasser, who denounced the British and French role in the Middle East, turned toward the Soviet Union for economic and, in 1955, military support. He resented the United States for its close ties to Israel, which it had been quick to recognize in 1948, and spurned Britain's defensive pact with Turkey and Iraq (the Baghdad Pact, 1955). This pact was directed against the Soviet Union, which sought to increase its reach in the Middle East by capitalizing on considerable dissatisfaction among Arab nationalists with the role of the United States in the construction of a Middle East treaty association similar to NATO. The Soviet government signed an agreement with Egypt, promising to exchange weapons for Egyptian cotton. Egypt planned to construct the Aswan High Dam on the Upper Nile River, which Nasser believed would help modernize the Egyptian economy. The World Bank had agreed to finance the construction of the dam if Britain and the United States would contribute. But the U.S. government was increasingly suspicious of British goals. Indeed, the British government was planning Nasser's overthrow. On July 19, 1956, the United States suddenly withdrew its offer of a loan when it seemed that the Egyptian government would accept a Soviet offer to finance the dam's construction. On July 26, Nasser announced the nationalization of the Suez Canal, with the assurance, however, that shareholders would be compensated.

The British government, pushed by Conservatives who feared that Nasser would undermine British interests throughout the Middle East, decided on armed intervention. France, too, wanted Nasser out of power because of French interests in the canal. More than this, Nasser supported the Algerian National Liberation Front, which sought Algerian independence from France. The U.S. government sought to diffuse the crisis through negotiation.

The government of Israel, which was still technically at war with Egypt since 1948, was also concerned about emerging ties between Egypt and the Soviet Union. Moreover, the arrival of Soviet arms in Egypt raised fears of a possible Egyptian invasion of Israel. In October 1956, the British government came around to the French view that they should agree to an Israeli invasion of Egypt, which would provide both powers with an excuse to intervene militarily and occupy the Suez Canal Zone. (The U.S. government was kept unaware of these difficult negotiations.) Israel sent an invasion force into Egypt on October 29. The Egyptian army put up stiff resistance. A Franco-British ultimatum then demanded that Israeli and Egyptian forces both withdraw to ten miles from the canal. The Israeli government halted the military drive within Egypt. An Anglo-French force then occupied the Canal Zone after Nasser ordered the scuttling of ships to block the canal. On November 3, the General Assembly of the United Nations called for a cease-fire (supported by both the United States and the Soviet Union) and a day later authorized a peacekeeping force. On November 5, British and French troops parachuted into Port Said, followed by troops put ashore the next day. Britain agreed to accept the cease-fire. Pressure on both Israel and Egypt from the United States and the Soviet Union (which had reason to be pleased that the world's attention could be diverted from Hungary, where Russian tanks were crushing an anti-Communist revolt; see Chapter 29) brought an end to the Suez crisis. U.S. pressure proved decisive, particularly with Britain, as the U.S. government refused to support British sterling, and the currency fell dramatically in the face of fears of a cut-off of oil from the Middle East. British and French troops withdrew. The Suez Canal crisis had demonstrated that European Western powers could no longer impose their will on the Middle East. Thereafter, the process of decolonization proceeded rapidly.

In Britain, Prime Minister Sir Anthony Eden (1897–1977) suffered a nervous breakdown and resigned from office in January 1957. Conservative Harold Macmillan (1894–1986), who succeeded Eden as prime minister and who had been a proponent of the Suez action, then undertook what one of his colleagues called the "most spectacular retreat from Suez since the time of Moses." Following the salvaging of the forty ships that Egypt had sunk in the canal, the Suez Canal reopened in April 1957 under Egyptian control. British influence in the Middle East continued to decline. A year later, British ally King Faisal II was assassinated in Iraq. When the island of Cyprus gained its independence in 1960, Britain lost its last base in the Middle East.

French Decolonization

France, too, lost its colonial empire in the post-war era, but not without bloody struggles. The French had begun their conquest of North Africa in 1830, and in Southeast Asia had held modern-day Laos, Cambodia, and Vietnam since the 1880s. The French left Syria and Lebanon in 1946 by agreement with the United States and Britain. In 1947, French troops put down a massive insurrection in Madagascar, with an enormous loss of life. The island finally received its independence in 1960, one of fourteen former French colonies in Africa.

In Vietnam, Ho Chi Minh (Nguyen Tat Thanh or Nguyen Ai Quoc, or "the Patriot," 1890–1969) emerged as a Vietnamese Communist leader. His father was an official under the French who had resigned from his position because of his Vietnamese nationalism. Ho Chi Minh himself worked as a kitchen helper on a French passenger liner before becoming a Communist activist. In 1929 he founded the Indochinese Communist Party. Following condemnation to death by the French government, Ho was saved by the refusal of the British government in Hong Kong to turn him over to French authorities. Nonetheless, the British arrested him in 1931, and he remained in prison in Hong Kong for two years. During World War II, he led the Viet Minh, an organization of Vietnamese Communists.

During World War II, Vichy France had held Vietnam as a colony until Japanese forces took control in 1945. When Vietnam proclaimed its independence, France attempted to re-conquer its former colony. In November 1946, the French army attacked the port of Haiphong, killing 6,000 Vietnamese, and captured Hanoi, the Vietnamese capital. The French military restored the nominal authority of a playboy emperor, Bao Dai (1913–1997). Yet Vietnam remained a colony. War between Ho Chi Minh's Vietnamese army, which held most of the countryside, and the French continued. Ho, supported by the Chinese, prophesied, "You will kill ten of our men, but we will kill one of yours and you will end up by wearing yourselves out." The Korean War increased U.S. interest in the ongoing struggles in Vietnam, bringing U.S. military assistance to the French effort. In 1954, the French army suffered a crushing defeat at the hands of the Vietnamese at Dien Bien Phu. Pierre Mendès-France (1907–1982), the new Socialist premier, succeeded in extracting France from war in Vietnam (he would later prove less successful in encouraging the French to drink milk instead of wine, a more hopeless task). At the Geneva Convention that year, France agreed to the division of Vietnam into two states. North Vietnam became a Communist regime led by Ho Chi Minh; South Vietnam became a republic run by a succession of leaders who carried out U.S. policy in exchange for a free hand.

(*Left*) A Viet Minh fighter is taken prisoner by a French soldier in 1952. (*Right*) A French patrol in Vietnam in 1954.

The end of French colonialism was even more wrenching in North Africa. There were 1.2 million French citizens in Algeria, 300,000 in Morocco, and 200,000 in Tunisia. They were called *pieds noirs* ("black feet") because of the black boots worn by French soldiers. Morocco and Tunisia were French protectorates, although nominally ruled by a sultan and bey (sovereign), respectively. Algeria, in contrast, was directly administered as a colony by French officials. During the inter-war period, a small nationalist movement developed in Algeria. In 1945, French troops put down an uprising in Algeria at the cost of 40,000 Algerian lives. During the early 1950s, movements for national independence continued to develop in France's North African colonies.

The writer Albert Camus, born in Algeria, summed up the difficult choices for some French families who lived there; he said that if given the choice between justice and his mother, he would take his mother. Many of the French living in North Africa had become wealthy, successfully developing land taken from the Arab population over the past century. Others were of modest means, including café owners in Algiers, government functionaries, and farmers with small plots of land.

In 1954, the National Liberation Front (Front de Libération Nationale, the FLN) called for Algerian independence. An uprising for independence began just four months after the French defeat at Dien Bien Phu. Fearing that the movement might spread to Tunisia and Morocco (where, in fact, some fighting followed), the French government granted virtual independence to both states in 1956, despite the protests of French residents and the vigorous opposition of the French officer corps.

As guerrilla actions and bombings increased and losses mounted, many people in France began to accept Algerian independence as both inevitable and desirable. In February 1956, French residents in Algiers rioted against the government when French Premier Guy Mollet (1906–1975), who had at first been willing to negotiate with the FLN, came to introduce his newly appointed governor of Algeria. In October, the newly crowned king of Morocco met with leaders of the FLN, enraging the French right. Mollet, fearing the political consequences of the war, then ordered the kidnapping of Ahmed Ben Bella (1919–), a leader of the Algerians, and launched a repression in France of critics of the French Algerian policy. In November 1956, France joined Britain in the ill-fated Suez expedition in part because of French anger at Egyptian support for the Algerian insurrection. French troops undertook a brutal campaign that included torture against militants and civilians alike, culminating in "the battle of Algiers" fought in the Arab quarters of the Algerian capital. In France, the left increasingly demanded an end to the war; intellectuals, like the philosopher Jean-Paul Sartre and the novelist Camus, denounced the torture of Algerians by the French army. In the meantime, casualties mounted in the French army (which, unlike the French war in Vietnam, included conscripts). Throughout the Algerian war of independence, the FLN successfully played off Cold War rivalries, using mass communication and building support in Algerian communities abroad, while winning international support. Their campaign helped isolate France internationally.

After humiliating defeats at the hands of the German army in 1940 and by the Vietnamese at Dien Bien Phu in 1954, some French military officers

French riot police throw back stones, as well as tear gas bombs, at demonstrators in Algiers in 1960, during the Algerian war of independence.

saw the fight in Algeria as a last stand for their honor. Early in 1958, by which time French troops in Algeria numbered 500,000, French planes attacked FLN camps on the other side of the border with Tunisia. A new premier was rumored to be willing to negotiate with the insurgents. On May 13, 1958, a demonstration by French settlers in Algiers protesting against any compromise turned into a military-led insurrection against the French government. A "Committee of Public Safety" of rightists seized power, led by General Jacques Massu (1908–2002). On May 24, another right-wing group seized power in Corsica. A military coup d'état seemed possible on the mainland of France.

Charles de Gaulle, who had been waiting in self-imposed exile for something like this to happen, announced that he was ready to serve France again. Many politicians believed that de Gaulle alone could prevent chaos. On May 29, 1958, President René Coty appointed de Gaulle prime minister, a move approved by the National Assembly early in June. The general accepted on the condition that he could rule by emergency decree for six months and could then ask the nation to approve a new constitution. The right, which counted many army officers among its ranks, was delighted with de Gaulle's return to power, thinking that the general would never allow Algerian independence.

The new constitution greatly increased the authority of the president, whose term was set at seven years. Presidents under the Fifth French Republic would conduct foreign policy, appoint prime ministers, and dissolve the French parliament. In September 1958, 80 percent of French voters approved the new constitution.

But what about Algeria? De Gaulle went to Algiers and, in a remarkably noncommittal speech, told the settlers in June 1958, "I have understood you, I know what you have tried to do here." But he had already decided that the costs of continuing the war in Algeria were too great, too divisive. He removed the generals responsible for the coup in Algeria from their posts. For a man whose French nationalism underlay his political philosophy, it seemed an astonishing turnaround.

To some officers, de Gaulle's actions seemed an incredible betrayal, a stab in the back by a fellow military man. As the Dreyfus Affair had revealed in the 1890s and the Vichy years had confirmed, a right-wing anti-democratic tradition survived in the officer corps. Many officers now felt betrayed not only by de Gaulle but also by much of the population in France. They enjoyed some support among rightist parties. When de Gaulle recalled General Massu to Paris in January 1960, right-wing riots took place in Paris. In Algeria, *pieds noirs* began a general strike and put up barricades. De Gaulle rallied French public opinion to what had clearly become a policy of allowing Algerians to decide their own future.

Negotiations between Algerian leaders and de Gaulle's government began in the spring of 1961. In the meantime, a secret group within the army, the Secret Army Organization (OAS), had formed in January 1961, determined at all costs to keep Algeria French. In April it staged a coup d'état and held power in Algiers and in the city of Oran for three days, yet it did not win support of the entire army. Political parties of the left and center threw their support to de Gaulle. The general assumed emergency powers, this time for a year. The OAS twice tried to assassinate de Gaulle and once nearly succeeded, riddling his car with machine-gun fire. Members planted bombs in Algerian cities and in Paris to terrorize the civilian population. Given the chance to vote on their future, the Algerians opted for independence; in France, the vote for Algerian independence in July 1961 was 15 million to 5 million. On March 19, 1962, the Algerian War officially ended, with the French people overwhelmingly ratifying the peace terms. In July 1962, Algeria became independent. However, France continued to maintain considerable prestige in the Third World.

Decolonization in Sub-Saharan Africa

At the end of World War II, only Liberia, Ethiopia, and Egypt had achieved independence in Africa. Nationalist groups in Africa were less organized than had been their counterparts in India and Southeast Asia. But in the subsequent decades, British rule ended in one African colony after another. In 1957, Ghana (formerly the Gold Coast) became independent. Others soon followed, including Nigeria in 1960, Sierra Leone and Tanganyika in 1961, Uganda in 1962, and Kenya in 1963. Sixteen states in Africa became independent in 1960, including the Ivory Coast, Senegal, and Cameroon, all former French colonies (see Map 28.1).

British determination to hold onto its East African colony of Kenya—presented under the guise of the mission to "civilize" people that they considered inferior—was particularly bloody. In the late nineteenth century, British colonialists obtained huge estates in fertile central Kenya in what they called the "White Highlands." They were followed by other white settlers of more modest means. Livestock farming, coffee growing, and the production of cereals enriched many of them, as Kenya became known as a fitting home for privileged British gentry, a "colony for gentlemen." In 1914 almost 5,500 European settlers were in Kenya and, aided by a government campaign after World War II to encourage immigration there, in 1948 about 30,000 whites resided there (compared with an African population of 5.3 million and almost 100,000 Asians). By the early 1950s there were at least 40,000 Europeans. Many benefited from good land that could be purchased or leased for very little, government subsidies, and cheap African labor, working at wage rates set by the colonial government.

The Kikuyu people, who had lost enormous amounts of land to the settlers and been forced to work for and pay onerous taxes to the British, did not profit from the economic boom generated by World War II. The Kikuyu launched a campaign for self-determination. Jomo Kenyatta (1889–1978), who had studied in London, emerged as an effective, charismatic leader of

MAP 28.1 DECOLONIZATION The map shows movements for decolonization in Africa, Asia, and the Far East, giving the dates at which each of the colonies achieved independence.

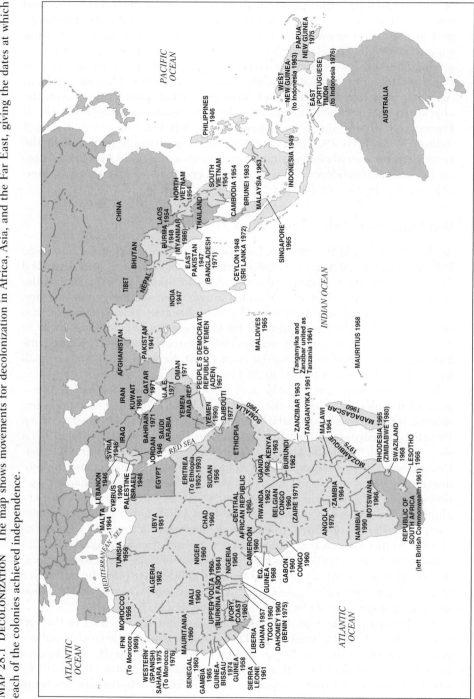

the Kenyan African Union, which by the early 1950s encompassed almost the entire Kikuyu population. What became known to the British as the "Mau Mau" rebellion (the origins of the term are mysterious but the rebels called themselves the "Land and Freedom Army") began in 1952, with violence directed at British settlers, thirty-two of whom were killed in the rebellion. Kenyatta's arrest, trial, conviction, and imprisonment for his role in the Mau Mau insurgency (despite no evidence) helped make him an international symbol of Kenyan resistance.

The British government declared a state of emergency and detained perhaps as many as 1.5 million people, virtually the entire Kikuyu population, in what amounted to a mass gulag. At the same time, the Mau Mau exacted bloody revenge against loyalist Kenyans with guerilla attacks. The British portrayed the struggle as one between civilization and savagery. British forces, including the Home Guard of white settlers recognized as part of the security forces in 1953, and indigenous loyalists killed tens of thousands of people, not counting thousands who perished in the detention camps or were shot when allegedly trying to escape. The counter-insurgency included terror, atrocious brutality, and widespread torture, most of which the British government succeeded in keeping secret. About 1,000 Kikuyu were hung after being convicted in British courts. British authorities enacted collective punishments against villagers who refused to cooperate with them, seizing livestock and closing down markets for months. The bloody struggle lasted until 1957, when British forces succeeded in breaking apart the Mau Mau armies.

Mau Mau soldiers training in Kenya, 1963.

However, the British government appeared in an increasingly bad light as word got out of the detention camps and conditions within them. In the meantime, Britain had accepted decolonization as inevitable. Prime Minister Harold Macmillan put together a "balance sheet of empire," which screamed out in red ink. He took the decision to end British colonial rule in Africa. Emergency rule ended and Kenyatta was freed in 1959. Majority rule followed. White settlers were allowed to sell their land under favorable conditions. Kenyatta's Kenya African National Union established a government after an overwhelming victory in elections in 1963. Britain granted Kenya independence later that year. Kenyatta earned his reputation as "the reconciler" and became president in 1964.

The Republic of South Africa left the British Commonwealth in 1961. With a white population of 21 percent in 1950 (and 68 percent African, 2 percent of mixed race, and 2 percent Asian), South Africa maintained a system of apartheid, an official policy of racial inequality and segregation implemented in 1948. It was supported by the white Afrikaner population of Dutch origin. In 1965 Rhodesia, which had been a self-governing colony, declared its independence from Britain. It did so, in part, so that its white minority would not have to share power with the black majority population. The British government then led a campaign of international economic sanctions against the white regime of its former colony. In 1980, Rhodesia was divided into the independent states of Zambia and Zimbabwe.

In the Belgian Congo in central West Africa, the Belgian government first tried to placate nationalists with concessions in the late 1950s and then to repress them following rioting in 1959. A year later, the Belgian government suddenly pulled out of its former colony (although the Congo's army retained Belgian officers), declaring the Congo independent. Civil war began between two nationalist leaders, a bloody conflict complicated by ethnic and tribal loyalties. Soldiers mutinied against their Belgian commanders and began to attack Europeans remaining in the Congo. The Congo's wealthiest province, Katanga, which has great mining resources such as cobalt, copper, and uranium, then declared its independence. At the request of the Congo's premier, the United Nations sent troops to restore order. After a year, the civil war ended. Katanga's secession lasted until 1963. Two years later, Colonel Mobutu Sese Seko (1930–1997) imposed military rule in Congo, which was known as Zaire between 1971 and 1997. After nationalizing his country's wealthy mines, Mobutu set about amassing enormous personal wealth.

Portugal's colonies were many times its size. It faced insurrections in its African colonies of Angola and Mozambique, which lie on the southwestern and southeastern coasts, respectively, beginning in 1961. Following years of bloody fighting, the new Portuguese government, which a year earlier had overthrown the dictatorship that had ruled Portugal for decades (see Chapter 29), recognized the independence of Angola and Mozambique. In both new states, horrendous civil war raged between left-wing and right-wing groups. In Angola, Cuban funds and soldiers helped the left-wing Popular

Movement, which emerged victorious. In Mozambique, too, the left won, despite assistance to the right by the South African government and a campaign of terror. Ordinary people suffered famine and slaughter.

Independence in many cases proved to be no panacea for the new African nations. Many post-colonial administrations proved unable or unwilling to provide a decent quality of life to their people. Some new states, like Angola and Mozambique, and more recently, Sudan, fell into bloody and debilitating civil wars. These conflicts were compounded by the multiplicity of ethnic groups, tribalism, and a lack of political experience—problems that still stand as major impediments to the construction of modern political systems in developing nations. Even with the departure of colonial governments, European companies still controlled valuable natural resources. Moreover, some African rulers have abused their power by enriching themselves at the expense of their people, while adopting, as in the case of Robert Mugabe (1924–) of Zimbabwe, anti-colonial rhetoric to justify their plunder. Appalling poverty and inadequate health care remain daunting challenges.

Conclusion

The end of European overseas empires was accompanied by significant political changes on the European continent as well. The late 1960s brought waves of student protest in many Western European countries and a movement for reform in Communist Czechoslovkia, which threatened Soviet orthodoxy before being crushed by Russian tanks. Dictatorships subsequently fell in Greece, Spain, and Portugal. And then, in a dramatic sequence of remarkable events, Communism collapsed in Central and Eastern Europe and the Balkans in 1989, followed by the break-up of the Soviet Union itself in 1991. Europe entered a new age.

CHAPTER 29

TRANSITIONS TO DEMOCRACY AND THE COLLAPSE OF COMMUNISM

After almost two decades of growing prosperity and relative political and social calm, domestic political conflict erupted in Europe—above all, in France—and the United States in 1968. The social, political, and cultural revolts that exploded that year seemed to pit young people, especially students, against those entrenched in power. Many "baby boomers" born after the war saw their revolt as one of an entire generation against its elders. They blamed them for a world that seemed unresponsive to demands for social justice and political change on behalf of the underprivileged and the oppressed. Many felt alienated (a word then much in vogue) from materialistic, industrial, bureaucratic society, and from the universities where they studied. Feminism, too, was a significant undercurrent during the protests of 1968, but it largely remained a movement of middle-class intellectuals and students.

Demonstrations and protest brought political reaction. The turmoil in France ended amid government repression and a conservative show of force. Demonstrations subsided elsewhere in Western Europe, although they continued in the United States against the war in Vietnam. In Western Europe, conservative or centrist parties dominated the governments of Britain, the German Federal Republic, and Italy for most of the 1970s and 1980s, while Socialists held power in France between 1981 and 1995. And, in southern Europe, democratic rule came to Portugal, Spain, and Greece.

A period of détente between the United States and the Soviet Union in the 1970s was followed by a chill that began as a result of Soviet intervention in Afghanistan in 1979. Then in 1989, dramatic change occurred in

Eastern Europe. Mikhail Gorbachev (1931–), the leader of the Soviet Union, had undertaken a dramatic series of reforms in the mid-1980s that liberalized the economy and political life in the Communist state. His bold moves encouraged further demands for reform and stimulated nationalist movements in the Soviet Union's republics. The impact was soon felt in Eastern Europe. As campaigns for liberalization revived in Poland and Hungary, it became clear that the Soviet leadership would not intervene to crush movements for reform, as Gorbachev indicated that he viewed reform in Eastern Europe as desirable.

Throughout Eastern Europe, one Communist government after another fell. These revolutions ranged from the "velvet revolution" in Czechoslovakia to the violent overthrow of Nicolae Ceauşescu in Romania, until there were no Communist regimes left in Eastern Europe (although in Bulgaria, Romania, and Albania, former Communists retained power). Overall, the fall of communism was achieved through a remarkably peaceful process of change. However, in 1989, Yugoslavia began to break apart in a cacophony of ethnic hatred generated by the very question that the polyglot state's creation after World War I could not resolve: the national question. In Bosnia, civil war raged. The Soviet Union itself collapsed in 1991. The U.S. official George Kennan's prediction in 1947 that the Soviet system "bears within it the seeds of its own decay" turned out to be correct.

Adulation of Mikhail Gorbachev in Stuttgart, West Germany, for his bold moves toward reform and liberalization in the Soviet Union.

POLITICS IN A CHANGING WESTERN WORLD

During the late 1960s, a loosely connected movement for political and social change swept across university campuses in a number of Western countries. Youth increasingly trumpeted sexual freedom, aided by the availability of birth control (notably the pill, beginning in the 1960s and 1970s) and the legalization of abortion in some countries. Based largely but not exclusively in the surging generation of baby boomers born after World War II (in the United States, the student-age population increased from 16 million in 1960 to 26 million in 1970), the youth revolt challenged long-established hierarchies, party politics, and even consumerism. From Berkeley, California, to Paris, Berlin, and Amsterdam, students protested against American involvement in the Vietnamese civil war, where, despite government claims of a high-minded struggle against communism, the United States seemed to be supporting a corrupt political regime against determined nationalists, albeit Communists. In the United States, particularly, the movements of the 1960s were closely tied to the civil rights movement, as students protested against social injustice and racism. Long hair, sexual freedom, rock music, and marijuana seemed part of the idealistic youth rebellion against the state and capitalism. The British impact on popular culture was never greater than in the 1960s, when the Beatles, Mick Jagger and the Rolling Stones, and the Who, among other rock groups, became phenomenally popular across much of the globe. In France, student demonstrations, insurgency, and strikes shook the country, challenging the government of President Charles de Gaulle. Demonstrations also rocked Italy, West Germany, and other Western European countries.

Western European states began to turn away from U.S. foreign policy domination. De Gaulle, who believed that France had a special historic mission and never doubted for a moment the part he was to play in it, feared the domination of Europe and France by Britain and the United States. He insisted that France maintain an independent nuclear capability; the country's first nuclear bomb was tested in 1960. Moreover, ending decades of animosity, the close partnership between Germany and France formed the cornerstone of the new Europe. However, de Gaulle refused to cooperate with the other Western powers. In 1966, France left NATO's military command, forcing it to transfer its headquarters from Paris to Brussels. U.S. Army and Air Force bases in France were closed. De Gaulle angered the U.S. government by refusing to support its policies in Vietnam. He also outraged many Canadians during a state visit in 1967 by shouting, "Long live Free Quebec!" (Quebec, predominantly French-speaking, has had considerable sentiment for independence.) Although de Gaulle remained vehemently anti-Communist, he wanted France to provide leadership as a third force that stood between the Soviet Union and the United States.

Other European governments also no longer automatically accepted U.S. Cold War rhetoric, which had encouraged the arms race. They reasoned that if the two superpowers went to war, the battlefields (in conventional warfare) or the targets (in case of "limited" nuclear warfare) would be in Europe.

Student Protests Challenge Gaullist France

In the spring of 1968, demonstrators took to the streets of Paris, protesting the rigid, overcrowded, and under-funded French university system, which largely remained the preserve of the elite. Intellectual ferment was heightened by opposition to the war in Vietnam. In France, students rebelled against those in political power, inequality, and even modern technology, which seemed to them dehumanizing. Graffiti in the Latin Quarter (where students attended university) proclaimed, "Comrades, the Revolution is daily, it is a festival!"

Early in May 1968, a student radical was expelled from the University of Paris. In protest, students and some young faculty members occupied university buildings at the Sorbonne. After the police entered the university and began arresting students, the demonstrators fanned out and were joined by more students. Several students were killed and hundreds injured when police attacked hastily improvised barricades.

Unlike in the United States, where most workers found student demands too radical and many supported U.S. participation in the war in Vietnam, French workers took to the streets in support of the students. A general strike began on May 13 in protest against police brutality, the largest wave of French strikes since 1936. Strikers demanded raises, better working conditions, and rights of self-management. Union organizations and the Communist Party, which had considerable prestige among industrial workers, had little to do with the movement. The tail seemed to be wagging the dog. If anything, trade union and Communist leaders tried to bring the movement under their control in its first days. Gaullist Prime Minister Georges Pompidou (1911–1974) hurriedly returned from a state visit to Afghanistan to confront the growing crisis.

After a hurried flight to West Germany, presumably to assure himself of the loyalty of French army units stationed there, de Gaulle dissolved the National Assembly on May 30 and announced that new elections would be held on June 23. Gaullists organized counter-demonstrations in support of the government, capitalizing on the hostility of many middle-class citizens and peasants in traditionally conservative regions to the turmoil in Paris. The strike movement ebbed, in part because the government and many companies agreed to raise wages. This left the students standing alone.

After dismissing Pompidou as prime minister, de Gaulle won what amounted to a referendum on his rule. However, his towering presence seemed increasingly anachronistic. Speeches about national "grandeur" rang hollow as French influence in the world declined. De Gaulle's answer to a general crisis of confidence was to call for more "participation" in the

An outnumbered policeman during the massive protests in Paris in May 1968.

political process, as a way of expressing French "national ambition," which he believed was slipping away. "The French think of nothing but increasing their standard of living," he once complained. "Steak and French fries are fine. A family car is useful. But all that does not add up to national ambition." In 1969, the president announced another referendum, this one on local administrative reform. This seemed an unlikely issue for de Gaulle, who believed in an efficiently centralized state and cared little about regional liberties (he once asked rhetorically how one could govern a country with several hundred different kinds of cheese). De Gaulle lost what turned into a plebiscite on his government and retired from political life.

The contentious year 1968 also brought student demonstrations and riots to Italy and West Germany, where Berlin was the center of the student movement. The University of Rome had been built to accommodate 5,000 students but that year enrolled 60,000 students. Thousands of university graduates were frustrated because they could not find jobs. But Italian students found no support from workers, and the movement quickly collapsed.

Shifts in Western European Politics after 1968

During the 1970s, European domestic politics underwent a shift from the right to centrist governments. This change was apparent not only in the German Federal Republic and Britain (where Labour was in power from 1974 to 1979) but also in France. In Italy, the strikes of 1968 and 1969 generated further political instability, although the Christian Democrats, forming a series of center-left coalition governments, continued to dominate Italian politics. In West Germany, the Christian Democrats refused any negotiations of consequence with the German Democratic Republic or the Soviet Union. However, following waves of student protest, Social Democrats bucked the tide and came to power in 1969. They were helped by an alliance with the centrist Free Democrats, who abandoned their Christian Democrat allies. Willy Brandt (1913–1992), who had fled Nazi Germany and fought with the Norwegian resistance during the Second World War before becoming mayor of Berlin, took office as chancellor. In 1970, Brandt signed a nonaggression pact with the Soviet Union, paving the way for the development of trade between the two states. He signed the Treaty of Warsaw, which recognized the frontier between Poland and East Germany as redrawn after the war. While echoing his predecessors' commitment to NATO, Brandt improved relations with the German Democratic Republic, calling for an "opening toward the East." Millions of people were allowed to cross the wall to visit the other side, overwhelmingly most were West Germans allowed to visit East Berlin.

Brandt resigned in 1974 following the discovery that one of his aides was a spy for East Germany. Helmut Schmidt (1918–), a more conservative Social Democrat, became chancellor. Schmidt weathered political storms, but drew the wrath of environmentalists and anti-nuclear groups in 1979 when he asked the United States to station medium-range nuclear missiles on West German soil to counter similar Soviet missiles. Schmidt and centrist French President Valéry Giscard d'Estaing (1926– ; president 1974–1981) believed that Germany and France had to become the center of Western Europe. However, economic recession, rising unemployment, and Schmidt's refusal to reduce welfare payments led to the return to power in 1982 of the Christian Democrats. They were led by Helmut Kohl (1930–), who cut taxes and reduced government spending. However, in September 1998, elections swept the Social Democrat Gerhard Schröder into the chancellorship, based on a coalition between Social Democrats and the German ecological party, known as the Greens, replacing Kohl, who resigned two years later as chairman of the Christian Democratic Party in the wake of a financial scandal. In 2005, Angela Merkel (1954–), a Christian Democrat who had grown up in the Communist German Democratic Republic, became the first female chancellor of Germany.

In Britain, under the pressure of the oil crisis and following bitter mining strikes, the Conservative government fell in 1974. But the subsequent Labour governments of Harold Wilson (1916–1995) and James Callaghan (1912–2005) were buffeted by soaring inflation, which was exacerbated by a series of major union victories in prolonged strikes during the Callaghan government.

Upper- and middle-class Britons turned against Callaghan, claiming that the unions now held their country hostage. In 1979, Conservative leader

Margaret Thatcher (1925–), the daughter of a prosperous grocer from the English Midlands, became prime minister. She was the first woman to hold the position, although she vociferously repudiated feminism.

Thatcher was committed to putting into effect a tight monetary policy ("monetarism"). She promised to slash government expenses with cutbacks. Within three years, 1 million jobs in manufacturing had disappeared. The Conservative government eliminated some of the health and education measures Labour had implemented. "The Iron Lady" reduced inheritance and capital taxes and waged war against the trade unions. The government sold off some nationalized industries, notably the rail system, with disastrous results for service. Without government subsidies, many factories closed down and unemployment continued to rise. By 1983, Britain had 3 million unemployed workers (about 12 percent of the workforce). Cuts in housing subsidies left hundreds of thousands without adequate places to live. Thatcher had, after all, once advised Britons to "glory in inequality."

In May 1982, the military government of Argentina, seeking to reverse a decline in its popularity at home, invaded the Falkland Islands. Although the British occupied the sparsely populated Falklands, which lie about 300 miles from the coast of Argentina in the Atlantic Ocean, Argentina had claimed them since the nineteenth century. British forces easily recaptured the islands. The short war boosted the prime minister's standing at home. Furthermore, the British economy began to recover in the early 1980s and inflation slowed down. The Conservatives rolled to another impressive victory in the general elections of 1983 over the bitterly divided Labour Party. In 1985, she outlasted a long strike by coal miners. However, fearing the revival of the Labour Party, Conservative leaders unseated Thatcher in 1990, replacing her with the bland John Major (1943–), who became prime minister following elections two years later. Meanwhile, Tony Blair (1953–) moved the Labour Party toward the center—what he called "New Labour." Turning away from the class politics of the old Labour Party, "New Labour" reached out to liberals and even moderate conservatives. Blair emphasized a commitment to economic progress and to practical policies in place of shrill rhetoric. In sharp contrast to most Conservatives, Blair made clear that he believed Britain's future lay with Europe. The sweeping victory of "New Labour" in 1997 brought Blair to 10 Downing Street as prime minister, where he remained for ten years.

Blair's policies increasingly could have been confused with those of his Conservative rivals. In 2001, Blair's Labour Party swept to another easy victory in Britain, leaving Socialist or Social Democratic parties in power in nine of the fifteen member states of the European Union.

In the meantime, the death of Princess Diana (1961–1997) in a high-speed car crash in a Paris tunnel on August 31, 1997, plunged Britain into mourning. This was just the latest of a series of reverses for the British monarchy, including Diana's separation and then divorce from Prince

Charles in 1996. Despite the attachment of many people to the monarchy as an institution and the fascination with the royal family perpetuated by coverage in tabloid newspapers, to some British subjects, the monarchy seemed an expensive and irrelevant atavism. Yet, to fervent British royalists, Prince William (heir to the throne after his father, Charles) and his younger brother, Harry, offered hope for the future. Increasingly unpopular because of Britain's involvement in the Iraq War (see Chapter 30), Tony Blair resigned in 2007, succeeded by Gordon Brown, under whose leadership the Labor Party's popularity in Britain plunged to an all-time low.

In France, the economic slump that began with the oil crisis of 1973 and financial scandals undercut the presidency of the centrist Valéry Giscard d'Estaing, a technocrat committed to economic modernization. In 1981, the pragmatic Socialist François Mitterrand (1916–1996) won election as president. Social Democratic parties maintained power in Scandinavia. Andreas Papandreou (1919–1996), became Greece's first Socialist premier in 1981. Italy and Spain also had moderately left-wing governments. As in Britain, Socialist and other leftist governments in France and other countries governed with moderation, abandoning traditional agendas of the left in the interest of practical politics. In the meantime, the influence of unions declined along with the number of industrial workers. Abandoned factories in the German Ruhr region, northeastern France, northern England, and the Czech Republic stood as rusty symbols of an industrial world that was disappearing.

By nationalizing large corporations and more banks and initiating ambitious social reforms, French President Mitterrand confronted determined opposition from the business community. The French franc plunged on the international currency market; people of wealth began to remove their assets from France. A year after taking office, the Socialist government was forced to devalue the franc and freeze prices and wages. Pressure from the right mounted from the Gaullists and their ambitious leader, Jacques Chirac (1932–), the mayor of Paris. The inability of the Socialist government to revive the economy undercut its popularity.

In the 1986 elections for the Chamber of Deputies, the right triumphed, leading to an awkward period of government known as "cohabitation." Mitterrand selected a rightist premier, Chirac, with ministers drawn from the right and center. The new government sold off some nationalized banks and businesses and ended wage and price controls.

Given a slight majority in the elections for the National Assembly in 1988, Mitterrand appointed Socialist prime ministers, but the right swept into power in 1993. When his second term ended in 1995, Mitterrand had become the longest serving head of state in France since Napoleon III (emperor 1852–1870). Chirac was elected president in 1995. He began his presidency by authorizing the resumption of French nuclear testing in the South Pacific, leading to considerable international opposition, particularly in Australia, New Zealand, and Japan. Facing a high unemployment rate and a growing economic deficit, reductions in health, retirement, and other benefits followed. Strikes forced the government to make some concessions. In 1997, however, Chirac called elections a year early in hopes of receiving a sweeping mandate. Socialists dominated the elections, forcing Chirac to name the Socialist Lionel Jospin as prime minister, bringing another uncomfortable period of "cohabitation" with a conservative president and a Socialist prime minister.

In Italy, instability and corruption continued to characterize political life. Despite a general increase in prosperity, inflation and high unemployment left many Italians still dissatisfied with all political parties. The government of Bettino Craxi (1934–2000) from 1983 to 1986 was the longest and in many ways the most stable of the post-war period. Socialists replaced the Communists as Italy's second largest party, forcing the Christian Democrats to accept them as coalition partners in 1986. Craxi himself was convicted of corruption, however, and fled in 1993 to Tunisia. Giulio Andreotti (1919–), Christian Democrat prime minister on six different occasions, stood accused not only of corruption, but was eventually found guilty of arranging the murder of a journalist who had uncovered evidence of wrongdoing. More than 2,500 Italian politicians and businessmen were arrested for corruption over an eighteen-month period. Campaigns against the Mafia have been periodic (most energetically following the assassination in 1992 of a public prosecutor who had devoted himself to the difficult legal war against the Mafia). In the 1994 elections, conservative financier and media tycoon Silvio Berlusconi (1936–) became prime minister of Italy. His new right-wing party, Forza Italia, came out of the elections as Italy's most successful party, with two parties of the extreme right as allies, both denouncing the increase in the immigrant population: the Northern League, which campaigned on a program of independence for northern Italy, provocatively describing the south as a weight around the neck of the north, and the neofascist National Alliance. Cynicism and mistrust of politicians became even more prevalent in Italy.

In every Western country, a new political force began to be felt. "Green" parties, political groups of militant environmentalists angered by the deterioration of the environment, emerged in Western Europe during the 1980s. In the German Federal Republic, the Greens, Europe's largest environmental party, were alarmed by industrial pollution, which was slowly killing their country's forests. Environmental parties stridently opposed nuclear power, even before a deadly Soviet nuclear disaster at Chernobyl in Ukraine in 1986. Greens helped push for agreements that have led to some cleaning up of the Rhine River and Mediterranean beaches.

Finally, in almost all Western states, economic slumps have accentuated complaints that state-subsidized programs are too expensive. In Sweden and Denmark, Social Democratic parties were ousted after decades of rule by conservatives calling for sharp reductions in the tax rates that financed

A nuclear power plant dwarfs a more traditional source of power.

cradle-to-grave social programs. With the recession of the early 1990s reducing tax revenue, Western European governments reduced social benefits, such as unemployment payments.

The Transition to Democracy in Southern Europe

During the 1970s, three southern European dictatorships became democracies: Greece, Portugal, and Spain. Greece, the cradle of democracy, had been controlled by a series of right-wing governments since its civil war in the late 1940s. In 1967, military officers overthrew Greece's first post-war government of the left, ruthlessly crushed dissent, and imprisoned, and tortured political opponents. The military dictators planned to seize the island of Cyprus, which lies off the coast of Turkey and which both Greece and Turkey had claimed for centuries. Relations between Greece and Turkey had often been extremely tense. Now bitter disagreements over the form of a new constitution in Cyprus led to fighting between Greeks and Turks. The Greek Cypriot National Guard overthrew the government of Cyprus. At the same time, the Cypriot Turks defeated the Greeks and declared the northeastern, predominantly Turkish part of the island to be independent. Further fighting ended in a cease-fire. Meanwhile, in Greece, the power of the generals, who had not sent help to the Greek Cypriot insurgents, collapsed in 1974. Greece became a republic in which conservative and Socialist parties took turns in power.

In Portugal, authoritarian leaders, notably Antonio Salazar, dictator from 1932 to 1968, struggled inefficiently with economic backwardness. Thousands of Portuguese went abroad as seasonal workers each year or emigrated permanently to other countries in Western Europe or in the Western Hemisphere. At the same time, the dictatorship, determined to hold on to Portugal's African colonies at all costs, became entangled in a long, bitter war with nationalist rebels in its African colonies of first Angola, beginning in 1961, and then Mozambique, conflicts that Portugal could neither afford (at the annual cost of half the nation's budget) nor win (see Chapter 28). In April 1974, a group of liberal army officers overthrew the dictatorship. The Socialist Party emerged victorious in elections the following year and Angola and Mozambique became independent, lapsing into bloody civil wars. Despite another coup two years later by a group of officers, the Portuguese transition to democracy occurred without bloodshed. However, political turmoil forced the government to abandon a program of state nationalizations and some agricultural collectivization in 1976. That year, Mário Soares (1924–) took office as the first democratically elected prime minister in Portugal in fifty years, and he dominated Portuguese political life into the 1990s.

In Spain, General Francisco Franco survived as dictator long after his friends Hitler and Mussolini had gone to their graves. After World War II, the United States prevented the United Nations from imposing economic sanctions against Spain because of Franco's support of the Axis powers. Franco maintained Spain's authoritarian political structure. While repudiating secular values, he accepted economic modernization, with the help of the United States.

In the late 1960s, opposition to Franco's regime mounted in Catalonia and the Basque country, Spain's most industrial regions, each with an entrenched separatist movement. Franco struck hard against Basque and Catalan separatists; the Catalan language, for example, remained illegal in print. But Franco retained popularity in traditionally religious regions, such as Navarre and his native Galicia.

Franco agreed that Juan Carlos (1938–), the son of the heir to the throne before the civil war, would succeed him as head of state and that Spain would remain an authoritarian state. Within the Spanish government, however, many officials already believed political reform inevitable, even desirable. Socialist and Communist parties existed, although they were illegal. Government censorship itself became more lax in the 1970s.

Upon Franco's death, Juan Carlos became king in 1975. He accepted the transformation of Spain into a constitutional monarchy with a democratic political structure. Spain emerged from authoritarian rule and international isolation. Spectacular economic growth and increasing prosperity helped the centrist Adolfo Suarez (1932–) keep a series of governments afloat through skillful political negotiation, even without a parliamentary majority. The charismatic Felipe González and the Socialists swept Suarez aside in the 1980s. In 1996, José Maria Aznar became Spain's first conservative prime minister since the time of Franco.

Religious and Ethnic Conflicts

Compared to the sixteenth, seventeenth, and eighteenth centuries, religious conflicts have diminished in modern Europe, with several notable exceptions. In Northern Ireland, the bitter centuries-old rivalry between Catholics and Protestants brought violence. Although the Catholic Republic of Ireland obtained independence in 1922, Northern Ireland is primarily Protestant (two-thirds of the population) and remains part of Britain. The Irish Republican Army (IRA), claiming to represent Ulster Catholics, struck at the British army and Protestants alike. Several weeks of disturbances in 1969 unleashed decades of violence, "the troubles" that took at least 3,500 lives. Secret Protestant paramilitary organizations, claiming that the British army inadequately protected Protestants, struck back against Catholics. Ian Paisley (1926–), a Protestant clergyman, heightened tension by speaking out provocatively against any compromise. On January 30, 1972—"Bloody Sunday"—British troops killed thirteen demonstrators in the Northern Irish town of Londonderry.

The economic crisis of the 1970s compounded Northern Ireland's problems, making Catholics even more disadvantaged compared to Protestants. The IRA, buying guns on the world weapons market with money stolen from banks or contributed by sympathetic Irish Americans, struck not only in Northern Ireland but also in England. Cease-fires in 1994 and 1996 could not still the violence that continued periodically, particularly during the

The aftermath of a bomb planted by the Irish Republican Army in Belfast, Northern Ireland, 1972.

period of the traditional Protestant summer marches. On April 10, 1998, Protestant and Catholic representatives signed the Belfast Agreement (or Good Friday Agreement), which provided for a National Assembly for Northern Ireland in which both religions would be represented. The people of Northern Ireland and of the Irish Republic overwhelmingly approved the Belfast Agreement. In December 1999, the British Parliament granted substantial power to the Northern Ireland Assembly, with a Catholic moderate as deputy first minister and David Trimble, a Protestant, as first minister. However, in February 2000, the British government suspended the Catholic and Protestant power-sharing government of Northern Ireland when the IRA refused to establish a timetable for the disarmament of its members.

The situation then began to improve dramatically. The IRA gradually abandoned the tactics of violence, and the Catholic political organization Sein Fein emerged as a force for conciliation. The expanding economy in Northern Ireland, as in the Republic, gave more people a stake in peace. Even Paisley now accepted compromise, becoming first minister of Northern Ireland in 2007.

Demands by ethnic minorities for independence surfaced in several countries. In Spain, Basque separatists (the ETA), sometimes hiding in the French Basque country, have moved across what they considered an arbitrary frontier to attack Spanish government, army, and police installations and to carry out assassinations. Popular support for the separatists in the Spanish Basque region waned in the 1980s, after the constitution of 1978 recognized "autonomous communities" within Spain. However, the violent ETA campaign has continued off and on. On the Mediterranean island of Corsica, violent groups opposed to French rule have planted bombs and carried out occasional assassinations, even as they feuded among themselves.

THE FALL OF COMMUNISM

In 1975, the leaders of European states gathered in Helsinki, Finland, to sign the Helsinki Accords, which concluded the first Conference on Security and Cooperation. All European states, with the exception of Albania, signed the accords, which recognized as valid the national borders drawn up after World War II. The thirty-five signatories also pledged to respect human rights and to cooperate in economic and scientific matters. To some critics, the Helsinki Accords seemed to recognize Soviet domination of Eastern Europe since the war. To other observers, they were a significant step forward because the heads of Communist states agreed in principle to respect human rights. The accords seemed a healthy pause in the renewed tension between East and West.

Hardly anyone at the time could have anticipated the fact that, fourteen years later, communism would collapse in Eastern Europe, bringing about an end to the Warsaw Pact two years later, or that the Soviet Union would

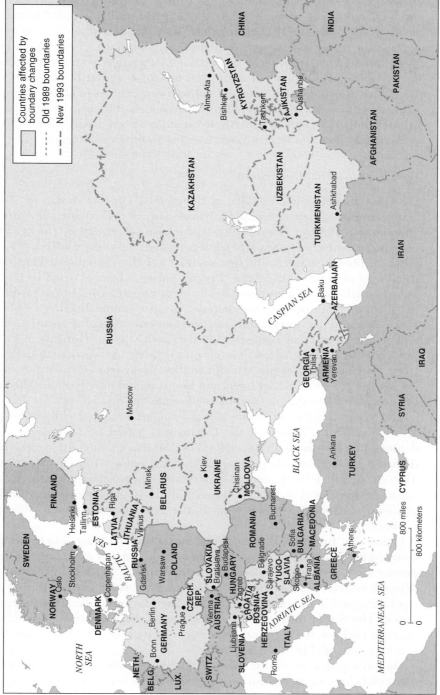

Map 29.1 THE FALL OF COMMUNISM IN EASTERN EUROPE AND THE SOVIET UNION, 1989–1991 With the fall of communism came the reunification of Germany and the breakup of the Soviet Union.

break up in 1991, leaving communism behind. However, the euphoria that arose from the realization that the Cold War had suddenly ended proved to be brief. New challenges and problems, among them those that had beset Europe for centuries, presented themselves. Decades of Communist rule had prevented the emergence of parliamentary political structures. Civic society in most Communist countries remained seriously undeveloped. Changing from planned economies with varying degrees of collectivization to free-market economies would prove extremely difficult. In Yugoslavia, ethnic conflicts exploded, and ethnic divisions also complicated the fall of communism in Romania, Hungary, Czechoslovakia, and Bulgaria.

Resistance to Soviet Domination

Calls for change echoed loudly in Communist Czechoslovakia in 1968. Intellectuals and writers accused the leadership of the Communist Party of clinging to Stalinism. The party leadership also acknowledged the need for change. In January 1968, party leaders named Alexander Dubček (1921– 1992), a liberal Slovak, to be first secretary of the Communist Party, and thus head of state. During the "Prague Spring," Dubček tried to implement "socialism with a human face" by instituting reforms, but as he did so he glanced anxiously over his shoulder toward Leonid Brezhnev's Soviet Union. Crucial to these reforms was a democratization of decision making and greater freedom of expression. But, as in the case of Hungary in 1956, the Soviet leadership feared that, despite Dubček's assurances to the contrary, Czechoslovakia might attempt to move away from the Warsaw Pact. On August 21, 1968, Soviet tanks and troops moved rapidly across the border and rolled into Prague, ending the Prague Spring.

The Soviet invasion of Czechoslovakia initiated another chill in Soviet-Western relations. Moreover, the Communist parties of Italy and France denounced the invasion. In the mid-1970s, Western Communist leaders, particularly in Spain and Italy, began to call themselves "Euro-Communists." They stressed their independence—for example, by collaborating with Socialists and other left-wing parties. However, Euro-Communism proved unable to slow the decline in membership in the Communist parties of Western Europe.

Under the "Brezhnev Doctrine," the Soviet leadership tried to justify the invasion of Czechoslovakia and left open the possibility of future intervention in any of the satellite states of Eastern Europe. With the exception of Albania, which remained closed to virtually all foreign contact during the rigid dictatorship of Enver Hoxha, only Yugoslavia retained real independence. The Soviet invasion of Czechoslovakia disenchanted liberal Communists in Eastern European countries. Many no longer believed that communism could be reformed.

Opposition to Communist rule and Russian influence grew in all of the Eastern European states during the 1980s. The overwhelming economic

(*Left*) Communist leaders meet shortly before the Russian invasion of Czechoslo-vakia. Participants include Walter Ulbricht and Erich Honecker of East Germany (first two on the left), and Soviet Communist Party chief Leonid Brezhnev confer-ring with Premier Alexei Kosygin (on the right). (*Right*) Soviet armies occupy Prague, 1968.

failures of the Communist regimes grew ever more apparent. Television and radio carried images of the consumer culture of the more prosperous people in the West. In the meantime, Eastern European Communist states continued to borrow massively from the West, which merely patched over huge problems without bringing economic reform. Debt owed by Eastern European countries in hard currency rose from 6 billion dollars in 1971 to 66 billion dollars in 1980 and more than 95 billion dollars in 1988. Well-developed social services could not compensate for economic inefficiency and massive demoralization. Membership in the Communist Party declined, particularly among young people, while the age of the leadership increased dramatically.

Within the Soviet Bloc, resistance was most developed in Poland. In 1976 a variety of opposition groups unified, publishing underground books and newspapers and organizing strikes and demonstrations. Massive unrest led to strikes in Poland in 1970 and the organization of a Committee for the Defense of Workers. Edward Gierek (1913–2001), who had become head of the Polish United Workers' (Communist) Party in 1970, made some conces-sions while attempting to stimulate economic growth. However, despite massive foreign loans and credits, by 1976 Poland again had lapsed into eco-nomic stagnation, and another wave of strikes followed. In the meantime, the Catholic Church, which retained considerable influence (unlike in Czechoslovakia) helped mobilize opposition to the Communist government, particularly after the election in 1978 of Polish Pope John Paul II and his visit to his homeland in 1979. Strikes began in July 1980, and the following month Solidarity, a new illegal organization of trade unions, organized. Led by Lech Walesa (1943–), an electrician from Gdańsk, Solidarity put forward twenty-one demands for reform. Much more than a trade union, Solidarity's membership reached 10 million and came to represent opposition to communism. In the meantime, underground publishing had since the late 1970s emerged as a huge dissident industry undertaken by Polish intellectuals, who published more than 2,000 titles. In 1980, strikes and riots in protest of living conditions spread rapidly in industrial areas, particularly in the vast shipyards of Gdańsk. The Polish government agreed to tolerate the creation of new unions as long as they did not engage in political activity. Solidarity represented the first major challenge to the Communist system since the "Prague Spring" of 1968.

In September 1980, the Communist Central Committee responded to the ongoing crisis by forcing Gierek to resign as head of state. Two months later, the government officially recognized Solidarity's existence. However, accommodation between the government and the non-Communist trade unions did not last long, particularly after Solidarity members called for free elections. In December 1981, General Wojciech Jaruzelski (1923–), the new head of state, imposed martial law and replaced key Communist Party officials in government with military officers. He suspended Solidarity and put hundreds of leading dissidents under arrest, including Walesa. Troops brutally crushed strikes that broke out in response to the repression. In 1982, the government declared Solidarity illegal again. Although martial law ended a year later, the murder of a militant priest by policemen in 1984 generated enormous popular anger and protest.

In the meantime, East Germany, Bulgaria, and Czechoslovakia were the Eastern European nations that were most loyal to the Soviet Union. The German Democratic Republic's chief, Erich Honecker (1912–1994), who came to power in 1971, proved absolutely intransigent to reform. The Stasi, the East German secret police, employed 90,000 people and had about twice that number as informers. The Lutheran Church provided a center for some dissidents, organizing weekly "prayers for peace" in Leipzig. In Czechoslovakia, the state campaign against dissidents was more intense. In 1977, about 1,200 writers, philosophers, intellectuals, and musicians signed a protest against government limitation of freedoms in an attempt to force the government to respect the Helsinki human-rights convention it had signed. Despite the fact that this was anything but a revolutionary document (those who signed pledged not to engage in political activity), members of the "Charter 77" group suffered repression.

Gradual economic liberalization helped make Hungary the second (after the German Democratic Republic) most prosperous of the Eastern bloc countries. The gradual development of a market economy and a private agricultural sector helped stabilize the Communist regime, with the help of Soviet subsidies. In 1985 Hungary became the first Communist state to declare political pluralism to be an ideal. However, Hungary had no organized and tested opposition force such as Solidarity.

In sharp contrast, no liberalization of any kind took place in Romania. Nicolae Ceauşescu (1918–1989), head of the Romanian Communist Party, had brazenly adopted a position of relative independence, or "national communism," with respect to the Soviet Union, criticizing the Soviet invasion of Czechoslovakia, remaining neutral in the Sino-Soviet conflict, and refusing to participate in Warsaw Pact military maneuvers. Ceauşescu forged ahead with grandiose plans to generate industrial development. The results were disastrous. Romania became, after Albania, the poorest country in Europe while caught in the increasingly mad grip of Ceauşescu's "cult of personality." The dictator ordered 1,500 villages in Transylvania razed to the ground. These were largely in areas where many Hungarians resided, whom he targeted while trying to garner support from Romanians with nationalist appeals. He also ordered some of old Bucharest torn down to forge enormous boulevards that would lead to his reviewing stand.

The Gorbachev Era

In the Soviet Union, in the meantime, Leonid Brezhnev reinforced the powers of the oppressive Soviet bureaucracy and the prestige of the army and the KGB (the secret police). Reflecting the chill in relations with the United States, the Soviet Union, like its rival, poured more money into the manufacture of arms. After Brezhnev died in 1982, he was succeeded by Yuri Andropov (1914–1984), who, despite his long years in the KGB, was somewhat more liberal than Brezhnev. Andropov acknowledged that there was widespread inefficiency and corruption in Soviet economic planning and government. He called for greater popular participation in economic decision making and purged incompetent party hacks from important positions. Following Andropov's death in 1984, his successor, Konstantine Chernenko (1911–1985) was quite ill when he came to power, and both he and the Soviet state treaded water until his death the following year.

Mikhail Gorbachev (1931–) became general secretary of the Communist Party and thus head of the Soviet Union in 1985. Gorbachev had worked his way up in the party youth organization and studied law at the University of Moscow. Both his grandfathers had been arrested on false charges during the Stalin era. Gorbachev assumed responsibility for Soviet agriculture. Less instinctively xenophobic than other Soviet leaders, he was the first Soviet leader since Lenin to have a university degree. Relatively young, charming, flexible, and determined, Gorbachev was a master of Communist Party machinations.

Gorbachev began by exorcizing some ghosts from the Stalinist past. Like a number of optimistic party officials and intellectuals, Gorbachev believed that the Prague Spring could come to Moscow, but that the Communist Party should continue to dominate political life in the Soviet Union. He embraced a policy known in Russian as *glasnost*: openness in government combined with a greater degree of free expression. He put some liberals in positions of responsibility and ordered the relaxation of censorship. Artists and writers brought forth new work, including strident criticisms of the Soviet regime.

Gorbachev insisted that "we need a revolution of the mind." He espoused *perestroika*: a restructuring of the Soviet system to make it more efficient and responsive to the needs of Soviet citizens. The Soviet leader spoke openly about the failure of economic planning without sufficient material incentives for workers. Centralized state agricultural planning would have to be scrapped in favor of a free-market economy. He summarily cashiered some corrupt or incompetent local party officials and launched a full-fledged campaign against alcoholism, which had taken on epidemic proportions in the demoralized Soviet Union. But Gorbachev remained convinced that communism could be rescued by necessary reforms once the inefficiency and brutality of Stalinism had been completely eliminated. His model may well have been Lenin's implementation of the New Economic Policy in 1921 (see Chapter 23), which had revived the Soviet economy without sacrificing Communist authority.

In 1987, he reduced the role state corporations played in the Soviet economy, paving the way for increasing economic privatization. The state accepted private cooperatives and permitted state companies to sell their products on the open market (which encouraged luxury goods more than daily necessities). Furthermore, Gorbachev sought foreign investment in the Soviet Union. However, decades of economic inefficiency would clearly have to be overcome. Black marketeering remained a way of life for millions of people. The enormous costs of social programs weighed heavily on the sagging economy. The Communist countries of Eastern Europe, which had been exploited to economic advantage during the immediate post-war period, now represented an expensive drain on Soviet finances because of subsidy commitments and the cost of maintaining Soviet bases there.

In 1988, Gorbachev began to sponsor a series of remarkable political reforms. Dissidents within the Communist Party or even non-Communists could now be elected to the Congress of People's Deputies. He expressed determination to renew the "thaw" with the West that had ended during the Brezhnev era.

Three factors converged in the late 1980s to prepare the fall of communism and the end of the Soviet Union. First, nationalist movements gained momentum within the Soviet Union, particularly in the Baltic states of Lithuania, Latvia, and Estonia, and in Moldavia, Armenia, and Georgia, where in 1989 soldiers bludgeoned to death nineteen demonstrators demanding independence. Nationalists in Ukraine celebrated their culture by passing manuscripts written in Ukrainian from hand to hand. These movements, encouraged by the growing vulnerability of the Soviet state to a weak economy, were not placated by the belated toleration of greater cultural autonomy. In some of the republics, long-festering conflicts between nationalities began to surface violently, further undermining Soviet authority, for example, in Azerbaijan between Muslim Azerbaijanis and Christian Armenians.

Second, in 1989, a forceful democratic opposition emerged, led in Russia by the Nobel Prize–winning Russian physicist Andrey Sakharov (1921–1989), who had helped develop the hydrogen bomb. Gorbachev's encouragement of participation in public life increased the ranks of Soviet citizens demanding reform. For many people, brutal tales of the Gulag became increasingly compelling, having been brought to light by works of the Russian writer Alexander Solzhenitsyn (1918–2008), first in his novel *A Day in the Life of Ivan Denisovitch* (1962) and then in *The Gulag Archipelago* (1973). Moreover, the campaign for human rights, led by Sakharov, discredited the regime, even if the Gulag itself no longer existed. The Helsinki Accords, signed by the Soviet Union as well as by the Western powers in 1975, encouraged dissidents. Increasingly, the Russian opposition reached a large audience through the circulation of handwritten, typed, or clandestinely printed manuscripts, as well as through the medium of Western radio broadcasts.

Third, the aggravation of the economic crisis beginning in 1988 increased the number of Soviet citizens convinced that a Communist government simply could not bring about a meaningful improvement in the quality of their lives. At the same time, television broadcasts from Finland day after day showed the advantages of a free-market economy. Gorbachev vacillated between free-market policies and traditional Communist state controls. The result was a further weakening of the economy, replete with shortages and undermined by enormous military spending.

Gorbachev determined that the Soviet Union could not afford to continue the arms race with the United States. He therefore moved to improve relations with the U.S. government. In the early 1980s, Soviet-U.S. relations had continued to sour dangerously. Following the U.S. ban on the export of oil and gas to the Soviet Union after the Soviet invasion of Afghanistan in 1979, the U.S. government had tried to prevent the Soviet Union from constructing a long pipeline that would bring Siberian natural gas to Central Europe by threatening sanctions against any state or company that assisted the endeavor. Then U.S. President Ronald Reagan (1911–2004) backed a plan to construct a space-based missile-defense shield, dubbed "Star Wars" (Strategic Defense Initiative), provoking an outcry by the Soviet Union and by some U.S. allies as well. In 1983, a Russian fighter shot down a South Korean passenger plane that had entered Soviet air space, killing 169 people, including Americans. The Soviet Union boycotted the 1984 Olympics, which were held in Los Angeles, as the United States had done four years earlier in Moscow.

Gorbachev now resumed arms-limitation negotiations with the United States, but he refused to sign an agreement because Reagan would not include the "Star Wars" experiments in the negotiations. Highly successful visits to Washington, D.C., and New York in 1987 gave the Soviet leader considerable global television exposure, leading to enormous personal popularity. That year the United States and the Soviet Union agreed to reduce the number of medium-range missiles, and two years later they signed another arms-control agreement. In 1988, the Soviet Union recalled troops from Afghanistan after nine years of bloody fighting against rebels there. For the first time in anyone's memory, government publications admitted the severe economic and social problems that troubled the Soviet Union. The Soviet Union began to allow Soviet Jews to emigrate abroad in greater numbers than ever before. In 1989, almost 70,000 Jews left, most for Israel or the United States.

In 1986, the most serious nuclear accident in history occurred in Ukraine, when a nuclear reactor exploded at Chernobyl, near Kiev, sending radioactive material pouring into the atmosphere. Thousands of people in the vicinity were killed or suffered grave illnesses. A nuclear cloud passed over Ukraine, Russia, and the Scandinavian states, among other countries. Following an initial official attempt to deny the seriousness of the disaster, Gorbachev discussed the situation with unexpected openness.

Early in 1989, some reform-minded government officials joined opposition leaders in Poland and Hungary in the belief that economic and political liberalization was urgent. Communist rule slowly floundered under the weight of economic decline and popular dissatisfaction. In Czechoslovakia, East Germany, Bulgaria, Romania, and Albania, Communist leaders sought desperately to hold on to power. The East German and Czech governments reverted to force in an attempt to halt popular movements for change.

A crucial factor made the outcome of this wave of demands for reform in Eastern Europe in 1989 different from those occurring earlier (in East Germany in 1953, Hungary in 1956, and Czechoslovakia in 1968): the Soviet government no longer was determined to preserve its empire. Indeed, the shout "Gorbi, Gorbi, Gorbi!" rang out from the ranks of Eastern European protesters. Even if the Communist leadership in Czechoslovakia, East Germany, and Romania, particularly, were determined to overwhelm dissent, Soviet tanks would no longer back them up. In a speech to the Council of Europe in Strasbourg in July 1989, Gorbachev made clear that he rejected the "Brezhnev Doctrine" that had brought Soviet intervention in Czechoslovakia in 1968. The Soviet leader called events in Eastern Europe "inspiring," adding, "What the Poles and Hungarians decide is their affair, but we will respect their decision whatever it is."

Transition to Parliamentary Government in Poland and Hungary

Poland became the first test case for the new Soviet relationship with its former satellites. Since its creation in 1980, the trade union organization Solidarity had virtually achieved the status of an unofficial opposition party. The Catholic Church remained a source of organized opposition to communism. But although these organizations exerted some pressure on the government, it was the continued pitiful performance of the economy that fatally undermined communism. In 1987, the government held a referendum, asking Poles to support price increases. When they were overwhelmingly voted down, the government imposed them anyway. Demonstrations and strikes followed, and renewed calls to legalize Solidarity were made, amid widespread shortages and a grotesquely inflated currency. The government could no longer meet the interest payments on its massive debt to Western banks. General Jaruzelski had no choice but to accept some reforms. In August 1988, the government invited Solidarity to negotiate. The opposition agreed to participate in exchange for government recognition of the legal status of Solidarity as the legitimate representative of Poles opposed to Communist rule. Negotiations between Solidarity representatives and the government in 1989 led to the creation of a senate and the position of president of Poland. In the first relatively free elections in Poland since the immediate post-war period, Solidarity candidates swept to victory in the Senate. In the lower chamber, negotiations had led to 65 percent of the seats being reserved for Communists and 35 percent for the candidates of Solidarity. Still, General Jaruzelski confidently believed he could orchestrate liberalization on his own terms.

Solidarity's candidates swept to victory. The extent of Communist humiliation was such that candidates supported by Solidarity (with the support of the Catholic Church) won all 161 of these parliamentary seats. Moreover, Communist candidates won only two of thirty-five seats in elections in which they ran unopposed. When the United Peasant Party began talks with Solidarity and left the government coalition, the Communist majority collapsed. The Communists could not put together a government acceptable to Solidarity. When parliament elected Solidarity leader Tadeusz Mazowiecki (1927–) Poland had the first non-Communist government in Eastern Europe since 1948, although Communists retained several important ministries. However, Solidarity leaders, still wary that popular momentum once again could lead to heavy-handed repression, supported the election by the Polish parliament of General Jaruzelski as president.

In 1990, the Communist era ended in Poland when the Polish Communist Party changed its name and espoused pluralist politics. In the wake of a split within Solidarity between the followers of Mazowiecki and those of Lech Walesa, the latter was elected president in December 1990. The Democratic Union, a party formed by Mazowiecki's followers within Solidarity, won the largest number of seats in the lower house and the senate. Economic reforms, aimed at introducing a full-fledged free-market economy, were slow to take effect, however. Poland began a long struggle for economic stability with mounting unemployment and a dramatically increased crime rate.

In Hungary, the Hungarian Democratic Forum and several smaller opposition groups began to emerge in 1988 out of café and living-room gatherings of longtime dissidents. Gorbachev's reforms in the Soviet Union

Border guards cut down the Hungarian "Iron Curtain."

greatly encouraged opposition groups. But with the economy floundering under declining productivity and rampaging inflation, liberal Communists ousted longtime leader János Kádár from power, intent on reforming Hungary. Opposition groups, with the memory of Soviet intervention in 1956 still looming large, hesitated to call the legitimacy of the Communist regime into question.

In the summer of 1989, the Hungarian opposition formed an "Opposition Round Table" and negotiated with the government. Candidates of the Democratic Forum won free elections. Faced with continuing popular mobilization, the Communist leadership decided to try to outbid the Hungarian liberals by initiating reforms. In May 1989, the government ordered the removal of barbed wire that defined the border with Austria. In June, the Communist Party itself admitted that the 1956 trial and execution of reform leaders had been illegal. The former premier Imre Nagy, who had been executed after the 1956 insurrection, was reburied with national honors. The Hungarian Communist Party changed its name to the Hungarian Socialist Party. It espoused democratic principles and encouraged the development of opposition parties, accepting a new constitution proclaimed later that year. The transition from communism to multiparty parliamentary rule in Hungary was therefore peaceful, with the Hungarian Democratic Forum leading a subsequent coalition government.

The Collapse of the Berlin Wall and of East German Communism

As pressure for change mounted in Poland and Hungary, East Germans fled the German Democratic Republic in record numbers. Many traveled to the German Federal Republic via Czechoslovakia and then Hungary, whose government in May 1989 had opened its border with Austria. About 150,000 East Germans reached the West during the first nine months of 1989. However, eschewing the reforms undertaken by Gorbachev in the Soviet Union, East German Communist leader Honecker in June 1989 praised the Chinese army and police for crushing the prodemocracy demonstrations in Beijing's Tiananmen Square. While other Communist governments negotiated with determined reformers, the East German leadership stood firm until it was too late. Honecker demanded that Hungary return fleeing East Germans to their country, as specified in an old treaty between the two Communist states. The Hungarian government refused to do so. When the East German government gave permission to East Germans on a train passing through Dresden and Leipzig to emigrate to West Germany, other East Germans frantically tried to climb aboard the train. About 1.5 million East Germans now applied for exit visas.

When Gorbachev visited East Berlin early in October 1989, demonstrators chanted his name, which had become synonymous with opposition to the East German regime. When demonstrations spread to other major cities, Honecker ordered the police to attack demonstrators, but Egon Krenz, responsible for state security, refused to do so. On October 18, 1989, Honecker, old, ill, and ignored, was forced out in favor of Krenz, more moderate, but no reformer. In Leipzig, anxious opposition leaders and fearful Communist officials had met and resolved that peace must be maintained at all costs.

On October 23, 1989, Soviet Foreign Minister Eduard Shevardnadze (1928–) declared that each country in Eastern Europe "has the right to an absolute, absolute freedom of choice." Such words further encouraged demonstrations and meetings in East Germany. On November 4, Krenz announced that East Germans were free to leave for West Germany via Czechoslovakia. A wholesale exodus began. On November 9, Krenz capitulated to the inevitable, announcing a sweeping change in government and promising to initiate legislation that would grant East Germans the right to travel where and when they wanted. He ordered that the Berlin Wall, which had divided East Berlin from West Berlin since August 1961, be torn down. Around 3 million East Germans (out of a population of 16 million) poured over the demolished wall, or crossed into West Germany at once-forbidden checkpoints. An East German poet remarked, "I must weep for joy that it happened so quickly and simply. And I must weep for wrath that it took so abysmally long."

When Egon Krenz announced that East Germans could travel where and when they wanted, people gathered at the Berlin Wall to forge openings with whatever tools they had.

Krenz still hoped that his promise to hold free elections would keep the Communists in power. But lacking popular support, Krenz's government fell on December 3 and was succeeded by a series of committees until elections were held in March 1990. Conservatives favoring German reunification (led by the equivalent of the West German Christian Democrats) won an easy victory over Social Democrats and the remnants of the (now renamed) Communist Party. A number of East German leaders already expressed eagerness for German reunification. Here, again, there would be no Russian opposition to what had seemed for decades to be unthinkable because of Russian fear that one day a united Germany might again threaten the peace. In the meantime, the German Democratic Republic began selling off state-owned companies and the West German mark became the currency of both Germanys. In September, Britain, France, and the United States, viewing reunification as inevitable, renounced their rights in Berlin. Unification took effect on October 3, 1990. In December, the first elections in the newly unified Germany returned the Christian Democrats to power. The former German Federal Republic would for years have to allocate a substantial part of its budget to modernize the former Communist state and to provide public services to new citizens (including unemployment benefits in the wake of the collapse of state-run industries). In 1999, Berlin again became the capital of Germany.

The "Velvet Revolution" in Czechoslovakia

In Czechoslovakia, where the Communist leadership resisted the forces for change as vehemently as their counterparts in East Germany, the regime was swept aside in ten days. As news arrived of the fall of the Berlin Wall, the number of determined dissidents rapidly swelled. Czechs and Slovaks alike signed petitions calling for reform. On November 17, 1989, students staged a demonstration in honor of a student executed by the Nazis fifty years earlier. But speakers quickly ignored the program censors had approved and began to call for academic freedom and respect for human rights. Then the crowd started to march toward the giant St. Wenceslas Square in the center of Prague. A squad of riot police moved in, throwing canisters of tear gas and beating students with clubs.

The next day, a crowd assembled on the spot where police had beaten protesters. Students called for a general strike to begin ten days later. As the demonstrations continued to grow, the minister of defense announced that the army was "ready to defend the achievements of socialism." Yet, without the support of the Soviet Union, the Czechoslovak Communist government took no steps to repress the movement for freedom. On November 19, 1989, the entire Politburo resigned. A group of leading dissidents formed the "Civic Forum," calling on the government to negotiate with them over four demands: the resignation of two Communist officials blamed for the police attack two days earlier, the establishment of a commission to investigate the police attack, the release of political prisoners, and the resignation of Communist leaders responsible for the Soviet invasion in 1968. Civic Forum was led by Václav Havel (1936–), a popular Czech playwright whose plays had been banned by the government but circulated in manuscript) and a veteran of "Charter 77." Havel had been imprisoned several times for dissent, once nearly dying from mistreatment.

On November 21, 1989, the elderly Alexander Dubček, the Slovak reformer who led the Communist Party of Czechoslovakia during the 1968 events, addressed a throng assembled in St. Wenceslas Square. The crowds, however, did not want any kind of socialism. Students went to factories in search of support from workers. Crowds poured into the streets almost every day, waving national flags and calling for freedom of speech, the release of political prisoners, and the end of communism. They lay wreaths on the spot where a Czech student burned himself to death in 1968 in protest of the Soviet invasion. On November 24, 1989, the Communist Central Committee narrowly voted against using the army to put an end to demonstrations. In Slovakia, intellectuals formed an organization called "Public Against Violence," the Slovak equivalent of the Czech Civic Forum.

The Communist government now had no choice but to negotiate with its opponents who demanded free elections. Yet, unlike Poland and Hungary, where political opposition was well developed within the constraints of the system, there were virtually no reform-minded Communists in

Czechoslovakia. From Moscow, Gorbachev advised the Czechoslovak leaders not to use force. Negotiations between the government and Havel and other representatives of Civic Forum began on November 26. That day, more than half of the top leadership within the party was purged. Two days later, Civic Forum demanded the formation of a new government.

The Communist-dominated Federal Assembly voted to end the party's domination of political life. On December 10, the first cabinet in Czechoslovakia since 1948 not dominated by Communists was sworn in. The general strike ended, and more than a third of the members of the Communist Party resigned during the first two weeks of December. The Federal Assembly unanimously elected Havel president of Czechoslovakia. What Havel called a "velvet revolution" had succeeded, led by writers, actors, and students. Free elections gave Civic Forum and its allies a majority of seats. Price controls ended. Havel quickly announced that Czechoslovakia "must return to Europe," suggesting that its future lay with the West.

The new government of Czechoslovakia immediately faced not only the problem of creating viable democratic institutions and establishing a market economy, but also of tensions between Czechs and Slovaks. Although the two peoples shared seventy years of common political history, much separated them. The Czech part of the state was more urban, prosperous, and Protestant than Slovakia, which was more rural and Catholic. Slovak nationalists, particularly on the right, called for the creation of an inde-

Václav Havel, leader of the Civic Forum and first president elected under free elections in Czechoslovakia after the fall of the Communists in 1989, reads the names of members of Czechoslovakia's first non-Communist government since 1948.

pendent Slovakia. On January 1, 1993, the "velvet divorce" took place: the Czech Republic and Slovakia became separate states.

Revolutions in Bulgaria, Romania, and Albania

Communist regimes also fell in Bulgaria, Romania, and Albania, the three Eastern European states without significant reform movements. In Bulgaria, long-suppressed unrest began to emerge in response to pressure for reform in other Eastern European countries. Todor Zhivkov (1911–1998), the first secretary of the Communist Party of Bulgaria since 1954 and the head of state since 1971, could boast a record of modest economic growth until the late 1970s. He also had orchestrated several cover-ups of the misdeeds of his family members (including the implication of his hard-drinking and -gambling son in the death of a television announcer). When a Bulgarian airliner crashed at the Sofia airport, killing most passengers, Zhivkov ordered that his jet leave at once for his Black Sea vacation, flying over the burning plane. Furthermore, the Bulgarian secret police had achieved international notoriety, blamed by some for an attempt to assassinate Pope John Paul II in Rome in 1981, as well as for a James Bond–like murder of a Bulgarian dissident killed by the deadly jab of a poison-tipped umbrella in London. The Bulgarian economy faltered badly in the late 1980s. Bulgarian exports (principally agricultural produce and light manufactured goods) had difficulty finding markets, particularly as the economic crisis deepened in the Soviet Union. Rural migrants poured into Sofia and other Bulgarian cities in search of work.

As the economy deteriorated, Zhivkov and the Communist leadership sought to displace popular anger in the direction of the country's large and rapidly growing Turkish minority. From time to time during the past several decades, the Turks had been the target of discriminatory government measures, including a law in 1984 requiring them to adopt Bulgarian names and forbidding the practice of Islam (the religion of most Turks). Just what the Bulgarian government hoped to achieve by such measures remains unclear (although this was hardly the first time in the often violent history of the region that an ethnic group had been targeted for discrimination in the hope of deflecting public opinion). After launching a harsh campaign against Turkish customs, Zhivkov's government encouraged the ethnic Turks to emigrate to Turkey, which further destabilized the Bulgarian economy. More than 300,000 of them left for Turkey within three months in 1989. Many soon returned, however, disappointed that conditions of life in Turkey seemed even worse than in Bulgaria.

With news of dramatic political changes occurring in the other Eastern European states, the Bulgarian Politburo surprised Zhivkov by suddenly demanding his resignation in November, the day after the Berlin Wall had fallen. The ease with which this was accomplished suggests that some party bureaucrats, army officers, and even members of the notorious government security force now believed change to be inevitable. The new government purged Stalinists and welcomed back Turks, contributing to a nationalist backlash among many Bulgarians. Zhivkov was tried for misuse of government funds and sentenced to prison.

In January 1990, the Communist monopoly on political power ended, and the Bulgarian Communist Party changed its name to the Bulgarian Socialist Party. However, in June, the former Communists, capitalizing on resurgent ethnic rivalries and fear of change in the countryside, won a majority of seats in the New National Assembly. A new constitution followed in October 1991. The Bulgarian Socialist Party and the Union of Democratic Forces remained the two largest parties, confronting a poor economy and the lack of foreign investment, although loans from the World Bank then helped stabilize the Bulgarian economy.

In Romania, the fall of the Ceauşescu clan and communism was anything but bloodless. Ceauşescu, who had enriched his family (at least thirty of whom held high office), vowed that reform would come to Romania "when pears grow on poplar trees." He awarded himself titles such as "Genius of the Carpathians" and the "Danube of Thought." His wife, Elena, fraudulently claimed to be a brilliant chemist, presenting papers at academic conferences that had been prepared by Romanian scientists, and then refusing to answer questions about them. On the occasion of a state visit to Britain, when the Queen of England for whatever reason knighted the Romanian leader, Ceauşescu and his wife virtually pillaged a suite at London's Buckingham Palace, carting away everything of value they could. In order to begin paying back $10 billion in foreign loans, Ceauşescu cut back food imports, increased food exports, rationed electricity, and banned the sale of contraceptives in the hope of increasing the Romanian population.

Ceauşescu's downfall began in 1989 in the Transylvanian town of Timisoara, where ethnic Hungarians resented second-class status. Ceauşescu had ordered the razing of 8,000 largely Hungarian villages and the relocation of their residents. Crowds rioted, smashing store windows and burning Ceauşescu's portraits. Romanians joined Hungarians in the protests. Army units refused to fire on demonstrators. The feared security forces (the Securitate, 180,000 strong) stepped in, shooting three army officers for disobeying orders and firing on crowds.

Discontent spread rapidly. As another cold Romanian winter approached along with the usual severe food and fuel shortages, Hungarian and Yugoslav television showed events rapidly transpiring in other Eastern European countries. Demonstrations now spread to other towns. In December, Ceauşescu called for a massive demonstration of support in Bucharest. Orchestrated cheers from the crowd soon became jeers, drowning out the dictator's pathetic speech blaming riots on Hungarian nationalists. From the safety of his palace, Ceauşescu ordered troops to fire on the crowds below. But most units refused to obey and, as a result, the minister of defense was executed on Ceauşescu's orders. The hated secret police eagerly fired on the assembled crowds, and tanks crushed protesters in a scene hauntingly reminiscent of Beijing's Tiananmen Square earlier that year. After soldiers battled the security forces outside the presidential palace, hundreds of bodies lay in the streets.

Several of the dictator's top officials now decided that Ceauşescu's days of iron rule were numbered. Ceauşescu and his wife left their stately residence on December 22, 1989, through secret tunnels,

A Romanian prays for countrymen executed on the orders of dictator Nicolae Ceauşescu in Timisoara, Romania.

and then commandeered a helicopter. They were captured and immediately charged with murder and embezzlement of government funds. On Christmas Day, they were tried by a hastily convoked tribunal—which, in fact, had no legal authority—and condemned to death. They were then taken behind the building and shot, their bloody bodies left lying stiffly in the snow for a worldwide television audience to see. More than 1,000 people died during the revolution that overthrew Ceauşescu and ended communism in Romania.

Communism was swept away even in Albania, which had remained largely isolated from change in Eastern Europe by sealed borders. In Europe's poorest country, where food shortages had generated sullen anger, the fall of Ceauşescu in December 1989 emboldened dissidents. As a crisis mounted, President Ramiz Alia (1925–) announced greater openness in the selection of government leaders and a larger role for workers in choosing managers. Agricultural cooperatives would be allowed to sell surplus produce. Alia then announced the right to travel abroad and the abrogation of the long-standing ban on "religious propaganda." A group of Albanian intellectuals demanded the end of the Communist monopoly on power and students went on strike. Like other Communist leaders, Alia believed that he could maintain control by placating Albanians with minor reforms.

Confronted by demonstrations that began in December 1990, Alia announced that henceforth the Communist Party would cease to be the only approved political party. The Democratic Party quickly constituted itself, and opposition newspapers began to publish, although the Communist Party of Labor retained control of radio and television. In February 1991, a crowd of 100,000 demonstrated in Tirana, pulling down a large statue of former strongman Hoxha, who had died in 1985. In early March, 20,000 Albanians tried to force their way onto boats departing for Italy. This event, which focused international attention on Albania, produced a

Communist backlash, particularly in the countryside, where Hoxha had been a cult figure. In elections, the Communists won 68 percent of the vote. Despite this victory, the handwriting was on the wall. In June 1991, the Communist government resigned. For the first time since 1944, a coalition government came to power. Elections in 1992 gave the Democratic Party a majority of the seats in the National Assembly, and Alia resigned as Albania's president. For the next decade, the Democratic Party and the Socialist Party battled it out against the background of economic hardship, the arrival of tens of thousands of refugees from Kosovo, political corruption and assassination, and the bizarre events of 1997 when a series of pyramid investment schemes collapsed on naive purchasers, leading to riots and a period of total chaos. Greek troops had to intervene to maintain peace. Despite some periods of relative political stability, Albania has changed very little in some ways: between 1991—the fall of Communism— and 2008, more than 9,000 people had been killed as a result of blood feuds between families.

The Collapse of the Soviet Union

As one by one the former Eastern European satellites of the Soviet Union abandoned communism, unhappiness with the system became more vocal within the Soviet Union itself. In March 1990, the Communist government voted to permit non-Communist parties in the Soviet Union, and created the office of president. State restrictions on religious practice ended. That month, the Congress of People's Deputies elected Mikhail Gorbachev president of the Soviet Union, a significant change, since previously the head of the Communist Party was the titular head of state.

Pressure for the breakup of the Soviet Union mounted from the republics. In Estonia, Latvia, and Lithuania, a human chain of more than 1 million people formed to support the independence of their nations. In June 1990, the Russian Republic declared that laws passed by its legislature could override those of the Soviet Union. The other republics followed suit with similar legislation. Gorbachev's attempt to enhance government decentralization fell short of what nationalists in the republics sought. In June 1990, Lithuania unilaterally declared its independence from the Soviet Union; Gorbachev responded by ordering an embargo on Soviet oil and gas shipped to the Baltic state.

Gorbachev still wanted to maintain a role for the Communist Party in the new era, and he wanted to ensure the existence of the Soviet Union itself. Moreover, he probably still believed that Soviet influence over its former satellites in Central and Eastern Europe could continue even after the fall of communism in those states. In 1990, he appointed several hard-line government officials and ordered a crackdown on nationalist movements in the Baltic states. This led to the dramatic resignation of Shevardnadze, the popular foreign minister.

In Russia, the charismatic, hard-drinking, impulsive Boris Yeltsin (1931–2007) had risen to positions of authority in the Communist Party as an efficient and honest administrator. Claiming that Gorbachev was not truly committed to reform, he challenged the latter's authority and the legitimacy of the Soviet state. As chair of the Supreme Soviet, the state's highest legislative body, he announced that henceforth Russia would be a sovereign, independent state. Yeltsin had no illusions about the survival of communism and had grave doubts that the Soviet Union itself would survive. He was willing to ally with the other republics against Gorbachev. When reactionary Communists attempted to unseat Yeltsin as chairman in the Russian Parliament, several hundred thousand Moscovites turned out to express their support for him.

Gorbachev now seemed to move away from reform, possibly encouraging right-wing officials within the Communist Party, army, and KGB, who believed their positions were threatened by a reduction in hostility with the United States. The hard-line group had begun putting pressure on Gorbachev in September 1990, and the army began mysterious maneuvers around Moscow.

In January 1991, Gorbachev may have approved an attempt to overthrow the democratically elected government of Lithuania, which began with an attack on a television installation in the capital of Vilnius. The clumsy plot, which involved army and KGB agents pretending they were a Lithuanian dissident group, failed miserably. A month later, in a referendum deemed by the Soviet government to be illegal, 90 percent of those voting in Lithuania expressed their support for independence, as did 77 percent of those voting in both Estonia and Latvia—the difference explained by the fact that more Russians lived in Estonia and Latvia.

In a nationally televised speech in February 1991, Yeltsin called for Gorbachev to resign. Gorbachev, in turn, ordered troops to surround the Kremlin in a show of force. However, Yeltsin had begun to undermine the army and security forces, where he had followers. Gorbachev's turn toward conservatives cost him supporters.

Gorbachev's conservative retrenchment proved short-lived. In April, he abandoned his commitment to preserving the Soviet Union at all costs and accepted the idea of autonomy for the republics. In June 1991, Yeltsin was elected

Atop a tank in front of the Russian Parliament building, Boris Yeltsin urges the Russian people to resist the coup d'état of August 1991.

president of the "Russian Federation," another sign of how quickly the Soviet Union was changing. The Communists now had little support in Russia, by far the Soviet Union's largest republic. Gorbachev announced a new Communist Party platform, which eliminated Marxism and Leninism in favor of "humane and democratic socialism." He then left for an August vacation in Crimea.

Intransigent Communists were now firmly convinced that Gorbachev's policies threatened the existence of the Soviet Union. In August 1991, hard-liners within the Communist Party, army, KGB, and some members of Gorbachev's own cabinet placed the Soviet leader under house arrest in his Crimean residence in an attempted coup d'état that looked more like a comic opera. Setting up an "Emergency Committee," the conspirators apparently hoped that they could convince or force Gorbachev to use his prestige against reform by declaring a state of emergency. Gorbachev agreed to do so, but only if such a move were approved "constitutionally" by the Supreme Soviet. The conspirators then publicly declared the president to be "incapacitated."

In Moscow, Yeltsin stood on a tank outside the Russian Parliament and encouraged resistance. The coup fell apart, its leaders having underestimated the strength of both Yeltsin's and Gorbachev's popular support. The Soviet army remained loyal to Gorbachev. Yeltsin mobilized people in Moscow by calling for resistance and the restoration of Gorbachev as the legitimate Soviet leader. This appeal to constitutionality revealed how much had changed in a very short time.

In August, Gorbachev returned to Moscow a hero, and again took a more reformist stance. Even as Gorbachev continued to defend the Communist Party before the Supreme Soviet, Yeltsin suspended the Communist Party and its newspaper *Pravda*. These bold moves amounted to the dismantling of communism in Russia.

The failed coup accelerated the collapse of the Soviet Union. Gorbachev appointed new people to key ministries. Some KGB officers were pensioned off, and television and radio were freed from the constraints of censorship. The Soviet government recognized the independence of the Baltic republics, just months after Gorbachev had insisted on retaining the structure of the Soviet Union. In late August 1991, the Supreme Soviet voted to put an end to the extraordinary powers previously accorded Gorbachev and to suspend the Communist Party in the entire Soviet Union. Yeltsin quickly moved to initiate a market economy in Russia.

One by one, the republics left the Soviet Union, where Russians had constituted only about half of the population. Moldavia, Uzbekistan, and Azerbaijan declared their independence. In December 1991, Ukraine followed, after 90 percent of the population voted to leave the Soviet Union. By the end of the year, thirteen of the fifteen Soviet republics had declared their independence. The Soviet Empire was no more. Yeltsin and the presidents of Belarus and Ukraine declared the Soviet Union dissolved. Gorbachev, too, acknowledged that the Soviet Union no longer existed. Symbolically, Leningrad again assumed its old name of Saint Petersburg. On December 25, 1991, Gorbachev resigned, closing one of the most remarkable political eras in modern European history.

The end of communism in Europe did not guarantee an easy transition to parliamentary democratic rule. The lack of democratic traditions, the economic turmoil, and the deep ethnic rivalries posed daunting challenges. Nowhere are the stakes higher for a peaceful transition to democracy than in Russia. The president of Ukraine put it this way: "When there's frost in Russia on Thursday, by Friday there's frost in Kiev." In 1993, Yeltsin declared a "special presidential regime," dissolving the legislature and overriding opposition to his reform program. Yeltsin insisted that the Russian presidency should have considerable authority, whereas the Congress of People's Deputies feared too much presidential power, remembering well the dictatorship of the Communist Party. In 1996, Yeltsin became the first democratically elected president of Russia. In ill health, his resignation at the end of 1999 led to the election of Vladimir Putin (1952–), a former KGB officer, as president of Russia. Putin provided some badly needed stability to Russia after considerable turmoil during the 1990s.

The Disintegration of Yugoslavia

The story of the disintegration of Yugoslavia most tragically illustrates the complexity of national identity, the impact of ethnic politics on the post-Communist era in Eastern Europe and the Balkans, and the challenges and hopes for the future. Marshal Josip Broz ("Tito"), a Croat, believed that communism in Yugoslavia could end ethnic rivalries and Serb domination. Yugoslavs lived in relative harmony, and following Tito's death in 1980, a collective presidency that rotated every year among the republics governed Yugoslavia. But tensions persisted between Serbs and Croats, the country's two largest ethnic groups. They shared a common spoken language (though Serbs use the Russian Cyrillic alphabet and Croats use the Latin alphabet). Yugoslavia's capital, Belgrade, was also that of Serbia. Serbs enjoyed disproportionate representation in the Communist state bureaucracy.

Regional disparities in economic development and prosperity compounded ethnic divisions. In the north, the republic of Slovenia, which was by far the most ethnically homogeneous of Yugoslavia's republics, enjoyed a standard of living not far below that of its neighbors, Austria and Italy. In the south, Macedonia and Bosnia remained backward and relatively impoverished. Within Bosnia, 85 percent of the population of the territory of Kosovo was Albanian and Muslim. Yet the minority Serbs—only about 10 percent of the population—viewed Kosovo as sacred Serb soil, because the Ottoman Turks had defeated them there in 1389 and Kosovo had become part of Serbia during the Balkan Wars (1912–1913). In the meantime, ethnic Albanians claimed the right to be the seventh Yugoslav republic.

In the mid-1980s, the Serb-run Yugoslav government launched a brutal repression of Albanians living in Kosovo, claiming that Albanian nationalism posed a threat to communism. In April 1987, Slobodan Milošević (1941–2006), the leader of the Serb Communist Party, provocatively told Serbs and Montenegrins that Kosovo was theirs and that they should remain at all costs.

Milošević turned the Communist Party and state apparatus into instruments serving Serb nationalist interests. He undertook what amounted to a military occupation of Kosovo, ending its administrative autonomy. In 1989, fighting broke out in Kosovo between ethnic Albanians and Serbs and Montenegrins, inflaming Serb nationalism.

Yugoslavia quickly disintegrated (see Map 29.2). The movement for political reform began in January 1990 in Slovenia. New parties formed in each of the six republics, including Serbia, where Communist leaders still opposed reform. Non-Communists won a majority of the parliamentary seats in Bosnia-Herzegovina, Croatia, Slovenia, and Macedonia. The Communist Party changed its name to the Socialist Party and won a majority in Milošević's Serbia and in Montenegro, Serbia's ally.

In December 1990, Slovenes voted overwhelmingly for independence. In Croatia, the nationalist Franjo Tudjman (1922–1999), won a clear electoral victory, accentuating tensions between Croatia and the Yugoslav state. Milošević loudly espoused the creation of a Greater Serbia that would include all territories populated by Serbs. In May 1991, Serbia prevented the succession of a Croat to the rotating presidency of Yugoslavia. In Slovenia, intervention by the Yugoslav army was met by determined resistance and was short-lived. But when Croatia declared independence from Yugoslavia in June 1991, as did Slovenia, violent conflicts between Croats and Serbs intensified. Serb militias, supported and armed by Yugoslav army units, began occupying large chunks of Croatia that had sizable Serb populations. Within several months they held about one-third of Croatian territory, driving Croats from their villages and killing thousands of people. From the heights above, Serbs shelled the walled Croatian city of Dubrovnik on the Adriatic coast, severely damaging one of Europe's most beautiful cities. Croatia became independent in January 1992, although parts of Croatia remained under Serb control.

Macedonia declared its independence in September 1991. In Bosnia-Herzegovina, ethnic rivalries also brought violence. The Yugoslav army occupied parts of Bosnia, allegedly to protect Serbs. In March 1992, a majority of Bosnian Muslims and ethnic Croats voted for the independence of Bosnia-Herzegovina. However, Bosnian Serbs refused to recognize the legality of the plebiscite. They declared their own independence. A bloody civil war broke out in Bosnia-Herzegovina. Bosnian Serbs carried out "ethnic cleansing," a term they invented. Serbs forced at least 170,000 non-

MAP 29.2 THE DISINTEGRATION OF YUGOSLAVIA, 1995   The fall of the Communists in Yugoslavia led to the breakup of the Yugoslav federation and to civil war between Croats, Serbs, and Bosnian Muslims. This map reflects the settlement reached in the Dayton Peace Accords, signed in November 1995.

Serbs from their homes and drove them away or imprisoned them. Bosnian Serb militias perpetuated atrocities against Bosnian Muslims, including rapes and mass executions. They massacred 8,000 men and boys in fields outside the town of Srebrenica. In the meantime, in predominantly Croat parts of Bosnia, Croats also carried out brutal measures against Muslims, some of whom reciprocated against Serbs and Croats.

Milošević, presiding over what remained of Yugoslavia (now including only Serbia and Montenegro), eliminated constitutional guarantees given by the old Yugoslav republic to the provinces of Kosovo and Vojvodina (a region of northern Serbia). Although Yugoslav armies withdrew, fearing international intervention, Bosnian Serb forces, supplied by the Yugoslav army, surrounded Sarajevo, the Bosnian capital, lobbing mortar and cannon shells from the heights above and killing civilians. In response to assistance given

(*Left*) A Kosovo Albanian refugee released from the custody of the Yugoslav army collapses. (*Right*). Yugoslav President Slobodan Milošević brandishes a mace, a gift from his supporters.

the Bosnian Serbs by Milošević's government, the United Nations placed an economic embargo on what was left of the Yugoslav state. However, the NATO alliance failed to act, thus allowing Serb nationalists to conquer more than 70 percent of Bosnia-Herzegovina. "Europe is dying in Sarajevo," warned a poster in Germany. To make things even worse, Croats and Muslims in Bosnia now began to fight each other.

The Bosnian conflict took a terrible toll, creating hundreds of thousands of refugees. Croatia also entered the conflict with an eye toward taking Bosnian territory that nationalists considered Croatian. Another full-scale Balkan war loomed.

Early in 1994, a cease-fire agreement took hold. Bosnian Muslim and Croatian leaders met in Washington, D.C., forming a Muslim-Croat Federation within Bosnia-Herzegovina. However, the Bosnian Serbs refused to respect either the cease-fire or an international plan for peace. The arrival of blue-helmeted UN peacekeepers in the first international attempt ever to stop ethnic cleansing at first made little difference. NATO launched air strikes against Serb targets in Bosnia. In August 1995, the Croats recaptured Krajina, contested territory bordering on Bosnia that Croatian Serbs had declared to be independent in 1991. Now tens of thousands of Serbs from Krajina took to the roads as refugees, heading toward Serb strongholds in Bosnia.

By the Dayton Peace Accords orchestrated in 1995 by the U.S. government, Bosnia was to be a single state that included a Bosnian-Croat federation and a Serb republic. This agreement would be supervised by a NATO peacekeeping force, including U.S. troops. However, Bosnian Serbs overran free zones that NATO forces had established to protect Bosnian Muslims. Mass murders perpetrated against Muslims in 1995 (including thousands in a so-called UN-protected safe zone) led to the indictment of Bosnian Serb leader Radovan Karadzić (1945–) by the International Criminal Tribunal, a UN tribunal that was established in The Hague (in the Netherlands) to judge those accused of crimes against humanity and genocide. (Karadzić was finally captured in Belgrade in 2008 and put on trial.) Europe's bloodiest conflict since World War II went on. Ethnic cleansing in Bosnia, overwhelmingly by Serbs, took more than 200,000 Bosnian lives, and by the end of the war about 2.1 million Bosnians were without homes.

In Kosovo, Albanians had formed the Kosovo Liberation Army with the goal of obtaining freedom from Yugoslavia. In 1998 and 1999, Milošević unleashed Serb forces against ethnic Albanians in Kosovo. A cease-fire arranged by the United States in October 1998 quickly collapsed and Milošević refused to allow NATO peacekeepers into the province. Serb troops began ethnic cleansing, killing thousands of Muslims, and drove 860,000 Albanians into Albania and Macedonia. When Serb forces did not withdraw from Kosovo, NATO forces in March 1999 began attacking military targets in Serbia from the air. The bombing campaign forced Serb forces to withdraw from Kosovo and to allow 50,000 NATO peacekeepers into Kosovo. They oversaw the return of about 720,000 ethnic Albanian refugees to Kosovo. In the meantime, 50,000 Serbs now fled possible reprisals.

Milošević's government in Yugoslavia collapsed in October 2000 in the face of mass demonstrations. The Serb leader was arrested six months later to face charges of crimes against humanity and genocide at the International Criminal Tribunal in The Hague. He died unrepentant in 2006 during his trial. In the meantime, the new Yugoslav government worked quickly to end the international isolation brought about by Milošević's policies. The United States and other states ended economic sanctions against Yugoslavia. In 2003, the remnants of Yugoslavia became Serbia-Montenegro, the only two of the six republics of Yugoslavia that remained together. The assassination in March 2003 of the prime minister of Serbia, Zoran Djindjic (1952–2003), who had been one of the forces behind the ouster of Milošević in 2000, attested to the continuing volatility of Serbia. In 2008, Kosovo proclaimed its outright independence from Serbia, a move that Serbia and Russia refused to recognize.

Challenges in the Post-Communist World

While the West breathed a sigh of relief after the collapse of communism in Europe, the existence of nuclear weapons in several of the former states of the Soviet Union became a considerable concern. The 1986 Chernobyl disaster clearly demonstrated the vulnerability of the rest of Europe to nuclear disasters. Ukraine's nuclear arsenal and its claim to the remnants of the Soviet Black Sea Fleet docked in Crimea raised tension between Russia and Ukraine. In 1992, Ukraine, Russia, Belarus, and Kazakhstan all agreed that nuclear weapons stored on their territory would either be destroyed or turned over to Russia. In 1996, nuclear warheads were shipped to Russia for destruction. However, the problem of preventing the theft and sale of nuclear materials, particularly to potential terrorists, remains one of the most important concerns for the future.

The end of communism has left other problems. The rapid industrialization in East Germany, Romania, and Czechoslovakia under communism left horrendous pollution from coal-burning furnaces and virtually unregulated factories. Acid rain destroyed forests, killed rivers, and compromised public health.

Suddenly freed from Soviet domination, the newly independent states faced the challenge of putting their own foreign relations on a firm footing. For many of the former Soviet republics, relations with Russia are complicated by centuries of animosity, nowhere more so than in Ukraine and Georgia. Soviet rule had favored Russian interests, and in the Baltic states, for example, brought the settlement of large Russian populations, as well as troops (250,000 Soviet troops were stationed in Soviet republics other than Russia at the time of the Soviet Union's dissolution).

Like the Soviet Union, the Eastern European Communist states were largely atomized societies of one-party rule without political infrastruc-

A factory in Poland polluting the atmosphere.

tures, traditions of political parties, civic cultures, or adequately developed voluntary associations. Only in Poland and Hungary had non-Communist political leadership gradually emerged in the 1980s, providing the basis for the emergence of party politics following the dismantling of one-party rule. In 1989, Civic Forum in Czechoslovakia served the same function, and in Hungary a series of right-center and left-center coalitions implemented far-reaching economic reforms. In some former Communist countries, the problem of creating political institutions in which basically only party members had experience in public life was daunting.

In the first free elections held in Eastern Europe since the late 1940s, two distinct trends were seen in the 1990s. Nationalist right-center parties emerged victorious in eastern Germany, Poland, and Hungary, where the parties of the left, including those formed by former Communists (some of them, to be sure, converted reformers), fared badly. In Poland, Solidarity was defeated in 1991 in the first free elections held since 1926, leading to the arrival in power of several center-right coalitions. On the other hand, in Bulgaria and Romania, former Communist parties (hurriedly renamed and claiming the mantle of reform) came out better than any other parties. They did particularly well in the countryside, where reform movements had been largely absent and Communist officials maintained considerable prestige, as they were identified with the modest increase in living standards that had occurred during the decades since the war. In late 1995, the Communist Party emerged as the biggest winner in the legislative elections in Russia. Six years after the fall of the Berlin Wall, Bulgaria, Hungary, Lithuania, and Poland, where Lech Walesa was turned out of office in 1995, were now led by former Communists. Many of them benefited from being familiar faces able to draw on old political networks and from protest votes from people exasperated by growing economic disparities.

The former Communist states moved to create modern economic systems based on private enterprise. Western economic advisers provided some of the expertise as the nationalized sector of Eastern European economies was drastically reduced. This process proved easier in the more northern countries than in the Balkans, where elected leaders in the 1990s tended toward authoritarian rule amid continuing corruption. With the exceptions of Poland and Hungary, economic privatization was not easy in post-Soviet Central and Eastern Europe and particularly in the Balkans. As in the former Soviet Union, weak economies and a relatively low standard of living continued to generate political instability. Policy changes came with numbing speed. The utilization of free-market "shock therapy," including the end of price controls on most consumer goods, at first brought economic chaos to Russia and Poland, where Communists were returned to power in 1993. In the region as a whole, industrial production fell by between 20 and 40 percent. Widespread unemployment and the sudden end of the massive welfare system under which entire populations had grown up left hardship, bewilderment, and anger. The distribution of state-owned property engendered problems. In Hungary, foreign conglomerates bought up property that had been held by the Communist state. Former owners of property collectivized by Communist regimes demanded their lands back. Yet, at the same time, in the former Soviet satellite states, the attraction of joining the European Union itself encouraged economic and political reform. In some countries, members of the former Communist elite managed to get hold of valuable assets. The end of authoritarian rule led to major increases in violent crime, above all in Russia and Bulgaria, where organized crime has become powerful as one unstable government has followed another (including, remarkably enough, the period of 2001–2005 when the man who had in 1946 briefly taken the title of "tsar" of Bulgaria became prime minister). Belarus remained a virtual dictatorship, a throwback to another time.

Foreign investment was far from adequate. In the short term, galloping inflation (up to 20 percent a month in Russia and 40 percent in Ukraine) engendered bitterness. Despite the fact that its Western creditors in March 1991 canceled half of the debts owed by Poland, the economic outlook in that country seemed bleak. The Russian economy virtually collapsed in the 1990s, and by the end of the decade about 30 percent of the population of Russia was classified as impoverished. With taxpayers simply not paying up, Russia barely avoided bankruptcy in 1998 by postponing paying off $43 billion in short-term loans. Romania, Bulgaria, and Albania, in particular, were confronted by the ravages of decades of Communist economic policies, leaving a ruinous emphasis on heavy industry, compounded by old technology, combined with an inefficient agricultural sector. However, in 1997, the new Romanian government undertook major economic reforms with the help of loans from the World Bank and the International Monetary Fund. These included the reduction of state subsidies to companies and the privatization of many state-run businesses.

Nation-states, which many liberals long assumed were necessary before constitutional rights and equality could be assured, have not always turned out to be liberal and tolerant. Even if bilateral treaties officially ended long-simmering disputes over some territorial boundaries, such as those between Germany and Poland, Hungary and Romania, and Hungary and Slovakia, tensions still remain between Turks and Bulgarians in Bulgaria, Hungarians and Romanians in Romania, Slovaks and Hungarians in Slovakia, and Albanians and Macedonians in Macedonia. In the Czech Republic, the Republican Party denounced in shrill nationalist tones Germans and, above all, the minority population of gypsies (Roma) until the party was dissolved in 2001. In Hungary and Romania, too, right-wing racism has focused on Roma, as well as Jews. The potential for ethnic violence in Russia and the other former Soviet republics also remained. Twenty-five million Russians lived in other republics within the Soviet Union at the time of the latter's disintegration, 17 million of whom were in Ukraine. It was telling that in Estonia, no sooner had Communist rule ended than new governments established language tests to determine who was a "real" Estonian. The newly independent Baltic republics established laws that classified Russians as foreigners. In Russia, the extreme right-wing Liberal Democratic Party won almost a quarter of the vote in parliamentary elections in 1993. Aggressive nationalism and xenophobia have become more in evidence in Russia. Azerbaijanis and Armenians battled in the Armenian enclave of Nagorno-Karabakh in the early 1990s. Since 1994, Russian troops have battled nationalist Muslim insurgents in Chechnya (which lies north of Georgia and west of the Caspian Sea). The revolt, which has taken the lives of thousands of civilians, has generated harsh Russian repression while generating terrorist attacks orchestrated by rebels inside Chechyna and inside Russia. The Russian government proposed greater Chechen autonomy, but not independence. Russian troops captured Grozny, the capital of the breakaway republic, in February 2000. Chechen rebels on several occasions took hundreds of hostages, many of whom were killed when Russian troops stormed a theater and a school. Russian troops responded with frequent brutality.

Elected to a second term in 2004, Putin oversaw a vigorous resurgence of Russian presence and assertiveness on the international scene. In Ukraine, tensions between those who wanted close relations with Russia and those who did not destabilized the government. The status of Crimea, which became part of Ukraine during the Soviet break-up, remains highly contentious because the Russian government still considers Crimea to be Russian and also because of the importance of Sebastopol as a Black Sea naval port. In 2007, Russia ended its participation in the Conventional Armed Forces in Europe Treaty, which had been signed in 1990 at the very end of the Cold War. In 2008, Putin's chosen successor, Dimitri Medvedev, was elected president. He quickly named Putin prime minister, leaving the latter's enormous influence in Russia virtually intact and keeping open the possibility that Putin might one day again be president.

Resurgent Russian nationalism was apparent in August 2008. Amid rising tensions between Georgia and separatists in two autonomous regions of the country, South Ossetia and Abkhazia, that were seeking to break away, Russian forces invaded, allegedly to protect the minorities, some of whom had been provided with Russian passports. The Russians pushed into Georgia itself before a cease-fire was signed. Russia declared that its troops would remain as "peacekeepers" in the contested zones. A sign of modern times, the offensive against Georgia included cybernet attacks intended to destabilize Georgian web sites. Russian actions drew virtually unanimous international condemnation, chilling relations, in particular, between Russia and the United States, which counted the pro-American Georgian government as an ally and had encouraged Georgian defiance. Russian military action and the subsequent official recognition of both enclaves as independent states reflected Russian anger at the recognition of the independence of Kosovo by the United States and other Western states, as well as Russian apprehension that Georgia, as well as Ukraine, both bordering states, might be invited to join NATO.

In January 2009, benefiting from considerable riches in energy, Russia seemed to flex its muscles by cutting off the supply of natural gas to Ukraine after a bitter dispute over prices. The shutdown had the immediate effect of leaving many countries in eastern and southern Europe without much heat during a very cold winter until the dispute was resolved.

Conclusion

The Western European nations failed to act effectively to resolve the Bosnian crisis, but the cooperation between states in the former Soviet bloc and the West is reassuring. Russia and the United States signed an arms treaty in 2002 and have cooperated in space ventures, notably a space station.

Freed from Communist rule, some of the Eastern European states lobbied to join NATO. In 1997, NATO announced that it would expand its membership to include eventually Poland, the Czech Republic, and Hungary, hoping that the adherence of former Communist states would help consolidate democracy. Furthermore, it was also announced that a Permanent Joint Council in Brussels would bring together NATO members and Russia to consider joint actions, including arms control and peacekeeping. This is a remarkable turnabout, as NATO, which now includes twenty-six nations, had been originally established with the goal of containing the Soviet Union. This, too, has been a sign of new times.

CHAPTER 30

GLOBAL CHALLENGES: "FORTRESS EUROPE," EUROPEAN COOPERATION, AND THE UNCERTAINTIES OF A NEW AGE

The remarkable increase in the movement of peoples from one part of the world to another has been a dramatic dimension of globalization. After centuries of sending millions of European emigrants to other continents, the trend was reversed. Beginning in the 1960s, Asians and Africans seeking a better life began to arrive in unprecedented numbers in Western Europe. Moreover, with the collapse of communism in Eastern Europe and the Balkans, tens of thousands of immigrants began arriving in Western Europe. Yet while immigrants have contributed enormously to the economies of many European states, their presence and the cultural differences they bring with them have generated xenophobia in many states and an increase in the political influence of nationalist parties of the extreme right. Immigration thus poses a challenge to the new Europe, raising difficult issues of identity and the very question of what it means to be European.

Globalization has brought other difficult challenges as well. For example, the financial crisis—indeed the near collapse of the financial sector—that began in 2008, the worst international economic crisis since the Great Depression, itself reflected dimensions of globalization. First, the rapid

1219

rise in the price of oil had immediate worldwide consequences. Then the subprime lending crisis, the result of irresponsible mortgage lending, was followed by the bankruptcy of several major financial giants and the propping up of others by national governments. In the United States, hundreds of thousands of houses were foreclosed upon when purchasers could not make payments. Overall, the prices of housing plunged. This had an immediate catastrophic impact on the world economy, and thus on ordinary people who have reason to fear for the safety of their money. Investments and retirement funds went up in smoke. The financial meltdown revealed the scale of global interconnectedness. As the world economy went into recession and economic growth slowed down in the United States and Europe, China and India—the world's two new booming economies—faced lower demand for their goods. In Europe, despite considerable economic integration provided by the European Union, the absence of comparable political integration made it difficult for the leading states to come up with effective comprehensive policies that cut across national boundaries.

The world economic crisis strained relations between member states. Some governments retreated from free trade policies in the context of a single European Union market by providing subsidies with the goal of protecting certain industries (for example, France aiding its automobile companies), raising the specter of protectionism. Tensions emerged between the states whose economies were doing relatively well and those like Spain, Ireland, and Greece who were suffering the most; and between the older member states, who feared an increased economic burden being placed on them, and those poorer Eastern European nations recently admitted to the European Union.

Europe has ceased to be the center of global political concern and conflict, a title that has arguably passed to the Middle East. Globalization has made Europe, like other parts of the world, vulnerable to the tensions linked to conflicts in the Middle East. Terrorist attacks have carried the struggles in that part of the world to Europe itself. Moreover, following the collapse of the Soviet Union, European unity and the traditional Western alliance have been challenged by the domination of the United States. Yet the European Union (EU) in the 1990s carried cooperation between European states to a level barely imaginable a decade or two before. Within the European Union, a single market led to the inauguration of a single currency—the "euro"—in 2002.

Immigration to Europe

More than ever before, the world's population has been on the move. Millions of people have emigrated to Western Europe. Africans, Asians, Turks, and people from the Middle East have arrived, legally or illegally, in Western European countries. To be sure, immigration within Europe, particularly from the poorer countries of southern and eastern Europe, has also continued to be significant. The mass movement of people from the Third World, particularly from Africa and Asia, must be seen in the context of the rapid growth of the world's population. The population of Africa in 1950 was half that of Europe; by 1985, the two populations stood about even, and within several decades the population of Africa will probably be three times that of Europe. In some cases, it was newly independent colonies that sent immigrants to their former colonizers, as in the case of Indians and Pakistanis moving to Britain and of North Africans to France. Europe now has an estimated 18 million foreign workers.

Beginning in the late 1960s, foreign-born "guest workers" (as they are called in Germany) made up an increasing proportion of the workforce in every Western European state. Encouraged by European governments concerned about a labor shortage, they took up a variety of skilled but mostly unskilled work. The government of the German Federal Republic established recruiting offices in southern Europe and North Africa, hoping to encourage immigration. The number of foreigners living in Western Europe tripled in thirty years. In Switzerland, foreign workers make up about a quarter of the workforce. The ethnic composition varies from country to country. Turks have settled in Germany in great numbers because of the relative proximity and historically close ties between Turkey and Germany. Portuguese make up the largest non-French ethnic community in the Paris

North African immigrants captured by a patrol boat after trying to enter Spain illegally.

region, followed closely by Algerians, Moroccans, and Tunisians, and an increasing number of West Africans. In France, where the number of Muslim residents reached 5 million people, the number of mosques rose from 130 in 1976 to more than 1,000 twenty years later. The percentage of ethnic minorities living in Britain rose from 6 percent to 9 percent in the decade between 1991 and 2001. In the latter year, 1.5 million Muslims lived in England and Wales, representing more than 3 percent of the population. In 2007, 2 million of London's 7 million residents had been born outside of Britain.

Following the collapse of communism, the opening of Eastern European borders and the elimination of border controls between many Western European states increased the number of people trying to reach Western Europe. Kurds fled Iraq and Turkey for Europe, as North Africans left Algeria (ravaged by a bloody civil war following the army's seizure of power in 1992 and the rise of militant Islamic fundamentalist groups), Tunisia, and Morocco, trying to reach France via Spain, if they did not drown first. Between 1990 and 1993, 200,000 Albanians crossed the mountains to reach Greece. Thousands of others, desperately attempting to flee violence and economic ruin in their country, made the dangerous trip across the Adriatic Sea to Italy. Between 1980 and 1992, 15 million immigrants arrived in Western Europe. The number of people seeking asylum rose from about 65,000 in 1983 to over 500,000 in 1991—many from the ethnic conflict following the break-up of Yugoslavia, as well as from Romania and Turkey (see Table 30.1). By the early 1990s, at least 3 million clandestine immigrants were living in Western Europe, and probably many more.

In response, Western European governments have turned increasingly to new strategies and laws to try to reduce the number of immigrants, establishing tougher tests for claims of political asylum and sending illegal immigrants back to their countries. The percentage of asylum seekers whose cases are judged favorably by government authorities has been decreasing. With 7 percent of its population now made up of foreigners (60 percent of them non-European), France has turned away from its long-held belief that being born in that country was enough to become a French citizen; it now requires that children born in France to non-French parents must apply for citizenship between ages sixteen and twenty-one. The government has also made it more difficult for foreigners to acquire French citizenship through marriage. Yet massive migration to Europe will certainly continue. Referring to the smuggling of migrants into his country, the Austrian director of immigration put it memorably, "There are no distances any longer in this world. There are no islands."

Immigration became a politically explosive issue. When economic recession sharply reduced the number of available jobs, the political tide began to turn even more against foreign workers. The British government put laws restricting immigration (targeting nonwhite arrivals) in place in 1968 and 1971. In the former year, Enoch Powell, a Conservative MP, caused a

TABLE 30.1. FOREIGN-BORN POPULATION AND PERCENTAGE OF
TOTAL POPULATION, 1995

Country	Foreign-Born Population	Percentage
Austria	724,000	9
Belgium	910,000	9
Denmark	223,000	4.2
Finland	69,000	1.3
France	3.5 million	6.3
Germany	7.1 million	8.8
Ireland	96,000	2.7
Italy	991,000	1.7
Luxembourg	138,000	33.4
Spain	500,000	1.2
Switzerland	1.3 million	18.9
United Kingdom	2 million	3.4
United States	24.6 million	10

Source: *World Book, 1998* (Chicago: World Book, 1999), p. 245.

storm when he warned that unchecked immigration would swamp Britain. When the economic recession began in the mid-1970s, other European states began to enact more restrictive immigration policies. While many foreign-born workers, recruited as single young men before the economic recession, became permanent residents of the countries where they worked (and became citizens), they were joined by hundreds of thousands of undocumented clandestine workers.

Nations put into effect stricter border controls in an attempt to reduce illegal immigration. EU nations have continued to build on the Schengen Agreement (1985), which initiated the exchange of information about immigration, moving toward common policies of border policing to crack down on illegal immigration.

At the same time, the birthrates of many countries continued to decline. Early in the twenty-first century, fourteen countries are no longer reproducing their populations (with Italy and Spain leading the way, followed by Germany and Sweden); in other countries, population growth is zero, or not far above that. At the end of the twentieth century, economic uncertainty was closely related to the continued fall in the number of births. The birthrate now shows few signs of reversing the trend of decline. Many Western European countries will lose population without significant immigration, and their economies will continue to require the labor of immigrants, legal and otherwise.

Many Europeans felt themselves overwhelmed by immigrants. In 1987, foreign and minority prisoners accounted for one-third of those locked up in France, Belgium, and Switzerland. In the 1990s, riots by—but also against—immigrants (principally Indians, Pakistanis, Bangladeshis, and

West Indians) rocked several northern industrial cities and London. As in the inter-war years, economic weakness has encouraged hostility to those some consider to be outsiders, and a perceived lack of security against crime became a central focus of electoral campaigns. The severe recession of the early 1990s contributed to this dangerous situation, bringing high unemployment rates (in 1993 over 10 percent in the European Union). Polls have reflected popular fears (without any foundation) that the quality of education declines when too many immigrants and asylum seekers are present in the classroom. Many Europeans believe that immigrants abuse existing social welfare programs (indeed, they are more apt to draw disproportionately upon them), and that most of those asking for political asylum were fleeing economic hardship, not the political persecution that would make them eligible for refugee status. At the same time, the emigration of many educated people with special training deprives poor countries of much-needed talent.

Rising intolerance, racism, and xenophobia—hallmarks of the rise of fascism during the inter-war years—have become apparent in Europe, orchestrated by extreme right-wing nationalist parties and directed against foreign workers and their families. Brutal and even murderous attacks against foreigners proliferated in Germany, France, Britain, Belgium, and Russia, among other countries. Right-wing political parties, such as the National Front in Britain (founded in 1967) and the party of the same name in France (founded in 1972) adopted aggressive anti-immigrant stances. In Germany, the German People's Union denounced legal changes in 1999 that made it somewhat easier for longtime foreign-born residents to become citizens. Xenophobia has also been seen in such traditionally liberal, open-minded countries as Sweden and Denmark. In Belgium, the right-wing Vlams Belang (Flemish Interest) has made anti-immigration a central part of its appeal, while challenging Belgian unity. Russia has seen a spate of murderous attacks on foreigners, particularly those from Central Asia and Africa.

In France, Jean-Marie Le Pen (1982–) emerged as the leader of the far-right National Front. Le Pen, who had been accused of torture after a stint in the army in Algeria and who described the death camps as "a minor detail" of World War II, won as much as 17 percent of the vote as a candidate in three presidential elections. In 2007, Nicolas Sarkozy (1955–) was elected president of France by borrowing the anti-immigrant language of the National Front and appearing to make it respectable. In Austria, Jörg Haider (1950–2008), head of the Austrian Freedom Party, became prime minister after making immigration a central issue and allying with the conservative People's Party. In the Netherlands, long a haven of toleration for immigrants, Pim Fortuyn, a candidate for the post of prime minister, caused an uproar by stating that his country had been saturated by immigration and that there was no room left (he was assassinated in 2002). In

A prayer demonstration by Muslims to protest opposition to the construction of a mosque in Nice, France—an example of cultural tensions across a multicultural Europe.

Switzerland, too, a party of the extreme right made its mark, as the Swiss People's Party gained almost 25 percent of the votes in 1999. The Danish People's Party, the Norwegian Progress Party, and the Flemish Bloc in Belgium reflect the close association of extreme right-wing parties and anti-immigrant sentiments.

Indeed, acceptance of multiculturalism has been slow in coming. (In the United States, the very term "multiculturalism" in general has a positive sense, but in Germany it means "a disarray of cultures, in which each individual culture is stripped of its richness and uniqueness.") While some foreign workers have been assimilated in their countries of residence, many have not and have maintained the customs of their homelands while living in ethnic enclaves in their new countries. In the first years of the twenty-first century, more than 12 million Muslims lived in Western Europe. In Britain, France, and Germany, Muslims have been viewed with suspicion. Difficulties in learning the language of the new country of residence—as well as outright discrimination—have made it harder to find work. This has often put the younger generation of foreign workers, born in their countries of residence, in the uncomfortable position of being excluded from mainstream life where they reside and not wishing to return to their parents' country of origin, to which many feel no real connection. In France, when Muslim schoolgirls went to school wearing the traditional headscarf, they were expelled. A lengthy court process ensued until a new law reaffirmed the ban. In 2008, French authorities refused citizenship to a Muslim

1226   Ch. 30 • Global Challenges

woman who made clear her strong religious beliefs. Riots in October and November 2005 in French suburbs reflected the isolation and alienation of North and West African Muslim minorities, particularly young people.

European Community, European Union

In the hope of enhancing economic cooperation and coordination, the European Community (EC) was created in 1967, when the European Atomic Energy Community, the European Coal and Steel Community (ECSC), and the European Economic Community (the EEC, or European Common Market) merged. The original members were Belgium, France, West Germany, Italy, Luxembourg, and the Netherlands (see Map 30.1). The government of Great Britain had first been disinclined to join the EC, fearing the flooding of its internal market by less expensive agricultural produce. Moreover, French president Charles de Gaulle had forcefully opposed Britain's membership. There were other reasons, as well, arguing against Britain seeking to join. The British government considered itself a great power, and this status seemed incompatible with membership in the EC. Moreover, Britain feared that the pound, once considered "as good as gold," might suffer. The government did not want to be necessarily constrained by policies favored by other European states. Many British subjects agreed with a Labour Party leader who warned that a "thousand years" of British history would be lost if the country joined the EC. However, British public opinion changed. Voters overwhelmingly approved their country's application for membership and Britain joined the EC in 1973. Edward Heath, a Conservative who believed that his nation's future lay with Europe, took Britain into the EC. However, Harold Wilson, Heath's Labour successor as prime minister, sought to renegotiate the terms of Britain's membership. Britain remained a hesitant, even skeptical member. The advent of staunchly Conservative and vigorously anti-European Margaret Thatcher as British prime minister in 1979 put her country's membership at risk, until an urgent EC meeting agreed to reduce British financial contributions.

In the meantime, the close relationship between France's president Valéry Giscard d'Estaing and West Germany's premier Helmut Schmidt lent stability to the EC. Denmark and Ireland had also joined the EC in 1973, followed by Greece in 1981, and Spain and Portugal in 1986.

The EC eliminated troublesome tariffs, aiding the most efficient producers, who were able to sell their products abroad easily. But it put smaller producers at a disadvantage. The Danish dairy industry profited greatly from sales of milk and cheese to other member countries, as did their French counterparts; but dairy farmers elsewhere often found that they could not compete with larger competitors. The problem of wine revealed the challenges posed by EC agricultural policy. New members Spain and Portugal produce great amounts of wine, threatening vintners producing inexpensive

ICELAND

NORWAY

SWEDEN
1995

FINLAND
1995

BALTIC SEA

ESTONIA
2004

LATVIA
2004

RUSSIA

LITHUANIA
2004

*NORTH
SEA*

DENMARK
1973

IRELAND
1973

KALININGRAD
(Russia)

BELARUS

GREAT
BRITAIN
1973

NETH.

1990

BELG.

GERMANY

POLAND
2004

UKRAINE

*ATLANTIC
OCEAN*

LUX.

CZECH REP.
2004

SLOVAKIA
2004

MOLDOVA

FRANCE

SWITZ.

AUSTRIA
1995

HUNGARY
2004

SLOVENIA
2004

CROATIA

YUGOSLAVIA

ROMANIA
2007

PORTUGAL
1986

SPAIN
1986

ITALY

BOSNIA-
HERZEGOVINA

ADRIATIC SEA

BULGARIA
2007

MACE-
DONIA

ALB.

GREECE
1981

MALTA
2004

MEDITERRANEAN SEA

CYPRUS
2004

EC members, 1970

Subsequent members
(with date joined)

0   400 miles

0   400 kilometers

MAP 30.1 MEMBERS OF THE EUROPEAN COMMUNITY   The original six members of
the European Community—France, West Germany, the Netherlands, Belgium,
Luxembourg, and Italy—were later joined by twenty-one other countries.

wine in southern France. Wine producers protested the arrival of Italian wine by blocking roads at the frontier.

Jacques Delors (1925–), a former minister of finance, became president of the European Commission in 1985. Delors led the campaign for a unified Europe that could compete with Japanese and U.S. economic strength. In 1986, member states signed the Single Europe Act. Calling for the termination of all obstacles to the free movement of capital, goods, workers, and services, it pointed toward the anticipated establishment of a single market within member states. Moreover, Delors believed that the EC should include a "social dimension" that would protect the rights of ordinary people.

Delors had in 1988 indicated his hope that in the future a single currency could be used by member states, further accentuating trade within the EC while eliminating fluctuations in the value of individual currencies. From the outset, Thatcher and British Conservative "Euro-skeptics" opposed the plan, partially out of fear that Germany's then-booming economy and currency would dominate the other EC members. Thatcher's departure from office in 1990 did not end vehement opposition from British Conservatives to any thought of abandoning sterling.

The Treaty of Maastricht, signed in that southern Dutch city in 1992 by the twelve members of the European Community, transformed the EC into the European Union. The new name took effect in 1993 when the single market began operation. France barely approved the treaty in a referendum called by President Mitterrand in late 1992, and it took a second vote to obtain the same result in Denmark. The European Union opened all borders within the European Community and committed the European Community to "economic and monetary union" by 1999. In 1995, Austria, Norway, Sweden, and Finland joined, while Norway turned down membership.

The European Commission became the executive institution of the European Union. Headquartered in Brussels, it consists of members appointed by each member state. It is headed by a rotating president and proposes legislation to the Council of Ministers, whose members are also delegated by each member state and which also has a rotating presidency. Each participating state elects representatives to the European Parliament, which has its headquarters in Strasbourg and can reject a proposed budget. The European Court of Justice rules on disputes between member states and between individual plaintiffs and the European Union. The European Council consists of the heads of each member state and meets twice a year (or more), along with the president of the European Commission. The European Union even has a small army, established by virtue of the Amsterdam Treaty of 1999.

The European Union, comprising 370 million people in fifteen member states, now accounts for about 20 percent of the world's exports, more than that of the United States. One of the most daunting challenges of creating a single market has been to establish an effective agricultural policy that takes into consideration the tremendous variety of agricultural production within the member states. As part of the common agricultural policy, EU subsidies to farmers accounted for nearly half of the annual budget in 1995. Subsidies have protected member states by limiting the importation of products from outside the EU, but they also have generated overproduction, such that many farmers are paid not to produce, or for the surpluses they produce. Besides this, considerable European Union funds are diverted in the attempt to aid the continual development of the poorer member states, including Greece and Portugal, and disadvantaged regions within other countries, such as southern Italy and Sicily. For example, the admission of Poland requires sizeable subsidies for Polish agriculture, which in terms of efficiency lags considerably behind its Western counterparts, despite a booming economy in the first decade of the new century. In the meantime, the European Union maintains strict guidelines for agricultural producers (for example, on how cheese can be produced). An infusion of funds from the European Union has brought new roads and other benefits to new members. Beginning in December 2007 when borders were opened between nine new member states, one could travel from Estonia to Portugal without being stopped at any border, leaving some national authorities to worry whether such openness might aid illegal immigration and organized crime.

The problem of how the European Union can create a sense of legitimacy within the member states remains daunting. The institutions of the EU have to wrestle with the enormous challenge of creating a cultural

Irish farmers clog the streets of Dublin with their tractors to protest the reforms proposed by the Common Agricultural Policy of the European Union that would reduce their income.

"European" identity and "European" vision. This project is made even more difficult by over-bureaucratization, inefficiency, and corruption. Elections for the European Parliament cannot create European identity. Moreover, definitions of what it means to be European vary. People on the left who describe themselves as "European" tend to stress civic reasons for this identity, such as support for democratic political systems and the affirmation of social and human rights. Those on the political right are more apt to emphasize a common European cultural heritage.

Member states of the European Union are required to keep their budget deficits down to no more than 3 percent of gross domestic product. In 1998, the European Central Bank began operation, charged with managing the European Union currency, setting interest rates for the euro zone of eleven nations, and working to keep down inflation. The euro was launched as an accounting currency in 1999, but without the participation of Britain, Sweden, and Denmark, or of Greece, which failed to meet the financial criteria for monetary union that the EU had set for member states. The euro became the official currency in participating member states on January 1, 2002. A relatively smooth transition was made possible by considerable preparations, including effective publicity campaigns by governments, banks, and shopping centers, the conversion of machines accepting bills and coins, and assistance to the elderly, immigrants, and other groups. The euro soared in value, rapidly surpassing the U.S. dollar, weakened by the soaring U.S. trade deficit.

The European Union includes 27 member states and thus close to 500 million people. It has engendered not only feelings of ambivalence toward supranational economic and political organizations but also a nationalist response. Many ordinary people believe themselves disconnected from the workings of Brussels. Even some farmers who receive subsidies from the EU are unaware that they come from Brussels and not their own ministries of agriculture. In 2005, the European Union suffered a blow when votes in France and the Netherlands rejected approval of the proposed constitution, which had been promulgated the previous year. This led to the Treaty of Lisbon in December 2007. Its goal was to reform the original treaty that created the European Union by streamlining its administration by, for example, creating the position of president of the European Council. However, the rejection of the new treaty in a referendum in Ireland in June 2008 cast a new shadow over the functioning of the European Union.

Despite continuing operational challenges, however, new members can indeed look to the example of Ireland, whose economy has received a major boost from its EU membership, largely through the biotech revolution. High unemployment, low agricultural productivity, the necessity of institutional reform, and the great cost of becoming a member of the European Union, as well as the extremely limited democratic experience of some of the new members, poses challenges to new members and to the European Union itself. The economic gap between the wealthiest countries—Britain, France, and Germany—and the states of Central and Eastern Europe seeking the advantage of greater access to markets remains considerable. The possible admission of Turkey has generated great debate, in part because of some doubts that the country, which still bridges Europe and Asia, is really European. Successes of fundamentalist Islamic groups in elections in a country that is overwhelmingly Muslim but not militantly Islamic challenged the stridently secular basis of Turkey. In 2008, the country's highest court turned aside legislation inspired by the prime minister that would have allowed female students in state universities to wear head scarves, conforming to their Muslim religion.

Yet the number of citizens of countries within the European Union who describe themselves as feeling "European" has increased, despite continuing loyalty to nation-states based on ethnic identity and long-standing traditions of citizenship and a sense of shared values. However, the European Union has encouraged regionalism, assisting the revival of such languages as Catalan and Welsh in Spain and Britain, respectively. Such a process in the long run may help reduce ethnic tension and conflicts. Moreover, many Europeans hope that the European Union will guarantee the rights of individuals through its Charter of Fundamental Social Rights of Workers. Indeed, the EU allocates considerable funds to worldwide humanitarian causes.

The European Union has worked to protect member states by maintaining standards for the importation of agricultural and food products. For example, "mad cow" disease, which struck cattle in Britain in the 1990s and infected a few human beings with a degenerative disease of the brain, led not only to the slaughter of millions of animals in Britain but also to the European Union's ban on the import of British beef on the continent for thirty-two months. In 1997, the EU began labeling products made from genetically modified soybeans and corn. Such imports, principally from the United States, are more resistant to damage by insects, but the long-range effect of their consumption is still unknown. Environmental groups, as well as many scientists, strongly oppose their use.

OPPOSITION TO GLOBALIZATION

Globalization itself became the target of protests and demonstrations in the 1990s, for example at the gathering of leaders of the eight leading industrial powers—the G8 (the United States, Great Britain, France, Italy, Germany, Russia, Canada, and Japan). Giant companies and banks, multinational in their structure and interests, have enormous economic power. Huge sums can be sent, traded, or invested with the push of a button. Global finance has brought volatility to the world economy, accentuated by the enormous U.S. trade deficit. The sharp decline in the U.S. stock market that began in 2000 followed wild speculation on dot.com companies. International dependence on oil, too, has increased, with prices rising and falling, often in tune with international events. The dizzying rise in the price of oil in 2008 jolted world economies, contributing to rapid inflation.

To its critics, globalization could be identified with corporate greed and indifference to the fate of the poor of the Third World. A French farmer (who had spent part of his childhood in California), José Bové (1953–), became a symbol of protest when in 1999 he led an attack on a McDonald's in a southern French town, damaging the fast-food restaurant as a means of calling attention to globalization. Cases of corporate greed and deception— such as that of the giant Enron corporation in the United States, whose corporate officers had lied and deceived, then unloaded their shares before the fall, leaving employees with virtually nothing—cast a shadow over big multinational corporations. Demonstrations became riots during the meeting of the World Trade Organization in Seattle in 1999, and in Nice in 2000 during the European Union summit meetings. During the summer of 2001, protesters demonstrated and some battled police at the summit in Gothenburg (Sweden) and then in Genoa (Italy), the site of the G7 meeting, an informal association of the world's leading industrial nations.

Damage to the environment is itself linked to global interconnectedness. The oceans have become veritable highways for the shipment of oil in huge tankers, a good many of which are old and badly maintained. Periodic oil

The 1999 meeting of the World Trade Organization in Seattle, Washington, was greeted with protests against the negative effects of globalization.

spills have damaged coasts catastrophically, such as that off the Atlantic coast of Spain in 2003. The diffusion of nuclear power (to say nothing of the threat of nuclear weapons) presents great risks, for all the advantage in generating electricity. By the end of the twentieth century, nuclear reactors, many of them old, generated about one-third of Europe's electricity. France led the way in adopting nuclear technology to produce electricity and by the end of the twentieth century nuclear reactors produced 75 percent of it. Nuclear power generated 60 percent of Belgium's electricity and 45 percent of Sweden's. The horrendous explosion at Chernobyl in Ukraine in 1986 further mobilized opposition to nuclear power. And as the threat from international terrorism becomes more real, nuclear reactors stand as potentially inviting targets for terrorists intent on taking as many lives and causing as much damage as possible. The international organization Greenpeace has actively opposed potential threats to the environment by nuclear power.

Opposition to globalization has also centered on the profits Western-based companies earn by selling products produced at low wages in, for example, Southeast Asia. Caps or jerseys with logos from NBA basketball teams, brand-name tennis shoes, and T-shirts with the names of U.S. universities became part of popular culture around the globe. Some of the products that are sold for high prices in the West are produced by destitute people in Asia (or elsewhere) for pitiful wages.

Globalization has helped the spread of AIDS. The disease has ravaged Europe (although not nearly to the same extent as Africa, where it is now the number one killer) and increased the cost of health care. As of 2003, more than 60 million people worldwide have been infected by the HIV virus, at least a third of whom have died. Although many AIDS victims live longer than before, no cure has yet been found.

THE THREAT OF TERRORISM

During the 1970s and 1980s, small groups on the extreme left and right turned to political terrorism. Violence seemed to them the only means of destabilizing political elites in the hope of taking power. Some terrorist groups were militant nationalists seeking independence from what they considered foreign occupying powers. Such groups included factions within the Irish Republican Army committed to ending British rule in Northern Ireland, militant Basque separatists (the ETA) in Spain, and Kurdish rebels in Turkey.

Between 1969 and 1982, political terrorists killed more than 1,100 people, including the bombing by fascists of the railroad station of Bologna in 1980 in which 85 people died. In the early 1970s, left-wing extremists (organized into perhaps as many as 100 separate groups) launched deadly attacks. The Red Brigades, founded in 1970, kidnapped and killed former Italian Premier Aldo Moro in 1978. But by the early 1980s, Italian terrorism had ebbed, the campaigns at political destabilization having failed.

Italian politicians put aside their usual differences long enough to back a vigorous campaign that led to the arrest of militants. In the German Federal Republic, small groups of left-wing terrorists lashed out with bombings, bank robberies, kidnappings, assassinations, and even a plane hijacking. The most notorious of these groups, the Baader-Meinhof gang, had links to terrorist groups in France and other Western countries.

Indeed, terrorism has posed an increasing threat in Western Europe, as extremist political groups and Islamic fundamentalist groups launched attacks. Notorious attacks included the massacre of Israelis by Palestinian militants at the 1972 Olympic Games in Munich and the seizure of a cruise ship in 1985. A terrorist bomb in 1989, probably planned in Libya, blew up a U.S. passenger jet over Lockerbie, Scotland, killing all 259 people aboard. In 1995, an Algerian Islamic fundamentalist group claimed responsibility for placing deadly bombs on subways and underground trains in Paris.

On a day of horror, September 11, 2001, hijackers commandeered four U.S. jetliners shortly after they took off from several airports early that morning. Two were crashed into the World Trade Center in lower Manhattan in New York City and a third into the Pentagon outside Washington, D.C. The fourth airliner plunged to earth in eastern Pennsylvania. Nearly 3,000 people were killed, the vast majority perishing in the World Trade Center, both towers of which collapsed in a heap of rubble. A massive manhunt began for the Saudi Arabian–born Osama bin Laden (1957–), leader of the Al Qaeda ("The Base") movement, which claimed responsibility for the attacks. Many of its members had trained in Afghanistan, which was ruled by an Islamic fundamentalist militia called the Taliban. Late that fall, the United States launched massive air strikes against Taliban installations in Afghanistan, and troops on the ground searched the rugged mountains near the border with Pakistan. An interim government took power in Afghanistan, backed by U.S. forces, facing the chronic problems of tribalism and poverty. The Al Qaeda organization had spread almost worldwide, with cells in Germany, Italy, France, and Britain, as well as in Malaysia and the Philippines. European states supported and assisted the U.S. campaign to uproot the structure of the Al Qaeda network in their countries. International police cooperation led to the arrests of Al Qaeda members in Germany, France, Spain, Britain, and Italy, but the search for others continued.

Islamic fundamentalist groups based in the Middle East have been actively recruiting adherents in European states that have large concentrations of Muslims. In March 2004, terrorist bombs detonated on several commuter trains in Madrid, killing almost 200 people and injuring 1,800 others. In July 2005, suicide bombers who had grown up in Britain detonated explosives in subway cars and on a bus in London, killing 50 people and wounding many more.

One of the consequences of globalization has been the increased vulnerability of Europe, as well as the United States, to political struggles and

A security alert in London, July 2005, not long after the explosion of terrorist bombs in three subway trains and on a bus.

events occurring far away, and to the terrorism these events have generated. Terrorists detonated cars packed with bombs in front of U.S. embassies in Dar es Salaam, Tanzania, and Nairobi, Kenya, in the summer of 1998, killing 213 people and wounding more than 5,000 in the latter attack. Islamic fundamentalists were also responsible for terrorist attacks in Arab states where fundamentalists wanted to impose strict religious rule.

Islam is not the only religion in which aggressive fundamentalism has emerged. In Israel, Jewish extreme nationalist groups, in coalition with the Likud party, have helped shape Israeli hard-line policies toward Palestinian demands for an independent state. The Palestinian question divides public opinion in Europe. The Palestinian minority in Israel demands an independent Palestinian state. Groups of Palestinian militants have undertaken murderous attacks on Israelis. In a cycle of violence that has become tragically common, the Israeli government often responds by razing villages or by further restricting the rights of Palestinians. The assassination of Yitzhak Rabin by a right-wing Israeli in 1995 was a blow to peace in the Middle East, which in some ways hinges on the Palestinian situation. In 1996, the Palestinian leader Yasir Arafat struck from the Palestine Liberation Organization's charter the call for the destruction of Israel. However, the "peace process"—as U.S. officials refer to it optimistically—began to break down in 2000.

A United States Empire?

The collapse of the Soviet empire left the United States as the world's single superpower. The U.S. maintains what constitutes an informal empire, influenced by financial might and vast if over-extended armed forces, including more than 700 military bases abroad. Conservative, or "Neo-Con," exponents of exerting forceful U.S. domination operate under the principle that what seems good for the United States is good for the world. In the late 1990s, a more aggressive U.S. foreign policy increased fears in Europe about U.S. foreign unilateralism and a rush to use force. On a continent ravaged by two devastating world wars, this has not gone down well. The U.S. refused in 2001 to sign the Kyoto Protocol, an agreement that requires countries to reduce the harmful greenhouse gas emissions that have caused global warming. In 2002, the U.S. government announced that it would not accept the jurisdiction of a proposed new international court, which was being set up to try those accused of crimes against humanity. Five years later, the U.S. government announced its intention of placing a missile defense system in Poland and the Czech Republic intended, in principle, to defend against any attacks launched by Iran, which the U.S. accused of working to build nuclear weapons. Such a plan outraged Russia, which fears the presence of such a system in neighboring states.

European Responses to U.S. Policy

In the wake of the attacks of September 11, 2001, the administration of U.S. President George W. Bush turned its attention to Saddam Hussein (1937–2006), Iraq's dictator, arguing that he was continuing to produce and hide "weapons of mass destruction" and that he had links to Al Qaeda. Neither assertion was correct. While British Prime Minister Tony Blair (despite popular opposition to the war) and a number of other states actively supported the U.S. position, Germany, France, and Russia opposed the Bush administration's position. In the meantime, UN weapons inspectors found no "weapons of mass destruction." Moreover, the Iraqis began to destroy missiles whose range exceeded that permitted by the United Nations following the Gulf War of 1991, when U.S. troops drove Iraqi forces from Kuwait, which Saddam Hussein had invaded.

The United States and Britain launched an invasion of Iraq in March 2003, quickly defeating the Iraqi army. The United States set up military authority in Iraq, along with a British zone in the south, anticipating that it would eventually give way to some sort of democratic Iraqi government (assuming religious, ethnic, and other tensions could be overcome). However, no weapons of mass destruction were ever found. This left the impression in much of Europe that some of the U.S. and British intelligence documents used to reach the conclusion that the regime of Saddam Hussein posed an immediate threat to the region or to U.S. interests—thus justifying the invasion—had been exaggerated, misrepresented, or even simply fabricated. (Moreover, President Bush's rhetorical evocation of a "crusade" against terrorism called to mind the bloody campaigns by European Christians against Islam during the Middle Ages.)

The Iraq crisis threatened the prestige and effectiveness of the United Nations, because of the determination of the U.S. government to go it alone. The outpouring of European sympathy and goodwill toward the United States following the terrorist attacks in New York and Washington, D.C., dissipated. Iraq descended into chaos. Insurgents rose up (aided by arms shipped from Iran) against the occupying forces. Terrorist attacks—the war brought Al Qaeda into Iraq—became a daily occurrence and Iraq plunged into civil war. Probably about half a million Iraqis have perished since the U.S. invasion and more than 2 million are refugees.

The C.I.A. operated secret prisons and undertook illegal kidnappings in Europe, sending several suspects off to probable torture in their countries of origin. Images of prisoners mistreated by their U.S. captors in Abu Ghraib prison flashed across televisions and computer screens across the globe, along with reports of the C.I.A. torturing prisoners and Iraqi civilians being gunned down by private U.S. security contractors. At the U.S. prison at Guantanamo Bay in Cuba, prisoners were held year after year without knowing the charges against them and denied access to any kind of legal representation. The president's acceptance of interrogation techniques considered to be torture further sullied the United States's reputation. Even as the security situation improved in Iraq in late 2007 and in 2008, President George W. Bush no longer seemed to represent the high moral standard long projected by the United States. When asked in 2008 whether

British Royal Marine Commandos guarding Iraqi prisoners of war, 2003.

a new president could restore American credibility, the foreign minister of France spoke for many, if not most, Europeans when he said, "It will never be as it was before. . . . The magic is gone." However, the election of Barack Obama in 2008 was overwhelmingly greeted with a sense of optimism by most Europeans.

CONCLUSION

As Europe moves through the first decade of the twenty-first century, its influence over the rest of the world has been reduced. Yet Europeans now for the most part live in peace, a situation that seems likely to remain for the foreseeable future. Their quality of life has continued to improve, thanks to ongoing advances in medicine and the production of food. Europe still confronts the challenges of finding enough safe energy while protecting the environment. In 2007, leaders of the EU agreed to try to reduce emissions of carbon dioxide by 20 percent by 2020, by which date renewable energy sources such as wind and solar power are to make up one-fifth of energy consumed.

As in other regions, European economies must continually adapt to the challenges of globalization. Following the failure of Communist states in Europe, even China has embraced some aspects of a market economy, and China and India have become economic giants. High unemployment rates in Europe still suggest the vulnerability of many people to the vicissitudes of the market. Young people in particular are affected by unemployment. Confrontations between young people and the police in Athens, as well as in other cities, in December 2008 followed the shooting death of an adolescent by a policeman. Many students and other young men and women are disaffected, fearing they will not find jobs and that they will be the first generation in the post-war period to do worse economically than their parents. Finding an appropriate balance between the free market and state intervention remains essential. Determined protests against globalization reflect the fact that global interconnectedness has not benefited everyone; millions of desperately poor people in Asia and Africa, and on other continents as well, have been left behind.

Human rights around the world remains a European concern more than sixty years after the adoption of the Universal Declaration of Human Rights by the United Nations. Amnesty International has been a force for identifying countries in which human rights are not respected, as has Human Rights Watch. European states were among those that put enormous pressure on South Africa in the 1970s and early 1980s, as it defied the world by maintaining its now dismantled official system of racial apartheid. Genocide in the African nation of Rwanda in the 1990s, ethnic cleansing in Kosovo, starvation in Ethiopia, massacres in the Darfur region of Sudan, and the explosive situation in the Middle East have also been the focus of human-rights groups, as well as of European states. The European Union has made support of human rights one of its priorities.

Europeans have many reasons to be optimistic about the future. German unification was achieved peacefully. Two old enemies, Germany and France, stand as a stable center for the continent's future. Despite divisions over policy toward Iraq, NATO adapted to the fall of communism and expanded toward the east, as has the European Union. Signs of greater toleration can be found in Eastern Europe and the Balkans, as well. In 1997, for the first time, ethnic Hungarians living in Romania could use their own language in their dealings with government officials and in education. And in 2000 the Bulgarian government finally allowed the state television network to broadcast a weekly news program in Turkish. While in most of Europe, nationalist irredentist claims have largely subsided, ethnic and religious rivalries have by no means been eliminated.

The Cold War is no more, and in Europe there is seemingly little risk of a hot one, at least of European-wide dimensions. The European Union has brought a single market to much of Europe and will continue to expand, with the help of its single currency, the euro. This in itself has made the continent smaller, making it even easier for people to travel and giving them increasingly more in common. Moreover, arguably the most important success of the European Union has been to make war between member states unlikely. All this should carry Europe into an even more prosperous future, one that can be built on lasting peace.

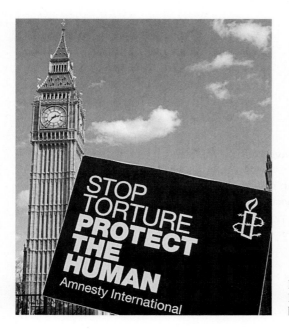

Protest outside Parliament in London against alleged torture by U.S. forces in Iraq.

FURTHER READINGS

GENERAL

Feroz Ahmad, *The Making of Modern Turkey* (1993).

Benedict Anderson, *Imagined Communities: Reflections on the Origins and Spread of Nationalism* (1991).

Geoffrey Best, *War and Society in Revolutionary Europe, 1770–1870* (1982).

David Blackbourn, *The Long Nineteenth Century: A History of Germany, 1780–1918* (1997).

Jerome Blum, *The End of the Old Order in Rural Europe* (1978).

Raymond Carr, *Spain, 1808–1975* (1982).

Owen Chadwick, *The Secularization of the European Mind in the Nineteenth Century* (1976).

S. G. Checkland, *British Public Policy, 1776–1939: An Economic, Social, and Political Perspective* (1985).

Richard Clogg, *A Concise History of Greece* (1992).

Gordon A. Craig, *Germany, 1866–1945* (1978).

John Darwin, *After Tamerlane: The Global History of Empire since 1405* (2008).

David Brion Davis, *The Problem of Slavery in the Age of Revolution, 1770–1823* (1975).

Jan de Vries, *The Industrious Revolution: Consumer Behavior and the Household Economy, 1650 to the Present* (2008).

Christopher Duggan, *A Concise History of Italy* (1994).

Norma Everson, *Paris: A Century of Change, 1878–1978* (1979).

Niall Ferguson, *Empire: How Britain Made the Modern World* (2003).

———, *Empire: The Rise and Demise of the British World Order and the Lessons for Global Power* (2002).

William Ferguson, *Scotland: 1689 to the Present* (1968).

R. F. Foster, *Modern Ireland, 1600–1972* (1988).

Derek Fraser, *The Evolution of the British Welfare State: A History of Social Policy since the Industrial Revolution* (1973).

Ute Frevert, Men of Honor: A Social and Cultural History of the Duel (1995).

———, *Women in German History: From Bourgeois Emancipation to Sexual Liberation* (1989).

Peter Gay, *The Cultivation of Hatred: The Bourgeois Experience: Victoria to Freud, Vol. III* (1994).

————, *Education of the Senses: The Bourgeois Experience: Victoria to Freud*, Vol. I (1999).

————, *The Tender Passion: The Bourgeois Experience: Victoria to Freud*, Vol. II (1999).

John Gillis, *Youth and History: Tradition and Change in European Age Relations, 1770 to the Present* (1981).

Patrice L. R. Higonnet, *Paris: Capital of the World* (2002).

William I. Hitchcock, *The Struggle for Europe: The Turbulent History of a Divided Continent, 1945–2002* (2003).

E. J. Hobsbawm, *The Age of Extremes: The Short Twentieth Century, 1914–1991* (1994).

Barbara Jelavich, *History of the Balkans* (2 vols., 1983).

Charles and Barbara Jelavich, *The Establishment of Balkan National States, 1804–1920* (1977).

Tony Judt, *Postwar: A History of Europe since 1945* (2005).

Anastasia Karakasidou, *Fields of Wheat, Hills of Blood: Passages to Nationhood in Greek Macedonia, 1870–1990* (1997).

Tom Kemp, *Industrialization in Nineteenth-Century Europe* (1985).

Ben Kiernan, *Blood and Soil: A World History of Genocide and Extermination from Sparta to Darfur* (2007).

V. G. Kiernan, *European Empires from Conquest to Collapse, 1815–1960* (1982).

E. H. Kossman, *The Low Countries, 1780–1940* (1978).

Andrew Lees and Lynn Hollen Lees, *Cities and the Making of Modern Europe, 1750–1914* (2007).

F. S. Lyons, *Ireland since the Famine* (1971).

Michael Marrus, *The Unwanted: European Refugees in the Twentieth Century* (1995).

Arno Mayer, *The Persistence of the Old Regime: Europe to the Great War* (1981).

Mary Jo Maynes, *Schooling in Western Europe: A Social History* (1985).

Mark Mazower, *The Balkans: A Short History* (2000).

————, *The Dark Continent: Europe's Twentieth Century* (1998).

Peter McPhee, *A Social History of France, 1780–1880* (2004).

John M. Merriman, *The Stones of Balazuc: A French Village in Time* (2002).

John Merriman and Jay Winter, eds., *Europe 1789 to 1914: Encyclopedia of the Age of Industry and Empire*, 5 vols. (2006).

————, *Europe since 1914: Encyclopedia of the Age of War and Reconstruction*, 5 vols. (2006).

Kerby A. Miller, *Emigrants and Exiles: Ireland and the Irish Exodus to North America* (1988).

Norman M. Naimark, *Fires of Hatred: Ethnic Cleansing in Twentieth-Century Europe* (2001).

P. K. O'Brien and C. Keyser, *Economic Growth in Britain and Europe, 1780–1914* (1978).

Pamela M. Pilbeam, *The Middle Classes in Europe, 1789–1914: France, Germany, Italy and Russia* (1990).

Leon Plantinga, *Romantic Music: A History of Musical Style in Nineteenth-Century Europe* (1984).

Roy Porter, *London: A Social History* (2001).

Donald Quataert, *The Ottoman Empire, 1700–1922* (2007).
David Reynolds, *The World Divisible: A Global History since 1945* (2000).
Pierre Rosanvallon, *The Demands of Liberty: Civil Society in France since the Revolution* (2007).
Christopher Seton-Watson, *Italy: From Liberalism to Fascism, 1870–1925* (1967).
Frank Snowden, *The Conquest of Malaria: Italy, 1900–1962* (2006).
Hugh Seton-Watson, *The Russian Empire, 1801–1917* (1967).
James Sheehan, *German History, 1770–1866* (1990).
———, *Where Have All the Soldiers Gone? The Transformation of Modern Europe* (2008).
Adrien Shubert, *A Social History of Modern Spain* (1990).
Timothy Snyder, *The Reconstruction of Nations: Poland, Ukraine, Lithuania, Belarus, 1569–1999* (2003).
Charles Tilly, *Coercion, Capital, and European States, AD 990–1990* (1990).
Isser Woloch, ed., *Revolution and the Meanings of Freedom in the Nineteenth Century* (1996).

CHAPTER 12. THE FRENCH REVOLUTION

Nigel Aston, *Religion and Revolution in France, 1780–1804* (2000).
Jean-Paul Bertaud, *The Army of the French Revolution: From Citizen-Soldiers to Instrument of Power* (1988).
T. C. W. Blanning, *The French Revolutionary Wars, 1787–1802* (1996).
Howard G. Brown, *Ending the French Revolution: Violence, Justice, and Repression from the Terror to Napoleon* (2006).
Richard Cobb, *The Police and the People: French Popular Protest, 1789–1820* (1972).
William Doyle, *Origins of the French Revolution* (1988).
Marianne Elliott, *Partners in Revolution: The United Irishmen and France* (1982).
Alan Forrest, *Conscripts and Deserters: The Army and French Society during the Revolution and Empire* (1989).
———, *The French Revolution and the Poor* (1981).
Francois Furet, *Interpreting the French Revolution* (1992).
David Garrioch, *The Making of Revolutionary Paris* (2002).
Dominique Godineau, *The Women of Paris and Their French Revolution* (1998).
Carla Hesse, *Publishing and Cultural Politics in Revolutionary Paris, 1789–1810* (1991).
Patrice Higonnet, *Sister Republics: The Origins of French and American Republicanism* (1988).
Lynn Hunt, *The Family Romance of the French Revolution* (1992).
———, *Politics, Culture, and Class in the French Revolution* (1984).
Peter Jones, *The Peasantry in the French Revolution* (1988).
Georges Lefebvre, *The Coming of the French Revolution* (1989).
Peter McPhee, *The French Revolution, 1789–1799* (2002).
Sarah E. Meltzer and Leslie W. Rabine, eds., *Rebel Daughters: Women and the French Revolution* (1989).

Mona Ozouf, *Festivals and the French Revolution* (1988).

R. R. Palmer, *The Age of the Democratic Revolution: A Political History of Europe and America, 1760–1800* (2 vols., 1959–1964).

———, *Twelve Who Ruled: The Year of the Terror in the French Revolution* (1989).

Jeremy D. Popkin, *Revolutionary News: The Press in France, 1789–1799* (1990).

George Rudé, *The Great Fear of 1789* (1973).

William H. Sewell, Jr., *A Rhetoric of Bourgeois Revolution: The Abbé Sieyès and "What is the Third Estate?"* (1994).

Donald Sutherland, *France, 1789–1815: Revolution and Counterrevolution* (1986).

Timothy Tackett, *Religion, Revolution, and Regional Culture in Eighteenth-Century France: The Ecclesiastical Oath of 1791* (1986).

———, *When the King Took Flight* (2003).

Isser Woloch, *The New Regime: Transformations of the French Civic Order, 1789–1820s* (1994).

CHAPTER 13. NAPOLEON AND EUROPE

David A. Bell, *The First Total War: Napoleon's Empire and the Birth of Warfare as We Know It* (2007).

Louis Bergeron, *France under Napoleon* (1981).

Michael Broers, *Europe under Napoleon* (1996).

———, *The Politics of Religion in Napoleonic Italy: The War against God, 1801–1814* (2002).

Philip Dwyer, *Napoleon: The Path to Power* (2007).

Steven Englund, *Napoleon: A Political Life* (2004).

J. Christopher Herold, *The Age of Napoleon* (1985).

Gunther Rothenberg, *The Art of Warfare in the Age of Napoleon* (1978).

Alan Schom, *One Hundred Days: Napoleon's Road to Waterloo* (1992).

Paul Srathern, *Napoleon in Eqypt* (2007).

Jakob Walter, *The Diary of a Napoleonic Foot Soldier* (1991).

Stuart Wolfe, *Napoleon's Integration of Europe* (1991).

D. G. Wright, *Napoleon and Europe* (1984).

CHAPTER 14. THE INDUSTRIAL REVOLUTION

Anna Clark, *The Struggle for the Breeches: Gender and the Making of the British Working Class* (1995).

Deborah Cohen, *Household Gods: The British and Their Possessions* (2006).

Leonore Davidoff and Catherine Hall, *Family Fortunes: Men and Women of the English Middle Class, 1780–1850* (1991).

James S. Donnelly, Jr., *The Great Irish Potato Famine* (2002).

Michel Foucault, *Madness and Civilization* (1973).

Colin Heywood, *Childhood in Nineteenth-Century France: Work, Health, and Education among the Classes Populaires* (1988).

E. J. Hobsbawm and George Rudé, *Captain Swing* (1975).

Gareth Stedman Jones, *Languages of Class: Studies in English Working-Class History* (1983).

David J. V. Jones, *Rebecca's Children: A Study of Rural Society, Crime, and Protest* (1989).
David Landes, *The Unbound Prometheus: Technological Change and Industrial Development in Western Europe from 1750 to the Present* (1976).
Lynn Hollen Lees, *Exiles of Erin: Irish Migrants to Victorian London* (1979).
David McLellan, *Karl Marx: His Life and Thought* (1977).
Joel Mokyr, *The Gift of Athena* (2003).
Claire Goldberg Moses, *French Feminism in the Nineteenth Century* (1984).
William H. Sewell, Jr., *Work and Revolution in France: The Language of Labor from the Old Regime to 1848* (1980).
E. P. Thompson, *The Making of the English Working Class* (1963).
Louise A. Tilly and Joan W. Scott, *Women, Work, and Family* (1978).
Clive Trebilcock, *The Industrialization of the Continental Powers, 1780–1914* (1989).
Dror Wahrman, *Imagining the Middle Class: The Political Representation of Class in Britain, c. 1780–1840* (1995).
William Weber, *Music and the Middle Class: The Social Structure of Concert Life in London, Paris and Vienna* (1975).

CHAPTER 15. LIBERAL CHALLENGES TO RESTORATION EUROPE

Michael Brock, *Great Reform Act* (1973).
Clive H. Church, *1830 in Europe: Revolution and Political Change* (1983).
Gordon A. Craig, *The Triumph of Liberalism: Zurich in the Golden Age, 1830–1869* (1988).
Friedrich Engels, *The Condition of the Working Class in England* (1993).
Eric J. Evans, *Britain before the Reform Act: Politics and Society, 1815–1832* (1989).
Norman Gash, *Aristocracy and People: Britain, 1815–1865* (1979).
Hugh Honour, *Romanticism* (1979).
Clara M. Lovett, *The Democratic Movement in Italy, 1830–1876* (1982).
Harold Perkin, *The Origins of Modern English Society, 1780–1880* (1972).
Barbara Taylor, *Eve and the New Jerusalem: Socialism and Feminism in the Nineteenth Century* (1983).

CHAPTER 16. THE REVOLUTIONS OF 1848

Maurice Agulhon, *The Republican Experiment, 1848–1852* (1983).
T. J. Clark, *The Absolute Bourgeois: Artists and Politics in France, 1848–1851* (1973).
István Deák, *The Lawful Revolution: Louis Kossuth and the Hungarians, 1848–1849* (1979).
Ted W. Margadant, *French Peasants in Revolt: The Insurrection of 1851* (1979).
Peter McPhee, *The Politics of Rural Life: Political Mobilization in the French Countryside, 1845–1852* (1992).
John M. Merriman, *The Agony of the Republic: The Repression of the Left in Revolutionary France, 1848–1851* (1978).
Jonathan Sperber, *The European Revolutions, 1848–1851* (1993).

———, *Rhineland Radicals: The Democratic Movement and the Revolution of 1848–1849* (1991).

CHAPTER 17. THE ERA OF NATIONAL UNIFICATION

David Blackbourn and Geoff Eley, *The Peculiarities of German History: Bourgeois Society and Politics in Nineteenth-Century German History* (1984).
István Deák, *Beyond Nationalism: A Social History of the Habsburg Officer Corps, 1848–1918* (1990).
Lothar Gall, *Bismarck: The White Revolutionary* (2 vols., 1986).
Denis Mack Smith, *Cavour* (1985).
———, *Cavour and Garibaldi, 1860: A Study of Political Conflict* (1985).
———, *Victor Emanuel, Cavour, and the Risorgimento* (1971).
Helmut Smith, *German Nationalism and Religious Conflict: Culture, Ideology, Politics, 1870–1914* (1995).

CHAPTER 18. THE DOMINANT POWERS IN THE AGE OF LIBERALISM: PARLIAMENTARY BRITAIN, REPUBLICAN FRANCE, AND TSARIST RUSSIA

Robert Anderson, *Education and Opportunity in Victorian Scotland* (1983).
Abraham Ascher, *The Revolution of 1905* (2 vols., 1992).
Jeffrey A. Auerbach, *The Great Exposition of 1851: A Nation on Display* (1999).
Edward Berenson, *The Trial of Madame Caillaux* (1992).
Victoria E. Bonnell, *Roots of Rebellion: Workers' Politics and Organizations in St. Petersburg and Moscow, 1900–1914* (1983).
Asa Briggs, *Victorian Cities* (1977).
———, *Victorian People* (1954).
Jeffrey Brooks, *When Russia Learned to Read: Literacy and Popular Literature, 1861–1917* (1985).
Michael Burns, *Dreyfus: A Family Affair, 1789–1945* (1992).
David Cannadine, *The Decline and Fall of the British Aristocracy* (1990).
G. Kitson Clark, *The Making of Victorian England* (1962).
H. J. Dyos and Michael Wolff, *The Victorian City: Images and Realities* (2 vols., 1983).
Catherine Evtuhov and Richard Stites, *A History of Russia: People, Legends, Events, Forces* (2004).
Michael Freeman, *Railways and the Victorian Imagination* (1999).
David M. Goldfrank, *The Origins of the Crimean War* (1994).
Sudhir Hazareesingh, *From Subject to Citizen: The Second Empire and the Emergence of Modern French Democracy* (1998).
E. J. Hobsbawm, *The Age of Capital, 1848–1875* (1976).
Steven L. Hoch, *Serfdom and Social Control in Russia: Petrovskoe, a Village in Tambov* (1986).
Michael Howard, *The Franco-Prussian War: The German Invasion of France, 1870–1871* (1981).
Paula Hyman, *From Dreyfus to Vichy: The Remaking of French Jewry, 1906–1939* (1979).

William Irvine, *The Boulanger Affair Reconsidered: Royalism, Boulangism, and the Origins of the Radical Right in France* (1989).

Gareth Stedman Jones, *Languages of Class: Studies in English Working Class History, 1832–1982* (1983).

James F. McMillan, *Napoleon III* (1991).

Roger Price, *The French Second Empire: An Anatomy of Political Power* (2001).

Lucy Riall, *Garibaldi: The Invention of a Hero* (2001).

Norman Rich, *The Age of Nationalism and Reform, 1850–1890* (1970).

Séamas Ó Síocháin, *Roger Casement: Imperialist, Rebel, Revolutionary* (2008).

Alan Sked, *The Decline and Fall of the Habsburg Empire* (1989).

F. M. L. Thompson, *The Rise of Respectable Society, 1830–1900* (1986).

Robert Tombs, *The War against Paris, 1871* (1981).

Martha Vicinus, *Suffer and Be Still: Women in the Victorian Age* (1973).

Eugen Weber, *Peasants into Frenchmen: The Modernization of Rural France, 1870–1914* (1986).

G. M. Young, *Portrait of an Age: Victorian England* (1980).

Reginald E. Zelnick, *Labor and Society in Tsarist Russia: The Factory Workers of St. Petersburg, 1855–1870* (1971).

CHAPTER 19. RAPID INDUSTRIALIZATION AND ITS CHALLENGES, 1870–1914

Lenard Berlanstein, ed., *Rethinking Labor History* (1993).

David Blackbourn, *Margingen: Apparitions of the Virgin Mary in Bismarckian Germany* (1993).

Alain Corbin, *Women for Hire: Prostitution and Sexuality in France after 1850* (1990).

Michael Freeman, *Railways and the Victorian Imagination* (1999).

Nancy Green, *The Pletzl of Paris: Jewish Immigrant Workers in the Belle Époque* (1986).

Ruth Harris, *Lourdes: Body and Spirit in the Secular Age* (1999).

Stephen Heathorn, *For Home, Country, and Race: Constructing Gender, Class, and Englishness in the Elementary School, 1880–1914* (2000).

David P. Jordan, *Transforming Paris: The Life and Labors of Baron Haussmann* (1995).

Thomas A. Kselman, *Miracles and Prophecies in Nineteenth-Century France* (1983).

William C. Lubenow, *Parliamentary Politics and the Home Rule Crisis* (1988).

John Lukacs, *Budapest, 1900: A Historical Portrait of a City and Its Culture* (1988).

Mary Jo Maynes, *Taking the Hard Road: Life Course in French and German Workers' Autobiographies in the Era of Industrialization* (1995).

Patricia M. Mazón, *Gender and the Modern Research University: The Admission of Women to German Higher Education, 1865–1914* (2003).

Patrick McDevitt, *May the Best Man Win: Sport, Masculinity, and Nationalism in Great Britain and the Empire, 1880–1935* (2004).

Michael B. Miller, *The Bon Marché: Bourgeois Culture and the Department Store, 1869–1920* (1981).

Alan S. Milward and S. B. Saul, *The Development of the Economies of Continental Europe, 1850–1914* (1977).

Leslie Moch, *Moving Europeans: Migration in Western Europe since 1650* (1993).

Jonathan Schneer, *London, 1900: The Imperial Metropolis* (1999).

Bonnie G. Smith, *Ladies of the Leisure Class: The Bourgeoises of Northern France in the Nineteenth Century* (1982).

Gareth Stedman Jones, *Outcast London: A Study in the Relations between Classes in Victorian Society* (1992).

Judith R. Walkowitz, *City of Dreadful Delight* (1992).

———, *Prostitution and Victorian Society: Women, Class, and the State* (1983).

CHAPTER 20. POLITICAL AND CULTURAL RESPONSES TO A RAPIDLY CHANGING WORLD

Steven E. Aschheim, *The Nietzsche Legacy in Germany, 1890–1990* (1992).

Philipp Blom, *The Vertigo Years* (2008).

Peter Gay, *Freud: A Life for Our Time* (1988).

———, *Modernism: The Lure of Heresy, from Baudelaire to Beckett and Beyond* (2008).

Ruth Gay, *The Jews of Germany: A Historical Portrait* (1992).

Steven C. Hause and Anne R. Kenney, *Women's Suffrage and Social Politics in the French Third Republic* (1984).

James Joll, *The Anarchists* (1981).

John Merriman, *The Dynamite Club: How a Bombing in Fin-de-Siècle Paris Ignited the Age of Modern Terror* (2009).

———, *The Red City: Limoges and the French Nineteenth Century* (1991).

Peter G. Pulzer, *The Rise of Political Anti-Semitism in Germany and Austria* (1988).

Charles Rearick, *Pleasures of the Belle Époque* (1985).

Carl E. Schorske, *Fin-de-Siècle Vienna: Politics and Culture* (1980).

Roger Shattuck, *The Banquet Years: The Origins of the Avant-Garde in France 1885 to World War I* (1988).

Debora L. Silverman, *Art Nouveau in Fin-de-Siècle France: Politics, Psychology, and Style* (1989).

Mikulás Teich and Roy Porter, eds., *Fin-de-Siècle and Its Legacy* (1990).

Eugen Weber, *France, Fin-de-Siècle* (1986).

CHAPTER 21. THE AGE OF EUROPEAN IMPERIALISM

Imran Ali, *The Punjab under Imperialism* (1988).

W. Baumgart, *Imperialism: The Idea and Reality of British and French Colonial Expansion 1880–1914* (1982).

Henri Brunschwig, *French Colonialism, 1871–1914: Myths and Realities* (1966).

Antoinette Burton, *Burdens of History: British Feminists, Indian Women, and Imperial Culture, 1865–1915* (1994).

David Cannadine, *Ornamentalism: How the British Saw Their Empire* (2001).

Richard Drayton, *Nature's Government: Science, Imperial Britain and the "Improvement" of the World* (2000).

Adam Hochschild, *King Leopold's Ghost: A Story of Greed, Terror, and Heroism in Colonial Africa* (1998).

Alan Hodgart, *The Economics of European Imperialism* (1977).

Isabel V. Hull, *Absolute Destruction: Military Culture and the Practices of War in Imperial Germany* (2006).

Dane Kennedy, *Hill Stations and the British Raj* (1996).

————, *Islands of White: Settler Society and Culture in Kenya and South Rhodesia, 1890–1939* (1987).

Patricia M. E. Lorcin, *Imperial Identities: Stereotyping, Prejudice and Race in Colonial Algeria* (1995).

Timothy Mitchell, *Colonizing Egypt* (1988).

Bernard Porter, *The Lion's Share: A Short History of British Imperialism, 1850–1983* (1984).

Edward Said, *Orientalism* (1979).

Megan Vaughan, *Curing Their Ills: Colonial Power and African Illness* (1991).

Gwendolyn Wright, *The Politics of Design in French Colonial Urbanism* (1991).

CHAPTER 22. THE GREAT WAR

Stéphane Audoin-Rouzeau, *Men at War, 1914–1918: National Sentiment and Trench Journalism in France during the First World War* (1992).

Jean-Jacques Becker, *The Great War and the French People* (1985).

Margaret H. Darrow, *French Women and the First World War: War Stories of the Home Front* (2000).

Modris Eksteins, *Rites of Spring: The Great War and the Birth of the Modern Age* (1989).

Niall Ferguson, *The Pity of War: Explaining World War I* (1999).

Fritz Fischer, *Germany's Aims in The First World War* (1967).

Paul Fussel, *The Great War and Modern Memory* (1975).

Peter Gatrell, *A Whole Empire Walking: Refugees in Russia during World War I* (1999).

Martha Hanna, *Your Death Would Be Mine: Paul and Marie Pireaud in the Great War* (2006).

David G. Herrmann, *The Arming of Europe and the Making of the First World War* (1996).

John Horne and Alan Kramer, *German Atrocities, 1914: A History of Denial* (2001).

Michael Howard, *The First World War* (2002).

Samuel Hynes, *A War Imagined: The First World War and English Culture* (1990).

James Joll, *The Origins of the First World War* (1992).

John Keegan, *The First World War* (1998).

George F. Kennan, *The Fateful Alliance: France, Russia, and the Coming of the First War* (1992).

Paul Kennedy, *The Rise of Anglo-German Antagonism, 1860–1914* (1980).

Alan Kramer, *Dynamic of Destruction: Culture and Mass Killing in the First World War* (2007).

Vejas G. Liulevicius, *War Land on the Eastern Front: Culture, National Identity and German Occupation in World War I* (2000).

Lyn Macdonald, *1915: The Death of Innocence* (1993).
———, *Somme* (1983).
Arthur Marwick, *The Deluge: British Society and the First World War* (1966).
———, *Women at War, 1914–1918* (1977).
Justin McCarthy, *The Ottoman People and the End of Empire* (2001).
Erich Maria Remarque, *All Quiet on the Western Front* (1929).
George Robb, *British Culture and the First World War* (2002).
Victor Rudenno, *Gallipoli: Attack from the Sea* (2008).
Gary Sheffield, *The Somme* (2003).
Kenneth Silver, *Esprit de Corps: Avant-Garde Art and the First World War in France* (1990).
Leonard V. Smith, *Between Mutiny and Obedience: The Case of the French Fifth Infantry Division during World War I* (1994).
Leonard V. Smith, Stéphane Audoin-Rouzeau, and Annette Becker, *France and the Great War* (2002).
Nigel Steel and Peter Hart, *Passchendaele: The Sacrificial Ground* (2000).
Norman Stone, *The Eastern Front, 1914–1917* (1998).
Hew Strachan, *The First World War* (2003).
Mark Thompson, *The White War: Life and Death on the Italian Front, 1915–1919* (2008).
John W. Wheeler-Bennett, *Brest-Litovsk: The Forgotten Peace* (1971).
J. M. Winter, *The Great War and the British People* (1986).
———, *Sites of Memory, Sites of Mourning: The Great War in European Cultural History* (1995).
J. M. Winter and Jean-Louis Robert, *Capital Cities at War: Paris, London, Berlin, 1914–1919* (2 vols., 1997 and 2007).

CHAPTER 23. REVOLUTIONARY RUSSIA AND THE SOVIET UNION

Abraham Ascher, *The Revolution of 1905* (2 vols., 1992).
Paul Avrich, *Kronstadt, 1921* (1991).
Victoria E. Bonnell, *Roots of Rebellion: Workers' Politics and Organizations in St. Petersburg and Moscow, 1900–1914* (1983).
Orlando Figes, *Peasant Russia, Civil War* (1989).
———, *The Russian Revolution, 1917–1932* (1982).
Sheila Fitzpatrick, *The Russian Revolution, 1917–1932* (1982).
Tsuyoshi Hasegawa, *The February Revolution: Petrograd, 1917* (1981).
Peter Holquist, *Making War, Forging Revolution: Russia's Continuum of Crisis, 1914–1921* (2002).
John L. H. Keep, *The Russian Revolution: A Study in Mass Mobilization* (1976).
Diane Koenker, *Moscow Workers and the 1917 Russian Revolution* (1982).
W. Bruce Lincoln, *Red Victory: A History of the Russian Civil War, 1918–1921* (1999).
Alexander Rabinowitch, *The Bolsheviks Come to Power: The Revolution of 1917 in Petrograd* (1978).
S. A. Smith, *Red Petrograd: Revolution in the Factories, 1917–1918* (1983).
Richard Stites, *Revolutionary Dreams: Utopian Vision and Experimental Life in the Russian Revolution* (1988).

CHAPTER 24. THE ELUSIVE SEARCH FOR STABILITY IN THE 1920s

Ivo Banac, *The National Question in Yugoslavia* (1985).

Manfred Franz Boemetie, Gerald D. Feldman, and Elizabeth Glaser, eds., *The Treaty of Versailles: A Reassessment after 75 Years* (1998).

Patrick Cohrs, *The Unfinished Peace after World War I: America, Britain, and the Stabilization of Europe, 1919–1932* (2008).

Peter Gay, *My German Question: Growing Up in Nazi Berlin* (1998).

———, *Weimar Culture: The Outsider as Insider* (1968).

Robert Graves, *Goodbye to All That* (1960).

Robert Graves and Alan Hodge, *The Long Week-End: A Social History of Great Britain, 1918–1939* (1963).

Adrian Gregory, *A Silence of Memory: Armistice Day, 1919–1946* (1994).

Helmut Gruber, *Red Vienna: Experiments in Working-Class Culture, 1919–1934* (1991).

Pierre-Jakez Hélias, *The Horse of Pride: Life in a Breton Village* (1978).

Martin Kitchen, *Europe between the Wars: A Political History* (1988).

Richard F. Kuisel, *Capitalism and the State in Modern France* (1983).

Gregory M. Luebbert, *Liberalism, Fascism, or Social Democracy: Social Classes and the Political Origins of Regimes in Interwar Europe* (1991).

Charles Maier, *Recasting Bourgeois Europe: Stabilization in France, Germany, and Italy in the Decade after World War I* (1975).

Sally Marks, *The Illusion of Peace: Europe's International Relations, 1918–1933* (1976).

Walter A. McDougall, *France's Rhineland Diplomacy, 1914–1924* (1978).

Detlev J. K. Peukert, *The Weimar Republic* (1989).

Antony Polonsky, *Politics in Independent Poland 1921–1939: The Crisis of Constitutional Government* (1972).

Antoine Prost, *In the Wake of War: "Les Ancien Combattants" and French Society* (1992).

Steven A. Schuker, *The End of French Predominance in Europe: The Financial Crisis of 1924 and the Adoption of the Dawes Plan* (1976).

Alan Sharp, *The Versailles Settlement: Peacemaking in Paris* (1991).

Daniel J. Sherman, *The Construction of Memory in Interwar France* (1999).

Dan P. Silverman, *Reconstructing Europe after the Great War* (1982).

Denis Mack Smith, *Italy and Its Monarchy* (1989).

A. J. P. Taylor, *English History, 1914–1945* (1965).

Mark Trachtenberg, *Reparation and World Politics* (1980).

Piotr Wandycz, *France and Her Eastern Allies, 1918–1925* (1985).

CHAPTER 25. THE EUROPE OF ECONOMIC DEPRESSION AND DICTATORSHIP

William Sheridan Allen, *The Nazi Seizure of Power: The Experience of a Single German Town, 1922–1945* (1984).

P. M. H. Bell, *The Origins of the Second World War* (1986).

R. J. B. Bosworth, *The Italian Dictatorship: Problems and Perspectives in the Interpretation of Mussolini and Fascism* (1998).

Karl Dietrich Bracher, *The German Dictatorship: The Origins, Structure, and Effects of National Socialism* (1970).

Gerald Brenan, *The Spanish Labyrinth: An Account of the Social and Political Background of the Civil War* (2001).

Robert Conquest, *The Great Terror: A Reassessment* (1990).

Victoria De Grazia, *How Fascism Ruled Women: Italy, 1922–1945* (1992).

Richard J. Evans, *The Coming of the Third Reich* (2003).

———, *The Third Reich in Power* (2005).

Orlando Figes, *The Whisperers: Private Life in Stalin's Russia* (2007).

Sheila Fitzpatrick, *Everyday Stalinism: Ordinary Life in Extraordinary Times: Soviet Russia in the 1930s* (1999).

Robert Gellately, *Backing Hitler: Consent and Coercion in Nazi Germany* (2001).

Geoffrey Hosking, *The First Socialist Society: A History of the Soviet Union from Within* (1993).

Gabriel Jackson, *The Spanish Republic and the Civil War, 1931–1939* (1974).

Julian Jackson, *The Popular Front in France: Defending Democracy, 1934–1938* (1988).

Eric A. Johnson, *Nazi Terror: The Gestapo, Jews, and Ordinary Germans* (1999).

Ian Kershaw, *Hitler* (2 vols., 1999–2000).

———, *The "Hitler Myth": Image and Reality in the Third Reich* (1991).

Charles Kindleberger, *The World in Depression, 1929–1939* (1986).

MacGregor Knox, *Common Destiny: Dictatorship, Foreign Policy and War in Fascist Italy and Nazi Germany* (2000).

———, *Mussolini Unleashed, 1939–1941: Politics and Strategy in Facist Italy* (1982).

Rudy Koshar, *Social Life, Local Politics, and Nazism: Marburg, 1880–1935* (1986).

Stephen Kotkin, *Magnetic Mountain: Stalinism as a Civilization* (1995).

David Clay Large, *Between Two Fires: Europe's Path in the 1930s* (1990).

George Mosse, *Fascist Revolution: Toward a General Theory of Fascism* (1999).

George Orwell, *Homage to Catalonia* (1980).

Detlev J. K. Peukert, *Inside Nazi Germany: Conformity, Opposition, and Racism in Everyday Life* (1987).

Anthony Read and David Fisher, *The Deadly Embrace: Hitler, Stalin and the Nazi-Soviet Pact, 1939–1941* (1989).

Joachim Remak, *The Origins of the Second World War* (1979).

Denis Mack Smith, *Mussolini: A Biography* (1983).

Robert Soucy, *Fascism in France: The First Wave, 1924–1933* (1986).

———, *Fascism in France: The Second Wave, 1933–1939* (1995).

Fritz Stern, *The Politics of Cultural Despair: A Study in the Use of the Germanic Ideology* (1974).

Hugh Thomas, *The Spanish Civil War* (2001).

Adam Tooze, *The Wages of Destruction: The Making and Unmaking of the Nazi Economy* (2006).

Henry A. Turner, Jr., *German Big Business and the Rise of Hitler* (1985).

———, *Hitler: Thirty Days to Power* (1996).

Gerhard L. Weinberg, *The Foreign Policy of Hitler's Germany: Diplomatic Revolution in Europe, 1933–1936* (1970).

————, *Starting World War II, 1937–1939* (1980).
Susan Zuccotti, *Under His Very Windows: The Vatican and the Holocaust* (2002).

CHAPTER 26. WORLD WAR II

Omer Bartov, *Hitler's Army: Soldiers, Nazis, and War in the Third Reich* (1992).
Anthony Beevor, *Stalingrad* (1998).
Marc Bloch, *Strange Defeat* (1968).
Norman Davies, *No Single Victory: World War II in Europe, 1939–1945* (2006).
Richard J. Evans, *The Third Reich at War, 1939–1945* (2008).
Sarah Farmer, *Martyred Village: Commemorating the 1944 Massacre at Oradour-sur-Glane* (1999).
Paul Fussell, *Wartime: Understanding and Behavior in the Second World War* (1989).
Robert Gellately, *Backing Hitler: Consent and Coercion in Nazi Germany* (2001).
Jan Tomasz Gross, *Neighbors: The Destruction of the Jewish Community in Jedwabne, Poland* (2001).
Raul Hilberg, *Perpetrators, Victims, Bystanders: The Jewish Catastrophe, 1933–1945* (1992).
Peter Hoffmann, *The History of the German Resistance, 1933–1945* (1977).
Julian Jackson, *France: The Dark Years, 1940–1944* (2002).
Eric T. Jennings, *Vichy in the Tropics: Pétain's National Revolution in Madagascar, Guadaloupe, and Indochina, 1940–1944* (2001).
H. R. Kedward, *In Search of the Maquis: Rural Resistance in Southern France, 1942–1944* (1993).
John Keegan, *The Second World War* (1989).
————, *Six Armies in Normandy* (1982).
Martin Kolinsky, *Britain's War in the Middle East: Strategy and Diplomacy, 1936–1942* (1999).
Walter Laqueur, *The Terrible Secret: Suppression of the Truth about Hitler's "Final Solution"* (1980).
David Clay Large, *And the World Closed Its Doors: One Family's Struggle to Escape the Holocaust* (2003).
Michael Marrus, *The Holocaust in History* (1988).
Arthur Marwick, *The Home Front: The British and the Second World War* (1977).
Ernest R. May, *Strange Victory: Hitler's Conquest of France* (2000).
Mark Mazower, *Hitler's Europe: How the Nazis Ruled Europe* (2008).
————, *Inside Hitler's Greece: The Experience of Occupation, 1941–1944* (1993).
Alan S. Milward, *War, Economy, and Society, 1939–1945* (1977).
Robert O. Paxton, *Vichy France: Old Guard and New Order, 1940–1944* (1972).
Robert O. Paxton and Michael R. Marrus, *Vichy France and the Jews* (1981).
Lyn Smith, *Remembering: Voices of the Holocaust* (2005).
Jonathan Steinberg, *The Axis and the Holocaust, 1941–1943* (1990).
John F. Sweets, *Choices in Vichy France* (1986).
Donald Cameron Watt, *How War Came* (1989).
Gerhard L. Weinberg, *A World at War: A Global History of World War II* (1994).

CHAPTER 27. REBUILDING DIVIDED EUROPE

Paul Ginsborg, *A History of Contemporary Italy: Society and Politics, 1943–1988* (1990).

Stanley Hoffmann, *Decline or Renewal? France since the Popular Front: Government and the People, 1936–1986* (1988).

Michael J. Hogan, *The Marshall Plan: America, Britain and the Reconstruction of Western Europe, 1947–1952* (1987).

George F. Kennan, *The Nuclear Delusion: Soviet-American Relations in the Atomic Age* (1983).

Paul Kennedy, *The Parliament of Man: The Past, Present, and Future of the United Nations* (2006).

Lothar Kettenacher, *Germany since 1945* (1997).

Richard Kuisel, *Seducing the French: The Dilemma of Americanization* (1993).

Andrew Marr, *A History of Modern Britain* (2007).

Arthur Marwick, *British Society since 1945* (1982).

Vojtech Mastny, *Helsinki, Human Rights, and European Security* (1986).

Alan S. Milward, *The European Rescue of the Nation-State* (1992).

———, *The Reconstruction of Western Europe, 1945–1951* (1984).

Kenneth O. Morgan, *Labour in Power, 1945–1951* (1984).

———, *The People's Peace: British History, 1945–1990* (1991).

Norman M. Naimark, *A History of the Soviet Zone of Occupation, 1945–1949* (1995).

Robert A. Pollard, *Economic Security and the Origins of the Cold War* (1985).

Henry Rousso, *Vichy Syndrome: History and Memory in France since 1944* (1991).

William Taubman, *Khrushchev: The Man and His Era* (2003).

Henry A. Turner, Jr., *Germany from Partition to Reunification* (1992).

CHAPTER 28. THE COLD WAR AND THE END OF EUROPEAN EMPIRES

David Anderson, *Histories of the Hanged: The Dirty War in Kenya and the End of Empire* (2005).

Franz Ansprenger, *The Dissolution of Colonial Empires* (1989).

P. J. Cain and A. G. Hopkins, *British Imperialism: Crisis and Deconstruction, 1914–1990* (1993).

Muriel Evelyn Chamberlain, *Decolonization: The Fall of the European Empires* (1985).

Matthew Connelly, *A Diplomatic Revolution: Algeria's Fight for Independence and the Origins of the Post–Cold War Era* (2002).

Jacques Dalloz, *The War in Indochina* (1990).

Caroline Elkins, *Imperial Reckoning: The Untold Story of Britain's Gulag in Kenya* (2005).

Prosser Gifford and William Roger Louis, eds., *Decolonization and African Independence: The Transfers of Power, 1960–1980* (1988).

John D. Hargeaves, *Decolonization in Africa* (1988).

Alistair Horne, *A Savage War of Peace: Algeria, 1954–1962* (1978).

Bruce R. Kuniholm, *The Origins of the Cold War in the Near East: Great Power Conflict and Diplomacy in Iran, Turkey, and Greece* (1994).

Robert J. Lieber, *Oil and the Middle East: Europe in the Energy Crisis* (1976).

CHAPTER 29. TRANSITIONS TO DEMOCRACY AND THE COLLAPSE
      OF COMMUNISM

Paul Arthur and Keith Jeffery, *Northern Ireland since 1968* (1988).

Timothy Garton Ash, *In Europe's Name: Germany and the Divided Continent* (1993).

———, *The Polish Revolution: Solidarity, 1980–1982* (1983).

Ivo Banac, *Eastern Europe in Revolution* (1992).

Corelli Barnett, *The Pride and the Fall: The Dream and Illusion of Britain as a Great Nation* (1987).

Serge Berstein, *The Republic of De Gaulle, 1958–1969* (1993).

George W. Breslauer, *Gorbachev and Yeltsin as Leaders* (2002).

David Caute, *The Year of Barricades: A Journey through 1968* (1989).

David Childs, *Britain since 1945* (2001).

Robert Darnton, *Berlin Journal: 1989–1990* (1991).

Karen Dawisha and Bruce Parrott, *Russia and the New States of Eurasia: The Politics of Upheaval* (1994).

Milovan Djilas, *Fall of the New Class: A History of Communism's Self-Destruction,* ed., Vasilije Kalezić (1998).

Milovan Djilas, *The New Class: An Analysis of the Communist System* (1957).

Paul Ginsborg, *Italy and Its Discontents: Family, Civil Society, State 1980–2001* (2001).

Václav Havel, *Art of the Impossible: Politics as Morality in Practice: Speeches and Writings, 1990–1996* (1997).

Václav Havel, et al., *Power of the Powerless: Citizens against the State in Central-Eastern Europe* (1985).

Robert O. Keohane, Joseph S. Nye, and Stanley Hoffmann, *Europe after the Cold War* (1993).

Stephen Kotkin, *Armageddon Averted: The Soviet Collapse, 1970–2000* (2001).

David Kynaston, *Austerity Britain, 1945–1951* (2008).

Walter Laqueur, *Europe since Hitler* (1983).

Carol Skalnick Leff, *The Czech and Slovak Republics: Nation versus State* (1997).

Paul Lendvai, *One Day That Shook the Communist World: The 1956 Hungarian Revolution and Its Legacy* (2008).

Anatol Lieven, *The Baltic Revolution: Estonia, Latvia, Lithuania and the Path to Independence* (1999).

Martin E. Malia, *The Soviet Tragedy: A History of Socialism in Russia, 1917–1991* (1993).

Kenneth Maxwell, *The Making of Portuguese Democracy* (1995).

Paul Preston, *Franco: A Biography* (1993).

———, *The Triumph of Democracy in Spain* (1986).

Peter Riddell, *The Thatcher Era and Its Legacy* (1991).

Alan Sked and Chris Cook, *Postwar Britain: A Political History* (1990).

Gale Stohes, *The Walls Came Tumbling Down* (1993).

Ronald Grigor Suny, *The Revenge of the Past: Nationalism, Revolution, and the Collapse of the Soviet Union* (1993).

George Weigel, *The Final Revolution: The Breaking of Communist Europe* (1991).

CHAPTER 30. GLOBAL CHALLENGES: "FORTRESS EUROPE," EUROPEAN COOPERATION, AND THE UNCERTAINTIES OF A NEW AGE

Martin Baldwin-Edwards and Martin A. Schain, eds., *The Politics of Immigration in Western Europe* (1994).

Rogers Brubaker, *Citizenship and Nationhood in France and Germany* (1992).

Desmond Dinan, *Ever Closer Union? An Introduction to the European Community* (1994).

François Gaspard, *A Small City in France* (1995).

Daniel Gros and Niels Thygesen, *European Monetary Integration* (1992).

Alec G. Hargraves, *Immigration, Race, and Ethnicity in Contemporary France* (1995).

Bernard Lewis, *Islam and the West* (1993).

Barbara Marshall, *The New Germany and Migration in Europe* (2000).

Jorgen Nielsen, *Muslims in Western Europe* (1992).

John Pinder, *The Building of the European Union* (1998).

Larry Siedentop, *Democracy in Europe* (2001).

Derek Urwin, *The Community of Europe: A History of European Integration since 1945* (1995).

John Wrench and John Solomos, eds., *Racism and Migration in Western Europe* (1993).

CREDITS

Frontispiece: Philadelphia Museum of Art, Purchased: Lila Dowin Peck Fund

Part Four (p. 432) Bildarchiv Preussischer Kulturbesitz, Berlin/Art Resource, NY; **Part Five (p. 644)** Private Collection/The Bridgeman Art Library; **Part Six (p. 860)** Bettmann/Corbis; **Part Seven (p. 1104)** AP Photo

Chapter 12: p. 439 (left) Musée Carnavalet, Photographie Bulloz; p. 439 (right) Versailles Museum, Photographie Bulloz; p. 443 (left) Musée Carnavalet, Photographie Bulloz; p. 443 (right) Abbé Sieyès, Photographie Bulloz; p. 444 Bibliothèque Nationale; p. 446 Giraudon/Art Resource, NY; p. 450 Giraudon/Art Resource, NY; p. 454 Trustees of the British Museum; p. 455 © cliché Bibliothèque Nationale de France, Paris; p. 456 © cliché Bibliothèque Nationale de France, Paris; p. 457 (left) Classic Image / Alamy; p. 457 (right) Mansell/Time Life Pictures/Getty Images; p. 459 (left) Bridgeman-Giraudon / Art Resource, NY; p. 459 (right) Tate Gallery, London/Art Resource, NY; p. 461 Photographie Bulloz; p. 463 © cliché Bibliothèque Nationale de France, Paris; p. 466 Photographie Bulloz; p. 468 Hulton-Deutsch Collection/Corbis; p. 472 © cliché Bibliothèque Nationale de France, Paris; p. 475 The Trustees of the British Museum

Chapter 13: p. 480 Giraudon/Art Resource, NY; p. 484 Bettmann/Corbis; p. 487 Giraudon/Art Resource, NY; p. 489 Stapleton Collection/Corbis; p. 492 Patrick Lorette/Bridgeman Art Library; p. 494 Alinari/Art Resource, NY; p. 499 Print collection, The New York Public Library, Astor, Lenox, and Tilden Foundations; p. 501 Alinari/Art Resource, NY; p. 506 Bavarian Army Museum, Munich; p. 507 (left) National Gallery, London; p. 507 (right) Gianni Dagli Orti/Corbis; p. 508 Warder Collection; p. 510 Mary Evans Picture Library / Alamy

Chapter 14: p. 514 Lauros/Giraudon/Bridgeman Art Library; p. 521 Mary Evans Picture Library; p. 523 Collection David Artis; p. 527 The Manchester Public Libraries; p. 528 The Art Archive/Bibliothèque des Arts Décoratifs Paris/Dagli Orti; p. 533 Martin Buhler/Oeffentliche Kunstsammlung, Basel; p. 534 Osterreichische Galerie, Wien; p. 536 Private Collection; p. 539 Statens Museum fur Kunst, Copenhagen; p. 540 Warder Collection; p. 542 Courtesy Museum of Fine Arts, Boston; p. 544 Graphische Sammlung Albertina; p. 545 The Granger Collection, NY; p. 548 British Library; p. 552 Snark/Art Resource, NY; p. 555 The Granger Collection, NY; p. 557 Hulton Archive/Getty Images; p. 558 Hulton Archive/Getty Images; p. 562 © cliché Bibliothèque Nationale de France, Paris; p. 565 Mary Evans Picture Library; p. 567 Musée Carnavalet, Photographie Bulloz

Chapter 15: p. 570 Historisches Museen der Stadt Wien; p. 572 Hulton Archive/Getty Images; p. 578 Adoc-photos / Art Resource, NY; p. 584 Giraudon/Art Resource, NY; p. 585 Bettmann/Corbis; p. 587 Private Collection/Archives Charmet/The Bridgeman Art Library; p. 589 Ludwig Burger, Wartburg Festival, Staatsbibliothek, Berlin, Bildarchiv, Preussischer Kulturbesits; p. 590 Giraudon/Art Resource, NY; p. 592 INTERFOTO Pressebildagentur / Alamy; p. 595 Art Resource, NY; p. 597 Erich Lessing/Art Resource, NY; p. 598 Versailles Museum, Photographie Bulloz; p. 602 Archives Charmet/Bridgeman Art Library; p. 606 Trustees of the British Museum; p. 610 © Her Majesty Queen Elizabeth II/Royal Collection Enterprises Ltd.; p. 611 Bettmann/Corbis

Index